A Social History of Disability in the Middle Ages

What was it like to be disabled in the Middle Ages? How did people become disabled? Did welfare support exist? This book discusses social and cultural factors affecting the lives of medieval crippled, deaf, mute and blind people, those nowadays collectively called "disabled." Although the word did not exist then, many of the experiences disabled people might have today can already be traced back to medieval social institutions and cultural attitudes.

This volume informs our knowledge of the topic by investigating the impact medieval laws had on the social position of disabled people, and conversely, how people might become disabled through judicial actions; ideas of work and how work could both cause disability through industrial accidents but also provide continued ability to earn a living through occupational support networks; the disabling effects of old age and associated physical deteriorations; and the changing nature of attitudes towards welfare provision for the disabled and the ambivalent role of medieval institutions and charity in the support and care of disabled people.

Irina Metzler studied Classical and Medieval History, gaining a doctorate from the University of Reading, honorary research affiliations with the universities of Bristol and Swansea, and was awarded a Wellcome Trust fellowship (2012). She has published widely on cultural, religious and social aspects of disability in the European Middle Ages.

Routledge Studies in Cultural History

A Social History of Disability in the Middle Ages

Cultural Considerations of Physical Impairment

Irina Metzler

Routledge
Taylor & Francis Group

NEW YORK   LONDON

First published 2013
by Routledge
711 Third Avenue, New York, NY 10017

Simultaneously published in the UK
by Routledge
2 Park Square, Milton Park, Abingdon, Oxon OX14 4RN

*Routledge is an imprint of the Taylor & Francis Group,
an informa business*

© 2013 Taylor & Francis

The right of Irina Metzler to be identified as author of this work has been asserted in accordance with sections 77 and 78 of the Copyright, Designs and Patents Act 1988.

Library of Congress Cataloging-in-Publication Data
Metzler, Irina, 1966–
    A social history of disability in the middle ages : cultural considerations of physical impairment / by Irina Metzler. — 1st Edition.
        pages cm. — (Routledge studies in cultural history ; 20)
    Includes bibliographical references and index.
    1. People with disabilities—History—Medieval, 500–1500. 2. People with disabilities—Legal status, laws, etc.—History—Medieval, 500–1500. 3. Social history—Medieval, 500–1500. I. Title.
    HV1552.M487 2013
    305.9'080940902—dc23
    2012039017

ISBN13: 978-0-415-82259-6 (hbk)
ISBN13: 978-0-203-37116-9 (ebk)

Typeset in Sabon
by IBT Global.

Printed and bound in the United States of America on sustainably sourced paper by IBT Global.

To my family

Contents

Introduction

For a long time, as Jacques Le Goff pointed out, historians used to believe the human body had no history since it belonged to nature and not to culture. More recently, historians have recognised that the body does indeed have a history, and is even an integral part of history to the extent of shaping it—much as economic or social structures as well as intellectual or spiritual representations do—so that the body is simultaneously both the product and the medium.[1]

While my previous book provided a theoretical framework to set the scene for discussions of disability in the Middle Ages, the aim here is to tease out from the many disparate sources some inkling of the 'lived experience'. Normative texts, such as the natural-philosophical, medical, theological and hagiographical material, may provide the intellectual theory and tell us how non-disabled people thought about the disabled, but the economic, social and even the legal texts collected, analysed and discussed here go some way further in presenting a picture of what challenges a medieval disabled person may have encountered. Even if historians are still a long way short of having at their perusal autobiographical accounts of medieval disabled people, the sources used here come closer in approximating the reconstruction of daily life and quotidian experience of physical impairment in the Middle Ages.[2] Transferring the analogy of the social model of disability to the historical disciplines, after a fashion, we, the modern researchers, historians and even medievalist specialists, are disabled by our lack of distinct, neatly arranged bodies of sources and struggle to find materials. And as in the social model of disability, where disability is seen as a construct, so as a discipline too medievalists need to recognise that an apparent lack of sources is a construct of the rigorously mono-disciplinary school of thought prevalent until fairly recently.

It is commonly assumed, even by luminaries such as Le Goff, that:

> the medieval west was full of blind people with sunken eyes and empty pupils who would come to stare out at us in the frightening picture by Breughel; the Middle Ages were full of the maimed, hunchbacks, people with goitres, the lame, and the paralysed.[3]

If disability in the Middle Ages was truly so prevalent, visible and omni-present, where then in both the sources and the historiography are the disabled? In documenting the paradoxically "absent presence" of disability in history, a work on the new vogue for disability history mentions one central reason for the previous "elision of disabled people from the historiography", in that historians may be assuming a paucity of primary sources for disability history.[4] The older style of writing disability history (derived from early twentieth-century medical historians, whereby random references to 'handicapped' persons from throughout history were collected only to list them in chronological order, with the briefest of commentaries regarding social or cultural context) served primarily to emphasise the 'despiteness' of such individuals: despite impairment, these characters overcame their 'handicap' and reneged their 'disability'. Even in the 1980s health care professionals working in the field of rehabilitation were churning out such exhortatory lists.[5] A sign of the changes within historiography itself is the amendment of a key textbook of (modern) Disability Studies, *The Disability Studies Reader*. In its first edition from 1997 this still included as one of the few historical essays looking beyond the modern and into the 'deep past' an article that in its subtitle referred to "Dread and Despair", as if those were the main things to note about the social situation of disability in past times. By the third edition of 2010, this essay had been dropped and replaced by one on blindness in the Middle Ages.[6]

But not just the apparent paucity of sources, also the multifarious aspects of disability that do not allow themselves to be neatly aligned against established academic disciplines might be regarded as problematic, since, as Catherine Kudlick said:

> disability is so vast in its economic, social, political, cultural, religious, legal, philosophical, artistic, moral, and medical import that it can force historians to reconsider virtually every concept, every event, every "given" we have taken for granted.[7]

However, taking a multidisciplinary approach, recent scholarly investigation, by the author and a growing number of others in this emerging field, is rapidly beginning to uncover references, which previous scholars thought non-existent, to medieval disabled people everywhere. Or as distinguished medievalist Anne Hudson concluded in the context of research into Lollardy: "I do not think that enquiry must be defeated by lack of material."[8] From a modern standpoint, accustomed as we are to autobiographical sources witnessing each and every event in a person's life—even more so with the advent of the Facebook generation—the study of disability in the Middle Ages has always been problematic due to its distinct lack of such sources. How can we know anything about the lives and experiences of disabled people in medieval Europe when virtually nobody who was disabled (with some very few notable exceptions) wrote about their condition, and even less about their emotional state concerning disability? Even such a rare example as the story of a deaf-mute man in the later thirteenth century found in the *Miracles of St. Louis* presents a misleading path for the modern reader on the hunt for 'genuine' autobiographical material, since although this narrative purports to tell an individual story, describing the 'real-life' fate of one disabled person, it is transmitted through the lens of hagiographical and legalistic conventions.[9] During the European Middle Ages other social and demographic groups, such as women, children or peasants, shared with disabled people the problem of lack of visibility in the sources, in that they tended not to leave personal testimonials that can be used as primary sources. As the successful study of women's history, peasant history and more recently children in history has demonstrated, it is possible to reconstruct the social and cultural history of groups previously deemed historically invisible. Of course, for medieval disabled persons we have hardly any personal writings, so that we cannot approach their early history from the same focus on identity and personal testimony that drives modern sociological approaches.[10] Nevertheless, just as, for instance, women's voices can be found in the predominantly male discourse of ancient and medieval documents and literature,[11] so too can the story of medieval disabled persons be unearthed from texts pertaining to legal history, from philosophical treatises, from works of literature and from social and economic sources (wills, tax rolls, municipal accounts, to name but a few). As I have previously emphasised, the reliance on, even deliberate seeking out of, 'identity history' is a futile approach when trying to study people who allegedly 'do not have a history'.[12] Richard Evans has pointed out that it is possible to write the history of 'invisible' groups, since "the idea that each group in society writes its own history breaks down in practice."[13] If solely the members of a particular group wrote that group's history, then, according to Evans: "In the end, no history would be possible, only autobiography."[14]

The problem of using non-autobiographical sources for disability is similar to that of sources for old age, as Shulamith Shahar has noted. The writings of medieval authors on old age, which could just as easily apply to disability, appear to be based on familiarity with and observation of the elderly, but encapsulated in "the concepts, the attitudes, the images and anxieties . . . that were prevalent in their culture."[15] Therefore, knowing a society's attitudes towards its disabled people:

> broadens and deepens our understanding of its nature. Knowing the views and attitudes of Medieval society will help to shed light on its historical uniqueness, as well as on the issues of continuity and change in Western society from an additional viewpoint.[16]

This study of disability in the Middle Ages follows that approach, in being a cultural history, a study of mentalities, focusing on social attitudes rather than on personal testimonies and identities.

A few words about methodology and terminology. This book uses both synchronic and diachronic approaches. 'Synchronic' refers to structures, ideas or cultures that exist now, in the present, whereas 'diachronic' refers to concepts and/or structures existing in time and changing over time. The terms are, of course, derived from Ferdinand de Saussure,[17] who suggested that one should find the infrastructure of a language that is common to all speakers on an unconscious level, which he referred to as 'deep structure', something that may stand outside of historical evolution. Hence, structuralism is concerned with the synchronic rather than the diachronic. 'Disability' is a term that only makes cultural sense in the present, so one could theoretically only discuss disability from a synchronic approach. But the people who made up the group nowadays collectively referred to as 'the disabled' existed even when the terminology did not—the crippled, blind, deaf and dumb of earlier ages would become the disabled of today. Hence, disability is also diachronic, because social and cultural concepts of who or what constituted disabled changed over time.

For reasons of falling into deep anachronisms, modern terminology is not apposite here. The mapping of modern terms like 'disability' or even 'disease' onto the past is intensely problematic. Words that may be offensive to the modern reader, such as 'cripple', were the words that medieval people employed to describe certain other people. While this may not be in accord with modern sensibilities, from the standpoint of cultural history to gloss over medieval terminology would be to lose a system of indispensable observations and insights—the very fact that the Middle Ages had no single term approximating to the modern 'disabled' or 'disability' already speaks volumes about medieval mentalities.

Medieval terminology relating to what we would now call 'disability' was notoriously vague, unless mentioning very specific physical conditions such as, in medieval parlance, the cripple, contracted or paralysed person, or the sensory impairments of blind, deaf and dumb.[18] One might see a fourteenth-century attempt in reaching a more precise definition in the article *Corpus humanum*, on the human body, in the encyclopaedic text *Omne Bonum* (possibly by James le Palmer), which states:

> If one has a useless limb, for instance, a leg, or a withered or powerless hand, or a blind eye, this can be called debility.
>
> (*Siquis habet membrum sed inefficax puta crus vel manum arridam vel impotentem vel oculum cecum, hec potest dici debilitas.*)[19]

Most frequently people are simply referred to as the 'infirm', which can encompass physical impairment such as an orthopaedic one or paralysis, as well as the effects of old age. The 'debilitated' or 'weak' would mean similar categories of people; as would the 'impotent' (made powerless through lack of physical ability),[20] but additionally encompassing more widely those suffering from poverty (made powerless through lack of economic ability). Modern terminology is, in fact, not much better. 'Disability' is often used to encompass all and sundry, whether or not the writer is referring to an anatomical phenomenon or to a social reaction. To enable a better correlation between medieval and modern terms, I prefer to use the terminology introduced by the social model of disability, formulated by the discipline of Disability Studies, where (physical) 'impairment' equates to the medical or anatomical phenomenon, while 'disability' describes the social construct loaded upon the former; hence, disability is culturally specific, and variable over time and space.[21] An application of the social model of disability is given by Moshe Barasch, in the context of blindness, who asks if blindness has a history. As a physiological, hence natural condition:

> blindness knows little change . . . But while blindness as such remains unchanged, our understanding of blindness, our views concerning its "meaning," are matters of culture. . . . As matters of culture, the interpretation of blindness and the social attitude toward the blind are, of course, prone to historical change.[22]

Therefore, what twenty-first-century Europe considers disability is not invariably what our medieval predecessors considered disability.

Some of these attitudes were shaped by concepts of health and illness, prompting the question where disability fits into this dyad. Is disability an 'illness'? Liminality, in its meaning of being on the border, in-between, not one or the other, has already proved a useful concept when discussing medieval medical notions of (physical) impairment.[23] But it is necessary to revisit this topic in connection with how such notions informed social and legal notions as well. What is crucial for my argument is the liminal state of the disabled person: neither ill nor healthy, they fit in neither category. This liminality has a knock-on effect on how law, charity and the work-ethic regard the impaired—hence the themes of the following chapters.

One may define the difference between illness, sickness or disease, on the one hand, and impairment or disability, on the other hand, as the difference between dynamic and static states. This point of view sounds surprisingly modern, but the first element of it was in fact voiced by Arnau of Villanova (c. 1240–1311), who studied and taught medicine at Montpellier. In his *Lecture on the Text "Life Is Short" (Repetitio super canonem "Vita brevis")*, Arnau stated that illness has an evolution, "for every illness from which someone recovers passes from onset (*principium*), through intensification (*augmentum*), to stasis (*status*), to recovery (*declinatio*)."[24] By this definition, illness is a dynamic condition, changing and evolving to take one or the other course. Impairment, irrespective of causes, whether accidental, acquired or congenital, is a static condition, unchanging and permanently present. This static aspect of disability made it more the proper concern of miracle rather than medicine in the medieval mind. The theologian Thomas

Aquinas, writing maybe a generation prior to the physician Arnau of Villanova, explained that alone God:

> can act outside the order of secondary [natural] causes, as by healing those who cannot be healed by the working of nature, or by doing certain things of this kind which are not in accordance with the order of natural causes.[25]

Therefore, it is fitting that only God, or the saints through whom God works, can perform miracles. Modern society finds the static condition, even incurable aspect, of disability deeply unsettling and problematic, since 'miracles' may no longer be the domain of religious thaumaturgy but are firmly ensconced in our beliefs in science and medicine: not for nothing do we frequently cite the 'miracles' of modern medicine. But in modern, Western medicine the predominant view is that illness, and hence disability, according to the medical model, has to follow a "restitution narrative":

> An example of this would be, "yesterday I was well, today I am ill, but tomorrow I will be better". This has been extended into the field of disability such that the "natural" reaction to a disabled person is to attempt to search for a cure, remove the deviation and recreate "normality".[26]

Medieval concepts of health and illness in relation to physical impairment have shown that the impaired body was neither sick nor healthy, since according to medical thinking the course of an illness was to either improve, in which case the patient was deemed healthy, or to take a turn for the worse, resulting in the death of the patient. The disabled person fits neither model, since the functional loss renders a body not truly 'healthy', yet the disabled person never recovers that loss. They are forever stuck in-between the two states proposed by the Hippocratic model. The influence of this model persists unto this day:

> The long term physically impaired are neither sick nor well, neither dead nor well, neither dead nor alive, neither out of society nor wholly in it. They are human beings but their bodies are warped and malfunctioning, leaving their full humanity in doubt. They are not ill, for illness is transitional to either death or recovery . . . The sick person lives in a state of social suspension until he or she gets better. The disabled spend a lifetime in a similar suspended state. They are neither fit nor foul; they exist in a partial isolation from society as undefined, ambiguous people.[27]

Or as liminal people. Such a medical mentality can be observed in the regulations of the hospital of Saint John at Hildesheim, which in 1440 only offered one night's lodging to a healthy pilgrim, but a sick pilgrim was assured of care until "he got better or died".[28] A 'disabled' pilgrim, for instance, an orthopedically impaired but otherwise 'healthy' person, would of course not fit either category—or would they? The challenge is to delve into what little medieval evidence there is and try to ascertain if, and when, those kinds of people our modern society terms 'disabled' were bracketed with the 'healthy' or the 'ill' category. In extreme cases some individuals were even described as being neither dead nor alive,[29] and therefore liminal. Liminality may also lead to special status and/or powers for an impaired person, such as people with magical powers like the witch (Old High German *hagazussa* meant 'the sitter or rider on the fence'),[30] whereby status is either defined by or acquired from literally being between two places, and metaphorically being between two worlds. The present volume will at times draw attention to specific examples and question if and how such concepts are relevant for medieval bodies of difference.

Liminality is not to be equated with exclusion, nor is it the same as marginality: in contrast to the "formalized marginality" inflicted on groups such as Jews, there is a more transient position, where people "find themselves outside normative family and social structures"—this is the liminal condition.[31] I have chosen liminal over marginal, since it better describes the in-between phase that physically impaired people found themselves in, since they are *between* normatively fixed positions (such as healthy or ill, alive or dead, male or female) rather than completely *outside* of traditional structures. In this I have followed the previous analysis of liminality derived from anthropological studies, notably in the work of structuralist Victor Turner in the late 1960s on rites of passage. Turner had categorised such rites according to three phases:

1) A pre-liminal or separation phase, where the initiate is spatially separated from their society, often accompanied by the physical removal of status signs such as clothing.
2) A liminal or transition phase, where the initiate is between states, not fully an initiated person but spatially and conceptually standing at the threshold.
3) A post-liminal or reincorporation phase, coming after the individual has been initiated and returns to their society, but occupying a different social status to the one they held prior to the rite of passage.[32]

Turner had focussed on the second, liminal phase as the most crucial one in most cultures that practised rites of passage, for it is during this phase that the initiate is, in effect, a kind of cultural wild card, removed from one status, but not yet inhabiting another one, and opening the possibility to any outcome. Hence traditional societies took particular care in ordering, supervising and directing the middle, liminal stage of a rite of passage. Notably, the liminal phase was intended to be temporary. "Initiates . . . are to be distinguished from marginals, who permanently form a group on the edges of society."[33] Herein lies the problematic nature of liminality: societies tend to expect a degree of permanence and stability with regard to status, yet with regard to physical impairment liminality may be fluid, a fleeting interval or a constant position.

One may apply Turner's structuralist anthropological analysis to an episode of blindness narrated, in fact, in the New Testament. On the road to Damascus Saul famously transforms into Paul,[34] struck to the ground by a light from heaven, which rendered him blind for three days, during which time also he neither ate nor drank. Disregarding theological exegeses, in anthropological terms what we have here are the classic features of an initiation ritual, a rite of passage that Saul must go through to become Paul. Abstaining from food and drink are well-recognised hallmarks of many initiations, but it is the temporary blindness that is of most interest here in the interpretation of Saint Paul as an initiate, corresponding with the second, liminal or transition phase according to Turner's categories. In his discussion of Paul's blindness, Moshe Barasch had already noted that Paul is not 'punished' by being struck blind, but had interpreted the significance of his blindness as lying in "the sharp break between two stages of his life."[35] Paul's blindness is a "pause", a "short stretch of time which separates the two parts of his life", and "the realization of nothingness, and therefore is fitting to stand for the total break."[36] Without labelling it as such,[37] Barasch is in fact describing the Turnerian liminal phase of an initiation ritual. Pertinent for my interpretation of 'liminality' is here, of course, the fact that Paul's liminal phase is manifested not in a spatial, temporal or other separation, but in physical difference, in what in other circumstances would be called a disability.[38]

This distinction between 'liminality' and 'marginality' (or exclusion) is not always made clear by modern historical or archaeological scholarship; all too often the two terms are used interchangeably, whereas they are neither verbally nor conceptually identical.[39] For instance, in a metaphysical sense, derived from its religious symbolism, the medieval hospital was also located "on the boundaries between heaven and earth",[40] which was reinforced by the liminality of the terrestrial positioning, at the intersections between territories, between town and country, so that it "was used to control and observe stigmatised groups . . . but was in addition used to *display* bodies classified through stigma."[41] Therefore, with regard to physical impairment, one might say that while disease can initiate a "pattern of separation, transition, and reintegration"[42], impairment permanently locates the affected person at the transition stage of this sequence.

Limen, originally meaning 'shore' in Latin, came to mean any thing or person on the boundary. Hence the liminality in the following case is very literally liminal. According to an Icelandic text, the *Landnámabók* (Book of Settlement), one of the earliest Christian settlers on Iceland expressed her wish to be buried on the seashore (*flöðarmálet*) in order to avoid burial in unconsecrated ground. Since the shore was not consecrated, but neither was it pagan ground, it was both geographically as well as theologically neutral territory.[43] The notion of legal liminality may be encountered in enforced liminal burial for outcasts, miscreants and other deviants. An example of such legal liminality can be found in the place-ment of a deformed or severely disabled child, according to Nordic law codes, at the boundary between land and water, that is the tide mark—the *forve*. The earliest Norwegian laws stem from the early eleventh cen-tury, even though they were not written down until the thirteenth. The Old Christian law of the *Borgarthing*, section I.1, mentions the severity of deformities which would cause a mother not to give food to the child but instead to take the child to a *forve* and there place it in a cairn. The deformities include heels being where the toes should be, and toes where heels, a chin between the shoulders, the nape of the neck sticking out from the chest, calves at the front of the legs, or eyes at the back at the nape of the neck. In other words reversal of the normal position of body parts, a back to front arrangement, or the symmetrical opposition of the deformed body to the hale and hearty body. Hence in the *Borgarthing* law the *forve* where such a monstrous child is to be placed is also described as "the forve of the evil one".[44] Many different Nordic texts copied from one another, so the meaning of *forve* as a tidemark of floodmark is possibly derived from another legal text, the *Gulathing*, a Norwegian royal law code of the eleventh century, where the meaning is also that of the meet-ing place of sea and green, i.e. of land and sea at the shore. The *Gulathing Law* had stated:

> Every man when he is dead should be brought to the church and bur-ied in consecrated ground. Except for wrongdoers, traitors, perjurors, thieves and those men who take their own lives. Those whom I have named should be taken out to the country and buried on the edge of the tideline where the sea and the green come together.[45]

Here too the meeting of land and sea, the convergence of two different topographies, embodies a liminal location.

Having thus already touched on legal matters, the first chapter will now take a closer look at medieval law and disability, in particular how through the effects of legal proceedings the law itself was making bodies disabled, through judicial mutilations. The term 'judicial' is used in the widest sense, so that not just corporal punishments as the result of (crimi-nal) trials are discussed, but also the deliberate use of impairment as part of military actions inflicted by the victors on the vanquished. Mutilation literally inscribed a record of misdemeanour on the body of the defeated or convicted criminal; thus, how a person with disabilities sustained through judicial mutilations might be affected socially will be explored as best as the meagre source material allows. A disabled body could stand under the suspicion of association with a criminal body.

The second chapter looks at how work came to define dis/enabled bodies. Since one of the main reasons for acquired disability—as opposed to congenital disability—was accident or injury, work-related disability, what we would now call industrial accidents or occupational disability, together with compensation for loss of earnings form one of the themes of this chapter. Another section examines how the social support system during the medieval period may have functioned in such cases by looking at guild and fraternity benefits. Common interests led to the creation of mutual aid societies, which throughout the medieval period remained, however, more of a club with clearly defined membership than a provider of universal benefits for all citizens, as in the modern welfare state. "Many social groups . . . [from merchants via artisans to beggars] . . . defined their identity and acquired some modest insurance against illness and disaster by forming confraternities."[46] A critique of the view that disability, in contrast to impairment, was something that only arose as the product of industrial capitalism had been made by Anne Borsay.[47] In an article looking at disability in relation to early eighteenth-century mercantilism, the work imperative and economic rationalities in advance of the Industrial Revolution, Borsay had argued, in response to disability concepts defined by Vic Finkelstein,[48] Michael Oliver[49] and Deborah Stone,[50] that 'disability' had then already been linked to the in/ability to work. I argue that this concept already applied to certainly the later Middle Ages if not earlier. The difference between rural and urban patterns of labour and its implications for disability is addressed, and the chapter concludes with an explosion of the myth that one particular group of disabled people, dwarfs and fools, were stereotyped as courtly entertainers.

The third chapter, 'Ageing', describes how previously able bodies become disabled through pathological physical and mental changes in old age. Contextualised case-studies of disabled old people across a range of social groups (peasants, urban populations, men and women of the church, with a few nobles and rulers) are used in conjunction with normative texts (medical, philosophical, scientific, religious) to investigate notions of disability in old age and to provide a picture of medieval mentalities and attitudes concerning what it meant socially to be old and disabled. The particular abhorrence of the old female body is highlighted, while less gendered themes include the practical aspects of care provisions for the elderly in the form of pensions and corrodies, concluding with an overview of the hitherto neglected topic of senile dementia and depression.

The final chapter, 'Charity', ties together the previous strands of law, work and age as defining factors for the social status of disabled persons, but it also looks at the question of how 'deserving' disabled bodies were deemed to be. "Contemporary concerns with welfare and social policy have led scholars to become interested in the study of poverty and the poor in western Europe during the Middle Ages."[51] Amongst such themes the disabled occupied a special role, and even underpinned changing medieval notions of the idioms of charity. The very powerlessness, literally impotence, of disabled bodies, both socially and economically, permitted their almost unquestioned inclusion among the truly 'needy' and deserving poor—unless accused of fraudulently manipulating and faking their impairments.

1 Law

This chapter investigates medieval laws and the effects of judicial actions.[1] Notions and perceptions of physically impaired people as presented in legal texts can inform us about the status, social position and rights (or restrictions) impaired people may have had. Similarly, the 'evaluation' of impairments in legal discourse can illuminate societal attitudes. Laws imposed restrictions on disabled people, but also protection in some cases, while injury, especially during the earlier Middle Ages, was often dealt with through compensation law. These topics have been discussed specifically in relation to permanent injuries, leading to physical impairments.[2] Conversely, through judicial mutilation in punishment, the law was actually causing impairment. The quantitative statistics surrounding judicial maiming, i.e. the question of how frequently people were physically impaired through punishments and judicial torture, are deliberately disregarded, since there is some controversy as to the extent of these practices which cannot be answered in an overview such as here. The questions of how prevalent physical mutilation really was, in which regions and in which epochs, and where more so than others, also to which extent the practical, 'real' application of written, 'theoretical' law codes was actually carried out, one cannot endeavour to answer with certainty.

The following may serve as illustration of the problem to which extent, at what times, under which circumstances or with what authority such penalties were enacted. In the laws of Cnut (compiled 1020–1023) there seemed to be a reluctance to execute criminals outright; instead there was a sliding scale of judicial mutilation. This followed a principle similar to the modern notion of 'three strikes and you're out'. An accused man, who could be accused of any criminal act although the majority mainly related to theft, had three chances of conviction, with a harsher penalty in each instance: the first conviction could still be resolved by a compensation payment and through wergild, but the second and third instances required corporal punishments:

> [30.4.] And on the second occasion there is to be no other compensation, if he is convicted, but that his hands, or feet, or both, in proportion

to the deed, are to be cut off. [30.5] And if, however, he has committed still further crimes, his eyes are to be put out and his nose and ears and upper lip cut off, or his scalp removed, whichever of these is then decreed by those with whom the decision rests; thus one can punish and at the same time preserve the soul.[3]

Note that in hierarchical terms of impairments, the second level of punishment caused the convicted criminal to have an orthopaedic impairment, while the third level inflicted sensory impairments. Note also the clause denying legal responsibility, in that although it was likely that the third-degree punishments would lead to the death of the convicted man, his death would not have been directly caused by capital punishment, which the laws of Cnut expressly tried to avoid for the sake of "preserv[ing] the soul". In late tenth-century and eleventh-century Anglo-Saxon England, the use of physical punishment was a means to reveal both the crime and its recompense on the body, so that the body was the 'text' for both crime and punishment.[4]

During the Carolingian period mutilation as a form of punishment had been on the increase, but in conjunction with crimes such as arson and theft, which used to carry the death penalty; hence by contemporaries mutilation was regarded as a more lenient approach.[5] Conversely, some crimes were treated more harshly, such as perjury or fraud, which prior to the Carolingian period had been compensated by monetary fines.[6] Throughout the medieval period, mutilating punishments were on the rise, the argument goes. While in twelfth-century Germany hacking off the hand was still the only mutilating punishment, by the thirteenth century a variety of mutilations such as blinding,[7] cutting off ears and so on were now being used.[8] Nevertheless, compensation payment as an alternative to mutilation continued to remain an option,[9] one which was of course more readily available to the wealthy than to the poor. Thus in German historiography, the late Middle Ages were seen as the period when physical punishments, from the amputation of hands to cutting off ears, became an integral part of the judicial process.[10]

It is certainly the case that during the later Middle Ages corporal punishments were coming to be favoured over other punitive measures, such as monetary fines or imprisonment. For instance, around 1500, within a two-week-stretch alone in Nuremberg two men were hung, a charcoal burner was beheaded, an eighty-year-old peasant had both eyes gouged out and a maid who had "stolen much" (*vil gestoln*) had her ears cut off.[11] Judicial practices perhaps echoed or reflected wider social mentalities, so that:

> one of the defining features of this Christianized, late medieval 'paradigm' of punitive justice, namely, a distinctive mode of *judicial spectatorship*, fretted with the visual habits and devotional attitudes unique to this period.[12]

Hints are occasionally provided by the documentary record that mutilating punishments were not necessarily carried out but instead commuted to fines.[13] From a study of the archives of Bruges in the fifteenth century, Malcolm Letts had drawn the conclusion that:

> a large number of offences, which we might expect to be punished by loss of liberty or by mutilation, were dealt with at Bruges by fines only. Fines were imposed for larceny, housebreaking and burglary, threats to murder, wounding, violent and aggravated assaults, adultery, forcible entry, common theft, for *wapeldrink*, a curious ducking offence which was regarded very seriously in Flanders at this time, and for various offences against the peace, which would seem in any age to have merited more serious treatment.[14]

More recently, according to Robert Mills, it seems, too, that "judicial violence was exercised selectively and acquittals and reduction of sentences were often the order of the day"[15] across late medieval Europe. Social historian John Bellamy had put forward the argument that physical punishments, such as judicial mutilation or branding, were relatively rare in England in the high Middle Ages, as compared with either the first century after the Norman conquest or with the fifteenth century and following.[16] Miri Rubin in turn, however, commented that the study of maiming through judicial punishment and torture was hindered by the paucity of medieval sources.[17] The 'classic' portrait of the later Middle Ages as especially 'barbaric' and full of violence (judicial and otherwise) is derived from the opening chapter—"The Violent Tenor of Life"—of an influential volume originally published in 1919, Huizinga's *The Autumn [Waning] of the Middle Ages*.[18]

By the early thirteenth century the Church was becoming more concerned about its clergy being involved in the shedding of blood (i.e. through warfare, practising surgery or by being present at judicial ordeals). Not for nothing were heretics handed over to the secular arm for punishment. The insistence at the council of 1215 that clerics should have no blood on their hands occurred at a time when secular justice was becoming increasingly bloody. Religious and secular legal codes came to differ quite sharply. Canon law had developed gradually from late antiquity through the early Middle Ages, but was substantially collected and systematised around 1140 in Gratian's *Decretum*. By the middle of the thirteenth century this collection had been added to by various papal decrees, coming to be known as *Corpus iuris canonici*. In terms of antecedents, canon law emerged from the old Roman law tradition as well as the early medieval penitentials, the penances in which were almost always non-mutilating (mainly prayer, fasting, etc.). The laws of Cnut did indeed make a claim for spiritual efficacy, but one ought to bear in mind these predated the emergence of formalised canon law by some half century. So once canon law emerged in fully developed form (and in the very early thirteenth century the former lawyer turned pope Innocent III embodied the apogee of this development), the distinction between bloodless canon law and blood-shedding secular law became more apparent.

> As execution and mutilation grew in importance, edging out earlier systems based on compensation, the priest and the clerk found that the rules of their order and the practices of the secular courts were increasingly discordant.[19]

Whereas the older legal systems, both secular and clerical, had tried to avoid bloodshed and mutilation, by the thirteenth century secular legal proceedings began to deviate more strongly from such sentiments which canon law nevertheless still entailed. Interestingly, the re-emergence of Roman law appears to have driven the increased use of judicial mutilation, if the argument presented by Patrick Geary is anything to go by; Roman law had liberally employed "torture, mutilation, and execution . . . both for the interrogation of unfree witnesses and as punishment for a wide range of offenses."[20] An alternative argument made by a number of historians is that with the abolition in 1215 of trial by ordeal, other methods of establishing the 'truth' in a criminal case had to be found, so that interrogation and confession of a suspect became the primary tools of the judiciary.[21] One important question for further research therefore might surround the apparent increase in judicial corporal punishments during the later Middle Ages.

'Judicial' can be interpreted in a very wide sense: the victors assailing the vanquished undoubtedly thought they were acting judiciously and within the moral and legal codes of the day. Thus while injury of combatants in direct battle will be covered in the next chapter, as part of the occupational hazards and disabilities concerning soldiers, here the disabling of non-combatants or of defeated and/or captive soldiers is treated as part of judicial mutilation. According to the thinking of medieval military commanders, the physical mutilation of enemies, and even downright massacre, was considered part of useful, if not always acceptable, military strategy.[22] Despite—or possibly because—many victims did not survive mutilations such as having their eyes gouged out, these tortures were used to demoralise the enemy. Since most victims of such actions tended to be non-combatants, it is more appropriate to consider their fate under 'judicial' mutilation than under occupational disabilities, even if that is stretching the definition of 'judicial' somewhat for modern sensibilities. Having said that, once soldiers ceased to be combatants, in that they were defeated and taken prisoner, they could suffer a similar fate to civilians. "Vanquished warriors but also defenceless peasants needed to reckon with the loss of eyes, noses, hands and feet."[23] This is exactly what happened in 1067 or 1068 at Exeter, when, according to Orderic Vitalis, William the Conqueror had one of his hostages blinded at the gates, that is, within sight of the inhabitants, of the town.[24] Mutilation of the vanquished happened again in 1098 during squabbles between the Armenians and crusaders under Baldwin I in Edessa, when Baldwin ordered that some of the participants in an attempted uprising were to be blinded and others were to have their noses, hands and feet cut off before being banished[25]—hence the assumption, at least on Baldwin's part, that some of the latter might in fact survive these mutilations[26]; otherwise there appears little point in using banishment as an additional sanction.

During the conflict between Bulgarians and Byzantines in the early ninth century, one Bulgarian ruler slit the noses of his Byzantine prisoners before sending them home. Not to be outdone, the Byzantine emperor retaliated "by blinding the great majority of his Bulgarian captives; leaving a handful of one-eyed men to lead the victims back Bulgaria."[27] Byzantine rulers seemed to have a predilection for this kind of mutilation, since in 1014, according to the chronicler Michael Glycas, after another battle against the Bulgarians, the emperor Basileios II Bulgaroktónos (Bulgar-slayer, 976–1025) ordered all the Bulgarian prisoners to be blinded, allowing just one man in every hundred to keep one single eye, so that he could lead his companions home.[28] The first incidence of this form of mutilation was mentioned in Byzantine chronicles with regard to the blinding of Kallinikos, the Patriarch of Constantinople, in 705 on orders of the emperor Justinian II.[29] Other examples include the blinding of general Symbatios, who had led a revolt against Emperor Basil I (867–886).[30] Byzantine sources described three types of blinding: the removal or complete destruction of the eye(s) by mechanical means such as with a dagger or other sharp tool; the destruction of the eye(s) by heat such as with a red-hot iron, or more rarely by boiling oil or vinegar; and a combination of these two methods.[31] The death of the victim was often a "characteristic" result of this form of mutilation, most likely due "to hardship and the possible infection of his wounds".[32] Where the victim survived this ordeal, the eye(s) would have been bound, although this appeared to have been performed more for aesthetic reasons than for medical ones.

> The binding of the eyes after blinding with special bandages, which is mentioned by Anna Comnena [in the *Alexiad*], was not to prevent infection but for the sake of appearances. That is, in order to cover the deformity caused by the usual careless blinding practices.[33]

As will be seen in the following (Chapter 4), in western Christendom also the (public) appearance of deformed and disabled persons did not always elicit sympathy or understanding but could result in aversion, with judicial measures taken to force deformed or mutilated people to cover up and in effect 'hide' their signs of disfigurement.

At the siege of Crema in 1159 during Emperor Frederick I Barbarossa's campaigns against the Lombard towns, the defenders cut off the hands and feet of one of Frederick's captured knights, leaving him to crawl in the streets.[34] According to the chronicler Rahewin, this spectacle of the mutilated and disabled imperial soldier provided "a wanton jest".[35] After the annexation of Cyprus in May 1191 by King Richard (the Lionheart), some Byzantine inhabitants were still resisting, upon which Richard

> was beside himself with fury. He had as many of our people as he could seized and had one of their eyes put out, or their nose cut off, or an arm or a foot mutilated, exacting whatever revenge he could to soothe his rancour.[36]

Two cases from the Albigensian Crusades of the early thirteenth century may illustrate the fact that neither of the opposing parties in a war was squeamish about using mutilation as a punitive measure against defeated soldiers, as well as employing it as a form of psychological warfare to demoralise the enemy. In 1209 Simon de Montfort captured the castle of Bram, and, perhaps aware of the actions of the Byzantine emperors some centuries earlier, mutilated the entire garrison, by cutting off the nose and upper lip, and excising their eyes, except for one man left with a single eye "to guide them to the next fortress that Montfort planned to besiege."[37] And after an ambush against French soldiers in 1228 the Count of Toulouse took as many as two thousand prisoners, wrote Roger of Wendover.

> After they had all been stripped to the skin, the count ordered the eyes of some to be torn out, the ears and noses of others to be slit, and the feet and hands of others to be cut off; after thus shamefully mutilating them, he sent them to their homes, a deformed spectacle to their fellow Frenchmen.[38]

According to Matthew Paris, at Carpaccio in 1246 the emperor Frederick II had the captive leaders of his opponents blinded,[39] and in the Holy Land atrocities were not just something committed between Christians and Moslems but among Christians themselves, such as the blinding of prisoners by Bohemund VII (1261–1287), nominal prince of Antioch and count of Tripoli, in his conflict with Guy of Jebail.[40] On 30 August 1255, the council of Siena (Consiglio della Campana) discussed the methods of punishment to be used against the occupants of the castle of Torniella in Val di Merse, who had rebelled against Siena. As in the aforementioned cases, these were not criminals in the conventional sense but defeated (political) enemies. Some councillors wanted to blind the inhabitants, others to put out one eye of each, some to cut off their hands and feet, others to cut off just one hand and foot each, others still to hang them all.[41] What this catalogue of potentially impairing mutilations demonstrates is, regrettably, the readiness of contemporaries to apply penal mutilations in political and/or military situations. Further cases motivated by political reasons, directed against opposing factions,[42] reinforce this point. In Siena in 1315, the *podestà* attempted to amputate a foot from each of six men who had entered the city in violation of a biased law.[43] Mutilation was actually carried out in 1435 at Nuremberg, when one Ulrich Swurl, who had been banished for a certain period, returned earlier to the city than the terms of his exile allowed, and the executioner cut off two of his fingers.[44]

Urban conflicts escalating into violence had a long history: in eighth- and ninth-century Italy the resolution of power struggles could include "actual and attempted blindings", for example, the case of Constantine, a layman who had been forcibly consecrated as pope, was rapidly deposed in 769 and later blinded.[45] "A vicious purge then followed, with mutilation, blinding or death being meted out"[46] to supporters of various popes and anti-popes in the 760s and 770s. Even the papal chamberlain Paul Afiarta joined in the partisan action, and had his rival, Christopher, a powerful bureaucrat (*primicerius*) of the Lateran, blinded and killed.[47] Then in April 799 two further papal officials, *primicerius* Paschal and the *sacellarius* Campulus attacked Pope Leo III, "attempted to blind him and confined him in the monastery of S. Erasmo."[48] The vogue for blinding did not end here, for in the 790s a spate of political mutilations was plaguing the Byzantine Empire. Emperor Constantine VI had the eyes of his uncle Nikephoros put out and the tongues of his father's four half brothers cut off, and he blinded the Armenian general Alexios Moselè. In a twist to the fate of his victims, the emperor himself was eventually blinded by supporters of his own mother, Irene, in 797; he died from his wounds a few days later.[49] All this violence was connected with the upheavals known to history as the iconoclast struggle, centred on the distinction between the veneration and adoration of images. It is perhaps no coincidence that the eyes were those body parts that were especially targetted, since one needed eyes to see images in the first place, so what more fitting punishment for those who regarded images in the wrong way than to deprive them of the physical capability of doing so. Furthermore, imperial power and the sun's rays were equivalents, according to the chronicler Theophanes; hence "blinding was chosen at Byzantium as the mutilation irreconcilable with the possession or expectation of supreme power."[50]

In times of weak central authority private feuding could also lead to private meting out of so-called justice, when rival and power-hungry nobles did not shy away from mutilating their opponents, as happened in mid-eleventh-century Normandy, where William Talvas, the son of William de Bellême, cut off William Giroie's eyes, ears and genitals after inviting him under false pretences to a wedding feast.[51] Orderic Vitalis recounted that a near-namesake, Robert of Bellême, had the unsavoury habit of blinding men and cutting off their hands and feet in order to obtain ransoms, leaving his unfortunate victims "deformed" and "useless",[52] something which was apparently practised, too, by Count Raymond of Toulouse as late as 1188, who was accused of deliberately targeting wealthy Aquitanian merchants, "blinding and castrating some and imprisoning others, presumably to get ransoms from them."[53] Orderic Vitalis also recorded the despicable tit-for-tat treatment of hostages, when Eustace, the son in law of Henry I, held the son of Ralph Harenc as hostage, for which in return Henry I held his own granddaughters, the daughters of Eustace, hostage; Eustace proceeded to blind the son of Ralph, upon which Ralph approached Henry I and asked to be handed over the (grand)daughters, whom in an act of vengeance Ralph then had blinded in turn, plus had the tips of their nostrils cut off.[54]

In the early twelfth century Waleran of Meulan, only slightly less a villain than Robert, while in open revolt against Henry I captured peasants who were hiding out in the forest and cut off their feet[55]—presumably since peasants were royal 'resources' that could be targeted primarily in an attempt to damage Henry I economically without even considering the plight of the thus disabled peasants. A similar attack on the non-combative population with the aim of using mutilation as an extreme form of economic plunder is recounted during the Albigensian Crusade. A heretic couple belonging to the local nobility, Bernard of Cazenac and his wife, allegedly left 150 men and women "with arms or legs amputated, eyes gouged out or other members cut, mutilated by the aforesaid tyrant and his wife" at the Benedictine monastery of Sarlat; even the wife participated in these atrocities, cutting off the breasts of poor women or tearing away their thumbs "thus rending them incapable of work."[56] The last point emphasises that behind all the lurid descriptions of mutilations often lurked an even more disagreeable rationale for carrying them out in the first place: the powerful employing a scorched earth approach on the bodies of the powerless subjects of the enemy.

For all the preceding examples we have only textual sources to go by for the deliberate mutilation of non-combatants,[57] if one discounts the many representations of the biblical Massacre of the Innocents. But from the very end of the medieval period there is one shocking depiction of a mutilated civilian. In 1514 Urs Graf, a Swiss artist who himself had been a mercenary, engraved a young woman standing against a wonderfully detailed, even romantic landscape.[58] However, the fashionably dressed woman has no arms, a peg leg substitutes for her right leg and she appears to be blind in one eye. Whether the maimed woman was a camp follower or an unfortunate civilian, her mutilations horrifically confront the viewer with the brutality and violence of late medieval warfare.[59] According to David Nicolle, "mutilation persisted longer in fringe areas like Ireland than elsewhere".[60] Space and scope of this chapter does not permit a headlong canter into the wider debate as to whether the 'chivalric' code really did have an impact on the conduct of combatants or not,[61] suffice it to point out that warfare remained a brutal affair—as it still is—and contributed greatly to the sheer numbers of physically disabled persons, mainly men, left in its wake.[62]

Maiming, as threat or actual punishment, was a useful disciplinary tool. During King John's conflict with the barons in the winter of 1215–1216 a man who had stolen a cow from a churchyard had a hand cut off on orders of the marshal of John's army;[63] this may just be a regular criminal act finding its way into the court records, but if the man was a member of the Royal Army it may also indicate attempts to enforce military discipline. Although as a mutilated one-handed person the man in question would hardly have been able to participate in further military campaigning. King John's older brother, Richard I, had issued decrees at Chinon for the behaviour of the sailors who were to ship him and his troops on Crusade, among them a stipulation for the loss of a hand in the event of brawling attacks which drew blood.[64] Before a battle during his Crusade, Richard threatened that any soldier "who ran away on foot should lose a foot".[65] Nearly a century earlier at the siege of Ascalon in 1099 Duke Godfrey had similarly used mutilation as a threat and pronounced that any crusaders who "touched booty before battle" should have their ears and noses cut off.[66] Using mutilation, or the threat of it, as a means to enforce military discipline was apparently also practised by Henry V on the eve of the battle of Agincourt: if any of his men below the rank of yeoman made any noise that would give their location away to the enemy, their right ear would be cut off.[67] Ironically, in his speech to the troops just before the battle, Henry V then accused the French of intended mutilation, in that they had threatened to cut off three fingers off the right hand of each archer, to render them incapable of any future archery.[68] Based on alleged prior experience with one's opponent, accusing the enemy of mutilation, amongst other atrocities, was a useful propaganda tool.[69]

Mutilation needs to be understood in the light of medieval legal thinking overall. The kind of mentality expressed by the *usatges* of Barcelona is typical:

> Since the rendering of justice in regard to criminals—namely, concerning murderers, adulterers, sorcerers, robbers, rapists, traitors, and other men—is granted only to the rulers, thus let them render justice as it seems fit to them: by cutting off hands and feet, putting out eyes, keeping men in prison for a long time and, ultimately, in hanging their bodies if necessary.[70]

It has been argued that as the use of the death penalty increased, compared to the earlier and high Middle Ages, so did judicial mutilation, which was seen as the compromise solution between enforcing and upholding the law and showing leniency.

> Clemency meant commuting the death penalty to mutilation: eyes, noses, ears, hands, feet and testicles were the most frequent payments for life; in many cases, mutilation was the standard, mandatory sentence.[71]

For example, an English collection of legal articles compiled around 1110–1135 stated that eyes should be gouged out and testicles cut off rather than

killing or hanging the culprit.[72] The *Laws of Henry I* were no less dra-
conian, in that the penalty for moneyers minting fake coins was to have
their hand cut off.[73] According to the mid-twelfth-century treatise known
as *Glanvill*, the crimes of killing of one's lord, concealment of treasure,
breach of the king's peace, homicide, arson robbery, rape and falsifying
(i.e. forgery) were all to be "punished by death or cutting off of limbs",
while judgment over whether to carry out this penalty in criminal pleas was
reserved to royal clemency.[74] These developments in England had followed
on from earlier commutation of the death penalty to mutilation elsewhere
in Europe. Already the Visigoths in the early seventh century punished
criminals by blinding rather than applying the death sentence, especially in
an article formulated in relation to rebels under the rule of Chindaswinth
(642–653), where nevertheless loss of eyesight is explicitly treated as substitute for capital punishment:

> But if perhaps out of the promptings of piety his life should be spared
> by the prince, let this not happen unless his gouged-out eyes are taken
> in place of his life, so that he may not see the damage by which he has
> wickedly been lured.[75]

In 818 Emperor Louis the Pious neglected to include his nephew Bernhard
in discussions about partial rule of his territory, so that Bernhard rebelled,
was initially sentenced to death but had that sentence commuted to blinding—which in fact he did not survive.[76] During an uprising at Mainz in 866
against Archbishop Liutbert some of his men were killed, but the perpetrators were caught and justice was meted out "with great severity", so that
"some were hanged, others had their fingers and toes cut off, or were even
blinded".[77] And in 885 Godafrid (Gottfried), one of the Danish kings, and
Hugh of Lotharingia were blinded for their conspiracy against Emperor
Charles the Fat, an ordeal which they survived, spending the rest of their
days under house arrest in the monastery of Fulda.[78] In this context it is
interesting to note the use of a claustral site for elite political prisoners.

Orderic Vitalis mentioned the English rebels defeated in 1075 all had
their right foot cut off, regardless of rank.[79] During the reign of Henry
I, a chamberlain who had tried to assassinate the king was blinded and
castrated, rather than being hung, which would have been the normal
penalty for this deed, according to Suger.[80] In 1221 one Thomas of Elder-
sfield was blinded and castrated instead of being hung in a demonstration
of judicial 'leniency'.[81]

Sometimes leniency related to age, as underage culprits were not to be
physically punished. According to the statutes promulgated by the city
of Cologne in 1083, relating to the Peace of God initiative,[82] one should
refrain from hacking off the hands of a peace-breaker who was less than
twelve years old—presumably boys over twelve were considered capable
of bearing arms and therefore merited the same treatment as adults.[83] The

early thirteenth-century *Sachsenspiegel* echoed these sentiments, also stating that neither capital nor mutilating punishments were to be inflicted on children.[84] Leniency of sorts was shown toward pregnant women, too. In Brünn during the fourteenth century two women had been accused of trying to sell a child to the Jews, and the punishments were meted out accordingly, so that one woman was buried alive, but the other, who was pregnant at the time, had her sentence commuted 'only' to blinding.[85]

Mutilation may have, if the victim was able to survive the ordeal, been more 'lenient' than capital punishment, but different kinds of mutilation existed in a hierarchy of shame as well as severity. Castration, for instance, may initially not appear to be as 'disabling' as loss of eyes, hands or feet (all of which would seriously impair the victim's ability to function in daily life), but could at times be regarded as a worse mutilation, as this anecdote from Liudprand of Cremona's *Antapodosis* makes clear. In the tenth century Tedbald, marquess of Spoleto, had taken captive some warriors sallying from a fortress and threatened to castrate them in punishment; the wife of one man argued successfully that Tedbald may rob their cattle, and even remove the noses, eyes, hands and feet of the captives, but not their testicles, since, she argued wittily, the other body parts belonged to the men, but the testicles rightfully to the women, as without these the women could have neither pleasure nor children.[86] Physical 'functioning' in medieval terms is therefore not just about being able to have unimpeded mobility, or intact sensory perception, but also connected to gender, fertility and procreative ability.[87]

The desired effect of judicial mutilation was to act as a visible deterrent, at least in theory, but in a more practical if not brutally direct fashion mutilation prevented a law-breaker from committing the same crime again. Already between 688 and 694 the laws of Ine, king of Wessex, had stipulated:

> 18. If a commoner, who has often been accused, is at last caught [in the act], his hand or foot shall be cut off. . . .

> 37. If a commoner has often been accused of theft and is at last proved guilty, either in the ordeal or by being caught in the act of committing an offence, his hand or foot shall be struck off.[88]

A thief who had had his hand cut off was hardly in the physical position to continue a career as a pickpocket, even if of course it did not mean that the mutilated thief was incapable of other criminal activities. More problematic as a measure of crime prevention is the mutilation of recidivist thieves by 'cropping' their ears, a legal right which the bishop of Paris maintained throughout the later Middle Ages,[89] and which was also a custom in the Bordeaux and Bayonne regions during the fourteenth and fifteenth centuries.[90] Simply cutting the outer ears would not physically prevent someone from being capable of carrying out theft, nor did it actually cause significant hearing impairments, since the inner ear would not be damaged by this action, but it did 'mark' the person as a convicted criminal, with the consequence that such people were often likely to be set further on a downward spiral of delinquency. As Lisi Oliver has noted with regard to the 'barbarian' compensation tariffs, the:

> regulation of the ear presents the converse to that for the eye: if the ear has been struck off but hearing is not damaged, the fine is half what it would be for striking off the ear and causing deafness.[91]

At Bruges in the fifteenth century offenders were sometimes nailed by their ears to the pillory so that they had to tear themselves free.[92] In various late-medieval German cities, too, the amputation of ears was "almost a universal punishment for small thieves" and other minor crimes, an attitude exemplified by the burghers of Nuremberg, who named that place where corporal punishments were meted out the "ear pillory" (*Ohrenstock*), after the most frequent type.[93] Legal records from Bamberg mention one Hans Lobeles, a cook originating from Worms on the Rhine, who in 1424 was caught red-handed cutting off people's moneybags. As punishment he had his ears cut off, was branded on both cheeks and was banished permanently from Bamberg.[94]

Apart from punishment through the immediate pain of mutilation, the future visible damage to the ears was intended to permanently inscribe the misdemeanour on the body of the convicted criminal. Particularly mutilations to the faces of women seem to fall into this category, such as the penalty for adultery of cutting off the woman's nose, which can be found in the earliest laws of the kingdom of Jerusalem, the canons of the council of Nablus (1120).[95] Already in the fifth century Gaiseric, king of the Vandals, ordered his Gothic wife's nose and ears mutilated, having accused her of plotting against him.[96] In literature, too, one finds the imagery of facial mutilation as a trope for the punishment of women's disobedience, in particular marital insubordination, for instance, in the tale of *Bisclavret* in the twelfth-century *Lais* of Marie de France; there the werewolf Bisclavret, betrayed by his wife, attacks her and tears her nose from her face; exiled from the court, she lives on to conceive female offspring born without noses.[97] Nasal mutilation can be especially associated with women's deviant behaviour. The fourteenth-century books of banishment (*Achtbücher*) of Augsburg mention a "noseless whore from Ulm"; cutting off the nose was an Augsburg penalty affecting prostitutes found soliciting in forbidden places or at forbidden times.[98] Valentin Groebner states *denasatio*, the cutting off of the nose, is particularly loaded with sexual connotations: "Medieval scholars described strong links between a person's nose and his or her sexual activities."[99] But the nose, as the most prominent part of the face, also served as a more general indicator of the aesthetic and even moral qualities of a person, to such extent that both Albertus Magnus in the thirteenth century and the municipal authorities of the Alsatian town of Kaysersberg in 1485 could agree that removal of the nose was an act of disfigurement affecting the whole person.[100] As far as visible corporal punishments were concerned, removal of the nose was the most immediately apparent mutilation, observable on the body of the convicted by others before they may have noticed blinded eyes or absent hands. It seems, then, that corporal mutilation was intended primarily as highly visible and immediate reminder of the powers of justice, although more refined secondary considerations could enter into the justification:

> Other times the intent [of judicial mutilation] was more subtle: at least one early medieval source justifies blinding so that the guilty party could not see the damage he had wrought, and so take no satisfaction in it.[101]

In terms of punishment for politically motivated transgressions (revolts and uprisings) the authorities also realised the deterrent effects of mutilation as a highly visual statement to reaffirm the status quo and prevent further insubordination. For instance, the rebellion of Norman peasants in 977 was described by Wace in the *Roman de Rou*, concerning the deeds of Rollo, Duke of Normandy. The peasants secretly held assemblies, swore oaths of mutual assistance and in effect tried to form a commune, which Rollo brutally repressed, pulling out the teeth of many, impaling others, having the eyes torn out or the fists cut off of yet more.[102] The poet described that those, who, presumably, survived the ordeal "were hideous to look at. / They could not been [*sic*] seen in that place from then on / Without being well recognized."[103] Everyone in the area therefore was reminded of the failed uprising and the ensuing seigneurial vengeance by the aspect of these maimed peasants. To address the historical balance, it is worth pointing out that sometimes revolting peasants were not the victims but themselves the perpetrators, as occurred in the following case during the fifteenth century: the prior of the Benedictine monastery of Merseburg was attacked while collecting tithes, and the peasants "cut off both his [upper and lower] lips, his nose and most of his right ear".[104]

Judicial mutilation was sanctioned not just by temporal law, but it was also underpinned by religious notions. Many hagiographical narratives mention the intervention of a saint to physically punish a miscreant; such punishments often resulted in physically impairing conditions such as loss of limbs or eyes. Just one example may suffice as illustration. Anglo-Norman records mention a pickpocket who was caught in the act of thieving by Saint Ecgwin and who was subsequently punished by the saint, who caused the thief's hand to be trapped in the purse from which he was trying to steal and then made the hand shrivel up.[105] Saints of course did not just punish; they helped the victims of judicial mutilation, too—miracles are a bit of a double-edged sword in the narratives. Saint Swithun miraculously restored to health and physical integrity a man who had been judicially mutilated (in error, one does well to note) so that he was scalped and blinded, and his nose, ears, hands and feet were all cut off:

> At the command of the glorious king Edgar, a law (*lex*) . . . was promulgated throughout England, to serve as a deterrent against all sorts of crime . . . that if any thief or robber were found anywhere in the *patria*, he would be tortured at length (*excruciaretur diutius*) by having his eyes put out, his hands cut off, his ears torn off, his nostrils carved open and his feet removed; and finally, with the skin and hair of his head shaved off, he would be abandoned in the open fields dead in respect of nearly all his limbs, to be devoured by wild beasts and birds and hounds of the night.
>
> (*Rex Eadgarus ob coercenda furta lege sanxit, ut in furto deprehensus oculis privaretur, auribus, manibus pedibusque praecisis, cute capitis nudaretur sicque feris et avibus laniandus obiceretur.*)[106]

Since this is the complete list of all the mutilating punishments, bar removal of testicles, that might be carried out individually, it seems Saint Swithun's miracle provided blanket coverage for a hypothetical miscarriage of justice case.[107] In the miracle narrative, the innocent man was rescued by his friends and relatives, but he had to languish for some three and a half months in this condition before he was cured by the power of the saintly relics. Commenting on the removal of hands and feet, eyes and testicles in English legal practice of the thirteenth century, one historian believed that:

> the popularity of stories in which a St Wulfstan of Worcester or St Thomas of Canterbury makes whole again the mutilated felon is some indication of the frequency of these horrible punishments.[108]

In 1170 a man called Ailward had failed to prove his innocence in trial by ordeal, so that now his eyes were put out and he was castrated for good measure, too; through his devotion to Saint Thomas Becket both his eyes and testicles were later restored.[109] And saints could themselves become the victims of judicial, in this case politically motivated, mutilation. A seventh-century example concerns Saint Leudegar, bishop of Autun, who became embroiled in a royal Frankish power struggle, resulting in his lips being cut and his tongue amputated by Ebroin, the *maior domus* of one of the rival kings, so that his ability to officiate as bishop became compromised.[110]

Even heretics, ironically often themselves the victims of judicial mutilation, could argue that the principle of mutilation as perfectly acceptable judicial penalty was justified. A Cathar heretic and Vaudois deacon, Raymoind de Sainte-Foix, said in reply to questioning by the inquisitor Jacques Fournier in 1321 "that it is permissible for secular authority to put to death

or to mutilate malefactors, for without such actions there would be neither peace no security amongst men".[111] The belief in the deterrent effects
of mutilating punishments appears to have been so prevalent that even
endangered groups themselves supported the arguments for their efficacy
in upholding law and order.

By the later Middle Ages torture had joined judicial mutilation as
accepted legal means, in this case to extract information or confession
rather than primarily as punishment, although of course the physical
and mental effects were little different.[112] In France, Italy and Germany
torture had become part of the judicial armoury by the thirteenth century, and during the fourteenth "it was common procedure."[113] Torture
seems to have had some supporters, but one may also hear voices warning against its widespread usage, for instance, the statutes of Vercelli
(Italy), which restricted torture to "known criminals, thieves or men of
ill-fame", while the statutes of Bologna made it difficult for any citizen
of that city to be subjected to torture. In 1254 Louis IX of France forbade the torture of "honest people of good reputations, even if they are
poor."[114]. By the fifteenth century, the gruesome subject of torture came
to be used as a tool in nationalistic propaganda, as when the eminent
writer in praise of English jurisprudence, Sir John Fortescue, chastised
the French judicial system for the inhumanity of using tortures, basing
his criticism on the argument that its use perverted the course of justice,
since the accused wretches were compelled by irresistible torments alone
and not the truth of the matter (*miseri faciunt, non veritatis causa, sed
solum urgentibus torturis arctati*).[115] If the alleged criminal survived torture, and was perhaps even acquitted, permanent physical impairment,
never mind mental scars, was a likely outcome, what with distorted
limbs and fractured bones due to the process. For example, according to
William of Tyre, during the siege of Jerusalem in 1099, Gerard, a Frankish cleric who administered the hospital that would later be known as
the Hospital of Saint John, was subjected to torture while in prison, "so
terrible that the joints of both his hands and feet were wrenched apart
and his limbs became practically useless."[116] And after the failure of the
Seventh Crusade in 1250 Joinville described a form of torture, the *barnacle*, nearly inflicted on King Louis IX of France, in which a person's leg
was placed between two pieces of wood fitted with teeth, so that when
weighted down, the planks caused multiple fractures in the leg; the process was repeated after three days "when the legs have become inflamed,
they put the swollen limbs back into the *barnacle*, and crush the bones
all over again."[117]

Judicial mutilation is, of course, also a question of status. While the
wealthy, powerful and noble were generally able to make compensation
payments, the poor, impotent and, especially in the earlier Middle Ages,
unfree were more likely to be subject to violent punishments. According to
Frankish law, mutilation punishments could usually be transmuted into a

monetary fine and only if the accused could not pay was the corporal punishment carried out in practice.[118]

Physical violence covered not just judicial mutilation for offences such as theft, but also the intimation of mutilation to keep *servi* and other lower orders in their place. In the ninth century Saint Gerald of Aurillac "threatened his servi with mutilation to end their indolence", and Gregory of Tours stated King Childebert II had the ears (and the hair—perhaps scalp?) of his *servus* Droctulf cut off.[119] After the slave of one Sichar tried to revolt, by grabbing his master's sword and wounding him with it, the slave had his hands and feet cut off in punishment.[120] An anonymous Carolingian poem, the *Carmen de Timone comite*, composed in Bavaria in the mid-ninth century, sums up the types of judicial mutilation facing criminals:

> Therefore, when the count arrives, he orders that thieves be hanged,
> And that the cheeks of robbers be forever branded.
> That criminals be disgracefully maimed by having their noses cut off;
> This one loses a foot, and that one loses a hand.[121]

Another Carolingian poem, the *Comparison of Ancient and Modern Laws* by Theodulf of Orléans, presented such punishments in even more gruesome detail:

> Modern law takes away the eyes, the source of begetting beautiful offspring, a leg and hand at the same time. They order that backs be cut with brands, lead be poured into the mouth, that ears, noses and all that is beautiful be cut off. They order that swift feet be amputated and that with a rope around it, the neck, suspended from a high pole, should bear the weight of a thief.[122]

Licit violence sanctioned by the rulers was (and still is) employed to curb the illicit. In England in 1222, the ringleader of a riot that had erupted after a wrestling match had turned too boisterous was executed, while his companions in the riot had their hands and feet amputated in punishment, according to Roger of Wendover.[123] Violence among private individuals was punished by violence enforced by the authorities in the Crusader states, too, such as the amputation of both hands followed by banishment for men accused of being compatriots to a murderer.[124]

A special punishment was reserved for slander and blasphemy. The ninth-century laws of Wessex had already demanded cutting out the tongue as penalty for slander, unless the perpetrator was wealthy enough to redeem it by paying a fine instead.[125] At Bruges during the second half of the fifteenth century, "blasphemy and seditious and evil speaking were punished by piercing the offender's tongue or cutting off a piece of it."[126] In 1484 a woman called Martine was punished for blasphemy by being branded with red-hot irons, bound to a stake and finally a piece of her tongue was cut off, after which she was banished for six years for good measure as well. In 1477 Gisbrecht Wauters had his tongue bored through with a red-hot iron for the same offence.[127] The Castilian Cortes of 1462 imposed amputation of the tongue among a range of penalties for blasphemy.[128] The Estates of Provence announced the following punishments for blasphemy in 1472: a first offence merited a day in the stocks followed by a month in prison, the second offence was punished by the splitting of the upper lip, a third offence caused splitting of the lower lip and in a fourth the entire lower lip was severed, while finally the tongue would be cut out completely.[129] Branding the lips of a blasphemer, as happened in France for repeat offenders, would result in destruction of the lips, leaving the victim with an appearance that mimicked leprosy, thus adding an extra dimension to the physical mark of punishment for a crime.[130] In Germany, the tongue might be split in punishment for blasphemy. Antecedents were already found in the laws of Alfred, dating from the 890s, which promulgated cutting out the tongue as punishment for slander.[131] Such a 'telling' punishment, of course, is meant to reflect the nature of the crime, with that body part being mutilated that the person had employed to commit the crime in the first place. A similar notion seems to have been present in the early thirteenth-century *Sachsenspiegel*, when cutting out the tongue is promulgated as punishment for not adhering to royal bans and if the culprit is unable to, literally, loosen his tongue with payment of a fine.[132] In an extreme version of the 'telling' punishment, during the period of the Crusader kingdoms, even a medical practitioner who "was convicted of malpractice so that a free man was maimed or disabled by substandard treatment"[133] might suffer penal mutilation, at Cyprus the amputation of the entire hand, while if he was lucky enough to be a physician in Jerusalem then just the right thumb; in both cases the principle of punishing the offending person or the agent of their offence (the surgeon's hand) was carried to its utmost logical conclusion.

An example from a literary text demonstrates how far the mentality of support for judicial mutilation, its acceptance as the lawful, just and correct punishment for a variety of criminal acts, penetrated into medieval consciousness. In the mid-thirteenth century Wernher der Gartenaere (the Gardener), a Bavarian or Austrian author, composed the satirical verse epic *Meier Helmbrecht*, in which the eponymous protagonist, an upwardly mobile peasant, attempts to live like a lord but ends up only in becoming a brigand, torturing and murdering his fellow peasants; eventually he gets apprehended by the lord's bailiff and for his just desserts has the same kind of punishment inflicted on him that he had inflicted on the peasants he stole from. The executioner put out Helmbrecht's eyes and cut off one of his hands and one of his feet, so that now as a blind and crippled man the former robber had to use a stick and be guided by a boy, thus wandering around the countryside. No peasant he encountered failed to shout at Helmbrecht: "Ha ha! Helmbrecht the robber! If you had stayed on the farm like me you would not be being led around blind" (*hâhâ, diep Helmbreht!*

/ *hêtest dû gebûwen alsam ich, / sô züge man nû niht blinden dich!* [lines 1818–20]).[134] The peasants' admonitions highlight not just an element of *Schadenfreude*, but reinforce acceptance of the principle of the punishment emulating the crime. In England, the satirical-political early fourteenth-century *An Outlaw's Song of Trailbaston* conveyed some critical sentiments towards the tendency of official law to mete out harsh punishments. The anonymous author threatens bad jurors who will not reform with the same mutilations as they were wont to proclaim: "I will teach them the game of Trailbaston and will break their backs and their rumps, their arms and their legs. it would be reasonable; I will cut out their tongues and their lips as well."[135]

Once a person had been tried, convicted and received judicial mutilation, their body was forever 'marked' by their crime and their punishment. What did it mean to be so 'marked', and how did that set a disabled person apart from 'ordinary' impaired people? Such a person's future life was dangerous, since the very visibility of their corporal markings proclaimed 'convicted criminal' to all and sundry.

> If such tortures and punishments really were handed out on a regular basis by those in power at the time, then it might be expected that a significant proportion of the population would have suffered disability or disfigurement of some kind.[136]

How a person with disabilities sustained through judicial mutilations might be affected socially should thus be explored as best as possible, even if the sources are rather reticent. Automatic conviction could ensue if a 'marked' person was apprehended. This is embodied in the sentiments of the municipal laws of Goslar, which stated that even in cases of very minor theft (normally not subject to capital punishment) a thief should be hung if "on his person he carries those signs that wrong-doing people commonly have."[137] By the sixteenth century this concept was still present, as Franciscus Vellesius, physician to Philip II of Spain, could state: "If two people fall under suspicion of crime, let him be put to torture first who has a deformed aspect."[138] A disabled body had come to be associated with a criminal body.

The sources very occasionally provide hints as to the mental or psychological effects of encounters with the law, such as the story of one Sebald from Nuremberg, whose wife, Susanna Previgne Leonardi *piliatoris*, originally from Vienna, sought annulment of their marriage in 1480. Apparently, Sebald changed his character for the worse, so that because of his crimes he was mutilated and his nose, ears and upper lip were cut off. One should note that it was due to his behaviour, and not his physical appearance, that Susanna asked for annulment.[139] The disabled need not only be the victims of judicial punishments, but could sometimes be active agents of criminal deeds, as a curious case from Cologne in 1486 shows. Two disabled men, the cripples Hans van Spire and Johann van Coellen, were the perpetrators of an apparent homicide. Hans accused Johann of having strangled a night watchman and then having strung him up by his armour (*Harnisch*), an act which the court found would have been impossible for a cripple to be physically capable of—the night watchman had probably committed suicide. During the trial both Johann and his wife were put to torture (*versoicht ind swairlich gepinget*) but remained steadfast and would not confess. Then Hans was tortured and quickly confessed that he had made the accusation out of hatred and spite. The upshot was that Hans was sentenced to death for false accusations as if he had carried out the homicide which never was one.[140]

From the trial of the so-called 'Coquillards' gang in Dijon in 1455 a number of individuals with 'incriminating' names can be sourced, that is, with names that indicate a physical characteristic that the person in question was likely to have sustained through mutilation, more often than not of the judicial sort. They included "The One-eyed Burgundian, Simon le Double, whose upper lip is split, Godeaul, who has only one ear" and their "earlier encounters with the law are attested in these split lips and lopped ears".[141] Late medieval German records, too, reflect the effects of judicial mutilation in the (nick)names given for some people, such as "Walburg with the stump", "the handless tailor" or "Ellen the earless".[142] The Augsburg books of banishment (*Achtbücher*) of the fourteenth century mention a "noseless Anna".[143]

With both the visible marks of mutilation and disreputable names signifying prior encounters with the judiciary, it is not surprising that other disabled people went to great lengths to prove that the impairment or deformation they had was *not* due to a corporal punishment. In England during the reign of Edward I a man called John de Roghton was accidentally mutilated when a horse kicked him so that he lost his left ear. He obtained "a certificate stating that the injury in question had not been sustained as punishment for any crime."[144] And, regrettably without mentioning further details, Carole Rawcliffe asserts:

> The loss of an ear (frequently sustained by those who had been nailed to a post or pillory) constituted such a mark of shame that soldiers who suffered this type of injury in warfare reputedly asked for letters explaining their appearance, lest they be taken for criminals.[145]

In 1445 the Hospitallers issued "certificates of mutilation" to men who had to have a hand amputated,[146] following Mamluk attacks on the island of Rhodes, and who as war casualties were not to be mistaken for common criminals. In Germany in 1393 a letter was issued by the mayor and the council of the town of Recklinghausen in support of one Johannes Marten. In the course of a feud between Count Dietrich von der Mark (†1398) and Archbishop Friedrich von Saarweden of Cologne (†1414), Marten had fought on the count's side. Unfortunately he was captured by the archbishop's men and was blinded in an act of revenge, since earlier the count had ordered the eyes be put out of any captured archiepiscopal supporters. In addition to blinding, during his captivity Marten suffered from frostbite so that one of his feet had to be amputated. The letter of good conduct emphasised that Marten had not been mutilated thus due to any misdemeanour, adding that he was now reliant on begging or on being accepted into a hospital. This statement of having been made disabled without any fault was a lifesaving necessity for Marten.[147]

Measures to 'clear one's name' included providing eminent or honourable witnesses who could affirm the non-judicial cause of a disability. An English example is provided in 1285, when Peter Peverer of Essex felt compelled to notify the authorities that he had lost his eyes through disease and not punishment.[148] In Germany, pigs presented troublesome factors, as occurred in the case of a man who had an ear bitten off by a pig when he was still a child.[149] With pigs running loose in urban streets this must have been a not unusual incident, and a number of cases involving children suffering accidental attacks by pigs are known from the sources. Here are just two. On 14 May 1420 in Lübeck young Arnold produced five well-known persons who

> appeared before the council, and after swearing the oath with upright fingers and uplifted arms made the sworn testimony, that Arnold, son of Johannes Heyzen, had in early childhood been bitten by a pig on the street which with bestial bite had removed part of his right (external) ear and that he did not lose this part of his ear in any other way.
>
> (*[5 namentliche genannte Personen], vor dem Rat erschienen, haben nach Ableistung des Eides mit aufgereckten Fingern und Erhebung ihrer Arme die eidliche Aussage gemacht, dass dem Arnold, Sohn des Johannes Heyzen, im frühen Kindesalter auf der Straße ein Schwein mit viehischem Biss einen Teil seiner rechten Ohrmuschel abgebissen hat und dass er diesen Teil seiner Ohrmuschel auf keine andere Weise eingebüßt hat.*)[150]

In 1455 a woman called Anna from the diocese of Basle presented the following case to the papal curia. As a small girl Anna had lost her left hand, which pigs came and ate off, but now as an adult she had been kept encloistered after the fashion of the Benedictine nuns, even hidden away, since her parents and friends felt awkward about her missing hand.[151] The anxiety could relate to unwelcome associations of one-handedness with judicial mutilation. The story then took a few dramatic turns. Anna was moved to another convent and forced to beg, so she rebelled and ran away from the cloister, returning to a secular life. Like all good stories, this one had a 'happy ending' of sorts, since the last we hear of Anna is that she had married and become a mother—it was at this point in her life that she had written to the curia asking for dispensation. Her missing hand turned out to be neither a romantic nor a legal impediment to marriage,[152] and she went on to lead a fulfilled life within the limits of what was generally deemed desirable for medieval women (marriage and motherhood).

So far I have provided examples of how people could be deliberately impaired through the application of violence and physical force in the course of legal proceedings. However, even where no one was judicially mutilated as part of carrying out a sentence, or assaulted and maimed during attacks on non-combatants in times of war, people could sometimes still end up with a lasting impairment as a result of being imprisoned. Medieval prisons were notorious for being dark, damp and cold places, even when they were not the stereotypical underground dungeons, whose aim was to keep the incarcerated out of sight and out of people's mind—"it was no accident that by the fourteenth century jails in French castles were known as *oubliettes*".[153] The longer the term of imprisonment, the more likely that the prisoner suffered some form of ill-health leading to permanent impairment, most commonly partial or temporary blindness and impaired vision, due to lack of (sun)light. There is anecdotal evidence that incarceration in the infamous Bottle Dungeon at Saint Andrews Castle was responsible for permanent blindness, "presumably a fate shared by others kept for long periods in similar conditions."[154] During the reign of Henry III the assizes held at Ludinglond recorded:

> The jury present that William le Sauvage took two men, aliens, and one woman, and imprisoned them at Thorlestan, and detained them in prison until one of them died in prison and the other lost one foot, and the woman lost either foot by putrefaction.[155]

So even if the medieval judicial system did not always actively (materially and physically) mutilate people, other facets of the law had the side effect of disabling them almost by chance. It is little wonder, then, that tending to prisoners came to be considered one of the Seven Corporal Acts of Mercy. However, as a recent study has demonstrated, north Italian prisons in an urban context "were far from dumping grounds"[156] and underwent modifications throughout the late thirteenth and fourteenth centuries that in some cases included the provision of rudimentary medical care for inmates. Over the course of these centuries prison terms in Italy came to be longer (incarceration was beginning to be used in what was to become the modern sense of penal confinement), which meant that some prisoners could be expected to suffer sickness and disability. During the later Middle Ages in Venice, which did not possess a prison infirmary as such until 1563, "sick prisoners could be released[157], separated or kept under ameliorated conditions",[158] although the authorities soon came to ensure that any periods of incapacity did not count towards the overall length of the sentence.

The hospital of Santi Pietro e Paolo catered in part to wounded soldiers but also to thieves whose hands had been cut off, according to a description of charitable institutions made by the Milanese ambassador to Venice in 1497.[159] To deter violence among inmates in 1355 the Florentine authorities threatened amputation of an arm to any prisoner who injured another and did not "pay the condemnation within eight days",[160] which demonstrates that even once the idea of confinement as punishment in itself was beginning to take hold, mutilation was still regarded as part of the judicial armoury when lesser measures were deemed ineffective. In Florence, which in the Stinche possessed the "flagship prison of late-medieval Italy",[161] a physician was hired, who, interestingly enough, had among his remits "the supervision and post-traumatic care of punitive amputations",[162] which leads us full circle back to disablement through judicial mutilation, only this time under official medical supervision.

Medical or social care of sorts was also provided by some of the German cities, such as Frankfurt, where those who had their eyes gouged out were permitted to remain in the civic hospital to be healed before they were sent out onto the highway,[163] or at Hildesheim, where in 1407 the authorities ordered the executioner to have linen cloths at the ready for binding the eyes of those men who had theirs gouged out.[164] In fifteenth-century Nuremberg men whose ears had been amputated were given a guide to accompany them for four days.[165] Already around the year 900 the notion of helping those who were suffering from the effects of judicial mutilation may be encountered. The Anglo-Danish laws of Edward and Guthrum stated:

> If a criminal who has been mutilated and maimed (*limlaeweo lama*) is abandoned, and three days later he is still alive, after this time [has elapsed] he who wishes to have regard to his wounds and his soul may help him with the permission of the bishop.[166]

Although it may appear strange to the modern mind, even schizophrenic, that the law may first mutilate someone and then help with their wounds, justice, according to such a medieval concept, was not malicious, and once the culprit had received his appropriate punishment further suffering was deemed not only unnecessary but inhumane.

Hence, lastly I shall consider the question of medieval critiques of penal mutilation. Perhaps unsurprisingly in the light of the preceding documentation this is rather thin on the ground. In the Carolingian poem *Paraenesis ad judices* (Address to Judges), Theodulf of Orléans had documented a range of mutilations:

> The law commands that the evil heads of the condemned be cut off, their legs, genitals, eyes, backs, hands; to burn their limbs, to fill their mouths with molten lead, or whatever else human laws demand.[167]

But Theodulf deliberately labelled these examples of "human laws", contrasting them with religious exhortations to Christian compassion. In his *Comparison of Ancient and Modern Laws*, Theodulf voiced even stronger criticism against what he regarded as 'modern' violence, as opposed to the biblical punishments which demanded restitution and compensation. According to Theodulf, if "he who steals a beautiful lamb from the flock restore it twice over to him who took it" is sufficient for biblical justice, then "it is unknown except in our own day that the apprehended thief is punished by death".[168] Both theological and sociological counter-arguments to the severity of judicial mutilation were used by Theodulf, although he did not go so far as to object to the principle of corporal punishment *per se*.

While the *Codex Justinianus* (6.1.3) had still advocated that fleeing slaves, if recaptured on their flight to enemy territory, were to either be mutilated by cutting off one of their feet or be sent to work in the mines,[169] during the Middle Ages the legal justification for such treatment came under scrutiny. Already the Visigothic laws promulgated by King Reccesvinth in 654 forbade even the great landholders to mutilate their slaves in any way; although one should note this applied only to actions taken without due legal process:[170]

> If any master or mistress, without a preliminary investigation in court, should openly and wickedly deprive their slave of his nose, lip, tongue, ear, or foot, or should tear out his eye, or should mutilate any other part of his body . . . he or she shall be sentenced . . . to three years in exile.[171]

By the thirteenth century Saint Thomas Aquinas pointed out that the Bible had already stipulated a punishment for those people who mutilated their slaves, instead advocating their release,[172] an argument which Aquinas elaborated and upgraded for his contemporary times to cover physical mistreatment of wage-earners by their employers. Judicial mutilation, however, was part and parcel of the legal process, and while regarded as such, it could only ever be questioned to the degree of its application and not according to its principle. Hence "cruelty is an exaggeration of legal punishment",[173] but cruelty is not defined as the punishment itself. "The disregard for cruelty in legal discourse is not surprising because legal violence is never perceived as cruel from within the system."[174]

One of the main troubles with mutilation as judicial punishment is, of course, that the law is not infallible: the forces of law and order will have 'got the wrong man' on a number of (unquantifiable) occasions. Once physical punishment and/or torture had commenced mutilation of a person, there was no turning back, no regrowing hacked-off limbs or reinserting gouged-out eyes. At Bruges the authorities admitted such miscarriages of justice, as when "compensation was paid in 1464–1465 to an unfortunate man whose limbs had been broken by mistake."[175] It is precisely the irreversibility of judicial mutilation that is the focus of the key modern criticism against it (as it is against capital punishment)—you cannot reverse a decision if the innocent accidentally gets punished or executed—but this rarely seems to have been considered in medieval times.

2 Work

Since the previous chapter discussed the disabling effects of legalised violence on non-combatants, it seems apposite to commence this chapter with a section on the 'occupational disabilities' of combatants and how 'professional' soldiers injured in war were provided for. Warfare and the 'occupational risk' of the professional soldier is a story that has been around since antiquity and the first quasi-professional, standing armies.[1] Nevertheless, the Athenians were apparently "the only Greek people *known to us* who made special provision for their poorer disabled citizens—perhaps originally those disabled in war",[2] in that an allowance mentioned for the fourth century BC may have been "designed originally for those disabled by war" during the time of radical democracy under Pericles in the fifth century.[3] In his *Athenian Constitution* (49, 4) Aristotle stated:

> There is a law which lays down that those who possess less than three *minae* [300 *drachmae*] and who are physically maimed so as to be incapable of work are to be examined by the council and to be given two obols a day for maintenance at public expense.[4]

For modern comparison with the effects of warfare on the actual combatants, one need only look to the aftermath of World War I, when hundreds of thousands of soldiers on both sides of the conflict returned home shell-shocked, blinded, amputated and dreadfully mutilated in too many ways to describe.[5] In any contemporary region where warfare is encountered, no matter on what scale, whether involving large numbers of personnel and the latest military hardware or small bands of guerillas, so, too, are the disabled victims of warfare.[6]

Medieval warfare had its share of disabled casualties, too. However, the sources, whether historical, financial or literary records, only seldom mention the impairment of knights and other warriors of all ranks as resulting from combat.[7] An intriguing image in a manuscript of Boccaccio's *De Casibus Illustrium* of 1461–1462 under the aegis of the Wheel of Fortune depicts the apparently interlinked fate of a crippled beggar on crutches and a soldier being mutilated, his limbs hacked off, by an enemy army.[8] But such references, whether visual or textual, remain scarce. "There were undoubtedly those who did suffer serious wounds despite their armour, leaving them with permanent disabilities of one sort or another, although these are rarely recorded."[9] From a literary text stems the example of Onund Tree-leg, an Icelandic man mentioned in *Grettis saga*, who had lost his leg just below the knee in a battle at Hafunsfiord and had to wear the wooden leg, which gave him his nickname, for the rest of his life—a life which significantly entailed active fighting in further battles, so that Onund became celebrated as "the bravest and nimblest one-legged man" ever to live in Iceland.[10] From historical sources a few more: the significantly named Sigibert the Lame († c. 508), king of the Ripuarian Franks, had one of his knees destroyed during a battle against the Alamanni at the fortress of Zülpich but continued to act as military leader thereafter.[11] Count Eudo, hero of the siege of Paris in 885, lost his right hand during battle, but, according to the account of the siege by Abbo (verse composition 897), Eudo had his missing hand replaced by an artificial one of iron which was hardly less mobile and stronger than his own hand had been.[12] The Norman knight Robert Fitz Hamon (c. 1045–1107), a member of William the Conqueror's entourage in 1066, rewarded with the county of Glamorgan and great estates in Gloucestershire and founder in 1092 of Tewkesbury Abbey, accompanied Henry I on campaign to Normandy in 1105, where he was wounded by a blow to the temple at the siege of Falaise. It is possible that Robert received medical treatment from Abbot Faricius of Abingdon, since Robert made a gift of land to the abbey. Because of this head injury he became brain damaged, although he survived for another two years, managing to hold on to all his estates.[13]

In Ireland, during the rebellion of Richard Marshal against the English king in 1233, Richard de Burgh attempted to grapple with him, but Marshal cut off de Burgh's hands with one single stroke of his sword.[14] Wounds sustained during warfare such as de Burgh's would have led to permanent impairment—if the soldier survived, since many would have died through heavy blood loss or infected wounds,[15] conditions which needed rapid treatment that was of course not always possible in the chaos of a battlefield or siege. Nevertheless warriors did survive injury and continued to fight another day as veteran, experienced individuals. An early example of a disabled warrior comes from Walter the Chancellor, a chronicler of the Crusades, who mentions that one of the Muslim leaders, Al-Ghazi of Aleppo, sustained a wound to the head in a battle in 1121, which a year later still left him "afflicted by a kind of paralytic illness".[16] When Berwick fell to the Scots in 1318 the Englishman Roger de Horsley lost an eye due to an arrow but survived; also in the Scottish wars Archibald, Earl of Douglas, lost an eye in 1402 (again due to an arrow, this time shot by an English archer at Humbleton Hill), which did not 'disable' him to the point of giving up active combat; instead he is found fighting on the side of the Percys at Shrewsbury a year later, 1403, where he lost one of his testicles, surviving this, too, "only to be killed by the English in France at Verneuil, 1424."[17] During the very varied course of the career of Mathieu d'Escouchy (1420–1482)—provost, bailiff and chronicler at different stages in his life—he was taken prisoner at the battle of Montlhéry (1465), returned ennobled and then maimed in a later campaign.[18]

In his study of armies and warfare, Michael Prestwich asserted: "There is surprisingly little information on the wounds incurred in battle."[19] This may be true of the documentary record, but the archaeological record tells a different and fuller story. Archaeological evidence gained from the examination of human bones on the sites of a number of medieval battle-fields indicates that the majority of wounds identified in palaeopathological evaluation "were actually old, healed lesions rather than fresh cuts made at the time of death. This suggests that they were sustained in previous battles and that the soldiers survived their injuries."[20] In the 1930s a detailed study of the palaeopathological evidence for battle injuries was made by Swedish archaeologists. They focussed their analysis on the mass graves resulting from the battle of Wisby, fought on the Swedish island of Gotland in 1361. Swords or axes were responsible for injuries to 456 skeletons, while arrows and spears had caused wounds in 126 skeletons. The sort of injuries to the bone and which body parts they affected were compiled into the following statistics: of the total location of wounds, 6.71 per cent were cuts to the humerus (upper arm), 3.35 per cent cuts to the radius (one bone of lower arm), 4.88 per cent cuts to the ulna (other bone of lower arm), 12.2 per cent cuts to the femur (upper leg), 56.4 per cent cuts to the tibia (front of lower leg) and 16.46 per cent cuts to the fibula (back of lower leg).[21] Had these soldiers survived the battle, the statistics indicate that they would predominantly have been orthopedically disabled, with the lower limbs most severely affected. As Piers Mitchell summarises, "the evidence from these medieval excavations suggest that weapon injuries in battle were most common in the skull, the forearms and the outer aspect of the lower leg."[22] Mitchell conducted osteological research at the castle of Jacobs Ford (Metzad 'Ateret) in Galilee, which was destroyed by Saladin's troops in 1179, concluding that while a variety of sword and arrow injuries proved fatal, e.g. deep cranial wounds and limb amputations, more superficial sword blows would be survived by the combatants.[23] Modern palaeopathological research has indicated that the most common site for medieval head wounds, known as the left precentral gyrus, is also the area of the brain responsible for controlling the motor functions of the right side of the body.[24] The laterality of this kind of injury was presumably caused by right-handed soldiers striking their opponents' left side of the head, and since the majority of soldiers were right-handed, the frequency of this trauma is consistent with the handedness of combatants. Of the recently discovered English archaeological sites for examining medieval warfare and wounding the best known is probably at Towton, where 1461 saw a particularly nasty engagement during the Wars of the Roses. Of thirty-seven individual remains from a mass grave that the excavators managed to reassemble, most victims died when they were in the range of between twenty-six and thirty-five years old, while two men were over forty, giving a mean age of thirty for the entire group. As such the average age of the soldiers killed at Towton is considerably older than that of burials in comparative mass graves dating to either the US in 1812 or Korea in the 1950s.[25] "This difference is not unexpected and highlights the contrast between medieval and modern warfare."[26] It also allows for the possibility that some of the combatants were the veterans, and hence survivors, with or without wounds and impairments, of previous engagements. This is exactly what a number of finds from Towton demonstrated. Twelve of the thirty-seven individuals displayed healed fractures, of which 29 per cent constituted fractures of the lower limbs, which "could have been sustained while fighting or training to fight during late adolescence".[27] The men buried at Towton were highly active in life, and some had bone changes especially to the upper limbs which are concomitant with "strenuous activities commenced in youth", possibly deriving from "the use of unimanual weapons and the bow. Taken in conjunction with the evidence of having sustained previous injuries, some may have developed these conditions in military pursuits."[28] One individual, whose skeletal remains have been labelled Towton 16, had received a wound to the left side of his jaw, while another, Towton 41, had sustained a cut to the top of his cranium, both of which were well healed without any signs of having been infected.[29] The type of these earlier injuries also suggest that the men had been involved in violent actions, possibly other battles, prior to the one in which they were killed. However, at Towton not all disabilities were the result of previous military action. One individual had a fusion of the right side of his sacrum and pelvis, resulting in a distortion of the pelvic shape, which possibly meant that in life this man limped.[30] Nevertheless he was regarded as 'fit for action'.

Occasionally the rare situation is encountered where material remains and textual evidence corroborate each other. The skeletal remains of one known individual, Sir Hugh Hastyngs (†1347), a Norfolk landowner and participant in a number of military encounters during the Hundred Years' War, have been examined by archaeologists and analysed osteologically. Sir Hugh was aged less than forty when he died, but he already had signs of osteoarthritis, probably due to continuous practice with a broad sword or other heavy weapon, and his body showed general wear and tear that was possibly due to repeated campaigning in France. In addition, he had marked dental deterioration, including the complete loss of some five or six front teeth sustained through a blow to the jaw.[31] Professionals like John Talbot (1384/7–1453), an important English military commander during the Hundred Years' War known as "Old Talbot" who survived more than one military encounter, will have had lasting evidence of countless wounds sustained in dozens of battles. Carole Rawcliffe surmises that in 1374 about a quarter of recruits serving in the Provençal army were badly scarred on the hands or face; and that many English soldiers mutilated in the wars with France returned home in a parlous condition to beg.[32]

This statement highlights an important aspect of life for soldiers and mercenaries, particularly for the lower ranks: the question of how to make a living *after* combat had ceased, either because military action was over anyway or because the individual soldier was injured and no longer fit for future battles—a disabled invalid. It appears from the scattered references in the sources that more often than not a severely or permanently injured and hence disabled soldier became reliant on alms and begging.

A few cases illustrate this social situation as a diachronically recurring event. One knight returning home from a Crusade after 1177 was fortunate enough to have been issued with a kind of warrant for 'invalidity benefits', to paraphrase it in modern parlance. He was given a letter by the grandmaster of the Order of Saint John, i.e. the Hospitallers, which recommended him as a martyr, since he had been gravely wounded and spilt his blood for the cause of Christ, and therefore as someone deserving of all the assistance, charity and sustenance those he presented the letter to would give, on account of his truncated and lacerated body, which made him unable (*impotens*) to labour and useless for work.[33] The case of one Thomas Hostell, who had been involved with the siege of Harfleur in 1415, demonstrates what consequences repeated injuries sustained in the course of military duties could entail. There he received a head injury, lost one eye and broke his cheekbone; then at the battle of Agincourt he was badly wounded again. Now, at the time of writing a letter of supplication to Henry VI in order to, presumably, obtain some pension or other material assistance, he was enfeebled, very old and impoverished, in debt and unable to help himself.[34] Some hospital foundations appear to have catered especially to veterans, for example, the unnamed institution at Eagle (Leicestershire), founded 1136–1148, perhaps by King Stephen, for sick and aged Knights Templar.[35] The Holy Roman Emperor Louis the Bavarian allegedly founded a hospital at the convent of Ettal in 1332 to cater specifically to fifteen veteran soldiers.[36] It is attested that the hospital on Rhodes of the military Order of Saint John, the Hospitallers, treated war casualties in 1445.[37]

Coming home from war as a disabled veteran could potentially lead to a downward slope of loss of former working ability and poverty, and hence descent into criminal activities, as the case of one Jehannin Machin, nicknamed Court-Bras (that is, Short-Arm), demonstrates. He had worked as a baker and pastry cook in Paris until he took part in the military campaign of July 1388, "from which he returned with a crippled arm."[38] Physical impairment resulting from warfare will not at all have been unusual.[39] In his case he was prevented from practising his former trade. Instead he tried

a stint at being a porter at the gates of Paris but then started petty thieving and begging for a living, degenerating to joining a band of vagabonds
until he was convicted in 1390 of thefts and of kidnapping people.[40] It is
impossible to quantify the number of disabled beggars who were former
soldiers, but, as such incidental references make clear, disabled veterans
of warfare could end their days eking out a living in poverty and reliant
on alms. How many of the maimed beggars were accused of fraud by the
later Middle Ages (on which topic see Chapter 4, this volume) we cannot
know; certainly many of the genuinely disabled veterans will have come to
be regarded with suspicion by this period, as they increasingly were in the
early modern period.[41]

Fictional literature, so full of knights fighting in all sorts of martial
encounters, is significantly silent on the 'fallout' from all this combative
action: disabled knights hardly figure. A case in point is the consolatory
text by Christine de Pisan, *Epistre de la prison de la vie humaine*, which
was addressed to Marie de Berry, duchess of Bourbon and Auvergne, and
written between 1416 and 1418;[42] in this epistle the battle of Agincourt is
not mentioned by name, but the text contains oblique references to the loss
that Marie, and women in general, had suffered due to the damaging effects
of the battle, naming some of those men who were killed or captured.[43]
Note that Christine mentions those combatants killed or captured but not
the maimed, mutilated and subsequently disabled. Warfare is presented as a
clean, neatly defined activity with only two outcomes: instant death or captivity, but no lingering invalid state, no permanent impairment, no disabled
soldiers returning home—no liminality, in fact. In his *Book of the Order of
Chivalry*, Ramon Llull had made it very clear that the chivalric body needs
to be whole and sound, without blemish, and essentially perfect in proportion and appearance. A man

> ouer grete or ouer fatte [. . .] lame of ony membre [. . . or] that hath
> ony other euyl disposycion in his body [is not] dygne ne worthy to be
> receiued in to thordre of chyualrye.[44]

Disability may just about be mentioned in a theoretical context, as in the
Art of Courtly Love of Andreas Capellanus in the 1180s, where one of the
didactic dialogues opines that a lady should not reject her lover "because
of some deformity resulting from the common chance of war" (*quae ob
deformationem solito belli contingentem eventu*), citing the loss of an
eye as an example of the "deformity of the members which naturally and
inevitably results from this bravery" (*membrorum deformitas, quae natu-
raliter ex audacia ipsa inevitabili procedit eventu*),[45] but not as a real-life
event affecting flesh-and-blood veterans. One aspect of the early Crusades
can be cited as a further example of the subsumption of the chivalric ideal
pertaining to physical integrity, namely, that until 1213, theoretically at
least, embarking on a Crusade had only been allowed for able-bodied men,

whereas thereafter, due to the populist vision of Pope Innocent III, previously unsuitable people such as "little children (*parvulos*), old men, women, the lame, the blind, the deaf, [and] lepers" could take up the cross.[46] This statement reflects something of the injured pride of the 'proper' crusader nobility at allowing the rabble to get in on the action.

The reason for this invisibility of the disabled soldier in literary texts, especially courtly romance literature, has been suggested to concern matters of status and class: such literary texts were written primarily for an elite audience, and most of the characters described in such texts also stemmed from the elite. Even when a courtly epic does start narrating the 'nasty side' of war, depicting the sometimes very serious wounds that the heroes sustained, they either recover or die: life or death are the only alternative outcomes.[47] Disability in its liminal aspects, as an in-between state between life and death, fits uneasily into such binary schemes. Heroes in epics do not make for very good heroes if they become disabled and have to beg for a living. The social realities as described in epics or courtly literature concern social elites, and in the real world these elites were the ones who, in battle, were more likely to be captured and held for ransom than to be maimed or mutilated. Although difficult to ascertain quantitatively, the evidence seems to indicate that the experience of disability was something that was far more likely to affect the lower ranks, and in particular the common foot soldier, than the mounted knights or commanders. The bloody rout and probable massacre of a group of soldiers at the Battle of Towton, which modern archaeological techniques have been able to reconstruct so meticulously, speaks greater volumes about medieval warfare than textual sources.[48]

Norbert Ohler has pointed out that common practice during sieges was for the defenders to throw, tip or pour all sorts of damaging substances onto the attackers, ranging from stones to boiling oil and pitch to the dust of unhydrated lime—the latter was particularly effective at blinding warriors trying to scale the walls.[49] And sometimes accidents during times of war arose for the most mundane of reasons, although still connected with military activities in the wider sense even if not due to actual combat. According to Galbert of Bruges, warfare continued to simmer throughout the whole of Flanders in the year after the murder of Count Charles the Good in 1127. During that time fatalities included "a fall from a horse, a slip while climbing a wall, the collapse of a ceiling and too much enthusiasm in blowing a horn".[50] All of which could have been caused by completely 'normal' peacetime activities as well. Thus it is apposite to now turn attention to industrial accidents or occupational disabilities in the more commonly understood sense.

Many histories of labour and workers tended to be first compiled in the period between the 1870s and 1914, a time when labour issues, trade unionism and social and political movements had brought the concept of 'work' to the fore.[51] Thereafter the interests of medieval historians had shifted into more general economic and social history,[52] so that topics of work, guild regulations and guild membership had been subsumed by histories of charity or gender history. More recently, labour and theology, especially the value of labour, have been of interest to researchers.[53] Work as an activity in and of itself and hence for an individual the ability to work were of considerable importance, whether in the religious-theological sense (work as the 'work of God', *opus Dei*) or in the purely material sense of making a living.

Disability that may have prevented one's ability to perform either kind of work, religious works or secular ones, was therefore a condition that was regarded as profoundly negative. Even in artistic representations, according to Livio Pestilli, the pairing of the blind and lame carried with it symbolic and theological meanings that reflected "on a practical level . . . the common inability of the blind and the lame to have a productive role in society."[54] The many miracle healings that narrated cures of disabled people not infrequently alluded to the reduced working capacity of the supplicants visiting healing shrines.[55] When such people with impaired working ability were forced to beg or to rely on other charitable handouts, they not infrequently highlighted the involuntary aspects of their begging as one of their main predicaments besides their physical disability. Connected with the enquiry into the miracles of Saint Louis in the 1280s are the following two cases of disabled people whose working ability was reduced and who would have been entitled to beg (since they could be classified as 'deserving' poor) but who tried their utmost to labour with their own hands. A woman called Jehanne of Serris, living in Paris at the time of the enquiry, became ill so that she could no longer stand or use her feet and legs, becoming housebound. Having been taken the Hôtel Dieu by her husband, she was given crutches by the nuns there, which returned limited mobility to her, but she still had to drag her left foot behind her. Forced to beg outside her local parish church, she heard about the miracles at the tomb of King (soon to become Saint) Louis IX. "And since she wanted to live by her own means when she went to the tomb, she spun some yarn until she gained three sous, which she carried with her."[56] The story makes two points: not only did Jehanne feel compelled to earn her own means of support, but her disability (impaired mobility of the legs) did not prevent her from performing wage-earning manual work. In the second case associated with the miracles of Saint Louis

> the mother of a crippled girl believed that 'God would be more favorable to them' if they lived by their own labor while they waited at Louis IX's tomb for a cure, and thus she did not want alms to be given to her daughter.[57]

Hence, even the lower strata of urban society had subsumed the elite intellectual (clerical) discourse on the intrinsic value of labour that was coming to be propounded from the latter part of the thirteenth century onwards.

Being able to perform physical, manual work was valued long before the so-called Protestant work ethic of post-Reformation times. In the case of one relatively minor, localised saint, the point about the "suggestive construction of a polarized, laboring body" is clearly made.[58] Saint Walstan was an East Anglian noble (975–1016) with a shrine at Bawburgh, Norfolk. What is of interest here is that in his *vita*, the emphasis of miracles is placed on the cure of impairments as a means to re-enable work. When an angel announced his imminent death to Walstan, he took this news placidly and only asked "that any laborer who prayed to him after his death should be healed of any infirmity or bodily disability that prevented his or her labor."[59] As (local) patron saint of agricultural workers, Saint Walstan exemplified the importance of being physically—and mentally—capable of work as a means to earn one's livelihood. The cult of Saint Walstan appears to have been especially popular in the fifteenth century. Miracles include a lame weaver from Canterbury, who first tried the normally far more efficacious shrine of Thomas Becket but then had to journey to Norfolk to be cured by Saint Walstan; or a carter who was crushed during harvest time by a cart laden with wheat and was so eager to return to work once cured that he did not even tarry at the saint's shrine but rushed back to his village.[60] "The usual charisma associated with saintly bodies here gets a contemporary coloring, allowing the injured worker to return to his or her productive work as soon as possible".[61] There is a social factor in all this, in that it is ironic that the religious miracle cure prevents the injured labourers from receiving the secular compensation they might be entitled to—quick cures mean rapid return to work, and cured workers make social security and benefit schemes redundant.

In 1406 William Taylor, a Wycliffite reformer, preached a sermon on the themes of poverty, charity and work. In his text he proposed an extreme work ethic that contained elements of the sort of thinking behind the rapid return to work notions in Saint Walstan's miracles. Taylor alluded to the healing miracles of Christ in the Gospels (Mark 10:46, Luke 18:35 and John 9:8) and proposed that the miracles were not just about healing for the sake of it (or even to enable greater faith), but expressly so that these impaired "clamorous beggeris" who "weren nedid to sitte at 3atis and biside weies, and crye and begge" should no longer be reliant on alms.[62] Allegedly motivated by a loathing of begging as much as by spiritual reasons, Christ performed these miracles to enable the disabled to earn their living through work:

> And in tokenynge þat Crist loþide sich begging, he heelide siche men not oonly in soule but also in body, þat þei my3ten gete þat hem nedide bi her bodily labour.[63]

William Taylor valorised and elevated work as a virtue in itself, a tool against poverty and even as a 'cure' for disability, generating "the astonishing argument that Christ healed the sick so that they could be put to work."[64]

In the real world, where miracles were a scarce commodity available only to the select few, injured and disabled workers had to find alternative means to ensure that they could survive once their working capacity had been impaired. In many, although not all, cases of injury, illness or old age the wages of labouring people ceased once they had become incapable of work, as has been argued for England in the fifteenth century with its relatively high wages.[65] Exceptions to cessation of wage payments were found in individual contracts between employer and worker, especially among some of the more important master masons in charge of large and prestigious building projects (see the following). An impaired worker need not have become spontaneously destitute, since a variety of organisations had developed in the course of the Middle Ages which may not have paid wages but nevertheless provided a primitive type of social security in the form of more or less regular charitable aid. Hence the importance to the topic of this chapter of guilds, fraternal associations and mutual aid societies.

A modicum of awareness of the risks involved in certain types of occupation and the possibility of what we now term industrial accidents must have been around for as long as human beings have existed. No doubt prehistoric hunter-gatherers already employed risk-minimisation strategies. More relevant to the medieval period is the fact that the key Christian text, the Bible, already drew attention to measures to prevent accidents and injury. In the Mosaic law of Deuteronomy 22:8, an 'employer' was held responsible for the welfare of building site workers: "When thou buildest a new house, then thou shalt make a battlement for thy roof, that thou bring not blood upon thine house, if any man fall from thence".[66] Perhaps deriving from this passage, one of the so-called 'barbarian' law codes, the Edict of Rothair dating from 643, picks up the topic and obliges building contractors to be responsible for any occupational injuries sustained by the masons employed by them and to pay compensation.[67]

It took until the early twentieth century for awareness of industrial injuries as a cause of chronic illness and impairment.[68] In connection with his survey of medieval and early modern guilds Georges Renard stated:

> Workmen and workwomen had suffered from the imperfection of the tools they had used, and from the craft which they carried on; for generations they had contracted diseases and infirmities which were a trademark.[69]

The various bans on working at night,[70] issued partly by the guilds themselves and partly by municipal authorities, did not just lead to a healthier and quieter urban environment for all burghers, but also to better-made goods (poor lighting conditions predispose to shoddy workmanship) and most importantly to better working conditions with less industrial accidents. Almost all persons encountered in the records with regard to industrial accidents are men, which reflects the reduced visibility of working women in the sources rather than the assumption that women invariably had less risky occupations than men—plenty of household accidents attest to that.[71] In fourteenth-century Ghent the notion that single women could very well be expected to earn their own living is apparent from those situations where they might no longer be able to do so, as in the case of Kateline Racorts, who was so severely mutilated in an accident (regrettably not further detailed) that "she may never again be able to earn her living"[72]— whatever the precise cause of the accident, she had become disabled in the modern sense of the term, that is, impaired to the extent that she was hindered from pursuing her 'normal' life. For Paris, a series of fiscal sources from the tax rolls of 1421, 1423 and 1438 indicate the reduced income affecting women who had suffered "misfortune and ordinary ruin"— exemptions were granted to nine women out of sixty, one of whom was described as blind.[73]

Petrus Hispanus (Peter of Spain, later Pope John XXI, †1277) wrote about accidents in his *Tractatus bonus de longitudine et brevitate vitae* (in the section known as *Liber de morte et vita* dealing with old age and the causes of death). He stated that "the causes of death with regard to external injury by chance accidents, like being hit, are unlimited, without certain number, and escape scientific understanding."[74] This philosophical, even stoical, approach to accidents as literally due to chance, without human influence and unpredictable is reflected in more prosaic texts such as the ordinances of English parochial guilds,[75] where social benefits in the form of financial and material support are provided to disabled members who suffered accidental injury, poverty or unemployment (a topic discussed more fully in the following). The notion of 'accident' as something purely happening by chance but nevertheless being part of the accepted (and expected) natural order of things is found, for instance, in the phrase "by auenture of ye world" in the fourteenth-century fraternity of Saint Christopher at Norwich.[76] Poverty, illness and disability (often collectively called "mischief" in such texts) were therefore regarded as natural occurrences and not intentional, divinely caused punishments. As such these conditions were subject to human alleviation, hence the provision of benefits to disabled guild members.

An incident from the later Middle Ages may illustrate just how mundane and quotidian accidents could be. An agricultural worker from Colmar had his leg run over by a farm vehicle and was so badly injured that the leg needed to be amputated. To perform treatment, the man was sent to the hospital of Saint Anthony in nearby Isenheim (founded around 1300), since the surgeons attached to this Antonite hospital had experience in amputations, gained from the treatment of people suffering from the effects of ergotism, which was the order's predominant role.[77] If the farm worker survived the amputation, his work-sustained accident will have left him permanently impaired. From a chronicler recording sundry events on an almost daily basis at Bruges between 1477 and 1491 we glean the following random examples of accidental injury and death: a workman killed by a falling wall, a 'traffic accident' when a carter ran down and killed a child at the corner of the Rue Flamande and the bellringer of the church of Saint Sauveur who climbed the tower (presumably in the course of his duties) and fell from the cross into the streets below.[78] According to Idung of Prüfening, a mid-twelfth-century Cistercian, bellringing itself could cause back injury in those pulling the bell ropes, due to the sheer weight of some of the bells.[79]

Climbing and subsequently falling off ladders appear to have been frequent reasons for industrial accidents. In an urban context, an old workman in London in the last quarter of the fourteenth century "climbed a ladder to examine the wall, was injured and died that night."[80] Rural areas were not without their hazards, either. A peasant, described as older than fifty, fell down from the ladder he had climbed to pick peas and died three days later from the injuries he had sustained.[81] An old woman in her seventies climbed a ladder to get to her storage of straw to obtain some kindling and slipped, falling to the ground so that she, too, was killed.[82] In France a man called Guillaume Audoyn fell off a ladder in 1403 and hit his head so that he became mentally disabled, considered an 'idiot' who was out of his senses and had lost his memory for two years until he struck his wife with a pitchfork, thinking she was mocking him "because he was stupid and idiotic through lack of sense, angered and incensed".[83]

In the thirteenth-century Bedfordshire coroners' rolls a number of deaths by misadventure were caused by what we may now term industrial accidents. The largest number concerned accidents on building sites: people working on the demolition of walls or pulling down of walls, resulting in their collapse onto the labourers.[84] Sometimes masonry already suffered from structural weaknesses and collapsed onto passers-by.[85] A Bedfordshire man died after falling from a ladder, another fell off a beam, a third fell off the belfry of the church he was doing repair work on and a fourth was the victim of earth collapsing onto him in a chalk pit that he was excavating.[86] In these instances the injuries were fatal—the workers died immediately or within a few days—but similar accidents could lead to permanent disability. In Yorkshire a victim of building site injury, William of Gloucester, who had been contracted by the archbishop of York, Roger Pont L'Evêque (†1181) to lay water-pipes on the archbishop's estates near Churchdown, was buried by a fall of earth. William's rescue through a miracle of Thomas Becket is narrated in seven of the stained glass panels in Canterbury Cathedral.[87] The activity of brewing beer could cause lethal accidents, as when two Norwich women in the late thirteenth century accidentally "fell into vats with hot barley malt, one dying within the day, the other taking over a week to expire."[88] Domestic servants were at risk, too, as the case from Norwich in 1274–1275 of one Horengia shows, who was sent by her master to fetch water from a pit or pool and was drowned, dragged to the bottom by the weight of her water container after the cord for pulling it up broke.[89]

Constructing wells and repairing them had obvious hazards: at Norwich in 1278–1279 a labourer died after the rope holding the bucket he was sitting in snapped and he fell to the bottom.[90] Workers in ports and the mariners on vessels themselves were obviously at risk from drowning, too, for example, when at least ten fatalities occurred in 1343 at Norwich after a boat carrying passengers as well as a cargo of goods capsized during a stormy night.[91] All sorts of mundane, routine tasks associated with everyday work could therefore pose hazards and potentially disabling accidents.[92]

Occasionally it was disabled people themselves who were the cause of accidental injury or even death in others. Two cases from English coroners' rolls concerning disabled 'babysitters' or childcarers and their young charges may illustrate in particular the dangers faced by infants and small children becoming the victims of accidents. During the latter half of the fourteenth century a Norfolk peasant mother had an epileptic fit and the child she was nursing slipped from her lap into the fire.[93] In a case from Cambridgeshire in the 1370s a blind peasant woman was looking after Maude, the daughter of William Bigge, while Maude's mother was visiting a neighbour, but the blind woman was negligent and Maude was found drowned in a ditch.[94] In such cases it seems the childcarers were generally not blamed, but a verdict of misadventure was recorded by the coroners.

As early as 1155 an individual work contract made between Sergius, a physician in Genoa, and Romualdo, presumably a kind of 'medical assistant', demonstrates awareness of the potential for injury and accident while at work, even in the not generally very hazardous métier of the *medicus*. Sergius promised "to place any disputed burden or injury to Romualdo before some good men who would arbitrate the matter",[95] thereby acknowledging at least the hypothetical event of injury and seeking to establish ground rules should the event occur in actuality. Towards the end of the period under consideration, in 1459 the craft guild of butchers in the southern German town of Memmingen made provision for accepting impaired artisans into its membership, apparently deliberately encouraging workers who were unable to exercise any other craft (*kein ander handwerk treiben*) to join this profession—which does however leave open the question what sort of physical impairment one could have and still carry out the physically strenuous job of butcher.[96]

Building sites in the Middle Ages were (and still are in the twenty-first century), besides mines, the most high-risk locations for workers.[97] The following two stories may suffice as just a selection of the countless examples that illustrate the dangers. During the construction of Hexham priory, a young man named Bothelm fell from a pinnacle of great height, was dashed upon a stone pavement below and broke his arms and legs, with his limbs all out of joint. The masons thought he was dead and carried him outside on a bier at the behest of Bishop Wilfrid (†709), who prayed together with the workmen and gave his blessing, so that the boy recovered. Doctors then bound his fractures with bandages and his condition improved day by day.[98] Here a mixture of miracle and medicine helped a potentially disabled labourer. Others were less fortunate. At Bologna in 1254, during building work for of the new convent church of San Francesco, two of the vaults then under construction collapsed, killing twelve labourers and two friars, while many other people on-site at the time received fractured skulls or broken limbs, including Brother Andrea, the master of works, who broke both his legs.[99] Apart from informing us about the risks, this episode also gives some hint as to the sheer numbers of people working on (or simply viewing?) a major building site.

The mobility of medieval building workers, which covered not just the masons, but also the carpenters, roofers and, in the case of prestigious building programmes such as cathedrals, the sculptors, painters and associated artists, was due to the temporary nature of the work: once a project, especially a large one, was completed, skilled and specialised building trades moved on to the next available project and to a different site. Medieval terminology often referred to masons and carpenters together as 'builders', so that "architects were simultaneously *carpentarii et lapidarii*, carpenters and masons, and building workers were often entitled *operarii lignorum et lapidum*, workers in wood and stone."[100] On a typical larger project such as building a cathedral, the site itself and overall work was under the command of a master (*magister operis*), with often as not a master specifically in charge of the masons (*magister lapidum*); these two formed the leadership of workers attached to the masons' lodge (in German often called 'builders' lodge' [*Bauhütte*]), of which some workers remained part of the lodge until completion of the project, while others, dependant on the nature of the trades and the timing of certain activities, could change personnel in the middle of a phase of building activity. Help and support in cases of industrial accidents could therefore not be restricted to a single locality, as the regular urban craft and artisanal guilds were, but had to cover persons rather than places. Hence masons' guilds were some of the first to develop a system of mobile and transferable security for their membership.

Because provision in disability, sickness and old age was of concern to medieval masons, yet the mobile nature of their work did not always facilitate support by localised guilds, another solution was to stipulate individual contracts of employment. Thus King Louis IX of France gave sick pay to a mason employed at Royaumont Abbey who had broken his leg in 1234, while at Urgel in Spain the mason Raymond the Lombard managed to negotiate a pension agreement that was the monetary equivalent of a cathedral canon's entitlement. Furthermore, in 1351 William de Hoton, mason for the minster, agreed with the chapter of York Cathedral that if he became "incapacitated by blindness or other disease" then half of his salary should go towards paying for a deputy, the "second master of the masons" (while presumably the remaining half was to be used for his own sick pay);[101] and in 1368 Robert de Patrington, successor to William at York, arranged for a contract stipulating he was to receive a pension if he was prevented from working through blindness or infirmity, as long as he was still able to fulfil an advisory role on-site.[102] A contract made in 1359 between the clergy of Hereford cathedral and the mason John of Evesham stated that where illness prevented him from working for one or two weeks, then he should continue to draw his full pay, but if his absence from work was going to be more prolonged, then his wage should drop from three shillings to twelve pence per week, although no time limit was imposed.[103]

If no contract was in place specifying the terms and conditions of work and 'sick benefits', the compensation in cases of disabling accidents could be rather meagre, as was the situation for a "stone mason who fell from a great height and hurt himself badly while working for the monks" at Norwich in 1420–1421, who was only given a gratuitous payment of two pence by the hostilar.[104] Possessing a written contract was therefore a way of securing some advantage. Master Richard Beke, who was appointed as master mason and buildings officer by the chapter of Canterbury Cathedral in 1435 "to have control of all their works of masonry", had a clause in his contract stipulating that he was to receive four shillings per week, a house, clothes, a fuel allowance and a pension if he became blind or bedridden.[105] The contract with John Bell, hired in 1488 by the prior and chapter of Durham Cathedral, stated that if he had "continuall infirmities or great age so that he may not wirke nor labour, nor exercise hys craft and cunnyng", then he should receive a pension of four marks per annum instead of his usual salary of ten marks.[106] This variety of contractual arrangements simply highlights the fact that 'social security' in cases of physical impairment was down to an individual mason to negotiate, with experience, qualification and reputation presumably being the deciding factors that increased a mason's bargaining position.

Journeymen had less security than master masons, and less negotiating power for contracts. In Strasbourg, the mason's lodge put aside one *Pfennig* a week for each worker, but this did not entail an automatic right for assistance for each mason.[107] Nevertheless, compensation for industrial accidents was sometimes paid on building sites, for instance, at Koblenz in 1278 a boy who was injured by a mason received twelve *denarii*; in 1279 a mason himself was injured and also received twelve *denarii*; and another mason who fell off a gate in 1278 so that he was off work on sick leave for several days received thirty-six *denarii*, which is approximately a week's wages for a mason.[108] Continuous pay during illness or injury was, however, not the norm, so that at Xanten during the week 14–26 January 1375 in which master William was incapable of working because he had wounded himself in the foot, the account book records that nothing was paid to him (*nichil operati sunt quia magister Wilhelmus vulneravit se ipsum in pede*).[109]

Of course, another method by which to ensure a modicum of social security in the event of accident, or simply age-related disability, was to earn enough while working and put aside funds for the purchase of a corrody later on. This appears to have been the case with Robert de Beverley, described as a master mason in the accounts of Westminster Abbey during the mid-thirteenth century, and frequently occurring in witness lists during that period, who received a full monk's corrody, either purchased from his savings or in compensation for the work he had provided for the monastery.[110]

Various measures were developed to protect workers on building sites and to minimise the risk of injury or ensuing disability. Early forms of eye protection included strips of wood or bone that had a narrow slit in them,[111] which were tied a small distance in front of the eyes (snow goggles used by many Arctic-living traditional cultures are of a similar design); face masks made from fine wire mesh in the shape of a veil were employed; and to prevent inhalation of masonry (and other) dust or noxious fumes face cloths and sponges were used, sometimes made from animal bladders or membranes.[112] Dangerous works were recognised, so that sometimes extra or additional pay was made to labourers employed on jobs more perilous than most, such as roofing work or placing stones at great heights above ground level.[113] In later medieval York, according to a study of building craftsmen between c. 1300 and 1534, the "elevated position in which they worked, particularly when '*in campanile*' perhaps warranted extra payment."[114] This reflects a certain risk awareness of the greater potential for injury, and hence the greater potential for loss of earnings in the event of accident and disability.

The carpenter's guild in London (Gilda Carpentar) had a passage in their statutes, dating from 1389, concerning mutual aid to be provided by the guild to sick members. Such stipulations are part and parcel of numerous other guild regulations and nothing unusual; what is unusual, however, is the mention of specific events leading to sickness, namely, what we would now term industrial accidents:

> Also it is ordained that each brother and sister of his fraternity shall pay to the helping and sustaining of sick men which have fallen in disease, as by falling down of an house, or hurting of an axe, or by diverse sicknesse, twelfe pennies per year.[115]

One must assume that for a carpenter falling off a height while working on a house (think of all those timber-framed buildings being erected in London) and sustaining an axe injury (the axe being one of the carpenter's most important and hence frequently used tools) will have represented two of the most typical work-related accidents for that particular profession. In contrast, the guild of York carpenters, in their 1482 statutes,[116] make no mention of industrial accidents but simply state they will provide help for members fallen into poverty or who had become blind—the normal state of affairs:

> Also it is ordained that if any of the said fraternity fall into poverty, so that they may not work, or happen to be blind, or to lose their goods

by 'unhap of the world', then the foresaid brotherhood to give them 4d every week, as long as they live, by way of alms, so that he that is so fortuned have truly fulfilled the ordinances above written.[117]

One of the most famous incidences of accidents on a building site leading to disability concerns William of Sens, the master mason (or what one might term 'architect-cum-project manager') who worked on the rebuilding of Canterbury Cathedral. In the autumn of 1178, while clambering around on scaffolding to inspect the progress of work at height, the scaffolding collapsed beneath him and William fell some fifty feet to the ground, breaking his legs. He was injured such by masonry and wooden beams that he remained disabled—"he was rendered helpless alike to himself and for the work", and was removed from the site, compelled to return to France. Project leadership was assigned to William the Englishman for completion of the job, recorded Gervase of Canterbury, the monk who narrated this episode.[118]

Riding was another fairly high-risk activity. According to modern British medical experts, horse riding, which nowadays is almost exclusively undertaken as a leisure activity, is one of the most dangerous sports.[119] Back in the Middle Ages, riding accidents might be sustained by all sorts of travellers, on private as well as official business. A random selection of members of the nobility alone who are known to the historical record to have suffered death or disability through riding includes the Carolingian West Frankish king Louis III (hit his head while chasing a girl on horseback);[120] King Alfonso I of Portugal (severely injured in a fall from his horse in 1167 during a battle); Fulk of Jerusalem (died from fatal injuries received after falling from his horse while hunting in 1143 and struck on the head by his wooden saddle which dislodged in the fall); Serbian king Stefan Dragutin (broke his leg in 1282 after falling off his horse, became lame and subsequently had to surrender his rule to Stefan Milutin); and Philip of Burgundy (died 1346 after a peasant's horse had kicked him).[121]

An early story relates the 'sporting accident' that befell Abbot Heribald, when in the exuberance of youth he raced his horse against those of other members of Bishop John of Beverley's clergy in early eighth-century Northumbria, sustaining a head injury causing temporary paralysis. Heribald's "spirited horse took off in a powerful jump across a hollow in the path", he fell "and at once lost all feeling and power of movement as though [he] were dying"[122]—note the liminal situation. Heribald cracked his skull, lay as though dead, unable to move from midday until evening as "motionless as a corpse", until he revived slightly but remained speechless all night.[123] Needless to say, through the intercession of Bishop John—and that of a surgeon who bandaged the crack in his skull—Heribald was cured. A further example that occurred about the year 968 concerns Abbot Purchard I of Saint Gall, who, while out riding near Rickenbach, fell off his horse and broke his leg.[124] One may assume that the abbot was taken back to the monastery of Saint Gall on some kind of stretcher (perhaps improvised from a table or a bed), his leg bandaged. Since the current *hospitalarius* of Saint Gall was Notker II (c. 905–975), a famed physician, one may also assume that the abbot received the best treatment and care that medical knowledge could provide at the time, which, however, may have exacerbated the condition of Purchard's leg, since if Notker applied Hippocratic treatment for fractures, the bone will have set in such a way as to leave his leg shortened.[125] Apparently Purchard did remain disabled thereafter and needed two crutches to enable him to walk, while he also had to delegate some of his work to an assistant, finally resigning his abbacy in 971.[126] In the following centuries of the Middle Ages, debilitating accidents while 'on the road' were also a recognised occupational hazard for Franciscan and Dominican friars. "Friars might spend months or years in inhospitable climates, becoming weak from hunger, ill from dysentery, depressed, lonely, or crippled with frost bite."[127] Reminiscent of the fate of Purchard, Stephen of Auvergne, the Dominican prior provincial of Provence, had to resign from his office in 1250 after suffering serious injury while travelling.[128] However, a priest from Franconia, Johannes Kyslings in the diocese of Würzburg, received a papal dispensation in 1480, which allowed him to continue officiating despite having a wooden leg; in his supplication he stated he had fallen off his horse, breaking his shin, and following advice from experienced surgeons, and after many other treatments were unsuccessful, he had allowed the damaged leg to be sawn off (i.e. amputated), so that instead of the missing shin he had himself made a wooden apparatus, with which he now walked.[129] A Portuguese carpenter called Vasco Lourenço fell from his horse, after it had stumbled, in such a way that he broke his right leg and hip, which would have left him disabled had he not been fortunate enough to become subject of a thaumaturgic miracle at the priory of São Domingos at Lisbon in 1432: after drinking holy water in the name of Christ and washing his leg and hip with it, he awoke the next morning to find his leg whole and his hip well. And like the good labourer in the miracles of Saint Walstan mentioned earlier, he "got up straightaway the next morning and went to work as he had done before".[130]

One would expect a significant number of accidents among 'professional' riders, the same way as in modern times professional drivers, by virtue of the greater frequency of using roads, are statistically more likely to be involved in traffic accidents than infrequent, occasional drivers. One group of such professional riders will have been messengers, especially royal or papal messengers, who sometimes had to ride at speed, even through the night, on matters of urgency; also those messengers employed regularly by the great merchant families (such as the Bardi) in the later Middle Ages. The English royal messenger service can be reconstructed through sources drawn from medieval accounts of expenses and has been well studied, so one would imagine to find at least one despatch rider crippled through falling from his horse. For post-medieval periods, a certain Major Wheeler-Holohan "remarked of the later king's messengers that scarcely a year passed without an application for sick leave, as a result of riding or carriage accidents or of illness brought on by hardship."[131] Unfortunately for the medieval period it is impossible, according to Mary Hill, to judge how many of the claims for sick pay were due to accident and how many due to disease, and her survey only discovered references to 'illness' in general. It is tempting to think that the sick pay John Piacle received in 1296 for a duration of seventy-seven days was due to an accident like a fractured limb rather than an illness such as an infectious disease, since fractures take quite a while to heal, and limbs would have to have healed completely before John could sit in the saddle again.[132]

Therefore, excluding the occupational risk to professional soldiers during war, in peacetime the occupations with the highest risk of accidentally induced disability would, not surprisingly, have been those of persons in the building trades and riders. Contrary to the common assumption that medieval kings and the higher nobility were most at risk from active participation in battle, recent research by Achim Hack into the causes of disabling or life-threatening events has come to the

> particularly surprising conclusion that Carolingian rulers had more to fear from accidents, like building collapses and falls from their horses or other incidents while riding or hunting, than from war.[133]

Any activity that involves the risk of falling from a height, which need not be a great height, either, has the potential for disabling accidents. Occasionally physical evidence is found in palaeopathological analyses of medieval human remains. One example comes from the crusader cemetery at Caesarea in the Holy Land, where one individual was found to have "two healed wedge fractures of lumbar vertebral bodies in the spine."[134] According to modern expert medical opinion, this kind of injury can be the result of a fall from a height, and it leaves the affected person with a kyphosis, that is, an angled spine, therefore with a bent back.

> Medieval scenarios that might cause this include a knight falling from a horse, a farmer falling from his cart, or even a disturbed burglar jumping from an upper window of a house to escape arrest.[135]

But even the genteel and physically not overly strenuous occupation of apothecary, for example, could have its health risks. The handling of sometimes dangerous, because poisonous, corrosive or acidic substances, in the process of manufacturing pharmaceutical recipes could expose apothecaries to not insignificant risks of accidental injury. The eyes especially needed protection, since many substances could cause if not total blindness, then severe eye injuries. Much like the masons on building sites, pharmacists employed protective clothing, namely, various kinds of masks to protect their eyes and faces.[136] Other trades that worked a lot with certain chemicals were also prone to eye injuries and even complete blindness as the result of accidents at work—tannic acids and lime were the main culprits. Lime used on building sites could be dangerous, as the following individual case of a monk demonstrates: he was involved in renovation works at his monastery in Germany when a fellow monk threw building lime at his face 'for a laugh', which permanently impaired his vision.[137] Tanners in particular and leatherworkers in general were affected by such injuries, as were fur sellers, all of them crafts which used tannic acid or lime to prepare the skins, furs and leather. Woodworkers were exposed to the hazards of sharp tools, dust and wood shavings getting into their eyes, and even needlework endangered vision by causing eye strain.[138] Roger Bacon had noted that the eyes of those who worked in hot environments, like blacksmiths and bakers, were prone to "softening",[139] and the encyclopedist Bartholomaeus Anglicus commented on the dangers of (urban) production activities for the health of one's eyes, since industrial pollution caused by smoke "greuyth yghen and maketh hem droppe out teeres and greueth the sight notabelyche".[140] The Byzantine monk John Moschus (Ioannes Moschos, c. 550–619) had in his *Pratum spirituale* already mentioned that glassblowers are prone to blindness due to the heat of the fire they worked with.[141] The guild of goldsmiths in London asked for extra funds of the king in 1341 to help "blind, weary and infirm" brothers who had been "blinded by the fire and smoke of quicksilver, and some worn out by manual work and oppressed and debilitated with various infirmities".[142] And an individual case of eye injury concerning a fifteenth-century priest who asked for dispensation due to canonical irregularity has come down to us: the priest was soldering the handle of his knife with lead (a case of clumsy DIY?) when a drop of lead splashed into his left eye, with which he no longer saw anything at the time of supplication. But the case emphasised that this injury was not obvious to others.[143] The question of physical integrity as a requirement for the priesthood goes beyond the scope of this present volume, but suffice it to draw attention to a single issue: visibility to others of an impairment. Humbert of Romans, Master General of the Dominicans during the thirteenth century, had argued:

> people who are disfigured in this way are debarred from the Lord's service in Leviticus [21:17] and similarly the church has banned them from public office for fear of popular scandal and ridicule.

> (*Ecclesia removit huismodi a solemniter officiis propter derisionem et scandalum populare.*)[144]

This emphasises in/visibility as a measure by which people were judged fit, or not, to be a priest, something which the priest with his unfortunate molten lead incident was also keen to point out.[145]

Awareness of alleviating or preventative measures in the form of what we might nowadays term 'benefits for workers' was not unheard of during the Middle Ages. At Constance there is indirect evidence, in the shape of a mural of c. 1300 in the *Haus zur Kunkel* for the provision of warming-rooms and steam baths (saunas) for the female linen workers who were the prime manufacturers of the product (*tela di Costanca*) which made the town rich. Twenty-one red-and-green images on the second storey of the building depict scenes from the process of textile manufacture, including plucking, spooling and weaving, but also show the women after work in the warming and steam rooms. To achieve high quality, textiles such as linen or silk had to be woven in a relatively damp environment. The explanation for this practice lies in the underlying laws of physics: textile fibres become electrostatically charged the drier the air is, causing them to move apart, while in damp air the static charge is diminished. The finer the thread to be spun was desired, the damper the air had to be.[146] For the workers, prolonged exposure to such working conditions could result in impairment through rheumatic joints and similar disorders, never mind constant respiratory diseases. Such warming rooms were therefore essential to prevent or alleviate occupational disabilities. The plight of female textile workers has found its place in literary texts of the high Middle Ages, notably in *Yvain* of Chrétien de Troyes, where the complaint is voiced by one of the women weavers about their condition in the Castle of Pesme Avanture. She says they only receive four *deniers* for every piece of work that is actually worth a *livre*, and although most of them do twenty *sous*' worth of work or more each week, what they earn from that is not enough to keep themselves adequately nourished let alone clothed (ll. 5306–17), and they are persecuted by a hard master (ll. 5338–44).[147] Hartmann von Aue, in his version of *Iwein*, expanded on Chrétien's original passage, describing a workhouse

> whose architecture resembled that of a dwelling for poor people . . . he saw a good three hundred women working; they were young, miserable, and poorly clad . . . All suffered from need, for their work hardly brought them more than constant hunger and thirst. They got just enough food and drink to permit them to survive in weakened condition. Haggard and pale, they suffered extreme want in both body and dress.[148]

In the context of female textile workers one must cite here one poignant exception: the case of a blind man mentioned in the miracles of Saint Bertin, dating from the end of the ninth or early tenth century. He was brought up from childhood at the court of a nobleman near the monastery of Saint Bertin (Sithiu, Saint Omer), where he worked in the workshop for female textile workers, the *gynaeceum*, having been trained in sewing (*nendi*), embroidery (*cusandi*), weaving (*texendi*) and all the works of women's art (*omnique artificio muliebris operis*).[149] What makes this story especially interesting is that here we have a man, who just happens to be visually impaired, who is spatially and therefore perhaps also socially positioned with the women in their textile workshop—is this an example of the emasculation of the disabled male body? Or just an example of finding the 'best' work placement for a disabled man who could not be warrior, farmer or priest?

From archaeological material excavated in urban and/or industrial sites we can tell that a number of the palaeopathological bone changes must have been caused by occupational injury.

> Activities such as spinning, weaving, leather working, carpentry and carving carried with them a high risk of RSI as well as ongoing trauma. Burns, scalds, hernias and respiratory disorders occasioned by the inhalation of dust, smoke and pollutants must have been equally common.[150]

An osteological case-study from Saint Bride's Church cemetery, London, has been interpreted as the result of "pressure and intermittent trauma exerted on [the femoral] muscle by members of the shoemaking community . . . who used their thighs as lasts."[151] Incidentally, in 1240 the shoemakers' guild of Bremen made a contract with the Deutschordenspital for the taking in and care of poor, aged or sick artisan members who therefore could not work or sustain themselves.[152] Osteological evidence for industrial injury may not easily be separated from evidence for trauma caused by other activities, but "doubtless some of the trauma, particularly fractures, evident in skeletal assemblages reflects the consequences of certain occupational factors."[153]

Mining was, as it still remains now, one of the occupational activities carrying the highest risks.[154] Despite these risks, the surviving literature mentions next to nothing concerning occupational hazards, accidents and diseases affecting miners during the medieval period, with dedicated texts covering the subject only from the early sixteenth century onwards.[155] The argument has been put forward that it was only with certain new technical developments by the end of the fifteenth century, which allowed both riskier mining by driving mine shafts deeper down and greater commercial exploitation, that occupational health and safety became an issue and hence a topic to be discussed in advice manuals.[156]

However, by organising into groups for self-help and mutual aid, miners themselves provide evidence that awareness of the risks existed already during the medieval period. In the central German mining regions, such as Harz (with silver mining, e.g. at Goslar since 968), Erzgebirge (between 1100 and 1300) or Fichtelgebirge, miners still worked independently ('free') in the twelfth century but had formed voluntary fraternities (*Bruderschaften*) for mutual aid as well as economic benefits. This development had started as early as the thirteenth century in Bohemia, where silver mines were opened from that century onwards, and Austria with the formation of primarily religious brotherhoods among the mine workers, but from the fourteenth century onwards organisations (*Knappschaften*) that

come close to the modern idea of labour unions can be found in the Erzgebirge, which by the fifteenth century "used strikes, go-slows and collective
absence without leave to push forward their demands" for better working
conditions, including increased benefits in the case of injury and disability.[157] An example of industrial action, i.e. a strike, occurred in the Gießhü-
bel iron ore mine at Pirna, southeast of Dresden, in 1483, when in a dispute
over pay the miners destroyed countless tools and machinery.[158]

In Goslar a hospital for the miners was attached to the church of Saint
Johannes by 1050,[159] and in 1260 the brotherhood of miners linked to the
church-cum-hospital was already providing for sick members. This brotherhood or guild was confirmed by the bishop of Hildesheim on 28 December 1260, with the document placing special emphasis on invalid miners:

> For that reason we confirm . . . their fraternity that they . . . have salu-
> briously founded for the support of poor and sickly persons who are
> sorely oppressed by mining work . . . by exhaustion of their bodily
> strength and by lack of livelihood.

> (*Deshalb bestätigen wir . . . ihre Bruderschaft, die sie . . . zur Unterstüt-
> zung armer und kränklicher Menschen, die durch Bergwerksarbeit . . .
> durch Erschöpfung der Körperkräfte und mangelnden Lebensunterh-
> alt schwer niedergdrückt sind, heilsamerweise gegründet haben.*)[160]

The fraternity had as its aims to aid the poor and the weak, who are
impeded by bodily infirmities and material needs through their work in the
mountain of Rammelsberg.[161] In 1473 a new brotherhood of Saint Barbara
was formed, incorporating both the employers of miners (*Gewerke*) and
the miners (*Bergknappen*) themselves, to which the miners had to contrib-
ute part of their weekly wages "for the honour of God" (i.e. for charitable
works), according to an ordinance of 1476.[162] The Erzgebirge, too, where
silver ore had been found at Freiberg in 1168, saw the foundation of a
church-cum-hospital named after Saint John, in this case confirmed 1224
but open to other people besides miners, to cater to accidents and illnesses
sustained while working.[163]

Awareness of the risks specific to mining is especially expressed by German authors of tractates on the subject. From slightly beyond the chronological limits of this books stems the *Schwazer Bergbuch* (Schwaz is a
mining site near Salzburg), a manuscript written in 1556, on the protection
of miners at work and how to make mines safer. The high phase of extract-
ing ore in Schwaz probably began at the start of the fifteenth century, and
already by 1430 the town of Markt Schwaz had developed into a European
centre for silver and copper production, while the Tyrol region in general
saw the appearance of mining fraternities in the fourteenth century with
their respective traditions and organisations, so that many of the items discussed by the *Schwazer Bergbuch* will have been valid for the late medieval

period as well. The sixteenth section of this tract discussed hospitals and welfare provisions for the miners, including an illustration of the so-called *Bruderhaus*, the fraternity hospital carried financially, through monthly contributions of one *Kreuzer* from each worker, by the commonality of all the miners for sick brethren, which significantly depicts a crippled miner having to support himself on two crutches in front of the hospital building. The accompanying text states:

> Since the mine has stood for many years [prior to 1556] and many labourers and persons come together and are often injured by their work in the mine shafts, also otherwise fall sick, so that they may no longer perform their work and have no sustenance, there have according to counsel and much thought formed a common society.
>
> (*Als nun lange Jahre her das Bergwerk gestanden viele Erzknappen und Personen dabei zusammen kommen und oftmals an ihrer Arbeit in den Gruben geschädigt, auch sonst krank geworden, daß sie ihre Arbeit nicht mehr auswarten mögen und keinen Unterhalt gehabt, da haben allsdann gemeine Gesellschaft nach Rat und gut Bedenken.*)[164]

The alleged antiquity of the corporation lent a certain air of respectability. From other German-speaking regions we also have texts by Ulrich Ellenbog († 1490s), who in 1473 wrote a pamphlet on poisonous vapours and smoke for the miners and goldsmiths near Augsburg,[165] plus in the sixteenth century Agricola (*Vom Berg- und Hüttenwesen*, 1556) and Paracelsus (*Von der Bergsucht und anderen Bergkrankheiten*, 1533–1534) composed influential works on miners' diseases, discussion of which would, however, go far beyond the scope of this present chapter.[166]

Punishment for working on a Sunday was treated as a kind of 'religious accident', a form of industrial injury brought about by transgression.[167] Stories abound in various hagiographical narratives. In Gregory of Tours one already finds three cases of disciplinary action for breaking the Sabbath, which occurs "in the form of physical affliction visited upon the slaves, such as paralysis or blindness",[168] but not on the masters. An Irish legal tract of the early eighth century, *Cáin Domnaig*, treats the Law of Sunday, listing which tasks were permitted (medical emergencies, tracking criminals, tending to cattle) and which tasks were not (financial transactions, craft or servile work, and no sexual activity of course).[169] Interestingly enough, the mining activity discussed in the preceding was sometimes exempt from the prohibitions against Sunday work for technical reasons connected to working underground and the natural geological or engineering difficulties associated with such environments, mainly the need to continually pump water out of the mines. For instance, the town of Sulzbach in Franconia, Germany, was granted a papal privilege in 1460, by which the town received dispensation, since the iron ore mines had to be freed from the uninterrupted flow of water threatening to flood the mine.[170] Such measures not only allowed ore production to go on round the clock on a 24/7 basis, but also reduced the risk to miners' safety while working underground.

The social support network, i.e. the development of a type of 'social security' in the form of benefits for members of guilds and fraternities, and if and when they concern themselves with the disabled person, will now be examined more closely.[171] The importance of guilds and their activities is considerable. Economic historian Boissonade had estimated that in England over the course of the Middle Ages the guilds had been responsible for the creation of around 460 charitable institutions.[172] Looking back on the high Middle Ages as a kind of 'golden age' for the urban labouring classes, Boissonade praised the solidarity that enabled such charitable institutions to be formed.

> The workers possessed in the highest degree the spirit of brotherhood and of charity, which was enshrined in their fraternities or *amitiés*, their hospitals, and their organization of help for the sick and for widows and orphans.[173]

Early precursors of the fully fledged (craft)guilds, for instance, the *coniurationes* or *confraternitates* mentioned in the earlier medieval sources, sometimes provided for insurance against falling sick outside of the locality that the guild covered (this need not mean abroad but simply outside of the jurisdictional realm of the 'guild').[174] Two guild statutes survive from Exeter around the year 1000 and from Abbotsbury around the mid-eleventh century which both mention the transport home of sick guild members.[175] Guilds of merchants can be regarded as the next stage in the development toward craft guilds and religious fraternities; these, too, such as the guild of merchants of King's Lynn provided in its statutes (article 6), dated before 1300, for the support of members fallen into poverty or sickness, or the statutes (article 12) of Berwick dating to 1238, which provide for old age, poverty or incurable sickness of members, especially if they possess no property or cannot support themselves by their own means. There is also the mercantile guild of Southampton with its fourteenth-century statutes providing care during illness.[176] At Venice, the guild of crockery-makers had by 1301 arranged for its members to receive payments on a weekly basis should they fall ill or become unemployed.[177]

For Paris at the end of the thirteenth century it has been estimated that around twenty of the 101 registered craft guilds made explicit statements in their statutes to provide charitable aid, both to guild members who had fallen on hard times as well as to the needy in the wider community; that the other eighty guilds did not specify such aims in their statutes is not evidence for lack of collective support but simply evidence for a perceived superfluity to record such statements of intent in writing.[178] According to the *Livre des metiers*, between 1261 and 1271 Parisian guilds such as those of the tailors, glove makers, roasters, cobblers and vair (squirrel fur) curriers provided assistance to elderly or impaired members, as a form of insurance policy against inability to work, while the goldsmiths' guild even built a hospice in 1399 for their aged membership.[179] Various examples of London guilds need not stand behind their Parisian colleagues, for example, the guild of Lorimers, who in 1260 had an alms box to support those members fallen into poverty; the carpenters who provided sick brothers and sisters with two pence a day; the white tawyers who paid one pence a day to old or sick members or to the widows of members (provided they did not remarry); the goldsmiths who founded an almshouse "for the poor, aged sick of their crafts" in 1341; and at York the mercers who also established a hospital for their membership in the later fourteenth century.[180]

The thirteenth-century polymath Roger Bacon had already advocated measures that were somewhat akin to modern notions of welfare-state-funded 'social security'. He was concerned about the 'needy' and had recognised the association between poverty and old age, proposing

> that the ruler create a special fund with some of the fines paid to the treasury, as well as the confiscated properties of rebels, to sustain those who for reasons of illness or old age could not support themselves.[181]

Special shelters to house them were to be built (foreshadowing the Victorian poorhouse, perhaps). Some of the funding for this scheme would have been available in part by another measure in Bacon's proposal, namely, that all the able-bodied people were to be compelled to work, and if "they failed to do so, they were to be expelled from the country."[182]

For some modern commentators the guild "assured a refuge against misery and distress, the certainty of assistance in times of trouble, illness, old age, or misfortune."[183] Within the wider social setting of the high and later Middle Ages, guilds were a vital part of urban life. Guild members heard sermons on the virtues of charitable giving as much as the rest of the urban population, imbuing them with the notion that charity was to be given to the 'deserving' poor' (disabled, widows and orphans) as much as to guild members. "Collective works of charity aided distressed guild members, but frequently the guild attended to the needs of the urban poor as well."[184] For example, the Parisian guild of goldsmiths maintained "a box belonging to the confraternity (*confrarie*)" into which was deposited all the silver earned by members of the guild who had illegally worked on Sundays, according to a strictly regulated rota; then at Easter the donations were given to the Hôtel Dieu to feed the poor and sick resident there.[185] And certain events within the guild could be associated with external charity, such as when a brother or sister of the guild of fullers at Lincoln died, the other guild members donated a halfpenny each in order "to buy bread to be given to the poor, for the soul's sake."[186]

Guild membership tended to mean fully qualified and accepted masters, so not apprentices or journeymen and certainly not day labourers. Whatever charitable aims and functions a guild had enshrined in its statutes therefore revolved purely around the full members of the guild—an exclusive club. The problem of not being a member of a guild and becoming incapable of earning one's living, through sickness and/or disability, is exemplified by the plight of several young men who came to Paris as migrants in the later thirteenth century and whose stories survive in the miracle collection of Saint Louis: blindness, lameness, paralysis, muscular failure and leg injury leading to incapacitating infection are all cited as cases whereby these young migrants could no longer work, but because they had not been resident for long enough, nor were they old and experienced enough to become full guild members, they were forced to beg for a living.[187]

The smiths of Modena were concerned about guild members who might become ill or impoverished and advocated assistance in such cases, but left it down to individual guild members to decide how much aid each would provide; according to the statutes of 1244 the guild officials were to inform the brothers at their monthly meeting of a member who continued to be on 'sick leave' for any length of time, "so that all should offer help and assistance, each of them as they wish".[188] The guild of tailors mentioned at Lincoln in 1328/1388 provided seven pence per week to its needy members.[189] And the guild of the Blessed Virgin Mary at Hull, founded in 1357, provided its members in the following:

> If it happen that any member of the Gild becomes infirm, bowed, blind, dumb, deaf, maimed, or sick, whether with some lasting or only temporary sickness, and whether in old age or youth, or be so borne down by any other mishap that he has no the means of living, then for kindness' sake, and for the souls' sake of the founders, it is ordained that each shall have out of the goods of the Gild, at the hands of the Wardens, sevenpence every week; and every one so being infirm, bowed, blind, dumb, deaf, maimed, or sick, shall have that sevenpence every week as long as he lives.[190]

In later medieval Norwich the guild of tailors provided support of one penny a day to members who had become disabled, here especially suffering back problems and blindness, no doubt caused by working conditions involving poor light and cramped, sedentary postures; the tailors helped those who had fallen "en pouerte, croked, blyn, be the grace of Godes sonde, out-taken yef [unless] he be a theff proued".[191]

Guilds and fraternities more often provided assistance to members during time-limited episodes of incapacity, such as illness, which raises questions as to how much impact they had on provisions for disabled members, considering that disabilities are by definition distinct from illness by their permanence. A study examining the charters of 507 guilds in existence in 1389 demonstrated that 154, that is, around one-third, provided benefits during illness and other finite personal crises, sometimes for a few months or at most a couple of years.[192] "They were intended to cover a temporary crisis or terminal illness rather than prolonged retirement."[193] Some fourteenth-century French guilds even went so far as to 'screen' potential members before allowing them to be admitted in an attempt to avoid welfare cases who came to rely on charity.

> Some rules stipulated that persons suffering from a 'loathsome' or incurable disease could not be admitted, but only persons who were 'healthy of body and capable of supporting themselves by their labours'.[194]

Similar attitudes may have been taken toward apprentices. In taking on apprentices, a master promised to treat them "well and decently in sickness as in health", although some contracts apparently qualified this to mean "provided that the illness does not last longer than a month."[195] A person with a chronic illness or an impairment would therefore have had little chance of being taken on as an apprentice in the first place, if the sources and their subtext are to be believed. One guild at least made it explicit that they would not admit disabled apprentices at all, namely, the London guild of carpenters, whose ordinances of 1455, dealing with control over the membership of the guild, laid down that every master shall present a prospective apprentice to the other masters and wardens to ensure "that he be not lame croked ne deformed".[196]

Even among religious groups the notion of screening prospective 'apprentices', i.e. novices, as a requirement for admission can be found. In 1346 Jean de Hubant, founder of the College of Ave Maria in Paris, declared that any adolescents who had "a physical deformity" were not to be given scholarships there[197]—note, however, the subtle difference between complete exclusion, which is not mooted here, and exclusion from financial benefits, the scholarships. It is interesting to note that amongst the mendicant orders similar 'health and fitness' requirements existed. So, for instance, an amendment of 1239 to the Franciscan statutes made it clear that any candidate who "had any sort of incapacity in addition to mutilation" would not be received into the order.[198] And a Franciscan statute from the French province ordered in 1337: "Novices must publicly acknowledge and witness that they are not concealing any latent illness they have, otherwise the Order shall not have any obligations to them."[199] The earliest constitution of the Dominican order prescribed that a panel of three friars should examine potential novices concerning their health, character, legitimacy and education, with the question on health specifically asking whether the candidate had any "hidden infirmity".[200] Ostensibly such screening of potential recruits to the orders was intended to reduce the burden on money and resources, but there is an undertone of more general notions of bodily perfection expected of those who were to set spiritual as well as practical examples to the wider Christian community.

Even if an apprentice was not impaired when first entering into an agreement with a master, someone becoming impaired during the term of their apprenticeship will have been at the mercy of their master's good will and charity, since the master was under no further (legal) obligation to maintain and train an apprentice beyond the terms of the contract. The contractual terms worked both ways, since if a master became victim to "a long and serious illness" that situation too nullified the agreement, and the apprentice would ideally return home to their family.[201] Apprentices and journeymen may, therefore, sometimes have been provided with some security by the 'in sickness and in health' clause of their contracts to cover illness, injury and accident, or may have even relied on verbal agreements between master and apprentice, but casual workers or day labourers who were not covered by such contracts or agreements had nowhere to turn to in cases of incapacity other than the general charity and almsgiving of the populace.[202]

Since masters did not always honour their agreements to provide for them, journeymen in Germany had begun to form their own associations by the later thirteenth century, specifically motivated by the lack of care in times of illness in the master's household.[203] For instance, in 1372 the journeymen furriers of Stendal had a special 'chest' (*Büchse*) which they paid into to cover cases of sickness,[204] and the accounts of the journeymens' guild of furriers at Braunschweig between 1441 and 1453 mentioned a surgeon's fee for the amputation of a hand[205]—the affected journeyman would have remained disabled irrespective of whether the cause was work-related accident or unrelated to labour activities. In Germany, provision for journeymen appears to have been referenced, if rather obliquely, in the *Sachsenspiegel* of 1225, where masters were obliged to keep on journeymen and pay them (part of) their wages even if these were incapable of working due to an (industrial) accident;[206] nevertheless, such provisions found their way into the civic laws of Hamburg in 1270 (further redactions 1292/1370) and of Bremen in 1303/1428.[207] Journeymen, therefore, were granted a modicum of job security in cases of industrial injury and disability. Fear of competition by the journeymen's guilds may have induced the craft guilds run by and for the masters to also start supporting sick journeymen; from the second half of the fourteenth century onwards, for instance, the guild of smiths at Flensburg's statutes after 1400 mention the "miserable" (*elenden*) journeymen who may have already arrived in a state of illness.[208] A concrete example of the masters' guilds' provisions for the journeymen they employed can be found in the statutes of the guild of coopers at Strasbourg, dating from 1355. If one of the journeymen (*knechte*) should become incapacitated, the masters would loan him three *schillinge* weekly up to a maximum of eighteen *schillinge*, and in the event of his demise, the journeyman was to buried in the same way as if he were one of the masters.[209] The guild of millers' journeymen at Basle stated in their statutes of 17 May 1427:

> 16. In such a case that God should allow infirmity and sickness to be brought upon a journeyman of this fraternity, so that he were incapable of working and earning his livelihood, one should from the treasury loan the sick journeyman 10 *Schilling Pfennige* according to his desire and his reputation. But if he remained infirm and bed-ridden for longer one should, if he demands it, loan him 1 pound *Pfennige* from the treasury against his security, if so much is available in the treasury. And the securities of the sick journeyman shall be kept unsaleable for a whole year, without exception.

> (16. *In dem Falle, dass Gott über einen Gesellen dieser Bruderschaft Siechtum und Krankheit kommen ließe, so dass er nicht arbeiten und seinen Unterhalt verdienen könnte, soll man dem kranken Gesellen auf sein Begehren und auf seine Redlichkeit aus der Büchse 10 Schilling Pfennige leihen. Würde er aber länger siech und bettlägrig, so soll man ihm, wenn er es verlangt, auf sein Pfand aus der Büchse 1 Pfund Pfennige leihen, wenn so viel in der Büchse vorhanden ist. Und die Pfänder des kranken Gesellen sollen ein ganzes Jahr lang unverkäuflich aufbewahrt werden, ohne Ausnahme.*)[210]

Thus support in times of incapacity is here made in the form of a loan, which is granted against a pledge of security by the journeyman. Such loans will not always have been recovered by the craft guilds, for example, in those cases where the journeymen died from whichever sickness they had suffered, or if they remained chronically ill[211]—or became too disabled to continue even with a reduced level of work. Another coopers' guild, this time at Cologne, contained a clause (number 12) in their statutes of April 1397 to the effect that members who were incapacitated by impairments (lame, blind, old age) and could no longer have customers, and therefore no income, were to be maintained at the guild's expense, provided the guild's treasury had enough capital to do so:

> If one of the brothers should have become lame, blind or so old that he became poor and could no longer win customers . . . so they need, and the guild officials shall give to the lame, blind or old, sick brothers because of their brotherhood all days, from the treasury [shrine], if it contains so much or if something else is to be taken from the commonality, namely to each eight *Mörchen* [= 16 *Pfennige*], for as long as God gives them life, and without any impediments.

> (*Wenn einer von den Brüdern lahm, blind oder so alt geworden ist, daß er arm wurde und keine Kunden (mehr) gewinnen konnte, . . . so*

begehren sie, und es sollen die Amtsmeister den lahmen, blinden oder alten, kranken Brüdern von ihrer Bruderschaft wegen aus ihrem Schrein (Kasse), wenn da so viel drin ist oder anderes aus dem 'gemeinligen' zu nehmen ist, alle Tage geben, und zwar jedem acht 'Mörchen', solange jenen Gott das Leben gibt, ohne jedwelche ('allerlei') Hindernisse.)[212]

Old age is qualified at the second mention to mean sick old age; hence, being old of its own was not regarded as an impairment and did not necessarily qualify the guild member for payment of support (a theme further discussed in Chapter 3). The egalitarian character of the guild towards its members is also apparent, since payments are to be made to all members "without any impediments", that is, irrespective of the status or reputation of that person and based purely on the criteria of lameness, blindness or incapacitated old age. And at Strasbourg the boatmen working along the Rhine followed the by now standard examples of mutual aid and made provisions for their incapacitated members, documented in statutes dating from the fifteenth century:

If one or several of the brothers fell into poverty due to infirmity or sickness, so that he suffered dearth of his bodily nourishment and he asked and desired that one should help him for God's sake, then the four treasurers should come together and consult, and they should include two or four reputable men who are also members of the fraternity, and agree amongst each other which contribution they want to give the poor brother, through God, as assistance from the treasury.

(Wenn einer oder mehrere der Brüder durch Siechtum und Krankheit in Armut fiele, so dass er Mangel an seiner Leibesnahrung litte und dieser bäte und begehrte dann, dass man ihm um Gottes willen zu Hilfe komme, so sollen die vier Büchsenmeister zusammenkommen und beraten, und sie sollen noch zwei oder vier redliche Männer hinzuziehen, die auch Mitglieder der Bruderschaft sind, und miteinander einig werden, welchen Beitrag sie dem armen Bruder, durch Gott, als Beihilfe aus der Kasse geben wollen.)[213]

In a number of other northern cities, too, outside of Germany, fraternities of journeymen had managed to negotiate certain privileges, e.g. in Saint Omer provision was made after 1412 to journeymen in need through guild contributions and the right of journeymen bakers in Riga to obtain admission to the Hospital of the Holy Spirit when they became too incapacitated to work, while some organisations even erected their own hospitals, such as the bakers of Venice, who provided a hospital for their infirm or unemployed members (albeit in a less salubrious district of the city).[214] During the fifteenth century, the Venetian tailors, silk throwsters and painters all had hospitals for use by their members.[215]

Many guilds formulated similar pledges of mutual aid and assistance in their statutes. What constituted a novel approach by the guilds to providing for the sick and others incapable of working was that the payments made by the later medieval German guilds to their members was based on the amount that an individual had paid in previously; in other words, payments were linked to the level of prior earnings, a concept not far removed from the social security regulations in many modern European states.[216]

Masters, the self-employed and employers of others, were for most of the medieval period not deemed to require incapacity benefits paid for by the guilds, since their workshop or business could continue to operate without the master necessarily participating in manufacturing himself, as long as there were enough qualified journeymen and apprentices to do the actual, physical work. Hence, some guilds, like the barbers of Riga in 1494 or the goldsmiths of Lübeck in 1492, simply acted as employment agencies for the individual master by sending a suitable journeyman to an incapacitated master (whom the master had to pay wages out of his own business profits) so that productivity could continue.[217] Exceptions to this form of economic solution to a master's physical incapacity were found in the masons' guilds, who did start paying sickness and incapacity benefits to masters; in part this was due to the highly migratory nature of (stone)masons' work, mentioned earlier. So, for instance, the stonemasons of Strasbourg stipulated in 1459–1464 that henceforth masters of the guild should also receive incapacity benefits, since they often worked abroad.[218] In 1439 at Colmar the master stonemason employed by the municipality was assured around twenty-three *gulden* in case of being unable to work due to incapacity,[219] and in 1478 the guild of carpenters at Strasbourg aided members who had suffered an occupational accident.[220] In 1491 at Basle the master of the well (that is, the person responsible for the municipal water supply and hence a figure of some importance) was entitled to almost seventeen *gulden* in case of incapacity, or a third of his full wages.[221]

Alongside the craft guilds discussed so far one need also mention the support provided by parish guilds. Parochial guilds primarily had a religious function, such as acting as a burial club for their members or paying for a priest to say masses, but sometimes they also encompassed the function of a "benefit society",[222] in the sense of helping members during episodes of sickness or poverty. One-off payments could be made, for instance, the six shillings and eight pence that the Trinity Guild of King's Lynn gave to a man with a broken back in 1373[223]—whether this impairment was the result of an industrial accident is not clear from the records. Aims and functions of English parish guilds can be analysed according to a list of ordinances, constitutions and guild customs submitted in 1389 on request to the royal chancery. Of a total of 507 guild returns, only 154 guilds (less than 31 per cent) were concerned with providing help in cash or kind, which was given with great individual variation. Some guilds stated the actual amounts their members might benefit from, some just made a general statement of intent and others said that the level of aid depended on available funds, while in yet more guilds the money doled out varied according to the number of people simultaneously seeking support. Finally, some guilds qualified entitlement to support depending on the length of individual membership.[224] Even then the vast majority of those 154 guilds with any form of function as a benefit society only very generally stated their intention to help those members fallen into poverty or suffering from the vague and non-specific 'sickness'—disability as a more or less specific condition, whether as result of work-related accident or physiological deterioration, hardly gets a mention in most of the guild returns. Those few that do are summarised in Table 2.1. It is interesting to note that one guild (at Stretham) explicitly connects disability with the inability of a member to work, while another (at Wisbech) highlights the theological concept of the accidental nature of disability as something caused by God.

Table 2.1   Support by Parish Guilds in Cases of Disability[225]

Certificate Number	Town	Associated Church	Foundation Date	Benefits Provided
5	Cambridge	Church of Holy Trinity	1384	Pays six pence per week to members impoverished due to sickness or accident.
31	Stretham, Isle of Ely, (Cambridgeshire)	Church of Saint James	1350	Pays three pence per week to a brother deprived of eyes, feet or other limbs and so unable to work.
43	Wisbech (Cambridgeshire)	Holy Trinity	1379	Ten pence per week to a brother "if by act of God he be paralysed, dumb or blind" so that he would have to beg.
45	Chesterfield (Derbyshire)	Saint Mary	?1218	"A brother in poverty by reason of old age, loss of limbs or leprosy, to be helped by those who are able in turn or they shall procure a dwelling for him."
59	Walden (Essex)	Corpus Christi	1377– 1378	Eight pence a week in accidental poverty, sickness or other mishap.

(continued)

Table 2.1 (continued)

Certificate Number	Town	Associated Church	Foundation Date	Benefits Provided
141	Lincoln	Church of Saint George	1377	Three pence a week from a collection in cases of poverty, old age or false imprisonment.
190	London	Saint Lawrence Jewry	1370	"14d. a week in infirmity by reason of mutilation of limbs or old age, etc., but the brother helped must have paid his quarter-age for 7 years."
308	Norwich	Chapel of Saint Mary *de campis*	1350	"And also it ys ordeyned, be þe Alderman and alle the breþeren, þat who-so falle at meschief, en pouerte, croked, blyn, be þe grace of Godes sonde, out-taken 3ef he be a theffe proued, he ssal han seuene penes in þe woke, of þe breþeren and sisteren, to helpen hem withe."[226] Associated with the Tailors' Guild.
342	Upwell (Norfolk)	Saint John the Evangelist	1382–1383	"In poverty, paralysis, blindness, etc., ¼ d. a week from each brother."
450	Kingston-on-Hull (Yorkshire)	Saint John the Baptist	No date	"Help given to the infirm and needy."

Sentiments concerning the deserving status of members expressed by the parish guilds were given stronger emphasis in some than in others. The guild of Garlekhith (London), founded in 1375, provided weekly relief in times of old age or 'feebleness' but only for members with a minimum of seven years' standing: "Also, 3if eny of þe forsaide broþerhede falle in such meschief þ[a]t he hath noght, ne for elde oþer mischief of feblenesse, help hym-self".[227] At Cambridge the guild of the Blessed Virgin Mary (associated with Saint Botolph's) ruled that:

If any brother comes to want by *mishap* [my emphasis] or sickness, so
that it is not through plunder by harlots, or through any other bad way
of life, and he has not the means of living, he shall have 7 pence a week
during life, from the Gild, and a new gown every year. If two brethren
are at the same time in want, then 4 pence per week each.[228]

This shows what a small organisation the guild was, in that finances would
be stretched if more than one member required assistance. Entitlement to
material support was therefore means tested, and the character and lifestyle
of the guild member mattered as much as the accident. This is even more
apparent in the guild of Holy Trinity, associated with Saint Botolph's at
Aldersgate in London, which was originally founded in 1374 as a guild
of Corpus Christi. According to the 1389 chancery returns for this guild,
financial help of fourteen pence per week in cases of sickness and poverty
due to old age were assessed by criteria such as inability to help themselves and the accidental nature of the situation (i.e. guild members had not
brought it upon themselves):

2. Also, yif it so bifalle that any of the brotherhede falle in pouverte,
or be anyentised thurwy elde, that he may nat helpe hymself or thurwy
any other chaunce, thurwy fyr or watir, theues or syknesse, or any
other hap, so it be nat on hymselue alonge, ne thurwy his owne wrec-
chednesse, he schal haue in the wyke xiiij d.[229]

One of the fullest description of disabilities and the aid given in such cases
found in guild ordinances stems from the guild of the Blessed Virgin Mary
at Kingston-upon-Hull (Yorkshire), which was founded in 1357. Since the
clauses relating to social benefits in this guild's statutes set the model for a
number of other local fraternities,[230] they are worth citing in full:

If it happen that any of the gild becomes infirm, bowed, blind, dumb,
deaf, maimed, or sick, whether with some lasting or only temporary
sickness, and whether in old age or in youth, or be so borne down by
any other mishap that he has not the means of living, then, for kindness' sake, and for the soul's sake of the founders, it is ordained that
each shall have, out of the goods of the gild, at the hands of the wardens, sevenpence every week; and every one so being infirm, bowed,
blind, dumb, deaf, maimed, or sick, shall have that sevenpence every
week as long as he lives.[231]

Not only do these ordinances list the more or less complete range of physical
impairments recognised in the later Middle Ages, but they still emphasise
that aspect of charity which concerns the reciprocal relationship between
the soul of the donor and the recipient (a topic more fully explored in
Chapter 4). And it is clearly emphasised that there is no time limit imposed

on the guild's financial help, but that disabling conditions require continuous support. Such support was necessary for chronic and incurable ailments, something another guild, the Palmers at Ludlow, founded in 1284, also recognised.

> But if any one becomes a leper, or blind, or maimed in limb, or smitten with any other incurable disorder (which God forbid), we wish that the goods of the gild shall be largely bestowed on him.[232]

In providing continuous, lifelong support, these particular parish guilds differed from many of the regular craft guilds, whose support was only intended for quantifiable periods of temporary illness.

Looking after one's sick or impaired members required a certain level of resources. The wealthier guilds had more capital to provide assistance in times of medical need or to provide financial aid to impoverished members. Many guilds had a chest, in other words, a fund maintained by members' subscriptions or voluntary donations but also by fines imposed on delinquent members, to raise the required capital. At Paris, members of the goldsmith's guild took it in turn to keep one shop open every Sunday and the proceeds of sales from that shop were divided "among the needy of the town and the widows and sick of the guild."[233] Georges Renard stated that at Florence the guilds of the carpenters and the stonemasons were able to maintain their own hospital.[234] For Alsace, Renard mentions the bakers' fraternities, who had bylaws regulating the support given to sick members in hospital, who

> were to be given confession, communion, a clean bed, and with every meal a jug of wine, sufficient bread, a good basin of soup, meat, eggs, or fish; and all were to be treated alike.[235]

The regular security provided by guilds and fraternities may have needed to be 'topped up' by external benefactors. Jean de Joinville mentioned that among the men whom Louis IX had helped with donations and charity were "artisans who were unable to work at their crafts on account of old age or illness".[236]

Having examined loss of working ability through impairment, the following section of this chapter will turn to what one may term the time and work controversy,[237] considering questions such as: did medieval economic realms allow greater 'freedoms' to less able people? Was it more likely for disabled people to fulfil a 'useful' economic function? And did the developing proto-capitalism of the urban high Middle Ages hinder the integration of disabled workers? The time and work controversy stems from Le Goff's thesis[238] that greater regulation of working time (i.e. merchant time derived from the technological innovations of church time[239]), as opposed to the flexible time of agricultural work (i.e. peasant time) curtailed the integration of disabled workers, who under the older, more flexible sense of time had been able to structure their working day as they saw fit. Furthermore, E. P. Thompson's seminal essay 'Time, Work-Discipline, and Industrial Capitalism' suggested that clock-discipline became the dominant way of structuring time in the industrial period,[240] but more recent work has postulated that this dominance has been overstated, and rather that evidence seems to indicate to a variety of multiple and competing sources of time-sense which continue into modern contemporary society.[241]

With regard to measuring time as opposed to experiencing time, Harald Kleinschmidt has argued:

> in the early Middle Ages and up to the thirteenth century, there were few general 'objective' standards regarding time and equally few instruments for the precise measurement of time. Instead, in the Middle Ages up to the thirteenth century, preference was given to natural rhythms like day and night, the seasons, the sequence of harvests, or the revolutions of the moon as indicators of the process of time, and local groups of settlers in villages were accustomed to control their own time rather than being controlled by it.[242]

This is essentially the argument Le Goff had put forward, namely, that earlier, more 'natural' forms of measuring or experiencing time permitted a predominantly rural workforce to be in charge of their own structuration of time and associated activities.[243] "Rural time was principally that of the *longue durée*", and "entailed waiting, putting up with things . . . slowness".[244] The lack of means to measure time, however, also meant that those who did possess such means were able to dominate those who did not. As Le Goff put it: "The masses did not own their own time and were incapable of measuring it. They obeyed the time imposed on them by bells, trumpets, and horns."[245] A combination of the development of precise time measurement in monastic as well as urban spheres led by the late thirteenth and early fourteenth century to the standardisation of measurement units.[246] "Hence, the hours came to be measured at equal length throughout the year, irrespective of seasonal variations."[247] Pioneered in the Italian cities, public clocks came to be installed, followed in the mid-fourteenth century by town halls in north-western Europe, and with the clocks came the expectation to 'keep time'—urban inhabitants, from artisans and merchants to clergy and university students, organised their activities according to the new regularised system of measurement. For instance, in 1355 the town of Aire-sur-la-Lys in the Artois built "a belfry whose bells would chime the hours of commercial transactions and the working hours of the textile workers."[248] The governor of the county of Artois granted this right because of the "cloth trade and other trades which require several workers each day to go and come to work at certain hours."[249] The workers were expected to begin and end their work in time with the regulated hours of the bells—a prefiguration of modern industrial work practices ('clocking on/off'). However, one may also interpret the adoption of the technology of the new mechanical clock as an accommodation into existing structures, rather than necessarily being oppositional or antagonistic to them; in that sense the 'clocking on/off' might have benefited workers by limiting the maximum length of the working day, and might have been something the labourers themselves welcomed as a means of curtailing arbitrarily fixed working times by their employers.[250] Nevertheless, according to Le Goff, the new system of urban labour of the thirteenth century onwards was marked, most importantly, by "the definition, measurement, and use of the working day".[251] As this author of an early fifteenth-century Middle English religious text commented: "In monasteries, religious men and women follow the candle and the clepsydra and, in cities and in towns, men and women follow the strikes of the mechanical clock".[252] The disciplined, reliable worker was and remains one of the prerequisites for capitalist economic enterprises.[253]

A disabled worker was less likely to keep up the same rate of production during a precisely measured unit of time as a non-disabled worker; so even if disabled people were participating in various economic activities, which was likely (at least for those with minor disabilities) considering the medieval patterns of work in artisan and craft guilds, then proto-capitalist manufacturing processes where work was paid for according to measured output will have disadvantaged the earning power of the disabled—or even excluded them as too unproductive. Under a system of payment for piecework, where the actual items produced held economic value rather than the length of time for which workers hired out their labour, a disabled person could be economically active, albeit at perhaps a slower pace than an able-bodied worker, but under a system of contracts for specified hours of work (which was beginning to develop in urban areas in the later thirteenth century[254]) a disabled worker posed a less attractive investment for an employer. As Herzlich and Pierret have pointed out with regard to modern society in the context of their study of illness and social attitudes:

> In a society in which we define ourselves as producers, illness and inactivity have become equivalents. That is why today we have come to perceive the sick body essentially through its incapacity to "perform", rather than through the alteration of its appearance.[255]

With regard to work, then, one's ability or in/dis-ability to perform work of all kinds has become the measuring stick by which degrees of impairment, disability or 'need' were defined. Being able to "perform" in society has become crucial. Some of the most interesting studies of how disability, both past and present, fits into this model of social performance have come from the discipline of geography, rather than sociology, let alone history, notably in the work of Imrie and Gleeson.[256]

Furthermore, the capacities of impaired people were devalued with the development of capitalism when the worth of individual labour was appraised in terms of average productivity standards, so that 'slower', 'weaker' or more inflexible workers were devalued in terms of their potential for paid work. In contrast to Gleeson, German historian Walter Fandrey argued that because the primarily agrarian mode of production in the Middle Ages made greater demands on people's physical capabilities, the situation for physically impaired people was actually worse[257]—lack of physical strength and stamina would have been noticed as a negative trait by contemporaries, and someone unable to 'pull his weight' during activities such as the harvest was a drain on resources. Conversely, many activities required for effective work in the modern industrialised world, such as fine motor skills and precise vision, would have been, according to Fandrey, of lesser importance in such a pre-industrial environment, where lack of motor skills could be compensated for by brute strength and accurate vision was not as necessary for many tasks.[258] Medieval disabled people, in this analysis, were in an ambiguous situation with regard to labour, productivity and socially expected norms.

Besides labour processes there is the question of spatial issue, of the removal of the site of production from home to a separate workplace, which was further disabling. Modern studies of disability and space have looked at the marginalisation of disabled people, linked by social geographers such as Gleeson, especially in the industrial city, to "the new separation of home and work, a socio-spatial phenomenon which was all but absent in the feudal era."[259] While industrial modes of production, with their emphasis on competitive, regulated productivity (one may think here of the factory worker at the conveyor belt), certainly marginalised what Karl Marx had already called an "incapable" social stratum,[260] it would be too simplistic to apply such analyses wholesale to the premodern past. By "incapable" social stratum Marx meant the latterly infamous term "Lumpenproletariat", which he coined to include, besides the criminal elements he was primarily referring to, also widows, the elderly, orphans, the sick and "the mutilated and the victims of industry" (i.e. people disabled in industrial accidents).[261] Ironically, for a medievalist, this reads almost like any list of 'deserving poor' from the ubiquitous moral and religious tracts of the later Middle Ages. With regard to the meanings of bodies as physical, material entities, Terry Eagleton made some interesting observations on the proletariat within premodern society, a group formed by "those who were too poor to serve the state by holding property, and who served instead by producing children as labor power"; furthermore, being a member of the premodern proletariat is at once a gendered and dehumanising condition, since they "have nothing to give but their bodies. Proletarians and women are thus intimately allied . . . The ultimate poverty or loss of being is . . . to work directly with your body, like the other animals."[262] This is not a new interpretation. In 1406, the Wycliffite reformer William Taylor had preached that the bodies of the poor are "waastid" and are "use[d] as beestis",[263] thus already drawing the same conclusions as Eagleton would some six centuries later. But an impaired body, in this line of thinking, has become so useless that it can no longer even be exploited like that of an animal; hence, the impaired are not even fit for a place within the proletariat and are instead relegated to the Lumpenproletariat.

So much for a brief excursion into the body's place within (proto)capitalism. But even the most developed mercantile or proto-capitalist regions of Europe, for instance, the northern Italian city-states or the Flemish towns, lacked the infrastructure and institutions, such as workhouses and of course the determinant factories, that characterised a fully industrialised society.[264] The disablement caused by capitalism and industrialisation has been regarded as the antithesis of the "power for self-creation" of the old, 'feudal' peasant society, where the impaired body was believed to be "an autonomous creator of social space".[265] Concerning the hypothesis that medieval work patterns lacked regimentation, regulation and were more fluid than modern structures, Christopher Dyer has observed that in

> this interpretation of medieval labour, it is emphasized that people tended to work slowly and inefficiently, and to stop whenever possible. It is said that their activities were not measured or timed accurately, and they worked until the job was completed. . . . To use modern phraseology, they were 'task-oriented' rather than 'time-oriented'.[266]

According to this model of labour in the Middle Ages as an activity less subject to the pressures of time or production than modern industrial societies,[267] it would appear that disabled persons were more likely to find a socially acceptable role as workers. If this model of work were correct, then it would have meant a greater accommodation of disabled people and their 'style' of working than possible in modern times. Hypothesising a blind person who was dexterous enough to work as a basket-weaver, such an artisan would have been able to not only work as a self-employed person, in their own time and using their own tools and equipment, but the stereotypical basket-weaver will have been in charge of their pattern of work, speed at which they laboured, daily output, time off and so forth. Other than perhaps producing less 'units' per day than an able-bodied basket-weaver, and therefore earning less money, the blind basket producer will have had no *institutional* disadvantage under the pre-industrial mode of working— simply producing less units, or working at a slower pace, did not disqualify the impaired worker from work *per se*, as long as the worker could be in charge of how they structured their working pattern.

In connection with this theme, one may look at how impairments may (or may not) have affected the working ability of individual people. Since examples of individual case-studies from the medieval period as such are few and far between, at least within the limits that the present author has been able to discover in the sources, it is appropriate to take a brief excursion into the early modern period, to Norwich in the 1570s, from where stems a particularly rich and precise set of records in the shape of a population census. The aim of the census was for the authorities to establish who in Norwich was entitled to poor relief, so one may assume a bias in favour of exaggeration of the potential working abilities and self-sufficiency of persons listed in the document, undoubtedly in an attempt to save 'public' money. Even so, Margaret Pelling, author of a number of studies on poverty, sickness and population in early modern England, commented that with regard to the Norwich census, "the sick and disabled were not necessarily excluded from social and economic life",[268] instead retaining the possibilities of interaction with others. If this was still the case for the early modern, post-Reformation period with its Protestant 'work ethic', then one would assume all the more economic interaction for the medieval period. Hence the census-takers recorded Elizabeth Mason, a widowed woman aged eighty who was lame and one-handed, as able to work for her living.[269] The concept that an elderly and (to modern minds) disabled woman was deemed quite capable of working clearly demonstrates the different notions of 'disability', in this case even a "severe disability", as Pelling terms her condition. Yet Elizabeth Mason could perform spinning and winding yarn sedentarily and single-handedly.[270] In short, the concept of what was regarded as economic activity in the 1570s and what the industrialised twenty-first century regards as such are not identical. Another woman in her fifties was described by the census record as "lame but able", yet she did not work, living instead from alms and off her friends (for which, one gets the impression, she was labelled as one of the 'undeserving' poor); in contrast, a blind man worked as a baker and a blind woman aged eighty supported herself by knitting, while another blind man had a fatherless child of twelve to lead him around[271]—note the mutual support among these 'deserving' poor: the orphan acting as guide for the blind. Both old age and disability were not invariably factors defining a person's capability to perform work: three widows aged seventy-four, seventy-nine and eighty-two years old were described as "almost" past work but still deemed (just) capable of work, as were "almost" lame or blind people in the Norwich census.[272] Such women in their seventies "who were blind, weak or lame-handed continued to knit, card, and spin" to make a living.[273] Incidentally, at Norwich a century earlier, the poor, sick and infirm in the local hospital of Saint Giles were kept busy, to the best of their abilities, with spinning wool: in 1479 two stones of wool were brought onto the hospital premises from the hospital-owned flock of sheep.[274] And, as was mentioned earlier, in 1276 one of the protagonists of a miracle alleged to Saint Louis, Jehanne de Serris, worked with her hands at spinning while she was paralysed in her legs, awaiting a thaumaturgic miracle at the shrine at Saint Denis, "since she wanted to live by her own means when she went to the tomb".[275] In some German towns, the municipal authorities tried to ensure a regular income for disabled people by employing them for certain tasks, in the 'public sector' as the modern equivalent would have it, for instance, in late medieval Frankfurt, where lame and blind (!) men were given jobs as guards and watchmen.[276] That the disabled, in an urban setting, were indispensable in times of crisis emerges from a late thirteenth-century chronicle of Cologne, which remarks that during an uprising against the bishop in 1262 the church bells were rung in hierarchical order, first the bell "Wellin" of the cathedral to alert all able-bodied militia, then the bell "Stürzkuppe" of Saint Martin, "which made even the lame hasten", and thirdly all the other alarm bells, which brought out the women with their distaffs[277]—note that the womenfolk were ranked below lame men.

One may therefore conclude that disability exists in an assumed system-specific functionality. This concept revolves around the functionality attributed to disabled people in any given society. The disabled need not be totally disfunctional for their overall functionality to be questionable. Generally, the difference of a given disability challenges just a partial aspect of societal standards, or rather just some functions and expectations of the disabled person are deemed insufficient, but the more central the values attached to such functions are to the value system of a society overall, and the greater the deviation from normalcy, the greater the 'threat' of a disabled person is deemed to be.[278] With regard to work and productivity, the disabled especially do not fulfil the "strategic functional achievements" of industrial society, with functionality being closely linked to the actual process of work and methods of production.[279] In that sense some of the later medieval urban production processes (e.g. wage earners working for an artisan/craft master, 'clocking on/off' of the workforce) are already premonitions of the later production methods of early industrial and mercantile systems, such as that promulgated in the seventeenth century by French minister Colbert, and even Taylorism.[280] In essence, therefore, the more highly 'work' and 'productivity' are rated within the overall value system of a given culture, the less the non-working and non-productive (or simply slower) members of that culture will themselves be valued. Conversely, in cultures where other abilities are accorded a higher value than 'labour', for instance, where fertility and childbirth are highly esteemed, someone with impaired fertility who could otherwise work perfectly well, like a hermaphrodite, is devalued.[281] Perhaps, with regard to the position of medieval disabled persons as labourers, as active participants in the various crafts, trades and occupations, one should place greater emphasis on the difference between urban and rural patterns and systems of work, a difference that became greater with the growth of markets and towns from the high Middle Ages onwards.

Under the (older) rural system of labour a greater flexibility of time existed, which allowed medieval people, including and especially the peasantry, to structure their working day as they saw fit—the exceptions being the 'boon' days when they were obliged to work for the lord's demesne.

According to this theory, expanded from Le Goff's original thoughts on medieval time and work by Gleeson, the dis/abilities of an individual peasant's body determined how much and how long they would work. "Feudal temporality was a significant contributor to somatic flexibility in the peasant labour process."[282] The implication for disabled people would therefore be that their 'disability' as far as rural work was concerned would be relatively negligible, although of course this still left the issue of 'cultural' disability, with all its multiple layers of positive as well as negative meanings. Attractive though Gleeson's theory might be at first sight, it nevertheless presents too simplistic a picture of an idealised 'feudal' rural past, described through the proverbial rose-tinted lenses. One may take a closer look at the practice of gleaning, which Gleeson himself did to underpin his thesis—arguing for the reservation of gleaning for old and disabled people as part of pre-clock time—to examine how the differing abilities of the disabled may or may not have been accommodated into medieval labour systems.

Gleaning was the name given to the activity of collecting the ears of corn that were left after the bulk of the harvest had been brought in. A time window of around five to seven days existed for gleaning after the reaping had finished, since thereafter the stubble was turned over to the animals for pasture. Medieval harvesting techniques—by hand—meant that there would be a reasonable amount of corn left to be gleaned once the 'professional' harvesters with their scythes and sickles had been to work on a field. Gleaners were as necessary as the reapers and binders during harvest time, especially for crops such as oats and barley, which were mown close to the ground and with short stalks, so that much remained to be gleaned after the sheaves had been gathered. According to agrarian historian Ault, "children and grown-ups too old or too feeble for such heavy labour [as harvesting] might glean; there was work for everyone."[283] Ault then cited an eighteenth-century authority as estimating that a gleaner could earn almost as much in a day as a reaper.[284] Whether this was the case for the medieval period, too, is open to question, but what certainly was the case is that medieval agrarian regulations and laws ensured that nobody who was physically capable of harvesting, i.e. reaping, was allowed to glean. Misdemeanours by people who were caught gleaning when they should have been reaping were fined in the manorial courts, hence the source of our evidence via manorial court rolls, such as this example from the manor of Newington (Oxon.), where proceedings were held in 1322 against one Alice King, who had "transgressed in gleaning".[285]

From these English manorial bylaws stems evidence for the reservation of gleaning for the poor, the elderly and the impaired, in other words, for those people who were incapable of participating in the 'professional' harvesting activities. For instance, the bylaws of Newton Longville in Buckinghamshire stated in 1290 that any labourer hired for a wage (in this case a penny per day with meals or two pence daily if self-catering) at harvest time was forbidden from gleaning.[286] Christopher Dyer posits that such legislation "developed during the thirteenth century and then spread from place to place" in part to protect the material needs of the vulnerable (such as elderly, widows, disabled persons) but presumably primarily to protect the interests of the landowners in securing enough labour to get the precious harvest in without mishap due to delays.[287] The onus of defining who was regarded as able-bodied was apparently placed on the reeves of royal manors, as in this instance from 1282:

> Let it be established that the young, the old, and those who are decrepit and unable to work shall glean in the autumn after the sheaves have been taken away, but that those who are able if they wish to work for wages will not be allowed to glean.[288]

The definition of who was classed as 'disabled' (decrepit, infirm, impotent, old, young, widowed) therefore hinged around the possibility of being hired for harvest work—if someone regardless of impairment was hired as a labourer, they were strictly forbidden from gleaning. Definitions of able-bodied versus disabled could also be made on an individual case-by-case basis according to a bylaw from Brightwaltham, Berkshire, in 1340 (see Table 2.2).

Table 2.2 English Manorial Documents on Gleaning and Dis/Ability[289]

Manorial/Village Bylaw	*Doc. no.*	*Date*
No one on the manor of Newington (Oxon) "shall accept any one as a gleaner who is capable of doing the work of a reaper."	5	1286
"Item that no one be allowed to glean who is able to earn a penny a day with food or two pence without food." Newton Longville (Bucks)	8	1290
"Item it is granted by the same that no one shall go about gathering grain [i.e. gleaning] who can earn half a penny a day and his food." Great Horwood (Bucks)	22	1305
"That no one of them male or female shall be allowed to glean who is able to earn his food and a penny a day for his work." Great Horwood (Bucks)	38	1322
"It is agreed and ordered in full court by the whole homage of the town of Great Horwood that no one among them shall be allowed to glean who is able to earn his food and a penny a day for his labour." Court roll of Great Horwood (Bucks)	203	1323
"And that no one shall glean who is able to earn a penny a day and food." Halton (Bucks)	41	1326

(continued)

Table 2.2   (continued)

Manorial/Village Bylaw	Doc. no.	Date
"It is granted and ordered by the whole homage of the town of Newington that no one be given leave to glean anything in the said town if he can find any one who wishes to hire him for his food and a penny a day." Newington (Oxon)	43	1329
"It is ordered by the lord's bailiffs and by the consent of the whole homage both free and customary that no one shall glean who is able to earn a penny a day and food." Court roll of Halton (Oxon)	205	1329
"Item Agnes Wat' (3d.) would not reap and was able to reap, therefore, in mercy." Newington (Oxon)	45	1330
"No one shall accept any gleaners, male or female, who are able to reap and earn a penny a day and food." Newton Longville (Bucks)	48	1331
"It is granted and ordained by the whole township of Horwood that no one shall be allowed to glean who can earn his food and a penny a day if there is anyone who wishes to hire him." Great Horwood (Bucks)	51	1332
"Item that no one shall be admitted to glean who is able to earn his food and 1d. a day if it is found that there is someone who wishes to hire him." Court roll of Newton Longville (Bucks)	199	1332
"Item that no one shall be allowed to glean who is able to earn food and 1d. or 2d. without food if there is any one who wishes to hire him thus." Great Horwood (Bucks)	55	1335
"And that no one shall be allowed to glean in autumn who is able to earn 1d. a day and food." Newton Longville (Bucks)	59	1339
"At this court all the tenants granted that no inhabitant [*intrinsecus*] shall glean grain within this liberty unless he be under age or over age." Brightwaltham (Berks)	61	1340
"Nor shall he allow anyone, male or female, to glean who is able to earn 1d. a day and food." Newington (Oxon)	67	1345
"It is agreed by all the lord's tenants free and customary that none of them shall go gleaning who is able to earn food and 1d. a day under pain of 40d." Great Horwood (Bucks)	72	1349
"It is agreed among all the lord's tenants free and customary that no one among them shall go gleaning who is able to earn a penny and a half or 2d. without food under pain of 2s." Great Horwood (Bucks)	76	1356

(continued)

Table 2.2 (continued)

Manorial/Village Bylaw	Doc. no.	Date
"It is agreed by all the lord's tenants free and customary that no one in the coming autumn shall go gleaning who is able to earn 1d. a day and food or 2d. without food under pain of 12d. every time he is found trespassing against this ordinance." Great Horwood (Bucks)	77	1357
"By the assent of the whole homage it is ordered that no one henceforth shall go gleaning in autumn who is able to earn 1d. a day with food under pain of 2d. for each default." Newton Longville (Bucks)	90	1387
"It is ordered by the assent of the whole homage that no one shall go gleaning in autumn as long as the lord or any other wishes to pay him for his labour 1d. a day with food." Newton Longville (Bucks)	92	1388
"And no one shall go gleaning in autumn who is able to earn 1d. a day with food under the aforesaid pain [40d.]." Great Horwood (Bucks)	94	1389
"And that no one shall glean [*coligat spicas*] in autumn if there is any one who wants to hire him at 1d. a day and food under the pain aforesaid [40d.]." Podnigton (Beds)	103	1395
"And that no one shall glean [*conspicabit*] through the whole of autumn who is able to earn 1d. a day and food under pain of 12d." Houghton (Hunts)	110	1405
"And that no one shall glean through the whole of autumn who is able to earn 1d. a day and food under the aforesaid pain [12d.]." Upwood (Hunts)	111	1405
"That no one shall go about gleaning [*transiet ad spicandum*] who is able to earn 1d. a day and food under the aforesaid pain [6s. 8d.]." Great Horwood (Bucks)	113	1406
"And that no one who is able to earn 1d. a day and food shall glean under pain of 4d. for each transgressor." Newton Longville (Bucks)	114	1406
"Item it is ordained that no one who is able to earn 1d. a day and food in autumn shall go gleaning under pain for each transgressor of 3d." Great Horwood (Bucks)	115	1407
"And that no one shall gleam in autumn who is able to earn 1d. a day and food under pain each one of 12d." Wistow (Hunts)	118	1410
"That no one shall be allowed to glean who is able to earn 1d. a day." Newington (Oxon)	119	1410
"And that no one shall glean in autumn who is able to earn 1d. a day and food under pain of 12d." Warboys (Hunts)	120	1411

(continued)

Table 2.2   (continued)

Manorial/Village Bylaw	Doc. no.	Date
"And that no one shall glean through the whole of autumn who is able to earn 1d. a day and food under the afore-said pain." Burwell (Cambs)	122	1411
"Item that no gleaner shall gather grain in autumn who is able to earn 1d. a day and food under pain of each trans-gressor paying the lord 4d." Elmley Castle (Worcs)	123	1412
"And that no one shall glean through the whole of autumn who is able to earn 1d. a day and food under the afore-said pain [12d.]." Upwood (Hunts)	124	1412
"To present that if there be anyone who is able to earn 1d. a day and food in autumn time and refuses this and goes about gleaning." Newington (Oxon)	130	1416
"And that no one shall glean who is able to earn 1d. a day and food under pain of 12d." Upwood (Hunts)	135	1428
"And that no one shall glean who is able to earn 1d. a day under pain of 12d." Warboys (Hunts)	138	1430
"And that no one shall glean who is able to earn 1d. a day and food under pain of 6d. to the lord and 6d. to the church." Wistow (Hunts)	139	1430
"And that no one shall glean who is able to earn 1d. a day and food under pain of 6d." Upwood (Hunts)	140	1430
"Item it is ordered that no one ought to glean in autumn time who is able to earn 1d. a day and food." Elmley Castle (Worcs)	145	1439
"And that no one shall glean who is able-bodied [*potens est*] and can earn 1d. a day and 1 ½ d. [*sic*] if any one within this demesne wishes to hire him." Leighton Buzzard (Beds)	160	1469
"It is ordained by the assent of the lord's council and of his tenants that none shall enter the sown field in autumn time to gather grain or spears with rakes or by hand if they are capable of earning 2d. a day, under pain for each one doing contrary to this ordinance of 3s. 4d." Hitchin (Herts)	162	1471

How in practice a person's dis/ability might be judged comes from Basing-stoke (Hants.) in 1389: "The impotent passed by view of the bailiff and constable with the assent of two or three of the tenants may commence gleaning from the beginning of the harvest."[290] A kind of assessment or 'means-testing' of individuals therefore took place involving members of the community (both officials as well as 'ordinary' tenants), which designated someone as "impotent". In fact, here we encounter the closest notion in the Middle Ages to the concept of 'accredited disability' that is prevalent in contemporary modern society. An official examination of the physical dis/abilities of a person decides whether they are permitted to perform a certain activity or not. This medieval manorial custom is conceptually not far removed from the modern custom of obtaining so-called expert statements (generally of a medical nature) labelling a person as disabled and hence entitled to certain welfare benefits.

Ault had simply commented that it was surprising that no other example of this kind of 'means-testing' had been found, but he postulated that doubtlessly some such provision will have been made elsewhere on other manors, too. Apparently at the time Ault was researching this topic, no roll of any English manor court had yet been found which recorded a dispute over the matter of whether someone was rightly or wrongly adjudged 'disabled'.[291] Interestingly, there is no suggestion in any of the numerous bylaws on gleaning which suggests that the poor, needy or disabled had a *right* to glean, nor is any mention of such concepts made in the thirteenth-century treatises on agriculture, e.g. in Walter of Henley. Brendan Gleeson had misinterpreted Ault's findings to believe that gleaning was an activity *specifically* reserved for the physically impaired members of a village or manorial community, but it is evident from a close reading of the bylaws that no such concept can be discerned in them; instead the agrarian rules are simply concerned with ensuring that the reaping gets performed properly and quickly before valuable human resources are allowed to be expended for gleaning. "When anyone was received as a gleaner in those days it was by consent of the landlord and on his terms."[292]

Like exemptions granted for gleaning, special provision could occasionally be made in cases of severe illness, as this example dating to 1251 from the manor of Hartest, in the bishopric of Ely, demonstrates. If a customary tenant

> should become so infirm within the harvest or without it that he shall have been confessed and given communion, then he shall be quit of his works for one month only. But nevertheless he shall do his ploughing outside harvest and his boonworks in harvest. And if he shall be infirm for more than one month then he will not be quit any more. And if he should be so ill for eight days that he shall have been confessed, then he will in the meantime be quit. And if he afterwards recovers from that illness then he will be quit for two days only. And if it should happen a second time he is no more quit.[293]

What this source is implying is basically a meticulously detailed scheme for various degrees of 'sick leave', to bring a modern comparison, during which the tenant is exempt from the demesne work normally expected, but if the period of illness becomes 'long-term sick leave' (i.e. anything beyond one month) the tenant no longer qualifies for exemption. It is not spelled out how the tenant is meant to perform the boonworks, but comparison with other sources on the handing over of tenancies and their associated duties in case of incapacity due to old age (see Chapter 3, this volume) suggests this is the likely course of action. Impaired tenants who were so disabled that they were unable to perform work after more than one month would presumably fall into the category of 'long-term sick' who were nevertheless required to fulfil their customary obligations. As an aside, the act of confessing and taking communion may be equated to the modern doctor's certificate or 'sick note', namely, the expert statement required by the modern employer/medieval landlord to validate a worker's/tenant's claim to the benefits/exemptions associated with sick leave.

Connected with the theme of work is the notion of a particular type of occupation for certain physically impaired people, which includes stereotypes such as the blind minstrel or the blind basket-weaver. However, it is important to remember that in anthropological studies it has been shown that there seems to be no *single* role or group of roles to which disabled people are limited—contradicting the stereotypical assumptions by researchers that in traditional societies the disabled usually function as shaman, priest, prophet and so on.[294] The exception to such stereotypes is begging. Begging has been found in many traditional societies to be the most common role for the unemployed, widows, orphans, unmarried mothers, the sick and the disabled[295]—and the Middle Ages do play up to this stereotype (see Chapter 4, this volume)—since all of these groups tend to be without the protection of their kin and community and lack social alliances. Furthermore, in anthropological literature one may find evidence that some cultures limit specific occupations or trades, so that, for instance, in a number of traditional societies hunting is not permitted to members of the group who are mobility impaired.[296] For examples from Jewish and Christian culture one need only think of the prohibitions in Leviticus that proscribe certain occupations, notably the priesthood, to physically impaired people.

Hence the question arises if there were particular jobs that were predominantly performed by disabled people. There is evidence that the medieval period tried to accommodate the (dis)abilities of workers in relation to specific tasks and duties. One may encounter an early example in the *Rule* of Saint Benedict, which stated that work should be "suited to both the physical and the intellectual capabilities of the individual monk."[297] Thus:

> weakly or sickly brethren should be assigned a task or craft of such a nature as to keep them from idleness and at the same time not to overburden them or drive them away with excessive toil.[298]

The physically fit were to be allocated tasks according to this principle just as much as the sick or impaired, so that if "it happens that difficult or impossible tasks are laid on a brother" and after due reflection "he sees the weight of the burden altogether exceeds the limit of his strength, let him submit the reasons for his inability to the one who is over him".[299] Although one was in the first instance expected to accept the burden of work, the *Rule* also expected each individual to recognise and take responsibility for their capabilities, and if capabilities were exceeded, to bring this to the attention of one's superior.

There is, therefore, precedent for the provision of 'tailoring' jobs according to individual (dis)abilities. Outside of the monastic realm, 'tailoring' of jobs for certain people was often advocated as something to be done by status: people of a lesser status were more suited to the mechanical and physically demanding tasks than people of higher status, who were suited for careers in intellectual work. Thus Robert Kilwardby opined in his *De ortu scientiarum* (a product of his early Oxford career between 1246 and 1250) that "physical activity is more suited to insignificant and common people, the peace of meditation and study to the noble elite; in this way, everyone has an occupation fitting his station of life".[300] Some definitions of what was meant by 'status' may be found in the so-called *sermones ad status* of Kilwardby's contemporary thirteenth-century preachers. These models for sermons were directed at particular socio-economic groups the preacher might encounter in his audience. According to the hierarchic classification given by Jacques de Vitry (c. 1165–1240), among the laypeople the following identifiable groups could be found: "hospitallers and custodians of the sick; lepers and other sick [persons]; paupers and afflicted [persons]",[301] as well as the more familiar categories of pilgrims, burghers, merchants, farmers, artisans and mariners. People in potentially disabling circumstances were therefore treated as having a distinct status in de Vitry's sermon models.

Furthermore, the general concept of specific jobs for certain types of people existed right through the Middle Ages. The question, then, of interest here is to ascertain if such a concept carried across to physically (and mentally) impaired persons. Bluntly put: were there any stereotypical careers that were deemed suitable or appropriate for the disabled?

One stereotypical occupation for the physically (and mentally) disabled immediately springs to mind, namely, the figure of the disabled person as (court) dwarf and fool, which appears to be more a creation of modern historians than medieval reality, there being very few references to dwarves at noble courts as fools or jesters before the sixteenth century. While some medieval aristocratic households did include people who may broadly be classed as 'entertainers with a physical difference', their appearance in the typical records—account books—on which most historians have based their argument for the frequency of disabled people as courtly entertainers is in fact much rarer than the inference from sporadic or isolated references. The topic of the disabled as entertainers at the courts of the nobility and the upper echelons of the bourgeoisie, of physically impaired people as dwarfs and mentally impaired people as fools, would fill a chapter in itself if not another monograph,[302] but under the rubric of types of work specifically performed by the disabled I will outline some of the key aspects here.

Fools were not invariably mentally disabled people in the Middle Ages. The modern notion of calling someone a fool, in the sense of being an idiot, as an insult to their mental capacities, real or alleged, was not a feature of the medieval mindset. Medieval fools were called fools because of their behaviour and not because of their lack of cognitive and other mental skills.[303] The medieval and early modern period therefore distinguished between 'natural' fools (who were those persons coming closest to the modern notion of the mentally disabled) and 'artificial' fools (who were professionals acting out a role they had voluntarily taken on). Both natural and artificial fools could function as courtly and public entertainers. The question to what extent, however, being a fool became the career 'of choice' for mentally or physically disabled persons during the Middle Ages is regrettably answered hastily and all too often by ill-informed modern writers perpetuating age-old inherited stereotypes of both the brutish and 'dark' medieval period as of the inevitable degradation and discrimination allegedly suffered by the disabled at all times prior to the modern era.[304] Thus an academic account in a leading journal of Disability Studies can bluntly state:

> During the Middle Ages, and thereafter, people with deformities and mental disabilities were frequently displayed for money at village fairs on marketing days, and peasant parents are known to have toured the countryside displaying for money recently born infants with birth defects.[305]

There appears to be little actual evidence for these assumptions. Medieval infants with birth defects were 'toured' in the sense that they would be taken to healing shrines in the hope of a cure, rather than exhibited at fairs.[306] References to the public display *à la* freak show of mentally or physically impaired people at fairs and markets are few and far between— although the abuse of blind beggars in staged spectacles involving them trying to club a pig to death, whilst accidentally hitting each other for the amusement of the sophisticated urban audience, is known from the later fourteenth and fifteenth centuries.[307] Perhaps the influential theories expounded in Mikhail Bakhtin's *Rabelais and His World* have something to answer for with regard to the perpetuation and dissemination of the idea that there is an association of the disabled with fools and laughter.[308] For Bakhtin, the medieval body was the grotesque body *par excellence*, so that the spectacles, carnivals, farces and other popular entertainments of the Middle Ages were marked by concepts of the body as grotesquely realistic.[309] Attractive as these musings may sound to modern philosophical and literary approaches to medieval culture, without evidence firmly based in medieval source material the received idea that the most common 'career' for a disabled person was to become a fool or a spectacle for entertainment just does not hold water.

There are, of course, a few examples of the physically or mentally disabled performing at public events. A rare narration of the occupation of a disabled person as public entertainer can be found in a chronicle of Cologne for 1343, where a cripple from Oberland who was lame in both hands attracted many audiences to the town hall, where he astonished them by using his feet as if they were hands: he played chess with his toes, took a small spoon between his toes and with that knocked down any chess figure the audience told him to; furthermore, with a knife he could hit any point in a board set up in front of him, he balanced a tankard on his head and filled it with wine by using his feet, achieving this without spilling a drop, and he threaded a needle and made a knot in the thread so that he could sew any stitch.[310] The chronicle's enunciation of this man's various skills points more to an admiration *for* his achievements than to a Bakhtinesque laughter *at* his person.

People with all sorts of mental and physical impairments, not just the 'natural' fools, could therefore sometimes—but neither always nor exclusively—find employment as entertainers in courtly circles. For example, during the years 1304–1328 the accounts of Countess Mahaut of Artois and Burgundy mention the presence of a dwarf and a 'fool' of diminutive stature.[311] And according to the *Marienburger Tresslerbuch*, between 1399 and 1409 the court of the Grand Master of the Teutonic Knights played host to a stuttering herald, a blind poet or minstrel, some dwarfs, various cripples and a lame man who demonstrated how he moved himself about on two wheels (perhaps a wheeled trestle reminiscent of the hand trestles so often depicted as used by mobility-impaired people?).[312]

Besides the fools, natural or artificial, one other group of persons whom we would now call disabled were often associated with courtly entertainments: the dwarfs.[313] And, as with regard to fools, it is not clear to what extent being an entertainer was the main or even the only occupation possible for medieval dwarfs, since their story, too, has been popularised and bowdlerised by amalgamation with that of the fools and jesters. As a critic rightly pointed out, many writers have been discovered "facilely assuming a widespread custom of maintaining dwarfs in the Middle Ages" as courtly entertainers, citing from literary texts and from each other's secondary literature without providing any medieval evidence—a classic case of a self-perpetuating trope.[314]

The search for medieval dwarfs as 'real' disabled persons is not helped, either, by the copious and therefore misleading literature, both medieval and modern studies thereof, on dwarfs in legends, folktales, romances and epics.[315] The dwarfs featured in medieval literature, portrayed sometimes as magical, even strong, characters, but often as devious, cunning and downright nasty, have little counterpart in real life. Using the dwarfs of myth and legend as examples to gain an understanding of 'real' medieval disabled people is like studying modern garden gnomes in comparison to contemporary people of short stature.

One important difference between fools and dwarfs is that while medieval fools may be 'natural' or 'artificial', dwarfs of all epochs are always 'natural', since it is their unfakeable physical characteristics, which cannot be manipulated, that define them. While 'artificial' fools are simply acting out a role, dwarfs are living their role. A few words about the anatomical phenomenon of dwarfism are in order to provide context. According to modern medical thinking, there are two types of dwarfism, caused by different aetiologies. One type of dwarfism is classed as an endocrine disorder, due to a deficiency in the function of the pituitary gland (hypopituitarism), and it limits the growth of people so that they only reach a very short stature in adulthood, but their body and limbs are of the same proportions as those of a 'normal'-size person, so that besides being small their physical appearance is no different to what is deemed normal. In contrast, the other type of dwarfism is a congenital disorder and results in disproportionate development of trunk and limbs, that is, the stunted development of the post-cranial skeleton (achondroplasia), so that the head and torso appear too large in relation to arms and legs. Although there is little from medieval medical, natural-philosophical or other 'scientific' sources that concerns dwarfs, a few authorities do mention them. Around 1245 Walther (also Gauthier/Goussoin) of Metz made some very interesting relativistic remarks, pondering the fact that the giants who are in certain places marvel very much to see us and how short we are compared to them, but we do the same with regard to those who do not reach half our height.[316] From a handful of medieval texts it does appear that some distinction was made between the two types of dwarfs as recognised by modern anatomists. In the thirteenth century Albertus Magnus, for instance, placed pygmies between humans and apes, but also made another distinction between pygmies and 'true' dwarfs (by which he probably meant achondroplastic dwarfs). He furthermore described a nine-year-old girl whom he had seen in Cologne who had not yet reached the height of a one-year-old boy; he followed the 'scientific' argument of Avicenna, explaining the cause for a lack of growth was due to the fact that at the moment of conception only a part of the paternal seed had reached the maternal uterus.[317] A hint that proportionate dwarfs were not considered 'true', that is, achondroplastic, dwarfs is given in the *Chronicles* of Matthew Paris. In the year 1249:

> a sort of mannikin, eighteen years old, John by name, was found in the Isle of Wight. He was not a dwarf, for his limbs were of just proportions; he was hardly three feet tall but had ceased to grow. The queen ordered him to be taken around with her as a freak of nature to arouse the astonishment of the onlookers. The length of his tiny body is sixteen times that of this line.[318]

Hence we also receive the hint that at least this particular person was treated as a spectacle in courtly circles, albeit as an object of wonderment and not of ridicule. Towards the later Middle Ages we do obtain more references to the presence of court dwarfs,[319] but then the sources in general become more verbose and descriptive of courtly pomp and display. It is worth taking a step back, in time, and briefly reflecting on how the stereotype, and its justification, arose of the dwarf as eminently suited for entertainment.

Aristotle, in *Parts of Animals*, had classified all animals, with the exception of humans, as "dwarfish" (ναυωδησ), by which he meant not deformed, but the natural arrangement of disproportionate weight and stature in the upper trunk, and inadequate parts below, i.e. the lower limbs, so that upright posture is simply biologically not possible for animals, whereas four-footedness was intended by nature. However, because of their dwarfish structure, for Aristotle animals are less intelligent than humans:

> This [dwarfish construction] is why all the animals are also more stupid than human beings. For even in humans—for instance children as compared with men and those who are natural dwarfs among the adult population, even if they have some other strength to an unusual degree, yet as regards possession of intellect they are lacking. The explanation, as was said before, is that the source of the soul is excessively hard to move and encumbered with body.[320]

Quadruped animals and human dwarfs (as well as children) therefore share a common 'defect', in that, for perfectly 'natural' reasons of course, they are unable to attain the same levels of intelligence as adult human males. These kinds of sentiments, irrespective of the 'scientific' language they are couched in, set the future course for treating dwarfs as pet-like entertainment and curiosity. The patronisation of certain human members of a household, such as children, women, servants and entertainers—and thus dwarfs and fools—has been compared to the abuse of power that is also exercised over non-human creatures, commonly referred to as pets; all of these could simultaneously be highly valued and severely controlled, trained to be obedient, entertaining playthings while also held in some affection.[321] That the same attitude could be shown toward pets and people, specifically courtly fools, emerges from an edict passed at the Reichstag held at Augsburg in 1500, which ordered that all those persons who kept fools should ensure that they keep them in such a fashion that they did not bother or molest other people[322]—an order that might just as easily have been passed concerning the keeping of domestic animals such as dogs. But pets are of course held in affection by their owners. An example of the affection, in the loosest sense, for dwarfs as valued companions at court might be found in the following anecdote. When Barbara, the daughter of Albrecht, Elector of Brandenburg, was ordered to return home to Ansbach in 1481, her mother, Electress Anna of Brandenburg, wrote to her, saying that she was to bring with her no more than six of her servants and attendants, which included a male (*Zwerg*) and female (*Zwergin*) dwarf; the two dwarfs were named first, before the doorman, tailor or cook, even the lady-in-waiting received lesser mention, as she was to be allocated to Barbara by her mother on her return to Ansbach.[323]

What does appear to develop gradually, reaching its apogee really only during the Renaissance, is the notion of collecting 'wonders'.[324] In a sense, people with physical or mental differences can be constructed as 'wondrous', 'marvellous' or simply exotic, and the greater numerical presence of dwarfs, fools and other such 'entertainers' may be part and parcel of the desire to establish and augment collections of the strange and different that begins to appear in the fifteenth century in Italian courts (beginning with the *studiolo*-type cabinets of, e.g. Federico da Montefeltro at Urbino and Isabella d'Este at Mantua),[325] spreading from there to other courts of Europe, with a final and most extravagant flowering at the Dresden court of Augustus II the Strong, Elector of Saxony, in the early eighteenth century, whose famous *Grüne Gewölbe* includes among its objects a collection of pearls shaped like dwarfs, hunchbacks, cripples or other orthopedically impaired people. The real-life 'collection' of Augustus included his elite guardsmen of giant stature—both extremes of the scale, dwarf and giant, figuring as the exotic and noteworthy.[326]

Spain appears to have been at the forefront of such employment of dwarfs, since one Spanish court held an elaborate banquet in the thirteenth century at which the "centrepiece was a castle tower from which a dwarf appeared, waving a flag, blowing a horn, and reciting a welcoming poem."[327] Non-disabled minstrels and poets performed at court, too, so one wonders what all the fuss was about employing a person of short stature to recite a poem as an example of the restricted job choice for medieval dwarfs. Firmer ground for an entrenchment of the notion of dwarfs as courtly entertainers is reached two centuries later. For example, at the festivities held in Bruges in July 1468 on the occasion of the wedding of Duke Charles the Bold of Burgundy to Margaret of York, sister of the English king Edward IV, a female dwarf called Madam de Beaugrant rode to the feast on a lion, where she was lifted off the lion's back and onto the table by a knight and was presented to Margaret.[328]

The problem in disentangling the cultural narratives surrounding dwarfs (including the dwarfs of myth and legend) from the narratives surrounding disabilities is that apart from being of short stature, proportionate dwarfs are not, in fact, particularly impaired physically, although achondroplasia may sometimes but not necessarily cause concomitant cognitive impairments, as well as debilitating back pain. In terms of working ability, therefore, proportionate dwarfs were disadvantaged purely by lack of stature and/or physical strength but not necessarily by lack of agility, dexterity or intellectual skills. The notion that being a court jester or entertainer was the only labour acceptable for medieval dwarfs therefore becomes as ambiguous as the corresponding notion regarding fools. As a case in point, among early Eastern monasticism one encounters John the Dwarf, whose main claim to fame was that he was a proponent of basket-weaving as a form of useful work in the medicine cabinet of remedies against the sins of sloth and idleness (*accedia*).[329] No mention here that being short of stature was an impediment to living the life of a monk. At the other end of the epoch's temporal spectrum, in the mid-fifteenth century one encounters two dwarfs at the University of Oxford. These two were students of "exceptionally small stature", who only made it into the documentary record because an exception in the usual examinations procedure was made: they were allowed to determine as bachelors "in their own halls, instead of in the public schools, because of the embarrassment occasioned by their diminutive height."[330] Whether it was the university who was 'embarrassed' by their presence or the two dwarf students who were 'embarrassed' by having to appear in public is not known, but it does seem that by the fifteenth century the association between dwarf and public entertainer was strong enough to consider this aspect may have been a factor in allowing the two students to be examined in private. Nevertheless, what should not be forgotten with regard to this anecdote is that here were two dwarfs who were students and not remotely connected with any work as court dwarfs. Jumping to the *a priori* conclusion, as so many popular histories have done, that the only 'career' possible for a disabled person in the Middle Ages was as entertaining fool or court dwarf paints just too simplistic a picture.

3   Ageing

"Various sources suggest that many old people were either partially or totally blind. . . . Some were partially paralysed, and some were disabled by an accident which happened in old age."[1] Thus stated Shulamith Shahar in her book on old age, without providing any examples other than the single one of Margery Kempe's husband. It is the present writer's aim to fill in some of the lacunae and illustrate how physical and mental changes in old age could disable the elderly in medieval Europe. But illustration it will be, using select examples to highlight more general trends. As Joel Rosenthal, another historian of old age in the Middle Ages, has remarked, "No useful purpose is served by trampling through the records in search of every old man (and woman) we can find."[2] The historiography of ageing covers a number of works on the Middle Ages,[3] while wider essay collections of the historical understanding of old age in past societies range further afield.[4] On how changes due to transition from one stage of the life cycle to the next affected individuals in later medieval society, one may consult the collection of articles by McDonald and Ormrod,[5] in addition to the literature cited in the following. For a monumental treatment of old age throughout history according to the (now outdated) views held on ageing in the 1970s, see Simone de Beauvoir's *Old Age*, which already touched on many of the themes that later, more scholarly works were to cover, and for that reason still provides a useful introduction. Medical historian Mirko Grmek covered the development of gerontology from the perspective of the advances of medical knowledge.[6] For classical antiquity, as important cultural predecessor of medieval concepts of old age, see a number of recent studies on ageing in the Roman world, which also covers the reception of Greek texts on the subject.[7] Hellenistic society had incorporated the ideal of *kalokagathia*, a term encompassing the moral and political perfection of both body and soul of the free citizen, as antithesis to which art of the period had portrayed the unfree, the mentally impaired, the sick, the crippled or the bodies of farmers and fishers deformed through heavy labour as objects of derision[8]—and the aged body was similarly derided as ugly and defunct.

Ageing may be a natural process—in modern thought a biological phenomenon affected by genetics and cellular change—but although deemed natural the process has tended to be pathologised. In this respect old age shares some of the aspects of 'disability': it is seen as a biological derivation from the healthy norm. In past times, supposedly, old age had not been pathologised, but due to the increased medicalisation of society old age, "which has been variously considered a doubtful privilege or a pitiful ending but never a disease, has recently been put under doctor's orders", as Ivan Illich, a critic of the modern medical system, has argued.[9] But like the notion of disability according to the medical model, ageing is problematic. If ageing is a natural process, how can it simultaneously be a pathology? Does a natural process imply health? Where, if at all, are the boundaries between ageing as a natural process and ageing as a pathological condition? These queries are similar to those more general questions one may phrase around the distinction between health and impairment. "Consideration of ageing has long put in focus the question of what constitutes health or disease, and the difficulty of answering it."[10] Therefore, ageing starts to share many of the conceptual and theoretical conundrums of disability, in particular the aspect of incurability—even in the twenty-first century there is no cure for old age. In short, ageing is both a physical and mental phenomenon (as is impairment) and a cultural and medical construct (as is disability). Hence the validity of discussing some of the aspects of ageing in a study of disability, even more so when one considers that some of the direct effects of ageing (sensory reduction, loss of mobility, etc.) have the same anatomical effects on a person's body as so-called disabling conditions. In contrast to the powerful, beautiful or wise figures like Titurel in the eponymous poem of Wolfram von Eschenbach one encounters in medieval literature,[11] I shall concentrate here solely on the negative effects of old age. As Shulamith Shahar had observed, in whatsoever medieval texts one looks at (be they scientific and medical, moral writings and sermons or literary works) the "powerful and dignified old body belonged exclusively to the mythical heroes of the epics".[12] Thus Gregory the Great (pope 590–604) eloquently summarised the inevitability of disability through ageing:

> Our body is strong and robust in youth; when it begins to approach old age, it also begins to weaken through illness; and if it falls into a decrepit old age, these languishing remnants of life are no more than a continual weakening which tends towards death.[13]

And in the ninth century, Einhard, the biographer of Charlemagne, pointed out the not just semantic connection between illness and old age: toward the end of his life Charlemagne was pressed down by both sickness and senescence (*iam et morbo et senectute*),[14] having become blind amongst other ailments. Paul Dutton has observed that especially for Carolingian rulers sickness and general infirmity went hand in hand with notions of old age.[15]

Indeed, after one has often encountered descriptions of infirm old men and phrases like *debilitata senectus*, "crippled old age," in Carolingian sources, one begins to wonder what awareness of agedness the Carolingians had beyond the merely pathological.[16]

It is just these pathological, because disabling, aspects of old age that are of interest here.

The drastic effects of old age were felt by Emma, wife of the Carolingian ruler Louis the German, who suffered a stroke in 874 which left her unable to speak; she died two years later.[17] The same pathology is documented for Hepo, dean of Magdeburg in the later tenth century, who also suffered a stroke and subsequently remained lame and speech impaired (*Qui cum iam senex et in cunctis actibus suis maturus esset, paralisi subito percussus obmutuit*).[18] Conditions like stroke could not be treated; at best advice could be given how to prevent them (through correct diet, lifestyle and so forth). Hence medicine could only play a limited role. In his overview of the history of old age, Georges Minois hinted at the problem medicine faced with regard to ageing:

> For thousands of years, medicine has tried to understand the causes of ageing and to delay its effects, but, given their impotence before this natural fatality, doctors had ended by limiting themselves to enumerating the pathologies typical of old people, classifying them among the incurably sick. The old were uninteresting patients because incurable, and so were relegated to hospices.[19]

Disability due to old age therefore shares characteristics with disability in general—incurable, irreversible, liminally sited between health and disease. Joel Rosenthal has also highlighted the futility, according to the medieval mind, of trying to alter or adjust, let alone improve on, conditions perceived to be part of human 'nature', such as disability in general and ageing in particular: "The 'senio ac debilitate nature' lay beyond the medieval sense of human engineering, just as the incurable and irremediable were of little interest to either physicians or philanthropists."[20]

Old age in the medieval period, furthermore, sits problematically at the intersection of physical characteristics or impairments, such as blindness, bodily weakness and infirmity, with cultural and social concepts of charity, alms or working ability. Simply being old in years did not automatically entitle an individual to 'special treatment' as in the modern Western world, where old age measured in years qualifies a person for a retirement pension and other benefits. Medieval people saw "nothing in old age to necessitate any reassessment of priorities or resources"[21]; there was no moral or logical obligation to provide pensions for everyone. Therefore, the old age pensioner familiar to contemporary Western societies (but now in danger of becoming an endangered species due to threats to the notion of universal state pensions) did not exist as such in medieval Europe.[22] Pensions and retirement may have been granted sporadically and individually, but "the concept and institution of retirement [did] not spread more widely".[23]

In Carolingian times, for instance, being old and incapable of working was not sufficient reason for receiving charitable aid, as the following episode concerning an old man in Aix refusing to pray for restitution of his sight exemplifies. He argued that with miraculous reversal of his blindness he would lose his alms, which he received on account of his sightlessness and not his advanced years:

> Why do I need the vision I lost so long ago? It is worth more to me to be deprived of it than to have it. Blind, I can beg and none will repulse me. Rather, they hasten to attend to my needs. But if I got my sight back, it would seem wrong for me to beg alms even though I am old and weak and cannot work.[24]

How poverty, begging and the (in)ability to work were interlinked will be explored in Chapter 4; suffice it here to emphasise that, in contrast to twenty-first-century notions of ageing, old age as such did not constitute a special status during the Middle Ages, and that physical and mental incapacities, at whatever age a person was afflicted by them, were regarded as the primary criteria by which to allocate or refuse a particular status. Having said that, because medieval intellectuals and producers of culturally normative concepts, such as clerical authors, were well aware of the potentially disabling effects of old age, the old were often (but not invariably) considered to be part of the wider group of 'needy' and deserving persons, such as children, widows, orphans and the poor.[25]

The older in years a person becomes, the more likely the presence of physical or mental disabilities begins to affect them. That was the same situation in the Middle Ages as it is nowadays. The problem of disability sustained through the physical deteriorations of old age is hence of topical import to contemporary societies.[26] A sobering thought: with an increasingly ageing population, this will become an even bigger topic for twenty-first-century developed countries. The process, already in motion, of a growing proportion of the populations of developed countries living well beyond their sixties is accelerating at the beginning of the twenty-first century. "In 1900 about 7 per cent of the population of the United Kingdom was aged 65 or above; in 2000 about 18 per cent; from 2020 the percentage is projected to rise still further."[27] A combination of birthrates and death rates declining is the reason for increased numbers of old people. Contemporary attitudes are such that this apparent trend is regarded with cautious suspicion:[28] old people, being physically incapable, are unfit for work and so become helpless dependants, "imposing burdens of healthcare and pensions on a shrinking population of younger workers."[29] In Germany, public health professionals are becoming increasingly concerned over the lack of qualified carers in the face of the demographic trend toward an elderly majority population, with part of the reasons given for this lack being the negative associations in modern society of both 'care' and 'old age'.[30] The popularly received notion in the early twenty-first century is that in the past few people lived to an old age, and the further back in the past the shorter the life expectancy; therefore, since old people were few and far between, they were less of a drain on sparse resources and consequently were more "valued, respected, cherished and supported by their families as, it is said, they are not today."[31]

The misconception that there were few old people in past societies, and the further back one looked at the past, the less old people one was to find, is often based on a skewed interpretation of what social and economic historians define as 'life expectancy at birth'. Life expectancy is just that: an expectancy, not an accurate prediction of how old an individual may become. Life expectancy at birth may have been comparatively low in pre-industrial societies (averaging around forty to forty-five[32]) compared with our own, but this does not mean that everyone died before they reached middle age. In fact, what these statistical assumptions on life expectancy do tell us is that infant and child mortality was horrendously high compared to the modern Western developed world. "Those who survived the hazardous early years of life at any time in the pre-industrial past had a good chance of survival to 60 or beyond,"[33] and during the Middle Ages there were also not a few men and women who lived into their eighties and even nineties.[34] In a letter dated 27 April 1373, addressed to his friend Boccaccio on the subject of not permitting age to interrupt study, Petrarch corrects his friend's (and other learned folks') misapprehension that the ancients lived longer than people today, i.e. the fourteenth century. He cites the life spans of a number of notable figures of classical antiquity to point out that for "about two thousand years, and more, there has been no change in the length of human life",[35] ranging from the sixties to eighties, "whereas today in our cities we see this kind of longevity all around; octogenarians and nonagenarians are common, and no one is astonished".[36] Far from being unusual, for Petrarch such longevity in his own times is considered the normal course of things, and it is only centenarians that arouse curiosity, as one Romuald of Ravenna, who apparently reached the quasi-Methusalemic age of 120.[37]

An additional consequence of high child mortality was that, also contrary to received wisdom, it could not be guaranteed in the past that there were surviving children able to care for an elderly parent. The nostalgic view that in the past old people were predominantly cared for by their families needs adjusting. The following anecdote may stand as an example for the lack of care provided by the immediate family. In the mid-fifteenth century a very old woman called Agnes Wurmserin, who in her senescence was altogether decrepit (*in annis senilibus quasi in decrepitu constituta*), hence implying mental as well as physical debility, wanted to visit her two daughters, who were both nuns in the convent of Saint Clare "uff dem weyde" in front of the walls of Strasbourg; she wrote to the papal curia asking for permission to do so but was only allowed to visit during the day and not to spend any nights at the nunnery.[38] It is unclear whether Agnes had any other family living with her, but her two daughters were certainly not actively engaged with support or daily care of their senile mother. In northern Europe at least, it was not "the expected lot" of older people in pre-industrial times to receive "comfortable succour in the household of one's children"[39]; in southern Europe intergenerational living was more common, but due to poverty and economic circumstances as much as due to expectations placed on children.[40] That children may not always have fulfilled their duties toward their aged parents is demonstrated in the need to legislate on the neglect of elderly parents, enacted by some Italian communes.[41] In northern Europe, literary examples abound of the neglect and mistreatment of their parents by the younger generation, transmitted in folktales and courtly epics.[42]

How many were aged?[43] As an average or very broad generalisation, it has been estimated that not more than 8 per cent of the medieval Western European population were aged sixty or seventy and above, "and in some regions and periods it was not above 5."[44] The proportion of the elderly compared to the overall population appears to have increased in the later Middle Ages.[45] For instance, for fifteenth-century Tuscany it has been calculated that 9.5 per cent of the population were aged sixty-five or over.[46] This stands in contrast to the popular assumption that most people in the Middle Ages died young and that anyone over forty or even thirty-five was considered 'old'. For the eighteenth century, where we have more reliable and accurate statistics, it has been calculated that at least 10 per cent of the population of England, France and Spain were aged over sixty. Certain wide-reaching events, such as warfare, famine or plague, could affect the age-ratio in a population; the recurrent plagues of the fourteenth and fifteenth centuries tended to kill more young people than older people, so that in 1427 among the population of Florence 14.6 per cent, and in Ravenna 15.9 per cent, were aged over sixty.[47]

How old is 'old'? Different cultures held different views on this, but in a broad generalisation one may recognise a certain continuity of definition. In the ancient world, as well as the Middle Ages, the early modern period and even nineteenth-century North America, old age was believed to commence somewhere between the ages of sixty and seventy.[48] The *Justinian Code* stated that the age of senescence alone was no impediment to making a donation.[49] In the twelfth-century *usatges* of Barcelona, a knight who neglected his knightly duties was legally no longer treated as a knight, unless "when he is prevented by age" from performing those duties.[50] More precise chronological markers of exemption are given in other regions and at other times. A knight aged over sixty in the thirteenth-century kingdom of Jerusalem was excused from military service, as were all men of that age in the English kingdom of the same period, yet in contemporary Castile and Léon the age to exempt men from watch duty and war service commenced at seventy, as was the case for Florence, Venice, Modena and Pisa, who regarded that as the cut-off age for public service.[51] Exemption from the expectation to work in a physically demanding capacity was also generally granted to people from sixty years onwards.[52] This is not dissimilar to modern European countries, where pensionable age tends to start from a person's sixties. What does differ is the individual person's physical and mental capability. Some people have become decrepit already in their fifties or even forties, while others are robustly active into their eighties.

At a more general level, recognition of the debilities of old age could be found in the special provisions sometimes made for the aged in procedural events. This was the situation in the twelfth-century English law collection *Glanvill*, where accused men over the age of sixty might refuse trial by battle.[53] The thirteenth-century laws of Alfonso X of Castile stipulated that, contrary to regular legal practice, witnesses who were sick and aged could be questioned before the actual commencement of the trial, for fear that they might die in the interval.[54] Similarly, in circumstances of age and physical incapacity canon law allowed the court to come to the witness, rather than the witness having to travel, possibly some distance, to the location of the court.[55] In other legal cases, those who had become senile in their old age were not required to testify, even if they had been witnesses to the events being tried by a court. For example, in York in the 1360s a woman most likely identifiable with one Ellen Grigge was described as "now senile because of old age" and was not called upon to make a deposition even though she had allegedly been present at the events now under consideration.[56] Even in alleged cases of heresy leniency on the grounds of advanced old age and incapacity might be shown, as occurred in 1449 when John Yonge, priest of Temple Church in Bristol, was arrested by two canons charged by Bishop Thomas Bekynton of Bath and Wells with investigating Lollard heresy in the region. Because Yonge—despite his name—was an old man and totally blind, he was first placed under house arrest in the Benedictine abbey of Muchelney, then a few months later he was tried before the bishop at his manor house of Chew Magna, interrogated concerning his beliefs, pronounced a heretic and excommunicated. But, "considering the bodily weakness and great age of the said John," the bishop absolved him, although he had to renunciate his heretical opinions, a long list of which was read aloud to him "he himself being blind".[57] Undoubtedly his clerical status saved him from the stake as much as his old age, but the documents do emphasise the factoring in of his physical condition in the trial proceedings. The infirm elderly could be exempt from the wrathful actions of a ruler, as in the case of King John, who, in 1207, in protest at his disagreement with their election of Stephen Langton as archbishop, exiled all the monks of Christ Church in Canterbury except for those who were deemed old and sick.[58]

Cultural and social expectations are interesting here, in that the definition of when someone became 'old' was not so much according to the actual number of years they had attained as according to their individual physical or mental state. When someone was no longer capable of looking after themselves, for physical or mental reasons, that was when they became 'old'. An illuminating cross-cultural comparison of both exemptions due to age and care for the elderly may be cited from ancient China, where "the kings of the Three Dynasties" practised a kind of old age pension scheme according to different categories of old age:

> With the 80-year-olds one son does not have to serve the state; with the 90-year-olds the entire family does not have to. With disabled or sick people, who can not feed themselves without others, one person is exempt [of state service].[59]

It is these people, the ones who became physically (and to a lesser degree mentally) affected negatively by the ageing process who are the focus of this chapter. Bearing in mind the diversity of age at which an individual's physical deterioration came to have such consequences that they were impaired, it is not just the very old who feature in the present discussion, but the common thread across all ages is that the records and contemporary sources in one way or another ascribe the physical state of the person in question to the deteriorations of age. Hence temporary illness or congenital disabilities, although of course impairing a person, will not be discussed in the context of ageing.

In the Bible and in Jewish thought old age and degeneration had already been treated as a common theme. For instance, Moses in his old age of 120 years suffered from lack of mobility (Deuteronomy 31:2: "I can no more go out and come in"); old people with walking difficulties are pushed about by the crowd they are in ([apocryphal] III Maccabees 4:5: " A multitude of hoary-haired men, were driven along with halting bending feet, urged onward by the impulse of a violent, shameless force to quick speed"); old Isaac is blind (Genesis 27:1: "when Isaac was old, and his eyes were dim, so that he could not see"), as is the old Israel (Genesis 48:10: "the eyes of Israel were dim for age, so that he could not see") and the prophet Ahijah in his old age, too (I Kings 14:4: "But Ahijah could not see; for his eyes were set by reason of his age"); while Barzillai aged fourscore years cannot hear any longer and has lost his sense of taste (II Samuel 19:35: "can thy servant taste what I eat or what I drink? can I hear any more the voice of singing men and singing women?").[60] Laments about the trials and tribulations of old age are found in Psalm 88. And in a sense of Solomonic metaphor, old age is treated by Ecclesiastes (12:1–6), where you are warned of the timeliness to "remember now thy Creator in the days of thy youth, while the evil days come not, nor the years draw nigh, when thou shalt say, I have no pleasure in them". Ageing as one's personal lot was often interpreted away in biblical exegesis of the early Church, and it only became a topic of interest from the later twelfth century onwards.[61] Medieval rabbinic literature did not restrain the descriptions of decrepitude in the elderly, citing bad eyesight and legs, baldness, drooping eyelids which hinder sight or lack of ability to stand (which, in allusion to the passage in Maccabees, endangers the elderly in crowds of people); as with Carolingian literature, rabbinic texts often saw 'old' as synonymous with 'sick', and old men especially were simply a burden, while old women at least could still be useful for household chores.[62]

A well-known concept revolves around the Ages of Man, a division of a person's life cycle into 'ages', with all variations on this theme encompassing youth, maturity and old age. Individual medieval schemes could consist of as few as three or as many as seven or even twelve 'ages', depending on which context (scientific, medical, didactic, homiletic and literary[63]) they occurred in. Most age schema had a subdivision for old age, into an earlier active and fit old age and a later, final decrepit stage.[64] Isidore of Seville's influential *Etymologiae* had categorised two periods of (relative) decline in the human life cycle, which follow on from the peak of youth: an earlier, fifth age which "is not yet old age, but neither is it any longer youth", lasting from fifty to seventy years of age; this is followed by the sixth age, with no limit to the number of years after age seventy, except that the last part of this old age is "decrepitude".[65]

A ninth-century Arabic writer known to the West since the end of the eleventh century as Johannitius wrote in his *Isagoge* that old age follows after the fortieth year, when the vigour of the body begins to lessen and diminish "but still without loss of power";[66] this stage lasts until someone is fifty-five or sixty. It thus represents the first stage of the subdivision, the 'young' old age. "After that follows decrepitude, cold and moist through the gathering of the phlegmatic humour, during which a loss of power becomes evident; its years run to the end of life."[67] A similar subdivision into a more vigorous and a decrepit old age was advocated by Avicenna (980–1037), whose *Canon* found its way into Western medicine via the translation by Gerald of Cremona at the end of the twelfth century:

> Then there is an age of diminution in which power is not lost, and that is old age, which commonly lasts until the age of sixty. There is also another age of diminution marked by a manifest loss of power, and this is the age of decrepitude and the end of life.[68]

And writing in the thirteenth century Albertus Magnus (†1280) placed the two divisions of old age into a wider scholastic context, stating that there is "an age when power diminishes without loss of substance, and an age when substance as well as power diminishes."[69] Many medieval medical and scientific writers reckoned that mental incapacity only affected the very old in this latter stage of *senium*. Dante had argued in *Il convivio* that if Christ had not died on the cross at age thirty-three, but had lived out the natural span of his years, he would have died in his eighty-first year and hence have shared with the rest of humanity the age of decrepitude. But precisely because it was inconceivable that God embodied in Christ should enter a state of decline, residing in a degenerating human body, it was inevitable and essential for Christ's body to change from mortal to eternal at a time when he was at the height of physical perfection, strength and integrity, in his thirty-fourth year.[70] In the later fourteenth century, Petrarch subscribed to a five-part division of the Ages of Man, calling infancy and childhood the springtime, followed by adolescence as late spring and closest to summer, then youth the summertime of life, "succeeded by that riper season— old age, starting with the sixtieth year . . . this is like autumn", and "last is the winter of decrepitude, idle, cold, and desirous of peace and warmth".[71] However, a simple threefold division of the Ages of Man was proposed by Simon of Faversham, an English scholar active in the University of Paris around 1280, which negated the differences between an earlier, active, and non-degenerative old age and a later, passive decrepit old age. For Simon of Faversham there were only the stages of perfecting (infancy, childhood and youth rolled into one), upholding the status quo (adult maturity) and the descent into defectiveness (old age), termed by him *perfectus*, *status* and *defectus*.[72] Old age is clearly equated with inevitable degeneration and hence disability.

The Ages of Man were sometimes aligned in a chronological scheme with the macrocosmos, for instance, in correlating human ageing with the phases of a day (the "eleventh hour" being the "decrepit" or "veteran" age) or with the ages of the world (*aetates mundi*).[73] As a primary symbolic schema, the Ages of Man can tell us little about when medieval contemporaries actually experienced the onset of physical deterioration and disability due to old age. Legal sources, stipulating 'retirement ages', and medical texts serve better to inform us concerning social and biological criteria of ageing.

How then was this natural process viewed in the theological/ natural scientific and medical literature of the medieval period? Hippocrates (c. 460–c. 370 BC)[74] held a fundamentally humoral medical theory, according to which, due to the excessive bodily cooling and drying during old age, most people from their early sixties onwards were susceptible to suffer from

> difficulty in breathing, catarrh, difficult micturation, arthritis, nephritis, dizziness, apoplexy, itching, sleeplessness, watery discharge from bowels and eyes and nostrils, dullness of vision, glaucoma, and hardness of hearing.[75]

Hippocrates thoroughly pathologised ageing, considering his amalgam of maladies intrinsic to old age. In contrast Galen (129–c. 200/210) regarded ageing as a natural process. Galen agreed with Hippocratic theory in "the humoral interpretation of the ageing process, but regarded this as natural rather than pathological or necessarily having pathological effects."[76] Because ageing was influenced by the humours, he did not view ageing of itself as something that necessarily had to have pathological effects, yet simultaneously Galen believed there was no point in trying to influence this process. For Galen ageing was a natural process, but illness was contrary to nature, so old age intrinsically and of itself was not an illness:

> The impaired capacity of function determines health. Nor is weakness of function, strictly speaking, a sign of disease, but only what is contrary to nature . . . Such a man we should say has some disease, unless he suffers this on account of old age; and some say that this also is a disease . . . For all disease is contrary to nature, but such people are not contrary to nature, any more than the aged.[77]

What Galen is saying about old age could equally apply to 'disability' as defined by the modern social or cultural model—impairment, as in simple weakness of function, is not contrary to nature any more than ageing is. Galenic and Hippocratic medical knowledge circulated widely in late antiquity and hence was transmitted to the Middle Ages. Advancing age brought with it a weakening of functions, but since this was part of a natural event it was considered unnatural to try and prolong life, slow down ageing or ease the physical deteriorations.

Two classical authors, Cicero and Seneca, with their respective texts, *Cato maior de senectute* and *Epistulae morales ad Lucilium*, traditionally exerted strong influence on subsequent medieval literary receptions of the ageing process and the condition of old age as one of irreversible and inevitable decline but also one of wisdom. Isidore of Seville reckoned that "there are two things by which the bodily faculties are depleted, old age and illness",[78] so that one might regard him as a Galenist in this respect, treating age and illness as conjunct events but not as identical pathologies. To these texts may be added from the thirteenth century onwards the rediscovery of Aristotle[79] and the commentary on his *Rhetoric* by Averroes.[80] The humoral schemes of classical and medieval medicine found their way into some medieval theology, too, so that Saint Bonaventura, for instance, could distinguish between ultimate and immediate causes of ageing: the symptoms of old age (such as trembling, grey hair, abdominal swelling and decline of libido) he attributed to original sin as the ultimate cause, while an increase of phlegm and melancholy as the immediate causes were derived from humoral theory.[81] Bartholomaeus Anglicus associated humoral consumption with the failing eyesight and defective vision which the aged were forced to suffer.[82] Nevertheless, it is important to emphasise that most medieval physicians did not consider ageing a disease.

The psychosomatic unity of body and soul, as argued for in some medieval medical and natural philosophy texts, meant ageing was seen as a deterioration affecting both physical constitution and mental abilities.[83]

Changes in composition of the four humours, especially a decrease of the body's natural heat, led to the *accidentia senectutis*, the impact of age on the body and mind. The loss of natural body heat led, among other age-related ailments, to asthma, spinal deformities, senile dementia and hair loss, and because of its weakened state, the older body was less able to cope with more interventionist medical treatments like bleeding[84]; hence, physicians were to exercise caution when bleeding the elderly. Old men were not to undergo bloodletting, "particularly the more decrepit", according to the late thirteenth-century surgical treatise of Lanfranc of Milan ("although this rule is sometimes contravened, since there are certain old people whose forces [*virtutes*] are stronger than those of some young people").[85] The decline of natural heat also had mental consequences, forcing the return of a childlike state,[86] yet this was seen as a natural, morally neutral process, part of the unavoidable trajectory of ageing, just like the physical changes occurring.[87] Isidore of Seville had used the relatively colder temperature of blood in both infants and the aged to argue for the foolishness of both:

> The aged, *senis*, are thought by some to have been named from a diminution of sense, because through advanced age, men act foolishly. For physicians say that fools are men of colder blood, wise men of hot: hence, old men, in whom the blood has become cold, and children, in whom it has not yet become warm, have less wisdom. It is in this that old age and infancy are alike: old men lose their wits from advanced age, children do not know what they are about because of playfulness and immaturity.[88]

Similarly, Archbishop Wulfstan of York had commented in the *Institutes of Polity* that

> while it is never appropriate for distinguished old age to behave in too juvenile a fashion, it is nevertheless no shame if an old man acts like a child in foolish behaviour—in short, becomes senile—when he cannot help himself.
>
> (La, utan þæt geþencan . . . þæt soð is, þæt næfre ne gerised geþungenre ylde to geonclic wise ealles to swyðe; ne ealdan esne ne bið buton tale þæt he hine sylfne wyrce to wencle on dollican dædan oþþon on gebæran.)[89]

In general it was believed the descent into ageing commenced with physical decline and then progressed to mental incapacity caused by memory loss and senility. Loss of mental faculties, what we would now term senile dementia or specifically Alzheimer's disease, was considered a particularly worrying aspect of ageing already in the medieval period. Writing on the four Ages of Man around 1265 Philip of Novara emphasised the mental deterioration of the old: "There are some who say that the old have grown foolish and for-getful, and that they are changed and have lost what they were accustomed to knowing."[90] Among medieval Jewish thinkers, too, senile dementia was considered one of the most lamentable aspects of ageing. A rabbinic text compared communicating with the old person who had become senile to writing on a palimpsest, while teaching the child was like using ink on a fresh page.[91] The issue of senility went further than simply causing memory loss in the very old, so that a personal disability had religious/theological conse-quences, according to Gerald of Wales. Concerning a long period of senility in the old person (*diuturna nimis delira senectutis*),[92] he wrote that this men-tal disability "obliterated a person's entire past, the evil acts as well as the achievements."[93] Senility does not just wipe out a person's memory, affect-ing their character and consequently the relations they have with family and friends, but this disability also imposes an eschatological dimension, since wiping out the memory one had of the evil (or good) deeds one performed during one's lifetime postpones the punishment (or reward) one would be due in the hereafter. Not all old people, though, were afflicted with mental dis-abilities in the final stage of senescence, as Vincent of Beauvais argued, since individual differences between people, due to their disparate personalities (and presumably due to their individual humoral constitution) entailed that not all old men suffered from "the foolishness known as senile dementia" (*stultia que deliratio dicitur senium*).[94]

Already in his *Manual* Byrhtferth in the early eleventh century had com-mented on the elderly being "cold and snuffly: *flegmata*, that is expectora-tion or catarrh, afflict the aged and infirm (*swa byð se ealda man ceald and snoflig: flegmata, þæt byð hraca oððe geposu, deriað þam ealdan and þam unhalan*)."[95] Cosmas of Prague (c. 1045–1125) complained that the grand old age he had attained bent his back, disfigured his face with wrinkles, his chest heaved for breath like a snorting horse, his hoarse voice hissed like a goose and morbid senescence diminished his senses.[96] Bishop Marbod of Rennes (c. 1035–1123) composed his *Liber decem capitulorum* around 1102 on the range of human life, when he himself was approaching his seventieth decade; in Chapter 5, "De senectute", he concerned himself with old age. "Many inconveniences trouble old age, which proceed from its mortal nature (*Aetatem vexant incommoda multa senilem, / Quae de mortali procedunt condicione*)",[97] among which is the indignity of having to eat bread soaked in milk that has to be twisted into a toothless mouth and swallowed rather than chewed (5, 24–25), and speech becomes impaired because without teeth the mouth can no longer form words properly and instead the tongue dashes uselessly and lispingly against the lips (5, 28–29). The negative effects of ageing were sometimes positioned into a 'natural' scheme, whereby age was regarded as a 'neutral' state between health and sickness. Thus, according to Constantine the African's († 1085x98) eleventh-century redaction of the ninth-century summary of Galen's *Art of Medicine* by a Nestorian Chris-tian based in Baghdad, Hunayn ibn Ishâq (809–887), known to the West as

Joannitius, the qualities of the body can consist of health, sickness and a neutral state. Health is a balanced condition, and sickness is an imbalanced one, while the "neutral state is that which is neither healthy nor diseased", with three types of neutrality, the second of which is "[a state] such as obtains in the body of an elderly person, where not a single member remains that is not causing trouble or suffering".[98] Medical symptoms could point to the deteriorations of age, such as "thin urine, white in color", which according to the late twelfth-century treatise *On Urines* by Gilles de Corbeil signified "debility or childishness" in the elderly.[99]

Around 1240 Boncompagno of Signa, a professor at the University of Bologna, completed his last book, *De malo senectutis et senii*, a manual whose topics, significantly, were the sufferings and misery of old age and decrepitude.[100] Also in the mid-thirteenth century, Robert Grosseteste described the effect on the body of ageing, in his tract on the Decalogue, where he noted that children are sometimes embarrassed of their parents or even despise them, far from honouring them as stipulated by the fourth commandment. This is due to the defects commonly associated with old age: "The deficiency of the senses, the weakening of vigour, the wrinkly deformation of the skin, curvature of the back, trembling of the limbs, unsteady gait, stammering again like a child" are among the list of negatives.[101]

Roger Bacon presented some particularly well-expressed views on the subject of ageing and deterioration in his *Opus majus* (1266–1267)[102] and in a specialist tract *De retardatione accidentium senectutis cum aliis opusculis medicinalibus*,[103] written in 1239. The lists of ailments were similar but more fully detailed in *De retardatione*, where Bacon stated the normal concomitants of ageing were

> grey hair, paleness and wrinkling of the skin, weakness of the faculties and powers, diminution of the blood and spirits, bleariness of the eyes, abundance of mucus, putrid spittle, weakness of breathing, insomnia, anger and mental restlessness, and lesions of the instruments of the senses in which the *virtus animalis* works [i.e. the faculties of the brain].[104]

Interestingly Bacon added that these symptoms of ageing were incidental conditions (*accidentia*) which were only diseases if they occurred in younger persons. However, in the *Opus maius* Bacon argued for a hereditary character, in that the corruption of the fathers (especially if due to immoral activity which weakened the body) might be inherited by the sons,[105] so that unless a proper regimen of health was followed or education was used to suppress the natural vices of youth, degeneration would continue from one generation to the next.

John of San Gemignano († 1333) elaborated in his *Summa de exemplis* on the physical decline of old age:

While the eyes grow blind, the ears hear with difficulty, the hair falls out, the face acquires a pallor, the teeth are reduced in number, the skin dries up, breathing becomes laboured, the chest feels clogged, a cough roars, the knees tremble, swelling overcomes the ankles and feet.[106]

And Martin de Saint-Gilles, in his *Amphorismes Ypocras*, III.31, written at Avignon between 1362 and 1365, listed the following complaints:

in the decrepit age, there comes dyspnea, catarrh, cough, strangury, joint pains, back or kidney pain, vertigo, apoplexy, stones, scabies all over the body, melancholy, insomnia, humid stomach, flux of humidity through the nose and eyes, glaucoma, hardness of hearing.

(*en l'age decrepite, vienent dipnna, catarri, toux, strangurie, douleurs de jointure, douleurs des rains, advertin de teste, apoplexie, calthecie, mengne ou gratelle par tout le corps, melencolie, veilles, ventres moistes, flux de humiditez par le nez et par les yeulx, glaucité, deffaut d'oir.*)[107]

According to the *Puncta angelica* of Jacques Angeli (c. 1390–1455) who was chancellor of the medical faculty at Montpellier, humans needed natural heat, generated by their hearts, to enable them to walk upright, "therefore we see old people bend on account of the weakened natural heat."[108] Natural decline was also blamed by Arnald of Villanova, who, in a translation of a treatise by Galen, "observed that tremor appears in the old [*accidit tremor senibus*] because of their weakened virtus."[109] In the marriage booklet of Albrecht von Eyb (1472), the author lamented that few in his day reached the age of sixty years and if they did, they were tormented in heart and soul and beset by dull eyes, runny nose, deaf ears, black and rotting toes, loss of hair and trembling limbs, so that in general the old person groans and moans, is limp, constantly sad and distressed and sick.[110] It was not only physical disabilities that struck the old person; depression was another side effect of ageing.

Positives in the physical deteriorations of old age can, significantly, be found in religious and moral texts. For example, Saint Bernard of Clairvaux declared in his *Book on the Manner of Living Well* that "a healthy body, which leads man to infirmity of soul, is a bad thing: but an infirm body, which leads man to the health of his soul, is a good thing."[111] The preacher Bernardino of Siena said that the old become prevented from sin by these very deteriorations of their weak and decrepit bodies that formerly tempted them in their youth: loss of teeth means less unseemly laughter and less idle talk[112]; weakened eyesight means less gluttony, avarice and lust; and loss of hearing means inability to hear nonsense.[113] However, a body afflicted by pain, loss of function or decrepitude is also a body that can distract from spiritual pursuits. The sheer corporeality of the body firmly draws the spirit back down to material considerations, or, as the poet Maximian wrote in the fifth century: "I am conquered by an infirm body."[114]

Medical treatment to counteract or alleviate the physical effects of ageing may have helped in some cases; operations performed for cataract probably were the most effective.[115] Here we have one of those rare sources for medieval times, a personal account, in the *Annales* of Gilles le Muisit (1272–1353). Gilles was Benedictine abbot of Saint Martin in Tournai. He had lost his sight to cataracts in 1345, when he was already aged seventy-three, and by 1348 he was so visually impaired that he stopped celebrating the Mass because he could no longer see sufficiently. Then in 1351 he allowed himself to be operated on for cataracts by an itinerant surgical master from Germany, Jehan (Johannes) of Mainz.[116] After the procedure he recovered his sight, but with the limitations expected of an aged man:

> I saw not as in my young age but as my age demanded, because I was already an octogenarian, and I saw the sky, the sun, the moon, the stars, though not perfectly recognizing people, and I saw everything at a distance from me very well, but I was not able to write or read.

> (*Visum recuperavi et vidi, non sicut in etate juvenili, sed sicut etas mea requirebat, quia jam eram octogenarius, et videbam celum, solem, lunam, stellas, non perfecte cognoscens gentes, et in omnibus michi bene providebam, excepto quod scribere aut legere non valebam.*)[117]

Another real-life medical case concerning an elderly man ("he was a good sixty years of age") who had suffered a stroke is recorded in the early fifteenth-century casebook of a German postgraduate medical student, who jotted down the advice and treatment of two eminent Parisian physicians, Guillaume Boucher († 1410) and Pierre d'Ausson († 1409). The man had been struck down by a "serious paralysis or light apoplexy . . . so that he could not speak or move".[118] The physicians prescribed various dietary measures and herbal remedies, including clysters, but the case was regarded as "desperate", since the disease "can be broadly termed a debilitating apoplexy, which is a paralysis that completely disabled one whole side [of the body], namely in the right arm and right hand, and in the shin—in short, his whole right side was paralyzed."[119] Since the left side of the brain, which controls the right side of the body, also controls speech, the man was speech-impaired as well as paralysed. Thankfully the doctors had some success, since after eighteen days of treatment "[the patient] began to speak perfectly" and "walked about his room, and made some use of his paralyzed arm and paralyzed leg."[120] Whether this was down to the physicians' regimen or natural resilience we cannot assess, but the elderly man made at least a partial recovery.

Probably the most influential treatise on old age was by Lothario de Segni, the future Pope Innocent III, who wrote *De miseria humanae conditionis* (On the Misery of the Human Condition) while he was still in his thirties. He was strongly influenced by classical texts on the topic of ageing, in particular by Horace's *Ars Poetica*,[121] but amplified the force of the description of debilities affecting ageing. In concentrating on the physical aspects of the old body he had the following to say about the debilities and discomforts of old age:

> Should someone perchance reach the age of senescence, then his heart suffers often from its beatings, his head shakes, his face becomes limp and dull, his breath malodorous. The face becomes wrinkled and the posture bent, the eyes become dark and the fingers tremble, the nose runny and the flow of tears becomes unstoppable. Constant trembling impedes the sense of touch, and that which he intends to do fails. The teeth rot and the ears become deaf.[122]

The catalogue of physical and mental suffering presented here set the tone for numerous later essays on ageing. Furthermore, this tractate was not just a (pessimistic but arguably naturalistic) rendering of the physical effects of ageing, but a moral exhortation to develop contempt of the flesh.[123] A similar eschatological aim was pursued by Petrarch (1309–1374), in his philosophical treatise *De Remediis utriusque Fortune* (*On the Remedies to the Two Kinds of Fortune*), where in a dialogue between optimistic Joy and pessimistic Reason, the "degradation and increasing unloveliness of the body and the loss of physical pleasures are indicators of the fragility, impermanence and insignificance of this world."[124] Loss of mental reasoning, weakened memory and disturbed speech are some of the changes the old body has to endure, according to Petrarch. If an old person escaped these deteriorations, they should consider themselves lucky, according to epistle VIII, 1 of his *Letters of Old Age*, written on the morning of his sixty-third birthday (20 July 1366), and addressed to his good friend Boccaccio. Thus Petrarch argues

> there would be nothing disgraceful, and perhaps something prestigious; not in itself—for there is no prestige in being old—but if there is gravity of mind, steadfastness, the preservation of the senses, and, for one's age, a bodily appearance, which is neither decrepit nor unkempt as is the case with most old people.[125]

A year later, however, Petrarch wrote another letter on the topic of old age, this time extolling its advantages, in which he argued (presumably influenced by his classical reading) that age as such is not a disease, and other, underlying factors cause the loss of mental faculties. Here the ageing process is seen as something 'natural' that of itself does not cause senility; instead it is the person's condition in youth that influences the kind of old age they will experience:

Illness has taken away some people's intelligence and memory, but age does this to no one. Never has a wise youth gone crazy in old age. But often a foolish adolescent has recovered his senses because of old age. Therefore, any foolish and crazy old people you may see were silly youths. It is not the fault of age if it gives back what it received.[126]

Petrarch's acquaintance, the Benedictine prior of Nantes and Paris, Pierre Bersuire (1300–1362), shared these views, arguing in his *Dictionarium moralis* (or *Repertorium*) that lethal sin and corruption may be signified by the physical disfigurements of ageing, so that the aged were seen to possess their own particular vices.[127] In his preface to the English translation in 1340 of *Ayenbite of Inwyt*, Dan Michel of Northgate asserted the old person of seventy full years is blind and deaf and also dumb, but shall not be drawn to the ground for neither penny, mark nor pound (*Blind. and dyaf. and alsuo domb. Of zeuenty yer al uol rond. Ne ssolle by dra3e to þe grond: Vor penny nor Mark ne uor pond*).[128] So although by now disabled (blind, deaf and dumb) the old person is not accepting the inevitable outcome all living things must have and avoids the grave.

How to preserve the ageing body for as long as possible in an uncorrupted, quasi-youthful state, and to avoid the physical and mental disabilities that all too often affected advanced old age, formed the themes of a number of medical texts, in particular the *regimen sanitatis* type,[129] although 'geriatrics', in the modern sense of a specialist sub-branch of medicine dealing with the pathologies and their therapies specific to old people, was yet to be developed.[130] By the end of Middle Ages there was a small publishing boom in advice manuals and *regimina* for care of the elderly. The first printed monograph on old age, the *Gerontocoma*, written for Pope Innocent VIII by Gabriele Zerbi (1445–1505), was published in 1489 and included observations on the most common pathological and debilitating conditions affecting the old; the same year Marsilio Ficino (1433–1499) wrote *Liber de vita producenda sive longa* (The Book of Life) for the Medici,[131] while in 1500 Burchard Hornecke dedicated *De senectute conservanda* (On the Preservation of Old Age) to Archbishop Lorenz of Würzburg, intended so that he "may relieve man, if not from all—for this cannot be done by nature—then at least from some discomforts and grave miseries of old age".[132]

On a practical level, alleviating the effects of the physical deterioration in old age was attempted through mobility aids for the orthopedically impaired,[133] and there were even prosthetic devices for lost limbs.[134] In *De remediis utriusque fortunae* 2.93 (*De tristitia et miseria*) Petrarch praised the technological advances by which man has been able to overcome illness and infirmity:

Indeed, he sustains and conveys himself by all means: in order not to lose his members he has learned to devise wooden feet, iron hands, wax noses.

(*Denique modus sese omnibus adiuvat, attolitque, quin amissis artu- bus pedes ligneos, manus ferreas, nasos caereos, fabricari didicit.*)[135]

Most frequently associated with age-related debilities were visual aids (e.g. glasses). "Spectacles, whose invention is credited to Bacon, was one of medieval medicine's greatest boons to old age."[136] Space prohibits a fuller discussion of the development of visual aids, as there is a copious literature, stemming mainly from the older medical history school of retired practitio- ners writing,[137] or sponsored by the manufacturers of optical instruments,[138] but with some newer forays into the field.[139] Of particular relevance to the theme of disability in old age is the statement by Jean de Tournemire in the chapter 'De debilitate visus' of his treatise *Nonum ad Almansorum* of 1365, that "eyeglasses are necessary at the beginning of old age, around fifty-five years (*indigent bericulis in primo seni, in LV anno vel circa*)".[140] Petrarch, in his autobiographical 'Letter to Posterity', admits that although for a long time he had had very keen vision, this suddenly abandoned him "so that, to my disgust I had to resort to glasses."[141] In late medieval literary as well as pictorial arts the wearing of glasses hence was originally asso- ciated with old age and/or scholarly activities—with the scholar himself generally being an older man.[142]

The Middle Ages often displayed a misogerontic attitude in terms of the physical aspects of ageing. While attitudes towards the aged *person* were equivocal, regarding old people as possessing both positive (e.g. wisdom) and negative qualities (e.g. senility), attitudes towards the aged *physiog- nomy* were quite definite: the old body "had no positive valuation."[143] This view can be found across the full spectrum of types of texts, from scientific via religious to literary works. Although the body tended to be gendered, with medieval authorities focusing almost exclusively on the aged male body, "they drew no distinctions between various social classes".[144] At least in that sense the old body was an egalitarian body—in the deteriorations of old age, at least outwardly, the decrepitude of a king was the same as the disability of the lowest of his subjects. For such negative views of old age two examples, one each from the beginning and end of the Middle Ages, shall elucidate the pains, decrepitude and inconveniences of ageing. At the turn of the fourth to the fifth centuries Augustine had pointed out the mis- eries of ageing and the decrepitude of the old man:

> His eyes grow dim, his ears dull, his hair thins, his complexion turns pale, his teeth rot and disappear, his skin withers, his breath stinks, his chest is sunken, he breaks out in coughing fits, his knees shake and his heels and feet swell up.[145]

At the very end of the period under consideration Albrecht von Eyb, author of a German booklet on ideal marriage that was first printed in 1472, pon- dered the question what it was that a person actually stood to gain in dying at advanced old age over the person dying young, and reached the sobering conclusion that it was nothing more than worry, work, vexation, pains, illness and sin.[146]

Connected with the theme of trials and tribulations is the theme of the elderly as burdensome. They are burdensome because they require care and comfort when no longer able to make their own living, and their physical deterioration is not just limited to decrease of their faculties (loss of sight, hearing, immobility), but it also has disagreeable effects that irritate their friends or family. Bartholomaeus Anglicus, in his encyclopedia *De proprietatibus rerum*, described the old thus:

> The elderly man is despised by all, judged burdensome, and plagued by coughing, spitting, and other afflictions until the time when ashes dissolve into ashes and dust returns to dust.
>
> (*Senex ab omnibus vilipenditur, et gravis et onerosus ab omnibus iudicatur, tussibus, sputis et aliis passionibus fatigatur, quosque resolvatur cinis in cinerem, et pulvis in pulverem revertatur.*)[147]

At least this befalls the elderly only in the the second part of old age ('old' old age).

Arguably physical integrity and capacity was valued highly, particularly in earlier medieval society such as reflected in the Norse sagas, where the elderly were valued on condition that they were capable of independent mobility and "leading an active life".[148] Simone de Beauvoir had already drawn attention to the earlier Middle Ages as a period where physical prowess and a warrior ethic that valued fighting ability "compelled the aged man to withdraw" due to his physical decline.[149] Thus the earlier medieval "frequent laments about old age seem to have focused on frailty because it was prohibitive of the active life which was requested from the young as well as the old."[150] The old were occasionally categorised together with other "useless" (*inutiles*) persons, particularly in military contexts, for example, in early medieval Ireland, where a clan or tribe would send their 'undesirables' into situations when hostages were demanded, that is, the elderly, the sick, physically impaired, mentally ill or criminals.[151] Or at the siege of Demmin in 1147 during the Crusade against the pagan Wends, when Danish prisoners taken by the Wends were released, but only those who were old or otherwise useless militarily, while the people of a "more robust age" were kept prisoner.[152] More explicitly misogerontic and less opaque in its denigration of the inutility of the old and disabled was the calculation of the 'worth' of older people according to the early medieval so-called barbarian laws, although only one of these, the Visigothic laws, made direct mention of different ages.[153] The wergild ratios stipulated by the seventh-century laws of the Visigoths had a system of a sliding scale dependent on a person's gender and age: young and fecund women were rated at a higher wergild than both prepubertal girls or postmenopausal elderly women, and for men the death of a man over fifty was valued at only two-thirds of that of a man aged between twenty and fifty (the prime of warrior strength), while a man aged over sixty-five was only valued at the same rate as a boy of ten years.[154]

Once someone became incapable of living an active life, particularly a member of the social elite, their usefulness became questionable and they could be forced to relinquish positions of power.[155] According to the laws of the Bavarians

> the son of a chief must not seek to replace his father as long as the latter is [physically] powerful, can assist the king in person, lead the army, ride on horseback, bear arms and is neither deaf nor blind (*non est surdus nec cecus*).[156]

The notion of 'functioning' defines usefulness and the right of the *dux* to remain in his role, in contrast to later periods. During the high and later Middle Ages, as well as the early modern period "laws did not stipulate that functioning was the criterion for continued service, and there is certainly no reference to the right of a son to oust his father whose physical and mental capacities are waning."[157] However, early medieval rulers were required to be warriors; thus they were expected to be fit and physically able.[158] This does not mean that all old people were despised, but that, as outlined earlier, age in years was not given precedence over 'biological' age, so that if someone was chronologically old but showed no signs of physical deteriorations, their status could even be enhanced. As Kleinschmidt has argued, the view of a dignified, physically and mentally active old age valued for its ability to transmit "normative oral tradition" seems to have prevailed until the eleventh century, after which the elderly began to be stereotyped as frail, ill and dependent.[159] Ethnographic studies of more recent peoples have shown that in traditional societies with a predominantly oral culture, the elderly enjoyed considerable prestige, fulfilling a social role as the group's memory and providing cultural continuity; this state of affairs, according to some theorists, "was to be unceasingly challenged in the historical societies of the west."[160] By the later Middle Ages the reciprocal, contractual relationship between the generations seems to have evolved, whereby the children received nurture, education and upbringing in return for looking after their parents once they became old.[161] Caring for one's elders was almost a natural law, at least according to Peter Damian (†1072), who provided this didactic anecdote from the animal kingdom: when birds were no longer able to fly or to see due to their old age, then their offspring would out of pity pluck out their elders' feathers and warm their eyes with their young wings and stroke their whole bodies until the feathers had renewed themselves on the entire body of the old birds and they were invigorated again.[162]

But the opposite of care—neglect or even deliberate geronticide—requires a brief discussion. A study of modern ethical literature on the question of the direct killing of newborns and the "severely demented elderly" has found that, especially in cases where the elderly are considered voiceless and as such can be regarded to have "ceased to exist",[163] geronticide could be legitimated—the depressing conclusion to be drawn from such attitudes being that the less an old person was capable of 'functioning', the more likely they were to be dehumanised. For the medieval period, legitimisation of geronticide has allegedly been discovered on a number of occasions. Based on the so-called 'barbarian' laws Jacob Grimm had collected spurious 'evidence' in his *Deutsche Rechtsaltertümer* on the alleged killing of useless elders in Germanic barbarian times, stating that the fragility of old age was held in low esteem among the ancient Germans, the Anglo-Saxons and Nordic pagans.[164] Thus in northern Germany it was the custom to kill the aged and the sick by burying them alive or by drowning,[165] and the Wends supposedly even practised cannibalism, eating their murdered old people,[166] while the ancient Prussians murdered their old and weakened parents;[167] things only improved with the advent of Christianity to these pagan folk, since from that point on German history knew no example of where the deceased parents had been the victims of either voluntary or violent death.[168] The myth of geronticide has been countered by more recent scholarship[169]; however, one single piece of evidence from the high Middle Ages points to the theoretical permission, if not actual practice, of killing the elderly in times of extreme circumstances. This has been attested only for western Norway, where the law code *Gulatingsloven* (cap. 63) of c. 1250 stated that in times of dearth the old freedmen should sit in a grave in the cemetery awaiting their death, referring to them as *gravgangsmenn*.[170] Thus one can in no way speak of the Middle Ages as legitimising the routine killing of 'useless' and disabled old people; instead medieval attitudes were such that a variety of arrangements and measures were taken to accommodate declining physical or mental abilities in the elderly as best as possible within cultural norms and social and economic circumstances.

One notable aspect of medieval concepts of old age is that they were not just misogerontic, but specifically misogynistic. Old women were seen as especially negative, and that in an intellectual climate which regarded women *per se* as a defective aberration of the male norm, according to natural philosophical notions derived mainly from Aristotle.[171] In scientific literature of the high Middle Ages, old women have by nature (that is, through their humoral *complexio*) a malignant and pathological physiology.[172] When medical writers do indeed mention female bodies, which is rare, since most of the time their texts implicitly refer to the (mal)functioning of the male body, they emphasise the cessation of the menses. Menstrual blood was considered biologically necessary but extremely harmful, thus post-menopausal women were regarded as dangerous because they can no longer eliminate this dangerous substance in the monthly menses. A tract popularly but wrongly attributed to Albertus Magnus, *De Secretis Mulierum*, stated:

> The retention of menses engenders many evil humours. The women being old have almost no natural heat left to consume and control this matter, especially poor women who live on nothing but coarse meat, which greatly contributes to this phenomenon. These women are more venomous than the others.[173]

Post-menopausal women were believed to retain the noxious matter of their menses with polluting effects, eventually seeping out through other pores of the body, so that their 'evil eye' alone could kill children.[174] Even younger women posed threats; for instance, intercourse with a menstruating woman could result in the birth of a leprous child.[175] The reason why the human infant, unlike the infants of other animals, was so helpless shortly after birth was that it was nurtured on menstrual blood in the womb, from which it had not been easily cleansed, while other animals nurtured their young on a purer substance; hence the human infant at birth was incapable of standing, sitting, walking and talking.[176]

Old women's bodies were regarded as even more abhorrent than those of old men, so that depictions of old women in visual art are even more cruel and horrendously ugly than those of old men. One of the most denigrating and abhorrent depictions of the old women stems from the *Triumph of Death* fresco cycle in the Camposanto, Pisa, produced in the 1330s, where the allegorical figure of Death

> is not yet represented as a dried-out skeleton, symbolizing the human condition without any religious implications, as is the case in the later *Triumphs*. It is still felt to be a consequence of Original Sin and is therefore given demoniacal connotations: a horrible old woman with clawed hands and feet and batwings.[177]

Because Death is female, the bloated and deformed *vetula* portrayed in this fresco reminds the viewer that death entered the world through primordial sin; hence in a sense the old woman as Death is equivalent to the post-lapsarian, aged Eve, without whom there would have been no Fall, no Death, no misery in this world.

In an oft-quoted passage in Mikhail Bakhtin's text on the 'carnivalesque' elements in popular and folk culture, reference is made to a collection of Hellenistic terracotta figurines from Kerch (Ukraine) which depict "senile pregnant hags. Moreover, the old hags are laughing."[178] In the contrary imagery of birth and death, of "senile, decaying and deformed flesh" and fecundity, Bakhtin saw the embodiment of the grotesque concept *par excellence*. However, there may be a simpler interpretation of these figurines, albeit one that is likely to be less attractive to theorists. The only indication of the 'pregnancy' of these old hags is recognised by their distended bellies—but a distended belly is also a feature of the costumes worn by comedy actors often found in Hellenistic and Roman art, and hence can easily be made a feature of the *anus ebria*, the inebriated old woman.[179] Even old men are shown with potbellies on spindly little legs in derogatory caricatures dating from the same period.[180] The Kerch figurines could then be depicting nothing other than the inebriated laughter of the stereotypical drunk old hag, rather than any pregnant symbolism.[181]

In medieval literature one encounters a stark portrayal of the old female body, often in the guise of allegorical stereotypes.[182] In the *Roman de la Rose* of Guillaume de Lorris, the figure of Vielleice is a companion to the Vices (e.g. Avarice, Hatred, Envy, Sorrow). Her graphic description encompasses many of the signs of physical and mental deterioration and disability associated with the second, 'old' stage of old age.

> Old Age was pictured next, who was at least a foot shorter than she used to be, and so childish in her dotage that she could scarcely feed herself. Her beauty was quite spoiled, and she had become very ugly. All her head was white and bleached, as if with blossom. If she had died, her death would not have been important or wrong, for her whole body was dried up and ruined by age. Her face, once soft and smooth, was now quite withered and covered in wrinkles. Hair grew in her ears, and she had lost all her teeth, for she had not a single one left. She was so extremely aged that she could not have gone eight yards without a crutch. . . . she could no longer prevent herself from entering her second childhood, for I think indeed that she had no more strength or force or wit than a year-old child.

> (*Aprés fu Viellece portraite, / Qui estoit bien un pié retraite / De tel cum elle soloit estre; / A pene qu'el se pooist pestre, / Tant estoit vielle et radotee. / Mout ert sa biauté gastee, / Et mout ert lede devenue. / Toute sa teste estoit chenue/ Et blanche cum s'el fust florie. / Ce ne fust mie grant morie/ S'ele morist, ne grans pechiez, / Car tous ses cors estoit sechiez / De viellece, et anoientis. / Mout ere ja son vis fletis, / Qui fu jadis soés et plains. / Mes or est touz de fronces plains. / Les oreilles avoit mossues/ Et toutes les dens si perdues / Qu'el n'en avoit neïs nesune. / Tant par estoit de grant viellune / Qu'el n'alast mie la montance / De quatre toises sans potence. / . . . Ains retornoit ja en enfance, / Car certes el n'avoit poissance, / Ce croi je, ne force ne sen / Nes plusqu'uns enfes d'un en.*)[183]

In addition she has to wrap herself in furs to keep warm, since "it is the nature of all old people to be cold".[184] In illustrations accompanying the text, further emphasising the allegories of physical decrepitude and infirmity that come with advanced old age, we often find depictions of the aged body shown covered in a cloak to keep warm, using crutches, with a hunched back and in the dwindling stature of the very old.[185]

The portrayal of old women as particularly vile continues, for instance, in the extremely popular fourteenth-century *Le Pèlerinage de la vie humaine*, written by Guillaume de Deguileville and soon translated into major vernacular languages. Here the allegorical characters of the Vices, as well as Tribulation, Heresy, Disease and Old Age, are all represented by old women. In terms of impairing afflictions, Pride is described as a monstrously obese old woman, who, because of her bulk and swollen legs, cannot walk unaided but has to ride on Flattery; Envy is shrivelled and dried up, without flesh on her bones, and has to crawl like a snake; Old Age has legs of lead; and Disease significantly walks on crutches.[186] In some respects, the figure of Hypocrisy is the most derogatory: she cannot even be described properly, but is hidden under a cloak such as that "worn by old women to hide their ugliness and infirmities"[187]—the aged female body is so abhorrent that it may not even be made visible in the full extent of its deformities and impairments.[188]

In the *Ruodlieb* (written by a southern German poet in Latin around 1030), Ruodlieb's mother describes an old woman as like an ape, with wrinkled forehead, fading vision, dripping nose, sagging cheeks, loose teeth, slurred speech, pointed chin, open mouth, scrawny neck, pendulous breasts, greasy hair, scrawny fingers, dirty nails and faltering gait.[189] In *Il Corbaccio* (written c. 1355) Boccaccio also drew attention to the ugliness of the old woman by describing her sagging flesh, with misshapen breasts that drooped down to her navel "empty and wrinkled like a deflated bladder".[190] And in the fifteenth-century *Testament* François Villon has a once beautiful young woman now describing herself as "whitehaired . . . so poor, so shrivelled, so spare, so lean", with wrinkled forehead, hooked nose, hairy ears, thin lips, crooked shoulders, sagging breasts and covered in liver spots.[191]

If it is not their repugnant physical appearance, then it is their behaviour that demeans old and disabled women. For instance, in a Middle High German *mære* of the second half of the thirteenth century, *The Old Mother and Emperor Friedrich* (*Die alte Mutter und Kaiser Friedrich*), the old mother of the title has become hearing and visually impaired due to her age, but does not cease to tell all folk her opinions and boss them about, especially her only son.[192] Classen has commented that this poet treats

> the phenomenon age in that he depicts the deaf and almost blind old woman as a kind of domestic scold, who even in her severely disabled condition still wants to order her son about.
>
> (*das Phänomen Alter, in dem er die taube und fast blinde alte Frau als eine Art Hausdrachen zeichnet, die selbst in ihrem stark behinderten Zustand immer noch ihren Sohn herumkommandieren will.*)[193]

A summary overview of the representation of old women in medieval texts concludes that if positive images of old women do crop up, they cause a "big surprise".[194] If they are represented at all positively, at least one or several of the aspects of either femininity or ageing are suppressed: "they appear as either not quite old (like the saints), not quite women (like the virgins), or not quite positive".[195] One of the more 'harmless' depictions of the physical characteristics of an old woman can be found in the late thirteenth-century English fabliau *Dame Sirith*, where the eponymous dame describes herself as "old, and sek and lame", a "poure wif" who has fallen "in ansine", that is, one who has declined or failed in appearance, so that she is no longer able to wilfully control her limbs: "Ich ne mai mine limes on wold".[196]

In the real world, the world of verifiable historical source such as legal records, tropes associated with literary figures do occur, however—for instance, in the infamous connection between old women ('crones') and witchcraft. This was the case in 1464, when a ninety-year-old woman called Turlateuse, living in Thiart in the Auvergne region of France, "held and reputed to be a great sorcerer and a bad woman",[197] was accused of poisoning the wife of a notary. Whether or not this was the first historical instance of the henceforth long-standing association of old women with witchcraft is irrelevant to the argument here, suffice it to draw attention to the fact that the image of the old woman as witch was no mere literary topos.

Aged men feature more prominently in medieval literary texts. *Egil's Saga* recounts the life of Egil Skallagrimsson, who died in 990 aged in his eighties. His descent into disability in old age is recounted in the saga. No longer the strong, youthful hero, "in his old age he began to be heavy of movement, and he was dull both of hearing and sight; he began withal to be stiff of leg. . . . That was on a day that Egil walked out along by the wall and struck his foot and fell."[198] He is laughed at by the women for this, who tell him that it is over for him when he falls of his own accord. Egil describes his condition in these verses:

> Like hobbled steed I stumble;
> Bald scalp I'm like to fall on;
> Woeful weak is leg-berg's
> Wimble; and hearing's gone now.[199]

In addition he becomes blind. Not even inside the house can he find refuge, since when he goes to warm himself by the fire, he is shooed away by the housekeeper for being clumsy and in the way. The literary genre *sermones ad status*, popular from thirteenth century onwards, groups the elderly with women and children and characterises them as physically or mentally weak; in some sermon texts these groups are also classed with invalids, foreigners or the paupers, thus reinforcing their weaknesses.[200] The elderly are merciful toward others because, as weak persons themselves, both physically and mentally, they show pity toward others who are also weak, as Giles of Rome (c. 1247–1316) wrote in his didactic treatise for Philip the Fair of France.[201] In texts such as *Le regret du Maximian* (thirteenth century),

An Old Man's Prayer (c. 1310) or *God Send Patience in Our Old Age* (fifteenth century) the authors variously bewail the physical weaknesses, illnesses, gluttony and lechery of the elderly and urge patience as the antidote in accordance with classical traditions.[202] The *Pricke of Conscience*, an English fourteenth-century vernacular and didactic poem, described old age in dismal detail, primarily as a warning to sinners, and in the later fourteenth century the Dominican preacher John Bromyard's *Summa Praedicantium* included a sermon topic, *Senectus*, on the usefulness to the spirit of the physical miseries of old age; both of these texts included descriptions of the disabilities brought on by the physical decay of old age apparently derived from Lothario di Segni's treatise *De contemptu mundi*, in turn ultimately derived from Horatian ideas about old age.[203] Such a catalogue of crooked backs, trembling limbs, deafness and loss of sight is also found in *Cursor mundi*, another English work of the same period.[204]

In a fourteenth-century English verse, the *Parlement of the Thre Ages*, the character of Age, all dressed in black, is described as crooked and curved, cramped by age, all disfigured of face and faded hue, bald and blind and thick-lipped (hence implying impaired speech), toothless and painful:

> Croked and courbede, encrampeschett for elde;
> Alle disfygured was his face, and fadit his hewe, . . .
> He was ballede and blynde, and alle babirlippide,
> Totheles and tenefull, I telle ȝowe for sothe.[205]

In *Piers Plowman* Langland contrasted the old men "with white hair, who are weak and helpless" with the able-bodied, fraudulent and therefore undeserving beggars.[206] The elderly, because of their condition, were entitled to charity—as were women with child or the blind, bedridden and crippled (*Blynde and bedreden and broken hire membres*[207]), all groups who were deemed unable to work. In the final section of the B-Text of his work, Langland depicted hoary Old Age as a compatriot of Death and Plague, with Age in the vanguard of an allegorical army,[208] attacking the figure of Will the Dreamer, making Will bald, hitting him around the ear until he became deaf, battering his mouth so that his teeth fell out, afflicting him with gout and rendering him impotent.[209] Within the allegory resides the stereotypical description of the negative effects of ageing on the body. The poet John Gower (†1408) was himself experiencing the effects of old age in his later years, suffering especially from inferior eyesight, so much that by around 1400 he had become totally blind. In the *Prologus* to his *Confessio amantis*, completed 1390 in the first recension, he complained, "thogh I seknesse have upon honed / and longe have had" yet he would still try to write, although he was now aged around sixty and had retired from public life some fifteen years earlier.[210] Returning to this theme in the conclusion, he states that he tried his best "this bok to write as y behighte, / so as siknesse it soffre wolde; / and also for to my daies olde, / that y am feble and impotent".[211] A Scottish poem of the early fifteenth century, *Ratis Raving*, emphasises the return to childishness in the decrepit stage of old age, where reason has been worn away by time, so that like great youth has not yet attained reasoned understanding, so great age has lost this thing that it once knew:

> Fra tyme haif woirn awaye resoun,
> Sik is of eild conclusioun;
> as gryt 3outhed has na knaving,
> Richt sa grit eild has tynt þat thing
> That it eir knev. (ll. 1732–36)[212]

Also in the early fifteenth century, the play *The Castle of Perseverance* has a character summarise the stereotypical effects on the body of old age:

> I gynne to waxyn hory and olde.
> My bake gynnyth to bowe and bende,
> I crulle and crepe and wax al colde.[213]

Grey-haired and old, the back bowed and bent, the elderly person becomes less mobile but also colder, in allusion to humoral theories, perhaps, of the reduced natural heat during one's later years. With regard to intergenerational relations, Christine de Pisan, in her *The Treasure of the City of Ladies*, advised that the young should stand in awe of the old even if they are physically frail because they always have ways of correcting the young; hence the young should help them out of charity because the old are fragile and "there is no worse disease than old age".[214] However, in the final chapter of *Treasure of the City of Ladies*, while acknowledging that old age is a great affliction, Christine de Pisan has Lady Hope praise the physical decline of old age, and even the lack of friends in old age, asking what, after all, would friends be able to do for you since they "would never relieve you of your old age, nor would they increase your merit".[215] Instead, old age is a positive, bringing you closer to the end of your journey, and in that sense bodily decline can only be good for you!

In art one encounters the notion of the stages of life linked to the concentric circles of the sun, moon and planets, whereby Saturn, as the planet farthest away from Earth, corresponds to the last stage of life, old age.[216] In imagery of the Children of the Planets, the personification of Saturn is an old man supporting himself on a stick.[217] Such notions stemmed from Ptolemy's work on astrology known as *Tetrabiblos*, Book IV, chap. 10, where he described the seventh Saturnian age:

> Now the movements both of body and of soul are cooled and impeded in their impulses, enjoyments, desires, and speed; for the natural decline supervenes upon life, which has become worn down with age,

dispirited, weak, easily offended, and hard to please in all situations, in keeping with the sluggishness of his movements.[218]

And in manuscript illuminations of the Ages of Man the representation of old age is typically depicted as a white-haired or white-bearded old man supporting himself on a stick, sometimes shown bent over by the burden of advanced years.[219] Similarly, the illustration of the Wheel of Life from the De Lisle Psalter (so named after its first owner, Robert de Lisle [†1343]) contains three medallions depicting the old person on the path to disability and death: the old man leaning on a staff, the decrepit man now blind and led by a boy and the terminally ill man lying in his bed. The text surrounding these medallions reads:

> [Old man:] I take up my staff, almost acquainted with death.
> [Decrepit man:] Given over to decrepitude, death will be my
>   condition.
> [Sick man:] Given over to sickness, I begin to fall.
> *[Senex:] Sumo michi baculum, morti fere notus.*
> *[Decrepitus:] Decrepetati deditus, mors erit michi esse.*
> *[Infirmus:] Infirmitati deditus, incipio deesse.*[220]

These words surrounding the medallions are echoed in the words of a late fourteenth-century poem, '3ing and tender child I am:'[221] "[Senex:] Myn eyn be dymmer þan þey wer; clere sight is gon away. [Decrepitus:] On my cruche I lene me; I begyn to heelde. [Infirmus:] Ded me has doun dryven; þet makes my mykell elde."[222] And the physical degeneration of the old man is reiterated in a poem on the page preceding the Wheel of Life image in the De Lisle Psalter, where the 'old' old man says, "I support my limbs and step slowly with the help of a staff. [*Imbecillis: Artus sustento baculo gradiens pede lento.*]"[223] In the imagery and wording of these three texts, old age appears to be described in three stages: first the *senex* of 'young' old age; followed by the *decrepitus* of 'old' old age, who is already severely afflicted by physical deterioration; and thirdly the *infirmus* or *imbecillis*, bedridden by sickness in the final stage of old age before death. Interestingly, the term *imbecillis* sometimes used for this third stage implies the mental deterioration that affects the old—by having imbecility follow after physical disability (loss of sight, immobility), the poetic texts describe the trajectory of ageing according to medical or scientific texts, where physical disabilities strike first, to be later followed by loss of mental faculties.

Wishful thinking to counter disability in old age was probably best expressed in the Fountain of Youth, the notion of which appears to have originated in Hindu tradition.[224] Thus in the fourteenth century, Mandeville's *Travels* mention a Fountain of Youth situated somewhere in the jungles of India.[225] By the fifteenth century, the standard iconography depicted a civilised scene set within a courtly garden, with old people in various stages of physical decrepitude on one side and the rejuvenated on the other. For example, a fifteenth-century engraving on a bone comb depicts an old couple on the right, both leaning on crutches, who are gazing toward the Fountain of Youth depicted in the centre, where they are made young again, so that they emerge rejuvenated on the left of the image.[226] The direction of movement can vary: an image by the Master of the Banderole of around 1460 shows old people approaching the Fountain of Youth from the left.[227] Intriguing is the early sixteenth-century variation on this theme, the Furnace of Youth, where the old are baked in a furnace and emerge young again, perhaps in erudite humanist allusion to the classical myth of Medea, who boiled Jason's ancient father, Aison, in a cauldron, thereby rejuvenating him.[228] Yet sometimes such imagery only offered what appears to be a miraculous reversal of the debilitating effects of old age and not the plain fact of old age itself.[229] However, learned intellectuals were well aware that the Fountain of Youth was only a myth. In the quest for eternal youth and to prolong life most authors of medical and scientific tracts on the subject, although promulgating all sorts of elixirs, potions and recipes, generally held the more realistic assumption "that medicine could, at best, extend life to its furthest natural term— that is, to the inevitable extinction of the innate heat—and improve the quality of advanced age."[230]

The depiction of disability through old age in art and literary texts is problematic for gauging social awareness, let alone consequences.[231] As one scholar of literary studies has commented recently, while "disability is often equated with aging in the Middle Ages and through the sixteenth century in France,"[232] one must note that a literary text "provides a different experience of disability than real life",[233] in that literary texts have a tendency to stylise, exaggerate and view characters through a narrowly focussed lens in the aid of dramatic representation and interest. The mundane facts discussed in the following, that tenant X entered into a maintenance agreement with tenant Y for the provision of food, lodging and care in old age, may not make for the most exciting dramatic narrative, but they do shed rare light on social and economic circumstances of the 'old'—and perhaps 'disabled'—in that not all people chronologically 'old' were necessarily physically or mentally decrepit. Therefore, I will now turn to questions of what practical measures were taken to aid the disabled aged person and what examples of care provision may have been made for elderly disabled people.

One of the key issues when thinking about old age in past times is the question concerning

> the contrast between old people in modern times who 'enjoy' retirement and no longer work to earn their living, versus old people in premodern times who only stopped working when their physical health failed them completely.[234]

Unqualified, this issue becomes a red herring, since social and economic status determined the *need* to work, rather than chronological age; artisans, peasants and labourers had to work at any age of their lives, whereas the rich and powerful, such as propertied patricians, landlords and the nobility, regardless of personal age, never had to work in the strict sense of the word. Retirement then becomes less of a rite of passage, as it does in modern Western societies, no transition from active working life to leisurely underoccupation, and instead marks an individual choice, albeit a choice for some enforced upon them through physical or mental incapacity. In contrast, voluntary retirement, i.e. unenforced by debility, was sometimes entered into by members of the nobility who relinquished their military status and powers and withdrew into a monastery, occasionally in penance for sinful behaviour in their younger days,[235] but often in a combination of factors relating to ageing, being a widower, having grown-up heirs or for political reasons. Even rulers sometimes retired in this way, for instance, Emperor Lothar I (795–855), who lived out his life as a monk in the monastery of Prüm.[236] According to the Zwiefalter chronicles (completed 1138), a Swabian landholder, who toward the end of his life became lame in his feet, retired to a modest dwelling near the monastery of Zwiefalten, where he lived out his days with the conventual brothers.[237]

With regard to such persons of property and of the duties that were associated with holding property—covering functions of an administrative or governmental type, or even military command—Vincent of Beauvais in the thirteenth century believed they should relinquish their occupation and the management of their estates.[238] And Philip of Novara (c. 1200–c. 1270) declared that

> a man who has reached the age of 60 is relieved from serving. From this age on, having paid all his debts and discharged his duties to people near and distant, he need serve only himself, and if he has the means, avail himself of the service of others.[239]

Therefore, one cannot necessarily argue that "the Middle Ages had no concept of retirement, especially when we consider the social strata of wealthy merchants and patricians."[240]

In rural environments the problem of the elderly peasantry, especially widows, who could no longer physically fulfil the obligations resting on them with regard to cultivation of the lord's land, feature strongly. Here manorial records, in England especially, provide some evidence for the material circumstances surrounding physical or mental disability in old age. A seminal article by Elaine Clark had drawn greater attention to the private systems of social welfare in support of the elderly, with individually arranged 'pension plans' providing a case in point.[241] The best evidence of these rural pension plans is found in the records of manor courts, together with other mentions of where physical or mental disability had had an impact on a tenant's ability to perform the stipulated duties. In manorial courts, for instance, the "poor and disabled gave evidence about overdue rents and unpaid debts."[242] A case concerning a widow can be found in the court rolls of Durham Priory for 1345, which mention the following transaction:

> Agnes widow of Adam de Mora has taken a house and 50 acres of land which her husband Adam formerly held, paying annually for her life 33s. 4d. And there is remitted to her 16s. 8d. a year from the old rent on account of her age and weakness of mind.[243]

Agnes was granted 'special treatment' due to her age and mental condition; presumably she was suffering from senility. Another woman given special treatment was the widow of a smallholder at Ingatestone manor, Essex, who in 1415 was granted relaxation of the usual entry fine on account of her poverty (*propter paupertatem suam*); this widow had been given a cottage and one acre of arable land by her husband before he died, with the additional charge that she should care for his disabled (*decrepita*) sister for life.[244]

But from the lord's perspective such incompetent and disabled tenants posed a problem. "Certainly no lord would countenance his land being allowed to deteriorate in the hands of the infirm."[245] And the law was on the side of the manorial lord, since he could claim custody of those holdings of his tenants who were deemed to be "impotent, incompetent or of unsound mind".[246] As Shahar has pointed out, elderly peasants or widows who did not have dependent family available to help with their labour obligations could find it difficult to meet these, "from which they were not exempted by old age. Only the sick were exempted, and for not more than one month."[247] The onset of physical (or mental) degeneracy might therefore enforce the 'retirement' of peasants.

> Lords, in their concern for the asset value of the holding, might wish to ensure that servile tenants were replaced long before their physical decay set in or their rent-paying capacity was impaired, especially in circumstances where labour services were demanded for the operations of the lord's own demesne farms.[248]

Since the lord had an interest in keeping his land well tended and not allowing it to deteriorate, this presented elderly, no longer able-bodied peasants with a dilemma—either surrender the land back to the lord of the manor or enter into some kind of agreement for other, physically able people to carry out the obligations for them. In the case of an older married couple with children, this was relatively straightforward, in that the holding was tended by the children. However, if there were no (able-bodied) children, the consequence for elderly peasants was to either relinquish the holding they held of the lord of the manor—and risk becoming reliant on charity of relatives or neighbours since they no longer had the necessary land to sustain themselves[249]—or to hand over the land, its cultivation and associated obligations to some third party in return for food, clothing and shelter.[250] An example of a man who was old, but also poor and childless, turning his land over to another for maintenance is found in the court book of Barnet, Hertfordshire. John in the Hale surrendered his land to the lord, while another, John atte Barre, paid the necessary fine to the lord, taking over the holding while agreeing to "find for the aforesaid John in the Hale yearly so long as the same John in the Hale lives" various items of clothing, food and drink "decently as is proper", in return for which John in the Hale "will work for the same John and serve him in proper services to the best of his ability."[251] No leisurely retirement for poor John, but as an impoverished peasant he had to continue working for as long as he was able to.[252]

Corrodies were a kind of salary or expenses payment for manorial workers. From the account roll for the manor of Downton, in the bishopric of Winchester, a series of entries for expenses in the accounting period 1208–1209 relate to corrodies given to various manorial staff, including the bailiff of the manor; among these expenses is the "corrody (*corredium*) of Robert of Lurdon who was sick for 21 days, with his man, 5s. 3d."[253] Corrodies of this kind in the thirteenth century can be treated as a manorial livery, that is, regular payments made to manorial servants for services rendered.[254] Such corrodies (i.e. annuities in kind) and maintenance agreements went some way in providing regulated retirement arrangements for the elderly who were incapable of supporting themselves through work any longer. The difference between corrodies and maintenance agreements was that in the former the holder of a corrody had to purchase it (not dissimilar to a modern pension plan), while in the latter the recipient of maintenance surrendered part or all of a land holding in return for maintenance.[255] An elderly woman who bought a corrody in 1317 from Winchcombe Abbey for the phenomenal sum of £93 6s. 8d. is unlikely to have been a peasant, but in the same year the reeve of Hazleton, John of Staunton, paid £10 to Winchcombe for his corrody, which puts the price of corrodies in perspective—John had to declare readiness to work at whatever the abbot appointed for him, however, for which he was entitled to pottage with the other abbey servants.[256] Corrodies are also known from Germany, for instance, the agreement made in 1322 between the hospital at Villingen (Black Forest) and Hainrich Klucke and his wife; the couple handed over all their arable lands and meadows in return for the hospital managing the lands so that the couple were paid maintenance out of the revenues—the elderly couple could 'retire' from working their holdings while being guaranteed maintenance.[257]

The legally binding nature of such an agreement was reflected in the fact that on some English manors this transaction was recorded in the manorial court rolls.[258] The value of such retirement contracts as recorded in manorial records "lies in the glimpses they provide into the otherwise hidden lives of older people in the distant past".[259] Furthermore, by being enshrined and institutionalised in the proceedings of manorial courts, the perhaps also informal practice of maintenance arrangements for the elderly "became a matter of *public* concern",[260] and in the event of one party neglecting their duty to the aged, the old person could seek legal redress and enforcement of the contract.

The court rolls of the manor belonging to Hales Abbey for the later thirteenth century present especially detailed examples of maintenance cases, for instance, the agreement in 1281 between the elderly Agnes, widow of Thomas Brid, and her son Thomas: Agnes is to surrender all her holdings to Thomas, in return for which he must annually supply her "so long as she lives, honourably and fully" with specified quantities of wheat, oats, peas, five cart-loads of sea-coal, five shillings of "good money" and build own housing for her ("30 feet in length and 14 feet in width within the walls, of timber with three new doors and two windows").[261] To prevent any chances of Thomas not fulfilling his side of the agreement, detailed clauses were drawn up safeguarding what in effect amounted to the retirement plan, in dignity and comparative comfort,[262] of his aged mother. That such precise legal agreements among the peasantry were not unusual in high medieval England is evidenced from other manorial court rolls, the Hales rolls being exceptional only insofar as they stand out in their detail.[263] Among the tenants of Worcester Priory during the latter half of the thirteenth century obtaining a pension was the general rule rather than the exception, for instance, if a son took over a half-yardland holding, he had to provide his mother with specified amounts of rye, barley and oats.[264] The level of maintenance and support is, however, questionable. Formal maintenance agreements between children taking over holdings from their aged parents may have reflected the fact that "they related to the sustenance of old people without dependents, not to working peasants with families to support".[265] Nevertheless, Christopher Dyer has argued that in some cases the specified quantities of grain and other foodstuffs were so small that the elderly or incapacitated peasants "must have had alternative sources of support, such as small-scale production, or grants from relatives."[266] Clothing grants were often a part of such maintenance agreements, too, with varying degrees of quantity and quality,[267] again depending on the affluence of the old peasants concerned.

Physical disability had a direct impact on the ability in one's old age to manage an agricultural holding. Thus William de Toneville in 1286 agreed in the manorial court at Heacham in Norfolk to surrender his house and lands to his son, because his "old age, his physical disability and poverty" prevented him from working his land without the help of "friends" or his son.[268] Where an old person had, for whatever reason, not been capable of making a maintenance agreement before they became too afflicted by debility, "the lord could reclaim the property and make alternative arrangements for his or her care."[269] This happened at Hindolveston, Norfolk, in 1382, where a "poor little woman" who was "feeble of body and simple of mind" was no longer able to care for herself, nor to tend the lord's land that she held.[270] The lord therefore had a vested interest to obtain someone to take on the land and associated duties, so he ordered her "nearest heir" to support her for life as befitted a widow in return for the grant of land. In another Norfolk case from the later fourteenth century, the person on whose behalf the local lord acted was a woman judged mentally incompetent and worn out by age.[271]

The situation among the peasantry in Germany will have been similar. From the end of the thirteenth century onwards the practice of *Ausgedinge* came to be institutionalised, whereby maintenance agreements along the lines of the English manorial documents were drawn up, initiated by the lord of a manor, who ordered old peasants who were physically incapable of fulfilling their obligations to leave their manorial holdings while ensuring, in line with his charitable obligations as lord over his subjects, that they received lifelong support.[272]

A problem with the these kinds of sources is that generally they do not allow us to ascertain if the person entering into a retirement contract was doing so because they were already disabled (or close to becoming incapacitated), or whether they were 'planning ahead' for the eventuality of potential disability. "While it is the case that many of the contracts mention impotency or incompetence as reasons for the retirement, early fifteenth-century East Anglian contracts show that the retirees were far from incapacitated or eager to give up their independence."[273]

Property was the means for ensuring an old age 'pension', and additionally of ensuring that the younger generation cared for the older one: "In this way the old and infirm made the use of their property contingent on support."[274] The more property a person had, of course, the harder the bargain they could drive, and where and when land was scarce, as it was in the century before 1348, the amount of property needed not be all that great to make for a good bargain. But property was not available to all people at all times throughout the period. "As social polarization increased in the later Middle Ages, however, an increasing proportion of the population had no property with which to set themselves up in old age."[275] In his close study of the bishopric of Tréguier during the fifteenth century, Georges Minois encountered a number of old people who were not just impoverished, but also physically disabled, and who eked out the last years of their lives, such as Alain Quiener, "a poor sickly old man who lived in great poverty and misery; Alain Todic, "a poor old man of 100 years, sick in bed, whose wife earns his bread"; Jean Leguen, "80 years old, poor and crippled who goes hunting, and his wife is just as old and they live on charity"; Jean Pratezer, an "old and miserable person, unmarried and practically blind, who has become a beggar"; or Jean Madec's widow, a "poor woman of 70 years, racked with ill-health and physical weakness and lives on charity".[276] How a crippled man goes hunting poses an intriguing but unanswered question (perhaps by laying traps, rather than by more physically strenuous hunting methods). That aside, the picture of some elderly people living in tragic and isolated circumstances, due to disability and/or poverty, begins to emerge.

People of all ages, not just the elderly, had to diversify their strategies for survival, so that the landless poor would rely on a combination of paid work (where available and they were physically capable), help from family or friends, charitable hand-outs and ultimately begging. "Once included among the mass of the poor, the old man cannot be distinguished from his companions in misfortune. He belongs to the more general history of poverty."[277] For some old people, what charity may have been available was too little too late, and they may have died of starvation or neglect, for example, the "old stranger" who was discovered dead of cold and exposure in a cowshed in 1362.[278] As Peregrine Horden, in his review of the role of hospitals in later medieval Europe, has observed, the lack of charitable aid reaching those who needed it most may in part have been because of break-downs in the social structures surrounding institutional poor relief—some people were 'difficult to reach' or to 'engage with', as modern sociological parlance has it.[279]

Urban retirement differed only in locale. In Ghent during the fourteenth century, elderly people made arrangements with their children or other relatives along similar financial lines to the arrangements discussed in the preceding in relation to the peasantry,[280] so that ailing parents could not automatically expect to be cared for by their children unless there was an economic incentive. At Norwich the hospital of Saint Paul's took in fourteen poor men and women who were "decrepit with age, or languished under incurable diseases".[281] The hospital and almshouse at Sherborne, Dorset, present another example, where the elderly beneficiaries of the re-endowment in 1437–1438 were to be "poor, feeble and impotent", and of course of good character;[282] they were forbidden to beg and had to wear a badge denoting their status as recipients of municipal charity. Among hospitals in the Low Countries that did take in the elderly disabled were Saint Jacob's hospital in Leeuwarden, which was founded in 1478 for old, sick and 'needy' burghers of respectable origins, and Saint Elizabeth's hospital in Alkmaar, which in 1456 agreed to remain an institution for old, poor and mad women.[283] The citizens of Passau founded a hospital of Saint John at the beginning of the thirteenth century "to take in old men and women no longer capable of work."[284] A few institutions founded during the fifteenth century also catered to elderly people, such as the one founded in 1419 at Regensburg, where a *Bruderhaus* (brothers' hostel) for twelve old artisans who had fallen into poverty but who were without debts was established; by 1437 demand must have exceeded sup-ply, since a second *Bruderhaus* was founded for a further twelve artisans, but by 1444 these two hospices had been amalgamated into a single institution for twenty-four people, who, according to the foundation charter, were to be old artisans of Regensburg but also other burghers who could no longer earn their living.[285] Venice possessed the hospital of Gesù Cristo di Sant' Antonio, founded specifically for elderly mariners and former (naval) soldiers.[286]

Some other institutions dating from the fifteenth century were that founded in 1488 at Roubaix, which was to provide for twelve "feeble and listless" old secular women and thirty old nuns, and the hospital instigated by the bishop of Milan for old women.[287] Securing a place in a hospital appears, however, not to have been desired by everyone, if the sentiments voiced by an elderly Florentine widow are to be considered. Recorded in the 1427 *catasto*, a census taken for taxation purposes, is the following statement aimed at obtaining a reduced tax assessment or better still an exemption: "The said woman monna Filippa is at least sixty years old and is poor and has to earn her living by spinning and were she to fall ill she would have to go to the hospital."[288] Filippa was able to retain some small measure of economic independence while she was still capable of certain types of manual occupation, and she was worried should she become too disabled to perform this work. In early fifteenth-century Florence at least, having to go to the hospital was sometimes regarded as a measure of last resort, similar to the way many elderly people feel today who are forced to go into a care home after they are no longer able to live independently, whether that be for financial or for physical reasons. Another Florentine old woman, the long-standing servant of lawyer Francesco di Piero, was paid a kind of informal pension by her former employer, since Francesco could not bear to see his faithful old servant end her days in hospital as a pauper. He told the *catasto* recorders in 1427:

> Monna Fiore, aged 77 years: I have paid her expenses from 1415 onwards because she is blind and sick, and I owed her her wages from 1400 because she was with me [as my servant] and my soul would suffer to throw her into a hospital.[289]

Another old woman struggled to continue working despite finding it difficult to cope, having adapted to the circumstances enforced by economics and physical decline in a fashion that may also sound familiar to modern readers. "An eighty-year-old widow who had withdrawn to one room of her house" told the *catasto* officials that she lived from the rent of the rest of her house, and "with my arms I spin a little carded wool, and also I am so old that I cannot manage."[290] In general, for widowed women with little property the "risks of social decline intensified with the onset of old age, when illness and inability to work became more likely."[291]

It seems that in cases of wanting security in old age, rather than requiring immediate care provision due to accidents, individuals looked to corrodies in religious houses. As just one example here of an artisan retiring, in 1248 one Simon de Dene, a carpenter, retired to a religious house, the hospital of Saint Mark in Bristol, selling his tenement for a rent of one mark and the promise by the hospital to maintain him after the death of his wife.[292] Corrodies, however, were something of a double-edged sword with regard to social and economic provisions for the disabled. Corrodies became more common from the twelfth century, and they specified residence in a monastic house or hospital in return for a gift or inheritance.[293] In that sense they were similar to the rural retirement contracts. Corrodians paid a kind of entry fee to a hospital, plus subsequent annual boarding charges, similar to the model of the modern old folks' home. One change over time affecting the inclusion of sick persons in general and people with disabilities in particular was the late medieval growth in corrodies. Since corrodies were bought, they tended to be affordable only to the wealthier elements of medieval society. As more wealthy people bought themselves places as corrodians in hospitals, the poor, sick and disabled came to be nudged out—it was more attractive for the administrators of hospitals to gain a substantial income from corrodians, not all of whom were physically so decrepit due to age that they needed high levels of care, than to provide for the poor and sick. "Wealth drove the poor from hospital beds in fourteenth- and fifteenth-century Germany and the Low Countries, too, where townspeople bought life annuities that guaranteed a hospital place in their old age."[294] In the German towns of Lübeck and Goslar by this time these charitable institutions had been almost entirely taken over by the wealthy aged as retirement homes.

A fine example of this sort of developmental process can be observed from southern Germany in the hospital of the Holy Spirit at Constance, situated right on the marketplace, which was founded in 1225 by two burghers, Heinrich von Bitzenhofen and Ulrich Blarer, who were "inflamed by the fire of charity".[295] In line with their motivation this hospital initially catered to all "Christian poor", taking in poor and/or sick persons of all descriptions in its early days, including the disabled such as paralysed persons and the mentally ill. But it was already starting to accommodate an ever-increasing number of paying guests in the form of corrodians, who over the centuries of this hospital's existence began to take up more and more space to the detriment of provision for the sick.[296] By 1448 the governing body of the hospital felt it necessary to appoint an official, the *Siechenamtmann*, to raise awareness of the needs of the sick, but to no avail, since the select circle of those granted admission to the hospital became ever smaller; thus by the end of the fifteenth century any sick poor who had recovered their health had to leave the hospital immediately (freeing up bed-space, no doubt) while only the bedridden sick continued to receive the former benefits.[297] One explanation for the development of this particular hospital lies in its economic basis: since the citizens of Constance had played an instrumental part right from the beginning, richly endowing the hospital with donations and gifts, mainly lands and buildings, they could influence the type of person the hospital was meant to accommodate (i.e. their own class), which meant that already in the thirteenth century corrodians were becoming inmates despite the foundation's aims.[298] One might see here the effects of 'stakeholders' at work, to use a modern analogy, by which that group of people who made an economic investment was the group who controlled admission, with a tendency to select from its own ranks to the exclusion of others. At Constance, during their lifetime the corrodians remained the owners of the property they brought with them on admission; the property fell to the hospital on their death. In this way already by the fourteenth century married couples were taken on as corrodians rather than sick people, and corrodians were classified according to whether they were "free (*Herrenpfründner*)" or "obedient (*gehorsam*)": "free" corrodians were free from servile tasks, while "obedient" corrodians were duty-bound to fulfil a variety of labour services for the hospital[299]— activities that were economically valuable for the hospital as an institution but which were not necessarily within the (physical) means of impaired people, highlighting yet another reason why the disabled and acutely sick were gradually being supplanted by the able-bodied retired.

Another German hospital, Saint James at Trier, had also changed its clientele, so that by the fifteenth century it was predominantly a retirement home for corrodians. Nevertheless, as the account books which survive from the middle of that century demonstrate, the occasional sick or disabled person was admitted, for instance, Clais [Klaus] "uff den krucken" [with the crutches], a journeyman from Koblenz apparently in Trier for work, and whose travel costs for his repatriation the hospital paid for in 1466–1467; staff were also paid for looking after "dem blynden manne" [the blind man] who resided during 1473–1474.[300] An individual foundation was due to the widow of Count Ulrich IV of Württemberg, who in 1366 created a house to receive all the lame and the hungry people loitering about in the nooks and crannies of Stuttgart, as well as the impoverished aged people.[301]

The problem of corrodies being preferred by hospitals over caring for the sick was already raised by the Council of Paris in 1212; "the waste of resources and corruption of morals occasioned by the presence of so many idle dependants" were criticised.[302] In England, the papal legate and cardinal deacon of Saint Adrian, Ottobuono, opposed the sale of corrodies on the grounds that they diverted resources away from the sick and the poor, robbing these needy people of the leftover food and drink in particular. According to Barbara Harvey's interpretation, Ottobuono had argued at the Council of London in 1268 that "because corrodies were sold, fewer of the poor and the sick were cared for in monasteries—or, for that matter, in hospitals—and alms were deflected from their proper destination."[303] In England, a royal commission of enquiry in 1376 noted "the excessive award of corrodies" at Saint Lawrence's, Bristol, hindering the support of lepers "and other infirm persons" for whom the foundation had been intended.[304] Also at Bristol, the canons of Saint Augustine's abbey were to pay a corrodian forty shillings annually for life and to provide lodging for him and a servant according to the terms of a charter issued between 1221 and 1230;[305] another charter dated October 1254–October 1255 provided a very detailed corrody (including allowances for food, wine, ale, firewood for the hearth and half a mark per annum for clothing) to the widow Mary Curtelane, who granted land to the abbey.[306] Edward I's onetime servant in Wales and Gascony, Robert Tiptoft, obtained a chamber in the infirmary of Westminster Abbey as a corrodian—conveniently close to his official business in London—in 1297 at the latest, when the bill for repairs to his lodgings appears in the accounts.[307] And at Saint Mark's Hospital, Bristol, the intention of the original foundation in the early thirteenth century to feed one hundred poor persons daily had developed into a residential almshouse for twenty-seven select paupers; similarly at the hospital of Saint Cross, Winchester, the daily alms given out to one hundred poor required by the founder had been abandoned by 1373, when the institution instead housed four priests, thirteen clerks and seven choristers and the alms to the poor were restricted to thirteen residential paupers.[308] Exemplifying the decline of variation among inmates, the hospital at Kingsthorpe by Northampton was reduced to only two lay brothers by 1535.[309]

When it came to making agreements of transferring property in return for a promise of food, clothes and shelter, wealthier people could afford to simply sublet part of their property and live off the rental income, only selling off parcels of land as and when necessary. Christopher Dyer makes an interesting observation regarding the elderly hiring servants to care for them,[310] which one may take further and explore in terms of an 'economy of care', raising the question of how many servants employed in urban contexts may in fact have been employed specifically to provide help and care for infirm elderly burghers. The evidence from maintenance agreements, corrodies, hospital and almshouse charters and similar documents points to a situation whereby in practice the elderly were not always or exclusively relying on their immediate family for support and instead turning to 'third party' care provision—and even to 'professional' care, in the form of paid staff found in hospitals and almshouses, or possibly even hiring dedicated servants for those old people wealthy enough to remain in their homes. (With changing fortune, staff could of course easily become inmates as well, since hospital nurses who became ill or feeble with age might end up as patients themselves.[311])

The gender difference between servants and employers could cause trouble, as exemplified by the following request made to the papal curia (between 1447 and 1454) by seventy-year-old John Langley of Worcester, who employed Joan White, a woman aged over fifty, as his "handmaiden and servant", stating that "he cannot do without the service of the said woman without great danger of his person."[312] Another request to the curia concerned an eighty-year-old provost, who stated that since he was no longer in danger of succumbing to carnal temptations (*de incontinentia carnis suspectus non existat*), he would like to take a female 'nurse' into his home to care for him in his old age.[313] The records are not always very clear as to what the relationship between people was, for instance, the woman Matilda mentioned in 1335 as 'nurse' to Richard Erneys in records pertaining to the city of Chester. Richard had been mayor of Chester, last holding the mayoralty in 1330, so that he will have been elderly by then.[314] Was Matilda his 'nurse' from his infant days, in which case she will have been significantly older than Richard, or was she a nurse for his dotage?

While the previous chapter mentioned financial benefits given to workers temporarily incapacitated or younger workers accidentally disabled, here the focus is on permanent arrangements made for elderly people who were too old to work any longer. Examples of occupational old age 'pension' may be found Venice, where a decree of the Grand Council in 1362 "stated that the proceeds of a brokerage tax on pepper should be conferred on native Venetian marines age sixty and over because of their old age and incapacity"; furthermore, some social insurance provision was made by Venetian guilds "for ageing workers in the city's shipbuilding business."[315] A pension in the modern sense was granted to John Bandy, the sergeant of the chamber of the City of London in October 1477. He had "voluntarily resigned his office on account of old age" and as a former 'civil servant' had some entitlement to support.[316] And in Frankfurt am Main in 1488 a servant of the mayor was given a pension of thirteen *gulden* on account of the infirmity of old age, which was equivalent to a quarter of the wages paid to mercenaries.[317]

Many guilds and fraternities did support members who were sick or disabled, a category which included those members disabled due to old age, but it "was not assumed that every old person was necessarily sick or disabled, nor that every old person *per se* was entitled to help."[318] Pensions were therefore only reserved for 'special cases' and not automatically available for any member above a certain age. Most guilds simply subsumed the category of the 'aged' within the wider group of sick and disabled members. And even then most assistance to members was intended for temporary periods only, while the person was deemed to be 'in need', so that people who were disabled in the widest sense had to prove the lasting and chronic effect of their condition; sometimes disability due to old age exempted the claimant for assistance from the proviso of being in need.[319] The London guild of Holy Cross in Saint Laurence Jewry provided for its members "in infirmity by reason of mutilation of limbs or because of old age,"[320] while another London organisation, the fraternity of the hospital of Saint Katharine by the Tower, made provision for a *confrater* to make a single payment of ten shillings and four pence (or spread the subscription over seven years) for which he could expect in return a room, bedding and food in old age.[321] At Chesterfield the guild of the Blessed Mary supported those members who were disabled through age, loss of limb or by leprosy.[322] The Coventry guilds might help either a member who was "no longer capable of work by reason of illness, accident, or old age" or a member's widow "by considering the great age, nede, & pouverte that she is ynne".[323] Accidents might of course have only a temporary effect, but disability due to old age would render the person 'needy' for the rest of their lives. It is therefore difficult to understand how the guilds dealt with such cases, if they preferred to dole out assistance for time-limited periods only. Regulations are somewhat reticent as to how the disabled elderly were helped, only rarely stating "explicitly 'for the rest of his life' [*terminum vite sue*]."[324] Furthermore, old men tended to be in a better position than old women (unless they were relatively affluent), since not all guilds admitted the widows of guildmembers, for example, the Weaver's Hall at Ghent in the fourteenth century was open to old and disabled guilds*men* but excluded their equally incapacitated wives.[325]

Although guilds tended to concentrate their relief efforts on those members requiring short-term help, there are some examples of labourers and artisans 'planning ahead' to make arrangements for their retirement, such as the worker at Lyons in the later Middle Ages, who "pledged their assets to the hospital against the assurance that they would be looked after in their old age".[326] In London the guilds of vintners and salters established almshouses for their members in 1446 and 1454, respectively.[327] And in the latter half of the thirteenth century the Parisian guild of cooks stipulated that a third of the fines collected were to go into a special fund "for the maintenance of old men of the craft who lost their standing owing to a [failed] transaction, or old age".[328]

Outside of guilds, individuals too might 'plan ahead'. In a record of 2 June 1305 in the Barcelona archives a surgeon from Foix in the Pyrenées made an agreement with another surgeon from Gerona (Aragon) to teach him all that he knew about surgery, in exchange for which the younger surgeon would provide food and clothing. Knowledge is economic bargaining power, as this anecdote affirms, so much so that to make the offer more attractive the elder surgeon agreed to give all his books to the younger— with the exception of a book on surgery with the teachings of thirteenth-century Ugo of Lucca by his pupil Teodorico Borgognoni, which the elder surgeon insisted he would keep until he died.[329]

The canonisation proceedings for Werner of Oberwesel/Bacharach on the middle Rhine in 1428–1429 feature a seventy-year-old lawyer (*advocatus*) who was retired in the modern sense of the word, presumably involuntarily, in that he had had to relinquish his office due to age and debility (*senio et debilitate ab officio absolutus*);[330] one gets the impression this 'professional' man would have liked to continue working instead of languishing in the *otium* of enforced retirement due to age-related disability.

English royal servants and retainers, or simply people whom the king wished to reward for some service or other rendered in the past, could be the recipients of royal munificence, in the form of a 'pension' in the widest sense. It appears already from *Domesday Book* that the long-term infirm, that is, the disabled, were given a portion of royal land as a small estate to support them, if they were considered important enough personages by the king;[331] *Domesday Book* mentioned a cripple at Evesham (Buckinghamshire) who held a hide of land as a royal almsman, and a blind man at

Warsop (Nottinghamshire) who held a bovate, along with a smallholder and six oxen.[332] Over the next few centuries the sporadic reward given to royal servants developed into a more regular practice, so that by the later thirteenth century greater numbers of elderly and disabled people can be found in the records who were provided for by 'pensions'. In August 1237 Henry de Brusel, who had been King Henry III's changer at the exchange in London, was granted a one-off gift of one hundred shillings, due to the fact that he "being now infirm has gone to his own parts".[333] And in 1269 Henry III "awarded a pension to master William le Sauser, formerly a king's sergeant, 'who is overcome with age and hampered by such infirmity that he cannot remain longer in his service'."[334] One aged royal retainer, Richard Whitoc, was pensioned off in 1333 to a religious house, the convent of Stanley (Wiltshire), since he had been "butler to the king's household" and had "long and faithfully served the king."[335] Edward Skelton "in his decrepit age" was granted a life annuity of twenty marks per annum for "his long continued service" in 1486 by King Henry VII.[336]

In later fourteenth-century and fifteenth-century England, wills by the aristocracy sometimes recorded gifts of alms to their former servants who had now retired due to incapacity brought on by advanced years. For instance, Lord Grey of Ruthin gave a cottage "to John Cartere in alms" for his retirement.[337] At the other end of the scale were royal servants or retainers, which included men of noble or gentle rank, who were allocated places in hospitals as part of a 'retirement plan'. For example, in 1348 Edward III did not just found the Order of the Garter (for the able-bodied, active and young), but he also founded Saint George's Chapel at Windsor, intended for a number of clergy and for twenty-four "poor and infirm" knights, whose number was increased to twenty-six in 1351, which was overly optimistic since the number of actual resident infirm knights was generally only two or three at any given time, and then only a few of these "were even proper knights".[338] Saint George's Chapel in effect came to be used as a "small private almshouse chiefly for important royal servants", so that by the time of Henry VII it housed his retired barber, physician and French secretary.[339]

One group of royal servants who have been well studied are royal messengers. They have been identified as individual *nuncii* (mounted messengers) and *cursores* (runners) during the reigns of English kings from John to Edward III, together with their service record.[340] If messengers became too old and physically disabled, there were a number of options the royal administration resorted to, ranging from being allocated an easier job involving less strenuous travelling to an allowance, a grant of property or a pension in the form of a corrody at a monastery or hospital. Pensions for elderly and incapacitated messengers feature in the accounts, such as the king's request in 1310 to the abbot of Winchcombe to provide a 'retirement' place for "John le Blak the king's envoy, who has long served the king and his father and Edmund, late Earl of Cornwall, and who is now too infirm to work".[341] In 1313 the king requested similarly of the prior of Trinity church, London, that they will grant to Simon le Messager who long served the late king and is now blind, suitable maintenance for himself and a groom in food and clothing, to be received by him whether staying within or without their said house.[342]

This suggests that old and blind Simon possessed his own house and could, if he wished, benefit of a kind of 'day care', to use a modern analogy, while remaining in his own home. In 1339 Robert of Chester "who has served the king, his father and his grandfather and who is so broken by age" that he cannot undertake overseas journeys any longer, was recommended to the abbot of Leicester—this appears to have been a semi-retirement from the more strenuous travels involved, indicating that old age and concomitant disabilities did not always force complete removal from one's working life and career, but just a slower pace.[343] A total retirement was effected for John Pynchoun in 1353 "for long service to the king's father and the king and because he is so broken with age that he can labour no longer",[344] and in 1362 "Henry Croft one of the king's messengers, for long service and because he is now too old and infirm to labour in the office" was given a pension of four pence per day.[345] Especially the mounted messengers may have been prone to disabling conditions, although all messengers could be retired early, it seems, due to general, unspecified injuries, as did John Taverner, who retired for such reasons in 1348.[346]

Other royal servants, or simply well-connected people, could equally be provided with a pension. In 1270—or possibly earlier—Ralph de Heles was granted two robes a year for life (which cost the royal treasury thirty shillings per annum) because he had become blind in the king's service[347]—it is not clear whether this was a royal servant retiring due to old age which had caused his blindness, or whether the blindness was caused by some unspecified kind of work-related injury or illness. The same was probably the case for John le Hotter, who was assigned a place in the hospital of Saint Leonard, York, by the king in 1312 because "he is so broken by age that he cannot work for his food."[348] In Durham in 1378 the hospital of Saint Mary in Staindrop sheltered eighteen aged gentlemen and a number of other poor old men, who were "probably retainers and servants of the hospital's founder".[349] Changes in the function of such institutions meant that hospitals and almshouses that used to take in the 'needy' in general came to be specialised to cater to certain groups of people only.[350] Among such groups were the elderly, for instance, at the hospital of Arundel, Sussex, established by the Earl of Arundel in 1395, which was preferentially catering for his servants. Other magnates who founded institutions for their servants were: Ralph Neville, Earl of Westmoreland, at Staindrop in Durham (re-)founded 1408 for his staff (which included among its residents gentlemen, yeomen and grooms); Edward, Duke of York, founding Fotheringhay, Northamptonshire, in 1413–1422; Lady Hungerford for her servants at Heytesbury in 1472; and the intended but not realised foundation of almshouses at

Alkmonton by Lord Mountjoy in 1472, all of which catered primarily for the founder's household staff.[351] The almshouse founded for thirteen men in 1504 by Henry VII at Westminster Abbey was for royal servants of not especially high status, but it exemplified the tendency of these specialised institutions to concentrate on men rather than women.[352] A continental example of a lord providing 'pensions' in this wider sense to his aged servants and retainers may be encountered in the *Arme-Diener-Hof* (poor servants' court) at Cleves, an almshouse-type institution founded in 1444 on the initiative of Adolph I, Duke of Cleves, for five former servants of the court, who were aged, poor and incapable of sustaining themselves.[353] Being a royal servant did not, however, automatically guarantee a pension or secure one's financial position in old age. In France, for instance, a 1341 ordinance of Philip VI "abolished all the stipends of the royal officials, except for those who were sick or disabled, had served the king for many years, and the old."[354]

Ecclesiastical lords, too, provided for their former retainers in this way. Archbishop Simon Islip (1349–1366) rewarded his servant Philip de Milton with a corrody in the hospital of Saints Peter and Paul, Maidstone (Kent), since Philip was "declining into the feebleness of old age".[355] An analysis of the corrodies granted by the archbishops of Canterbury between 1313 and 1414 shows that fourteen corrodies were awarded for people termed 'old', twelve due to poverty, three due to blindness and one because of leprosy.[356] Staff at ecclesiastical institutions could sometimes expect guarantee of a retirement place, for instance, at the hospital of Saint Peter's at Bury Saint Edmunds, founded by Abbot Anselm in the time of Henry I, which kept secure places for aged and sick chaplains and wardens formerly working at these hospitals.[357] Cardinal Henry Beaufort enlarged a hospital for his former servants at Saint Cross, Winchester, in 1443–1446,[358] and Saint Katherine's almshouse, Exeter, founded c. 1450 served old servants of Exeter's cathedral clergy.[359] Bishop Edmund Stafford of Exeter (1395–1419) ensured that at least two elderly and disabled priests in his diocese were admitted to one local hospital.[360]

Why were special provisions made for old and/or disabled priests? Shulamith Shahar argued that "the church authorities viewed it as an indignity that old churchmen should be brought to the edge of starvation", and that such a sense of dignity and shame "led to the arrangements for pensions for retired clergymen, and for houses to accommodate them."[361] Already in 816 a church council had expressed concern over what would happen to sick and old secular canons, which resulted in the establishment of special accommodation for them, even though they were permitted possession of their own houses, so that in the special house other, able-bodied and younger canons could visit them and "look after them lovingly and compassionately".[362] And another church council, in 1261 in Mainz, intended to provide almshouses for aged and debilitated priests, "as it disgraced the priesthood if those who had served God were reduced to beggary."[363] In the early fifteenth century Bishop Robert Rede of Chichester ensured measures were in place to pay the pension of a retired priest "lest he be seen begging."[364] And retired clergy could sometimes, also, be the beneficiaries of private charity, as was former chaplain John Wright in 1433, who was now blind and impoverished so that he was left a legacy of a mark per annum for life by his benefactor, Thomas Ricard.[365]

Secular servants of the church could be rewarded with pensions, too. Of uncertain nature was the relationship between Matilda of Tiverton and Bishop Grandisson of Exeter, but in a letter addressed to the master and brothers of the hospital of Saint John at Exeter in 1329 he requested a place for her at that institution, describing her as old and ill; if there were no immediate vacancy for Matilda, then she was to be given the next place available and to be cared for with "sincere charity".[366] Fountains Abbey maintained "the olde mane howse" reserved for retired servants of the monastery.[367] Saint Giles hospital, Lincoln, which had originally been intended for the poor in general, seems to have been converted during the fourteenth century into a house for twelve poor ministers and servants of the cathedral.[368] Also in the diocese of Lincoln, Thornton Abbey had provided "certain alms called little corrodies, which were formerly wont to be given to serving folk and to friends of the canons who had fallen upon old age or loss of strength",[369] but by the fifteenth century these corrodies were being sold to higher bidders, so that it took an episcopal visitation to set matters right. However, a corrody sometimes entailed duties with it, such as the one granted to John Baker at the Carmelite Friary of Lynn, Norfolk, in 1367, where he was to serve the friary "except in extreme old age and in time of bodily infirmity".[370] One must remember that the provision of pensions to servants by secular or regular clergy "was an acknowledgement of a moral obligation to secure the old age of those who had served the monastery for many years: it was not a legal obligation."[371]

Conflict between monasteries and the demands of (royal) patrons sometimes erupted when patrons requested retirement places in such institutions for their own retainers, which reduced the number of available pensions for the monastery's own clerks and servants.[372] Kings and the higher aristocracy had dealt with their old and infirm gentlemen-in-waiting by sending them to monasteries as pensioners, especially if the monastery in question was under royal patronage. The peak period of royal exploitation of monastic corrodies was in the decades either side of 1300, starting under Edward I from c. 1290.[373] For example, Edward I forced the monks of Romsey Abbey in 1303 to provide a corrody for Edward's aged surgeon even though the abbey was already looking after two other aged former servants of the king.[374] And in 1317 Edward II requested a corrody at Westminster Abbey for his former laundress Matilda de Haukeseye, "on account of her long service";[375] hence she must have been considered aged or at least incapable of performing her former duties by this stage. Furthermore, in 1319 Edward II requested another corrody, consisting of food and drink, of the same abbey for John Lescurel, a serjeant-at-arms "said to have served both the king and his father at home and abroad but now to be old and weak".[376] However, pensions given to household servants of the nobility, in the form of places in almshouses, from the fourteenth century onwards indicated "a partial turning away from the practice of sending infirm servants to monasteries."[377] Instead, the larger and wealthier English hospitals were used for this purpose. For example, in 1309 Edward II "sent his disabled servant Robert of the Napery to be maintained at St. Mary without Bishopsgate London with food, clothing and a private chamber; other such pensioners were sent in 1330 and 1331."[378]

Edward II seems to have been a conscientious and good 'employer', since in 1314 he also sent one William of Grove, who had lost his hand in the Scottish wars, to Saint John's hospital, Brackley,[379] a rare case in the records where mention is made of a military invalid being provided for. The nominal hospital God's House at Ospringe in Kent was founded in the early thirteenth century by the English crown among other reasons to provide retirement facilities for royal servants.[380] King Edward III sent his retired servants to Durham Priory, where they were to be looked after until they died.[381] More controversial was the royal practice of sending infirm, disabled or elderly servants to leper hospitals, presumably if the endowment of these houses was especially good, since, according to the survey by Orme and Webster, healthy people tried to "infiltrate" some leper houses as soon as they were founded; they cite a case from 1315 where the "staff of the leper hospital of Saint Giles Holborn complained to the king that his household officers sent them infirm servants to maintain who were not lepers, and the king ruled that this should stop."[382] Pretense could also be made of other impairments, as did former chaplain William Lulleman, "who pretends to be deaf and for that cause has at the king's request been admitted to this hospital of Newton [Holderness]"; in 1342 the hospital lodged a complaint concerning William's "lunatic and mad" behaviour and managed to have him removed, only to be ordered four years later to "admit William Lulleman of Bernleye, chaplain, who is detained by severe sickness, and to give him maintenance for life."[383]

The tensions between rulers and hospitals that emerged in England over the king's practice of demanding 'retirement pensions' for his aged retainers is also evident from Germany. There since at least the thirteenth century the ruler had the right to request a corrody for senile or disabled persons, whom the king or emperor specified, from every ecclesiastical institution in the empire on one occasion during the period of his reign. For instance, in 1487 the imperial servant Hans Tekheler was provided with a (lower status) corrody at the hospital of Esslingen, which entailed certain duties of work for Hans; conflict between ruler and institution over the privileging of royal servants over local townsfolk, who had one place less available, meant that such corrodians were not always treated amicably, so that by 1492 the emperor and his senior staff had to request of the council of Esslingen that their protegé Hans Tekheler should no longer be subjected to such onerous work as hacking wood or similar.[384]

An example of an individual foundation that specified particular inmates is the famous Saint Nicholas hospital at Cues along the Moselle, founded in 1450 by Cardinal Nicholas Cusanus, which was specially intended for thirty-three 'needy' old men over the age of fifty who were incapable of working any more,[385] of whom a number, one must assume, had become disabled due to old age. That the elderly who had become incapable of working, so in effect had become 'disabled' in one way or another, could be perceived of as a burden emerges from an incidental note in the *Customal of Chartreuse*, compiled in the early twelfth century by Prior Guigues I, who mentions that the monastery had to increase the number of lay brothers (*conversi*) working on the estates because some had become economically redundant due to the decrepitude of old age: "Some of them, in effect, were old and frail, and they could no longer work."[386] Georges Minois believes that other monastic communities considered sending "their aged monks and nuns to return to their families" but regrettably fails to provide evidence for such considerations or attempts.[387] He does, however, cite Salvian of Marseille, who in the fifth century was opposed to the notion of returning redundant clergy back home.[388] Perhaps the 'problem' of what to do with those elderly people disabled by age was more of an issue in late antiquity or the earlier Middle Ages, before changes in social and economic situations or even religious attitudes led to consolidation of ideas about charity, care for and support of the needy.

One group of people who, particularly in the later Middle Ages, rarely received a pension, according to Shulamith Shahar, were those mercenaries whose contract did not cover their pay or retainment fee beyond the fixed terms set out; such men who may well have become disabled due to the injuries they had sustained in the course of their careers, as was detailed earlier, and if they reached old age at all, "were forced to beg for a living, unless they were lucky enough to receive help from some quarter".[389] An example of one aged soldier who received such informal help was given in an oblique reference by Joinville, in his *Life of Saint Louis*: the abbot of Cluny had "often given bread for the love of God" to a poor knight whom Joinville described as having to lean on his crutch.[390] Rarely, an institution provided dedicated support for veterans, such as Saint John's hospital, Winchester, founded around 1275 "for the relief of sick and lame soldiers, poor pilgrims, and necessitous wayfaring men".[391] Thomas More, in his famous *Utopia* of 1516, described the desperate condition of the maimed and mutilated former soldiers and mercenaries who were simply left to fend for themselves, in an allusion to real events after the ineffectual besiegement of Boulogne in October 1492 and the Cornish rebellion subdued in June 1497.[392] Another group of people who practically never received a pension were the widows of minor English royal officials,[393] although one fifteenth-century woman, Lady Lovel, was granted one by the English king, apparently, however, "in recognition of her own, not her husband's services", as a royal governess.[394]

In England we find the enforced retirement of those king's coroners who were too old or too infirm to do their job properly, which occurred as an apparent one-off case in the early years of the reign of Edward III (when 21 per cent of 275 coroners had been forcibly retired due to old age, sickness, blindness or paralysis),[395] and in some greater numbers during the middle of the fifteenth century.[396] For instance, between 1429 and 1435 alone some twenty-five coroners had to retire on the grounds of being "too sick and aged" or "too weak and too hampered with divers infirmities.[397] As individual example stands the case of William Hales of Kirketon, who was relieved off his office for being "too sick and aged to travail in the exercise of that office."[398]

In contrast, the urban 'professionals', such as bankers, merchants and artisans, as well as physicians, lawyers and notaries were independent 'self-employed' people, who, unlike royal officials or retainers of the nobility, generally could not be obliged to retire at either a fixed age or due to a disability.[399] An example of a craftsman who continued to work despite certain incapacities brought on by old age can be found from January 1344 at York. There an aged carpenter working on the minster was given special consideration, since "W. the carpenter is an old man and cannot work at high levels (*in altis*). It is ordered that another young man be employed in his place, and that the other old man shall supervise defects."[400] Hence transfer to a supervisory role, rather than complete cessation of work, was a likely route for the aged craftsmen no longer physically capable of competing with the able-bodied younger folk.

However, the opposite of enforced retirement, namely, almost an enforced expectation to continue in office until the death of the office-holder, occurred in some municipal authorities. For example, in York during the fifteenth century aldermen were normally elected in their mid-forties and then held office until death, so that one cannot speak of an official retirement age for these civic governing bodies; nevertheless, some individuals were forced to resign due to ill-health and age, which appears to have been granted reluctantly by their colleagues.[401] The York draper William Warde had to pay ten pounds in 1476 to secure his 'retirement' from office on account of his "grete age and sekenisse".[402] London was somewhat more accommodating of the physical and/or mental needs of its aged citizens, since men holding office were permitted to retire once they had reached the age of seventy, as in the case of one old man who was examined by a commission and found not just to be over seventy but also "afflicted with deafness".[403] In the House of Lords between the late fourteenth and early fifteenth centuries, two-thirds of those peers given permission to excuse themselves were granted this because of the disabilities of old age, such as Bishop Heyworth (†1447), who was excused in 1439 "by reason of his age and infirmities",[404] as was Bishop John Arundel of Chichester in 1474, due to "his debility and old age",[405] or Lord Vesci in 1456 who, aged about sixty-six, was permitted to relinquish his duties to "attend the sittings of the House on account of his age and infirmity".[406] Other secular peers were excused from attendance because they suffered from bad sight, incurable infirmity, age and weakness or old age and debility.[407] In France, ordinances of 1319 promulgated by Philip V permitted sick, impoverished or old vassals of the king to perform homage to a local official instead of having to travel in order to do so before the king's person.[408]

Sickness and disability in old age did not, of course, spare the clergy, even if many historians have tended to depict the institution of the Church as one "in which there was no illness and nobody grew old."[409] Holding office as a member of the clergy was in effect an open-ended contract: there was no upper limit of years that (dis)qualified a man from being in a clerical position. In practice, many clergy who were senior in years will have simply slowed down, depending on their individual physical or mental constitution, but did not automatically resign from their offices.[410] The complaint lodged by Hrabanus Maurus in his dedicatory epistle to Emperor Lothar at the beginning of his *Commentary* on Jeremiah exemplifies the disabilities forcing a less active life on him. He is infirm and debilitated and not so much physically ill as also restricted in his senses, and he is pressed down by grave illness. He spends more time lying in bed than he sits at the place of meditation in order to write or read:

> ipse infirmus et debilis et non tam corpore egrotus quam etiam sensu minutus pertinaciter quasi ad hoc idoneus temptarem aggredi. [. . .] qui gravi egritudine pressus iam sepius in lectulo accumbo, quam ad scribendum vel ad legendum in meditatorio sedeo.[411]

Elsewhere Hrabanus Maurus reiterates these sentiments, bemoaning the fact that although he had often been ill, due to the grand old age he had now reached he just wasn't the way he used to be (*propter corporis egritudinem et animi debilitatem; qui licet numquam aliquid fuerim, longe tamen propter grandevam aetatem modo aliud sum quam eram*), and had to lie down more often instead of mediating or teaching (*quoniam sepius suscipit me lectulus meus cubantem, quam cathedra tenet meditantem aut docentum*).[412] Alcuin, too, who had by 796 retired to the monastery of Saint-Martin in Tours, complained in a letter to his friend, Archbishop Eanbald of York, that "he was beset by the double burden of old age and infirmity."[413] A twelfth-century manuscript contains a passage appended to the main text, in which a letter by Saint Ambrose offered consolation to an infirm old monk who had been rendered decrepit by his advanced age.[414]

The sufferings of the (intellectual) writer beset by the miseries of old age remained a topos throughout the medieval period, not just among the clergy, so that in a letter Boccaccio could write to a friend:

My body is heavy, my step unfirm, my hand trembling; the pallor of death is in my face, I have no appetite, everything upsets me. The strength of my soul is failing, my memory almost gone, my genius turned to imbecility.[415]

And in a letter written around 1400 to Archbishop Thomas Arundel of Canterbury, John Gower "joins the club" of those who referred to themselves as aged and blind, sick in body, old and miserable in all.[416] The difference between the Carolingian clerics and the later medieval poet is simply that in the case of the latter we have enough biographical detail to prove that in his case he really was becoming blind in old age and suffering from other illnesses.

Physical (and mental) vigour was important to the clergy, too, not just the secular rulers, warriors or workers. According to Hrabanus Maurus, almost all physical strength vanishes in old people, and while wisdom alone increases, all else decreases, so that those things that a person (meaning here a cleric) required bodily vigour for, such as fasting, sleeping, receiving pilgrims, the defence of the poor, strong prayers, perseverance, visiting the languishing or manual labour, all had to be performed less and less.[417] The gradual slowing down of one's working pace affected the duties of the clergy as much as those of secular folk. Slowing down meant, for instance, travelling less frequently or less far if one was a bishop on visitation or other business around one's diocese, or on the way to councils. Roger de Meuland, bishop of Coventry and Lichfield, had been born c. 1215, become bishop in 1258 and was therefore already well into his seventies when, according to his registers, he reduced his travelling in 1280–1281, apparently due to illness.[418] He even had a coadjutor appointed to him by Archbishop Peckham. In 1288 another bout of illness further reduced his ability to perform visitations around his diocese. He died in 1295 aged around eighty.

Various measures were employed by the church to ensure the pastoral duties of aged and incapacitated clergy were not neglected. In some instances, as for Roger de Meuland, coadjutor clergy were appointed to help the aged incumbent in his daily affairs; this happened much earlier already in the case of Archbishop Adalgar of Hamburg (†909), who was too old to travel around his archiepiscopate so that the pope appointed the five neighbouring bishops to assist Adalgar, and in the case of Saint Boniface (c. 672–754), who was provided with an adjutant due to the decrepitude of his senescence which prevented him from ministering to his flock.[419] In 1309 William, vicar of Perran Zabulo, had Michael de Newroneck appointed by the bishop as coadjutor on two shillings a week salary because of William's age and infirmity.[420] Several cases of coadjutors in the diocese of York are known from the register of Archbishop William Melton of York: in 1322 Roger de Sutton, rector of North Collingham, who was paralysed and unable to carry out his duties, had William de Sutton appointed as his coadjutor; next in 1326 Elias de Coulton, canon of Southwell minster, who was almost blind and completely incapacitated, received a coadjutor; then in 1330 Ralph de Hertford, rector of Hockerton, who was blind and incapacitated; and, finally, John de Somerhous, rector of Rounton and old, totally blind and ill, had his brother Robert de Somerhous appointed as coadjutor.[421] Towards the end of the time period under consideration Reginald Calle, the provost of Glasney College in the diocese of Exeter, wrote to his bishop in 1374, asking for a coadjutor, since he sat "in the shadows, like the elder Tobias" and no longer saw "the light of the heavens", having become blind.[422] And one may cite the fifteenth-century dean of Irthlingborough College, diocese of Lincoln, who was "broken in health by reason of old age" and unable to continue with his office, so that other canons had to take over his duties of visiting the sick and of preaching the Sunday sermon.[423]

Lesser clergy, too, down to the level of parish priest, could, with permission of the local bishop, employ a curate or coadjutor,[424] whom they were responsible for paying for; therefore, only the economically more secure priests will have been in a position to 'retire' voluntarily, since many minor clergymen did not even have a benefice and instead received an annual salary.[425] Aged priests could resign and retire, with episcopal permission, as did the rector of Great Torrington in 1453 due to old age, weakness and blindness,[426] or if they were "broken down by age and weakened in sight by palsy of the eyes, and for many years incurably troubled with heavy sickness",[427] as had been a priest in the diocese of Chichester in 1414. In the same diocese Bishop Rede discovered the priest of Finden who "had been afflicted through many years continually and incurably with severe and diverse infirmities and particularly with the complaint of deafness as he is now notoriously afflicted, so that he is now rendered altogether useless for the cure of souls entrusted to him."[428] The rector of Saint Martin's by Loo, Cornwall, suffered great adversities to his health and debilities of his body, paralysis, infirmity and was aged ninety when he was finally able to retire (*tanta adversa valetude vesatus ac corporis sui debilitacione gravatur, eciam paralasium . . . infirmitatem . . . et nimiam senectute quia nonagenarius est*).[429] Among the seventy-seven clergy of Exeter diocese between 1300 and 1540 who received coadjutors, forty-six were termed "old", and of these aged priests ten suffered from blindness, while yet others among the aged were granted coadjutors because they had become senile and demented.[430] Advanced years and physical (or mental) disability in the local priest meant significant hindrances for the ability to provide proper cure of souls in the parish. Minor incapabilities ranged from being too old to sing matutins or too old to read the breviary any longer,[431] to more disabling conditions like blindness, deafness or severe mobility issues, such as paralysis.

The problem of a priest incapable of saying the Mass or of elevating the Host for the congregation to view, with its associated quasi-medicinal properties, went beyond just personal incapacity and questions of financial support (e.g. lack of employment as chaplains or chantry priests) to touch on the belief in the efficacy of liturgical ceremonial.[432] Thus disability was not just a personal problem for the aged priest, but also a wider issue for the local community.

> There were, moreover, some who wanted to retire, and should have done so, being old, sick, and sometimes senile, deaf or blind, but were not allowed to retire. That is evident from the complaints of parishioners, who frequently protested that their priest was no longer capable.[433]

Even where the financial means for retirement may have been readily available, there was a minimum age, in England at least. "Parish priests were neither allowed to retire nor forced into retirement (on the grounds that they were feeble, ill, semi-blind, deaf or senile) before they reached their 60s."[434] Nicholas Orme has observed, mainly for the diocese of Exeter, but with similar examples from other dioceses since the thirteenth century, that until the fifteenth century chronically ill and disabled clergy tended to have a coadjutor (or curate) appointed for them while they remained, in effect, in post officially, but from the fifteenth century onwards the use of coadjutors became rarer, becoming superceded by pensions.[435] At a personal level, this kind of attitude to age, debility and retirement could make life difficult. Bishop Thomas Spofford of Hereford had begun complaining of his age and incurable physical infirmities (in 1433: "par cause d'age come par privez et incurable infirmiteez"; in 1438: "corpore debilis ac senio confractis"), asking to resign his office for over decade, which was not granted to him by the papacy until 1448, on account of the delicate political situation in England—King Henry's minority—which apparently required older, experienced senior churchmen to remain in office until the young king had attained "greter yeres of discrecion."[436]

Sometimes secular clergy in effect retired by joining the regular clergy, since monastic communities, generally possessing an infirmary, were particularly well set up to cater to sick or disabled members.[437] Bishop Ansfried of Utrecht (†1010), who joined a monastery once he had become old and his eyes dim, 'retired' in this fashion—however, he continued to care daily for the poor and infirm even when he himself had turned blind.[438] During the twelfth century a number of French bishops in their seventies and eighties retired to monastic houses to spend the last years of their lives there.[439] Members of the regular clergy might move to an 'easier' order or to a different house. A number of Franciscan and Dominican friars are mentioned in papal letters of dispensation who had asked to move "to the less rigorous surroundings" of Benedictine or other regular orders, on the grounds of being physically incapable, due to the frailties of old age or due to chronic diseases, of sustaining the austerities of the mendicants.[440] In the later Middle Ages the prior of Blyth Priory left this monastic house completely when he retired due to old age and infirmity.[441] The former abbot of Peterborough retired to Markby Priory, where he was provided with lodgings which included his own personal fire-place and a privy, since he had become incapacitated "by reason of his want of strength and old age and the sore infirmities which he daily suffers and that daily grow upon him."[442] Abbots and priors of monastic houses who were deemed to have become incompetent at holding their office (due to old age, misdemeanour or general incompetence) could be 'persuaded' by the offer of a generous corrody to relinquish their duties and take early retirement.[443]

Mechthild of Magdeburg (1210–1297) was cared for and nursed by the nuns in the convent of Helfta during her final years, when she was old, sick and almost completely blind, to the extent that she had to dictate her works, actions which she praised in her mystic text *The Flowing Light*, where the nuns are described as her hands and eyes: "Thou now clothest and feedest me through the goodness of others . . . that since Thou hast taken from me the sight of my eyes, Thou servest me through the eyes of others . . . Lord! I pray thee for them (7, 64)".[444] Quite the opposite appears to have happened in 1385, when Joan Heyronne, a nun crippled with gout in the Benedictine convent of Saint Helen's Bishopgate, London, felt so badly treated by her convent that she had to secretly appeal to the pope against her prioress, so that she could obtain a pension paid to her out of the funds of the convent, a ruling which eventually had to be enforced by the dean and chapter of Saint Paul's.[445] Obtaining adequate care and a pension was therefore somewhat haphazard and dependent on individual circumstances, in particular the relations an aged person had with the people providing for them.

Retiring to a monastery could be a hit-and-miss affair, since some orders applied more rigorous discipline than others, so that life for an incapacitated elderly person may not have been as comfortable as they may have initially believed when they considered joining an order, as the following story makes clear. In 1485 a priest called Johannes de Thiner, from the diocese of Aquileia, asked the apostolic poenitentiary for dispensation from a vow; during a bout of sickness he had vowed to enter a monastic order if he were cured; now, although cured from that illness, he wanted release from his vows, since he felt he could no longer endure the harshness of a monastic rule, because at the age of sixty he presented a veritable catalogue of age-related disorders: he had been arthritic for a long time, had piercing pain around the spine along his back and hips downwards to his heels (*usque ad talos pedem suorum descendentes*)—perhaps ischaemia—so badly that sometimes he could hardly walk; furthermore, he suffered from rheumy eyes and often from pains in bladder, muscles and joints, and (as if that was not enough to convince the papal curia) he feared that in the future from day to day he would get even more illnesses.[446]

Life as a 'retired' cleric in a monastery will, however, not always have been a life of ascetic rigour and harshness. Special exemptions from otherwise binding rules were made for some people afflicted by the debilitating effects of old age, such as the early fifteenth-century priest who, "on account of his old age and bodily weakness", received papal dispensation to eat meat during periods of abstinence.[447] We know of one aged and disabled monk, Marculinus of Forli, a Dominican friar who died in 1397, who had a personal servant.[448] It is therefore not surprising that medieval contemporaries could occasionally make vociferous critique of elderly people wanting the 'easy life' who were joining monasteries at a late stage in their lives: old people may be refused entry to monasteries or forced to seek exemptions to switch orders from a harsher to a less rigorous monastic discipline. Already in the seventh century Fructuosus of Braga criticised "old novices" (*nouicii senes*) in his monastic rule for their motives on joining an order, since they chose to do so not for reasons of faith but because of their physical infirmity.[449] At the other end of the period in 1465, Johannes de Raickingen, an aged priest from the diocese of Trier, decided at age seventy to join the Carthusian order, but then reconsidered and put his decision on hold since he would rather wait a few more years (presumably because he did not feel ready just yet for the rigours of the discipline); but then, by now aged eighty and depressed by old age none of three Carthusian monasteries he applied for would accept him (*videntes eum adeo senio confractum et in octuagesimo sue etatis anno constitutum ipsum recipi recusarunt*).[450] Another priest aged seventy, and having recovered from an illness, vowed to enter a convent of Augustinian eremitics but he was ejected from that convent because he was deemed too old (*de quo propter eius senectutem deiectus fuit*); he managed to find acceptance among the Benedictines instead.[451] Other physically senescent people themselves realised the futility of trying to enter a monastic order at their advanced age and commuted any vows they had taken into other charitable deeds, for instance, the case of the man who had "flux in the head" and lost a third of his jaw together with the teeth therein.[452]

A number of high and late medieval monastic orders specifically stated that old age, disability and/or sickness were barriers to being accepted into the order, since rigours demanded of life in such an order would not be compatible with such a person's physical disposition. For instance, the rule dating to 1252 of the Poor Clares "stated that only such women would be accepted as were not disqualified by advanced age, ill health or 'fatuity'."[453] Already among the desert fathers of the fourth through seventh centuries a critical voice was heard, expressing scepticism concerning the (physical and/or mental) ability of an old man (*gerôn*) who wished to join a monastery to cope with the hard labour and very ascetic life.[454] Among the military orders physical and/or mental debility due to age will have been a particular issue: if the main reason for being a knight in a military order is to fight the infidels, protect the pilgrim routes and care for others, then becoming disabled would have put an automatic end to one's career as a Templar, Hospitaller or Teutonic knight. However, as the statutes of the Teutonic knights demonstrate, some orders at least felt the same moral obligation to provide for their staff as secular and ecclesiastical lords did:

The old brethren and the infirm shall be generously cared for according to their infirmity; they shall be treated with patience and diligently honored; one shall not in any way be rigorous as to the physical requirements for those who bear themselves honorably and piously.[455]

If brothers were unable to stand unaided or to genuflect, they were to stand behind the others during divine worship, or they were permitted to sit.[456] The Teutonic knights would send their old and sick members from the Holy Land back to Europe to spend their old age in such homes where "the sick are customarily cared for" according to the requirements of their illness, while the Hospitallers provided quarters for their incurably ill brethren in the order's general hospital.[457] At Fellin (Livonia) records of the Teutonic knights mentioned a *Spittler* in the fifteenth century, who was appointed to care for the sick and old members of the order.[458] Towards the end of the fifteenth century a German nobleman remarked that the Order of Teutonic Knights was the hospital and abode of the impoverished elderly among the German nobility.[459]

A special problem was presented by the condition of senile dementia. In 1390 the late lord of Eksaarde, Ghent, was posthumously declared to have been incompetent to manage his affairs and property in the years before his death, because "he was so aged that he was a child and had no control over his five senses".[460] An almost contemporary case of what appears to be senile dementia comes from France. There a remission letter was written to the king in 1387, asking to pardon "a man who had gone mad from old age, recovered his sanity, and then had a relapse during which he murdered his wife."[461]

Senile dementia, senile depression and suicide of the elderly disabled person could become contingent themes. In 1278 a man variously described as "well over ninety" or even allegedly one hundred years old named Philippe Testard, who had been prévôt to the archbishop of Paris, rose from his bed in the night to relieve himself but instead tried to commit suicide by throwing himself out of a window onto the street below; he survived for long enough to be carried back inside to his bed, where he stabbed himself. To prove that he had been afflicted by a fit of madness, rather than had willingly committed suicide, a posthumous trial was held, at which twelve witnesses declared he "did so many silly things that everyone said he was out of his senses."[462] His eccentric behaviour was said by all to have become worse in the weeks before his death, and some thought his 'madness' had started as much as five years earlier. The question whether Philippe Testard suffered from a severe case of senile dementia or whether he was still fully rational and voluntarily killed himself, or even whether it was a mixture of both, can of course never be answered. Insanity may well have been argued in cases of suicide, since if a person was deemed to have committed suicide, their property could be confiscated by the crown, but if it was ruled that at the time of suicide they had been mentally disturbed, insane or in the widest sense mentally incapacitated, then the person's property could be claimed by their relatives. Distinctions between differing motives for suicide had already been made in the early sixth-century *Lex romana visigothorum*, where the estate of a suicide would be confiscated unless it had been motivated by "a distaste for life [literally: tedium of life], by shame caused by debts, or by illness."[463] Similarly, at the other end of the chronological spectrum, the French jurist Jean Boutillier (†1395) opined in his *Somme rural* that in cases of suicide for reasons of sickness or madness the deceased "should not lose his wealth or his body".[464] It is hence not possible to know how many 'hidden' cases of suicide might lie behind people who turn up in the records who apparently killed themselves in a bout of madness.[465]

Suicide was often linked to the sin of *acedia*, that is, sloth, a sin arising out of despair of God's mercy or from spiritual dejection.[466] The Franciscan writer David of Augsburg (fl. mid-thirteenth century) described three kinds of *accidia*, of which the first was regarded as a

> certain bitterness of the mind which cannot be pleased by anything cheerful or wholesome. . . . It inclines to despair, diffidence, and suspicions, and sometimes drives its victim to suicide when he is oppressed by unreasonable grief. Such sorrow arises sometimes from previous impatience, sometimes from the fact that one's desire for some object has been delayed or frustrated, and sometimes from the abundance of melancholic humors, in which case it behooves the physician rather than the priest to prescribe a remedy.[467]

Note that a medical or 'scientific' explanation, and concomitant therapy, was being advocated here alongside a theological one! An early Dominican, Roland of Cremona, wrote a *Summa* while at the University of Toulouse in 1233, which incorporated a discussion of sadness (*tristitia*) and melancholy; he included medical as well as theological viewpoints, arguing that *tristitia* is a sin, which generates despair, but sadness can also be outside the bounds of reason and can be an involuntary response to stimuli (an argument based on humoral theory) in which case it is not a sin.[468] Saint Bonaventura in the thirteenth century had remarked on a kind of despair which frequently leads people to bring about their own death,[469] so that, with the caveat that we do not of course have absolute numbers of suicides for the medieval period, we can nevertheless gain a hint that 'despair' was a considerable motive. In the early thirteenth-century *Dialogue of Miracles* by the Cistercian Caesarius of Heisterbach, he remembers an incident (which may have occurred in 1221–1222) concerning a nun "of great age" who was "so severely afflicted with the vice of melancholy . . . that she fell into despair" and tried to drown herself.[470] Here we have another possible case of age-related depression.

Not necessarily elderly, but certainly despairing, was Michelet le Cavelier, another suicide mentioned by Georges Minois, who had been an embroiderer in Paris, but suffering terribly under an (unspecified) illness threw himself out of a window in 1423.[471] A man called Martel the Swineherd, described by the sources as "poor and sick" and living in great poverty and misery due to debt (so he may have been incapable of working due to his sickness/disability), committed suicide in 1411 in Regensburg, hanging himself with a rope on the gallows next to the corpse of an executed criminal.[472] And although I have tended to refrain from discussing leprosy, I will mention one case here, since the source the story is in sheds some further light on despair at one's illness, disability and social condition. At the Cistercian monastery of Villers, near Brussels, a *conversus* was afflicted by leprosy around 1300 and was put in isolation. Thus "separated from the community, living on his own, he found the weight and persistence of his sufferings too much to bear and began to lose heart."[473] He attempted suicide, barely able to leave his bed and with his legs giving way under him due to weakness, for reasons "as much by the tedium caused by ostracism as by the revolting nature of his disease" (*tum taedio solitudinis, tum foeditate morbi*).[474] In a number of miracle stories, the protagonist who later benefits from a successful healing is at first dreadfully wounded, sick or disabled, to the extent that he or she despairs.[475] The fact that the condition seems incurable, that there is no (earthly) hope for any betterment, appears to be the deciding factor influencing a person's state of mind. As Alexander Murray has observed:

> Thus in miracle stories *desperatio* is employed frequently in respect of a sickness thought incurable before the miracle. A sick man is *desperatus* by his doctor. Doctors *desperaverunt* a patient. A patient is 'desperately ill', and the weakest patients can be said to have 'despaired of life': *vitae . . . desperati.*[476]

Suicide out of complete and utter despair at one's failing health, deteriorating physical condition and reduced quality of life may have been more frequent than the sources show at first glance. Murray's study has discovered some five hundred cases of suicide from medieval England, France, Germany, the Low Countries and Italy, gleaned from judicial records,[477] among which are a number of suicides motivated by disability and/or decrepit old age (there may have been more but the sources do not always state details of age). Overall, for suicide motivated by illness/disease, Murray has found that the judicial sources, especially the English ones, suggest "that it was in fact a commoner motive for suicide than chronicles, miracles, or *exempla* would give us reason to believe."[478]

Age-related depression—or what the later medieval texts termed *melancholia*—is not the prerogative of the twenty-first century alone.[479] Seneca, much respected in the medieval period, had (for the medieval way of thinking) problematically argued that it was the height of folly for a decrepit person, suffering the worst physical deteriorations of old age, to carry on living, asking if a scrap of life was a more poignant loss than the freedom to end it.[480] A hint that suicide was a considered possibility, even a 'temptation', for disabled, sick and despondent old people, is given in literary texts.[481] Already Job in the Old Testament only wishes for his death once he has become sick and full of sores, a wish not expressed during all the trials he has withstood before. With his "flesh clothed in worms [literally: putrefied]" and broken skin, Job says "my soul chooseth strangling, and death rather than life. I loathe it [literally: I have despaired], I would not live alway".[482] But Augustine had already pointed out that "we detect weakness in a mind which cannot bear physical oppression",[483] elevating patience and endurance to the highest virtues. In the fifteenth-century *artes moriendi* one of the last temptations by the devil is to the sick man who is already lifting his dagger, ready to commit suicide: "Go ahead and kill yourself", the devil suggests.[484] In the English translation of Alain Chartier's original French work, *Le Livre d'Espérance* (1428), the narrator is visited by the allegorical figure of Lady Melancholy, a hideous old woman accompanied by three monsters (Defiance, Indignation and Despair), who eloquently bewail the world as it is and suggest suicide as the only bearable solution.[485] And in the poem *La Belle Heaumière* by François Villon, the decrepit and ugly old woman, looking back in vain on the days of her youthful beauty, laments that she is brought down so soon by old age, asking, "Who stays my hand, that I do not strike myself / This very moment and end my days?"[486]

The visual arts, too, occasionally represented the theme of the sick and disabled as longing for death to free them from their suffering, and to these must be reckoned the pathologically aged. The fresco cycle, formerly attributed to Orcagna but now to Buonamico Buffalmacco, of the Triumph of Death (Trionfo della Morte) in the Camposanto in Pisa depicting eight mainly elderly disabled people (including a blind man, a man on crutches, one using hand-trestles and possibly a leper with partly eroded nose) shows these unfortunate disabled people gesturing in desperation toward the winged figure of death, and also shows one of their group holding out a scroll (like a 'speech bubble') in which these miserable people ask for death as redeemer of their suffering.[487] "I only wish to extinguish life", reads the opening line.[488] In his book on blindness, art historian Moshe Barasch associates the fresco with Francesco Traini and states:

> Modern scholars are agreed on what this group [of "ugly and deformed cripples and beggars"] was meant to convey within the general theme of the Triumph of Death. While the figures belonging to most of the other groups are trying to escape Death's sickle, the unfortunate, suffering beggars and cripples wait for him[489] to come.[490]

The painter has visually offset these suicidal lost souls from the 'real' ascetics, depicted in another part of the fresco, who voluntarily chose their suffering and are content to observe the turmoil of the secular world from the distance of their desert solitude.[491] The dating of this fresco has been disputed by art historians, since it used to be thought that it embodies the change in attitudes following the catastrophes of the mid-fourteenth century, in particular the Black Death,[492] but more recently it has been argued that the fresco dates from between 1330 and 1342.[493] In another version of this iconographic narrative, the Trionfo della Morte formerly in Santa Croce, Florence (now preserved fragmentarily in the Museo Civico), one finds the same depiction of old and disabled people: the elderly blind and lame, the crippled, the leprous and beggars plead for death as redemption and are shown on that side of the fresco where the damned are located; hence their pleas are not only useless but the actual source of their damnation.[494] Both frescoes use the conventions of visual language to chastise the old and disabled for their un-Christian suicidal desires.[495]

Medieval literary and visual arts therefore occasionally concerned themselves with the theme of suicide, and historical records document cases of voluntarily ending of life. Potential and actual suicide among elderly and disabled people is therefore an unfortunate but real, if unquantifiable, event in the Middle Ages, albeit one that most historians have tended to either ignore completely or gloss over. We will probably never be able to untangle from the sources those cases of elderly people who committed suicide from the larger groups of those who were deemed to have acted out of 'insanity', or even from those whom the coroners declared to be the innocent victims of accidental drownings or falls.

And accidents could readily lead to mental or physical disability in the aged. Margery Kempe's account spares little detail of the trial and tribulations she felt she had after her husband became an incontinent dotard, most likely through an accident that befell him, lacking reason due to his return to childishness. When he was "of great age, over sixty years old", her husband had fallen down the stairs and injured his head, which healed, but he remained disabled until he died around six years after this incident. Margery had ceased living together with her husband at the time of the accident, but she returned to nurse him; the issues affecting many long-term carers in the modern world of elderly and/or disabled persons, especially emotional struggles, will not have been unknown to Margery.

> [Margery] had very much trouble with him, for in his last days he turned childish and lacked reason, so that he could not go to a stool to relieve himself, or else he would not, but like a child discharged his excrement into his linen clothes as he sat there by the fire or at the table—wherever it was, he would spare no place.[496]

It appears that although her husband was generally still physically capable of controlling when and where he relieved himself, a kind of demented stubbornness led him to behave the way he did, so that Margery Kempe complained her husband had "turnyd childisch a3en and lakkyd reson" in his senility. His mental incapacity meant, too, that he had to relinquish his role as head of the Kempe household, becoming instead a burden.

In other cases, accidents could lead to the death of the already elderly and disabled person.

> On 14 January 1267 Sabillia, an old woman, went into Colmworth to beg bread. At twilight she wished to go to her house, fell into a stream and drowned by misadventure. The next day her son Henry searched for her [and] found her drowned.[497]

This sorry incident tells a few stories: Not only was the woman so poor she had to beg for bread, but her eyesight may have been failing due to age, since she may have had extra difficulties finding her way home at twilight. The presence of her son in the records says no more than that she had relatives in the vicinity, but it does not inform as to how close the relations may have been, so that, with regard to the popular notion of old people in past times being looked after by their loving families, this does not appear to have been the case here. Another elderly widow, too, succumbed to drowning:

> About prime on 27 March 1270 Mariot, formerly the wife of Richard the Reeve of Pertenhall, who was infirm, feeble and old, lay in her bed in Pertenhall [while other household members were out at work]. She rose from her bed, took a pitcher in her hand, went to a well in her court-yard and tried to draw water, but, because she was feeble, she slipped and fell into the well and drowned by misadventure.[498]

Falls by the elderly were a big hazard then as now—trips and falls being one of the greatest factors leading to extended periods of hospitalisation among the old in modern times.[499] In 1326 Alice le Pusere wanted to descend from her solar down the stairs and "being of the age of 80 years and more, she accidentally fell from the top to the bottom, and was carried by her friends into the solar where she had her ecclesiastical rights" and then died.[500] In a tragic incident on 19 June 1472 during a big fire in Erfurt, which destroyed several churches and houses, a further story unfolded. A "very old" priest called Heinrich, lame and almost blind and helpless against the flames had asked another priest, Johannes Happeyner, to let him take shelter from the flames in Johannes's cellar (*introducite me in vestrum cellarium, ut possim salvari ab igne*) which Johannes did. However, aged Heinrich suffocated in the cellar due to the smoke, when this old and decrepit priest was left behind, while the (presumably) younger Johannes managed to leave the building and saved his own life only.[501] Was this simply a sad and regrettable accident highlighting how during the dramatic events of a town on fire the old and weak fell victim more readily? Or an example of the selfishness and drive for self-preservation of the young and able-bodied, who fled while they could?

Simply being old in years was not automatically regarded in the Middle Ages as also being 'over the hill', senile and disabled, although of course individual persons could and did suffer from the negative aspects of physical and mental deterioration that (often but not invariably) accompanied old age. The important aspect to consider, however, is that the old person was not equated *per se* with the disabled person. In the context of a series of late medieval hagiographical texts, Christian Krötzl has concluded: "The 'normality of old age' clearly emerges, age was not equated with senility or debility, and derogatory remarks concerning age or elderly people are completely absent in the sources studied."[502] In Joinville's description of the Seventh Crusade, he recounted the episode at Damietta in 1250, where a heavily pregnant Queen Margaret, living in constant fear of Saracen attack, was consoled by an aged knight, who held her hand without any amorous thoughts and assured her he would fulfil her request that in the event of an attack, he would cut off her head before the heathen could lay a hand on her.[503] Leaving aside the moral aspects of this anecdote, for our purposes it demonstrates that not only was an old man present on Crusade, still bearing arms, but also due to his age he could assume an additional role as a trusted confidant.

> In ancient and medieval Europe, as in the present, old people in general were not respected or despised by reason of the simple fact of their advanced age: those who continued to wield power at later ages could command respect by virtue of continuing mental or physical powers, or by possession of property or high position, as could others due to past achievements.[504]

So old age of itself is not a disabling condition during the Middle Ages; instead the individual physical or mental condition that characterised a person was the defining factor. Some old people, including some very old in years, would never have been disabled, since they were fortunate enough to live into their ripe old years in a fit, healthy and active state, while others of less years will already have suffered the aches and pains that eventually led to physical and mental deterioration, incapacity, consequently retirement from work or public life and dependency. The fact that retirement in the Middle Ages existed, albeit in sporadic, individual and both voluntary and involuntary forms, meant "some indication of special regard for debility and waning powers" was acknowledged.[505] With the advent of the sixteenth century and the early modern period, nothing much changed in the perception of old age:

> With crashing legs and dripping nose, bald, deaf and half blind the old person drags themselves out of the Middle Ages and, propped on crutches and under the ridicule of youth, crawls across the threshold to the modern age.[506]

4 Charity

This chapter is not intended as a general history of poverty in the Middle Ages. Volumes have already been written on the poor,[1] on charity and poor relief,[2] on the religious context of alms and on the causes of poverty in the medieval world.[3] Instead, this chapter will focus on one specific group of people who may not necessarily always have been among the poor, but who if they were then formed a very special subgroup within the ranks of the poor: the physically impaired, or who for convenience's sake we tend to call the disabled. It is important to recognise that "many poor people suffered from disability, but not all disabled people were poor."[4] A case in point is provided by the depiction on a fifteenth-century panel painting of a tenant farmer who, resting his amputated stump on a peg-leg and leaning on a crutch, proudly watches his farmhand feed the pigs, saying, "I am called Mair with the crutches of Riedee and have many sows and cows (*Bin ich genant Mair uf der stelzen von Riedee und han fyl der sawen und kyee*)."[5] However, those disabled persons who were impoverished brought a specific meaning to the medieval concept of poverty. As Miri Rubin remarked, understandings of poverty

> are constructed at the intersection of two processes: the process of economic, demographic and social change which refashions areas and forms of need on the one hand, and the cultural perceptions of need as they are translated into idioms of charity and evaluations held by diverse social groups on the other.[6]

Exploring the multiple layers and ranges of meanings that (physical) disability brought to such "idioms of charity" is the aim of this present chapter.

Semantically, the poor person tended to occur in a binary relationship with other linguistic terms. Antinomies of pauper could be *potens*, the person with influence, *miles*, the person with military might, *civis*, *burgensis*, the person with civil liberties or *dives*, the person with material wealth—different antinomic pairings of these concepts with pauper delineated different sections of the history of poverty in the Middle Ages.[7] Poverty could mean not just material, economic poverty (as we moderns primarily understand it), but also physical incapability and physical lack of means, i.e. relating to those wounded, sick, impaired and old persons. These people are often collectively termed *debiles*.

> 'Poor' are those people, who always or temporarily live in a state of weakness, of need, of lacking necessities, whereby concern is not just about the absence of physical strength and material goods (money, food, clothing), but about a more generalised lack of social 'power', which is the result of social standing and influence, of skill in wielding weapons and legal position, of being secure via social bonds, but also of knowledge and political power. That is why in the Middle Ages the 'poor' person (*pauper*) is not just contrasted with the 'rich' (*dives*), but also with the 'powerful' (*potens*).[8]

So, thirdly, poverty in the Middle Ages can mean the disempowered, the socially powerless person.[9] In his seminal, eponymously titled book on religious poverty and the profit economy, Lester Little made a similar point: "The essential meaning of 'poor' before the triumph of the commercial economy was 'weak' in relation to the powerful."[10] In this wider sense, all those persons are *pauperes*, contrasting with the *potentes*, who are lacking social ties or who are living without the protection of social superiors, which would include unmarried women, orphaned children, girls without a dowry, prisoners, travellers in foreign regions (therefore especially pilgrims). The contrasting notional pairing *potens–pauper* first appears in early medieval documents, such as the edict of Chlothar II of 18 October 614,[11] and then more frequently in Carolingian texts from around 800 onwards,[12] where *pauper* is primarily meant in a social context as powerless (including the minor free vassals) and not a material one[13]—the beggar is as yet absent from the explicit definition of pauper. This thesis, originally proposed by the German social historian Karl Bosl, that the early medieval meaning of *pauper* related only to the politically or socially poor,[14] but not to the economically poor, has been criticised as too generalising.[15] Every powerful person (*potens*) in early medieval society is also wealthy (*dives*), but the reverse (every *dives* is also *potens*) is not true; nevertheless, the conceptual pair *potens–pauper* must jointly consider the contrasting *dives–pauper*,[16] so that even for the earlier Middle Ages the notion of *pauper* contains an element of economic poverty.

Medieval means to combat economic poverty tended to be restricted to the giving of alms. Almsgiving was advocated as a charitable Christian duty throughout the entire Middle Ages, which was carried out both privately and institutionally. As late antiquity was becoming more Christianised, so the forerunners of medieval charitable institutions were emerging, such as the xenodochia, for instance, that founded in 398 at Portus Trajani near Ostia by Pammachius, a patrician Roman, in memory of his deceased wife, Paulina. Saint Jerome mentioned this hospice in one of his epistles, describing the condition of some of the sick poor and disabled:

> That blind man, who stretches out his hand and often laments where nobody is present, is now the heir of Paulina and co-heir of Pammachius. That cripple, who can no longer use his legs and who drags the entire weight of his body along, is supported by the tender hand of a maiden. The doors through which the visitors formerly streamed in are now besieged by poor people. This one is swollen from dropsy, sees himself facing death, another is speechless and dumb, and since he does not possess a tongue with which to beseech his begging appears all the more imploring. Another is debilitated from childhood and does not beg the gift for himself. A fourth has putrefied due to leprosy and outlives his own corpse, so to speak.[17]

According to the sixth-century *Rule* of Saint Benedict, the poor and needy had a special relationship with Christ, so that Christ came to be identified with alms and charity given to the pauper in his name. Thus Chapter 31 of the *Rule* admonishes the cellarer of a monastery to take care of the sick, the poor and children as well as guests in general, while Chapter 53 emphasises the likeness of the stranger or outsider with Christ (with referral to Matthew 25:35: "I was a stranger and you took me in").[18] The *Rule* had expressly ordered that hospitality was to be shown towards those who needed help, and that members of the monastic community should serve these needy people just as one should serve Christ himself,[19] since, as Christ had said: "I was sick and you have visited me" (Matthew 25:36).

Since Merovingian times some of the bishops' churches had kept lists (*matriculae pauperum*) of those poor people who were to receive alms; Saint Konrad, bishop of Constance, founded a hospital in the tenth century specifically to support the poor; and many monastic orders, starting with the Benedictines from the sixth century onwards, prescribed the care and support of poor and travellers (*pauperes et peregrini*).[20] In the early and high Middle Ages, the poor person who relied on the support of his fellow citizens did definitely not stand outside or even on the margins of society but instead was an integrated member.[21] This situation lasted until the twelfth century, with the physically impaired, the old, the sick and the otherwise needy surviving "through the charity of the parish and the monastery."[22] To be classed as poor, or rather as 'needy', even gave one the right to receive alms. In tenth-century northern Italy, the needy were defined as "widows, orphans, captives, defeated, infirm, blind, crippled and weak",[23] according to Bishop Rather of Verona (890–974). And, according to Maurice of Sully, a preacher active in Paris during the twelfth century, the authentic poor comprised the widow, the orphan, the sick, the exile and the destitute—but interestingly enough not the aged.[24]

In encompassing the sick, the impaired, the economically poor, the widowed and pilgrims, the earlier and high medieval collective of *pauperes* who had a need for assistance were a multiform category,[25] as we have seen. The register of Wolfger of Erla, bishop of Passau, includes a list of who received alms during the accounting year 1203–1204, which includes just these kinds of people: travelling folk (*vagi, girovagi*); poor (*pauperes, pauperculi*); aged (*vetuli*); sick (*infirmi*); blind (*caeci*); obese (*pingues*); pilgrims (*peregrini, wallerii*); penitents (*penitenciarii*); poor crusaders (*pauperes cruciferi*); wandering monks (*monachi, moniales*); poor clerics (*pauperes clerici, lodderpfaffi* [*Lotterpfaffen*]); scholars and students (*scolares*); plus one elderly canon (*vetulus canonicus*).[26] In addition, the alms expenditure register of bishop Wolfger included further long lists of people who later came to be regarded as not quite so deserving, namely, players (*ioculatores*); actors and mimes (*histriones, mimi*); fiddlers (*gigari*); singers (*cantores, discantores*); and female singers (*cantatrices*), including a girls' choir (*puellae cantantes*), thus exemplifying the earlier medieval mentality of indiscriminate charity.[27]

According to early thirteenth-century commentaries on the *Decretum*, a prime text of canon law, when times were hard any superfluous material goods and possessions were to be treated as "common property" and were to be shared among all those people in need—"superfluous property belonged to the poor in need".[28] The Church possessed property which it held communally as an institution, and which it, depending on the individual member of the institution, more or less liberally and frequently redistributed to those deemed deserving. At the Augustinian priory of Barnwell, Cambridgeshire, one of the earliest English foundations of this order, the almoner had the duty during the thirteenth century, much like a modern-day family doctor, to make 'home visits' to "old men and those who are decrepit, lame and blind, or are confined to their beds" and to "endow with more copious largess pilgrims, palmers, chaplains, beggars and lepers".[29] In 1250 Bishop Robert Grosseteste of Lincoln addressed the papal curia on the subject of clerical malpractice, and he pointed out that "the work of pastoral care consists not only in the administration of the Sacraments and the saying of canonical hours, and the celebration of masses" but also in the practical and material charity of the Seven Acts of Mercy, "in visitation of the sick and prisoners, especially of one's own parishioners, to whom the temporal goods of the churches belong."[30] Cardinal Hostiensis (†1271) argued this common property of the Church was to be used by the *pauperes*, who had a right to receive it; the Church was therefore not doling out charity but making "an established legal use of public property whose purpose was the maintenance of the common welfare and especially the sustenance of the needy poor."[31] We shall return to the question of who exactly the needy poor were deemed to be.

The rich were to give alms, while in return the poor were to pray for the souls of the donors.

The emphasis on the spiritual value of alms-giving encouraged the idea that the donors should avoid discrimination—who were mortal men to reject one beggar for another, because they cannot know who enjoys the favour of God?[32]

Already in the early sixth century Caesarius of Arles (bishop 502–542) had observed that if "nobody were poor, nobody could give alms and nobody could receive remission of his sins."[33] The contractual nature of this recipro-cal arrangement was expounded on in the sermons of Giordano da Rivolto (1260–1311), a Dominican preacher from Pisa. Even in the later Middle Ages, when, as shall be explained in the following, changing perceptions of who it was that *deserved* the receipt of alms came to curtail almsgiving, lone voices were occasionally still heard advocating the earlier style of indiscriminate charity. In a strong reaction to the growing trend for selective almsgiving, an English Carmelite friar, Richard Maidstone (†1396), argued that instead "painstaking inquisitiveness and consideration in this business is not only deadly—on the contrary, it is diabolical (*curiosa perscrutatio et discussio in hac materia est non solum peremptoria, immo diabolica*)".[34] Thus charity was not egalitarian. Furthermore, the older form of direct giving from per-son to person came to be institutionalised, so that alms were given less as a personal gift but more and more frequently through an intermediary institu-tion (almoner, hospital, civic/parochial poor relief), and hence the giver gave anonymously. It has been observed that the collection boxes for alms placed at hospital sites not only allowed the inhabitants of a town to donate money effortlessly and anonymously, but for the spiritual convenience of fulfilling "all of the Corporal Works of Mercy in one go",[35] since through the institu-tion, if not in the location, of a medieval hospital all these seven activities could take place: feeding the hungry, giving drink to the thirsty, clothing the naked, sheltering the needy, caring for the sick and the imprisoned and providing proper burial for the deceased. According to a charter of 1255 relating to the Heiligengeistspital at Wismar, the institution was to allow the weak and infirm to recuperate, paupers and those with tormented spirits to be consoled, the homeless to be hospitably received, the naked to be clothed and other proofs of charity,[36] all of course inspired by the Christian concept of the Seven Acts of Mercy. In modern times large televised 'fundathons', such as *Children in Need* or *Comic Relief* in the UK, exemplify this deper-sonalised charity. But in such modern fundraisers

the recipient of charity can not personally express thanks to the donor for the aid provided. Therefore the intermediary fundraising authority has to act as substitute for reciprocity to allow the donation to become a positive experience for the donor.[37]

Thus it should come as no surprise to read that material assistance was more readily forthcoming towards those people whom one knew than to complete strangers. The development of parish fraternities might be explained by this factor, among others. For instance, a number of Florentine people deemed 'needy' and worthy of receiving charitable doles were helped by the Orsanmichele fraternity; during October 1356 those whose conditions might be disabling included a woman called Nezetta, "who is old and sick"; Madonna Fiora di Lapo, "who is blind and pregnant"; Madonna Agnese, "a poor and infirm woman"; Monno Bice, "who is poor, old, and infirm"; and Monna Dolce, "a poor, old, and infirm woman" who nevertheless still cared for a girl recommended to her by the society.[38] Alms and other practical help for the chronically ill and/or disabled were therefore more likely to come from private charities than from Florentine hospitals.

At the top of the social scale royalty set an example of how to perform charity, while embodying the contractual nature of the arrangement. During the thirteenth century in England the distribution of royal largesse could lead to quite chaotic scenes, as an incident in 1236 at the coronation of Queen Eleanor showed: William of Beauchamp, the official who acted as hereditary almoner, left an account to the Exchequer, where he stated that his powers included

> jurisdiction over the quarrels and faults of the poor and the lepers, to this point, that if one leper strikes another with a knife, he may adjudge him to be burnt.
>
> (*ea die habet omnem jurisdictionem circa rixas et delicta pauperum et leprosorum; adeo quod si leprosus alium cultello percusserit, judicare eum ut comburatur.*)[39]

Agitation among the crowd of poor and potential outbreaks of violence were therefore expected by the thirteenth-century authorities, which led a twentieth-century historian to imagine "as the ordinary thing a horrible scramble in which the sick and the feeble took their chance among the jostlings of the greedy and the idle, or even of the leprous."[40] At other times the royal distribution of alms was more organised, perhaps having learnt lessons from dealing with large numbers of people. For instance, in 1243, when allegedly six thousand poor persons awaited their dole at Westminster, the infirm and the aged were ushered into the greater and lesser halls, those less disabled and the rest into the king's chamber and the children into the queen's chamber.[41] The English kings of the later fourteenth and early fifteenth centuries also employed a dedicated almoner, whose daily expenditures on alms distribution survive in the general wardrobe accounts for the period. There were two types: alms given directly to the poor and sick and alms distributed at shrines or donated to religious houses (which in England included hospitals). Under Edward III, Richard II and Henry IV the king's *elemosina statuta* had been formalised to amount to four shillings per day, which would have been roughly enough to provide for 336 meals per week.[42] In addition extra alms were distributed on special days, such as Good Friday.

> All three kings also maintained a number of paupers on a regular basis, giving them each 2d. a day: Edward III usually maintained about twenty, while under both Richard II and Henry IV it was twenty-four. They were called the poor 'orators' of the king—presumably they were meant to pray for his soul. Presumably, too, they must have followed the court continuously.[43]

Overall, the king's almoner distributed between 350 pounds and 700 pounds annually, even in "unexceptional" years, so the paupers who followed the court may not have been all that poor, as, according to Given-Wilson, this was a very large sum even if split between some one hundred persons, which could well have been the case, since the attraction of such 'official' and large alms would have drawn great numbers of poor and disabled people, especially on special occasions when extra alms were made available.[44] One gets the impression that the 'official' paupers following the royal household may well have been screened for suitability, but once accepted were treated similarly to the so-called *Hausarme* maintained by private citizens in German cities of the same period.

Therefore, royalty demonstrated to lesser subjects how the reciprocal arrangement between powerful and rich, on the one hand, and impotent and poor, on the other hand, worked, by providing a permanent soup kitchen in return for being followed by praying *oratores*. Nevertheless, this contractual arrangement may have been weaker in the later Middle Ages with the advent of chantry priests and chantry chapels from the fourteenth century onwards.[45] The exact correlation between the rise in popularity of the chantry chapel and the decline in direct material assistance given to the poor by private donors still needs to be assessed, but it is a startling coincidence that the hugely popular late medieval endowment of chantries occurs at the same period in time when the poor in general and beggars in particular came to be seen as somewhat suspect. The function of a chantry was to provide masses for the soul of the benefactor, to aid the passage of their soul through purgatory, so that at the very least a chantry priest had to be paid for, while more wealthy benefactors had chapels built for them. So-called 'caged' chantries, appearing in England during the fourteenth century, embodied the epitomy of architectural expression of care for one's soul. Note the singular: one soul, or at best a single family, was what was being cared for behind the gated perimeter of the caged chantry, the original 'gated community', to use a modern analogy. Hence to the late medieval mind the question might arise of why give money to dirty, smelly and offensive beggars in the hope they will pray for your soul in humble gratitude when you can have priests say proper masses in the refined setting of your own private chapel—and make a powerful architectural statement concerning your wealth and influence at the same time.

However, charity to the poor and giving alms did not die out overnight. Even some donors of chantries did still remember the poor in their endowments, as did Bristol merchant Edmund Blanket, who instituted a chantry in 1389 that "provided for the distribution of 5s. in money to the blind and lame paupers lying in their beds" at Saint Bartholomew's hospital.[46] Since the twelfth century the reciprocal concept of almsgiving and charity as linked to care for one's soul, but also as a Christian duty, was clearly expressed in contemporary thought.[47] Almsgiving, along with fasting and praying, was regarded as part of the process of penance, as *operis satisfactio*. The depiction in richly illuminated and costly books such as the eleventh-century Codex Epternacensis of sick, poor and crippled people being welcomed at the feast of the wealthy man exemplifies the self-imposed fulfilment of this duty by the monastic community which commissioned the work.[48] But imagery commissioned for secular *potentes* could just as well demonstrate their largesse and thereby their status and power, such as the depiction in the famous Manesse Codex of a group of *pauperes* being received at the home of Herr Hesse von Reinach (†1280).[49] These include a shaven-headed man with a crutch being lead by the lord of the house himself, followed by a blind young woman with a stick, a man on hand-trestles, a semi-naked man with a pair of crutches and four more people in the background whose disability is not obvious. By 1405, when Christine de Pisan published her *Treasure of the City of Ladies*, poverty may still (just) have been regarded as a virtue, but one to be endured with patience; by now the poor are those whom God loves but whom the world hates.[50] Poverty attacks the suffering poor with

> very great afflictions . . . namely frequent hunger and thirst, cold, poor shelter, a friendless old age, sickness without comfort, and besides that, the contempt, villainy and rejection of the world.[51]

Patience, rather than practical almsgiving, is the antidote to all this suffering, and especially so with regard to illness, which God wishes so.[52] The reward for all this patient suffering will be merits in heaven.

Not just the ever-present alms collection boxes in churches encouraged people to give, but also the world of images: the stained glass decorating church windows,[53] the panel paintings and altarpieces which time and again depict the beggar, often integrated into the sacred action taking place, be it as marginal figure in the background or as object of the action, in the form of a person receiving charity. Even when poverty had lost its status as a virtue, "the lame retained their place in the art of the fourteenth century as symbols of human misery and recipients of charity."[54] This iconographic tradition became even further entrenched, so that in the fourteenth and especially fifteenth centuries the orthopedically impaired person came to symbolise the deserving poor person *per se*. "It was at this time that the most common depiction of a beggar became the cripple who dragged his body through the streets with small wooden crutches to ask for charity from his benefactors."[55]

Besides the visual world of exhortations to charity there was the audible world: stories of the medieval period again and again admonished people to give alms.[56] Legends of the saints as well as secular textual material issued moral warnings about those people who were hard-hearted and refused to give alms to beggars.[57] In Langland's *Piers Plowman*, the allegory of Scripture preaches that when one makes a dinner or a supper, one ought to invite not friends, relatives or wealthy neighbours, but "the poor, the wretched, and the deformed".[58] Here the classic group of people one should definitely give alms to, the "worthy poor", that is, included "cripples and the blind".[59] In a preacher's handbook of the fourteenth century, the poor were themselves compared to cripples, for their dependency on alms is like that of the lame man (symbolising the materially poor but spiritually rich) who is carried to a feast by the blind man (symbolising the spiritually impoverished but materially wealthy), in return for which "the lame man taught the blind which way to go", but nevertheless the poor "who spiritually have a clear sight" can show their (spiritually) blind patrons "the way to the banquet of heaven".[60] According to the *Decretum* of Gratian, alms need not consist simply of a monetary value, but may be in the form of care, affection and devotion to one's fellow humans, which are accorded an even higher value.[61] "The acknowledgement of the positive right of the poor to expect charity is reflected in the parallel imperative on propertied people to act charitably."[62]

So much for the theory. In practice the medieval world had economic and social realities to contend with, where the lower orders were more often than not struggling for daily survival and the higher orders were ensconced in a feeling of superiority and dominance over their lesser contemporaries. Towards the later Middle Ages poverty was on the increase, as a sample of court records dating from 1370 to 1600 shows, where the proportion of offences that were reported in connection with poverty displayed a significant rise from the mid-fifteenth century onwards.[63] "If theologians saw the poor as living the life of Christ, ordinary people who encountered poverty and begging all around them were inclined to be less charitable."[64] Suffering might just as well elicit *Schadenfreude* as it might compassion.[65] Contradictory attitudes and ways of behaviour toward blind people, for example, demonstrate this ambivalence, since on the one hand people helped the blind through charity and alms, while on the other hand the same people could laugh at the misfortune of the blind in late medieval public spectacles.[66] The fight between blind beggars over a pig arouses our distaste, but by the late Middle Ages and the early modern period such spectacles were not unusual.[67] The 'entertainment' of blind people fighting for the delectation of the able-bodied is attested at Lübeck in 1386, where the *jeunnesse dorée* of the city, the sons of patricians, selected twelve strong blind men—note that visual impairment need not mean physical weakness—and gave them plenty to eat and even more to drink, then armed them with helmets, breastplates and weapons to make them fight for the pig in the marketplace; young and old, clergy and laity watched this spectacle, in which the blind injured themselves severely.[68] The fight over a sow is also attested in the Swiss confederation.[69] A chronicler recorded that at Stralsund in 1415 this spectacle was arranged as part of a carnival entertainment, which was so 'successful' that such laughter had not been seen before on a Shrove Tuesday (*Fastnacht*).[70] At Cologne in 1498 this spectacle was also arranged as part of a Shrove Tuesday entertainment, for which the *Koelhoffsche Chronik* provides a detailed description: an enclosure was erected out of wooden boards and the pig confined therein, and then five blind men, armed with cudgels, were led in to beat the pig to death, the 'amusement' for the spectators consisting of watching the blind men beat and injure each other.[71] Perhaps of greatest interest to the modern reader is the fact that when a similar event was organised as entertainment for Emperor Maximilian I at a Reichstag in Freiburg, also in 1498, the organiser was Kunz von Rosen, court fool to the emperor[72]—one 'disabled' person exploiting other disabled people to further his own career. Just in case one might think that these spectacles were a regional feature typical only of the German-speaking territories, it is worth pointing out that the Bourgeois of Paris mentions a similar fight at the château of Armagnac on the last Sunday in August 1425, which, with the stereotypical elements of blind men, pig and fight arranged in the lists as if intended for as 'proper' knightly tournament, may have become the prototype for later degrading spectacles.[73] On the evening before the spectacle, four blind beggars were led through Paris "all armed, with a great banner in front, on which was pictured a pig, and preceded by a man beating a drum".[74] Such a fight over a pig arranged as entertainment was also mentioned for Paris in 1450.[75] Thus the disabled, those blind, crippled or lame people, could simultaneously be the recipients of charity, pity and human kindness, as well as the objects of ridicule and gloating.

At this point it is apposite to enter into a brief excursion on the topic of comic representation of disability. The spectators at the pig-beating 'game' were laughing at the blind as well as laughing about the 'comedy' of the situation. The subtle difference between laughter *at* something and laughter *about* something was first defined in the eighteenth century, by Francis Hutcheson (1725), which in turn led to a differentiation between the comic and the ridiculous.[76] Since antiquity the comic was equated with the ugly (*deformitas*), something carried forward into medieval literary theory, and, according to theology, laughter was somewhat suspect, since it could also entail laughing about God's sacred ordering of the cosmos.[77] It is surprising, then, that not only do none of the sources mentioned for the (eye-witness) accounts of the pig-beating in any way voice criticisms of the event as something which arouses inappropriate laughter, but also that none of the religious texts, where one might expect a more critical attitude, to the best of my knowledge even mention such events.[78] For all the rhetoric that one should not put stumbling blocks before the blind (Leviticus 19:14), it seems that the Church was quite happy to turn a blind eye, so to speak, to popular entertainments of this sort. Blind beggars were easy game for the exploitation of their economically depressed state—the attraction of winning an entire pig, which could feed many people, may have outweighed the bruises and broken bones.

Interestingly, since we must not assume that all disabled people were poor or even beggars, there will have been cases of disabled people themselves being the givers of charity to others, to both able-bodied and disabled recipients. In the *Preloquia* of Benedictine monk and Bishop Rather of Verona (931–68) there is a chapter dedicated to beggars, where Rather argues that the state of poverty has no intrinsic value, and the poor person is just as culpable as other people; more to the point, beggars and even the sick and crippled are obliged to perform charitable acts themselves within the limits of their abilities.[79] But such charity given out by the physically impaired themselves would have been valued differently than charity given out by the able-bodied, according to the rationale of thirteenth- and fourteenth-century theology. Jacques de Vitry mentioned a man in his *exempla* who did not give any alms during his lifetime but left his worldly goods to the poor in his testament. When this man fell sick, "four kinds of almsgiving appeared to him in a vision: of gold, silver, lead and clay corresponding to almsgiving in youth, in old age, in sickness and after death."[80] A century later, in 1377, Bishop Thomas Brinton of Rochester retold this story and formulated the general rule that "almsgiving is more worthy and virtuous when it is done in health and during one's lifetime".[81] In a theological sense, therefore, charity performed by the disabled themselves was valued less highly than charity performed by the able-bodied—whether that is how the common person perceived it cannot be fathomed.

By the late Middle Ages beggars were ever-present: they could be found everywhere, on country roads, in the towns, in front of churches, in the marketplace. The traditional groups of widows, orphans and the physically impaired (the crippled, lame and blind)[82] had been augmented with a variety of new poor.[83] In late medieval society many people could be threatened with descent into poverty, so in addition to the elderly, the sick or weak, the mentally disabled and the physically impaired could be added runaway peasants, apprentices, servants and maids, travelling folk, prostitutes, prisoners and wounded veterans—in short those people who were either positioned at the bottom of the social hierarchy or were economically disadvantaged or who had no relatives or friends to support them.[84] But by the late Middle Ages the willingness of contemporaries to perform charitable acts had been much reduced over the earlier period.

If the New Testament had still praised poverty and compassion as two sides of the same coin, even as Christian virtues (*caritas*), towards the end of the Middle Ages one was far removed from this view in lived and everyday practice.[85]

Increasing poverty and larger numbers of beggars drastically changed the attitudes of late medieval society towards poverty and begging, but also the first attempts to develop a kind of institutionalised social security incrementally dislodged individual pity and personalised compassion.[86] The later Middle Ages were therefore a period of transition. "The new quantity and quality of poverty demanded a radical departure from the beaten tracks of medieval charity."[87] A number of notable historians have observed this development of a more discriminating attitude by donors towards 'the poor' from the thirteenth century onwards.[88]

More fundamentally, early and high medieval notions of poverty and of the poor differed from late medieval and early modern notions through definition: the earlier definition had understood poverty as the compulsion, the unavoidable need to perform work, whereas the later definition completely reversed this, so that work came to be understood as the means to combat poverty, and poverty was defined as being in a state of non-work.[89] Over time, medieval concepts of work came to encompass an evaluation of labour that rated it as an activity pleasing to God, part of a rational choice humanity took thanks to the gift of free will.[90] Labour thus became part of an ethics of merit, whereby people merited salvation due to their (good) works. As an early (and somewhat atypical) advocate of the theological benefits of 'work' (*labor*), Hrabanus Maurus had commented that Christ's healing miracles of the blind, lame and dumb (Matthew 9) were positive not just because he cured these people of their impairments, but also because, now able-bodied, they could, supported by faith, work well in divine service[91]—in other words, perform God's works. Although primarily thinking of *labor* as 'good works' in a religious sense, Hrabanus Maurus's comments could be extrapolated to encompass the wider sense of work in all its meanings (physical, intellectual and religious labours) as a benefit for attaining salvation.

What were the causes of the increase in poverty? Population growth, greater mobility which meant loss of the traditional support network of family and friends and famine and disease led to a dramatic rise in the numbers of the poor by the fourteenth century. This development was not without influence on the attitudes to beggars and led to a change in provisions for the poor. One argument, made by Peter Laslett, blames family structures: living in simple-family households, i.e. nuclear families, leaves many individuals without wider familial support, leading to the hypothesis that the more nuclear-family households there are in a given society, the more important support from other quarters will be, namely, from the collectivity, be that charitable organisations, the Church, municipalities or, in later times, the state. In northern and western Europe of the late medieval and early modern periods, charitable support was indeed provided predominantly through collective action, and kin-based support held less importance.[92] The development of medieval hospitals, in all their bewildering variety, may be cited here as an example of such collective action. The ordinances of 1400 for the hospital at Saffron Walden provided for thirteen people who were "lame, crooked, blind and bedridden".[93] In Spain, the hospital d'En Colom in Barcelona, based on the accounts extant for the period between 1375 and 1386, included among its patients a person lame in arms and legs, and one without hands, as well as many acutely sick (e.g. fevers, dropsy, respiratory diseases) and wounded (e.g. inflicted by fencing and lances).[94] The abbey of Saint-Antoine-en-Viennois possessed the healing relics of Saint Anthony, which some hermits in the Dauphiné had claimed in 1070 to have received from Constantinople; daughter houses of the abbey were established as far as Hungary and the Holy Land. Since the Antonite order tended to specialise in receiving the sick into their abbeys-cum-hospices, and especially those people lacking limbs, "their great hospital at St-Antoine-en-Viennois was called the hospital of the 'dismembered'."[95] However, whether or not a particular hospital accepted impaired people may well have been a relatively academic question, when one considers the small proportion of people compared to the overall population who were resident in any kind of institution. If one extrapolates the estimate given by Laslett for pre-industrial settlements in England, then only around 335 people out of a sample population of about seventy thousand resided in an institution (e.g. almshouse or hospital).[96]

The majority of impaired people would therefore have experienced little or no long-term contact with hospitals anyway, apart from the occasional charitable handout, so that the question of inclusion or exclusion starts to lose practical significance for the everyday lives of medieval disabled people. Janet Coleman has argued that the kind of changes that have been discussed in attitudes to poverty commenced

> from the mid-twelfth century when a growing population, increasingly conscious of social stratification, experienced the transformation of agrarian structures, the development of a money economy and urbanisation.[97]

These developments resulted in economic poverty, that is, involuntary poverty, as opposed to a voluntary spiritual poverty.

Medieval notions of poverty distinguished between voluntary and involuntary poverty. Voluntary poverty was understood as part of a religious vocation and was praised, while involuntary poverty was seen as resulting from a situation of social distress and increasingly came to be despised.[98] Commencing in the eleventh century, religious poverty movements came to be promulgated and practised by the mendicant orders originating in the later twelfth century, as well as female religious groups such as Beguines, conventual and lay sisters.[99] The phrase the 'poor of Christ' (*pauperes Christi*), meaning the religious poor, starts becoming increasingly frequent from the eleventh and twelfth centuries onwards.[100] Apostolic poverty was something to be imitated voluntarily by those people who according to their original status (think of Saint Francis, the wealthy merchant's son) were neither materially poor nor socially powerless; "voluntary poverty *can* be a religious response *only* to those with some wealth to renounce."[101] In the recent interpretation by Sharon Farmer, the involuntary, economically poor can be associated with the flesh, while the voluntary, religious poor can be associated with the spirit.[102] The binary emphasis of this analysis, however, is rather over-simplified in that it denies the very real lived poverty experienced by some of the religious embracers of pauperism.[103] Nevertheless, because the involuntary poor, who had not chosen to be poor, resented being in that state and desired change and improvement, in particular desired wealth, such desire, even if for just a modicum of possessions and money, endangered the spiritual health of the poor.[104] According to Thomas Aquinas:

> spiritual danger comes from poverty when it is not voluntary, because a man falls into many sins through the desire to get rich, which torments those who are involuntarily poor.[105]

Humbert of Romans (†1277) complained that the poor rarely went to church and rarely attended sermons or knew anything about how to attain salvation, instead, in their anger at being poor, they blasphemed God whereas it should have been important for them to at least learn the basics of what concerns all Christians and to confess and receive communion annually.[106]

In *Pèlerinage de la vie humaine*, a popular text translated into many European vernaculars, but originally written by the Cistercian Guillaume de Deguileville in 1331,[107] the pilgrim meets the allegorical figures of both "Willful [Voluntary] Poverty" and "Involuntary Poverty", where the former is described as cheerful due to her patience, while the latter is ugly to look upon, groans, frowns and is sad.[108] Hence it was argued by some medieval intellectuals that it was better to give alms to the voluntary poor, since they did not fall into the sin of cupidity by desiring wealth, whereas the involuntary poor were consumed by desire. Already in the fourth century the patristic authority Jerome had stated that it was preferable to give alms to the voluntary poor than the involuntary ones "among whose rags and bodily filth burning desire has domain."[109] In the thirteenth century both Dominican (Aquinas) and Franciscan (Bonaventure) mendicants cited this argument in favour of their own activities of alms-seeking to the detriment of the 'genuine' poor.[110]

But, thankfully for the economically and involuntary poor, not everyone agreed. By the third quarter of the thirteenth century there was already critique of the voluntary poverty lived by the mendicant orders.[111]

People who were capable of working, that is, who were able-bodied, as most mendicant friars were, should not beg alms of fellow Christians; this view was based on the admonition of Saint Paul "if anyone does not wish to work, neither should he eat".[112] Such critique from within the Church itself became more common.

> Although in the [high] medieval period voluntary poverty was considered commendable, by the early fourteenth century pontifical documents cease to refer to poverty as the greatest of virtues.[113]

James le Palmer, putable author of *Omne Bonum*, a fourteenth-century encyclopedia, was equally critical of friars begging, since he was disgusted at the idea that able-bodied men should not work: "Alms should not be given to mendicant friars who are able-bodied and capable of physical labour nor to any other able-bodied persons who can do physical labour."[114]

In vernacular texts, too, by the fourteenth century, religious voluntary poverty was being viewed somewhat ambiguously. In *Piers Plowman*, Langland satirised, "the friars and their hypocritical creed of voluntary poverty" in the character of Need, who states that the needy person (that is, someone hungry, poor or on urgent business) is entitled to take what they need.[115] From an analytical standpoint, voluntary, religious poverty also undermined the status of involuntary, that is, economic or circumstantial, poverty. As the great historian of poverty Bronislaw Geremek observed:

> The rule was that poverty could reach its apotheosis only as a spiritual value, while real, physical poverty, with its visible degrading effects, was perceived, both doctrinally and by society, as a humiliating state, depriving its victims of dignity and respect, relegating them to the margins of society and to a life devoid of virtue.[116]

While the cultural value of voluntary poverty increased compared with the loss in status of real, involuntary poverty, so similarly another religious development impacted on the views of physical impairment, that is, the growth of a concept of saintliness defined by asceticism, physical deprivation and corporal mortification. Ironically, as religious bodies, such as the body of Christ—with the institution of the new feast of Corpus Christi in the 1260s—and the bodies of saints started to matter more, the real, actual lived-in bodies of ordinary people started to matter less. As with the tension between voluntary religious poverty, deemed something to aspire to, and involuntary actual poverty, deemed something to be avoided, so a tension arose between the voluntary physical mortification (at times even mutilation) endured by saints, mystics and ascetics, and the involuntary physical impairment that ordinary people tried their best to avoid in the first place, or wished to be cured of once afflicted.[117] The key issue in this context is that one must not simply explain the changes in attitude toward the poor in the later Middle Ages as brought about by economic and other 'hard', measurable facts, but one ought not to underestimate the importance of such 'softer' factors as the cultural and religious shift in concepts of the body.

What worried medieval people most was the fake body, the body that pretends to be one thing but is in fact quite another:[118] the theatrical delusion of the fraudulent beggar's artificially disabled body. Regarded by modern scholarship primarily as a phenomenon of the later Middle Ages, the concern over fraudulent beggars actually possesses earlier antecedents. A Carolingian capitulary issued at Nimwegen in 806 had already forbidden almsgiving to those beggars who refused to work with their hands,[119] i.e. who were able-bodied, and around the year 820 Louis the Pious had ordered that supervisors were to be instated for beggars and paupers so that simulators might not hide among them.[120] In the early thirteenth century Peter the Chanter had dedicated the chapters *Contra eos qui dant non indigentibus* (against them who give to those not indigent) and *Contra dantes histrionibus* (against giving to those acting [like beggars]) of his *Verbum abbreviatum* to rail against improper charity,[121] and he had condemned beggars "who make themselves tremulous, and putting on the various forms of the sick, change their faces just like Proteus."[122] A generation later, Thomas of Chobham (a pupil of Peter the Chanter) in his manual for preachers, *Summa de arte praedicandi*, mentioned beggars who attended church primarily to "extort money through false tears and deceptions and many simulations."[123] Thomas was also the author of an influential manual for confessors, *Summa confessorum*, where with regard to beggars he wrote that they "frequently transfigure themselves into the appearance of the wretched, so that they seem more destitute [literally: have greater need] than they really are, and thus deceive others so that they will receive more."[124] And Godfrey de Fontibus, who taught at Paris around 1280, stated that altogether he who gives alms to those who are not indigent not only does no merit but furthermore a demerit.[125] One should, however, not regard these citations as representative: "Other theologians and moralists of the mid-thirteenth and early fourteenth centuries were less specific in their descriptions of the deceits of false beggars."[126]

There is some indication that these opinions of the learned clerics found their way into the minds of the non-elite, 'ordinary' population. Attitudes towards the benefits (spiritual and material) of manual labour, of earning one's living through the work of one's own hands and not relying on charitable doles, seem to have percolated into at the least the realms of the Parisian urban poor, as the following example from 1282 demonstrates. At the enquiry into the miracles associated with Saint Louis, a blind woman named Luce of Rémilly "pointed to the fact that she had never begged while she was blind as proof that she had not faked her condition."[127] The fear of being labelled a fraudulent beggar appears to have grown so strong that even the genuine 'needy' poor, in this case a blind woman, felt compelled to do everything possible to avoid begging and conversely to try as hard as possible to live by one's own labour.

By the fourteenth century the concern over fraudulent beggars was finding its way into literary texts.[128] In *Piers Plowman* Langland "speaks of professional beggars as harshly as the Statute of 1388 sought to treat them."[129] Langland accuses these beggars of even going so far as to mutilate their own (or other people's) children by breaking their backs and limbs in infancy, so that as artificially created cripples they would be more pitiable and therefore more profitable in extorting alms.[130] Unfortunately, as events were to prove some sixty or seventy years after Langland wrote, this appears not to have remained simply a horror-evoking literary device. In the region of Paris a criminal gang, of whom some were beggars and others murderers, robbers and highwaymen, was arrested during late 1448 and early 1449. They had apparently specialised in kidnapping young children and turning them into 'professional' beggars. Once they had stolen a child, the gang (which included a former butcher, but also a woman) would mutilate the child, putting out the eyes and cutting off a foot or a leg. Any child who survived this ordeal would then become a better beggar, they thought, by arousing greater degrees of pity and more generous alms.[131] This gang was extreme in its criminality, and should not be considered typical of 'fraudulent' beggars in general, most of whom did not resort to mutilating innocent children.[132]

But back to the less gruesome realm of fiction. The French poet Eustace Deschamps in the fifteenth century expressed strong views about lazy, fraudulent beggars deceiving people, which worried him so much that he was not prepared to give the benefit of the doubt to physically impaired people and was suspicious of the disabled in general.[133] In a miracle play of the early fifteenth century, *Miracles de Sainte Geneviève*, some beggars featured include a leper feigning convulsions; a paralytic who is pushed along in a wheelbarrow; a person afflicted with dropsy and many secondary aches, pains and illnesses; a hunchback; and a person suffering fever and a face-deforming toothache.[134] These figures "invariably constitute a comic element in medieval theatre" and generate suspicion as to the veracity of their impairments rather than arousing pity.[135] In *Jacob's Well*, too, readers are warned against beggars who wheedle money out of folk who have pity on them by seeming to be crooked, blind or sick but not being so.[136] These fake beggars spend their ill-gotten gains in taverns, so the advice to rich men is to let such "lollares" starve.[137] In 1509 Alexander Barclay made a loose translation of Sebastian Brant's *Narrenschiff* (1494), where a passage combines the stereotypes of both the voluntary faking of ailments and the involuntary mutilation of children by fraudulent beggars:

> Some array their legs and arms over with blood,
> With leaves and plasters though they be whole and sound,
> Some halt as cripples, their legs falsely up-bound;

Some other beggars falsely for the nones
Disfigure their children, God wot unhappily,
Mangling their faces and breaking their bones,
To stir people to pity that pass by.[138]

In literary works, the world of beggars is often portrayed as a world turned upside down, with its internal logic that the more disfigured, maimed or mutilated a person is, or pretends to be, the richer they are through greater income from alms, in contrast to the real world, where 'honest', hard work is the necessary prerequisite for material gains. The less able to work a fraudulent beggar is, the greater their aptitude for begging, so that in the reversed realm of fiction the *dis*abled become the *en*abled.[139]

In *Piers Plowman* there were many such deceiving types, for

> Langland knows them all, the guilers, lubbers, lollers, gadelings, false hermits, fobbes, faitors, bidders, leapers, lordains, lorels, mendinants, and their criminal associates the pissares, Robardsmen, Britonners, draw-latches and so on, creatures familiar enough in national and local ordinances and records.[140]

Langland described the 'shirkers' who "pretended to be blind, or twisted their legs askew, as these beggars can, moaning and whining on Piers to have pity on them."[141] They repeat the age-old 'social contract' of offering prayers in return for Piers's charity, but Piers does not believe they are truly impaired and admonishes them. "If anyone is really blind or crippled, or has his limbs bolted with irons, he shall eat" while the rest should work.[142] To put the fraudulent to a test, Piers sends in the figure of Hunger. "Then thousands of blind and bed-ridden folk suddenly recovered, and men who used to sit begging for silver were miraculously cured."[143]

In other regions and other types of secular texts, too, beggars came to be methodically differentiated, such as in the *Augsburger Achtbuch* of 1343, which divided beggars into nine classes: *Grantner*, who simulated epilepsy; *sinweger*, who were supposedly undergoing penance for the murder of a blood relative; *spanvelder*, who simulated an illness; *kappsierer*, who dressed up in clerical robes; *clamyerer*, who dressed up as pilgrims for Rome; *mümser*, who pretended to be sick monks; *scherpierer*, who dressed as pilgrims; *fopperinnen*, who were female beggars simulating a mental illness; and the *hurlentzer*, who said they were baptised Jews.[144] This set the tone for yet more derogatory categorisation of beggars: the register of beggars by Breslau chancellor Dietmar von Meckbach of around 1350;[145] then around 1450 the *Basler Betrügnisse* (Frauds of Basle) noted twenty-six categories of duplicitous beggars.[146] In 1475 the *Chronicle* of Matthias von Kemnat mentioned simulated impairments,[147] while the culmination is reached around 1510 with the publication of the *Liber vagatorum* of Mathias Hüt-lin, master of the hospital at Pforzheim, which reads like a police manual to detect and uncover the fraudulent practices of twenty-eight 'types'.[148] Of particular concern seem to have been beggars who disguised themselves a pilgrims, termed *Christianer und Calmierer* (Christians and swindlers) in the *Liber vagatorum*,[149] possibly because in a metaphysical way they were defrauding God and not just ordinary gullible folk. In Italy around 1485 Teseo Pini wrote a similar list of fraudulent and duplicitous mendicants and vagabonds, *De Cerretanorum Origine Eorumque Fallaciis*, including forty-three 'types' in his extremely popular treatise.[150]

Late medieval society accused the poor of fraud, duplicity and faking, assuming that they begged even though they did not have an actual need for it. Begging had to be legitimated through need, and physical impairment could be regarded as one such legitimation—even if the begging literature accuses people of faking impairments and illnesses, the texts demonstrate that those conditions were perceived as rightful need and therefore prone to simulation. Many depictions of the poor in fifteenth-century art therefore show the 'type' of the disabled, mainly the orthopedically impaired, beggar.[151] As the late medieval entitlement to beg and receive alms came to rely primarily on physical infirmity and impairment, so the body of the beggar gained fundamental importance for the overall appearance of the beggar.[152] Nevertheless, one should not assume that all strata of medieval society regarded the disabled beggar with suspicion, as one who fraudulently acted out a role. A rare occasion when the voice of an 'ordinary' person is heard, rather than the moralising writings of an intellectual, comes from the late-thirteenth century miracles of Saint Louis.[153] There Robert the Smith, one of the witnesses to the miraculous healing of a crippled and severely immobilised woman, states that it was "absurd to think that she could have feigned her malady, 'given the great labor and difficulty' that was required of her in order to move about."[154] Which goes to show that whatever elite texts said, common people readily believed the evidence of their own eyes and could quite pragmatically differentiate between a physical impairment that was genuine, because it was so disabling, and an acted performance by a fraud. Even the 'official examiner' of an alleged miracle could come to the conclusion that precisely because an illness or disability had lasted for a long time, in other words, was a chronic and permanent condition, it could not be feigned or faked. Thus Cardinal Peter Colonna of Saint Eustachio argued in the 1290s, when he was examining a miracle of Louis IX being considered as evidence for canonisation, stating that just because some witnesses had seen the protagonist, one Amelot de Chaumont, "walking as if she were disabled is not in itself incontrovertible proof of her disability",[155] neither was the fact she lay in bed feeling cold and pained, but the length of time she suffered in this condition was proof.

Those regions that became the most commercially developed early on were also the first regions to impose restrictive legislation on begging.[156] The north Italian city-states were the first to do so. As an ad hoc measure during a time of severe economic strain caused by food shortages in the thirteenth century, Genoa hired several galleys . . . as well as rowers who were paid, and then notice was given that all the poor should go to the shore and that they would receive bread from the commune. So many came that it was a wonder . . . all embarked.[157]

The Genoese authorities in effect exported the 'problem' of their poor to Sardinia, where, according to the same source, they were abandoned, although at least there was enough food to eat there. In statutes of 1288 Bologna described the "falsely crippled and the spuriously blind" as a "problem" that needed addressing.[158] The Florentines enacted a piece of legislation as early as 1294 whereby the poor blind were to be sent out of the city. "It is unclear how far this was put into practice, but it has been asserted that even in the 1320s the commune did not want the blind to beg openly in the city and only allowed those who could support themselves financially to live in Florence."[159] The Venetian republic decreed in 1300 "that *pauperes* should be institutionalized in hospitals rather than be allowed to beg through the city".[160] The Florentine Leon Battista Alberti in the 1440s had a very low opinion of physically impaired poor people. As a humanist and aesthete he was probably thinking of their affronting impact on the visual sense, such as when he stated that an important role for hospitals was to prevent the public visibility of disabled people: the poor and sick "should not disturb honest citizens uselessly with their begging and the fastidious with their repugnant appearance".[161] Furthermore, he approved the policy of certain "Italian princes who did not tolerate the presence in their cities of cripples, who with clothes in tatters walk from door to door asking for alms".[162]

In contrast to Alberti's views on the role of hospitals as a place for sequestration and confinement of the unaesthetic poor, in other regions and other times the admission to a hospital did not mean the end of begging for the inmates. Being admitted to hospital was the exception rather than the rule for the impaired, since they must be prevented by illness from 'going about' to ask for alms. Such sentiments were expressed in the thirteenth-century law redacted by Alfonso X of Castile, *Las Siete Partidas* (6.3.20), where charitable bequests were primarily to be given to "those unable to beg for themselves, such as abandoned children, the feeble, and those so crippled as to be unable to leave the hospital in which they are sheltered."[163] Although receiving regular rations of food, inmates of the famous institution in Paris, the hospital of Quinze-Vingts founded in the thirteenth century by Louis IX for three hundred blind people, were licensed to beg to supplement an income for the foundation.[164] Pope Clement IV had issued a bull (1265) permitting the beggars of the Quinze-Vingts to be welcomed in the parish churches of Paris.[165] So much so that already shortly after its foundation the poet Rutebeuf satirically commented on the "braying" of the inmates as they wandered daily around Paris in groups of three begging for alms for the "three hundred who cannot see".[166] Interestingly for this economic context, the Quinze-Vingts, which included sighted and otherwise non-disabled as well as blind residents, is referred to by contemporary accounts as the hospital of the *povres avugles*, emphasising the blind, so that the presence of the other types of people, gleaned from various records, becomes subsumed by the institution's prime focus. "In this case, by living with the blind, the sighted willingly became like the blind."[167] The point about the lack of an officially deemed necessity to curb begging as such is well made by Geremek: "So the creation of such a large, specialised refuge for a single category of beggars—for the blind were beggars *par excellence*—was not designed to prevent them from begging."[168] At hospitals in Troyes (statutes of 1263) and Angers (early thirteenth-century statutes), the

> chronically ill, permanently invalid and handicapped, would be turned away, as would be victims of epidemics who might otherwise flood the establishment. Not only lepers but also amputees (*demembrati*), the paralyzed or crippled (*contracti*), the blind, and those suffering probably from what is today known as ergotism (*ardentes*) had to find other venues for relief.[169]

The exclusion of the *demembrati* may have been due to their supposed capacity for work of some kind,[170] i.e. they could have supported themselves without reliance on the institution. The hospital of Saint Jacques in Valenciennes in 1434 excluded the aged, the paralysed, "phrenetics" and those with other incurable diseases—but then this was primarily a pilgrim's hostel catering for short-stay travellers.[171] Similarly, the anonymous thirteenth-century *Summa pastoralis*, a kind of handbook for archdeacons, made it very clear that almshouses should not support those with physical impairments:

> For the burgesses and very many others, not having God before their eyes, almost under a certain pretext of piety, are accustomed to burden houses of this kind, placing there certain members of their family or neighbours who are crippled, blind, old and powerless, even when the almshouses were not founded for this but for showing hospitality to the travelling poor and especially the sick until they convalesce.[172]

The disassociation of disability and illness, and its consequences for hospital admission, becomes evident in two cases from the miracles of Saint Louis: a woman called Jehenne de Serris, who had become paralysed, only stayed at the Hôtel-Dieu of Paris for so long "until the nuns at the Hôtel-Dieu were able to teach her to use crutches so she could go out begging," and a crippled man called Guillot de Cauz only made use of the same hospital during episodes of what we might term acute illness, i.e. "when fevers prevented him from going out to beg."[173]

Even when the hospital was specifically intended to admit people who could otherwise *not* beg, such as at the hospital of Cambrai, whose statutes of 1220 very significantly included a passage that stipulated only those people who were physically incapable of begging, that is, who were too sick to do so,[174] should be admitted, this reinforces the argument that begging *per se* was not condemned but seen as part of a legitimate means of making a living—provided of course that the beggar was legitimate in the first place.

From the fourteenth and fifteenth centuries onwards many German towns and cities started enacting legislation to protect the resident poor (*Hausarme*), who were to continue receiving alms, and to exclude the migratory, foreign poor who were expulsed or forbidden to beg.[175] Nuremberg pronounced the earliest German begging law (*Nürnberger Bettelordnung* 1370),[176] which forbade all begging outside of churches and condoned begging elsewhere only by registered beggars who were to be demarcated with a special sign or token,[177] just as Jews and lepers had to wear. An official was charged with issuing these tokens, which were limited to six months' validity, so that twice a year beggars had to be examined to establish if they genuinely qualified for their status as 'needy',[178] which they had to prove with two or three reliable witnesses, while those who were capable of working were to be denied issue of the begging token; foreign beggars were to be allowed only three days stay in the city of Nuremberg, after which they had to leave and were not permitted to return for a year.[179] At Regensburg, male beggars who faked illnesses and female beggars who faked pregnancies were to be put in the stocks, while beggars who were unable to recite common prayers were to be ejected from the city—one wonders how such a ruling may have applied to the speech-impaired—and if they could not pray because of mental disabilities, they were to be taught how to pray.[180] At Regensburg, it seems, it was not enough for the civic authorities to distinguish genuine from idle beggars, but their morals and their faith had to be improved upon, too. With regard to tokens as a means of regulating begging, there appears to be some literary evidence that from the thirteenth century onward the authorities tried to ensure that each individual beggar only received one handout at a time through the issuing of special tokens. Richard Fishacre, a Dominican at Oxford, mentions the distribution of tokens around the year 1240 in his commentary to the *Sentences*. He provides the example of a courtier who was ordered by the king to distribute to the poor little numbers made of tin, which entitled them to eat at the king's table on a certain day. Although employed in a theological text as a didactic example, the point is that Fishacre takes for granted the practice he describes and regards it as generally in use.[181] The issuing of tokens, whether real or a literary plot device, indicates how important were the means to discern legitimate and illegitimate beggars. The notion of discernment has been extended by Sharon Farmer to emphasise also the "conviction that able-bodied beggars should be clearly distinguishable from disabled beggars".[182] At Paris, the privileged residents of the famous hospital of Quinze-Vingts were granted the right in 1312 by Philip IV to wear the *fleur-de-lys*, hence a token of royal approval, on their cloaks while out begging in the city, thus legitimising them as opposed to rival beggars from other institutions.[183]

In terms of begging legislation other German cities quickly followed suit, like Constance (1388), Esslingen (1389), Cologne (1403 and 1435), Vienna (1442) and Augsburg (1491).[184] In Italy, Venice prohibited begging in the late fourteenth century and Genoa in the fifteenth.[185] Beggars congregated in particular locations, for example, in late thirteenth-century Paris "paralytic and lame beggars often frequented one specific place—usually their own parish church."[186] They had their traditional places in front of churches or even inside the buildings.[187] Because of such spatial concentrations, later medieval anxiety about begging in general turned its attention to the topography of mendicancy. In Regensburg, the begging laws of 1388 enacted by the council forbade beggars to ask for alms in the houses of burghers, and certain types of people (itinerant entertainers) were prohibited from entering the city at all.[188] Laws came to be enacted prescribing spatial restrictions on begging, with begging in churches singled out as a particular practice that needed curbing, such as at Cologne (Article 14 in a statute of Archbishop Henry II of 26 February 1330 prohibiting the donation of alms to beggars inside churches),[189] Basle (1429) or Augsburg (1459). At Regensburg beggars with contagious diseases were allowed to beg outside of, but not inside, churches, according to begging regulations from the fifteenth century onward.[190] However, at Cologne the blind specifically continued to beg outside of the cathedral, where they had their regular pitch and officially received alms, such as two shillings given by the hospital of Saint Revilien in May 1484.[191] But in general banishing beggars from the interior of churches withdrew them from clerical protection,[192] and it further severed the former link between charity, alms and compassion, on the one hand, and Christian duty rewarded by care for one's soul, on the other hand. By the time of the Reformation giving alms even became criticised *per se*, with the stereotype of the able-bodied, sturdy beggar (*starke Bettler*) used to specifically argue against alms.[193]

For England, the town of Chester provides an example of anti-begging legislation, details which emerge thanks only to a detailed study of local records by Jane Laughton. Chester enacted a series of bylaws after the general mood following the 1349 crisis had shifted to encompass stronger concern over beggars. The first recorded bylaw was enacted in 1393 to control the movement of beggars, which prohibited "men from roaming the streets without sufficient means on which to live";[194] this prohibition was repeated in 1404. Perhaps there was a connection between these anti-begging laws and the slightly earlier preaching legislation of 1391 and 1403 respectively—note the dates—which "re-iterated the principle that the poor should be relieved by the local community."[195] During the mid-fifteenth century accusations were made against Chester's tapsters of sheltering vagabonds and of keeping their doors open at night (i.e. running an 'open' or disorderly house), and at the same time the hermit of Saint James in Handbridge was accused of harbouring thieves and other malefactors, as vagrants may have sheltered at his hermitage. People of dubious religious reputation and economic undesirables were by this stage being bundled together by the authorities. The crunch came in the 1490s and early sixteenth century, when Chester's beggars were ordered to take up employment or to face imprisonment, while Chester's good citizens were fined if they offered them accommodation.[196] Thus by 1509 one encounters the first mention in Chester records of an able-bodied beggar who was deemed fit and healthy enough to work by the civic authorities, a man called Gilbert Beggar (!), resident of Love Lane within the Bars, an area of humble dwellings, who was fined for his offence of begging.[197]

What emerges from this overview of begging legislation and restrictions is that the physically impaired were almost always included amongst the category of legitimised beggars, the ones deemed truly 'needy', and retained some protection from the clamp-down against undesirable beggars enacted by many civic authorities of late medieval Europe.

Municipal restrictions on begging led to differentiation between resident (and thereby legitimate beggars) and outsiders, so that in some towns competition among the poor for the ever-scarcer resources of charity led to the development of guild-like organisations, of begging fraternities. One of the earliest seems to have been a begging fraternity for the blind, the Consorzia dei Ciechi, or *Congregatio orborum*, which existed at Genoa during the thirteenth and fourteenth centuries, while similar brotherhoods were founded in Venice (the Scuola degli Orbi in 1315) and Padua during the fourteenth century.[198] In Spain one encounters the confraternities of the blind at Barcelona and Valencia, dating from 1329 according to their statutes. A later document of 1442 records the "Confraternity of the Holy Spirit for the Lame, Blind, and Poor of the City of Barcelona that owned a house and some property and that could receive legacies."[199] Unlike most such corporations, and particularly in contrast to later fraternities, which were modelled on the religious fraternities extant in many cities,[200] the Barcelona and Valencia guilds provided for different forms of solidarity and mutual aid within the organisation, such as reciprocal loan of the guide for the blind (*lazarillo*), help in cases of sickness and the collective sharing out of the alms received.[201] In this context it is most interesting to observe that in late medieval Barcelona, the 'undeserving' or less deserving poor (*pobres captaires*) numbered blind and deaf beggars among their ranks,[202] presumably since these people were following a 'profession', i.e. begging, and therefore were deemed already sufficiently provided for.

Since we have now encountered mention of the *lazarillo*, the guide for the blind, a little excursion into the evidence for and presumptions of mobility aids for the blind is perhaps in order. The guide was for a blind person their prime 'mobility aid'. Besides the many literary treatments of the abuse the blind person receives through the deceit of their guide,[203] we have a few neutral examples from the lived experience of named individuals. In Guillaume de Saint-Pathus's *Les Miracles de Saint Louis*, composed in the 1280s, Agnés de Pontoise "went as blind people go, holding her hand on the shoulder of [her sister] who led her".[204] In one of his *Letters of Old Age* , Petrarch describes how Stramazzo di Perugia, "that old blind man who ran a grammar school in the town of Pontremoli", made his way to meet Petrarch at Naples by "leaning on the shoulder of his only son, a lad in his teens".[205] Blind people tended to be led by other people, preferably adults, since children (although cheap to employ) were deemed unreliable, as were dogs. The elusive hunt for medieval guide dogs for the blind has turned up a few isolated textual references and a couple of images. It seems guide dogs were regarded as a 'last resort', because of their unreliability, as emphasised in the mid-fourteenth-century Middle High German laudatory poem by Heinrich von Mügeln, *Der meide kranz* (ll. 765ff.): just as a king without sense or understanding (*âne sin*) misleads his people and misrules his realm, so a blind man is misled by a dog, a child or his staff for the blind.[206] Bartholomaeus Anglicus, *De proprietatibus rerum*, VII:19, also mentioned the unsuitability of dogs. The reason generally given is that dogs (and children!) are too readily distracted, so that if a dog, who is meant to be guiding a blind person, sees a bone, the dog will drag the blind person with him into the mud.[207] Art historian Moshe Barasch cites the early fourteenth-century marginal image in a Flemish manuscript of a blind man with his staff being 'led' on a rope by a dog, who is additionally holding the man's begging bowl in its muzzle, as an example of this presumption in favour of guide dogs[208]—personally I am inclined to regard this dog simply as a 'companion animal' or pet in the modern sense, and not in any way as a trained guide dog, since the blind man navigates primarily by use of his staff. The dog jumping away and dragging the unfortunate blind man with him is, as Barasch rightly points out, turning this visual mini-story into a tragi-comic episode. Also stemming from the fourteenth century, a literary source is employed by Barasch to argue for the 'ubiquity' of guide dogs for the blind. In Franco Sacchetti's *Trecentonovelle* one of the stories mentions three blind beggars from Florence and their dogs, who decide to go to Pisa for their customary stint of alms-collecting at the feast of Our Lady. "And each man being led by his dog, which was taught to hold the dish for alms, they set upon their way".[209] They need to take a room overnight at an inn, which the blind men enter "with their dogs held by leading-strings".[210] A fight over money taken from alms ensues among the three blind men, and they start hitting each other and their dogs with their sticks, resulting in a general commotion at the inn that Sacchetti milked for its comic effects. But, unlike the spectacle mentioned earlier of the 'entertainment' provided in towns with blind beggars enacting a 'joust' in a fight over a pig, Sacchetti's tale is slightly more sympathetic to his blind protagonists, since although sorely bruised and beaten, and cheated of their money by the innkeeper, the story ends with this passage:

And because, in addition to being blind, they were all wounded with their beating, so many alms were bestowed upon them at Pisa that not only were they consoled for these blows, but they would not have gone without them for all the world, by reason of the advantages they derived from them.[211]

Sacchetti was arguably offering "some observations of actual life, as he directly experienced it", presenting "an amusing story about a scuffle between the dogs of the different blind beggars, and its unfortunate and ridiculous consequences for those who depend on these dogs".[212] And last but not least, a historical record mentions what may be guide dogs: as part of the begging legislation which restricted who could beg and under what personal circumstances, between 1464 and 1506 the city of Strasbourg ordered on penalty of a fine that no beggar was in future permitted to keep or raise a dog, unless he was blind and therefore needed one.[213] It therefore seems that blind *beggars* may have sometimes kept dogs as a mobility aid, but everyone else who was visually impaired and could *afford to* would rather have employed a sighted human guide.

Thus appositely returning to begging organisations, at Venice one finds the begging fraternity of the Scuola dei Zotti, according to statutes or *Mariegola* founded in 1392.[214] That same year the Venetian Council of Ten legalised an association of *senes et impotentes*, ostensibly for "veterans who had served with the Venetian fleet in their younger days, and were now unable, on account of old age, to support themselves by their trades."[215] It is possible that the Scuola dei Zotti, which was based in the same parish of Sant' Anzolo as the veterans' brotherhood, "either succeeded or developed out of the veterans' association, although it was not initially stipulated that the aged ex-servicemen must be disabled as well as physically weak."[216] According to statutes dating from between 1392 and 1464, the *gastaldo* (chief officer) of the Scuola dei Zotti had to meet strict requirements for certain impairments but not others, since he must be a "capable beggar, who is lame or without a leg and not in any other condition, for he must not be without arms, or blind, or suffering from any other infirmity".[217] By 1551 the Scuola did admit "men without arms" (i.e. hands), but with the proviso that they must be so naturally and not due to judicial mutilation.[218] The Scuola also collected contributions from its members for a central fund (*basolo*) for the benefit of those who were "infirm", meaning acutely ill, and "cannot leave their homes in order to go out begging and earn a poor living for themselves".[219] One should note the small-scale operation of this fraternity: at a chapter meeting in 1493 only seventeen members voted.[220]

Local beggars, especially the blind and the lame, thereby formed associations that tried to fit in with the urban guild structure. In this they were different from the regular (non-begging, non-disabled) charitable fraternities that became common in the fourteenth and fifteenth centuries, which were concerned with providing for the foreign poor and sick, and organising their burials in the event of death,[221] since such fraternities effectively took a top-down approach,[222] whereas the true begging fraternities were formed *by* the beggars *for* the beggars themselves. An exception to the general rule concerning charitable fraternities seems to have been the London-based guild of the Holy Blood of Wilsnack, established in 1491, which stated in its ordinances that "when any brother or sister is sick, then shall *every* [my emphasis] brother and sister give a half penny every week to the sustentation and keeping of the said sick."[223] A corporation of the blind poor was founded at Strasbourg in 1411, which donated a candle and had a mass read for the soul of each deceased member;[224] and according to revised statutes issued in 1469 besides the blind poor other physically impaired people could join.[225] There was also the guild at Zülpich (Eiffel), in the territory of the archbishopric of Cologne, founded in 1454 and devoted to "poor people who live of alms such as cripples, blind and other folk".[226] This was a very organised begging fraternity founded specifically by the physically impaired, and as such was closer to the Barcelona/Valencia group than to any northern European guild, in its emphasis on solidarity of the brothers and sisters and mutual aid in times of need, which it made a duty in its exceptional statutes.[227] This fraternity existed primarily as a self-help organisation with wider regional importance but was also aimed at the social reintegration of marginalised people, as the involvement of the archbishop of Cologne and the town council of Zülpich demonstrate. The key points of the statute are worth citing. The mayor, officials and council of Zülpich announce that with the permission of Archbishop Diederich of Cologne and Johan van Melen, the provost of the church of Saint Peter in Zülpich, they have allowed that

> some poor people who live of alms such as cripples, blind and other poor people have formed a guild and confraternity for themselves and all poor people such as cripples and blind or other people who may come into this fraternity.

> (*dat etzliche arme mynschen, die der almoesen levend van kruppelen, blijnden ind andere arme lude eyne erffgulde ind broderschafft annomen hant vur sich ind alle arme lude van kruppelen ind blinden off ander lude, die noch in dise broderschafft komen moigen.*)[228]

On the third day before the feast of Saint Michael all crippled, lame and blind members of the fraternity and who lived within ten Cologne miles (approximately seventy kilometres) were to appear at Zülpich. Half the income of what a member had begged on that day was to be given to the fraternity. In the event that a brother or sister became ill and could not help themselves, that is, obtain their own alms, the fellow members of the fraternity should support them by begging alms for them; if the healthy brothers or sisters could not stay with the sick member for so long, then they should give the sick person four shillings, but if they were too poor and could not give so much, then the healthy members should give the sick two shillings for the sake of the brotherhood.

> *Vort were sache, dat eynich broder off suster dieser broderschafft in eynich lant, dorp off stat queme ind von den eynich dieser selver broderschafft broeder off suster krancklijgen ind sich nijt behelpen en kunden, as dann soelen die den krancken bijstendich sijn ind yme die almoesen echt dage vur bidden, ind en kunden die gesunden broedere off sustere nijt aslange bij deme krancken blijven, so sullen sij dem krancken vier schillinge geven, ind off die gesunder broeder off suster as arm werden ind yme des geltz nijt geven en kunden, so sullen sij ym zweene schillinge geben um der broderschafft willen.*[229]

Apart from the material mutual aid that the members agree to give to each other, what is interesting here is the notion, which was also held by the Venetian Scuola dei Zotti, that the crippled, lame or blind brothers and sisters are not 'sick'—being physically impaired is not *per se* a state of illness.[230]

Similar to the guild attested at Zülpich was another begging fraternity, officially based at Trier (Treves) but with supra-regional membership. This fraternity was founded in 1437 for blind and deaf members, under the patronage of the bishop of Trier, but rapidly expanded to include cripples, 'sick', lepers and non-disabled persons as well. Officials were elected according to strict protocol: two cripples, two blind men, one leper and one non-disabled person. The aims of this fraternity were, like that of Zülpich, to provide mutual assistance amongst members in times of dearth or sickness[231]—again, disability as such was not perceived to be an illness.

The necessity to differentiate among the poor and to exclude those able to work (the undeserving) from the claim to alms was emphasised by the church fathers as well as by many medieval theologians and canonists.[232] In the fourth century John Chrysostom "had been of the opinion that it was the Christian's duty to perform charitable offices indiscriminately",[233] but already in 382 the city of Constantinople, of which ironically he was patriarch, was to be rid of beggars, whereby checks were carried out to sort the sick (rightful) from the healthy (idle) beggars.[234] These measures were based on an edict *De mendicantibus non invalids*, which stated that

> all beggars were to be tested for soundness of body and vigour of years [*integritas corporum et robur annorum*]. Those beggars who had no signs of any physical disability, and who were found to be lazy, were to become the slaves of those who reported them and were taken off the streets.[235]

Ambrose of Milan also had already discerned between degrees of need:

Even in the distribution of largesse age and debility are to be considered, sometimes even the modesty that derives from free birth, so that you endow more generously the old who cannot obtain food any longer by their own work. The case is similar for physical debility, and for such things assistance should be most prompt.[236]

In the sixth century the Justinian legal code had continued to differentiate among the poor between those able and those unable to work.[237] In a charter of Pepin, dated 13 August 762, confirming the donation of property to the monastic hospital at Prüm (Eiffel) the link between legitimate receipt of charity and inability to work was already made clear:

> The aforesaid prebends for the twelve poor may however not be bestowed on healthy people or persons of means, who in other respects have [sufficient] to live or who can earn their bread by the daily labour of their hands: but they shall be given to infirm, blind, deaf and decrepit people, as has been ordained by the holy fathers. Whosoever should do otherwise, shall know that in that he would grossly insult God.[238]

By the high Middle Ages the notion of indiscriminate charity was becoming refined. High medieval canonical theory tried to make ethical differences: only the 'just', the 'honest' and the 'shameful' poor were to receive charity. As an example, the *Vita* of Raimundo Palmario of Piacenza (†1200) mentions that in his charitable activities he "began to seek out the needy around the city, those whom shame or disease prevented from begging".[239] The 'real' poor (*verecundi pauperes*) were the ones who modestly risked invisibility rather than 'offensively' or 'aggressively' begging. However, if someone was in a life-threatening situation then such differentials were to be ignored, unless a person was just plain idle. In principle, only those ready to be converted to a 'better' way of life and those ready to better themselves were to receive help. In such a way the giving of alms came to be connected more closely with exhortations to make oneself useful[240]—the notion of *utilitas* became more important, as expressed in the New Testament verse "who does not work shall not eat".[241] The canonist Rufinus of Bologna, commenting on Gratian's *Decretum*, wrote that

> if the man who asks is dishonest, and especially if he is able to seek his food by his own labour and neglects to do so, so that he chooses rather to beg or steal, without doubt nothing is to be given to him, but he is to be corrected . . . unless perchance he is close to perishing from want, for then, if we have anything we ought to give indifferently to all such.[242]

In the twelfth century the corpus of papal laws and decrees known as *Decretals* included a passage that prohibited the giving of alms to "followers of infamous professions".[243] The *Glossa ordinaria*, another canon law text and basic commentary on the *Decretum*, "cautioned against one who can work and earn his bread and chooses not to, but rather 'plays all day long with dies and cubes'."[244] Johannes Teutonicus, a contributor to the *Glossa Ordinaria*, stated that "the Church need not provide for those who can work. One must take into account wholeness of body (*integritas membrorum*) and strength of constitution (*robur membrorum*) when alms are dispensed".[245] Still in the twelfth century the *Summa elegantius*, a text based on the work of the canonist Rufinus, advocated this view of charity:

> In almsgiving there should be distinction between people. You had better give to your own than to strangers, to the sick rather than to the healthy, to ashamed rather than to aggressive beggars, to the have-not rather than to him who has, and amongst the needy, first to the just and then to the unjust. That is ordered charity.[246]

Correct guidance on charitable discrimination was provided in the account-book of the Cistercian monastery of Beaulieu Abbey, compiled 1269–1270, making adjustments especially according to time of year, so that during harvest time, when work was readily available, alms should not be given to the poor unless they were pilgrims, the old, children and those incapable of work.[247] In the same century, the compendium of law redacted by King Alfonso X of Castile prescribed that in the ordering of charity "the old and the disabled should be favored over the young and healthy".[248]

In literary texts, too, one encounters an echo of the increasing discrimination of charity. Interestingly, these literary sentiments pre-date the Black Death (again in contrast to a popular modern interpretation of the change in attitudes toward poverty as arising from the "calamitous" fourteenth century[249]). In the *Romance of the Rose* the character of False-Seeming mentions the man who is capable of body and yet asks for his bread. "One would do better to cripple him or punish him openly than to maintain him in such a malicious practice."[250] False-Seeming offers a list of people who are allowed to beg, based on the preaching of a thirteenth-century Paris master, William of Saint Amour (1202–1272)—in this the *Romance of the Rose* pre-empts the municipal legislation of the later Middle Ages. Included in this list are people who cannot work because of sickness, old age or dotage[251]—the classical configuration of the needy poor. However, it is from the fourteenth century onwards that texts in general start becoming more concerned with who the beggar is and start questioning the truthfulness of a beggar's claim to be needy. "Denunciation of false beggars appears frequently in vernacular literature" from the fourteenth and fifteenth centuries.[252] Interestingly, Langland, who has been cited here for his views on such fraudulent beggars, did encompass the notion of indiscriminate charity, at least as something the giver should do, placing the moral onus on the recipient to clear their conscience as to whether they are truly needy or not.

Yet Gregory the Great, who was a holy man, bade us give alms to all that ask, for the love of Him who gave us all things. 'Do not choose whom you pity,' he said, 'and be sure not to pass over by mistake one who deserves to receive your gifts; for you never know for whose sake you are more pleasing to God.' Nor do you ever know who is really in need—only God can know that. If there is any treachery, it is on the beggar's side, not on the giver's.

(*Ac Gregory was a good man, and bad us gyven all*
That asketh for His love that us al leneth:
Non eligas cui miserearis, ne forte pretereas illum qui meretur
accipere; quia incertum est pro quo Deo magis placeas.
For wite ye nevere who is worthi—ac God woot who hath nede.
In hym that taketh is the trecherie, if any treson walke -
For he that yeveth, yeldeth, and yarketh hym to reste.)[253]

Thus begging was regarded by Langland as a last resort, something the "tramps [*beggeres*]" should only do "in dire need [*gret nede*]".[254] His 'model' poor appear to have been those shame-faced poor, "the poorest folk who are our neighbours" described as "ashamed to beg, or tell their neighbours of their need."[255]

In German literature, an Alemannic didactic text known as *The Devil's Net* (Des Teufels Netz) of around 1420 describes how the Devil ensnares people of all estates, including the "worldly beggars", that is, healthy, able-bodied people who have sunk to begging out of idleness and now use all sorts of ruses to obtain alms.[256]

Literary texts, as well the theological or philosophical texts and the begging laws cited earlier, have in common that, almost without exception, they categorise the needy as either legitimate or fraudulent beggars, where the fake beggars are seen as bringing their condition on themselves due to idleness. But none of these texts address the possible economic or social mechanisms which could have led to impoverishment and in consequence to begging as a self-help action, nor do they question whether work would even have been a plausible alternative or been available. "Under critical scrutiny the sources mentioned document in the main a developmental process of prejudices toward the people mentioned, which in the final analysis are surviving to the present."[257]

In her study of charity in medieval Cambridge, Miri Rubin addressed the issue of deserving versus the undeserving poor. A record of poor relief can be found in the episcopal registers of the bishops of Ely. The register of John Fordham, bishop 1388–1425, qualified the status of some of the poor recipients of charity according to their physical well-being. Of seven recipients, one was a blind man (who received an indulgence on two occasions); another was "very infirm"; three were "mutilated", one of whom had been wounded in battle; and another was a tiler who had fallen off a roof. Apart from providing some indication as to the causes of (temporary or permanent) disability, this list uses disability to justify the charitable act. "This qualification of their state of need was an attempt to enter the recipient into the category of 'deserving' poor."[258] Religious guilds and fraternities, too, applied to the poor the criteria of need based on physical condition, such as the guild of Stretham-in-the-Isle, where the inability to work due to loss of vision or loss of a limb justified the receipt of charity by guild members.[259]

The increased specialisation and definition of the purpose of hospitals as providers of charitable care, whereby some institutions allowed one sort of people to enter, but others did not permit entry to the same group, can also be seen as part of the greater differentiation between the deserving and the undeserving poor during the later Middle Ages.[260] As Carole Rawcliffe described the situation with regard to English hospitals:

> relief moved from the general, relatively unselective hospitality of the *xenodochium* (hospital) to the stricter confines of the parish, where the needs and merits of the resident poor could more easily be assessed.[261]

The type of the earlier 'general' hospital may be exemplified by the institution founded near the cathedral by Bishop Aldrich of Le Mans (832–857), which was a hospice, hotel and hospital rolled into one, catering, amongst others, to lame, blind and other impaired persons.[262] Hospitals financed and to an extent administered by the communes broke with the ecclesiastical concept of providing free and indiscriminate charity, so that they were transformed from institutions providing a multifaceted programme of care into specialised houses which might cater to just one group (such as the mentally ill, lepers, orphans or the elderly).[263] With hospitals underlying individual donors' instructions, somewhat bizarre stipulations laid on the inmates could emerge not infrequently, for instance, the twelve poor old men who had to grow a beard in honour of Saint Anthony, according to the regulations set out by the hospital of the eponymous saint at Augsburg in 1410, as well as committing to pray fifteen paternosters daily at the grave of the founder.[264] The case of the hospital of Saint-Sauveur in Lille seems also to point towards a change in clientele, or at least toward increased pressure to change 'customers'. There the canons of Saint-Pierre noted:

> since this hospice was particularly intended for the relief of the sick and bedridden poor, and for the reception of pilgrims and travelers, we are absolutely determined that the said hospice avoid lodging travelers in good health . . . so that revenues intended for pilgrims and the bedridden sick can be fully reserved for them.[265]

Also age limits were introduced, e.g. sometimes no children or no elderly patients were to be admitted. For instance, at the Quinze-Vingts for blind residents of Paris, the hospital's "rule forbade the admission of blind or sighted children under the age of sixteen (art. 28), suggesting a desire to prevent families from depositing blind children at the hospital's gate."[266] The financial ups and downs of an institution throughout its existence will also have had an influence over who was admitted: less resource-demanding cases may well have been preferred during times of economic uncertainty. That hospitals themselves, not just their inmates, could fall on hard times is evidenced in the following anecdotes from Joinville's *Life of Saint Louis*:

> The king was so generous in giving alms that wherever he went in his kingdom he would distribute money to poorly endowed churches, to leper-houses, to alms houses and hospitals, and also to men and women of gentle birth in distress.[267] . . . In addition to this, every day the king used to give generous alms to poor monks and nuns, to ill-endowed hospitals, to poor sick persons, and to religious communities with little money.[268]

Obviously being generous in one's alms distribution was such a qualifying mark of the good and just king that Joinville found himself compelled to repeat the facts twice over.

The categorisation of persons according to their ability to work (begging forbidden) or inability (begging allowed) constituted a paradigmatic under-pinning of the discourse pertaining to concepts of deserving and undeserving poor.[269] In short, to that degree by which the value of work increased, the status of beggars decreased.[270] In the 1350s Richard FitzRalph, an Englishman holding the archbishopric of Armagh in Ireland, wrote several tracts on poverty, where he started developing an early form of work ethic;[271] poverty was now the result of sin, and wealth could be found in Paradise, culminating in his view that "he who will not work neither shall he eat".[272] In his sermon *Defensio Curatorum*, which he presented in 1357 before the papal curia at Avignon in defence of his attacks on the voluntary poverty and begging of the mendicant orders, FitzRalph also attacked secular beggars, whom he wished to see disqualified from the receipt of alms. The story of Christ's invitation of people to the feast, narrated in Luke 14:12–14,[273] became the lynchpin for FitzRalph's anti-poverty and anti-begging argument. FitzRalph repeated the Gospel story: "Whanne þou makest a feest clepe þou þerto pore men, halt & blynde, & þou shalt be blessed, for þei haueþ no3t wherof þie mowe quyte hit to þee",[274] but then he immediately glossed the passage, so that 'poor' in general came to be qualified as meaning those 'poor people who happened to be halt and lame':

> Þanne pore men þat beþ stalworþe and stronge schulde nou3t be cleped to þe feeste of beggers, for þei mowe quyte hit wiþ her trauail. Noþer riche feble men, noþer riche halt men, noþer riche blynde men schuld be cleped to þe feeste of beggers, for þei mowe quyte hit wiþ her catel.[275]

According to FitzRalph, then, only those people who were both impaired (feeble, halt, blind) and materially poor constituted the true, needy poor, since the able-bodied economically poor are capable of work; hence they can repay the charity of the feast, while the disabled rich have no need for material charity. Apart from providing an eloquent exercise in discriminatory charity, FitzRalph's statement, unusually for most medieval texts that mention physical impairment at all, allows for the possibility of rich disabled persons—quite in contrast to the stereotype of the medieval disabled beggar. Half a century after FitzRalph, in 1406 William Taylor, a Wycliffite reformer, delivered his own version of a sermon concerned with poverty, work and charity at Saint Paul's Cross. Influenced by FitzRalph's theology, Taylor was particularly concerned with "the legitimacy of begging, the correct practice of almsgiving, and the benefits of labour".[276] He too cited the invitation from the Gospel of Luke, and he too glossed "the text in order to assert that only the poor who are feeble, lame, and blind should be called to the feast."[277] But Taylor went one stage further in linking entitlement to charity with in/ability to work, in that he expanded the gloss to proscribe even the correct causes of impairment:

> For þe vndirstondyng of þis text Crist techiþ and specifieþ here þre bodily myesis þat vnabliþ a man to gete his liiflode bi his labour, þat is to seie feblenesse bi age or siiknesse, lamenesse þat is depryuyng of mannys lymes bi birþe, hap or violence as bi prysonyng, and þe þridde is blyndnesse.[278]

In a pre-figuration of modern disability legislation, which outlines the criteria for the means-testing of people and 'accrediting' recognised disabilities, Taylor narrowed the aetiologies of impairment down to acceptable categories. Only someone 'feeble' due to age or sickness, but not due to other factors should be entitled to alms. Similarly only those persons lame due to birth, accident or violence (but presumably here not due to sickness) fall into the acceptable category; only blindness is accorded a statutory carte blanche. And on top of delineating the causes of impairment, Taylor made it quite clear that what really mattered most was whether the alms-seeker was unable to work. He is "emphatic that the beggars deserve charity not primarily because they are 'mysesid,' but because these specific 'mysesis' 'vndisposiþ a man to labore'".[279] In the ideal scenario proposed by William Taylor, the blind beggar, for instance, would find gainful work as a basket-weaver or some such suitable occupation, and would thus no longer be needful of charity—the impairment alone (simply being feeble, halt or blind) is not enough to ensure 'needy' status, for that one has to be disabled in the modern sense and deemed incapable of working.

Nevertheless, most medieval commentators recognised physical impairment as one of the classic situations which prevented a person from working. An illustrative example can be found in the miracles of Saint Louis, that is, in the collection of posthumous miracles worked at the tomb of King Louis IX of France, occurring between 1271 and 1282. There a woman called Agnes of Pontoise is mentioned, who had been a domestic servant for many years until she was more than thirty years old, and as such had worked until 1271 when "she fell victim to an eye disease that rendered her blind and compelled her to beg for a living."[280] After some four years she was cured and was able to re-enter the job market by spinning wool for a bourgeois household. Another woman mentioned in the miracles was Aelés Malachine, who had worked as a wool comber, but after apparently suffering a stroke in 1268 which rendered her unable to use her right side, made her hand tremble, compelled her to use crutches and to rely on another woman's help with getting dressed, she was forced to beg due to her inability to work.[281] Begging by women was seen as particularly stigmatising by clerical authors, more so than begging by men, since women were ideally associated with the domestic and not the public realm.[282]

> When illness, age, or disability interrupted the work rhythms of these [labouring poor], they crossed the line from the working to the nonworking poor, joining the masses of beggars who congregated at parish doors.[283]

They also joined other public places in thirteenth-century Paris. An example of someone of a different sex (male) and of a different time (around a century later) demonstrates an alternative scenario of what could happen if a person became physically impaired and as a consequence unable to work. The French register of criminal cases of the Châtelet in Paris mentions one Jehannin Machin, nicknamed Court-Bras (Short-Arm), who was convicted in 1390 of thefts and of kidnapping people. This man had worked as a baker and pastry-cook in Paris until he took part in the military campaign of July 1388, "from which he returned with a crippled arm."[284] This injury prevented him from practising his trade, so first he became a porter at the gates of Paris, but then he started petty thieving and begging for a living, until he degenerated to joining a band of vagabonds, with whom he held people to ransom outside the town walls of Paris.[285] These potted biographies show that an acquired impairment which prevented practising one's trade could bring about the economic and consequent social descent illustrated here, which for this man, with his arguably violent military experiences, led to a life of crime as well as just mendicancy.

How in/ability to work affected the lived experience of common people can also be seen in the legislation issued by secular governments—again a phenomenon that is not just in evidence after the crisis of the Black Death. In the Hispanic peninsula, Ferdinand IV of Castile promulgated a requirement in 1308 that forced able-bodied, and therefore work-suited beggars to leave Burgos; in Valencia, James II was worried about false beggars in connection with legal cases from 1321; and by 1351 Peter I of Castile had enacted similarly repressive laws to the Statute of Labourers (coincidentally also dating from 1351) in England.[286] France became the third nation that year to instigate laws concerning begging, work and vagrancy, with an ordinance of John II of February 1351 concentrated on Paris and the surrounding region. People without work, idlers, beggars, of whichever sex, status or former trade, were to start work immediately or leave Paris and the region within three days—"only the crippled and the sick were excluded".[287] This royal ordinance recommended that preachers pass the message on in their sermons

> that those who wish to give alms should not give to people who are sound in body and limb, or to people who are able to do work by which they can earn their living, but they should give to people who are deformed, blind, impotent or to other miserable people.[288]

Interestingly the early medieval concept of 'impotent' is still apparent here, as in people who are powerless in their social and economic position. Under Charles VII in the mid-fifteenth century a further French ordinance aimed at beggars was passed. This repeated the injunctions against able-bodied persons begging but added a second part which attacked the alleged practices of false beggars, so all beggars were to be supervised by specially appointed people in an attempt to weed out the frauds.[289]

In England we find the aforementioned Ordinance of Labourers of 1349, which became statute in 1351: no alms were to be given to healthy and able-bodied beggars, and all able-bodied people under the age of sixty had to accept the first offer of work they received from an employer.[290] "Many able beggars [*validi mendicantes*], as long as they can live of alms-begging, refuse to work and laze in idleness and sins . . . thefts and deceit".[291] They allegedly waste the alms given to them, which would otherwise have been given to many genuine poor folk, such as lepers, the blind, the lame and people "oppressed with old age and divers other maladies".[292] The years around 1350 appear to have been a turning point in many ways, both for perceptions of who the 'truly' deserving were who should be assisted, and for political and legal developments in the treatment of the poor, with developments in essence originating at this time culminating in the early modern Poor Laws and the Dickensian workhouse.[293]

In England, as in the German towns and cities with their numerous begging legislations, there was also an anxiety over larger numbers of poor, and especially over vagrant poor people. People who were travelling and who relied on charitable handouts, such as pilgrims, no longer had the benefit of the doubt and needed legitimisation. Not being able-bodied was one such legitimisation, which because of its very visibility did not need documents.[294] A statute of Richard II enacted at Cambridge in 1388 "decreed that all persons claiming to be pilgrims who could not produce letters of passage stamped with a special seal were, unless infirm or otherwise manifestly incapable of work, to be arrested."[295] During the reign of Edward IV anxiety levels were raised even further. A Close Roll of 17 May 1473 stated:

> Forasmuch as this day many persons being strong of body to service in husbandry and other labours feign them to be sick and feeble . . . by means of which feignings, divers fall into the said beggings in cities, boroughs and other places, and so living idly will not do service but wander from town to town in vagabondage, sowing seditious languages whereby the country people be put in great fear and jeopardy of their lives and losses of their goods . . . Our sovereign lord . . . straitly chargeth and commandeth that no person able to do labour or do service live idly, but serve in husbandry and other business according to his laws.[296]

Furthermore, according to the 1388 statute, even when they were disabled, beggars were meant to remain in one place and not move about the country[297]—the once purely monastic *stabilitas loci* was now even required of secular beggars. In Cologne the municipal authorities stipulated in 1478 that all male and female beggars who were licensed to beg had to do work on non-feast days unless they were crippled, lame or blind.[298] And even in cases of private charity, such charity stipulated a form of means-testing the recipient. In a series of wills made between 1392 and 1421 by citizens of Paris who left legacies to the poor, the poor were to be carefully selected: before charitable handouts were to be publicly distributed, the testators asked that the beggars were to be screened, so that alms were only given to those who were genuinely unable to work.[299] Similarly, a bequest left in a will of 1427 by Oxfordshire man Thomas Mokking specified "26s. 8d. to be distributed among aged poor, blind, cripples, and those unable to work"[300]—here emphasis was placed not just on the earlier medieval category of the 'needy' as recipients of charity but specifically connected with the in/ability to work. In 1418 a former mayor of Norwich, Walter Danyell, made "bequests of one shilling each to the bedridden paupers in his own parish" plus "2d a week for one year to every old, blind, paralysed or otherwise infirm parishioner"—parochialism at its most obvious—and "of 4d to each sick person begging there", by implication censuring able-bodied beggars, and finally considering the "most deserving and crippled residents" of the remainder of Norwich with twenty shillings to be distributed every Friday for one year.[301] Another Norwich burgess, William Setman, left ten pounds in 1429 to "the poor and especially the lame, the blind or the severely disabled *residing continually in Norwich*" (original emphasis), thus also displaying a preference for localism.[302] And in a will proven on 20 November 1459, the Southampton burgess William Soper provided for gifts to be made to the poor on the day of his funeral, as long as these were "married men and women, the decrepit, blind and lame".[303]

By the fifteenth century in some instances opinion about the ability to work had become so refined that even the condition of being physically impaired was not necessarily a carte blanche for receiving charity. The Franciscan Francesc Eiximenis (†1409), no doubt thinking of his own domicile of Barcelona, argued against cities supporting beggars, since they could find work, even the disabled among them, so that the blind might make things with their hands (one is reminded of the stereotypical blind basket-weaver), while "lame folks could carry burdens on their shoulders" (one wonders how), and "those without feet could teach, write, or sell" (more plausible but dependent on educational circumstances).[304] Similarly, the Italian humanist Alberti thought that "even the blind can make themselves useful working in a ropemaker's workshop".[305] And in England by the early modern period, to provide an example of diachronic contrast to the Middle Ages, towns had begun to follow "continental practice and humanist precept in assuming that some form of work could and should be found even for the most disabled members of society."[306]

The analysis by Sharon Farmer of beggars' bodies in high medieval Paris led her to three strands of scholarly assessment: one was to look at the mind–body binary (and associated groupings of rational–irrational, male–female, rich–poor) according to which beggars (whether physically impaired or able-bodied) are placed firmly in the 'body' category; the second was to compare medieval didactic texts on the abuse of cosmetics by women with the fraud committed by (some) beggars in faking physical impairments; and the third strand concluded that women, especially if female saints, were reduced to "bodily signs" rather than embracing all facets of their individual characters.[307] While providing a useful insight into the study of gender stereotypes in the Middle Ages, Farmer's analytical premise does, however, neglect the wider meanings and connotations of poverty, beggars and physical impairment that medieval theory and practice demonstrated. So the use of cosmetics, which is generally condemned by medieval writers, is in fact expressly permitted to be used by women who are mutilated or physically impaired. None other than Thomas Aquinas had declared that, although he despised the use of cosmetics as such, in certain circumstances women were allowed to wear cosmetics "as a means to rectify unavoidable blemishes, especially those incurred by illness."[308]

Nevertheless, because beggars were believed to artificially modify their physical appearance, the poor who needed to beg were not trusted, and the elites therefore "thought it important to scrutinize the bodies of the poor carefully, for the truth of their abilities and disabilities—and hence of their proper roles in society—lay in their bodies".[309] While this may be valid for late thirteenth-century and early fourteenth-century French canonisation proceedings, the exact opposite started occurring in early fifteenth-century Germany. There, the begging laws of Cologne, enacted around 1435, forbade all able-bodied and healthy people to beg, but also required that those legitimate, the sick or impaired beggars covered themselves up[310]—they were not to annoy the good citizens with the smell and sight of their disgusting wounds and infirmities.[311] The city of Nuremberg, too, in a new version of its begging laws dating from 1478, stated that beggars were to keep their physical ailments under cover, particularly so as not to cause pregnant women to be affected through such sights[312]—this exemplifies the notion of the maternal imagination as impacting on the developing fetus. Probably influenced by nearby Nuremberg, the city of Regensburg also ordered beggars with contagious diseases, severe physical ailments or impairments to stay away from pregnant women.[313] Even in the narrative of the thirteenth-century miracles of Saint Louis studied by Farmer, the sight of a severely disabled person is something that contemporaries did not always welcome: Amelot of Chambly was so afflicted by her impairment (her body bent probably by spinal tuberculosis), that she could only crawl around Saint Denis, her head just held above the ground, which caused the children of the town to flee when they saw her coming.[314] Therefore, physical blemish or impairment had become something shameful that must be hidden, while conversely being the justifying factor for legitimate begging. With regard to their appearance, both their dirty, torn clothes and their physical condition, giving off a disagreeable odour and covered in pustulating sores, the begging poor person is sometimes described as *abiectus*, literally as abject, in the sources.[315] The abject situation of being both poor and disabled becomes even more apparent in the incidents Guy de Chauliac related in his eye-witness account from Avignon in 1348 of the Black Death:

> Many have speculated on the cause of this great mortality. In some places they believed the Jews had poisoned the world, and so they killed them. In others, they believed it was the mutilated poor, and so they drove them away.[316]

Needless to say, as an educated university graduate and personal surgeon to three of the Avignon popes, Guy de Chauliac dismisses 'their' arguments, 'they' being the ignorant masses, and places the causes for the plague firmly in the realm of scientific and medical paradigms—an active, universal cause based on astrological conjunctions, and a passive, particular cause based on "the disposition of each body, such as cachochymia [bad digestion], debility, or obstruction, whence it was that the working men or those living poorly died."[317]Abjection was a double-edged sword in this case, leading to both social and physical reactions, in that the persecution of the "mutilated poor" was added to the observation that they were more likely to succumb to the disease in the first place.

The importance of physical appearance, and specifically of physical impairment, for not just legitimated but also for successful begging, can also be understood from medieval literary texts, where the theme of the lame person who is miraculously healed against their will is a recurring topic. Some examples: in the *vitae* of Saint Martin of Tours, starting with the so-called Pseudo-Odon version dating to the turn of the eleventh to twelfth century, stories relating to the translation of the saint's relics from Auxerre to Tours can be found. Two lame men (variously referred to as *paralitici* in the Latin text, *kontret* in the twelfth-century rhymed *vita*, and *contrefaictz* in the fifteenth-century version) are terrified at the thought of being healed by the imminent miracle; one says to the other:

> Behold, brother, we live a life of soft leisure . . . and it is this infirmity by which we are cast down that lays claim to all of this for us. But— God forbid!—if we were to be cured, manual labour, to which we are unaccustomed, would weigh us down by necessity.

> (*Ecce frater, sub molli otio vivimus . . . hoc autem totum nobis vindicat infirmitas haec qua jacemus; quae si curata fuerit, quod absit, necessario nobis incumbet labor manuum insolitus.*)[318]

Because life lived off alms is so convenient, the two lame men decide to flee before the impending miracle might occur. In their haste they grab their crutches, with which they used to beg, fling them over their shoulders and run away: in this fashion the miracle does after all take place. In both the *Exempla* of Jacques de Vitry[319] and in the *Golden Legend* of James of Voragine,[320] as well as in a religious drama probably performed in Tours in 1441,[321] one finds a similar narrative, except that it is a blind and a lame man[322] who does not wish to be cured by the powers of Saint Martin, but all the other elements of the topos are present.[323] The physical impairment of each of them is their justification for obtaining alms, but they are afraid of physical labour; therefore, they try to avoid the miracle happening, but the crowd prevents them from escaping, and so they are healed against their will.[324] There is a suspicion in some medieval moralising texts that disabled beggars are making a better living by collecting alms than people think. Sharon Farmer has called this the theme of the avaricious beggar, who publicly begs but privately has hoarded a mass of wealth.[325] But secular literature, too, aroused this suspicion. In one of Franco Sacchetti's fourteenth-century stories "it is suggested that one of the blind men, having amassed a great amount of alms over the years, is actually rich, yet he continues to beg".[326]

In another fourteenth-century text, *Pèlerinage de la vie humaine*, the sin of avarice is treated. It was fashionable at the time to criticise in particular this sin, more so than others.[327] Avarice is described as an allegorical figure, surrounded by false images produced by her, e.g. Treachery and Deceivance. In *Pèlerinage*, once Avarice has tampered with the real, old images in churches, she visits all the fraudulent beggars in the land and has them pretend to be crippled and maimed, "orr deff and dowm".[328] These false cripples then come before one of the idols, itself a false image, made by Avarice, and cry out to be made well again—the third falsehood in this series now being a fake miracle as well. The idol which Avarice carries on her head is, significantly, described as itself having a broken back and a limp,[329] hence carrying resonances of the fraudulent disabled persons the idol pretends to cure. A manuscript illumination of this scene can be found in a fourteenth-century French copy of the *Pèlerinage*.[330] Michael Camille said of this illustration of a hunch back and a cripple kneeling before the false image:

> The two cripples are also figures meant to elicit not sympathy but censure, since they are 'professionals', like those in the *exempla* of the two lazy beggars, one blind and the other lame, who vainly try to avoid the relics of St. Martin so they may not be healed and lose their alms.[331]

Speaking in the modern language of the welfare state, these two men are benefit cheats, and as such pose a threat to real, genuine and accredited disabled people.[332] Perhaps it is no coincidence that when, not long after the publication of *Pèlerinage*, Parisian Jean Hubant founded a charitable institution in 1339, he was careful to ensure that preference was given either to the able-bodied who were willing to work or to 'accredited' disabled. The statutes of this foundation, Ave Maria College on the Left Bank of Paris, stipulated that preference should be given to those who work the soil or earn their bread by other work but not to false beggars or those living off fraudulent begging unless they were blind or otherwise debilitated or old and because of that it is necessary for them to beg.[333]

Disability was thus generally regarded as a prerequisite for legitimate begging and/or receiving alms. But other factors, namely, changes in judicial procedures, could impact on the recognition of impairment: with greater physical punishment for crimes, and more mutilation for ever-lesser offences, which became a trend during the later Middle Ages, there was also a greater possibility that a disabled person was seen to be in such a physical condition as a consequence of being a convicted criminal, of having suffered visible mutilation (a theme discussed in Chapter 1, this volume). This seems to have affected in particular people who had for one reason or another lost their ears, since cutting off the ears was a common punishment meted out for theft and other crimes we would now regard as relatively minor. Therefore, people went to great lengths to demonstrate that they were not disabled as a result of judicial mutilation. Similarly, in late medieval Germany a man whose ear had been bitten off by a pig when he was a child produced eminent and honourable witnesses who testified that his deformity was not due to the effects of corporal punishment.[334]

In summary, poverty, impotence and disability formed three strands of a unified theme. In theological terms of the twelfth to fifteenth centuries, poverty and the poor possessed neither dignity (*dignitas*) nor authority (*auctoritas*).[335] "Paupers, according to canon law, were those who passively received alms as a right",[336] which placed them at the bottom of the social hierarchy, and therefore without authority. Without authority, a person was also impotent. We have so returned full circle to the definition of pauper as the antithesis of *potens*.

How some of this concept may have filtered down from the refined intellectual circles of theologians and scholastics to 'ordinary' people can be seen in literary texts. In the thirteenth-century *Roman de la Rose*, for example, the crutch that the allegorical figure of Old Age has to employ is called "potence",[337] the Old French term deriving from the Latin *potens*. In Chaucer's *Troilus and Criseyde*, furthermore, the staff that is used as a crutch by a mobility impaired character is also called his "potente"[338]—this is a rare word in Middle English and probably derived from the Old French or Latin *potentes*. Interestingly, the T-cross used since the late twelfth century by the Antonite order as an emblem of St Anthony is in German also called the *Krückenkreuz* or Latinised as *potentia*.[339] Here the material prop used as a crutch literally becomes the thing that gives power to the person, in this case the power of movement: it empowers both physically and nominally. The opposite, where a person is described as *im*potent due to the lack of ability for movement, can be found in a near-contemporary will dated 2 August 1400, where Sir Richard de Scrop, lord of Bolton, left a sum of money to people who were "lame, blind or impotent, being bedridden".[340] And in a medieval will from Somerset "72 poor persons, impotent, lying in beds" were to be given lengths of cloth.[341] Impotent meaning powerless could also entail being incapable of fulfilling one's obligations. In this sense William Attetonneshend of Oakington (Cambridgeshire), one of the peasants on the estates of Crowland abbey, relinquished his holding due to his impotence (*propter impotenciam suam*), as he was no longer capable of working the land.[342] In the opposite meaning of the term, an agricultural bylaw from Leighton Buzzard in Bedfordshire, dating to 1469, referred to the able-bodied peasant as someone who is *potens*; such people were not allowed to glean during harvest time, which only the young, old and disabled were permitted to do.[343]

The impotent as a group also featured in a statute of Henry VII (1503), which stipulated that those in authority to punish beggars and vagabonds were entitled to diminish this punishment for men and women aged over sixty, pregnant women and for the sick and impotent of both sexes.[344] Henry also arranged for distribution of alms on his anniversary, which was endowed in 1504, and to be performed by Westminster Abbey, taking care to exclude 'sturdy beggars', so that of the total sum of twenty pounds provided on each occasion, sixteen pounds, thirteen shillings and four pence was to be given to "the blind, lame, impotent, and most needy persons among those actually coming to the monastery on the day in question", while the smaller part of three pounds, six shillings and eight pence was to be shared among the residents of the almshouses founded by the king in the precinct, and among the blind, lame, bedridden, and most needy residents in the monastery itself, the town of Westminster, or the city and suburbs of London who could not come for alms in person, and among prisoners in Westminster and London.[345]

So during a period generally seen as becoming harsher toward begging and the poor in general, the concept of the particularly deserving poor still existed and was defined according to their degree of *potentas* or rather lack thereof. Later in the sixteenth century, the English writer William Harrison classified the poor into three "degrees" and subcategories. Interestingly even in 1577–1587 the impotence of the poor was still something to be remarked upon. Harrison's categories were:

1   The poor by impotence
1.1   the fatherlesse child
1.2   the aged, blind and lame
1.3   the diseased person that is iudged to be incurable
2   The poor by casualty
2.1   the wounded soldier
2.2   the decaied householder
2.3   the sicke persone visited with grieuous . . . disease
3   The poor thriftless
3.1   the riotour that hath consumed all
3.2   that vagabund that will abide no where
3.3   the rog[u]e and strumpet[346]

In this scheme of categorisation Harrison was very much expressing (late) medieval concepts. Modern sociological concepts, in contrast, would focus on notions of poverty as caused by life cycle (orphans who are too young to work, widows with small children, the elderly) and accident (illness, injury, physical impairment).

   Physical impairment could also be seen as the uppermost of a sliding scale of moral and anatomical defects that push the pauper ever downward. The thirteenth-century preacher Peregrine of Oppeln, a Polish mendicant friar, opined that if at first the pauper is hungry, blind, lame, sick, smitten by leprosy, orphaned or old, then subsequently he declines to a state of dependency, baseness and contempt.[347] The concepts of the disabled as impotent and abject are thus only separated by degrees. Being poor and disabled is the prime cause for despondency leading to sins of desire, envy and hopelessness. But disability on its own need not carry a stigma. "In the medieval context, stigma was sometimes attached to disability alone, but it occurred much more frequently when poverty and involuntary begging were also involved."[348] This is also exemplified in a series of antifraternal and Wycliffite sermon texts from the beginning of the fifteenth century, where "a concrete and familiar definition of need" is entered into: "only the poor who are disabled should be called to the feast or rewarded with material goods."[349] Resonances of such late medieval concepts of poverty, charity and dis/ability are encountered in contemporary anxieties about the 'undeserving' recipients of welfare benefits. Kate Crassons makes the point most clearly in her comparison of medieval notions of poverty with its modern counterpart: by reminding us of "medieval labor laws and anti-fraternal discourse", we become aware of a "continued resistance to the notion of a legitimate form of able-bodied poverty" and recognise "the assumption that those capable of labor cannot be truly poor—a profound myth that has flourished in our cultural imagination thanks in no small part to the legacy of medieval poverty polemic."[350]

As Bronislaw Geremek has observed:

> The authentic poor were those for whom work was impossible; that is, the crippled, the sick, the old, widows and orphans. They constituted the approved and acceptable body of people receiving assistance. They alone were entitled to protection, to a place in a refuge or a hospital, to receive alms and to beg.[351]

However, Geremek's observation needs an important qualification with regard to charity and the elderly: old age on its own did not mean an automatic entitlement to charitable handouts. Already in the fifth century Salvian, a German convert to Christianity who first became a monk at Lerins and subsequently a priest at Marseilles, had qualified that it was the "wretched old", not just the old in general, who arouse us to pity in the same way as "weeping mothers" and "little children in tears".[352] So instead of all of the elderly being categorised as needy, only if the consequence of being old happened to entail for a particular person that they became impoverished or physically debilitated, then they would be covered by one or the other categories (crippled, sick) that Geremek believed medieval people recognised.[353] Nevertheless, the inability to work of many (but not necessarily *all*) disabled people led to their ambiguous position, especially in the Italian cities:

> Their impossibility to work often placed them on the margins of their communities as beggars who were seen as either the recipients of the Christian *caritas* or as the embodiment of the social parasite who was to be shunned or expelled from civic centres altogether.[354]

Being physically—and visibly—impaired was one way to be categorised among the 'classical' definition of the needy and truly deserving poor, together with widows and orphans. This acceptance of certain physically impaired persons among such groups that deserved charitable handouts is the nearest equivalent from the Middle Ages to the modern concept of special (material) needs of the disabled: in their perceived inability to work, the impaired become the disabled, and thus the deserving recipients of charity. A visual representation makes this point very succinctly: the manuscript illumination in Domenico Lenzi's fourteenth-century Florentine chronicle, *Specchio umano* or *Human Mirror*, which illustrates the role of the confraternity of Orsanmichele in distributing charitable resources during the dearth of 1329, depicts two blind and lame men together with a pregnant woman, sitting below the stall or office of the confraternity's official, as the very emblems of the anonymous mass of the 'deserving poor'.[355]

Conclusion

One story from the archives, a particular episode from the *Miracles* of Saint Louis,[1] may elucidate the cultural, social and economic aspects of disability that have been described in the preceding chapters, for in that single narrative, with the exception of ageing, all the multifarious strands (law, work and charity) of the social history of disability in the Middle Ages presented in this volume come together. The episode has already been discussed by Sharon Farmer,[2] but the interpretation given in the following highlights significant points either omitted or read differently. A formerly deaf and mute man known as Louis, who presented evidence at the panel investigating the miracles of King Louis IX of France sometime between May 1282 and March 1283, when he was in his early thirties, is the subject. Essentially, this text is an example of the hagiographical material encountered since the early thirteenth-century application of inquisitorial processes into investigations regarding sanctity, where miracles are no longer narrated in simple prose but concentrated on questions of who were the protagonists, what happened to them and what conditions were they in, where and when did events occur, which imparts a certain legalistic—even forensic—tone that to the modern reader lends such texts an aura of quasi-scientific authenticity. We, just as our thirteenth-century forbears, are more likely to 'believe' events if they are presented to us in a certain way: scientific in the twenty-first century, inquisitorial in the thirteenth.[3] For such reasons, these later, formalised miracle 'protocols' tend to provide much more incidental detail than earlier medieval texts about the cultural, social and even economic circumstances of individual protagonists. It is the details of this particular story that provide valuable insights into the cultural context of, at the very least, one disabled individual's social and economic condition.

Around 1257, when he was eight years old, Louis had been found alone, but not necessarily abandoned,[4] at Orgelet near Lake Geneva, and was taken in by Gauchier, the local smith. This is an example of the sometimes potential and in this case actual integration of the disabled, living in rural settings within a single household—*familia* being 'family' in the widest sense.[5]

Louis was both deaf and mute, a condition that the text asserts was tested repeatedly for veracity by various means (blasting a horn in his ear, hitting and slapping him to make him cry out, even throwing burning coals on his stomach "to prove whether or not he could speak and if he was truly mute"[6]). Louis remained with Gauchier the smith for twelve years, i.e. until he was around twenty years old, during which time he worked for him, at first blowing "on the fires of the smith to light the forge", then "when he had grown stronger he assisted the smith with a hammer and helped out in other ways in the house, having been shown what to do with signs."[7] This episode is especially illuminating with regard to perceptions of the working in/ability of disabled persons, both medieval and modern. Being deaf and mute was obviously no hindrance to Louis's training, in comparative fashion to a standard metalworking apprenticeship, in the art of smithing. The problem of the communication of deaf people during a period prior to both dedicated educational and linguistic measures is apparently not an issue in this story: physical tasks, which Louis was obviously capable of, could be communicated with signs, even if this limited communication did not permit the transmission of abstract concepts, such as cultural or religious practices.

On leaving the smith, perhaps after the customary length of apprenticeship, he went to Lyon with the countess of Auxerre,[8] where he started following the French king, Philip, living "on the alms of the king's court and of the other nobles" in Philip's entourage.[9] Becoming a kind of professional recipient of alms is just the kind of scenario for Louis in the thirteenth century that was described more anonymously for the later reigns of the English kings Edward III, Richard II and Henry IV, who maintained varying numbers of *oratores*, accredited 'poor' persons, like Louis, permanently trailing the court.

Following the court he came as far as Saint Denis, "where he viewed the entombing of the bones of the blessed Saint Louis, as he now recalls, now that he understands those events, because at the time he did not know what they were doing".[10] In this context the miracle text displays parallels to the notions of the cognitive disability of congenitally deaf persons in theological and legal texts. The miracle account is at great pains to make clear that simply because of his incidental attachment to the royal court as recipient of alms Louis the deaf-mute happened to find himself at what was to become the shrine of Saint Louis, and he entered the church because he was used to imitating what other people did in such a building, without actually *knowing* what he was doing. Three times in brief succession the text emphasises that he did so ignorantly, we might say subconsciously, because as yet

> he did not know or understand anything about God and his saints. However, when he was with Gauchier and his wife . . . he had often seen them go to church and pray there and have devotion, and kneel and raise their eyes with their hands joined together and raised to the sky. For that reason he now went to the church [of Saint Denis], but not because he knew what a church was or what devotion was . . . And

thus it happened that when the blessed king was entombed, because he saw the other men kneeling and praying at the tomb, he too knelt and joined his hands without knowing what he was doing.[11]

Toward the end of the narrative, after the miracle has occurred which enabled Louis to hear and speak, the point concerning this lack of knowledge, Louis's inability to understand the Christian faith, is picked up again by the panel at the investigative hearing. The inquisitors ask Louis why he believed he was cured through a miracle, "since at that time you had no belief or faith or devotion for him [Saint Louis], and you had come to the tomb by happenstance?"[12] Louis replied that "he knew of no other cause of his belief [in the potential miracle] except that he was in need of this benefit."[13] This makes an interesting statement concerning the condition of the supplicant: 'need' alone justifies the miraculous event, an attitude in stark contrast with later medieval thaumaturgic miracles, where the moral condition of the supplicant is as, if not more, important than physical need.[14]

Additionally, Louis apparently did not know what a king or barons were; hence, besides the religious ignorance—or innocence—already described he was also possessed of social ignorance. The miracle text therefore makes important observations concerning the ambiguous interaction of the disabled, especially the deaf, with the non-disabled. Louis can 'go through the motions', as it were, of social interactions, he can participate by imitation, he can 'fit in' superficially, yet all the while remaining unaware of what it is that he is doing. Louis is, arguably, a liminal figure, who is permanently situated at the borders of social and religious conventions: ostensibly he is an adult, but like a child he is incapable of speech and unaware of the meaning behind actions, objects or people's social status.

While at Saint Denis Louis turned to the abbey for alms "and thus, because of religious charity, he found enough to eat"[15]—a further reference to the different manifestations of charity as discussed in the eponymous chapter. On his last day at Saint Denis the miracle that 'cured' him occurred, and he suddenly found himself able to hear, an event that frightened him so much that he left Saint Denis the very same day, trying to make his way back to Orgelet by retracing the route he had come. The question of the veracity of this miracle has, unsurprisingly, attracted the attention of modern commentators. Sharon Farmer, for instance, has questioned the congenital origin of Louis's deafness, pointing out that "Louis must have been able to hear when he was born, since adults who have been deaf since birth cannot learn to speak, even if they do gain the ability to hear as adults",[16] a view concurred by modern linguistic science. More importantly, his ability to now "hear and perceive the voices of beasts and men and the sounds of other things" nevertheless did not lead to an equally sudden cognitive awareness: "However, he did not understand nor did he know how to judge what it was, because he had never before heard anything."[17] He had also been 'cured' of his muteness, but he could not employ this faculty as yet: "Nor could he speak, because he did not know how to speak or to form words, although from that time he had the capacity to learn to speak, if anyone would teach him."[18] Notably, this passage appears to precede the learned discussions concerning the acquisition of (verbal) language that were emerging from the university of Paris, in the works of Jean de Jandun, within a few decades of the miracle protocol being taken down.[19] It was recognised, both in the miracle text and the slightly later scholastic discussions, that verbal language was something that one could only learn if one was able to hear spoken words.

Louis, having retraced his steps back to Orgelet, returned to Gauchier the smith and his wife "and made them understand by the best signs that he knew to show them that he could hear. He did not know how to explain this well to the inquisitors", but the smith and his household "understood what he was indicating",[20] which implies that the signed form of communication Louis, Gauchier and *familia* had developed was probably similar to the autochthonous types of signing ('homesigns') described by modern linguists.[21] Interestingly, the text alludes that the inquisitors, i.e. the members of the learned and expert panel charged with investigating the miracles, appear to have been intrigued by this form of communication but seem to not have grasped the conceptual possibility of communicating a lengthy and complicated narrative by means of signed language. Louis may not have been able to explain well to the inquisitors how he could use signs to tell his story, but the people he had lived with for twelve years were quite capable of understanding what it was he was telling them, as the text admits in the very next sentence. Now that Gauchier and household knew Louis could hear, they "began to teach him in the way that very young children are taught, or even as people teach birds", focusing on individual nouns such as 'bread' or 'wine' (and presumably indicating the object in question) while getting Louis to repeat the spoken word. In this passage the association between (formerly) disabled person and child, even pet, evokes certain reminiscences with regard to dwarfs in Chapter 2 of this volume.

Concluding the story, Louis entered into the household of the countess of Auxerre at her request, and "to facilitate his learning to speak she placed him with her kitchen staff, so that he would be with several other people, and ordered that he be taught to speak."[22] Once his verbal language had reached a certain level, one allowing the comprehension of more complex content than simply naming objects, Louis "returned several times to the house of Gauchier, and there he learned from Gauchier and his wife and household that they had found him at the chateau [of Orgelet], and at what age".[23] Acquisition of speech, as well as of hearing, is what finally enables Louis to gain knowledge and understanding, not just of the world around him—his newly gained understanding of the meaning of religious rituals or correctly assigning kings and barons to a certain social status—but also knowledge of himself, of who he is and where he came from. While in his impaired condition, Louis had been disabled in more ways than one, since he was not just physically or sensorily impaired and thereby prevented from participating fully in the social and ritual environment; he was also disabled by being prevented from knowing himself.[24]

Old age has been discussed at length, but one may leave the reader with this extract from *Aucassin et Nicolette*, a thirteenth-century *chantefable*, where mockery of the poor, the old, the infirm and by extension the disabled alludes to several of the themes touched in this volume. The character of Aucassin claims that heaven holds no attractions for him because it is inhabited by such people:

> Those old priests and the aged lame go there and those who have only one arm and who crouch night and day in front of those altars and in those old crypts, and those with old, worn-out cloaks and wearing old rags, who are naked, bare-foot and bare-legged, who die of hunger, thirst, cold and privation. Those people go to heaven and I want nothing to do with them.

> (*Il i vont ci viel prestre et cil viel clop et cil manke qui tote jor et tote nuit cropent devant ces autex et en ces viés croutes, et cil a ces viés capes ereses et a ces viés tatereles vestues, qui sont nu et decauc et estrumelé, qui moeurent de faim et de soi et de froit et de mesaises. Icil vont en paradis: aveuc ciax n'ai jou que faire.*)[25]

Thus the old are despised by the young Aucassin, not for their age as such, but for what it entails, namely, physical debility and poverty. One must remember, however, that this type of satirical literary source skews the picture somewhat. The evidence presented here from the more mundane records of social, legal and economic sources points rather to the integration of both the old and the disabled. Even Le Goff was able to dismiss the disabled in a few well-trodden historiographical clichés:

> Other social outcasts were the sick in general, and above all the crippled and the maimed. In a world where sickness and infirmity were considered to be exterior signs of sin, those who were afflicted with them were cursed by God and thus by man too.[26]

One may counter this with a passage in *Piers Plowman*, where Langland has the figure of Reason advise that one should look at oneself before blaming others, since men cannot create themselves as they wish, for if they could, they would be faultless; instead "whether a man is handsome or ugly, it is no one's business to criticize the shape and form which God created; for all that God did was done well".[27] For Langland, the divinely created body is therefore always a good body, regardless of its physical appearance. Such a comparative approach to medieval texts allows us to gain a somewhat different picture to the rather simplified and stereotyped image of the disabled person as beggar marked by sin, which persisted in medievalist historiography until fairly recently.[28]

Finally, in response to comments and criticisms received following this author's earlier volume on disability, two points need clarifying.

One: the question of gender. Why did gender not feature more in discussions of medieval disability? And, to pre-empt the same question, why does it not feature strongly in this present volume either? After all, when dealing with social aspects, surely gender plays a vital role. The simple response is that the disabled body negates the sexed body. Disabled people are seen, especially in modern societies, as asexual, and are first and foremost defined by their impairment and not by their male or female traits. To the able-bodied, an orthopedically impaired woman is seen first as that gender-neutral being, a wheelchair-user, and only with second thoughts as 'woman'. With few exceptions the narratives from medieval sources presented here fall into the same neutralising mode concerning gender. Medieval disabled women featured as workers, old people and beggars as much as men did. Sharon Farmer had argued that there was a gendered difference according to which disabled people received support, from either their families or wider charitable organisations, so that more young disabled men than young disabled women were encountered as beggars because they were ineligible for such support.[29] However, this conclusion, interesting as it is, is based on a close reading of one single source, namely, on the thirteenth-century miracle stories of Saint Louis, and does not necessarily transfer across to other regions or centuries. Two significant differences concerned female experience of the law and old age: far fewer women than men appeared to be the victims of mutilating punishments, and the image of the old woman as somehow more disgusting, worse and more dangerous than the old man is certainly a gendered difference. Within the scope of this work it has not been possible to examine in detail the comic treatment of disabled persons in medieval literature, but one other gender difference suggested by Claudia Gottwald with regard to medieval and Renaissance texts, and also continuously from the seventeenth century onwards, indicates disabled men were almost exclusively the object of comedy, but not disabled women.[30]

Two: the distinction between illness and disability. It has been pointed out to me that my previous research did not look at illness enough, or that the distinction between illness and impairment had been painted as too drastic a picture. Modern disability theory still has problems in delineating exactly the boundaries between illness and disability, especially with regard to chronic illness.[31] There may sometimes be a more fluid relationship between illness and disability, but generally they are treated as two distinct conceptual and cultural categories. Even in the social and economic sources that have been drawn together here illness was seen as something quite separate from what we would now call 'disability'. To recall just one poignant example: the blind beggars of Zülpich stipulated in their fraternity statutes that blind members should help each other in times of sickness—being blind was emphatically *not* an illness. The incurable, by human agency at least, and permanent state of impairment is precisely what made it liminal, sits uneasily between categories of health and illness, and, in social, legal and general cultural terms, *sometimes* led to a 'special treatment' of medieval disabled persons.

Notes

NOTES TO THE INTRODUCTION

1. "In der Historikerzunft herrschte lange Zeit die Meinung vor, der Körper des Menschen gehöre zur Natur und nicht zur Kultur. Und doch hat der Körper eine Geschichte, er ist Teil von ihr, ja, gestaltet sie sogar, genauso wie die ökonomischen und gesellschaftlichen Strukturen es tun oder die geistigen Repräsentationen, deren Produkt und Vermittler er zugleich ist" (Jacques Le Goff and Nicolas Truong, Die *Geschichte des Körpers in Mittelalter*, trans. Renate Warttmann [Stuttgart: Klett-Cotta, 2007], 18).
2. The (over-)reliance on autobiography as a way of doing Disability Studies/ History was yet again emphasised by a series of essays which arose from the proceedings of a conference in 2004 trying to get to grips with disability in historical perspective. Medieval disability was conspicuous by its almost complete absence (the exception ratifying the rule being an article on the deafness of fifteenth-century nun Teresa de Cartagena), not surprisingly, since if autobiography is the only source deemed permissible for disability history, then disability history perforce cannot exist prior to the creation of such texts. See the special essay section in *Publications of the Modern Language Association of America* 120 (2005): 495–641.
3. Jacques Le Goff, *Medieval Civilization 400–1500*, trans. J. Barrow (Oxford: Blackwell, 1988), 240.
4. Paul K. Longmore and Lauri Umansky, eds., *The New Disability History: American Perspectives* (New York: New York University Press, 2002), 6.
5. A prime example is the article by Richard Stensman, 'The Paraplegic Viking and the Onearmed Pianist—Some Well Known Persons with Locomotor Disability', *Scandinavian Journal of Rehabilitation Medicine. Supplement* 9 (1983): 82–87, where the single medieval entry (at 82) is rather telling, both in its terseness as in the topics it addressed:

   > Ivar Beinlausi . . . who according to Encyclopaedica Britannica died in 873, was one of the sons of the viking chieftain Ragnar Lothbrok. He was tall, handsome and clever. His legs, however, "were like cartilage" and he was carried on a stretcher or a big shield. The cause of his handicap is not known. He became the most famous of the brothers.

   So 'despite of' his disability, Ivar Beinlausi (the epithet actually means "the bone-less") was handsome *and* clever, achieving fame above his siblings, while regrettably for the medical author no anamnesis or causality could be reconstructed. Case closed.
6. Margaret A. Winzer, 'Disability and Society before the Eighteenth Century: Dread and Despair', in *The Disability Studies Reader*, 1st ed., ed. Lennard

J. Davis (London: Routledge, 1997), 75–109; Edward Wheatley, 'Medieval Constructions of Blindness in France and England', in op. cit., 3rd ed. (2010). In fairness to Winzer, the available secondary literature at the time was pretty much restricted to the above-criticised progressivist tomes written during the late nineteenth century and the first half of the twentieth century.

7. Catherine J. Kudlick, 'Disability History: Why We Need another "Other"', *American Historical Review* 108, no. 3 (2003): 763–93; see also Douglas Baynton's classic 'Disability: A Useful Category of Historical Analysis', *Disability Studies Quarterly* 17 (Spring 1997): 82–96; and the review article by Julie Anderson, 'Voices in the Dark: Representations of Disability in Historical Research', *Journal of Contemporary History* 4, no. 1 (2009): 107–16. Lennard Davis's foundational analysis, *Enforcing Normalcy: Disability, Deafness, and the Body* (London: Verso, 1995), paved the way for recognition of the cultural construction of disability, while more recently disability theory is explicitly named as a parallel to queer theory, the obvious reference being to Robert McRuer, *Crip Theory: Cultural Signs of Queerness and Disability* (New York: New York University Press, 2006); his theory of compulsory able-bodiedness is the central concept.

8. Anne Hudson, *The Premature Reformation, Wycliffite Texts and Lollard History* (Oxford: Clarendon Press, 1988), 517.

9. Sharon Farmer, 'A Deaf-Mute's Story', in *Medieval Christianity in Practice*, ed. Miri Rubin, (Princeton, NJ: Princeton University Press, 2009), 207, claims "the narrative offers us an insider's view of what it was like to be deaf"; see discussion in the conclusion to this volume.

10. On the problem of historical identity, see L. L. Downs, 'If "Woman" Is Just an Empty Category, Why Am I Afraid to Walk Alone at Night? Identity Politics Meets the Postmodern Subject', *Comparative Studies in Society and History* 35 (1993): 416. In reaction to Barbara Ehrenreich's book, *Nickel and Dimed: On (Not) Getting by in America* (2001), on poverty in the contemporary US, a critic has complained that Ehrenreich's experience was somehow 'fake' because she only temporarily lived the life of the subjects of her book, stating her research method is "the journalistic equivalent of learning what it's like to be blind by closing your eyes" (cited in Kate Crassons, *The Claims of Poverty: Literature, Culture, and Ideology in Late Medieval England* [Notre Dame, IN: University of Notre Dame Press, 2010], 287). This neatly problematises the concept that one may only discuss those conditions, whether they be disability or poverty, which one experiences 'genuinely' and 'authentically'. According to this line of thinking, one could not do any form of historical research without a time-machine, since one wasn't there to 'experience' it firsthand.

11. Among a wealth of secondary literature a succinct introduction to the problem is given in L. E. Mitchell, ed., *Women in Medieval Western European Culture* (New York: Garland, 1999).

12. Irina Metzler, *Disability in Medieval Europe: Thinking about Physical Impairment during the High Middle Ages, c.1100–1400*, Routledge Studies in Medieval Religion and Culture 5 (London: Routledge, 2006), 27.

13. R. J. Evans, In *Defence of History* (London: Granta Books, 1997), 213.

14. Ibid.

15. Shulamith Shahar, *Growing Old in the Middle Ages: 'Winter Clothes Us in Shadow and Pain'*, trans. Yael Lotan (London: Routledge, 1997), 7.

16. Ibid., 11.

17. *Cours de linguistique générale*, published posthumously 1916 [*Course in General Linguistics*, ed. Charles Bally and Albert Sechehaye, trans. Roy Harris (La Salle, IL: Open Court Publishing, 1983)].

18. See the discussion in Metzler, *Disability*, 4–5. The multitudinous medieval terminology has also been emphasised by Walter Fandrey, *Krüppel, Idioten, Irre. Zur Sozialgeschichte behinderter Menschen in Deutschland* (Stuttgart: Silberburg-Verlag, 1990), 19.

19. *Omne Bonum: A Fourteenth-Century Encyclopedia of Universal Knowledge*, ed. Lucy Freeman Sandler. 2 vols. (London: Harvey Miller, 1996), I:100; compiled in the third quarter of the fourteenth century, *Omne Bonum* was discussing debility with regard to the question of physical defects and the un/suitability to clerical office.

20. Nicholas Orme and Margaret Webster, *The English Hospital, 1070–1570* (New Haven, CT: Yale University Press, 1995), 119.

21. Discussed in Metzler, *Disability*, 3–10.

22. Moshe Barasch, *Blindness: The History of a Mental Image in Western Thought* (New York: Routledge, 2001), 3.

23. See the discussion in Metzler, *Disability*, 31 and 68. On theories of liminality pertaining more generally to a medieval context, see Caroline Walker Bynum, 'Women's Stories, Women's Symbols: A Critique of Victor Turner's Theory of Liminality', in *Anthropology and the Study of Religion*, ed. Robert L. Moore and Frank E. Reynolds (Chicago: Centre for the Scientific Study of Religion, 1984), 105–25.

24. Given in Faith Wallis, ed., *Medieval Medicine: A Reader. Readings in Medieval Civilizations and Cultures XV* (Toronto: University of Toronto Press, 2010), 212; cf. M. McVaugh and L. García Ballester, 'Therapeutic Method in the Later Middle Ages: Arnau de Vilanova on Medical Contingency', *Caduceus* 11 (1995): 76–86.

25. *Compendium theologiae*, 1 chap. 136, in *Opera Omnia* 42 (Rome, 1979) 1–205, at 133, cited and trans. in D. L. D'Avray, *Medieval Religious Rationalities: A Weberian Analysis* (Cambridge: Cambridge University Press, 2010), 37.

26. Kathryn Hollins, 'Between Two Worlds: The Social Implications of Cochlear Implantation for Children Born Deaf', in *Madness, Disability and Social Exclusion: The Archaeology and Anthropology of 'Difference'. One World Archaeology 40*, ed. Jane Hubert (London: Routledge, 2000), 181; cf. A. Franky, *The Wounded Storyteller: Body, Illness and Ethics* (Chicago: University of Chicago Press, 1995).

27. R. Murphy, *The Body Silent* (London: Phoenix House, 1987), 112.

28. *Urkundenbuch der Stadt Hildesheim*, ed. R. Doebner, 8 vols. (Hildesheim, 1901; rpt. 1980), IV, 375–76 on the revised statutes of 1440, cited by Diana Webb, *Pilgrims and Pilgrimage in the Medieval West* (London: I. B. Tauris, 1999), 91.

29. Metzler, *Disability*, 156–57.

30. Old English had related terms such as 'hægtesse', from which derived the more familiar 'hag'. See I. Metzler, 'Responses to Physical Impairment in Medieval Europe: Between Magic and Medicine', *Medizin, Gesellschaft und Geschichte* 18 (1999): 29–30; also Claude Lecouteux, 'Hagazusa—Striga—Hexe', *Hessische Blätter für Volks- und Kulturforschung* 18 (1985): 57ff., according to whom the term dates from the tenth century. A summary of Old English notions of the 'hægtesse' can be found in Alaric Hall, *Elves in Anglo-Saxon England: Matters of Belief, Health, Gender and Identity. Anglo-Saxon Studies 8* (Woodbridge: Boydell Press, 2007), 175. The collective expression for Grendel and his mother in the Old English *Beowulf* is *mearcstapa*, 'the stepper on the margin', thus the monstrous can also be deemed the liminal, since being *on* the margin is being on the border, not beyond it. See also Joyce Tally Lionarons, 'Bodies, Buildings, and Boundaries: Metaphors

of Liminality in Old English and Old Norse Literature', *Essays in Medieval Studies* 11 (1994): 43–50.

31. Michael Goodich, ed., *Other Middle Ages: Witnesses at the Margins of Medieval Society* (Philadelphia: University of Pennsylvania Press, 1998), 221.

32. Victor Turner, *The Ritual Process: Structure and Anti-Structure* (London: Routledge and Kegan Paul, 1969), 94–95. Turner (at 96) called the liminal phase of rites "a 'moment in and out of time,' and in and out of secular social structure". For a medievalist's critique of Turner, see Caroline Walker Bynum, *Fragmentation and Redemption: Essays on Gender and the Human Body in Medieval Religion* (New York: Zone Books, 1992), 27–51, who, however, as implied in the subtitle, concentrates on gender without considerations of (non-gendered) health.

33. Patricia Baker and Han Nijdam, 'Introduction: Conceptualizing Body, Space and Borders', in *Medicine and Space: Body, Surroundings and Borders in Antiquity and the Middle Ages. Visualising the Middle Ages 4*, ed. P. A. Baker, H. Nijdam and K. van 't Land (Leiden: Brill, 2012), 12.

34. The story of Paul's conversion is given in three slightly differing versions: Acts 9:1–9, Acts 22:6–11 and Acts 26:13–18.

35. Barasch, *Blindness*, 58.

36. Ibid., 59.

37. Ibid., 60, actually refers to the episode as "chiastic" blindness, which in itself is interesting, since chiasma refers to a cross-shaped intersection, a cross-roads, hence a concept similar to the being-on-the-boundary of liminality.

38. In her dissertation for a doctorate of theology, Teresa Leann Reeve, *Luke 3:1–4:15 and the Rite of Passage in Ancient Literature: Liminality and Transformation* (PhD diss., University of Notre Dame, 2008, available at http://historiantigua.cl/wp-content/uploads/2011/08/Luke-3.1–4.15–and-the-rite-of-passage-in-ancient-literature.-Liminality-and-transformation.pdf, accessed 28 February 2012) had already explored ways in which Turner's anthropological model of rite of passage is useful for interpreting the portrayal of Saul's transformation from persecutor to witness in Chapter 9 of Acts, but had neglected the liminal aspects of blindness as an impairment/disability—in fact, the latter two words are not mentioned once in the entire thesis. Conversely, in his recent study of blindness as a disability, Edward Wheatley, *Stumbling Blocks before the Blind: Medieval Constructions of a Disability* (Ann Arbor: University of Michigan Press, 2010), frequently refers to the construction of disability but never once to the experience of Saul/Paul as a rite of passage.

39. Considering which of these terms is the better to use, one may point out that marginal groups were more likely to be excluded or persecuted than were liminal ones. The argument concerning a persecuting society with regard to the similarities between the treatment of Jews, heretics and lepers was made especially by R. I. Moore, who regarded the Fourth Lateran council of 1215 as a defining moment in creating, on the foundations of developments made during the preceding century, a "comprehensive apparatus of persecution", but which, significantly, did not extend to disability (R. I. Moore, *The Formation of a Persecuting Society* [Oxford: Blackwell, 1987], 66).

40. Carole Rawcliffe, *Medicine for the Soul: The Life, Death and Resurrection of an English Medieval Hospital* (Stroud: Sutton, 1999), 44. Adam J. Davis, 'Preaching in Thirteenth-Century Hospitals', *Journal of Medieval History* 36 (2010): 88, has also described hospitals to have a kind of liminal status, "betwixt and between" the earthly and heavenly worlds, but he acknowledges his debt to Victor Turner's anthropology.

41. Roberta Gilchrist, 'Medieval Bodies in the Material World: Gender, Stigma and the Body', in *Framing Medieval Bodies*, ed. Sarah Kay and Miri Rubin (Manchester: Manchester University Press, 1994), 49.

42. Goodich, *Other Middle Ages*, 223.

43. Anne Irene Riisøy, 'Outlawry and Moral Perversion in Old Norse Society', in *Bodies of Knowledge: Cultural Interpretations of Illness and Medicine in Medieval Europe. Studies in Early Medicine 1*, ed. S. Crawford and C. Lee (Oxford: Archaeopress, 2010), 23.

44. Could this be based on an association with the devil, or pre-Christian pagan deities? On this law, cf. R. Keyser and P. A. Munch, eds., *Norges gamle Love indtil 1387*, 5 vols. (Christiana: Trykt hus Chr. Gröndahl, 1846–1895).

45. *Gulathing Law*, chap. 23, trans. L. M. Larson, *The Earliest Norwegian Laws* (New York, 1935), 51, cited in Alexander Murray, *Suicide in the Middle Ages* (Oxford: Oxford University Press, 2000), II:571.

46. Brian Pullan, 'Support and Redeem: Charity and Poor Relief in Italian Cities from the Fourteenth to the Seventeenth Century', *Continuity and Change 3*, no. 2 (1988): 184.

47. Anne Borsay, 'Returning Patients to the Community: Disability, Medicine and Economic Rationality before the Industrial Revolution', *Disability and Society* 13 (1998): 645–63.

48. *Attitudes and Disabled People* (Geneva: World Health Organization, 1980).

49. *The Politics of Disablement* (Basingstoke: Macmillan, 1990).

50. *The Disabled State* (Philadelphia: Temple University Press, 1984).

51. James William Brodman, *Charity and Religion in Medieval Europe* (Washington, DC: Catholic University of America Press, 2009), 1.

NOTES TO CHAPTER 1

1. The literature on the origins, development and enforcement of various medieval laws, plus on the topic of the social effects of law, of crime and concepts of what constituted criminal activity, is of massive extent—for the sake of brevity I would like to point the reader to Susan Reynolds' excellent essay 'Medieval Law', in *The Medieval World*, ed. Peter Linehan and Janet L. Nelson (London: Routledge, 2001), 485–50, which does this vast topic more than justice (pun intended), tracing the prior historiography and including a valuable introductory bibliography.

2. I have elsewhere investigated to what degree legal differentiation was made; whether all impairments were simply bundled together as so-called disabilities or if physical impairments were hierarchised (e.g. was sensory impairment regarded as worse than orthopaedic impairment; was blindness regarded as worse than the loss of one hand?); what inheritance rights disabled people had; or under what circumstances disabled people were permitted to act in a court of law. Hearing impaired persons, for example, had to have a guardian appointed to act on their behalf. See Irina Metzler, 'Reflections on Disability in Medieval Legal Texts: Exclusion—Protection—Compensation', in *Disability and Medieval Law: History, Literature, Society*, ed. Cory Rushton (forthcoming: 2013); also 'Speechless: Speech and Hearing Impairments as a Medieval Legal Problem', in *Studies in Early Medicine 3*, ed. Sally Crawford (forthcoming, Oxford: Archaeopress, 2013).

3. *English Historical Documents, vol. 1 c. 500–1042*, 2nd ed., ed. Dorothy Whitelock (London: Eyre Methuen, 1979), 459. Cnut's laws may be following the example set by two Carolingian capitularies dealing with punishments for

theft, that of Herstal (from 779) and the *capitulare de Latronibus*, with the former stating that for a first conviction the thief should lose an eye, for a second the loss of the nose and death at the third offence (Lisi Oliver, *The Body Legal in Barbarian Law* [Toronto: University of Toronto Press, 2011], 173; Patrick Geary, 'Judicial Violence and Torture in the Carolingian Empire', in *Law and the Illicit in Medieval Europe*, ed. Ruth Mazo Karras, Joel Kaye and E. Ann Matter [Philadelphia: University of Pennsylvania Press, 2008], 81; G. M. Bruce, 'A Note on Penal Blinding in the Middle Ages', *Annals of Medical History* 3 [1941]: 369). Other Carolingian capitularies entitled royal agents to "flog or mutilate law-breakers among unfree (and sometimes also free) persons" and a person who persisted with feuding (*faidosus*) "would be punished by a heavy fine and the loss of a hand" (Janet L. Nelson, 'Violence in the Carolingian World and the Ritualization of Ninth-Century Warfare', in *Violence and Society*, ed. Halsall, 92–93); cf. *Capitularia Regum Francorum* I, 28.v, x, xxiii; 33.xxxvi; 44.v; 130.ii, ed. A. Boretius, MGH Legum Sect. II (Hanover, 1883), I, 51.

4. This notion is examined further in the article by Katherine O'Brien O'Keefe, 'Body and Law in Late Anglo-Saxon England', *Anglo-Saxon England* 27 (1998): 209–32, using evidence from the *Anglo-Saxon Chronicle*, the *Translatio et miracula S. Swithuni* by Lantfred and legal codes. "Mutilation designed for the living body serves multiple purposes. Whatever its function as deterrence, juridical mutilation produces a body about which things may be known . . . [C]onstruing juridical mutilation as a mercy, by making it a happy alternative to eternal death, makes the criminal a partner in his punishment . . . [extending] the power of the law (previously satisfied by external compensation) inward into the criminal's soul" (ibid., 230).

5. For example, in 870 Rastiz, a Moravian *dux*, was convicted of treason, but, due to the mercy of King Louis he was not killed, as the death penalty was the norm for a traitor. Instead he had his eyes put out (*The Annals of Fulda*, trans. Timothy Reuter, Ninth-Century Histories II [Manchester: Manchester University Press, 1992], 64). Under Charlemagne "the conspirators of the Thuringian revolt of 768 were condemned to be blinded, deprived of their honors, and divested of their property" (Geneviève Bührer-Thierry, '"Just Anger" or "Vengeful Anger"? The Punishment of Blinding in the Early Medieval West', in *Anger's Past: The Social Uses of an Emotion in the Middle Ages*, ed. Barbara Rosenwein [Ithaca, NY: Cornell University Press, 1998], 80–81, according to the *Annals of Lorsch*), and exile and blinding (*exilio et caecitate damnatis*) befell those supporting the revolt of Pippin the Hunchback in 792 (according to the *Annals of Fulda*). The seventh-century *Forum Iudicum* (§II, 1, vi) of the Visigothic laws stipulated that a traitor be blinded in both eyes "so that he may not see the wrong in which he wickedly took delight" (cited in Oliver, *Body Legal*, 173; trans. in S. P. Scott, *The Visigothic Code (Forum Iudicum)* [Boston, 1910]).

6. C. Hinckeldey, ed., *Strafjustiz in alter Zeit. Band III der Schriftenreihe des mittelalterlichen Kriminalmuseums Rothenburg ob der Tauber* (Rothenburg-o.-d.-Tauber: Mittelalterliches Kriminalmuseum, 1980), 152. The penalty for perjury was the loss of a hand, namely, of that very hand which one had held up in the gesture of oath-taking, as stipulated by the Saxon and Chamavan laws (Oliver, *Body Legal*, 141–42; and on amputating the hand generally at 172: "In all these cases, the hand is punished for the illegal deed which it performed, respectively, perjury, theft, or forgery"). See A. Harding, 'The Origins of the Crime of Conspiracy', *Transactions of the Royal Historical Society* 5th series 33 (1983): 93, and *Capitularia Regum Francorum*, ed. A. Boretius, MGH Legum Sectio II (Hanover, 1883), I, 124, for a capitulary of 805.

7. For an overview see Jan Ulrich Büttner, 'Die Strafe der Blendung und das Leben blinder Menschen', *Medizin, Gesellschaft und Geschichte* 28 (2009): 47–72.

8. Hinckeldey, *Strafjustiz*, 152. More recent scholarship has shown that this simplistic outline is not quite the case.

9. Exhibition catalogue *Der Sachsenspiegel. Ein Rechtsbuch spiegelt seine Zeit* (Oldenburg: Idensee Verlag, 1996), 42.

10. "Mit dem Spätmittelalter wurden die Körperstrafen vom Abhauen der Hand bis zum Abschneiden der Ohren Teil des Strafrechts" (Ernst Schubert, *Räuber, Henker, arme Sünder. Verbrechen und Strafe im Mittelalter* [Darmstadt: Primus Verlag, 2007], 100 and note 754, observes that *detruncatio*, the punishment of mutilation, already occurs in Tyrolean account books of the fourteenth century).

11. Schubert, *Räuber*, 39 and 104, for the eighty-year-old peasant, who had apparently betrayed three of his neighbouring peasants to the Westphalian enemy: "da stach man einem päuerlein, pei 80jarn, die augen auß, hat drei seiner nachpaurn gen Westvalen geladen"; see the city chronicle of the artisan Heinrich Deichsler, which covers the years up to 1487, in *Städtechroniken* Bd. 10: *Die Chroniken der fränkischen Städte. Nürnberg* Bd. 4 (Leipzig, 1872; rpt. 1961), 352.

12. Mitchell B. Merback, *The Thief, the Cross and the Wheel: Pain and the Spectacle of Punishment in Medieval and Renaissance Europe* (London: Reaktion Books, 1999), 128. For an earlier close study of this theme in seventeenth- and eighteenth-century Amsterdam, see Pieter Spierenburg, *The Spectacle of Suffering: Executions and the Evolution of Repression: From a Preindustrial Metropolis to the European Experience* (Cambridge: Cambridge University Press, 1984).

13. This was an option, albeit only one, of course, for those who could afford to pay it, already found in some of the earlier medieval Germanic/'barbarian' law codes. For instance, according to the Burgundian laws, a Jew who raised his hand against a Christian could redeem his hand (instead of having his right hand severed) "with a fine of seventy-five shillings and a payment of twelve to the public coffer"; similarly the Chamavan law and that of Alfred permitted redemption of the hand, and Lisi Oliver thinks it is likely the same situation existed for Saxony (Oliver, *Body Legal*, 142).

14. Malcolm Letts, *Bruges and Its Past*, 2nd ed. (Bruges: Desclée, De Brower and Co./London: A. G. Berry, 1926), 78.

15. Robert Mills, *Suspended Animation: Pain, Pleasure and Punishment in Medieval Culture* (London: Reaktion Books, 2005), 15.

16. See John Bellamy, *Crime and Public Order in England in the Later Middle Ages* (London: Routledge and Kegan Paul, 1973), 139, 182–83. More recently, Robert Bartlett, *Trial by Fire and Water: The Medieval Judicial Ordeal* (Oxford: Clarendon Press, 1986), has argued in support of this thesis, emphasising that in the high Middle Ages torture made an appearance in judicial systems as an alternative to the ordeal; in contrast, Patrick Geary, 'Judicial Violence', argues for the supplanting of Carolingian torture practices by the ordeal.

17. Miri Rubin, 'Medieval Bodies: Why Now, and How?', in *The Work of Jacques Le Goff and the Challenges of Medieval History*, ed. Miri Rubin (Woodbridge: Boydell Press, 1997), 209 and 217.

18. Many modern popular editions, including Johan Huizinga, *The Waning of the Middle Ages*, trans. F. Hopman (Harmondsworth: Peregrine, 1976); cf. Mills, *Suspended Animation*, 8–11, for an overview of how different historians have approached the "medieval penal imaginary" and how such notions

still influence the modern popular concept of cruel justice equalling medieval justice. Also Valentin Groebner, *Defaced: The Visual Culture of Violence in the Late Middle Ages*, trans. Pamela Selwyn (New York: Zone Books, 2004), 21–29 on modern popular and scholarly perceptions of justice and violence in the later Middle Ages.

19. Bartlett, *Trial by Fire*, 98.
20. Geary, 'Judicial Violence', 82, adding that it is an erroneous view to blame the 'barbarian' legal codes for this, instead judicial violence was inherited from the Roman tradition. See also Bartlett, *Trial by Fire*, 140. On punishments in classical Rome, see R. MacMullen, 'Judicial Savagery in the Roman Empire', in *Romanization in the Time of Augustus*, ed. R. MacMullen (New Haven, CT: Yale University Press, 2000), 204–17.
21. Esther Cohen, *The Modulated Scream: Pain in Late Medieval Culture* (Chicago: University of Chicago Press, 2010), 52–67, summarises the main arguments, noting especially John Langbein, *Torture and the Law of Proof* (Chicago: University of Chicago Press, 1977). The question and answer approach developed by canon law to deal—painlessly—with a variety of issues, from hearing individual confession to assessing heretical beliefs, was transferred to the secular realm where it became "a system of truth-finding by torture and pain masquerading as a system of truth-finding by question and answer" (Cohen, *Modulated Scream*, 67).
22. On the wider issue, beyond the scope of this chapter, of what constituted acceptable governmental violence and the justification for warfare in general as a means to impose justice and peace, see F. H. Russell, *The Just War in the Middle Ages* (Cambridge: Cambridge University Press, 1975); M. H. Keen, *The Laws of War in the Late Middle Ages* (London: RKP, 1965); and David S. Bachrach, *Religion and the Conduct of War c.300–c.1215* (Woodbridge: Boydell Press, 2003).
23. Norbert Ohler, *Krieg und Frieden im Mittelalter*. Beck'sche Reihe 1226 (Munich: C. H. Beck, 1997), 272: "Mit dem Verlust von Augen, Nasen, Händen und Füßen mußten unterlegene Kämpfer, aber auch wehrlose Bauern rechnen."
24. Orderic Vitalis, *The Ecclesiastical History of Orderic Vitalis*, ed. M. Chibnall, 6 vols. (Oxford: Clarendon Press, 1969–1980), II:212: "et unus ex obsidibus prope portam oculis priuatus est".
25. Piers D. Mitchell, *Medicine in the Crusades: Warfare, Wounds and the Medieval Surgeon* (Cambridge: Cambridge University Press, 2004), 126; the sources for this episode can be found in Albert of Aachen, *Historia Ierosolimitana*, ed. and trans. S. Edgington (Oxford: Oxford Medieval Texts, 2007), bk. 5, chap. 17, and Guibert of Nogent, *The Deeds of God through the Franks: Gesta Dei Per Francos*, trans. R. Levine (Woodbridge: Boydell Press, 1997), 71.
26. One person known to have survived blinding was Louis of Provence the Blind (†928), who was crowned king of Provence by Pope Stephen V in 890 and grabbed the title of 'Emperor of the Romans' in 901, but then during his invasion of Italy in 905 was blinded in the church of Verona by nobles following Berengar of Friuli. He returned to Provence, where he reigned for another twenty-three years.
27. David Nicolle, *Medieval Warfare Source Book*, vol. I, *Warfare in Western Christendom* (London: BCA, 1996), 247.
28. Ohler, *Krieg und Frieden*, 272. Glycas is cited by J. Lascaratos, 'The Penalty of Blinding during Byzantine Times: Medical Remarks', *Documenta Ophthalmologica* 81 (1992): 139: "The king after blinding the captive Bulgars, who were said to be approximately fifteen thousand and after ordering every

hundred of them blinded by heat in both eyes to be led by a one-eyed man, sent them to Samuel [the Bulgar king]. He was unable to bear the pathetic sight, grew dizzy, fainted and fell to the earth."

29. Lascaratos, 'Penalty of Blinding', 133.

30. Ibid.

31. Ibid., 134–35.

32. Ibid., 139. This was apparently the scenario in quite a few of Byzantine judicial blindings (ibid., 142).

33. Ibid., 141–42.

34. Sean McGlynn, *By Sword and Fire: Cruelty and Atrocity in Medieval Warfare* (London: Phoenix, 2009), 192; R. Rogers, *Latin Siege Warfare in the Twelfth Century* (Oxford: Clarendon Press, 1992), devotes pages 135–43 to the siege of Crema and mentions different perspectives of tactics, strategy and military technology but not a single word on the atrocities committed there—by both sides.

35. Jim Bradbury, *The Medieval Siege* (Woodbridge: Boydell Press, 1992), 92; cf. Otto of Freising and Rahewin, *Gesta Friderici Imperatoris*, ed. A. Waitz and B. de Simson, MGH Scriptores Rerum Germanicarum 12 (Hanover and Leipzig, 1912), 315: "grave ludibrium"; also Otto of Freising and Rahewin, *The Deeds of Frederick Barbarossa*, ed. C. C. Mierow and R. Emery (New York, 1953), 304. Earlier that century, after a battle between the Crusader state of Antioch and Aleppo in the summer of 1119, some of the captured Frankish knights had been subjected to a similar torture and been made into objects of public 'entertainment'. Taken to Aleppo by their Muslim captors, some knights had every one of their limbs cut off "before being thrown into the town square to die as a spectacle for the local population" (Mitchell, *Medicine*, 129). Walter the Chancellor, whose chronicle provided an eyewitness account of these atrocities, had cautioned that he would not recount all the details, since he did not wish Christians, by reading about them, to be able to emulate these terrible deeds; see Walter the Chancellor, *The Antiochene Wars*, ed. H. Hagenmeyer, trans. T. S. Asbridge and S. B. Edgington (Aldershot: Ashgate, 1999), 132–36. Unfortunately, as the events at Crema show, it seems that in the intervening forty years someone had been reading about such horrific mutilations for inspiration!

36. Richard de Templo, *Chronicle of the Third Crusade: A Translation of 'Itinerarium Peregrinorum et Gesta Regis Ricardi'*, trans. H. Nicholson (Aldershot: Ashgate, 1997), 193; quoted by Mitchell, *Medicine*, 130.

37. McGlynn, *By Sword and Fire*, 191. The justification appears to have been that Simon de Montfort's men had previously been at the receiving end of similar actions, when two of his knights had been mutilated by having their eyes gouged out, noses, ears, and upper lips cut, and sent back naked (in winter!) to him; see Baraz, *Medieval Cruelty*, 86–7; also *The History of the Albigensian Crusade: Peter of les Vaux-de-Cernay's Historia Albigensis*, trans. and intro. W. A. and M. D. Sibly (Woodbridge: Boydell Press, 1998).

38. Roger of Wendover, *Flowers of History (1066–1215 AD)*, ed. and trans. J. A. Giles, 2 vols. (1849; rpt. Felinbach: Llanerch, 1996), II:508, cited in McGlynn, *By Sword and Fire*, 135.

39. Bradbury, *Medieval Siege*, 332; cf. Matthew Paris, *English History*, ed. J. A. Giles, 3 vols. (London, 1852), II:187.

40. Bradbury, *Medieval Siege*, 313.

41. C. Frugoni, *A Day in a Medieval City* (Chicago: University of Chicago Press, 2005), 79. Frugoni notes, to our undoubted relief as modern readers, that "for once, the voice of moderation finally prevailed" (189, note 66), but without informing us in what way: were the inhabitants spared or simply killed

quickly? See L. Zdekauer, *La vita pubblica dei senesi nel Dugento* (Siena: L. Lazzeri, 1897), 98–99, minutes of council meeting printed in Appendix 4, at 184–86.

42. A nearly exhaustive survey of blinding used as a political tool has been conducted by Meinrad Schaab, *Die Blendung als politische Maßnahme im abendländischen Früh- und Hochmittelalter* (PhD diss., University of Heidelberg, 1955).

43. Trevor Dean, *Crime in Medieval Europe 1200–1550* (Edinburgh: Longman, 2001), 128. These men were fortunate, since they had partisan supporters in the city, which erupted in riot against the proposed mutilation.

44. The removal of fingers is symbolic, since fingers were used to make the gestures of oaths and swearing fealty. By breaking his imposed exile, Ulrich Swurl had in effect broken his oath and committed perjury. Schubert, *Räuber*, 124; see also Paul Sander, *Die reichsstädtische Haushaltung Nürnbergs, dargestellt auf Grund ihres Zustandes von 1431 bis 1440* ([Nuremberg?],1902), 649.

45. T. S. Brown, 'Urban Violence in Early Medieval Italy: The Cases of Rome and Ravenna', in *Violence and Society in the Early Medieval West*, ed. Guy Halsall (Woodbridge: Boydell Press, 1998), 79.

46. Ibid.

47. Ibid., 80.

48. Ibid., 81. Leo could be rescued the same day and famously went on to meet Charlemagne at Paderborn later that year.

49. Evelyne Patlagean, 'A New Byzantium in the Making?', in *The Cambridge Illustrated History of the Middle Ages Vol. 1 350–950*, ed. Robert Fossier (Cambridge: Cambridge University Press, 1989), 307–11.

50. Patlagean, 'New Byzantium in the Making', 310. The argument is made by Bührer-Thierry, 'Just Anger', 82–87, that the Carolingian rulers, influenced by Byzantine practices, were making a similar statement about the connection between imperial splendour and the light of the sun, hence the penalty of blinding was especially appropriate for punishing traitors and rebels.

51. McGlynn, *By Sword and Fire*, 46; see *The Gesta Normannorum Ducum of William of Jumièges, Orderic Vitalis and Robert of Torigni*, ed. E. Van Houts, 2 vols. (Oxford: Oxford University Press, 1992, 1995)—William of Jumièges completed his account about 1070. Also Klaus van Eickels, 'Gendered Violence: Castration and Blinding as Punishment for Treason in Normandy and Anglo-Norman England', in *Violence, Vulnerability, and Embodiment: Gender and History*, ed. Shani D'Cruze and Anupama Rao (Oxford: Blackwell, 2005), 94–108.

52. Bradbury, *Medieval Siege*, 78; Orderic Vitalis, *Ecclesiastical History*, IV:298: "Homines priuatione oculorum et amputatione pedum manuumque deformare paruipendebat", also at 160: "uel quod est peius debilitatis membris mancos uel loripedes uel orbatis luminibus inutiles reddidit".

53. Jean Dunbabin, *Captivity and Imprisonment in Medieval Europe 1000–1300*. Medieval Culture and Society (Basingstoke: Palgrave Macmillan, 2002), 89; see M. Strickland, *War and Chivalry: The Conduct and Perception of War in England and Normandy, 1066–1217* (Cambridge: Cambridge University Press, 1996), 51.

54. Orderic Vitalis, *Ecclesiastical History*, VI:212: "earum oculos in ultionem filii sui crudeliter effodit, nariumque summitates truncauit." Orderic then commented how cruelly innocent childhood had to suffer for the sins of the fathers: "Innocens itaque infantia parentum nefas proh dolor miserabiliter luit" (ibid.). In 1107 Robert, duke of Normandy and oldest son of William the Conqueror, was confined at Cardiff, and had his eyes put out following

an unsuccessful escape attempt. However, the mutilation was carried out in such a way as to avoid "noisome deformity" (R. R. James, *Studies in the History of Ophthalmology in England Prior to the Year 1800* [Cambridge: Cambridge University Press, 1933], 25, citing Holinshed's *Chronicle*). According to medical historian James, the use of penal blinding peaked under Henry I, declining after c. 1180, when Glanville's legal collection gained influence.

55. Bradbury, *Medieval Siege*, 78; Orderic Vitalis, *Ecclesiastical History*, VI:348.

56. The events are described in the chronicle of Peter of Vaux-de-Cernay, Petrus Vallium Sarnaii Monachus, *Hystoria Albigensis* 142, ed. Pascal Guébin and Ernest Lyon (Paris, 1930), II:225–26, cited by Daniel Baraz, *Medieval Cruelty: Changing Perceptions, Late Antiquity to the Early Modern Period* (Ithaca, NY: Cornell University Press, 2003), 87. The narration gains an added dimension in that it is the wife who assaults the poor women, thereby behaving in an even more inhumane fashion than her husband, since in other instances of cutting off the breasts it has always been male perpetrators acting on the female body; see the chapter 'Invincible Virgins' in Mills, *Suspended Animation*, 106–44, for a discussion of 'religious pornography' and gender in the context of depictions of female martyrs.

57. For further discussion of those people not participating in war but who are nevertheless affected by the actions of those fighting, see the chapter by Christopher Allmand, 'War and the Non-Combatant in the Middle Ages', in *Medieval Warfare: A History*, ed. Maurice Keen (Oxford: Oxford University Press, 1999), 253–72.

58. Urs Graf, *Armloses Mädchen mit Stelzfuß*, Öffentliche Kunstsammlung Basel, Kupferstichkabinett. On the artist, see Christiane Andersson, *Dirnen, Krieger, Narren: Ausgewählte Zeichnungen von Urs Graf* (Basel: GS-Verlag, 1978); also J. R. Hale, 'The Soldier in Germanic Graphic Art of the Renaissance', *Journal of Interdisciplinary History* 17, no. 1 (1986): 85–114.

59. And not just medieval warfare: a shocking criminal case occurred in Cornwall as recently as 2011, where a woman who became the victim of domestic violence was blinded by her 'boyfriend', who deliberately strangled her into unconsciousness so that he could then gouge her eyes out (http://www.bbc.co.uk/news/uk-england-cornwall-17701804, accessed 13 April 2012). Tina Nash survived the ordeal of this disturbing assault, but she was left completely blind.

60. Nicolle, *Medieval Warfare*, 247, although even in twelfth-century southern France there were references to captured sergeants and militiamen having a hand or foot cut off, while captive knights had their ears or noses slit. Michael Prestwich, *Armies and Warfare in the Middle Ages: The English Experience* (New Haven, CT: Yale University Press, 1996), 237, also discusses the Welsh and Scottish predilection for cutting off heads rather than taking prisoners of war.

61. Various military historians, David Nicolle included, have argued for a decrease in barbarity over time from the earlier to the later Middle Ages, and less wholesale massacre of the vanquished party in later times in favour of more hostage taking for the lucrative ransom business; more recently the notion of chivalric attitudes having any positive effect on the treatment of combatants and non-combatants alike has been convincingly challenged by McGlynn, *By Sword and Fire*. Occasionally rulers tried to limit the amount of violence and destruction, such as Edward III, who in 1346 on arrival in France "forbade attacks on the elderly, women and children, robbery of churches, and burnings of buildings" (Prestwich, *Armies and Warfare*, 180) although the effectiveness of such orders is debatable.

62. For modern times, one need only look back to the impact of the First World War, both for statistical evidence of impairment as well as the conspicuous legacy of disability; see Deborah Cohen, *The War Come Home: Disabled Veterans in Britain and Germany, 1914–1939* (Berkeley: University of California Press, 2001); also Joanna Bourke, *Dismembering the Male: Men's Bodies, Britain and the Great War* (London: Reaktion, 1996), 66, which provides a table of compensation rates not far removed in principle to those of the Germanic law codes. See also discussion in Metzler, *Disability*, 12.

63. McGlynn, *By Sword and Fire*, 229.

64. Prestwich, *Armies and Warfare*, 179; Mitchell, *Medicine*, 134. These decrees of 1190 became known as the Oleron laws and are mentioned in *The Annals of Roger of Howden, Comprising the History of England and of Other Countries of Europe from AD 732 to AD 1201*, trans. H. T. Riley, 2 vols. (London: H. G. Bohn, 1853), II:140–41.

65. Prestwich, *Armies and Warfare*, 180.

66. Albert of Aachen, *Historia Iherosolimitana*, ed. and trans. S. Edgington (Oxford: Oxford Medieval Texts, 2007), bk. 6, chap. 42, quoted by Mitchell, *Medicine*, 128.

67. Prestwich, *Armies and Warfare*, 5 and 180; *Gesta Henrici Quinti*, ed. F. Taylor and J. S. Roskell (Oxford: Clarendon Press, 1975), 69, 81.

68. Prestwich, *Armies and Warfare*, 314; *Chroniques par Waurin*, ed. W. Hardy, Rolls Series (London, 1868), ii, 203–4.

69. Ohler, *Krieg und Frieden*, 254; cf. the contributions by G. Braungart, M. Wolter and P. Segel in *Feindbilder: Die Darstellung des Gegners in der Publizistik des Mittelalters und der Neuzeit*. Bayreuther Historische Kolloquien 6, ed. F. Bosbach (Cologne: Böhlau Verlag, 1992).

70. Usatge 73, *The Usatges of Barcelona: The Fundamental Law of Catalonia*, trans. Donal J. Kagay (Philadelphia: University of Pennsylvania Press, 1994), 83.

71. McGlynn, *By Sword and Fire*, 13.

72. Article 10 from William I's *Ten Articles*: "Interdico etiam, ne quis occidatur aut suspendatur pro aliqua culpa, sed eruantur oculi et testiculi abscidantur" (Felix Liebermann, *Die Gesetze der Angelsachsen*, 3 vols. [Halle: Niemeyer, 1898–1916], I:488).

73. *Leges Henrici Primi*, ed. and trans. L. J. Downer (Oxford: Clarendon Press, 1972), 116, c.13,3: "Falsarii pugnum perdant et nullo modo redimant." McGlynn, *By Sword and Fire*, 13, mentions they were to have their testicles cut off as well.

74. "Que scilicet ultimo puniuntur supplicio aut membrorum truncatione", *The Treatise on the Laws and Customs of the Realm of England Commonly Called Glanvill.*, ed. and trans. G. D. G. Hall, Medieval Texts (London: Nelson, 1965), Book I, chap. 2, at 3; Book XIV, chap. 1, at 171 on clemency.

75. *Lex Visigothorum*, ed. Karl Zeumer. MGH Fontes iuris Germanici antiqui 5 (Hanover, 1894), 2.1.8: "Quod si fortasse pietatis intuitu a principe fuerit illi vita concessa non aliter, quam effosi oculis relinquatur ad vitam, quatenus nec excidium videat, quo fuerat nequiter delectatus'; cited in Bührer-Thierry, 'Just Anger', 78; also McGlynn, *By Sword and Fire*, 17.

76. Ohler, *Krieg und Frieden*, 313; Bruce, 'Note on Penal Blinding', 369; Bührer-Thierry, 'Just Anger', 81–82.

77. *Annals of Fulda*, 56.

78. Ibid., 98; Bührer-Thierry, 'Just Anger', 90. The *Annals* furthermore mention that in 873 "Charles, the tyrant of Gaul, put aside his paternal feelings, and had his son Carloman, who had been ordained deacon, blinded" (*Annals of*

Fulda, 70). That case is also cited in *The Annals of St-Bertin*, trans. J. Nelson (Manchester: Manchester University Press, 1991), 181.

79. Prestwich, *Armies and Warfare*, 237; see Orderic Vitalis, *Ecclesiastical History*, II:316.

80. McGlynn, *By Sword and Fire*, 17; the episode is related in Suger's biography of Louis VI; Suger, *The Deeds of Louis the Fat*, ed. and trans. Richard Cusimano and John Moorhead (Washington, DC: Catholic University of America Press, 1992).

81. McGlynn, *By Sword and Fire*, 24; Robert Bartlett, *England under the Norman and Angevin Kings, 1075–1225* (Oxford: Clarendon Press, 2000), 185.

82. On this movement, see, for example, Thomas Head and Richard Landes, eds., *The Peace of God: Social Violence and Religious Response in France around the Year 1000* (Ithaca, NY: Cornell University Press, 1992).

83. Ohler, *Krieg und Frieden*, 300; see *Quellen zur deutschen Verfassungs-, Wirtschafts- und Sozialgeschichte bis 1250*. Ausgewählte Quellen zur deutschen Geschichte des Mittelalters. Freiherr von Stein-Gedächtnisausgabe 32, ed. and trans. L. Weinrich (n. p., 1977), 144 Nr. 36 § 8. The question to which extent minors were legally culpable arose also in English legal practice, for instance, a case of c. 1338, where a thirteen-year-old maidservant had killed her mistress, was used by jurists to consider whether the accused person, technically a child, could act with premeditation ("malice") or know "how to distinguish evil from good"; the jurists pointed out that under the "old law no one under age was hanged or suffered judgment of life or limb" but recent case law had caused minors to be punished (from the *Year Books of Edward III: 11 & 12 Edward III*, in *Crime, Law and Society in the Later Middle Ages*, Manchester Medieval Sources Series, trans. and ed. Anthony Musson with Edward Powell [Manchester: Manchester University Press, 2009], 95–96). This episode is grist to the mill of the school of thought which believes that justice became more violent towards the later Middle Ages and punishments became more corporal compared with the earlier period.

84. Schubert, *Räuber*, 104; see *Sachsenspiegel* Landrecht 2.LXV.1, 111: "Kein kint mag binnen sinen iaren geton, da ez sinen lip mete verwerken muge." A child's guardian is liable for compensation payment instead. The *Schwabenspiegel* also included a similar clause, stating thieves under the age of fourteen were not to receive capital punishment unless their "wickedness" was too great (*Schwabenspiegel* Landrecht 177; CCC Art 164, ed. F. L. A. Freiherr von Laßberg (Tübingen, 1840), c. 177; Schubert, *Räuber*, 104, note 810).

85. Schubert, *Räuber*, 105; see Emil Franz Rössler, ed., *Die Stadtrechte von Brünn aus dem XIII. und XIV. Jahrhundert, nach bisher ungedruckten Handschriften herausgegeben* (Prague, 1852; rpt. 1963), 254, no. 537. Also by implication, according to Lisi Oliver's survey of the earlier medieval Germanic/'barbarian' laws, "judicial mutilation—or at least public scourging—was a punishment more commonly assessed for men than for women" (Oliver, *Body Legal*, 178).

86. *Antapodosis*, Bk. 4, chap. 10, in Liudprand of Cremona, *The Embassy to Constantinople and Other Writings*, trans. F. A. Wright, ed. J. J. Norwich (London: J. M. Dent, 1993), 105–6.

87. For a discussion on how inability to procreate, be it due to infertility, hermaphroditism or mutilation as in this case, may have been considered a disability in medieval times but not in modern Western society, see Irina Metzler, 'Hermaphroditism in the Western Middle Ages: Physicians, Lawyers and the Intersexed Person', in *Bodies of Knowledge: Cultural Interpretations of Illness and Medicine in Medieval Europe*. Studies in Early Medicine 1, ed.

S. Crawford and C. Lee (Oxford: Archaeopress, 2010), 27–39; an interesting cross-cultural comparison of how impotence and/or infertility are regarded as 'disabilities' by many non-Westernised traditional cultures is given in Dieter Neubert and Günther Cloerkes, *Behinderung und Behinderte in verschiedenen Kulturen. Eine vergleichende Analyse ethnologischer Studien*, 2nd ed. (Heidelberg: Edition Schindele, 1994), 41–44.

88. *The Laws of the Earliest English Kings*, ed. and trans. F. L. Attenborough (Cambridge: Cambridge University Press, 1922; rpt. Felinfach: Llanerch Publishers, 2000), 43 and 49; the laws of Alfred from the 890s (section 6 §1) made similar provisions for theft, especially theft from a church, although the accused had the option of redeeming his hand in return for payment of a wergild (ibid., 67 and 69). This passage from the laws of Ine is quoted by Wilfred Bonser, *The Medical Background of Anglo-Saxon England* (London: Wellcome Historical Medical Library, 1963), 107–8, who prompted an interesting aside, in that he compared palaeopathological evidence to the documentary record, citing the archaeological report by E. Horne, 'Anglo-Saxon Cemetery at Camerton, Somerset, pt. 2', *Proceedings of the Somerset Archaeological Society* 74 (1933): 41, which mentioned that grave number 83, containing an adult male under middle age whose right foot had been taken off at the ankle, with the end of the tibia being completely healed and rounded, demonstrated that whatever had caused the loss of the foot, the man had lived for long enough after sustaining this trauma for the bone to heal. The amputation looked as if performed professionally. One may wish to compare this case with other palaeopathological evidence for 'successful' amputations, successful in the sense that the afflicted person survived long enough for the cut in/through the bone to heal, and for the person to become disabled. D. R. Brothwell and V. Møller-Christensen, 'Medico-Historical Aspects of a Very Early Case of Mutilation', *Danish Medical Bulletin* 10 (1963): 21–25, looked at a similar period to the Anglo-Saxon, while S. A. Mays, 'Healed Limb Amputations in Human Osteoarchaeology and Their Causes: A Case Study from Ipswich, UK', *International Journal of Osteoarchaeology* 6 (1996): 101–13, provided a somewhat later medieval example. One cannot rule out the possibility that palaeopathological amputations such as these were the results of judicial mutilations. As Mitchell, *Medicine*, 114, observes, amputation as a result of juridical violence is suggested in the palaeopathology "if the cut is at right angles to the bone and more than one limb is amputated in a symmetrical manner."

89. The bishop "had in his high justice the power 'to have ears cropped in Paris, at the Croix du Tirouer.'" From the cartularies of Notre-Dame, cited by Simone Roux, *Paris in the Middle Ages*, trans. J. A. McNamara (Philadelphia: University of Pennsylvania Press, 2009), 40 and note 30. In 1355 a man convicted of theft had his ears cut and was subsequently banished from the jurisdictional area. In 1390 six people, and in 1391 two more people, had their ears cut off for theft on orders of the court of the Châtelet, while at Saint-Germain-des-Prés one person suffered this fate; the point of this exercise was to disgrace the criminal (Bronislaw Geremek, *The Margins of Society in Late Medieval Paris*, trans. J. Birrell [Cambridge: Cambridge University Press/Paris: Editions de la Maison des Sciences de l'Homme, 1987], 52–53, 56, 106).

90. Claudine Fabre-Vassas, *The Singular Beast: Jews, Christians, and the Pig* (New York: Columbia University Press, 1997), 102 and 338, note 8; see Francisque Michel, *Histoire des races maudites de la France et de l'Espagne* (Paris, 1847), II:211; and Marie-Laure LeBail, 'Le droit et l'image: sur un cas d'essorillage', *Médiévales* 9 (1985): 103–17.

91. Oliver, *Body Legal*, 93, also noting that since the site of a cut-off ear can be covered by hair, the loss is not immediately visible, whereas "there is no disguising the loss of an eye or the nose" (ibid., 95).

92. Letts, *Bruges*, 74; cf. L. Gilliodts-van Severen, *Inventaire des Archives de la ville de Bruges* (Bruges, 1871–1878), III:200.

93. Schubert, *Räuber*, 102; for reference to the *Ohrenstock*, see Hermann Knapp, *Das alte Nürnberger Kriminalrecht* (Berlin: J. Guttentag, 1896), 61. A woman who had been arrested ten times in Nuremberg and was repeatedly banned from the city kept returning, so that on different recidivist occasions she was branded, her ears were cut off and she was threatened with drowning, all to no avail, finally the civic authorities incarcerated her for life in a tower (Schubert, *Räuber*, 106, and Knapp, *Das alte Nürnberger Kriminalrecht*, 15).

94. Schubert, *Räuber*, 193–94, thought this harsh punishment was made because perhaps the cook was a repeat offender; see Heinrich Weber, 'Ein Bamberger Echtbuch (*liber proscriptionum*) von 1414–1444', in *Bericht des Historischen Vereins für die Pflege der Geschichte des ehemaligen Fürstbistums Bamberg* 59 (Bamberg, 1898), 47. The *Sachsenspiegel* had prescribed hanging for theft, unless the value of stolen goods was below three shillings, in which case clemency could be shown and the culprit simply punished "in skin and hair", that is, by flogging and cutting short their hair (*Sachsenspiegel* Landrecht 2.XIII1, 81).

95. Mitchell, *Medicine*, 128; Benjamin Z. Kedar, 'On the Origins of the Earliest Laws of Frankish Jerusalem: The Canons of the Council of Nablus, 1120', *Speculum* 74 (1999): 310–35.

96. Oliver, *Body Legal*, 95; J. B. Bury, *The Invasion of Europe by the Barbarians* (New York: Norton, 1967), 128.

97. For a discussion of disabilities in the *lai* of Bisclavret from the perspective of literary criticism, cf. Troy Vandeventer Pearman, *Women and Disability in Medieval Literature*. The New Middle Ages (New York: Palgrave Macmillan, 2010), 77–83.

98. Groebner, *Defaced*, 72.

99. Ibid., 73. Thus at Venice in 1462 and 1474, and at Florence in 1484 sodomy was punished by *denasatio*, rare cases as punishments for men, "since, as the sources note, the penalty was otherwise reserved for women" (ibid.).

100. Albertus Magnus, *Alberti Magni ... opera omnia*, ed. Auguste Borgnet (Paris, 1890), I:292: "Constat ... quod denasatio non dicit inesse ens ut accidens, nec est ens ut substantiae, quae est forma el materia vel compositum, sed solum ex defectu habitus debiti relinquit deformitatem et turpitudinem", cited by Groebner, *Defaced*, 75; the records of the town of Kaysersberg state that Count Hans von Lupfen had called cutting off a woman's nose by her attackers a particularly heinous crime "since the nose is a member on a person that, when removed, completely disfigures [*ungestalt*] the person", Archives historiques de Kaysersberg, FF 32, fol. 3v, cited by Groebner, *Defaced*, 76; furthermore, the "face is the most noble part of a human being ... and a person becomes *gantz ungestalt*, completely disfigured, utterly hideous, when his or her face is mutilated" (ibid., 12).

101. McGlynn, *By Sword and Fire*, 17.

102. Le Goff, *Medieval Civilization*, 302.

103. Wace, *Roman de Rou*, cited by Le Goff, *Medieval Civilization*, 302.

104. A. Esch, *Wahre Geschichten aus dem Mittelalter. Kleine Schicksale selbst erzählt in Schreiben an den Papst* (Munich: C. H. Beck, 2010), 148; see *Repertorium Poenitentiariae Germanicum*, vol. VI (papacy of Sixtus IV, 1471–1484), ed. L. Schmugge (Tübingen: Max Niemeyer, 2005), case no. 3643;

similar at *Repertorium Poenitentiariae Germanicum*, vol. II (papacy of Nicholas V, 1447–1455), ed. L. Schmugge (Tübingen: Max Niemeyer, 1999), cases no. 754 and 982.

105. McGlynn, *By Sword and Fire*, 10.
106. Lantfred, *Translation and Miracles of St Swithun*, cited by Patrick Wormald, *The Making of English Law: King Alfred to the Twelfth Century*, vol. I, *Legislation and Its Limits* (Oxford: Blackwell, 2001), 125. Latin text given in Liebermann, *Gesetze der Angelsachsen*, II, part II, 292–93, following *Miraculi S. Swithuni*, Acta SS, July 2. The idea of the innocence of a mutilated man found by another is also encapsulated in a section of the *Lex Salica Karolina* (XI [XLIII], 9), a Carolingian revision of the earlier sixth-century Salic law code: "If anyone finds a man at a crossroads without hands and feet whom his enemies have left mutilated [and he kills him], he shall be liable to pay four thousand denarii (i.e., one hundred solidi)"; *The Laws of the Salian Franks*, trans. and intro. Katherine Fischer Drew (Philadelphia: University of Pennsylvania Press, 1991), 181.
107. Lantfred had suggested this was a man whom the legislators had blinded: "de homine, quem legislatores cecaverunt", cited by Liebermann, *Gesetze der Angelsachsen*, II, part II, 292–93. Liebermann (ibid.) had already commented that this was "rather an exaggerated amassment of those penalties actually employed individually" (*eher eine übertriebene Häufung der im einzelnen wirklich angewandten Strafen*).
108. Alan Harding, *The Law Courts of Medieval England. Historical Problems: Studies and Documents 18* (London: Allen and Unwin, 1973), 57; cf. R. R. Darlington, ed., *The Vita Wulfstani of William of Malmesbury, Camden Society 3rd Series* (London: Butler & Tanner, 1928) for examples of miracle healings of felons.
109. McGlynn, *By Sword and Fire*, 33; see J. Hudson, *The Formation of the English Common Law: Law and Society in England from the Norman Conquest to Magna Carta* (London: Longman, 1996), 160. This story is narrated in the *Life of St Thomas* by Benedict of Peterborough: "Orbatur oculis, genitalibus mutilatur, et oculum quidam sinistrum statim integrum eruerunt. Dexter autem laceratus et in frustra concisus vix tandem effusus est" (cited by Bruce, 'Note on Penal Blinding', 370). The same story is also told in the *Life and Miracles of St Thomas* by William of Canterbury, ed. J. A. Giles (London, 1850), 185–86, who describes the healing of a felon after "oculorum loca jam fere desiccata et cilia clausa fuissent" (cited by Bruce, 'Note on Penal Blinding', 370).
110. The story is told in the *passio* of Saint Leudegar, who is miraculously healed but then executed in 678 by the same Ebroin; Baraz, *Medieval Cruelty*, 51; Bührer-Thierry, 'Just Anger', 77–78; and *Passio Leudegarii*, ed. B. Krusch, MGH Scriptores Rerum Germanicarum 5 (Hanover, 1919).
111. Cited by Philippe Contamine, *War in the Middle Ages*, trans. Michael Jones (Oxford: Blackwell, 1984), 295; *Le registre d' inquisition de Jacques Fournier, évêque de Pamiers, 1318–1325*, trans. J. Duvernoy (Paris: Mouton, 1978), I:83.
112. In the mid-thirteenth century torture was still a "new and double-edged weapon as part of a judicial investigation" (Andrew P. Roach, *The Devil's World: Heresy and Society 1100–1300* [Harlow: Pearson Education, 2005], 147). The first medieval records of the use of torture as a means to engender confession to a crime appear in the towns of north-east Italy, e.g. at Vercelli and Verona.
113. McGlynn, *By Sword and Fire*, 18. For the story of how torture came to be reintroduced into legal procedures in the thirteenth century (following classical Roman precedents), see the volume by Edward M. Peters, *Torture*

(Oxford: Blackwell, 1985); Peters's argument is succinctly summarised by Dunbabin, *Captivity*, 126—the main points being that the legal paradigm of an accusatorial system in the earlier Middle Ages (in which an accusation had to be made by the injured party before any further legal proceedings could take place) shifted to an inquisitorial system from the thirteenth century onwards (in which judicial proceedings came to reside in the hands of 'professionals'—judges and courts—who investigated, accused and deliberated away from the public space).

114. Quoted by Roach, *Devil's World*, 147.
115. Written in 1468–1471, at chap. XXII, *Sir John Fortescue: De Laudibus Legum Anglie*, ed., trans. and intro. S. B. Chrimes (Cambridge: Cambridge University Press, 1942), 50.
116. Cited in Mitchell, *Medicine*, 127; William of Tyre, *A History of Deeds Done beyond the Sea*, trans. E. A. Babcock and A. C. Krey, 2 vols. (New York: Columbia University Press, 1943), I:335.
117. [Jean de] Joinville and [Geoffroy de] Villehardouin, *Chronicles of the Crusades (The Conquest of Constantinople and The Life of Saint Louis)*, trans. M. R. B. Shaw (London: Penguin, 1963), 249; Mitchell, *Medicine*, 131–32. Another form of torture described by Joinville (255), which this time was carried out on the person of the eighty-year-old patriarch of Jerusalem, involved his hands being tied up so tightly "that they swelled to the size of his head and the blood started to flow from his nails". Mitchell shares his expert modern medical opinion with regard to the physical phenomena described by Joinville, suggesting that if compressed "for sufficient time the tissues would have been so damaged that at best the prisoner would have been left with scarred, paralysed hands while at worst the soft tissues may have sloughed off and resulted in his death" (Mitchell, *Medicine*, 132).
118. Hinckeldey, *Strafjustiz*, 152.
119. Ross Samson, 'The End of Early Medieval Slavery', in *The Work of Work: Servitude, Slavery, and Labor in Medieval England*, ed. Allen J. Frantzen and Douglas Moffat (Glasgow: Cruithne Press, 1994), 105; *Vita Geraldi* 2.11, PL vol. 133; Gregory of Tours, *The History of the Franks*, trans. Lewis Thorpe (London: Penguin, 1974), IX.38, 525.
120. Samson, 'End of Early Medieval Slavery', 106; Gregory of Tours, *History of the Franks*, VII.46, 428 and VII.47, 429. The unfortunate slave was subsequently hanged, so he did not live long enough for the mutilation to effect a disability.
121. Cited by Geary, 'Judicial Violence', 83.
122. Ibid., 84.
123. McGlynn, *By Sword and Fire*, 9; Roger of Wendover, *Flowers of History (1066–1215 AD)*, ed. and trans. J. A. Giles, 2 vols. (1849; rpt. Felinbach: Llanerch, 1996), II:441: "the justiciary went into the city with Falcasius and a body of soldiers, and seized on all who were discovered to be guilty of the said sedition, and committed them to prison, and after cutting off the feet of some and the hands of others, he permitted them to depart".
124. Mitchell, *Medicine*, 134; *Les Livres des Assises et des Usages dou Reaume de Jérusalem*, ed. E. H. Kauslet (Stuttgart: Adolf Krabbe, 1839), I:315, and *Assizes of the Lusignan Kingdom of Cyprus*, ed. N. Coureas (Nicosia: Cyprus Research Centre, 2002), 199.
125. *Alfred 32*, in *Laws of the Earliest English Kings*, 76–77; Oliver, *Body Legal*, 173.
126. Letts, *Bruges*, 74; see the city chronicle *Het Boeck van al 't gene datter gheschiedt is binnen Brugghe, 1477–1491*, ed. C. Carton (Ghent, 1859), 152 and 219.

127. Letts, *Bruges*, 74–75; see *Het Boeck*, 67–68.
128. Dean, *Crime*, 56–57.
129. McGlynn, *By Sword and Fire*, 23. Dean, *Crime*, 56, cites this hierarchy of repeat punishments for fourteenth-century France.
130. Carole Rawcliffe, *Leprosy in Medieval England* (Woodbridge: Boydell Press, 2006), 101, note 247.
131. *Laws of Alfred* 32, in *Laws of the Earliest English Kings*, 77.
132. *Sachsenspiegel* Landrecht 1.LIX.1, 62–3: "Wer bi koninges banne dinget unde den ban nicht en hat entphangen, der wettet sine zungen."
133. "If he crippled a Christian man or woman, reason adjudges that he should lose the right thumb", cited in Mitchell, *Medicine*, 173, discussion at 135 and 230; *Les Livres des Assises et des Usages dou Reaume de Jérusalem*, ed. E. H. Kauslet (Stuttgart: Adolf Krabbe, 1839), I:258 [extract in English given in Mitchell, *Medicine*, 232–4], and *Assizes of the Lusignan Kingdom of Cyprus*, ed. N. Coureas (Nicosia: Cyprus Research Centre, 2002), 182.
134. Cited in Le Goff, *Medieval Civilization*, 323; see *Peasant Life in the Old German Epics: Meier Helmbrecht and Der arme Heinrich*, trans. C. H. Bell (New York: Columbia University Press, 1931).
135. *Crime, Law and Society*, 253.
136. As Mitchell, *Medicine*, 136, concludes with regard to the eponymous period, but a historiographic trope that can be applied to northern Europe and to the later Middle Ages as much as to the Holy Land during the times of the Crusades. The only problem is that we do not have any statistics to back up such assumptions.
137. "Er sodane teken (Zeichen), de misdadighe lude phleget to hebbende, an sik hevet", cited by Schubert, *Räuber*, 101; see *Das Stadtrecht von Goslar*, ed. Wilhelm Ebel (Göttingen, 1968), 81.
138. "Si duo homines inciderunt in criminis suspicionem, is primus torqueatur, qui sit aspectu deformia", quoted by Sander L. Gilman, *Making the Body Beautiful: A Cultural History of Aesthetic Surgery* (Princeton, NJ: Princeton University Press, 1999), 26–27; William Armand Lessa, *Landmarks in the Science of Human Types* (New York: Brooklyn College Press, 1942), 1.
139. Mentioned in Esch, *Wahre Geschichten*, 35, note 68; see *Repertorium Poenitentiariae Germanicum*, vol. VI (papacy of Sixtus IV, 1471–1484), ed. L. Schmugge (Tübingen: Max Niemeyer, 2005), no. 3714.
140. Narrated in the *Koelhoffsche Chronik* and mentioned by Franz Irsigler and Arnold Lassotta, *Bettler und Gaukler, Dirnen und Henker. Außenseiter in einer mittelalterlichen Stadt. Köln 1300–1600* (Munich: DTV, 1989), 253.
141. Dean, *Crime*, 63. The gang also included Nicholas the stammerer, but he is unlikely to have had this speech impediment as a result of judicial encounters.
142. "Walburg mit dem Stumpf", "der handlose Schneider", and "Ellen die Orlos", cited in Gerd Althoff, Hans-Werner Goetz and Ernst Schubert, *Menschen im Schatten der Kathedrale* (Darmstadt: Wissenschaftliche Buchgesellschaft, 1998), 319.
143. Groebner, *Defaced*, 72.
144. Andrew McCall, *The Medieval Underworld* (New York: Dorset Press, 1979), 76.
145. Rawcliffe, *Leprosy*, 138.
146. Anthony Luttrell, 'The Hospitallers' Medical Tradition: 1291–1530', in *The Military Orders: Fighting for the Faith and Caring for the Sick*, ed. Malcolm Barber (Aldershot: Ashgate, 1994), 72.
147. K. P. Jankrift, *Mit Gott und schwarzer Magie. Medizin im Mittelalter* (Darmstadt: Wissenschaftliche Buchgesellschaft, 2005), 110; see Karl Rübel,

ed., *Dortmunder Urkundenbuch*, vol. 2 *1372–1400 Nachträge* (Dortmund, 1890; rpt. Osnabrück 1978), no. 324a–c, 349.

148. *Calendar of the Patent Rolls: Edward I, A.D. 1281–92* (London, 1893), 192; cited in Wheatley, *Stumbling Blocks*, 37.

149. Althoff, Goetz and Schubert, *Menschen im Schatten*, 347.

150. *Urkundenbuch der Stadt Lübeck*, Teil 6 (Lübeck, 1881), 245, no. 205, cited in Evamaria Engel and Frank-Dietrich Jacob, *Städtisches Leben im Mittelalter. Schriftquellen und Bildzeugnisse* (Cologne: Böhlau Verlag, 2006), 84.

151. "Als Anna ein Kind war, kamen Schweine und fraßen ihr die linke Hand ab. Da Anna nun keine linke Hand mehr hatte, brachten Freunde und Eltern sie an einen abgeschiedenen Ort, wo einige Frauen ein einsiedlerisches Leben nach Art des Benediktinerordens führten", Esch, *Wahre Geschichten*, 100; see *Repertorium Poenitentiariae Germanicum*, vol. III (papacy of Calixtus III, 1455–1458), ed. L. Schmugge (Tübingen: Max Niemeyer, 2001), case no. 130: "Anna filia Nicolai parvisartoris de Nuenburch".

152. Canonists and theologians had explored various conditions which provided physical impediments to marriage, e.g. congenital bodily defects relating to the genitalia, mutilation and sorcery. Robert of Courson (†1219) had said that the impossibility of intercourse was an impediment, which was sometimes caused by frigidity, sometimes by sorcery, sometimes by defect or vice (i.e. fault) of members and sometimes by poisonous abuse (i.e. homosexual practices): "Sequitur de alio impedimento matrimonii quod est impossiblitas coeundi que provenit multiplici de causa quia quandoque provenit ex frig[id]itate, quandoque ex malefico, quandoque ex defectu vel ex vicio membrorum, quandoque ex infectione abusionis . . ." (*Summa*, XLII, 16, fol. 142rb, Paris, Bibliothèque nationale, MS lat. 14524, cited in John H. Baldwin, *The Language of Sex: Five Voices from Northern France Around 1200* [Chicago: University of Chicago Press, 1994], 96 and 294, note 34). Since a missing hand is in no way anatomically related to one's ability to procreate, Anna was free to marry.

153. Dunbabin, *Captivity*, 129; see ibid., 120–29 for a general description of conditions in prison suffered by those folk who were neither wealthy nor important enough to warrant 'special treatment'.

154. Ibid., 37.

155. Cited in J. J. Jusserand, *English Wayfaring Life in the Middle Ages*, trans. Lucy Toulmin Smith (1889; rpt. London: Ernest Benn, 1950), 150. The Assizes "was loth to try them, because they were not attached for any robbery or misdeed for which they could suffer judgment. And so they were permitted to depart." But the source had no interest in detailing in what condition they "departed", nor how they were still able to.

156. G. Geltner, *The Medieval Prison: A Social History* (Princeton, NJ: Princeton University Press, 2008), 80.

157. At Florence, too, even before the foundation of the famous Le Stinche, prisoners were released, commonly on the grounds of infirmity and old age, for instance, in 1296 (ibid., 155, note 58).

158. Ibid., 16, e.g. with extended visiting rights for relatives of inmates, or limited medical aid, provided, for instance, in 1329 by one Master Ricobaldo, a surgeon who was himself impoverished, who tended to poor prisoners free of charge (ibid., 66 and 137, note 33).

159. Brian Pullan, "'Difettosi, impotenti, inabili": Caring for the Disabled in Early Modern Italian Cities', in *Poverty and Charity: Europe, Italy, Venice, 1400–1700*, ed. Brian Pullan (Aldershot: Ashgate, 1994), VI:10 and 19, note 37.

160. Geltner, *Medieval Prison*, 68.

161. Ibid., 17.
162. Ibid., 19, with the first mention of a "sickroom", a quasi prison hospital, in 1357 (ibid., 139, note 66). On parallel developments in law and medicine, see also M. Herzog, 'Scharfrichterliche Medizin. Zu den Beziehungen zwischen Henker und Arzt, Schafott und Medizin', *Medizinhistorisches Journal* 29 (1994): 309–31.
163. Schubert, *Räuber*, 117; Albrecht Keller, *Der Scharfrichter in der deutschen Kulturgeschichte* (Bonn/Leipzig, 1921; rpt. Hildesheim: G. Olms, 1968), 198.
164. The source gruesomely refers to the breaking out of eyes, "do he den mennen de ogen utbrak", Schubert, *Räuber*, 117; H. Deichert, 'Zur Geschichte der peinlichen Rechtspflege im alten Hannover', *Hannoversche Geschichtsblätter* 15 (1912): 154. The executioner was paid three and a half pounds and two shillings for this action, but then he had to be specially hired from elsewhere (Schubert, *Räuber*, 80); *Urkundenbuch der Stadt Hildesheim, Teil 5: Stadtrechnungen 1379–1415*, ed. Richard Doebner (Hildesheim, 1893; rpt. Aalen: Scientia, 1980), 299.
165. Schubert, *Räuber*, 117; *Die Nürnberger Ratsverlässe. Teil 2: 1452–1471*, ed. Martin Schieber (Neustadt an der Aisch: Degener, 1995), 71. The thorough late medieval integration of physical mutilation into not just the judicial, but also into the administrative process can be seen in the tariffs for payments to the executioner according to which mutilations he carried out: at Nuremberg the (frequent) lopping of ears warranted a salary of five shillings while the (comparatively rare) amputation of a finger was paid with thirty pence (Schubert, *Räuber*, 79); see Knapp, *Das alte Nürnberger Kriminalrecht*, 61.
166. *Laws of the Earliest English Kings*, 107.
167. Cited by Geary, 'Judicial Violence', 84.
168. Ibid.
169. *Codex Justinianus*, ed. and trans. Gottfried Härtel and Frank-Michael Kaufmann (Leipzig: Reclam Verlag, 1991), 121.
170. Luis A. García Moreno, 'Legitimate and Illegitimate Violence in Visigothic Law', in *Violence and Society in the Early Medieval West*, ed. Guy Halsall (Woodbridge: Boydell Press, 1998), 56; *Leges Visigothorum* VI.5.xiii, ed. K. Zeumer, MGH Leges I.1 (Berlin, 1902).
171. *Forum Iudicum* §VI, 5, xiii, cited in Oliver, *Body Legal*, 174.
172. Aquinas, *Summa theologiae*, I–II q. 105, a. 4, see Verena Postel, *Arbeit und Willensfreiheit im Mittelalter*. Vierteljahrschrift für Sozial- und Wirtschaftsgeschichte Beihefte Nr. 207 (Stuttgart: Franz Steiner, 2009), 145.
173. Baraz, *Medieval Cruelty*, 193, also 20–23 for a discussion of Aquinas's views on what constitutes cruelty.
174. Ibid., 27.
175. Letts, *Bruges*, 70.

NOTES TO CHAPTER 2

1. On disabled veterans of warfare in antiquity, see Loretana de Libero, 'Mit eiserner Hand ins Amt? Kriegsversehrte Aristokraten zwischen Recht und Religion, Ausgrenzung und Integration', in *Res publica reperta. Zur Verfassung und Gesellschaft der römischen Republik und des frühen Prinzipats. Festschrift für Jochen Bleicken zum 75. Geburtstag*, ed. Jürgen Spielvogel (Stuttgart: Franz Steiner, 2002), 172–91.
2. A. R. Hands, *Charities and Social Aid in Greece and Rome. Aspects of Greek and Roman Life* (London: Thames and Hudson, 1968), 100.

3. Ibid., 138.
4. Ibid., 202, document 61; the wording in Greek is literally the "incapables" (αδυνατους).
5. On the extent of disability among these veterans, see the chapter on the consequences of 'Mutilation', especially at 31–33, in Joanna Burke, *Dismembering the Male: Men's Bodies, Britain and the Great War* (London: Reaktion, 1996). Not surprisingly, the years immediately following World War I saw a glut of interest in and publications on disability. For the general tenor of such tomes this publication is of particular note: Arthur Keith, *Menders of the Maimed: The Anatomical and Physiological Principles Underlying the Treatment of Injuries to Muscles, Nerves, Bones and Joints* (London: Hodder and Stoughton, 1919)—the title says it all, the heroic efforts of medical men in 'curing' the crippled. This book did not even discuss any medical history prior to the eighteenth century, but the author clearly stated his aims: "surgeons are being called on to restore movement to thousands of men who have been lamed or maimed in war" (vii).
6. Rather than enumerate the all too depressing statistics of twenty-first-century civilian and military casualties, I will mention just one single example: the Cup of African Nations of Amputee Football, a sporting event last held in November 2011 in Ghana, where sport is used to raise awareness of the marginalised situation the victims of war often find themselves in, especially in countries like Angola, Liberia or Sierra Leone, which between them number tens of thousands people mutilated by landmines and machine guns; see Stephan Orth, 'Cup der Hoffnung', Spiegel Online (http://www.spiegel.de/sport/fussball/0,1518,798928,00.html, accessed 21 November 2011).
7. A general examination of how medieval literature treated the topics of warfare and mutilation may be found in Burkhardt Krause, 'Imaginierte Gewalt in der mittelalterlichen Literatur. Der fragmentierte Leib', in *Verstehen durch Vernunft. Festschrift W. Hoffmann*, ed. Krause (Vienna: Fassbaender, 1997), 201–26.
8. *De cas des nobles hommes et femmes*, Huntington Library HM 937, fol. 1, a translation into French by Laurent de Premierfait of Boccaccio's Latin original. I am indebted to Christopher Baswell for drawing my attention to this image.
9. A. King, '"According to the Custom Used in French and Scottish Wars": Prisoners and Casualties on the Scottish Marches in the Fourteenth Century', *Journal of Medieval History* 28, no. 3 (2002): 269.
10. Jessica L. Mou, '"Sumir Kallaðr Þat Meinsemd": Going Berserk in the Shadow of State Centralization in Old Norse Society', in *The Treatment of Disabled Persons in Medieval Europe: Examining Disability in the Historical, Legal, Literary, Medical, and Religious Discourses of the Middle Ages*, ed. Wendy J. Turner and Tory Vandeventer Pearman (Lewsiton, NY: Edwin Mellen Press, 2010), 98, citing chap. 11, *The Saga of Grettir the Strong*, trans. Bernard Scudder, in *The Complete Sagas of the Icelanders*, ed. Viðar Hreinsson (Reykjavik: Leifur Eiriksson, 1997), II:59. Other characters from Nordic culture who may be identified as orthopedically impaired by their names include Thorir Arnason (*Eyrbyggjasaga*, chap. 18), who lost a leg in battle in 981 and was known as Viðleggr (wooden leg), and Thorleif Kimbi (*Eyrbyggjasaga*, chap. 18), who also lost a leg in battle "and after this went about most often with a wooden leg"; see W. Bonser, *The Medical Background of Anglo-Saxon England: A Study in History, Psychology, and Folklore* (London: Wellcome Historical Medical Library, 1963), 101.
11. Gregory of Tours, *History of the Franks*, 153; *Historiarum Francorum Libri X*, cap. II, 37, ed. Bruno Krush and Wilhelm Levison, MGH Scriptores rerum

Merovingicarum 1, 87–88. Unless due to congenital causes (Metzler, 'Reflections on Disability in Medieval Legal Texts', in *Disability and Medieval Law*, ed. Cory Rushton [forthcoming: 2013]), physical impairment appears not to have been regarded as a 'disability' in a military leader.

12. Pierre Riché, *Die Welt der Karolinger*, 3rd ed., trans. C. Dirlmeier and U. Dirlmeier (Stuttgart: Reclam, 2009), 211; see Abbon, *Le Siège de Paris par les Normands*, trans. and ed. H. Waquet, (Paris: Les Belles Lettres, 1942; rpt. 1964), 64.

13. According to William of Malmesbury, *Gesta regum Anglorum*, Robert received a wound that caused him to lose his senses, in punishment for the firing of Bayeux; *Oxford Dictionary of National Biography*, eds H. C. G. Matthew and B. Harrison (Oxford: Oxford University Press, 2004), XLVII, 118.

14. Episode mentioned in the *Chronicle* of Roger of Wendover—*Chronici Rogeri de Wendover*, ed. H. Hewlett, iii (Rolls Series, 1889), 85–86; see M. Prestwich, 'Miles in armis strenuus: The Knight at War', *Transactions of the Royal Historical Society* 6th series 5 (1995): 212.

15. Ohler, *Krieg und Frieden*, 268.

16. Walter the Chancellor, *The Antiochene Wars*, ed. H. Hagenmeyer, trans. T. S. Asbridge and S. B. Edgington (Aldershot: Ashgate, 1999), 171, quoted by Mitchell, *Medicine*, 165–66; in contrast, Baldwin VII, Count of Flanders, received an injury to the brain during the attack on Arques in 1118 which proved fatal; see William of Malmesbury, *De gestis regum Anglorum*, ed. W. Stubbs, Rolls Series 90 (1897), II, 479.

17. King, 'According to the Custom', 269. More generally, see A. R. Bell et al., eds., *The Soldier Experience in the Fourteenth Century* (Woodbridge: Boydell and Brewer, 2011).

18. Huizinga, *Waning of the Middle Ages*, 28.

19. Prestwich, *Armies and Warfare*, 332. In terms of potentially disabling wounds, Prestwich cites the following horrific case: "in a fight against the Norwegians one English knight had his hip-bone cut away with a single blow from a battle-axe" (ibid.); see Giraldus Cambrensis, *Expugnatio Hibernica: The Conquest of Ireland by Giraldus Cambrensis*, ed. A. B. Scott and F. X. Martin (Dublin: Royal Irish Academy, 1978), 76–77.

20. Mitchell, *Medicine*, 111. Examples of such archaeological findings from battlefield sites include Visby (on which see the following); Aljubarrota (Portugal), where a battle took place on 15 August 1385; and the recent evaluations of Towton (fought 29 March 1461 during the War of the Roses); see E. Cunha and A. M. Silva, 'War Lesions from the Famous Portuguese Medieval Battle of Aljubarrota', *International Journal of Osteoarchaeology* 7 (1997): 595–99; A. Boylston, 'Evidence for Weapon-Related Trauma in British Archaeological Samples', in *Human Osteology in Archaeology and Forensic Science*, ed. M. Cox and S. Mays (London: Greenwich Medical Media, 2000), 357–80; and Veronica Fiorato, Anthea Boylston and Christopher Knüsel, eds., *Blood Red Roses: The Archaeology of a Mass Grave from the Battle of Towton AD 1461* (Oxford: Oxbow, 2000).

21. Information reproduced in Nicolle, *Medieval Warfare*, 256; after Bo E. Ingelmark, 'Skeleton Finds from the Warrior Graves outside Wisby', in *Armour from the Battle of Wisby, 1361*, ed. Bengt Thordeman (Uppsala, 1939; rpt. with intro. by Brian R. Rice, Union City, CA: Chivalry Bookshelf, 2001).

22. Mitchell, *Medicine*, 116.

23. Piers D. Mitchell, Yossi Nagar and Ronnie Ellenblum, 'Weapon Injuries in the 12th Century Crusader Garrison of Vadum Iacob Castle, Galilee', *International Journal of Osteoarchaeology* 16 (2000): 145–55.

24. Mitchell, *Medicine*, 165–66.
25. A. Boylston, M. Holst and J.Coughlan, 'Physical Anthropology', in Fiorato, Boylston and Knüsel, *Blood Red Roses*, 52 and 53.
26. Ibid., 53.
27. J. Coughlan and M. Holst, 'Health Status', in Fiorato, Boylston and Knüsel, *Blood Red Roses*, 72.
28. C. Knüsel, 'Activity-Related Skeletal Changes', in Fiorato, Boylston and Knüsel, *Blood Red Roses*, 116.
29. C. Knüsel and A. Boylston, 'How Has the Towton Project Contributed to Our Knowledge of Medieval and Later Warfare?', in Fiorato, Boylston and Knüsel, *Blood Red Roses*, 173.
30. Coughlan and Holst, 'Health Status', 72.
31. B. Hooper et al., 'The Grave of Sir Hugh de Hastyngs, Elsing', *Norfolk Archaeology* 39 (1984): 89–99.
32. Carole Rawcliffe, *Medicine and Society in Later Medieval England* (Stroud: Sutton, 1995), 3; cf. M. Hebert, 'L'Armée Provençale en 1374', *Annales du Midi* 91 (1979): 5–27.
33. "Presentium lator nobiscum viriliter agens fortiter dimicavit et graves vulnerum dolores pro Christo suscipiens et sanguinem suum copiose fundens inter Christicolas Christi martir triumphavit. [...] quia presentium lator passiones nostras nobiscum sustinuit et in Christi nomine robur et sanguinem suum offerens truncato ac lacerato corpore impotens laborum et morum opera inutili permansit, omnium ac singulorum rogamus pietatem, ut necessitates ipsius pie respiciatis, quatenus eleemosinarum vestrarum largitione iter possit peragere usque martirii et laboris sui nostrarumque orationum communionem." Cited by Achim Hölter, *Die Invaliden. Die vergessene Geschichte der Kriegskrüppel in der europäischen Literatur bis zum 19. Jahrhundert* (Stuttgart: J. B. Metzler, 1995), 65, from a manuscript in Wolfenbüttel, first mentioned by Julius Ficker, 'Invalidenpaß für einen Kreuzfahrer. Anno 1177', *Katholische Zeitschrift Münster* 2 (1852): 170–72.
34. Thomas Hostell had been "smyten with a springolt through the hede, lesing his oon ye, and his cheke boon broken; also at the bataille of Agincourt, and after the takyng of the carrakes on the see, there with a gadde of yren his plates smyten in sondre, and sore hurt, maymed and wounded; by meane wherof he being sore febeled and debrused, now falle to great age and poverty, gretly endetted, and may not helpe himself." Cited by Rawcliffe, *Medicine and Society*, 4; see also *Original Letters Illustrative of English History*, ed. H. Ellis, 3 series in 11 vols. (London, 1824–46), second series, IV. 95–96. Knüsel and Boylston, 'How Has the Towton Project Contributed?', 172–73, use Hostell as an example for the observation that "previously wounded, sometimes quite incapacitated individuals, continued to participate in warfare."
35. Edward J. Kealey, *Medieval Medicus: A Social History of Anglo-Norman Medicine* (Baltimore, MA: Johns Hopkins University Press, 1981), 155, entry 39.
36. Hölter, *Die Invaliden*, 66. Relying on the older research by W. Haberling, *Die Entwicklung der Kriegsbeschädigtenfürsorge von den ältesten Zeiten bis zur Gegenwart* (Berlin: Hirschwald, 1918), 21–30, Hölter (67) cites a number of cases where royal orders by German, English and French monarchs facilitated placement of invalid veterans as quasi-oblates within monasteries.
37. Luttrell, 'Hospitallers' Medical Tradition', 72.
38. Geremek, *Margins*, 105.
39. A historical account of society's response to disabled war veterans ranging from the earliest times through to the First World War can be found in

Edward T. Devine, *Disabled Soldiers and Sailors: Pensions and Training*. Carnegie Endowment for International Peace, Preliminary Economic Studies of the War, no. 12 (New York: Oxford University Press, 1919)—note the date of publication! For the chronologically varying interest in disabled war veterans see the discussion in Metzler, *Disability*, 12.

40. Geremek, *Margins*, 105.

41. Hölter, *Die Invaliden*, 62–97, discusses these themes in detail with many references to examples in European literature between the fifteenth and eighteenth centuries.

42. Translation of this text available as Christine de Pizan, '*The Epistle of the Prison of Human Life*', with '*An Epistle to the Queen of France*', and '*Lament on the Evils of the Civil War*', ed. and trans. J. A. Wiseman (London: Garland, 1984).

43. Anne Curry, ed., *The Battle of Agincourt: Sources and Interpretations* (Woodbridge: Boydell Press, 2000), 341–42; also Hölter, *Die Invaliden*, 430.

44. Ramon Lull, *The Book of the Ordre of Chyualry*, trans. William Caxton, ed. A. T. P. Byles, EETS o.s. 168 (London, 1926), 63–64. Conversely, in a real-life case, one John of Bella Aqua used his 'deformity' in 1346 as an excuse: he had refused an instruction of Edward III that he take up knighthood but was pardoned for his disobedience on account of having a malformed right foot; see Michael Prestwich, *Knight: The Medieval Warrior's (Unofficial) Manual* (London: Thames and Hudson, 2010), 26.

45. Andreas Capellanus, *The Art of Courtly Love*, intro., trans. and notes John Jay Parry (New York: Columbia University Press, 1960), Book II, 7, case XV, 174; Hölter, *Die Invaliden*, 430, gives the Latin.

46. Chronicler William the Breton (Guilelmus Brito), *Historia Philippi Augusti*, in *Recueil des Historiens des Gaules et de la France*, eds Martin Bouquet and Léopold Delisle, 24 vols. (Paris, 1738–1904), XVII, 108, s.a. 1214, cited in Gary Dickson, *The Children's Crusade: Medieval History, Modern Mythistory* (Basingstoke: Palgrave, 2008), 126. During preparations for the Crusade of 1241, described by Matthew Paris (*Chronica majora*, ed. H. R. Luard, Rolls Series, vol. 57/4 [London, 1877], 134), even women, old men, the sick and disabled and children took up the cross—although there was never a concrete expectation that these 'weak' people would actually venture to the Holy Land, since they could seek dispensation and send (and finance?) a 'proper' crusader as substitute, thus participating in the promise of the remission of sins granted to regular crusaders; see Shahar, *Growing Old*, 2.

47. Hölter, *Die Invaliden*, 66: "Selbst in der nach 1220 auch in der Dichtung immer vehementer vorgetragenen Kritik an den z. T. katastrophalen Kreuzzügen scheint im allgemeinen nur die Alternative Leben—Tod zu existieren, auch wenn die schwere Verwundung durchaus geschildert sein kann."

48. S. A. Novack, 'Battle-Related Trauma', in Fiorato, Boylston and Knüsel, *Blood Red Roses*, 100–101: "The analysis described in this chapter suggests that what we are seeing is merely the result of hand-to-hand combat in a brutal battle using very efficient weapons of war. Rather than seeing these individuals as anomalous casualties of war, the location and type of wounds in these bodies can reveal much about medieval warfare as experienced by the common soldier."

49. Ohler, *Krieg und Frieden*, 261.

50. Contamine, *War in the Middle Ages*, 256.

51. For instance J. E. Thorold Rogers, *Six Centuries of Work and Wages: The History of English Labour* (London: Swan Sonnenschein, 1886).

52. With regard to medieval artisans and guilds within the context of organisation and administration of the craft, trade connections and economic activities in general, see, for example, Heather Swanson, *Medieval Artisans: An Urban Class in Late Medieval England* (Oxford: Blackwell, 1989); a general overview is provided in the collection of essays edited by S. Todd Lowry and B. Gordon, *Ancient and Medieval Economic Ideas and Concepts of Social Justice* (Leiden: Brill, 1998).

53. For instance, the work by Postel, *Arbeit*.

54. Livio Pestilli, 'Blindness, Lameness and Mendicancy in Italy (from the 14th to the 18th Centuries)', in *Others and Outcasts in Early Modern Europe: Picturing the Social Margins*, ed. Thomas R. Nichols (Aldershot: Ashgate, 2007), 107.

55. See Metzler, *Disability*, 149–51, with pertinent cases from the miracles of Saint Foy (Hugh the master mason's legs crushed by a cart carrying stones from the quarry; ibid., 203), Saint Godric (youth injured on a building site whereby his spine is broken; ibid., 229) and Saint Elisabeth (man aged about thirty injured his knee with an axe; ibid., 241). Pestilli, 'Blindness', 108, remarks that in Italian art of the fourteenth and fifteenth centuries "the presence of the infirm is justified by their role as miracle-seeking supplicants".

56. "De quoi cele Jehenne qui voloit venir au dit tombel et vivre du sien propre, fila tant que ele gaaigna trois sous que ele porta", Guillaume de Saint-Pathus, *Les miracles de Saint Louis*, ed. Percival B. Fay (Paris: Champion, 1931), 134, cited by Sharon Farmer, 'Manual Labor, Begging, and Conflicting Gender Expectations in Thirteenth-Century Paris', in *Gender and Difference in the Middle Ages*, Medieval Cultures 32, ed. Sharon Farmer and C. B. Pasternack (Minneapolis: University of Minnesota Press, 2003), 265.

57. "Nolebant quod daretur ei elemosina, pro eo quod, sibi videbatur quod, si de suo labore hic [Louis's tomb] viveret cum filia sua predicta, magis esset propitius sibi Deus", H.-François Delaborde, 'Fragments d'enquête faite à Saint-Denis en 1282 en vue de la canonisation de Saint Louis', *Mémoires de la Société de l'Histoire de Paris et de l'Ille de France* 23 (1896): 49, cited by Farmer, 'Manual Labor', 277 and 287, note 55.

58. Kellie Robertson, *The Laborer's Two Bodies: Literary and Legal Productions in Britain, 1350–1500*. The New Middle Ages (Basingstoke: Palgrave Macmillan, 2006), 32.

59. Ibid.; cf. *Nova Legenda Anglie: As Collected by John Tynemouth, John Capgrave and Others, and First Printed, with New Lives, by Wynkyn de Worde*, ed. Carl Horstmann, 2 vols. (Oxford: Clarendon Press, 1901), II:412–15.

60. For an account of this and other miracles in the English life of the saint, see M. R. James, 'Lives of St. Walstan', *Norfolk Archaeology* 19 (1917): 264.

61. Robertson, *Laborer's Two Bodies*, 36.

62. 'The Sermon of William Taylor', *Two Wycliffite Texts*, 19; Kate Crassons, '"The Workman Is Worth His Mede": Poverty, Labor, and Charity in the Sermon of William Taylor', in *The Middle Ages at Work*, ed. Robertson and Uebel (Basingstoke: Palgrave Macmillan, 2004), 79.

63. 'The Sermon of William Taylor', lines 589–92; Crassons, 'The Workman', 79.

64. Crassons, 'The Workman', 79; also Crassons, *Claims of Poverty*, 164. Crassons compares the wider theory of discriminate almsgiving with Taylor's sermon as well as with an episode in the *Entry into Jerusalem* of the contemporary York Corpus Christi drama cycle, where the inclusion of an able-bodied poor man, alongside the blind and lame men healed by Christ, "acknowledges the reality of able-bodied need and thus refuses to accept the assumptions of antifraternal discourse and post-plague labor legislation"

(*Claims of Poverty*, 232); the *Last Judgment* part of the York cycle also "refuses to stipulate that the hungry, naked, and sick are legitimately needy because they cannot work. It does not confine need to physical disability, nor does it scrutinize the poor people's claim to charity" (ibid., 252).

65. Christopher Dyer, *Standards of Living in the Later Middle Ages: Social Change in England c. 1200–1520* (Cambridge: Cambridge University Press, 1989), 233; see D. Woodward, *Men at Work: Labourers and Building Craftsmen in the Towns of Northern England, 1450–1750* (Cambridge: Cambridge University Press, 1995), 160–62, for examples from early modern England.

66. Vulgate: "cum aedificaveris domum novam facies muram tecti per circuitum ne effundatur sanguis in domo tua et sis reus labente alio et in praeceps ruente".

67. F. Koelsch, *Beiträge zur Geschichte der Arbeitsmedizin*. Schriftenreihe der Bayerischen Landesärztekammer Bd. 8 (Munich: Bayerische Landesärztekammer, 1967), 76; *Edict of Rothair*, c. 144 and 145, in *The Lombard Laws*, ed. and trans. Katherine Fischer Drew (Philadelphia: University of Pennsylvania Press, 1973), 39–130.

68. For instance, a newly founded journal included amongst its first essays a look at the question of industrial injury from the distant past: (Sir) Thomas Legge, 'Industrial Diseases in the Middle Ages', *Journal of Industrial Hygiene* 1 (1919–1920): 475ff.

69. Georges Renard, *Guilds in the Middle Ages* (London: G. Bell and Sons, 1918; rpt. New York: Augustus M. Kelley, 1968), 119.

70. For instance, the act of 23 January 1248 in Genoa which prohibited the foil beaters (*batifolii*) from beating foil with hammers at night; see Steven A. Epstein, *Wage Labor and Guilds in Medieval Europe*. Chapel Hill, NC: University of North Carolina Press, 1991), 72.

71. Married women helping their husbands in the 'family business' commonly become invisible to the records, while single or widowed women are more likely to feature as individuals. Most women's work in towns was too low status or too unskilled to warrant the formation of craft guilds, and even where work was skilled (such as that of the London silk workers) women failed to gather together in a guild. On the problem of women labourers, see the essays by M. Kowalski and J. Bennett, 'Crafts, Guilds, and Women in the Middle Ages', and M. K. Dale, 'The London Silkwomen of the Fifteenth Century', in *Sisters and Workers in the Middle Ages*, ed. J. M. Bennett et al. (Chicago: University of Chicago Press, 1989); also relevant is David Herlihy, *Opera muliebra: Women and Work in Medieval Europe* (Philadelphia: Temple University Press, 1990).

72. David Nicholas, *The Domestic Life of a Medieval City: Women, Children and the Family in Fourteenth-Century Ghent* (Lincoln: University of Nebraska Press, 1985), 96; the source is Stadsarchief te Gent, Ser. 330, *Zoendineboeken*, Z 2,5, f. 18v.

73. Roux, *Paris*, 155.

74. *Liber de morte et vita* 2.3, in P. Osmund Lewry, 'Study of Aging in the Arts Faculty of the Universities of Paris and Oxford', in *Aging and the Aged*, ed. M. Sheehan (Toronto: Pontifical Institute of Medieval Studies, 1990), 31. In an ironic twist of fate the author himself was killed in a collapse of the roof of the new papal apartments at Viterbo.

75. However, by the late Middle Ages, when witchcraft and sorcery arrived on the scene to preoccupy the anxious, Johannes Nider, author in around 1437 of the *Formicarius*, could cite a case where an accidental trip on the stairs, leading to a head wound and consequently to insanity, was not so accidental after all but caused by the agency of the devil's sorcery; see Aleksandra N.

Pfau, *Madness in the Realm: Narratives of Mental Illness in Late Medieval France* (PhD diss., University of Michigan, 2008), 266–67.

76. *English Gilds: The Original Ordinances of More than One Hundred Early English Gilds*, ed. Joshua Toulmin Smith and Lucy Toulmin Smith EETS o.s. 40 (London, 1870), 24. The word 'adventure' in its medieval form, 'aventure' (and many versions thereof), meaning chance, hazard or risk, still retains closer proximity to the original Latin meaning of 'advenire', 'to come, arrive'—going on an adventure is leaving many things to chance.

77. Jankrift, *Mit Gott und schwarzer Magie*, 78; see Hans-Wolfgang Beyer and Adalbert Mischlewski, *Führer durch das Antoniter-Museum* (Memmingen: Stadt Memmingen, 1998), 27.

78. All incidents cited by Letts, *Bruges*, 127; see *Het Boeck van al' t gene datters gheschiedt is binnen Brugghe, 1477–1491*, ed. C. Carton (Ghent, 1859), 233, 136 and 166.

79. Julie Kerr, 'Health and Safety in the Medieval Monasteries of Britain', *History* 93 (2008): 5.

80. Shahar, *Growing Old*, 144; see *Calendar of the Letter-Books of the City of London, 1275–1498, Books A–L.*, ed. Reginald R. Sharpe, 11 vols. (London, 1899–1912), at *Letter-Book H. c. 1375–1399* (1907), 202.

81. Shahar, *Growing Old*, 155; see *Documents Relating to Cambridgeshire Villages*, ed. W. M. Palmer and H. W. Saunders (Cambridge: Cambridge University Press, 1926), 90, no. 5.

82. Shahar, *Growing Old*, 158; B. A. Hanawalt, *The Ties that Bound: Peasant Families in Medieval England* (Oxford: Oxford University Press, 1986), 237.

83. "Pour ce qu'il estoit sourt et ydiot par non sens, yré et courroucé de ce", Paris, Archives Nationales series JJ book 160 fo 70v no 91, cited by Pfau, *Madness*, 189; the case features in one of the remission letters sent to the French king asking for pardon on the grounds of insanity.

84. *Bedfordshire Coroners' Rolls*, ed. R. F. Hunniset (Bedfordshire Historical Record Society 41, 1960), numbers 103, 110, 140, 158.

85. Ibid., numbers 169, 232, 242.

86. Ibid., numbers 282, 250, 85, 253, 90.

87. For an illustration and description of the narrative cycle, see M. H. Caviness, *The Windows of Christ Church Cathedral, Canterbury*. Corpus Vitrearum Medii Aevi, Great Britain (London, 1981), II:213. The iconography closely follows the miracle accounts in William, *Miraculi sancti Thomae*, ed. J. C. Robertson, Rolls Series vol. 67 part i (London, 1875), Bk. III, chap. 1, and Benedict, *Miraculi sancti Thomae Cantuarensis, auctore Benedicto, abbate Petriburgensi*, ed. J. C. Robertson, Rolls Series vol. 67 part ii (London, 1976), Bk. VI, chap. 1.

88. Carole Rawcliffe, 'Health and Safety at Work in Late Medieval East Anglia', in *Medieval East Anglia*, ed. Christopher Harper-Bill (Woodbridge: Boydell Press, 2005), 146; see Norwich Record Office, NCR, 8A/2, mm. 2r, 2v.

89. Rawcliffe, 'Health and Safety', 144; Norwich Record Office, NCR, 8A/2, m. 3r.

90. Rawcliffe, 'Health and Safety', 144; Norwich Record Office, NCR, 8A/2, m. 3r. While sinking a well (or perhaps digging out a cellar) another Norwich labourer was buried alive, as was the owner of a property who was sinking a pit (ibid.).

91. Rawcliffe, 'Health and Safety', 144, note 71. To protect themselves from the consequences of accidents arising from the dangers of shipping, seamen from the high Middle Ages onwards founded confraternities or brotherhoods, generally in honour of one of the patron saints of mariners, such as Saint

Nicholas. For example, in Venice, one of the largest maritime powerhouses of Europe, several such confraternities existed before the mid-thirteenth century; see Karel Davids, 'Seamen's Organizations and Social Protest, c. 1300–1825', in *Before the Unions: Wage Earners and Collective Action in Europe, 1300–1850*. International Review of Social History 39 Supplement 2, ed. Catharina Lis, Jan Lucassen and Hugo Soly (Cambridge: Cambridge University Press, 1994), 149.

92. A recent ESRC-funded study of sixteenth-century coroners' reports by Steven Gunn, based at the university of Oxford, into accidents in Tudor England has found that summer was the most dangerous time, as it was the agricultural peak season, with cart crashes, dangerous harvesting techniques, horse accidents and windmill mangling all leading to fatalities among agricultural labourers; http://www.bbc.co.uk/news/education-17601616 (accessed 4 April 2012).

93. Hanawalt, *Ties that Bound*, 178; the extant Norfolk coroners' rolls cover the years 1363 to 1379, this case is in Just. 2/105 m. 1d.

94. Hanawalt, *Ties that Bound*, 177; the extant Cambridgeshire coroners' rolls cover the years 1374 to 1376, this case is in Just. 2/18 ms. 42d, 45.

95. Epstein, *Wage Labor*, 74; see M. Chiaudano and M. Moresco, *Il cartolare di Giovanni Scriba*, 2 vols. (Rome, 1935), II:259, supplement, no. 3.

96. Cited in Fandrey, *Krüppel*, 18; also Cordula Nolte, *Frauen und Männer in der Gesellschaft des Mittelalters* (Darmstadt: Wissenschaftliche Buchgesellschaft, 2011), 29.

97. On medieval building activity in general from the perspective of the labourers and the techniques rather than a purely architectural history, see F. B. Andrews, *The Medieval Builder and His Methods* (East Ardley: EP Publishing, 1976).

98. Eddius Stephanus, *Life of Wilfrid*, chap. 23, in *The Age of Bede*, rev. ed. trans. J. F. Webb (London: Penguin, 1988),129.

99. Angela Montford, *Health, Sickness, Medicine and the Friars in the Thirteenth and Fourteenth Centuries* (Aldershot: Ashgate, 2004), 227. The event is mentioned in three contemporary chronicles, all to be found in the collection *Corpus chronicorum Bononiensium*, ed. A. Sorbelli (Città di Castello, 1939), II:136.

100. Le Goff, *Medieval Civilization*, 207.

101. L. F. Salzman, *Building in England down to 1540: A Documentary History* (Oxford: Clarendon Press, 1952, reissued 1997), 45.

102. All examples in Nicola Coldstream, *Masons and Sculptors. Medieval Craftsmen* (London: British Museum Press, 1991), 19.

103. D. Knoop and G. P. Jones, *The Medieval Mason: An Economic History of English Stone Building in the Later Middle Ages and Early Modern Times*, rev. ed. (1933; Manchester: Manchester University Press, 1967), 86; Hereford Cathedral Archives 2372, cited by P. E. Morgan, 'The Effect of the Pilgrim Cult of St. Thomas Cantilupe on Hereford Cathedral', in *St. Thomas Cantilupe Bishop of Hereford: Essays in His Honour*, ed. Meryl Jancey (Hereford: Friends of Hereford Cathedral, 1982), 152.

104. Rawcliffe, 'Health and Safety', 149; Norwich Record Office, DCN 1/7/65.

105. Salzman, *Building*, 45.

106. Ibid., 46; also see Knoop and Jones, *Medieval Mason*, 86.

107. Coldstream, *Masons*, 19.

108. Günther Binding, *Baubetrieb im Mittelalter* (Darmstadt: Wissenschaftliche Buchgesellschaft, 1993), 148.

109. Ibid.

110. Barbara Harvey, *Living and Dying in England 1100–1540: The Monastic Experience* (Oxford: Clarendon Press, 1993), 241, Appendix V no. 8.

111. Koelsch, *Beiträge zur Geschichte*, 90.
112. All examples given by Koelsch, *Beiträge zur Geschichte*, 91; also in Volker Zimmermann, 'Ansätze zu einer Sozial- und Arbeitsmedizin am mittelalterlichen Arbeitsplatz', in *Mensch und Umwelt im Mittelalter*, ed. Bernd Herrmann (Stuttgart: Deutsche Verlags-Anstalt, 1986), 142, who mentions that the latter techniques were known since antiquity, e.g. face masks are mentioned by Pliny the Elder, *Natural History*, Book 33, on the subject of mining.
113. Binding, *Baubetrieb*, 148: in 1459 at Regensburg the journeymen carpenters received a bonus since they had worked high up above ("si haben in der hoch obenauff gearbait").
114. Heather Swanson, *Building Craftsmen in Late Medieval York*. Borthwick Papers 63 (York: St. Anthony's Press, 1983), 6.
115. Cited by H. Levy, 'The Economic History of Sickness and Medical Benefit before the Puritan Revolution', *Economic History Review* 13 (1943): 42. On the London carpenters' guild, see also the essay by M. A. Amos, 'The Naked and the Dead: The Carpenters' Company and Lay Spirituality in Late Medieval England', in *The Middle Ages at Work*, ed. Kellie Robertson and Michael Uebel (Basingstoke: Palgrave Macmillan, 2004), 91–110; from the printed edition of the statutes that Amos cites, one of the work-related injuries is not caused by an axe, but a more general "hurting of any eye" (at 97).
116. The statutes of this guild are printed in R. H. Tawney and E. Power, eds., *Tudor Economic Documents*, 3 vols. (London: Longmans, 1924), I:93.
117. *York Memorandum Book, Part II, 1388–1493*, ed. M. Sellers, Surtees Society 96 (1897), 279–80, cited in Woodward, *Men at Work*, 82; Crassons, *Claims of Poverty*, 267–69.
118. Gervase's account is cited in Salzman, *Building*, 373; also Coldstream, *Masons*, 19.
119. The BBC broadcast a documentary in 2003 which highlighted the "terrible toll of deaths and serious injuries in riding accidents", including a woman from Lincolnshire who became paralysed as a result of breaking her neck (http://www.bbc.co.uk/print/pressoffice/pressreleases/stories/2007/03_march/23/riding.shtml, accessed 26 April 2011). A leading British spinal consultant "concluded that riding a horse is 20 times more dangerous than riding a motorbike" (ibid.; see J. R. Silver and J. M. Parry, 'Hazards of Horse-Riding as a Popular Sport', *British Journal of Sports Medicine* 25 [1991]: 105–10).
120. Frederick S. Paxton, review in *Speculum* 87 (2012): 225, of Achim Thomas Hack, *Alter, Krankheit, Tod und Herrschaft im frühen Mittelalter. Das Beispiel der Karolinger*. Monographien zur Geschichte des Mittelalters 56 (Stuttgart: Anton Hiersemann, 2009).
121. See http://en.wikipedia.org/wiki/List_of_horse_accidents, accessed 17 April 2011.
122. Bede, *Ecclesiastical History of the English People*, rev. ed., vol. 6, trans. Leo Sherley-Price (London: Penguin, 1990), 273.
123. Ibid.
124. The event is discussed in Guenter B. Risse, *Mending Bodies, Saving Souls: A History of Hospitals* (New York: Oxford University Press, 1999), 87–91. Purchard had been born around 925, a premature baby, allegedly delivered by Caesarean, and was made an oblate to the monastery of Saint Gall; as a child he was sickly and bled frequently (he may have suffered from haemophilia). Invalid and sickly children could be regarded as being spiritually closer to God if they had been oblated, see H. Fichtenau, *Living in the Tenth Century: Mentalities and Social Orders*, trans. P. J. Geary (Chicago: University of Chicago Press, 1991), 264.

125. Risse, *Mending Bodies*, 101.
126. Ibid., 105; Johannes Duft, *Notker der Arzt. Klostermedizin und Möncharzt im frühmittelalterlichen St. Gallen* (St. Gallen, 1972), 48–49.
127. Angela Montford, 'Fit to Preach and Pray: Considerations of Occupational Health in the Mendicant Orders', in *The Use and Abuse of Time in Christian History. Studies in Church History 37*, ed. R. N. Swanson (Woodbridge: Boydell Press, 2002), 96, cites a source mentioning amongst others that eye, knee and thigh disorders and complete debility of the body could result: "Et cum dimidium miliare processissent, ceperunt oculi deficere, crura thabascere et genua infirmari a ieunio et toto debilitare corpore" (citing *Chronica Fratris Jordani* [OFM], ed. H. Boehmer, Collection d'études et de documents, VI [Paris, 1908], 26).
128. Montford, 'Fit to Preach', 96, note 7; a thirteenth-century Franciscan chronicler emphasised the ability to travel long distances as a prerequisite for becoming a friar (ibid., 102). Kerr, 'Health and Safety', 4, mentions a number of riding accidents involving monastic personnel.
129. Esch, *Wahre Geschichten*, 47; *Repertorium Poenitentiariae Germanicum*, vol. VI (papacy of Sixtus IV, 1471–1484), ed. L. Schmugge (Tübingen: Max Niemeyer, 2005), case no. 3102.
130. Iona McCleery, 'Christ Mightier than Galen: Medicine in Late Medieval Portuguese Miracles' (paper preseneted at 'Contextualising Miracles' conference, Wolfson College, Cambridge, 16 April 2011); see M. Martins, ed., *Laudes e Cantigas Espirituais de Mestre Andre Dias* (Lisbon, 1951), 291.
131. Mary C. Hill, *The King's Messengers 1199–1377* (London: E. Arnold, 1961), 57. Major V. Wheeler-Holohan published a *History of the King's Messengers* (London: Grayson & Grayson) in 1935.
132. Hill, *King's Messengers*, 1961 edition, 58.
133. Frederick S. Paxton, review in *Speculum* 87 (2012): 225, of Achim Thomas Hack, *Alter, Krankheit, Tod und Herrschaft im frühen Mittelalter. Das Beispiel der Karolinger*. Monographien zur Geschichte des Mittelalters 56 (Stuttgart: Anton Hiersemann, 2009).
134. Mitchell, *Medicine*, 122, with illustration at 121.
135. Ibid.
136. Zimmermann, 'Sozial- und Arbeitsmedizin', 145.
137. Esch, *Wahre Geschichten*, 48; *Repertorium Poenitentiariae Germanicum*, vol. VII (papacy of Innocent VIII, 1484–1492), ed. L. Schmugge (Tübingen: Max Niemeyer, 2008), cases no. 2433 and 2434. General mention of accidents in monasteries arising from building and repair work is made by Kerr, 'Health and Safety', 4, 6–8.
138. On injuries to the eyes for tanners, leatherworkers, furriers, carpenters and needleworkers, see Mark P. O'Tool, 'Disability and the Suppression of Historical Identity: Rediscovering the Professional Backgrounds of the Blind Residents of the Hôpital des Quinze-Vingts', in *Disability in the Middle Ages: Reconsiderations and Reverberations*, ed. J. R. Eyler (Farnham: Ashgate, 2010), 13 and 19–23.
139. Roger Bacon, *Perspectiva*, Book 2, chap. 3, see Wheatley, *Stumbling Blocks*, 188–89.
140. Bartholomaeus Anglicus, *On the Properties of Things: John Trevisa's Translation of Bartholomaeus Anglicus's De proprietatibus rerum*, ed. M. Seymour. 2 vols. (Oxford: Clarendon Press, 1975), I:562.
141. In the Latin translation by Ambrose Traversari of 1475: *De vitis patrum*, X: *Pratum spirituale*, PL, vol. 74, col. 156BC; Gudrun Schleusener-Eichholz, *Das Auge im Mittelalter* (PhD diss., University of Münster, 1975; 2 vols. Munich: W. Fink, 1984), I:497.

142. Lisa Jefferson, ed., *Wardens' Accounts and the Court Minute Books of the Goldsmiths' Mistery of London, 1334–1446* (Woodbridge: Boydell Press, 2002), 67, 71, cited in Wheatley, *Stumbling Blocks*, 60; Rawcliffe, 'Health and Safety', 150; T. F. Reddaway, *The Early History of the Goldsmiths' Company* (London: Edward Arnold, 1975), 6, 70 and 103.

143. Esch, *Wahre Geschichten*, 48; *Repertorium Poenitentiariae Germanicum*, vol. VI (papacy of Sixtus IV, 1471–1484), ed. L. Schmugge (Tübingen: Max Niemeyer, 2005), case no. 3225. Another priest was decorating the altar of Saint Dorothy with fresh leaves from trees and, while whittling a branch, something flew into his eye (Esch, *Wahre Geschichten*, 48; *Repertorium Poenitentiariae Germanicum*, vol. VII [papacy of Innocent VIII, 1484–1492], ed. L. Schmugge [Tübingen: Max Niemeyer, 2008], case no. 2327).

144. Cited by Montford, *Health*, 30; see *Opera de vita regulari*, ed. J. J. Berthier, 2 vols. (Rome, 1888–1889; rpt. Turin, 1950), II:406.

145. Visibility of one's impairment had also been of concern to King Alfred: according to his biographer Asser, Alfred was afflicted by an unspecified illness for many years, so that at one point he entered a church and prayed that his present malady might be changed for some lesser infirmity which should not appear outwardly in the body lest it should render him useless and despised; Asser, *Life of Alfred*, chap. 74, cf. discussion of this episode by Paul Kershaw, 'Illness, Power and Prayer in Asser's *Life of King Alfred*', *Early Medieval Europe* 10, no. 2 (2001): 201–24.

146. Koelsch, *Beiträge zur Geschichte*, 227.

147. However, some literary critics have argued that Chrétien was not drawing on real-life examples for these working conditions, e.g. Robert Hall, 'The Silk Factory in Chrestien de Troyes' *Yvain*', *Modern Language Notes* 56 (1941): 418–22. This analysis was mainly based on the assumption that in Chrétien's time, allegedly, so little money was in circulation that his audience would not have reacted to such references to pay and working conditions in the same way a modern, industrialised audience reacts. This line of reasoning seems somewhat outdated and detracts from the main point Chrétien is making concerning the hardship *per se*, irrespective of financial details, that female textile workers could face.

148. *Arthurian Romances, Tales, and Lyric Poetry: The Complete Works of Hartmann von Aue*, trans. with commentary by Frank J. Tobin, Kim Vivian and Richard H. Lawson (University Park: Pennsylvania State University Press, 2001), 301, ll. 6183–6221.

149. *Miracula St. Bertini*, Acta Sanctorum, c. 5, OSB III, 1, 131, cited in Franz Irsigler, '*Divites* und *pauperes* in der Vita Meinwerci. Untersuchungen zur wirtschaftlichen und sozialen Differenzierung der Bevölkerung Westfalens im Hochmittelalter', *Vierteljahresschrift für Sozial- und Wirtschaftsgeschichte* 57 (1970): 485–86.

150. Rawcliffe, 'Health and Safety', 146.

151. Charlotte Roberts and Margaret Cox, *Health and Disease in Britain: From Prehistory to the Present Day* (Stroud: Sutton, 2003), 237.

152. "Ut quicumque ex eis opus proprium fuerit operatus et postmodum tanta fuerit, infirmitate seu paupertate vel senectute sive alie quacumque necessitate depresus, quod nec operari valeat nec sustentari, in infirmarium domus Theotonice in Brema suscipiendus sit et enutriendus", D. Ehmck, ed., *Bremisches Urkundenbuch Band 1: Urkunden bis 1300* (Osnabrück, 1873), 246–50; "quam allutarii de paupertate et valetudine depressi in domo sancti spiritus nunc habent et hactenus habuerunt", Staatsarchiv Bremen 2–S.13.o.1, fol. 5v. I am grateful to Ivette Nuckel for providing this reference.

153. Roberts and Cox, *Health and Disease*, 241.

154. For an archaeological perspective on mining in general, see A. Bernard Knapp, Vincent C. Piggott and Eugenia W. Herbert, eds., *Social Approaches to an Industrial Past: The Archaeology and Anthropology of Mining* (London: Routledge, 1998), which, unfortunately, does not cover the Middle Ages but does mention techniques of extraction and the labour intensity of mining activities in non-European and in ancient societies, from which one may make interesting extrapolations as to the risks to mine workers in medieval society; similarly, the standard introduction to the economics of medieval mining, John U. Nef, 'Mining and Metallurgy in Medieval Civilisation', in *The Cambridge Economic History of Europe*, vol. II, *Trade and Industry in the Middle Ages*, 2nd ed., ed. M. M. Postan and E. Hatcher (Cambridge: Cambridge University Press, 1987), 691–761, makes no mention of industrial accidents or social welfare.

155. George Rosen, *The History of Miners' Diseases* (New York: Schuman's, 1943), 39.

156. Ibid., 47–48.

157. Jan Lucassen, 'The Other Proletarians: Seasonal Labourers, Mercenaries and Miners', in *Before the Unions: Wage Earners and Collective Action in Europe, 1300–1850*, International Review of Social History 39 Supplement 2, ed. Catharina Lis, Jan Lucassen and Hugo Soly (Cambridge: Cambridge University Press, 1994), 188; sources in Saxony and Austria mention such strikes prior to 1500, while miners' strikes in Central Europe can be documented for at least as early as the mid-fifteenth century, probably even prior to 1300 if the Bohemian *Iglauer Bergrecht* (*Constutiones Juris Metallici*) is anything to go by (ibid.).

158. R. Sprandel, *Das Eisengewerbe im Mittelalter* (Stuttgart: Anton Hiersemann, 1968), 244 and 350, citing that "etliche Haspeln, Kasten und Stempelin" were destroyed.

159. Dieter Schewe, *Geschichte der sozialen und privaten Versicherung im Mittelalter in den Gilden Europas*, Sozialpolitische Schriften 80 (Berlin: Duncker & Humblot, 2000), 111–12; the church had existed since 980–1000, while the hospital was enlarged in 1200.

160. Engel and Jacob, *Städtisches Leben im Mittelalter*, 125, cf. *Urkundenbuch der Stadt Goslar*, ed. Gustav Schmidt (Halle, 1878), II, 152f., no. 70.

161. "Die Hilfe für die Armen und Schwachen, die durch die Arbeit in dem besagten Berg von körperlicher Hinfälligkeit und materieller Not bedrängt sind", document no. 70 of 28 December 1260 in the *Urkundenbuch* of the city of Goslar, translated by Ulrich Lauf, *Die Knappschaft. Ein Streifzug durch tausend Jahre Sozialgeschichte* (St. Augustin, 1994), 27 and 28, cited in Schewe, *Geschichte*, 112. From the accounts of Goslar mining companies it is evident that as late as 1409–1410 monies were paid to "the poor" (ibid., 113).

162. Ibid.

163. Ibid., 114; between 1450 and 1500, as more sources of ore were discovered in the Erzgebirge, other towns formed miners' fraternities. Also at Dalarna in Sweden the miners had established a fraternity in the second half of the fifteenth century for mutual aid in case of accident or poverty. As an aside, one of the first 'industrial' strikes, prefiguring the great labour disputes of the nineteenth and twentieth centuries, took place at Geisingberg near Altenberg in the Erzgebirge in 1469; see Ulrich Lauf, *Die Knappschaft. Ein Streifzug durch tausend Jahre Sozialgeschichte* (St. Augustin: Asgard-Verlag, 1994), 13.

164. *Schwazer Bergbuch*, fol. 154r; fols 154v–155r deal with miners' health care provision; C. Bartels, A. Bingener and R. Slotta, eds., "*1556 Perkwerch etc.*" *Das Schwazer Bergbuch*, 3 vols. (Bochum: Veröffentlichungen des Deutschen Bergbau-Museum Bochum, 2006), I.

165. Ulrich Ellenbog, *Von den gifftigen besen tempffen und reuchen*, ed. Franz Koelsch and Friedrich Zoepfl, Münchener Beiträge zur Geschichte und Literatur der Naturwissenschaften und Medizin, II, Sonderheft (Munich, 1927).

166. Agricola and Paracelsus mention respiratory diseases, as well as joint disorders and crippling fractures resulting from falling rocks and breakages of ladders or other equipment as typical hazards affecting miners; Rosen, *History of Miners' Diseases*, 54–63; Metzler, *Disability*, 117.

167. For an overview, from late antiquity to the thirteenth century, of Sunday as the holy day when work is prohibited, see Epstein, *Wage Labor*, 159–63. For iconography of Christian prohibition on (most) forms of Sunday work, see Athene Reiss, *Sunday Christ: Sabbatarianism in English Medieval Wall Painting*, British Archaeological Reports 292 (Oxford: BAR, 2000), which covers the imagery depicting Christ with the tools that parishioners were forbidden from using on Sundays or holy days, otherwise they would have been breaking the Sabbath.

168. Samson, 'End of Early Medieval Slavery', 114; Gregory of Tours, *History of the Franks*, VIII.12, 442.

169. Niall Brady, 'Labor and Agriculture in Early Medieval Ireland: Evidence from the Sources', in *The Work of Work*, ed. Allen Frantzen and Douglas Moffat (Glasgow: Cruithne Press, 1994), 131; see V. Hull, 'Cáin Domnaig', *Ériu* 20 (1966): 151–77, for edition and translation of the Irish legal text.

170. Sprandel, *Eisengewerbe*, 245.

171. Among a copious literature, see especially *English Gilds*, reprinting guild ordinances from various parts of England; George Unwin, *The Gilds and Companies of London* (London, 1908); Lisa Jefferson, *The Medieval Account Books of the Mercers of London: An Edition and Translation* (Farnham: Ashgate, 2009); idem on the *Goldsmith's Company*; J. H. Round, *The Commune of London* (London, 1899); David J. F. Crouch, *Piety, Fraternity and Power: Religious Gilds in Late Medieval Yorkshire 1389–1547* (York: York Medieval Press/Woodbridge: Boydell Press, 2000); Virginia Bainbridge, *Gilds in the Medieval Countryside* (Woodbridge: Boydell Press, 1996); and Berent Schwineköper, ed., *Gilden und Zünfte. Kaufmännische und gewerbliche Genossenschaften im frühen und hohen Mittelalter*, Vorträge und Forschungen 29 (Sigmaringen: Thorbecke, 1985) a collection of essays covering social, economic and religous aspects of guilds and their development in Germany.

172. P. Boissonade, *Life and Work in Medieval Europe (Fifth to Fifteenth Centuries)*, trans. E. Power (London: Kegan Paul, 1937), 208.

173. Ibid., 224. The development of (craft)guilds in Flanders seemed to have been influenced by the English model dating from late Saxon times (Schewe, *Geschichte*, 72–73), while German guilds in the imperial territories were somewhat late in formulating a wider range of charitable support (ibid., 78–79). Flensburg, then in the Danish kingdom, had a guild statute (article 44) of 1200 which stipulated that if a brother or sister were to be ill, then lots should be drawn as to who of the other members should keep watch at the sick-bed (ibid., 89).

174. For an overview of the origin and early history of guilds, corporations and fraternities, see Anthony Black, *Guilds and Civil Society in European Thought from the Twelfth Century to the Present* (London: Methuen, 1984), 3–11; also M. Flynn, *Sacred Charity: Confraternities and Social Welfare in Spain, 1400–1700* (New York: Cornell University Press, 1989); Hincmar, archbishop of Reims in the ninth century, described some of the purposes of confraternities as being the duty of charity to both the living and the dead, cf. Peregrine Horden, 'The Confraternities of Byzantium', in *Voluntary Religion*,

Studies in Church History 23, ed. W. J. Sheils and D. Wood (Oxford: Blackwell, 1986), 30.

175. Schewe, *Geschichte*, 50–51.

176. Ibid., 54–55 and 159.

177. Gervase Rosser, 'Crafts, Guilds and the Negotiation of Work in the Medieval Town'. *Past and Present* 154 (1997): 28.

178. Roux, *Paris*, 159; for a close study of guilds in medieval Strasbourg using a social science approach, see Sabine von Heusinger, *Die Zunft im Mittelalter. Zur Verflechtung von Politik, Wirtschaft und Gesellschaft in Straßburg*, Vierteljahrschrift für Sozial- und Wirtschaftsgeschichte—Beiheft 206 (Stuttgart: F. Steiner, 2009).

179. Sharon Farmer, Young, Male and Disabled', in *Le petit peuple dans la société de l'Occident médiéval. Terminologies, perceptions, réalités*, ed. Pierre Boglioni, Robert Delort and Claude Gauvard (Paris: Publications de la Sorbonne, 2001), 439.

180. Edward Miller and John Hatcher, *Medieval England: Towns, Commerce and Crafts 1086–1348* (Harlow: Longmans, 1995), 373.

181. Shahar, *Growing Old*, 9; Roger Bacon, *Opus majus*, ed. J. H. Bridges, 3 vols. (London 1897–1900), II, pars 2, 251; *Opus majus*, trans. R. Burke, vol. 2 (Philadelphia, 1928), II, part 2, 661.

182. Shahar, *Growing Old*, 167; Bacon, *Opus majus*, ed. Bridges, II, pars 2, 251; *Opus majus*, trans. Burke, II, part 2, 661.

183. Renard, *Guilds*, 70.

184. Epstein, *Wage Labor*, 158 and 167.

185. Ibid., 162.

186. Ibid., 167.

187. Farmer, 'Young, Male and Disabled', 441; Guillaume de Saint-Pathus, *Les miracles de Saint Louis*, miracles 8, 14, 17, 18, 20. Farmer, 'Young, Male and Disabled', 445, points out that because of their 'alien' status, such young men could not benefit from the charities set up to support children of guild members, nor could they rely on the support of civic initiatives for orphans.

188. "Ita quod omnes prebeant auxilium et iuvamen quilibet prout volunt" (V. Franchini, *Lo statuto della corporazione dei fabbri del 1244: Contribuito alla storia della organizzazione del lavoro in Modena nel secolo XIII* [Modena, 1914], 50), cited by Epstein, *Wage Labor*, 166.

189. Schewe, *Geschichte*, 55 and 159.

190. C. G. Lewin, *Pensions and Insurance before 1800: A Social History* (East Linton: Tuckwell Press, 2003), 53, based on Cornelius Walford's, *The Insurance Cyclopaedia* (n.p., 1878), article on guilds.

191. Cited by Rawcliffe, 'Health and Safety', 150; *English Gilds*, 33–36.

192. H. F. Westlake, *The Parish Gilds of Medieval England* (London: SPCK, 1919), 137–238; B. Hanawalt and B. R. McRee, 'The Guilds of *Homo Prudens* in Late Medieval England', *Continuity and Change* 7, no. 2 (1992): 163–79.

193. Pat Thane, *Old Age in English History: Past Experiences, Present Issues* (Oxford: Oxford University Press, 2000), 87.

194. Shahar, *Growing Old*, 137; P. Adam, *La vie paroissiale en France au XIVe siècle* (Paris: Sirey, 1964), 16–17.

195. Renard, *Guilds*, 11. In Montpellier a contract of 1294 between a tailor and the mother of a fourteen-year-old female apprentice obliged the tailor to keep her "in sickness and in health" (Epstein, *Wage Labor*, 77), although some "cagey masters insisted that days lost to illness be added to the end of the term [of apprenticeship], but all masters accepted some level of caring for the physical health of their charges" (ibid., 111). From a series of studies of French

sources it emerges that one month of support was the standard expected of a master (Farmer, 'Young, Male and Disabled', 445). In England, after the Statute of Labourers of 1351, the situation appears to have been more regulated, in that contracts between employer and employee were always to last a full year, and if an employee (e.g. servant, apprentice, journeyman) became ill or incapacitated through no fault of their own, the employer was obliged to 'keep on' the hired labourer (Jeremy Goldberg, *Communal Discord, Child Abduction, and Rape in the Later Middle Ages*, The New Middle Ages [New York: Palgrave Macmillan, 2008], 46, citing the case of a wet nurse who contracted a fever).

196. Cited by B. W. E. Alford and T. C. Baker, *A History of the Carpenters Company* (London: George Allen and Unwin, 1968), 30; these ordinances are actually found written down in the *Court Book* of the guild from the sixteenth century, presumably repeated from the previous century.

197. Le Goff, *Medieval Civilization*, 322.

198. "Si infirmitate aliquem habeat vel praevam corporis qualitatem propter quam foret postea onerosus si membrum aliquod mutilatum habeat vel inefficax quoquomodo", Cesare Cenci, 'De fratrum minorum constitutionibus praenarbonensibus', *Archivum Franciscanum Historicum* 83 (1990): 76, cited in Montford, 'Fit to Preach', 103, note 35.

199. Michael Bihl, 'Statuta provincialia provinciae Aquitaniae et Franciae', *Archivum Franciscanum Historicum* 7 (1914): 485, cited in Montford, 'Fit to Preach', 95.

200. "Occultam habeat infirmitatem", cited by Montford, 'Fit to Preach', 98, see *The Constitution of the Dominican Order, 1216 to 1360*, ed. G. R. Galbraith (Manchester, 1925), 2141–5. If a friar did not disclose disabilities on application to join the order which were discovered later, the friar should not be ejected from the order against his will (Montford, 'Fit to Preach', 103–4). Also see Montford, *Health*, 30–33.

201. Renard, *Guilds*, 12.

202. Epstein, *Wage Labor*, 166.

203. Schewe, *Geschichte*, 117–18 and 123, with two examples from 1336 (Zurich) and 1337 (Duderstadt) of the kind of care provided in case of illness. Because of the mobility of journeymen, such gilds had to cover flexibility of membership and temporary contributions, which in terms of administrative and legal achievement placed them far in advance of the masters' (craft) guilds, with their membership fixed by locality and generally until a master's death. As such, according to Schewe, journeymens' guilds constituted the first medieval instances of personal insurance (ibid., 129: "Damit war die erste vollständige Personenversicherung des Mittelalters ins Leben getreten."). On early development of journeymen's guilds, see also W. Reininghaus, 'Die Migration der Handwerksgesellen in der Zeit der Entstehung der Gilden (14./15. Jahrhundert)', *Vierteljahrschrift für Sozial- und Wirtschaftsgeschichte* 68 (1981): 1–22.

204. Schewe, *Geschichte*, 129.

205. Ibid., 127; Wilfried Reininghaus, *Die Entstehung der Gesellengilden im Spätmittelalter* (Münster: Reininghaus, 1980), 341–42.

206. Schewe, *Geschichte*, 118; possibly based on a reading of *Sachsenspiegel*, II, article 39 § 2.

207. Ibid. According to James Farr, *Artisans in Europe, 1300–1914* (Cambridge: Cambridge University Press, 2000), 203, there were associations of journeymen coopers in Hamburg, Lübeck, Wismar, Rostock and Stralsund by 1321, and by 1400 *Gesellenvereine* for shoemakers, tailors, furriers, bakers and smiths were found in towns all along the upper Rhine.

208. Schewe, *Geschichte*, 131.
209. "Auch wurde der knechte eyner sych, so lyhen wir ime dry schillinge alse lange bis sin achtzehen schillinge schwerden; sturbet he, so begrabin wir in glichirwis also unser meystir eynen" (ibid.). The wool weavers of Constance in 1386 requested that a journeyman had to provide security for the loan in cases of incapacity, or to swear he would not leave the town until he had repaid the loan (ibid., 131–32).
210. Cited by Engel and Jacob, *Städtisches Leben im Mittelalter*, 359–60; see *Quellen zur Geschichte der Handwerksgesellen im spätmittelalterlichen Basel*, ed. and intro. Wilfried Reininghaus (Basel: Kommissionsverlag F. Reinhardt, 1982), Text 3, at 72 and 76.
211. Schewe, *Geschichte*, 132.
212. *Amtsbrief* of the Cologne coopers, dated 14 April 1397, in Heinrich von Loesch, *Cölner Zunft- und Gewerbeurkunden bis 1500* (Bonn, 1907), I:133, chap. 6, cited in Schewe, *Geschichte*, 159.
213. Statutes of the *Schiffsleute-Bruderschaft* of Strasbourg, cited in Engel and Jacob, *Städtisches Leben*, 126; see *Strassburger Zunft- und Polizei-Verordnungen des 14. und 15. Jahrhunderts*, ed. Johann Brucker (Strasbourg, 1889), 439.
214. Rosser, 'Crafts', 28–29.
215. Farr, *Artisans in Europe*, 230.
216. Schewe, *Geschichte*, 135.
217. Ibid., 142.
218. Ibid., 132.
219. P. Borscheid, *Geschichte des Alterns: 16.–18. Jahrhundert* (Stuttgart: F. Steiner Verlag, 1987), 44.
220. Schewe, *Geschichte*, 131.
221. Borscheid, *Geschichte*, 44.
222. Westlake, *Parish Gilds*, 40. Such fraternities existed in other parts of Europe, too; see J. Henderson, 'Confraternities and the Church in Late Medieval Florence', in *Voluntary Religion*, Studies in Church History 23, ed. W. J. Shiels and Diana Wood (Oxford: Blackwell, 1986), 69–83; Henderson concentrates purely on the administrative and organisational aspects.
223. Crassons, *Claims of Poverty*, 202; Ben R. McRee, 'Charity and Gild Solidarity in Late Medieval England', *Journal of British Studies* 32, no. 3 (1993): 215.
224. All these permutations had been identified by Westlake, *Parish Gilds*, 41.
225. Following *English Gilds* and data collated by Westlake, *Parish Gilds*, 137–238.
226. Full text given in *English Gilds*, 35.
227. Ibid., 5.
228. Lewin, *Pensions*, 53, based on Cornelius Walford's article on guilds, *The Insurance Cyclopaedia* (n.p., 1878). Other guilds mentioned by Lewin include the guild of Blessed Mary at Chesterfield (aid given to people for incapacity due to loss of limb) and the guild of Saint Katherine at Aldersgate ("help in poverty through old age, fire or water, theft or sickness"); on the latter, cf. *English Gilds*, 6, which also cites a London guild of Saints Fabian and Sebastian at Aldersgate (ibid., 9) with almost identical ordinances.
229. Cited in Westlake, *Parish Gilds*, 69.
230. The guilds of Corpus Christi (which mainly differs in that a weekly dole of fourteen pence was provided) and Saint John the Baptist, both at Kingston-upon-Hull (*English Gilds*, 161 and 162, respectively).
231. Ibid., 157.
232. Ibid., 194.

233. Renard, *Guilds*, 70.
234. Ibid., 43.
235. Ibid., 45.
236. Cited by Shahar, *Growing Old*, 136; see Jean Sire de Joinville, *Histoire de Saint Louis, credo et lettre à Louis IX*, ed. and trans. M. Natalis de Wailly (Paris, 1874), C. CXLII, 722, at 392. Saintly Louis, according to Joinville, furthermore had "a number of old and crippled men to dine or sup with him every day near his own table, and ordered them to be served with the same food as himself" (Joinville and Villehardouin, *Chronicles of the Crusades*, 342).
237. On the link between structuration of time and structuration of society, see Gerhard Dohrn-van Rossum, *History of the Hour: Clocks and Modern Temporal Orders*, trans. T. Dunlop (Chicago, 1996); on time in the Middle Ages according to intellectual concepts, see P. Porro, ed., *The Medieval Concept of Time: Studies on the Scholastic Debate and Its Reception in Early Modern Philosophy* (Leiden: Brill, 2001); on literary and linguistic concepts of time in medieval culture, see R. Glasser, *Time in French Life and Thought*, trans. C. G. Pearson (Manchester: Manchester University Press, 1972); on the link between Protestant work ethic and post-medieval concepts of time, see Max Engammare, *On Time, Punctuality, and Discipline in Early Modern Calvinism*, trans. Karin Maag (Cambridge: Cambridge University Press, 2010). On how the Protestant reformers of Geneva, France, London and Bern internalised a new concept of time and also for the change from antique to medieval notions of work, see Birgit van den Hoven, *Work in Ancient and Medieval Thought: Ancient Philosophers, Medieval Monks and Theologians and Their Concept of Work, Occupations and Technology*, Dutch Monographs on Ancient History and Archaeology 14 (Amsterdam: Gieben, 1996), especially the introductory chapter for a historiographic discussion of the development of 'capitalism' during the Middle Ages.
238. 'The Framework of Time and Space', in his *Medieval Civilization*.
239. The ecclesiastical calendar is in a sense the only calendar in the Middle Ages, and the imposition of ordered time on the inmates of monastic institutions, in the form of the various services and monastic hours, is the closest thing in this period to a kind of pre-capitalist structuration of time, of fixing and partitioning time according to set rules.
240. Originally published in *Past & Present* 38 (1967): 56–97, reprinted in *Essays in Social History*, ed. M. W. Flinn and T. C. Smout (Oxford: Clarendon Press, 1974).
241. It is useful to read Thompson's classic essay in conjunction with Paul D. Glennie and Nigel Thrift's paper 'Reworking E. P. Thompson's "Time, Work-Discipline And Industrial Capitalism"', *Time and Society* 5, no.3 (1996): 275–300; their ideas were later reformulated and expanded in Paul Glennie and Nigel Thrift, *Shaping the Day: A History of Timekeeping in England and Wales 1300–1800* (Oxford: Oxford University Press, 2009), with 43–47 summarising their critique of E. P. Thompson.
242. Harald Kleinschmidt, *Understanding the Middle Ages: The Transformation of Ideas and Attitudes in the Medieval World* (Woodbridge: Boydell Press, 2000), 18.
243. Jacques Le Goff put forward this thesis in articles originally published in the early 1960s (reprinted in Jacques Le Goff, *Time, Work, and Culture in the Middle Ages*, trans. A. Goldhammer [Chicago: University of Chicago Press, 1980]). Incidentally, another Jacques, French filmmaker Jacques Tati, was at the same time criticising and lampooning modern society and the hurried time imposed by technology and consumerism ('more, faster, bigger,

better') in his satirical films. Is this an example of *mentalités* in modern popular culture having perhaps some influence on the direction of academic medievalisms?

244. Le Goff, *Medieval Civilization*, 177.

245. Ibid.

246. Monastic timekeeping was important for observation of the liturgical hours and services (see ibid., 181), while urban time had to be measured more accurately in conjunction with mercantile and banking developments, although Le Goff has argued (ibid., 182) that even in the world of industry and commerce 'natural' time played a role, mainly with regard to the contrasts between night–day and summer–winter in corporation rules regarding work activity. For a readable overview of the technological development of clocks from antiquity to modern times, including the importance of individual clockmakers among the craftsmen involved in the process, see Carlo M. Cipolla, *Clocks and Culture, 1300–1700* (London: Collins, 1967); a more scholarly treatment of temporal concepts and the science associated with time is presented by Wesley M. Stevens, *Cycles of Time and Scientific Learning in Medieval Europe*, Variorum Collected Studies 482 (Aldershot: Ashgate, 1995); see also David S. Landes, *Revolution in Time: Clocks and the Making of the Modern World* (Cambridge, MA: Harvard University Press, 1983).

247. Kleinschmidt, *Understanding*, 26.

248. Le Goff, *Time*, 35, continues: "The communal clock was an instrument of economic, social, and political domination wielded by the merchants who ran the commune." At Florence, since the thirteenth century, the bell of the Badia rang at terce and none to mark the beginning and end of the Florentine working day, until replaced by a clock of 1354 (ibid., 43).

249. Source in G. Espinas and H. Pirenne, *Recueil de documents relatifs à l'histoire de l'industrie drapière en Flandre* (Brussels, 1906), I:6, cited by Le Goff, *Time*, 46.

250. Using examples from later medieval York, Chris Humphrey, 'Time and Urban Culture in Late Medieval England', in *Time in the Medieval World*, ed. Chris Humphrey and W. M. Ormrod (York: York Medieval Press/Boydell Press, 2001), 105–17, examines what impact clocks had on the regulation of the working day.

251. Le Goff, *Time*, 45.

252. *Dives and Pauper*, ed. P. H. Barnum EETS o.s. 275 (London, 1976), Commandment I, cap. XVIII, 120.

253. The disciplinary similarity between cloister and factory, in that both breed timely regularity, has been noted by Hubert Treiber and Heinz Steinert, *Die Fabrikation des zuverlässigen Menschen. Über die "Wahlverwandtschaft" von Kloster- und Fabrikdisziplin* (Münster: Westfälisches Dampfboot, 2005); among other factors the authors cite Cistercian mining activities (at 77–98) in a critique of Foucault's (*Discipline and Punish*) earlier approach to the topic. The historical development of a methodical way of life occurred long before capitalist society, namely, within Western Christian monasticism, famously organised according to Benedict's rule of *ora et labora*. The concept of the 'closed institution' described by Foucault for the modern period has antecedents in the institutional practices of medieval monasteries, where 'discipline' is organised, utilised and transmitted. Treiber and Steinert argue, furthermore, that these principles, which stood the test of time for centuries in the cloister, had not just religious/spiritual elements but strong economic ones, too, allowing them to be generalised in the nineteenth century for the requirements of the factory and industrial production.

254. Richard Sennett, *Flesh and Stone: The Body and the City in Western Civilization* (London: Faber and Faber, 1994), 205.
255. C. Herzlich and J. Pierret, *Illness and Self in Society*, trans. E. Forster (Baltimore, MD: Johns Hopkins University Press, 1987), 85.
256. Rob Imrie, 'Ableist Geographies, Disablist Spaces: Towards a Reconstruction of Golledge's "Geography and the Disabled"', *Transactions of the Institute of British Geographers* 21 (1996): 397–403; Brendan Gleeson, *Second Nature? The Socio-Spatial Production of Disability* (PhD diss., University of Melbourne, 1993); Brendan Gleeson, 'A Geography for Disabled People?', *Transactions of the Institute of British Geographers* 21 (1996), 391–92.
257. Fandrey, *Krüppel*, 11.
258. Ibid.
259. Brendan Gleeson, 'The Social Space of Disability in Colonial Melbourne', in *Images of the Street: Planning, Identity and Control in Public Space*, ed. Nicholas R. Fyfe (London: Routledge, 1998), 94.
260. Karl Marx, *Capital: A Critique of Political Economy* (Harmondsworth: Penguin, 1981), III:366.
261. "Der tiefste Niederschlag der relativen Übervölkerung endlich behaust die Sphäre des Pauperismus. Abgesehn von Vagabunden, Verbrechern, Prostituierten, kurz dem eigentlichen Lumpenproletariat, besteht diese Gesellschaftsschicht aus drei Kategorien. Erstens Arbeitsfähige. Man braucht die Statistik des englischen Pauperismus nur oberflächlich anzusehn, und man findet, daß seine Masse mit jeder Krise schwillt und mit jeder Wiederbelebung des Geschäfts abnimmt. Zweitens: Waisen- und Pauperkinder. Sie sind Kandidaten der industriellen Reservearmee und werden in Zeiten großen Aufschwungs, wie 1860 z.B., rasch und massenhaft in die aktive Arbeiterarmee einrolliert. Drittens: Verkommene, Verlumpte, Arbeitsunfähige. Es sind namentlich Individuen, die an ihrer durch die Teilung der Arbeit verursachten Unbeweglichkeit untergehn, solche, die über das Normalalter eines Arbeiters hinausleben, endlich die Opfer der Industrie, deren Zahl mit gefährlicher Maschinerie, Bergwerksbau, chemischen Fabriken etc. wächst, Verstümmelte, Verkrankte, Witwen etc. Der Pauperismus bildet das Invalidenhaus der aktiven Arbeiterarmee und das tote Gewicht der industriellen Reservearmee. Seine Produktion ist eingeschlossen in der Produktion der relativen Übervölkerung, seine Notwendigkeit in ihrer Notwendigkeit, mit ihr bildet er eine Existenzbedingung der kapitalistischen Produktion und Entwicklung des Reichtums." Karl Marx and Friedrich Engels, *Werke*, Volume 23, *Das Kapital*, Vol. I, Seventh Section (Berlin/GDR: Dietz Verlag, 1968), 673.
262. Terry Eagleton, *After Theory* (New York: Basic Books, 2003), 42.
263. 'The Sermon of William Taylor', *Two Wycliffite Texts*, 16; Crassons, *Claims of Poverty*, 153.
264. See Metzler, *Disability*, 25–26, for further reasons why the materialist model of socio-spatial disability, while perfectly suited to explain the situation in industrialised societies, is inadequate for understanding impairment in the medieval (or any premodern) period.
265. Brendan Gleeson, *Geographies of Disability* (London: Routledge, 1999), 97. From the perspective of disability studies Mike Oliver, similarly, argued that 'feudal' society "did not preclude the great majority of disabled people from participating in the production process, and even where they could not participate fully, they were still able to make a contribution" (Mike Oliver, *The Politics of Disablement* [Basingstoke: Macmillan, 1990], 27).
266. Christopher Dyer, 'Work Ethics in the Fourteenth Century', in *The Problem of Labour in Fourteenth-Century England*, ed. James Bothwell, P. J. P. Goldberg and W. M. Ormrod (York: York Medieval Press, 2000), 22.

267. Fandrey, *Krüppel*, 13, also emphasises a rural working environment dominated by natural rhythms and cycles.

268. Margaret Pelling, *The Common Lot: Sickness, Medical Occupations and the Urban Poor in Early Modern England* (London: Routledge, 1998), 13.

269. Margaret Pelling, 'Illness among the Poor in an Early Modern English Town: The Norwich Census of 1570', *Continuity and Change* 3, no. 2 (1988): 282, note 46; and Pelling, *Common Lot*, 75.

270. The census describes her as "of 80 yere, a lame woman of one hand, & spin & wynd with one hande", cited in Pelling, *Common Lot*, 161, note 26.

271. All examples from Pelling, *Common Lot*, 85.

272. Ibid., 141.

273. Ibid., 142.

274. Rawcliffe, *Medicine for the Soul*, 173.

275. Sharon Farmer, *Surviving Poverty in Medieval Paris: Gender, Ideology, and the Daily Lives of the Poor* (Ithaca, NY: Cornell University Press, 2002), 121; see Guillaume de Saint-Pathus, *Les miracles de Saint Louis*, miracle 42, at 131–34.

276. Fandrey, *Krüppel*, 18; Werner Moritz, *Das bürgerliche Fürsorgewesen der Reichsstadt Frankfurt im späten Mittelalter* (Frankfurt-am-Main, 1981), 52.

277. Gottfried Hagen, *Das Buch von der Stadt Köln*, in *Ritter, Bürger und Scholaren. Aus Stadtchroniken und Autobiographien des 13. bis 16. Jahrhunderts*, trans. and ed. Hans Joachim Gernentz (Berlin: Union Verlag, 1980), 49, rendered into modern German: "In das Glockenhaus des Doms / eilte sehr schnell Eberhard/ und läutete die Glocke Wellin, / die alle aus dem Haus trieb, / dann in Sankt Martin Stürzkuppe,/ die auch die Lahmen laufen ließ, / und schließlich alle Sturmglocken, / die die Weiber mit Spinnrocken/ in Bewegung setzten."

278. Disabilities "bedrohen im allgemeinen nur einen Teilbereich gesellschaftlicher Standards, bzw. genügen nur einigen Funktionen und Anforderungen nicht. Je zentraler diese Werte jedoch für das gesellschaftliche Wertsystem sind . . . und je größer die Abweichung ist, desto massiver wird die Bedrohung empfunden." S. Karstedt, 'Soziale Randgruppen und soziologische Theorie', in *Stigmatisierung*, vol. I, *Zur Produktion gesellschaftlicher Randgruppen*, ed. M. Brusten and J. Hohmeier (Neuwied: Luchterhand, 1975), 183, cited by Neubert and Cloerkes, *Behinderung*, 15.

279. Neubert and Cloerkes, *Behinderung*, 15.

280. Colbert regulated the guilds and quality of production, with sometimes unpopular measures (Charles Woolsey Cole, *Colbert and a Century of French Mercantilism* [London, 1964]). Taylorism was popular at the turn of the nineteenth century and concerned the 'scientific management' of the smallest movements of a factory worker to determine the minimum times necessary to perform a given activity—the factory worker as component of a machine; see Paul Glennie and Nigel Thrift, *Shaping the Day: A History of Timekeeping in England and Wales 1300–1800* (Oxford: Oxford University Press, 2009), 50–51.

281. On the value aspect of hermaphroditism in the Middle Ages, see the argument in Metzler, 'Hermaphroditism', 34–35.

282. Brendan Gleeson, *Second Nature? The Socio-Spatial Production of Disability* (PhD diss., University of Melbourne, 1993), 161.

283. W. O. Ault, *Open-Field Farming in Medieval England: A Study of Village By-Laws* (London: George Allen and Unwin, 1972), 28.

284. Ibid., 30.

285. Ibid., citing PRO, Eccl., 26–50, *m.* 2.

286. Dyer, 'Work Ethics', 32; Ault, *Open-Field Farming*, 27–34, 82–83.
287. Dyer, 'Work Ethics', 33. Ault's study showed that there was no record of proceedings in manorial courts prior to the 1240s as up until that date it had not been a regarded as general administrative practice (*Open-Field Farming*, 18–19); hence, it seems that these central decades of the thirteenth century introduced an administrative and legal innovation.
288. Ault, *Open-Field Farming*, 30, citing Cambridge University Library, MS Ee I.1, fol. 223v.
289. Following Ault, *Open-Field Farming*. Document numbers refer to Ault's publication. Ault's study concentrated on manorial or village bylaws, starting with records from the thirteenth century, in total encompassing the court rolls of thirty-one different manors across ten English counties. The original Latin text was published by Ault in 'Open-Field Husbandry and the Village Community: A Study of Agrarian Bye-Laws in Medieval England', *Transactions of the American Philosophical Society* 55, no. 7 (1965): 5–102.
290. Ault, *Open-Field Farming*, 31, citing F. J. Baigent and J. E. Millard, *History of Basingstoke* ([Basingstoke?], 1889), 217.
291. Ault, *Open-Field Farming*, 31.
292. Ibid.
293. *English Manor*, 52, document 4; original at Cambridge University Library, EDR G3/27, fols 162–65.
294. J. Sheer and N. Groce, 'Impairment as a Human Constant: Cross-Cultural and Historical Perspectives on Variation', *Journal of Social Issues* 44, no. 1 (1988): 29.
295. Ibid.
296. Ibid.
297. Van den Hoven, *Work*, 154; cf. *Regula Magistri* 50, 72–77.
298. *St. Benedict's Rule for Monasteries*, trans. L. J. Doyle (Collegeville, MN: Liturgical Press, 1948), chap. 48, cited by Patricia Ranft, *The Theology of Work: Peter Damian and the Medieval Religious Renewal Movement*, The New Middle Ages (Basingstoke: Palgrave Macmillan, 2006), 26.
299. Chap. 68, cited by Ranft, *Theology*, 26.
300. Robert Kilwardby, *De ortu scientiarum*, ed. A. G. Judy (Oxford: British Academy, 1976), 128–9, cited in van den Hoven, *Work*, 194.
301. Jacques de Vitry addressed 37 sermons to lay people, including "hospitalarii et custodes infirmorum; leprosi et alii infirmi; pauperes et afflicti" (van den Hoven, *Work*, 219, note 67).
302. Among the extensive historiography of fools and folly the following literature stands out as particularly poignant in relating fools and disability: Enid Welsford, *The Fool: His Social and Literary History* (London: Farrar and Rhinehart, 1935; rpt. 1968), the classic introductory study; Beatrice K. Otto, *Fools Are Everywhere: The Court Jester around the World* (Chicago: University of Chicago Press, 2001), for some necessary diachronic and transcultural comparisons; Clifford Davidson, ed., *Fools and Folly*, EDAM Monograph 22 (Kalamazoo, MI: Medieval Institute Publications, 1996), on how medieval and early modern fools either capitalised on their 'natural deficiencies' or deliberately turned themselves into professional clowns; Claudia Gottwald, *Lachen über das Andere. Eine historische Analyse komischer Repräsentationen von Behinderung* (Bielefeld: transcript Verlag, 2009), 72–115, on the cultural meaning of the comic and laughter elicited by fools—but treat with caution as the author's grasp of medieval history is not always accurate; John Southworth, *Fools and Jesters at the English Court* (Stroud: Sutton, 1998), for the English perspective up to the reign of James I; Clemens Amelunxen, *Zur Rechtsgeschichte des Hofnarren. Erweiterte Fassung eines*

Vortrags, gehalten vor der Juristischen Gesellschaft zu Berlin am 24. April 1991, Schriftenreihe der Juristischen Gesellschaft zu Berlin 124 (Berlin: De Gruyter, 1991), on the legal position of courtly fools; Yi-Fu Tuan, *Dominance and Affection: The Making of Pets* (New Haven, CT: Yale University Press, 2004), an interesting exposition of the shared characteristics of women, black slaves, fools, dwarfs, castrati and pets; Sergey A. Ivanov, *Holy Fools in Byzantium and Beyond*, trans. Simon Franklin (Oxford: Oxford University Press, 2006), for the topic of holy folly as a counterpoint to the conventional image of sainthood; on this also John Saward, *Perfect Fools: Folly for Christ's Sake in Catholic and Orthodox Spirituality* (Oxford: Oxford University Press, 1980); in conjunction with holy folly one should consider the stereotype of the fool based on Psalm 52 (the fool is the person who denies God), on which topic see, among others, Barbara Swain, *Fools and Folly during the Middle Ages and the Renaissance* (New York: Columbia University Press, 1932), as well as number of art historical studies, for instance, D. J. Gifford, 'Iconographical Notes towards a Definition of the Medieval Fool', *Journal of the Warburg and Courtauld Institutes* 37 (1974): 336–42.

303. Ernst Schubert, *Alltag im Mittelalter. Natürliches Lebensumfeld und menschliches Miteinander* (Darmstadt: Wissenschaftliche Buchgesellschaft, 2002), 177.

304. These biased views of both historians as well as scholars of Disability Studies were critiqued by Metzler, *Disability*, 8–9.

305. David A. Gerber, 'Volition and Valorization in the Analysis of the 'Careers' of People Exhibited in Freak Shows', *Disability, Handicap and Society* 7, no. 1 (1992): 57–58, apparently painting this dramatic and fanciful picture after Ottavia Niccoli, 'Menstruum quasi monstrum': Monstrous Births and Menstrual Taboo in the Sixteenth Century', in *Sex and Gender in Historical Perspective*, ed. E. Muir and G. Ruggiero (Baltimore, MD: Johns Hopkins University Press, 1990), 5.

306. On disabled or ill children being taken to shrines, see R. Finucane, *The Rescue of the Innocents: Endangered Children in Medieval Miracles* (Basingstoke: Macmillan, 1997), 55–99; Metzler, *Disability*, 153–83.

307. See Chapter 4, this volume, for references to the pig hunt.

308. Bakhtin, for instance, rather impressionistically, mentions the "parish feasts, usually marked by fairs and varied open-air amusements, with the participation of giants, dwarfs, monsters, and trained animals" (*Rabelais and His World*, trans. H. Iswolsky [Blomington: Indiana University Press, 1984], 5), without providing a single concrete example of such an event, let alone references or notes to it.

309. Bakhtin, *Rabelais*, 22–29.

310. Irsigler and Lasotta, *Bettler*, 127–28, quoting L. Ennen, *Geschichte der Stadt Köln* (Cologne, 1869), III:920–21; also L. Ennen and G. Eckertz, *Quellen zur Geschichte der Stadt Köln* (Cologne, 1860), I:342.

311. Farmer, 'A Deaf-Mute's Story', 207, source: Archives du departement de Pas-de-Calais, Series A, 316, fol. 14; Series A, 293, fol. 20.

312. J. Brandhorst, 'Spielleute—Vaganten und Künstler', in *Randgruppen*, ed. Hergemöller, 169, note 41.

313. The literature on dwarfs is not quite as extensive as that on medieval fools, but nevertheless large enough to here warrant selective references only. Setting the scene for influences on medieval concepts, an excellent study of dwarfs in antiquity, Véronique Dasen, *Dwarfs in Ancient Egypt and Greece*, Oxford Monographs on Classical Archaeology (Oxford: Clarendon Press, 1992), has been translated from the French; Erica Tietze-Conrat, *Dwarfs*

and Jesters in Art (London: Phaidon, 1957), and A. Enderle, D. Meyerhöfer and G. Unverfehrt, eds., *Kleine Menschen—Große Kunst. Kleinwuchs aus künstlerischer und medizinischer Sicht* (Hamm: Artcolor Verlag, 1992), are two studies of the depiction of dwarfs in Western art. Yet most treatments of dwarfs in the Middle Ages follow a literary line of enquiry, for example, V. J. Harward, *The Dwarfs of Arthurian Romance and Celtic Tradition* (Leiden: Brill, 1958), or Albrecht Classen, 'Außenseiter der Gesellschaft im späthöfischen Roman, Volksbuch und Volkslied: Eine literar-soziologische und ethnologische Untersuchung', in *Europäische Ethnologie und Folklore im internationalen Kontext. Festschrift für Leander Petzoldt zum 65. Geburtstag*, ed. Ingo Schneider (Frankfurt: Peter Lang, 1999), 351–66. There is to date no social history of medieval dwarfs.
314. Harward, *Dwarfs of Arthurian Romance*, 21.
315. See Josef Neumann, 'Der Zwerg in Sage und Märchen—Ursache oder Abbild der Mißgestalt des Menschen?', *Gesnerus* 43 (1986): 223–40, for an attempt to untangle literary dwarfs from science and anatomy.
316. "Les géants qui sont en certains lieux s'émerveillent beaucoup de nous voir si petits comparés à eux. Nous faisons de même vis-à-vis de ceux qui ne font que la moitié d notre taille", Goussoin de Metz, *Image du Monde*, ed. O. Prior (Lausanne, 1913), 132, cited in Claude Lecouteux, *Les nains et les elfes au moyen age* (Paris: Imago, 1988), 21.
317. Enderle, Meyerhöfer and Unverfehrt, *Kleine Menschen*, 34; cf. H. Balss, *Albertus Magnus als Zoologe* (Munich: Münchner Verlag, 1928), 15.
318. *Chronicles of Matthew Paris: Monastic Life in the Thirteenth Century*, ed. and trans. Richard Vaughan (Stroud: Sutton, 1984), 189–90. Another contemporary chronicler, Johannes de Oxenedes (probably based at the Norfolk monastery of Saint Benet), mentions a variant of this episode for the same year, except that here the dwarf is nineteen years old and is led with the queen as her prodigy: "Tempore sub eodem quidam homuncio aetatis habens annorum xviiij staturae fuit vix tripedalis, nomine Johannes, quem quasi prodigium regina secum duxit" (Harward, *Dwarfs of Arthurian Romance*, 24, note 18; Johannes de Oxenedes, *Chronica*, ed. Sir Henry Ellis [London, 1859], 180).
319. As Harward concluded: "Court dwarfs most certainly existed during the Middle Ages, but in what numbers it is difficult to tell. Although it is dangerous to make negative assertions, I suggest that the paucity of evidence indicates that they were relatively rare, at least in the earlier part of the Middle Ages" (*Dwarfs of Arthurian Romance*, 26).
320. Aristotle, *Parts of Animals*, 4.10, 686 b 23–29, in Catherine Osborne, *Dumb Beasts and Dead Philosophers: Humanity and the Humane in Ancient Philosophy and Literature* (Oxford: Clarendon Press, 2007), 115, who helpfully points out: "It is simply a physical disability, like disabilities in dwarfs: animal souls would be as intelligent as ours if they were put in suitably slender, upright bodies that would permit them to operate their higher faculties."
321. A topic first discussed by Yi-Fu Tuan, *Dominance and Affection: The Making of Pets* (New Haven, CT: Yale University Press, 2004).
322. Gottwald, *Lachen*, 82.
323. From a letter dated 21 May 1481, Anna of Brandenburg to her daughter Barbara, in *Deutsche Privatbriefe des Mittelalters*, ed. Georg Steinhauser, vol. 1 (Berlin, 1899), no. 336, cited by Klaus Arnold, ed. and trans., *In Liebe und Zorn. Briefe aus dem Mittelalter* (Ostfildern: Thorbecke, 2003), 151. In 1572 King Charles IX of France 'owned' nine dwarfs, four of whom had been given to him by King Sigismund-Augustus of Poland and three by Maximilian II of Germany.

324. On wonders, see especially Lorraine Daston and Katharine Park, *Wonders and the Order of Nature 1150–1750* (New York: Zone Books, 1998).
325. On collecting, see Paula Findlen, *Possessing Nature: Museums, Collecting, and Scientific Culture in Early Modern Italy* (Los Angeles: University of California Press, 1994).
326. The state finances of Augustus were allegedly ruined, amongst other factors, by his obsession with hiring extra-tall guardsmen, 'buying' them from other rulers' armies, as when he traded 151 pieces of Chinese porcelain for six hundred dragoneers with his neighbour the king of Prussia.
327. Betty Adelson, *The Lives of Dwarfs: Their Journey from Public Curiosity toward Social Liberation* (New Brunswick, NJ: Rutgers University Press, 2005), 13 and note 28.
328. Letts, *Bruges*, 54. Fifteenth-century Bruges was witness to two other (possibly) disabled entertainers. At a banquet in January 1430 on the occasion of the wedding of Duke Philip the Good to Isabella of Portugal a female fool or court jester, one Madam d'Or, was present among the fools, acrobats, dancers and actors (ibid., 48); at a court festival she was made to wrestle with the acrobat Hans, according to Huizinga (*Waning of the Middle Ages*, 24). And in 1468 at a feast held several days after yet another noble wedding, there were more spectacles partly based on a re-enactment of romance stories, including Master Peter, a dwarf, who led a 'giant' on a chain and tied him to a tree (Letts, *Bruges*, 55).
329. John the Dwarf is mentioned in the *Apothegmata Patrum*, in *The Sayings of the Desert Fathers*, trans. B. Ward (London: Penguin, 1975; rpt. 1984).
330. Alan Cobban, *English University Life in the Middle Ages* (London: UCL Press, 1999), 19; J. M. Fletcher, 'The Teaching of Arts at Oxford, 1400–1520', *Paedagogica Historica* 7 (1967): 443.

NOTES TO CHAPTER 3

1. Shahar, *Growing Old*, 42. Elsewhere Shahar assumes that "probably many [old people] were decrepit, chronically maimed and also mentally impaired" ('The Old Body in Medieval Culture', in *Framing Medieval Bodies*, ed. Sarah Kay and Miri Rubin [Manchester: Manchester University Press, 1994], 170).
2. Joel T. Rosenthal, *Old Age in Late Medieval England* (Philadelphia: University of Pennsylvania Press, 1996), 115.
3. Ibid., 191–92, lists the key works omitting only Shahar, *Growing Old*, which had not been published then; recent historiography also includes chapters by Albrecht Classen and Elisabeth Vavra in their respective introductions to the volumes they edited on the topic, providing many further references to recent scholarship in both German and English.
4. Paul Johnson and Pat Thane, eds., *Old Age: From Antiquity to Post-Modernity* (London: Routledge, 1998); P. N. Stearns, ed., *Old Age in Preindustrial Society* (New York: Holmes and Meier, 1982) with contributions from a sociological perspective.
5. Nicola F. McDonald and W. M. Ormrod, eds., *Rites of Passage: Cultures of Transition in the Fourteenth Century* (Woodbridge: Boydell Press, 2004).
6. Mirko D. Grmek, *On Ageing and Old Age: Basic Problems and Historic Aspects of Gerontology* (The Hague: Junk, 1958).
7. Karen Cokayne, *Experiencing Old Age in Ancient Rome* (London: Routledge, 2003); Tim Parkin, *Old Age in the Roman World: A Cultural and Social History* (Baltimore, MD: Johns Hopkins University Press, 2003),

mentions the notion that old people were useless (*inutilis*), based on the catalogue of physical disabilities given by many Greek and Latin authors; or
Mary Harlow and Ray Laurence, eds., *Age and Ageing in the Roman Empire*
(Portsmouth: Journal of Roman Archaeology Supplementary Series No. 65,
2007).

8. Paul Zanker, *Die Trunkene Alte. Das Lachen der Verhöhnten* (Frankfurt:
Fischer Taschenbuch Verlag, 1989), 65.
9. Ivan Illich, *Limits to Medicine. Medical Nemesis: The Expropriation of
Health* (Harmondsworth: Penguin, 1977), 89.
10. Pat Thane, 'Geriatrics', in *Companion Encyclopedia of the History of Medicine*, vol. 2, ed. W. F. Bynum and Roy Porter (London: Routledge, 1993),
1092.
11. See the essay by Rasma Lazda-Cauders, 'Old Age in Wolfram von Eschenbach's *Parzival* and *Titurel*', in *Old Age*, ed. A. Classen (Berlin: Walter de
Gruyter, 2007), 201–18.
12. Shahar, *Growing Old*, 37.
13. Gregory the Great, *Moralia in Job*, Book 34, cited in Georges Minois, *History of Old Age: From Antiquity to the Renaissance*, trans. Sarah Hanbury
Tenison (Cambridge: Polity Press, 1989), 116.
14. Einhard, *Vita Karoli* 30, ed. Oswals Holder-Egger, MGH Scriptores Rerum
Germanicarum 25 (Hanover, 1911), 34.
15. Paul Edward Dutton, 'Beyond the Topos of Senescence. The Political Problems of Aged Carolingian Rulers', in *Aging and the Aged*, ed. M. Sheehan
(Toronto: Pontifical Institute of Medieval Studies, 1990), 77, note 12, gives
further examples, e.g. in the writings of Candidus, Einhard, the so-called
Narratio clericorum Remensium, and in various letters, all published by the
MGH series.
16. Ibid., 77.
17. "Hemma quoque regina morbo paralisi correpta usum loquendi amisit." The
Annales Fuldenses sive Annales Francorum Orientalis, ed. G. H. Pertz and
Friedrich Kurze, MGH Scriptores Rerum Germanicarum 7 (Hanover, 1891),
83, mention this event, which is rare for a chronicle of the period to do in
such detail. Emma had been queen for thirty-nine years, so the assumption
must be, even if she married very young, that she was aged at least in her fifties when she died.
18. Mentioned by Thietmar of Merseburg, *Chronicon*, ed. Robert Holtzmann,
MGH Scriptores Rerum Germanicarum n.s. 9 (Berlin, 1955), 4, 65, at 204.
19. Minois, *History of Old Age*, 3.
20. Joel T. Rosenthal, 'Retirement and the Life Cycle in Fifteenth-Century England', in *Aging and the Aged*, ed. M. Sheehan, 173–88 (Toronto: Pontifical
Institute of Medieval Studies, 1990), 185.
21. Ibid., 187.
22. "Tatsächlich gab es ja keine "Rentner" im heutigen Sinn" (Hans-Werner
Goetz, 'Alt sein und alt werden in der Vorstellungswelt des frühen und hohen
Mittelalters', in *Alterskulturen*, ed. Vavra [Vienna: Verlag der Österreichischen Akademie der Wissenschaften, 2008], 21).
23. Rosenthal, 'Retirement', 183–84, ponders the question as to why there was
no institutionalised, universal pension during the Middle Ages, arguing that
it was not just down to simple economics (lack of the necessary resources) but
also due to scales of priorities (old age pensions ranking not especially high),
and "cultural dissonance between theories about life, age, and numbers one
the one hand, and observed reality on the other."
24. Cited by Minois, *History of Old Age*, 139–40; Riché, *Daily Life*, 249. In
contrast, an old man referred to as Petrus, in the canonisation proceedings

from 1378 onward for Saint Birgitta of Sweden, is described as very old and poor (*valde senex et pauper homo*), with one hand that was already very weak and blind for three years (*altera manu dolorose debilitatus et cecus per tres annos*), yet he prayed to Saint Birgitta for healing—which was successful (Christian Krötzl, '*Sexaginta vel circa*. Zur Wahrnehmung von Alter in hagiographischen Quellen des Spätmittelalters', in *Alterskulturen*, ed. E. Vavra [Vienna: Verlag der Österreichischen Akademie der Wissenschaften, 2008], 113).

25. The *vita* of Desiderius, bishop of Cahors, mentioned on the death of the saint in 655 that "Clerus nimirum plangebat patrem, abbates pastorem, parvuli nutritorem, senes tutorem, viduae protectorem, egeni adiutorem, pupilli defensorem" (*Vita Desiderii Cadurcae urbis episcopi* 37, in *Passiones vitaeque sanctorum aevi Merovingici*, ed. Bruno Krusch, MGH Scriptores rerum Merovingicarum 4 [Hanover, 1902], 593).

26. For a summary of the dual effects in modern societies of increased survival of (elderly) people with disabilities (due to improved medical prevention and treatment) and a declining birthrate (changing population structure from the traditional pyramid shape in to more of a column—"like Nelson's column but with an elderly woman at the top of it"), see Stephen J. Kunitz, 'Medicine, Mortality, and Morbidity', in *Companion Encyclopedia of the History of Medicine*, vol. 2, ed. W. F. Bynum and Roy Porter (London: Routledge, 1993), 1704–6.

27. Thane, *Old Age*, 1. According to a report for the Organisation for Economic Co-operation and Development, the cost of caring for the elderly in OECD countries could treble by 2050, with estimates that 10 per cent of people will be aged eighty years or over by that time (BBC News http://www.bbc.co.uk/news/health-13437528, accessed 21 May 2011).

28. On modern ageism, see, for instance, Todd D. Nelson, 'Ageism: Prejudice against Our Feared Old Self', *Journal of Social Issues* 61 (2005): 207–21.

29. Pat Thane, ed., *The Long History of Old Age* (London: Thames and Hudson, 2005), 9. In *Old Age*, 2, Thane argues that this attitude is due to an "influential social science narrative that has reinforced this belief in profound difference between then and now."

30. Interview with Prof. Stefan Görres, director of the Institut für Public Health und Pflegeforschung (IPP) at the university of Bremen, in *Highlights. Informationsmagazin der Universität Bremen*, no. 24 (July 2011): 7.

31. Thane, *Long History*, 9.

32. Ibid.

33. Ibid.

34. Shulamith Shahar, 'The Middle Ages and Renaissance', in *The Long History of Old Age*, ed. Pat Thane (London: Thames and Hudson, 2005), 71. On the question 'Did People in the Past Grow Old?', see the eponymous chapter in Thane, *Old Age*, 19–27.

35. Aristotle and Cicero both reached age sixty-three, Ennius and Horatius Flaccus both seventy, Virgil fifty-two—which is considered "a short time even in our [Petrarch's] age"—and Plato eighty-one (Sen. XVII, 2, *Letters of Old Age: Rerum Senilium Libri I–XVIII*, trans. Aldo S. Bernardo, Saul Levin and Reta A. Bernardo. 2 vols. [Baltimore, MD: Johns Hopkins University Press, 1992], II:650–51).

36. Ibid.

37. Ibid., 651.

38. Esch, *Wahre Geschichten*, 50; *Repertorium Poenitentiariae Germanicum*, vol. II (papacy of Nicholas V, 1447–1455), ed. L. Schmugge (Tübingen: Max Niemeyer, 1999), case no. 886.

39. Thane, *Long History*, 12; for north-western European family structures and the position of the elderly, see also Richard M. Smith, 'The Manorial Court and the Elderly Tenant in Late Medieval England', in *Life, Death, and the Elderly: Historical Perspectives*, ed. Margaret Pelling and Richard M. Smith (London: Routledge, 1991), 39–45.

40. D. Vassberg, 'Old Age in Early Modern Castilian Villages', in *Power and Poverty: Old Age in the Pre-Industrial Past*, ed. S. Ottaway, L. Botelho and K. Kittredge (Greenwood, CT, 2002), 156–57.

41. Deborah Youngs, *The Life Cycle in Western Europe, c. 1300–c. 1500* (Manchester: Manchester University Press, 2006), 182; Shahar, *Growing Old*, 90; Charles de la Roncière, 'Tuscan Notables on the Eve of the Renaissance', in *A History of Private Life II: Revelations of the Medieval World*, ed. Philippe Ariès and Georges Duby, trans. A. Goldhammer (Cambridge, MA: Belknap Press, 1988), 207.

42. See the discussion in Albrecht Classen, 'Old Age in the World of the Stricker and other Middle High German Poets: A Neglected Topic', in *Old Age*, ed. Albrecht Classen (Berlin: Walter de Gruyter, 2007), 241–47; also see Albrecht Classen, 'Der alte Mensch in den spätmittelalterlichen Mæren: Die Komplexität der Alterserfahrung im Spätmittelalter aus mentalitätsgeschichtlicher Sicht', in *Alterskulturen*, ed. E. Vavra (Vienna: Verlag der Österreichischen Akademie der Wissenschaften, 2008), 222–27, for the same topic in a thirteenth-century poem, *Der Schlegel* by Rüdiger der Hünkhover.

43. On this question, for a general overview, see the essay by demographic historian J. C. Russell, 'How Many of the Population Were Aged?', in *Aging and the Aged*, ed. M. Sheehan, 119–27; for a microhistory of age-ranges within one particular group, see the essay by Anne Gilmour-Bryson, 'Age-Related Data from the Templar Trials' in the same volume, 129–42.

44. Shahar, 'The Middle Ages', 79.

45. See the summary of demographic analyses and conclusions in Youngs, *Life Cycle*, 30–33.

46. David Herlihy and C. Klapisch-Zuber, *Les toscans et leurs familles* (Paris: Editions de l'Ecole des Hautes Études en Sciences, 1978), 371.

47. Shahar, 'The Middle Ages', 79.

48. Thane, *Long History*, 17.

49. *Codex Justinianus*, Book 8 titulus 53.16, at 185: "Das Greisenalter ist allein kein Hindernis, eine Schenkung zu machen" (Senectus ad donationem faciendam sola non est impedimento).

50. "Nisi senectum eum detineret", cited in Shahar, *Growing Old*, 181, note 66; see usatge 7, *Usatges*, 66.

51. Thane, *Long History*, 17; the sixties and seventies as medieval definition of old age are reiterated also by Shahar, 'The Middle Ages', 71 and 75.

52. Shahar, 'The Middle Ages', 75.

53. "Sit sexaginta annorum uel supra", *Glanvill*, Book XIV, chap. 1, at 173.

54. Shahar, *Growing Old*, 85; *Las siete Partidas del Rey Don Alfonso el Sabio*, ed. G. Lopez (Salamanca, 1555; rpt. Madrid, 1974), P. 3, t. 16, ley 2, at 74.

55. Mentioned by Goldberg, *Communal Discord*, 199, note 63, who also cites the case of one Lady Margery, aged seventy, giving evidence in the 1360s at her local parish church rather than the usual site of the court (ibid., 99); Pope Gregory IX, *Decretales*, Liber 2, tit. 20, Canon 8, in *Corpus Iuris Canonici, Pars Secunda: Decretalium Collectiones*, ed. Emil Ludwig Richter and Emil Friedberg, 2 vols. (Leipzig: Tauchnitz, 1879–1881).

56. Goldberg, *Communal Discord*, 5 and 180, note 4.

57. Cited by Joseph Bettey, *Morning Stars of the Reformation: Early Religious Reformers in the Bristol Region*. ALHA 8 (Bristol: Avon Local History and

Archaeology, 2011), 17; H.-C. Maxwell-Lyte and M. C. B. Dawes, eds., 'The Register of Thomas Bekynton (Bishop of Bath and Wells 1443–65)', *Somerset Record Society* 49 (1934): 458.

58. Shahar, *Growing Old*, 101.

59. "Wenn die Könige der Drei Dynastien Altersfürsorge betrieben, dann geschah dies auf Grundlage der (verschiedenen) Alters(kategorien). Bei den Achtzigern (Achtzigjährigen) braucht einer der Söhne nicht dem Staate zu dienen; bei den Neunzigern braucht es die (ganze) Familie nicht. Bei Behinderten und Kranken, die sich ohne andere nicht ernähren können, wird einer freigestellt." German translation from the ancient Chinese text *Lǐjì* given in Enno Giele, 'Staatliche Altersfürsorge im frühen China aus historiographischer Sicht', in *Über Himmel und Erde. Festschrift für Erling von Mende*, ed. R. T. Kolb and M. Siebert (Wiesbaden: Harrassowitz, 2006), 202. The same text differentiates state provision for the elderly, that is, people in their sixties and seventies, according to rank, so that noblemen no longer have to travel without a wagon, while aged commoners eat no meal without meat (ibid.). A citation from the year AD 117 of an older Chinese text mentions an ordinance relating to monthly activities performed by the state; here the activity for mid-autumn includes caring for the weak and the elderly, dispensing arm supports and crutches and feeding the aged with millet gruel (ibid., 203). And a further text from the Han period mentions the gift of "royal crutches" given on the occasion of a person's seventieth birthday (ibid., 204). In China, state provision for all of the 'needy' in a community seems to have been regarded as a duty from at least the fourth century BC onwards, with concrete measures, such as the communal feeding and donation of clothing and crutches, evidenced from the third century BC on (ibid., 207). These samples demonstrate the widespread notion, across different cultures and different times, of the somehow 'special' position of the elderly and, most importantly, of their physical requirements.

60. On the pathology of old age according to Old Testament sources, see I. G. Papayannopoulos, 'Information Revealed from the Old Testament Concerning Diseases of Old Age', *Koroth* 8, nos. 5–6 (1982): 68–71.

61. See Rolf Sprandel, *Altersschicksal und Altersmoral: Die Geschichte der Einstellungen zum Altern nach der Pariser Bibelexegese des 12.-16. Jahrhundert*. Monographien zur Geschichte des Mittelalters XXII (Stuttgart: Hiersemann, 1981).

62. Johann Maier, 'Die Wertung des Alters in der jüdischen Überlieferung der Spätantike und des frühen Mittelalters', *Saeculum* 30 (1979): 363.

63. Shahar, 'The Middle Ages', 71; according to the twelfth-century author of the *Tractatus de Quaternario*, the *physici* spoke of four ages of man, while the *philosophi* spoke of seven ages (J. A. Burrow, *The Ages of Man: A Study in Medieval Writing and Thought* [Oxford: Clarendon Press, 1986], 37). The *Kalendar of Shepherds* divided the ages of man into twelve, to tie in with the months of the year; October, November and December were the months equated to old age (Minois, *History of Old Age*, 160).

64. Thane, *Long History*, 22. On the ages of man theme see also U. Helfenstein, *Beiträge zur Problematik der Lebensalter in der mittleren Geschichte* (Zürich: Europa Verlag, 1952). Medieval Jewish thought also divided the human life span into various ages (three-, four- and seven-schema), whereby the age of senescence was often viewed as a time of degeneration, sometimes also subdivided and occasionally regarded as a positive through bringing about greater spiritual contemplation (see Maier, 'Wertung', 355–56). The transcendence of one's 'natural' age was viewed as a positive, in that one aimed to overcome the defects of a particular age, such as the immaturity

of childhood; the *puer senex*, the child who acts like a wise old man, based on the boy Jesus in the temple, is the prime example of this ideal, on which see Christian Gnilka, *Aetas Spiritalis. Die Überwindung der natürlichen Altersstufen als Ideal frühchristlichen Lebens*, Theophaneia 24 (Bonn: P. Hanstein, 1972).

65. "Quinta aetas senioris, id est gravitas, quae est declinatio a iuventute in senectutem . . . Senium autem pars est ultima senectutis, dicta quod sit terminus sextae aetatis." Isidore of Seville, [*Etymologiae*], William D. Sharpe, 'Isidore of Seville: The Medical Writings. An English Translation with an Introduction and Commentary', *Transactions of the American Philosophical Society* 54, no. 2 (1964): Book XI, chap. 2.7–8, at 49; Latin cited in Burrow, *Ages of Man*, 200–201. These are in part the effects of the exhaustion of the blood in old age "whence also tremor occurs in the elderly" (Book XI, chap. 1.123, at 46).

66. "Hinc succedit senectus, frigida et sicca, in qua quidem minui et decrescere corpus incipit, tamen virtus non deficit, quinquagesimo quinto anno vel sexagesimo persistens." Cited in Burrow, *Ages of Man*, 22–23.

67. "Huic succedit senium, collectione phlegmatis humoris frigidum et humidum, in quo virtutis apparet defectus, quod suos annos vite termino metitur." Cited in Burrow, *Ages of Man*, 23.

68. "Aetas minuendi cum virtus non amittitur, et haec est aetas senectutis, quae fere est usque ad annos lx. Et est aetas minuendi cum manifesta virtutis debilitate, et haec quidem est aetas senium et finis vitae." Cited in Burrow, *Ages of Man*, 23.

69. Albertus Magnus, *De Aetate*, Tractatus I, chap. II: "et in aetatem diminuendi virtutem sine diminutione substantiae, et in aetatem minuentem tam substatium quam virtutem." Cited in Burrow, *Ages of Man*, 24.

70. Dante, *Il convivio*, iv. xxiii. 10 and iv. xxiv. 6, 2nd ed., ed. G. Busnelli and G. Vandelli, rev. A. E. Quaglio (Florence: Felice Le Monnier, 1964); Burrow, *Ages of Man*, 143, points out that Thomas Aquinas, *Summa Theologica*, 3 q. 46 a. 9 ad 4, had already used the same argument; Metzler, *Disability*, 55–62, had discussed notions of physical perfection at the corporeal resurrection and hence the absence of disability in eschatological visions.

71. Letter XII, 1, *Letters of Old Age*, II:439, addressed to Giovanni [Dondi] da Padova, a famous physician.

72. "Nota quod etas viuencium distinguitur in tria tempora, scilicet in tempus perfectus, defectus, et status . . . est tempus defectus quando, scilicet, virtutes viuencium tendunt ad declinacionem, ita quod virtutes insite a generantibus vadunt ad corrupcionem." Cited in Lewry, 'Study of Aging', 36, from Merton College, Oxford, MS 292, fols. 396vb–401va, at fol. 398ra.

73. From Gregory the Great's treatise on the five hours as representing the five ages of the world, and these in turn connected to the ages of man, *XL Homiliarum in Evangelia*, Book I, Hom. 19, PL vol. 76, col. 1155: "Undecima vero hora ea est aetas quae decrepita vel veterana dicitur." On this theme see the chapter 'Time' in Burrow, *Ages of Man*; furthermore, see Simone de Beauvoir, *Old Age [La Vieillesse]*, trans. P. O'Brian (London: A. Deutsch and Weidenfeld and Nicolson, 1972), 138–39, who had already drawn attention to medieval intellectual's perceptions of the world they were living in as 'old'.

74. On ageing in the classical world, see, for example, Thomas M. Falkner and Judith de Luce, eds., *Old Age in Greek and Latin Literature* (Albany: State University of New York Press, 1989); Parkin, *Old Age*.

75. Listed in Thane, *Old Age*, 38; cf. Hippocrates, *Aphorisms*, ed. W. H. S. Jones (Cambridge, MA: Loeb, 1931), III.31.

76. Thane, 'Geriatrics', 1093.

77. Cited in Minois, *History of Old Age*, 104; Robert M. Green, *A Translation of Galen's Hygiene* (Springfield, IL: Charles C. Thomas, 1952), 7.

78. Isidore of Seville, *Etymologiae*, Book XI, Chap. 30, at 51.

79. The thirteenth-century introduction of Aristotle to the West, plus the translation of Arabic medical texts, led to a greater scientific discussion of ageing, based on humoral theory, which allowed for the vices of senescence to be balanced by its virtues, in that ageing could bring opportunities for spiritual perfection; Michael E. Goodich, 'The Virtues and Vices of Old People in the Late Middle Ages', *International Journal of Aging and Human Development* 30, no. 2 (1990): 119–27.

80. On the topic of old age in the medieval reception of Aristotle via Averroes, see Alexander Brungs, 'Die philosophische Diskussion des Alters im Kontext der Aristoteles-Rezeption des 13. Jahrhunderts', in *Alterskulturen*, ed. E. Vavra (Vienna: Verlag der Österreichischen Akademie der Wissenschaften, 2008), 98–107; on ageing in thirteenth-century university texts, see Lewry, 'Study of Aging', 23–38.

81. Luke E. Demaitre, 'The Care and Extension of Old Age in Medieval Medicine', in *Aging and the Aged*, ed. M. Sheehan (Toronto: Pontifical Institute of Medieval Studies, 1990), 9, note 25.

82. *De proprietatibus rerum* VII 19: "Aliquando propter humorum & spirituum consumptionem, vt est videre in senibus, quorum oculi primo caligant & defectum visus patiuntur", cited in Schleusener-Eichholz, *Das Auge*, I:496.

83. However, in his *Summa* Thomas Aquinas argued that the ages of the body are not detrimental to the ages of the soul (*corporales aetates animae non praejudicant*), cited in Mary Dove, *The Perfect Age of Man's Life* (Cambridge: Cambridge University Press, 1986), 48.

84. Youngs, *Life Cycle*, 184.

85. Lanfranc of Milan, *Chirurgia magna*, completed in 1296, cited in Wallis, *Medieval Medicine*, 283.

86. Honorius Augustodunensis, *De philosophia mundi libri quator*, PL vol. 172, L. 4, C. 36, col. 99; Vincent de Beauvais, *Speculum naturale*, in *Bibliotheca mundi seu speculum quadruplex* (Douai, 1624), L. 31, C. 87, col. 2360; Arnaldus de Villanova, *De regimine sanitatis*, in *Opera Omnia* (Basel, 1585), col. 372; Albertus Magnus, *Parva naturalia, de aetate sive de juventute et senectute*, in *Opera Omnia*, ed. A. Borgent (Paris, 1890), IX, tractatus 1, C. 6, 306–14. For a general treatment of senile dementia, see Herbert C. Covey, 'A Return to Infancy: Old Age and The Second Childhood in History', *International Journal of Aging and Human Development* 36, no. 2 (1992–1993): 81–90.

87. Vincent de Beauvais, *Speculum naturale*, in *Bibliotheca mundi seu speculum quadruplex* (Douai, 1624), L. 31, C. 88, col. 2361.

88. Isidore of Seville, *Etymologiae*, Book XI, chap. 2.27, at 50. Needless to say, women also had colder blood, and were therefore mentally subnormal compared to adult males, according to numerous medieval medical treatises.

89. Cited by Ashley Crandell Amos, 'Old English Words for *Old*', in *Aging and the Aged*, ed. M. Sheehan (Toronto: Pontifical Institute of Medieval Studies, 1990), 106, acknowledging that this passage may also be read in a contrary sense, but preferring the interpretation given in the preceding.

90. Cited by Minois, *History of Old Age*, 162; Philippe de Novare, *Des quatre tenz d'aage d'ome*, chap. 36.

91. "Wer ein Kind lehrt, wem gleicht es?—Tinte, auf neues Papier geschrieben; wer einen Greis lehrt, wem gleicht das?—Tinte, auf radiertes Papier geschrieben" (cited by Maier, 'Wertung', 363).

92. Giraldus Cambrensis, *Speculum duorum*, ed. Y. Lefèvre and R. B. C. Huygens, trans. B. Dawson (Cardiff: University of Wales Press, 1974), Distinctio II, C. 8, 206–7.
93. Shahar, *Growing Old*, 60.
94. Vincent of Beauvais, *Speculum naturale*, L. 31, C. 89–90, cols 2359–61, cited in Shahar, *Growing Old*, 56.
95. *Byrhtferth's Manual*, ed. S. J. Crawford, EETS o.s. 177, 1929, 12.
96. "Iam mihi annosa etas dorsum incurvat, iam rugosa cutis faciem deturpat, iam pectus velut sonipes fessus anhelat, iam vox rauca ceu anser sibilat, et morbida senectus meos enervat sensus" (Cosmas of Prague, *Cosmae Pragensis Chronica Boemorum*, ed. Berthold Bretholz. MGH Scriptores Rerum Germanicarum n.s. 2 [Berlin, 1923], 3, 59, at 237).
97. *Liber decem capitulorum* 5, 1–2, cited in Juanita Feros Ruys, 'Medieval Latin Meditations on Old Age: Rhetoric, Autobiography, and Experience', in *Old Age*, ed. A. Classen (Berlin: Walter de Gruyter, 2007), 180; *Marbodi Liber decem capitulorum: Introduzione, testo critico e commento*, ed. Rosario Leotta (Rome: Herder, 1984).
98. Joannitius, *Isagoge* 58, cited in Wallis, *Medieval Medicine*, 149.
99. Cited in Wallis, *Medieval Medicine*, 257; Gilles de Corbeil was born around 1140, and after studying at Salerno taught medicine at Paris until his death in 1214.
100. *De malo senectutis et senii: Un manuale duecentesco sulla vecchiaia*, ed. Paolo Garbini (Florence: Sismel, 2004).
101. "Sensuum defeccionem, virium inbecillitatem, rugose contraccionis in cute deformitatem, dorsi incurvitatem, membrorum tremorem, gressuum titubacionem, linguam iterum pueriliter balbucientem" (Robert Grosseteste, *De decem mandatis [de quarto mandato]*, Auctores Britannici medii aevi 10, ed. Richard C. Dales and Edward B. King [Oxford: Oxford University Press, 1987], 47).
102. "White hair, pallor, wrinkling of the skin, excess of mucus, foul phlegm, inflammation of the eyes and general injury of the organs of sense, diminution of blood and spirits, weakness of motion and breathing in the whole body" (Roger Bacon, *Opus majus*, ed. Bridge, II:206; English translation in Roger Bacon, *Opus majus*, trans. Burke, II:619).
103. Roger Bacon, *De retardatione accidentium senectutis cum aliis opusculis medicinalibus*, ed. A. Little and E. Withington (Oxford: Clarendon Press, 1928), 9, 29, 31, 80.
104. Demaitre, 'The Care and Extension', 10. For a Middle English translation of Bacon dating from the late fifteenth century, see Cambridge, Trinity College MS R.14.52, edited and discussed in M. Teresa Tavormina, ed., *Sex, Aging, and Death in a Medieval Medical Compendium: Trinity College Cambridge MS R.14.52, Its Texts, Language, and Scribe*, 2 vols. (Tempe: Arizona Center for Medieval and Renaissance Studies, 2006), I:133–248, where the second chapter gives an abbreviated list of the accidents of old age as "pallidnes of spirite, moche icchyng and cracchyng, short and stynkkyng breth, blerid eyen, slumber, wrath, and vnrest of soule, hurt of instrumentis of wittis in whom lifly vertu werkith" (ibid., 163).
105. "Et ideo patres corrumpuntur, et generant filios corruptos et habentes dispositionem ad mortis festinationem" (*Opus maius*, VI.xii.2, cited in Michael Goodich, *From Birth to Old Age: The Human Lifecycle in Medieval Thought, 1250–1350* [Lanham, MA: University Press of America, 1989], 152); Roger Bacon, *Opus majus*, ed. Bridges, II:204–5.
106. *Summa de exemplis et rerum similitudinibus*, VI. 52 (Venice, 1584), cited by Goodich, *From Birth to Old Age*, 147; also see Albrecht Classen, ed., *Old*

Age in the Middle Ages and the Renaissance: Interdisciplinary Approaches to a Neglected Topic, Fundamentals of Medieval and Early Modern Culture 2 (Berlin: Walter de Gruyter, 2007), 40.

107. Martin de Saint-Gilles, *Les Amphorismes Ypocras*, ed. G. Lafeuille (Geneva: Droz, 1954), 71, cited and trans. Julie Singer, *Blindness and Therapy in Late Medieval French and Italian Poetry*, Gallica 20 (Cambridge: D. S. Brewer, 2011), 161.

108. "Propter hoc videmus senes incurvari propter debilitatem caloris naturalis", cited by Demaitre, 'The Care and Extension', 11.

109. Ibid.

110. "Er erseufftzet, schlaffet vnd ist stetigs betrübt, bekumert vnd kranck", cited in Borscheid, *Geschichte*, 15; Albrecht von Eyb, *Ob einem manne sey zunemen ein eelichs weyb oder nicht*, ed. H. Weinacht (Darmstadt: Wissenschaftliche Buchgesellschaft, 1982).

111. Cited by Minois, *History of Old Age*, 170; Saint Bernard, *Oeuvres complètes*, trans. Abbé Dion, 8 vols. (Paris, 1867), VII:257.

112. On laughter as a moral danger, see Jacques Le Goff, *Das Lachen im Mittelalter* (Stuttgart: Klett-Cotta, 2004), and especially Le Goff, 'Kann denn Lachen Sünde sein?', *Frankfurter Allgemeine Zeitung*, 3 May 1989.

113. Shahar, 'The Middle Ages', 94; Bernardino of Siena, *De calamitatibus et miseries humanae et maxime senectutis*, in *Opera Omnia*, ed. Fathers of the Collegium of S. Bonaventurae (Florence, 1959), VII:253, 256–62, sermo 16. Elsewhere, Bernardino stated tersely that "old age is filled with numerous infirmities, labours, and complaints" (cited by David Herlihy, 'Age, Property, and Career in Medieval Society', in *Aging and the Aged*, ed. M. Sheehan [Toronto: Pontifical Institute of Medieval Studies, 1990], 144).

114. Quoted by Shahar, 'The Old Body', 178; G. Zerbi, *Gerontomacia: On the Care of the Aged and Maximianus' Elegies on Old Age and Love*, trans. L. R. Lind (Philadelphia: American Philosophical Society, 1988), 325, Elegy 1, line 257.

115. M. McVaugh, 'Cataracts and Hernias: Aspects of Surgical Practices in the Fourteenth Century', *Medical History* 45, no. 3 (2001): 319–40.

116. Gilles's biography is narrated by Wheatley, *Stumbling Blocks*, 204–5; Singer, *Blindness*, 138–42; with a unique illumination of Gilles undergoing cataract surgery accompanying his 'autobiography' in Brussels, Bibliothèque Royale de Belgique, ms 13076–77, fol. 50v.

117. Gilles le Muisit, *Chronique et Annales de Gilles le Muisit*, ed. Henri Lemaître (Paris, 1906), 307, cited and trans. Wheatley, *Stumbling Blocks*, 260, note 96.

118. Cited in Wallis, *Medieval Medicine*, 397, based on the edition of the text by Ernest Wickersheimer, 'Les secrets et les conseils de maître Guillaume Boucher et de ses confrères. Contributions à l'histoire de la médecine à Paris vers 1400', *Bulletin de la société française d'histoire de la médecine* 8 (1909): 89–91. In the sole surviving manuscript this Latin text is refered to as *The Secrets and Consultations of Drs Guillaume Boucher and Pierre d'Ausson (Secreta et consilia Carnificis et Danszon)*.

119. Wallis, *Medieval Medicine*, 398.

120. Ibid., 399.

121. George R. Coffman, 'Old Age from Horace to Chaucer: Some Literary Affinities and Adventures of an Idea', *Speculum* 9 (1934): 254–55.

122. *De miseria humanae conditionis*, Book 1, chap. 10, following the edition *Lotario de Segni*, 49.

123. Shahar, 'The Middle Ages', 84.

124. Ibid., 85.

125. *Letters of Old Age*, I:265. See J. D. Folts, 'Senescence and Renascence: Petrarch's Thoughts on Growing Old', *Journal of Medieval and Renaissance Studies* 10 (1980): 207–37.
126. Letter VIII, 2, *Letters of Old Age*, I:272. Some passages further on in the same letter, Petrarch explicitly states that he does not "agree with Terence's Chremes that old age itself is a disease, unless he were perhaps to add one thing that would make the idea more complete, namely, that old age is a disease of the body, but the health of the soul" (ibid., 278). In yet another letter, dated 27 April 1373, also addressed to his friend Boccaccio, Petrarch cites a classical maxim, "old age itself is a disease" (Terence, *Phormio* 575), with which he agrees in principle "provided that one point is added to it: that old age is a disease of the body but the health of the mind" (Letter XVII, 2, II:646).
127. *Dictionarium*, VI. 86–87, in Goodich, *From Birth to Old Age*, 147; this text was apparently first published in 1340 as a preaching aid.
128. Dan Michel, *Ayenbite of Inwyt*, new ed., ed. Richard Morris and Pamela Gordon, EETS o.s. 23 (London, 1866, reissued 1965), 1.
129. For medieval and early modern medical literature, cf. Peter Dilg, 'Arzneimittel *ad longam vitam* aus Mittelalter und früher Neuzeit', in *Alterskulturen*, ed. E. Vavra (Vienna: Verlag der Österreichischen Akademie der Wissenschaften, 2008), 361–87.
130. On the historical development of geriatrics, see Thane, 'Geriatrics', 1092–1115; for medieval medical literature, see Demaitre, 'The Care and Extension', 4–7.
131. Youngs, *Life Cycle*, 183.
132. Demaitre, 'The Care and Extension', 22. For advice manuals on the care and preservation of old age (*gerocomia*), cf. Daniel Schäfer, 'Gerokomien—eine vergessene Fachliteratur der Frühen Neuzeit', *Würzburger Medizinhistorische Mitteilungen* 21 (2000): 7–17.
133. Metzler, *Disability*, 169–78.
134. Simone Kahlow, 'Prothesen im Mittelalter—ein Überblick aus archäologischer Sicht', in *Homo debilis. Behinderte—Kranke—Versehrte in der Gesellschaft des Mittelalters*, ed. Cordula Nolte (Korb: Didymos-Verlag, 2009), 203–23.
135. Singer, *Blindness*, 149; Petrarch, *Opera quae extant omnia* (Basel, 1581), 185.
136. Thane, *Old Age*, 53.
137. For instance, Edward Rosen, 'The Invention of Eyeglasses', *Journal of the History of Medicine and Allied Sciences* 11, no. 1 (1956): 13–47 and 11, no. 2 (1956): 183–218; or James, *Studies*, who (at p. 26) mentions that in 1411–1412 the poet Hoccleve, in his English version of *De Regimine Principum*, stated that although by his age he had problems with his eyes he refused to wear glasses.
138. The best, and still useful, example is the monumental *Beiträge zur Geschichte der Brille. Sammlung wissenschaftlicher Aufsätze und Berichte über die Brille und ihre Geschichte*, ed. and pbl. by Carl Zeiss (Stuttgart: Oberkochen und Marwitz, 1958).
139. Some of which is summarised in Singer, *Blindness*, 150–52. For the archaeological evidence, see Geoff Egan, *The Medieval Household: Medieval Finds from Excavations in London* 6 (London: The Stationery Office, 1998), 277, fig. 213, with a particularly decorative example from Merton Priory; Judy Stevenson, 'A New Type of Late Medieval Spectacle Frame from the City of London', *London Archaeologist* 7, no. 12 (1995): 321–27.
140. Singer, *Blindness*, 151, citing Hermentaire Truc and Pierre Pansier, *Histoire de l' ophtalmologie à l' école de Montpellier* (Paris, 1907), 138.

141. Epistle XVIII, 1, *Letters of Old Age*, II:672, dated to 1370–1374.
142. Frank Rossi, *Die Brille. Eine Geschichte der Sehhilfen* (Leipzig: Edition Leipzig, 1989), 35, points out that during the first century after the invention of glasses it was primarily intellectuals and scholars who wore them, to aid their reading, so that glasses were *not* primarily intended for the correction of sight deficiencies more generally; thus, in early depictions spectacles were originally the symbols of the learned and wise person.
143. Shahar, 'The Old Body', 160.
144. Ibid., 161.
145. Cited by Minois, *History of Old Age*, 120; cf. Augustine, 'Des douze sortes d'abus', in *Oeuvres complètes de saint Augustin*, 32 vols. (Paris, 1873), XXIII:63.
146. "Nichtz dann mer sorg, arbeit, verdießen, schmetzen, kranckheit vnd sünde" (*Ehebüchlein*, cited by Borscheid, *Geschichte*, 14); Albrecht von Eyb, *Ob einem manne sey zunemen ein eelichs weyb oder nicht*, ed. H. Weinacht (Darmstadt: Wissenschaftliche Buchgesellschaft, 1982).
147. *De proprietatibus rerum*, VI, 1, in Elizabeth Sears, *The Ages of Man: Medieval Interpretation of the Life Cycle* (Princeton, NJ: Princeton University Press, 1986), 128 and note 40, following *Liber de proprietatibus rerum* (Strasbourg, 1505), L. VI, C. 1; also Bartholomaeus Anglicus, *On the Properties of Things*, I:293.
148. Kleinschmidt, *Understanding*, 298. In rare cases elderly people, as well as those deemed too young or too infirm to be useful, were killed during times of extraordinary events, as occurred in the year 1030, when, according to the *Annals of Saxo*, the Polish warlord Mieszko had such persons put to death: "Omnes ergo, quibus grandeva senectus vel tenera etas vel egretudinis infirmitas vires negaverat, armis interire precepit" (*Annalista Saxo* a. 1030, 367). On life cycle studies for Scandinavian regions, cf. Shannon Lewis-Simpson, ed., *Youth and Age in the Medieval North* (Leiden: Brill, 2008).
149. Beauvoir, *Old Age*, 130; see 127–30 for her views on the position of the aged in earlier medieval society.
150. Kleinschmidt, *Understanding*, 298.
151. Nerys T. Patterson, *Cattle-Lords and Clansmen: The Social Structure of Early Ireland* (Notre Dame, IN: University of Notre Dame Press, 1994). I am grateful to Sally Crawford for drawing my attention to this.
152. "Et de captione hominum relaxaverunt omnes senes et inutiles ceteris retentis, quos servicio robustior aptaverat etas" (Helmold of Hirsau, *Chronicon*, ed. Bernhard Schmeidler, MGH Scriptores Rerum Germanicarum 32 [Hanover, 1937], 1, 65, at 123).
153. Already in the Old Testament (Lev. 27:1–7) a sliding scale, degenerating according to age and gender, of valuation in silver shekels was stipulated, this time in connection with vows dedicating to God the value of a person; see Shahar, *Growing Old*, 5–6.
154. *Lex Visigothorum* VIII, 4, 16, at 248–49.
155. In epic literature, the old and therefore inactive King Hrothgar in *Beowulf* fails to protect Denmark from the onslaught of a monster; see Britt C. L. Rothauser, 'Winter in Heorot: Looking at Anglo-Saxon Perceptions of Age and Kingship through the Character of Hrothgar', in *Old Age*, ed. A. Classen (Berlin: Walter de Gruyter, 2007), 103–20.
156. Minois, *History of Old Age*, 141; *Lex Baiwariorum*, ed. Ernst von Schwind, MGH Leges I: Leges Nationum Germanicarum V.2 (Hanover, 1926), II.9, 302–3.
157. Shulamith Shahar, 'Who Were the Old in the Middle Ages?', *Social History of Medicine* 6 (1993): 335.

158. A number of works on images and expectations of medieval masculinities have been published in recent years, of which the most pertinent to the question of physical ability includes Gesine Jordan, 'Hoffnungslos siech, missgestaltet und untüchtig? Kranke Herrscher und Herrschaftsanwärter in der Karolingerzeit', in *Homo debilis. Behinderte—Kranke—Versehrte in der Gesellschaft des Mittelalters*, ed. Cordula Nolte (Korb: Didymos-Verlag, 2009), 245–62.

159. Kleinschmidt, *Understanding*, 305. Thane, *Old Age*, 7, also mentions the employment of old people, usually men, as legal advisors on ancient customs, for instance, in connection with property disputes. But the utility of the aged as arbiters of collective memory did not suddenly disappear overnight after the eleventh century, as a condensed reading of Kleinschmidt would lead one to assume. Shahar, *Growing Old*, 82–85, provides a number of examples from the thirteenth to fifteenth centuries of elderly men (and occasionally elderly women) "giving evidence on past customs and events". Rosenthal, *Old Age*, 11–13, discusses fourteenth- and fifteenth-century Inquisitions Post Mortem as example of legal proceedings where the memory and social standing of the elderly was valued, also on role of the elderly in Proofs of Age (34 and 43). And C. Phythian-Adams, *Desolation of a City: Coventry and the Urban Crisis of the Late Middle Ages* (Cambridge: Cambridge University Press, 1979), 93, points out that still in the fifteenth century in Coventry old men (that is, those in the stylised age of decrepitude, namely, over sixty) were the trusted repositories of local custom, and their memories and interpretations of such custom had legally binding status.

160. Minois, *History of Old Age*, 6.

161. Kleinschmidt, *Understanding*, 305.

162. "Hae siquidem volucres cum senili gravantur etate, ut iam nec volare valeant nec videre, filii parentibus suis pio compatientes affectu vetustas sibi pennas evellunt, eorumque oculos alis porpriis confovent, ac totum corpus undique velut obliniendo ac palpando demulcent, donec toto corpore renovati plumis undique reflorentibus adholescant" (Petrus Damiani, ep. 86, 479). In this context it is interesting to note that in his 1871 publication, *The Descent of Man, and Selection in Relation to Sex* (London: Penguin, 2004), Charles Darwin had observed a number of incidences of birds helping other, disabled birds: "Capt. Stansbury found on a salt lake in Utah an old and completely blind pelican, which was very fat, and must have been well fed for a long time by his companions. Mr Blyth, as he informs me, saw Indian crows feeding two or three of their companions which were blind; and I have heard of an analogous case with the domestic cock" (126). Modern studies of animal behaviour include the observation by ornithologist Kevin McGowan of healthy American Crows (*Corvus brachyrhynchos*) feeding sick family members, and "scientists in British Columbia recorded in detail how a crippled and partially blind Northwestern Crow [*Corvus caurinus*] was fed, and hence kept alive, by its group members" (J. M. Marzluff and T. Angell, *In the Company of Crows and Ravens* [New Haven, CT: Yale University Press, 2005], 190). There is furthermore the anecdote of a cat named Libby who would guide her elderly, deaf and blind dog friend, called Cashew, away from obstacles and lead him to food (Marc Bekoff and Jessica Pierce, *Wild Justice: The Moral Lives of Animals* [Chicago: University of Chicago Press, 2009], ix). And archaeology has uncovered evidence that very early hominids may have fed and cared for their elderly disabled. An article in *Nature* reported that fossils found in the Caucasus (at Dmanisi, Georgia) dating from 1.77 million years ago included the skull of a hominid well over the age of forty—a grand old age for the species—which was completely

toothless. This aged individual, who lost all teeth some years before death, would not have been able to eat the then normal diet of raw meat or fibrous plants, because of the inability to chew. The report suggested that the old hominid was kept alive through being fed choice soft morsels like brain, marrow and succulent berries. The researchers were unclear as to why the hominid was kept alive, but speculated that such preferential treatment may have been a) due to the kindness of the group, b) due to an ulterior motive as perhaps the individual may have been useful (helping to procure food, defend the group or care for their young) or c) because the individual could have been valued for cultural reasons, similar to the value attached to old people in modern hunter-gatherer societies, for experience and knowledge (reported by the BBC News website http://news.bbc.co.uk/1/hi/sci/tech/4418363.stm, accessed 7 April 2005).

163. Stephen G. Post, 'Infanticide and Geronticide', *Ageing and Society* 10 (1990): 317–18.
164. Jacob Grimm, *Deutsche Rechtsaltertümer*, 4th ed. 2 vols. (Originally published 1828. Leipzig, 1899; rpt. Darmstadt: Wissenschaftliche Buchgesellschaft, 1994), 669.
165. Ibid., 671.
166. Ibid., 672; accusations of cannibalism conform to the general stereotyping of the Other, in this case the barbarian and pagan Slavs, so as not to be taken very seriously.
167. Ibid.
168. "Die deutsche geschichte kennt kein beispiel, daß seit der Einführung des christenthums abgelebten Eltern ein freiwilliger oder gewaltsamer Tod widerfahren wäre" (ibid., 674).
169. For instance, in the essay by Dietz-Rüdiger Moser, 'Die Märchen von der Altentötung und das Altwerden im Märchen nach Beispielen in Volkserzählungen des späten Mittelalters', in Vavra, *Alterskulturen*, 203–18.
170. Peter Dinzelbacher, *Europa im Hochmittelalter 1050–1250. Eine Kultur- und Mentalitätsgeschichte* (Darmstadt: Primus Verlag, 2003), 139; *Kulturhistorisk leksikon for nordisk middelalder*, ed. Johannes Brønsted et al. (Copenhagen: Rosenkilde og Bagger, 1956), V:422–23.
171. A brief summary of high medieval scholastic views of the female body as disabled is given in Pearman, *Women*, 7–11. The ageing female body as especially 'disabled' is a theme also explored by Mikee Delony, 'Alisoun's Aging, Hearing-Impaired Female Body: Gazing at the Wife of Bath in Chaucer's *Canterbury Tales*', in *Treatment of Disabled Persons*, eds. W. Turner and Tory Vandeventer Pearman (Lewiston, NY: Edwin Mellen Press, 2010), 336–38.
172. "La vetula est une nature (*complexio*) physiopathologique maligne" (Jole Agrimi and Chiara Crisciani, 'Savoir médical et anthropologie religieuse. Les représentations et les fonctions de la *vetula* (XIIIe–XVe siècle)', *Annales Économies, Sociétés, Civilisations* 48 (1993): 1298); the authors also draw attention to the greater impressionability of *vetulae* and their greater readiness over old men to believe in fantastic apparitions.
173. Cited in Danielle Jacquart and Claude Thomasset, *Sexuality and Medicine in the Middle Ages*, trans. M. Adamson (Oxford: Polity, 1988), 75; also Shahar, 'The Old Body', 163; see *Secreta mulierum*, ed. Margaret Rose Schleissner (PhD diss., University of Princeton, 1987), ll. 2331–35.
174. Bettina Bildhauer, *Medieval Blood* (Cardiff: University of Wales Press, 2006), 112; see *Secreta mulierum*, ed. Schleissner, ll. 2319–25 and 2363–69.
175. Lotario de Segni, *De miseria humane conditionis [(Papst Innozenz III.). Vom Elend des menschlichen Daseins]*, Book 1, chap. 4, trans. C.-F. Geyer (Hildesheim: Georg Olms), 45–46.

176. B. Lawn, *The Prose Salernitan Questions* (Oxford: Oxford University Press/ British Academy, 1970), 155, Q. 228.
177. Chiara Frugoni, 'Altri luoghi, cercando il Paradiso (Il ciclo di Buffalmacco nel Camposanto di Pisa e la committenza domenicana)', *Annali della Scuola Normale di Pisa, Classe di Lettere e Filosofia*, s. III, XVIII (1988): 1583–84, cited in Lina Bolzoni, *The Web of Images: Vernacular Preaching from Its Origins to St. Bernardino of Siena* (Aldershot: Ashgate, 2004), 29.
178. Bakhtin, *Rabelais*, 25.
179. Comedy actors are routinely portrayed "deformed, with fat bellies, spindly legs, wrinkled and grimacing faces" (Zanker, *Trunkene Alte*, 23). For example, a Roman statue of a drunken old woman clutching her amphora of drink, a first-century AD copy of a Greek original, can be found in the Museo Capitolino, Rome; reproduced in Tim Parkin, 'The Ancient Greek and Roman Worlds', in *Long History*, ed. P. Thane, 53. Now in the Glyptothek, Munich, the Greek original of the *anus ebria* has been arousing controversy among art historians and critics since its discovery in the eighteenth century (Zanker, *Trunkene Alte*, 6–11).
180. Some examples are shown in Robert Garland, *The Eye of the Beholder: Deformity and Disability in the Graeco-Roman World* (London: Duckworth, 1995), plates 25, 34, 54.
181. In fact, Paul Zanker has argued that the Munich statue of the *anus ebria*, with whom he compares the Kerch terracottas (*Trunkene Alte*, illustrations 17 and 19, at 30 and 31), makes a satirical comment on the social decline of the aged former prostitute (*hetaera*) no longer capable of earning her fees.
182. On medieval misogyny expressed in the literary treatment of women in general, see R. Howard Bloch, *Medieval Misogyny and the Invention of Western Romantic Love* (Chicago: University of Chicago Press, 1991); on misogyny toward old women in particular, see the essays by Gretchen Mieszkowski, 'Old Age and Medieval Misogyny: The Old Woman', in *Old Age*, ed. Albrecht Classen, 299–319 (Berlin: Walter de Gruyter, 2007), and Karen Pratt, '*De vetula*: The Figure of the Old Woman in Medieval French Literature', in *Old Age*, ed. Albrecht Classen, 321–42 (Berlin: Walter de Gruyter, 2007). The *vetula* has been described as "a truly European phenomenon, appearing in all the major vernacular literatures of the West as well as in Latin poetry and exemplary fiction" (John V. Fleming, *The Roman de la Rose: A Study in Allegory and Iconography* [Princeton, NJ: Princeton University Press, 1969], 171–73). Having relinquished their own sexuality due to the ravages of age and a deteriorating body, old women often become procuresses and/or corrupters of young women in such texts. While the literature on the image of the old woman as witch is too vast to even hint at here, suffice it to mention that the physiognomy of the *vetula* was one of the misogynistic factors feeding into the discourse on witchcraft; for the antecedents to the topos of old women as sorceresses and witches, developing out of male criticism of old women's medical knowledge, via stereotyping of old women as ignorant, credulous and idolatrous, all set out in intellectual texts from the thirteenth century onwards, see Agrimi and Crisciani, 'Savoir médical', 1281–97.
183. Guillaume de Lorris and Jean de Meun, *Le Roman de la Rose*, ed. Daniel Poirion (Paris: Garnier-Flammarion, 1974), ll. 339–60 and 391–94; English trans. *The Romance of the Rose*, trans. and ed. Frances Horgan (Oxford: Oxford University Press, 1994), 7–8.
184. de Lorris and de Meun, *Romance*, 8 (*Le Roman de la Rose*, l. 405).
185. For instance, in the illuminations to a number of manuscripts in the National Library of Wales at Aberystwyth, see Alcuin Blamires and G. C. Holian, *The*

Romance of the Rose Illuminated: Manuscripts of the National Library of Wales, Aberystwyth (Cardiff: University of Wales Press, 2002), 59.

186. Guillaume de Deguileville, *Le Pèlerinage de la vie humaine*, ed. J. Stürzinger (London: Roxburghe Club, 1893), 229, 251–52, 255, 374, 407, 414.

187. Shahar, 'The Middle Ages', 87; for an analysis of the imagery employed in this text, see Susan K. Hagen, *Allegorical Remembrance: A Study of* The Pilgrimage of the Life of Man *as a Medieval Treatise on Seeing and Remembering* (Athens: University of Georgia Press, 1990).

188. See also Sarah Alison Miller, *Medieval Monstrosity and the Female Body* (London: Routledge, 2010), emphasising that although the female body is regarded as monstrous it is not subject to the usual marginalisations that other (literary) monsters undergo, while highlighting the "authoritative discourse" on the topic commencing with the Pseudo-Ovidian poem *De vetula*, via the treatise *De secretis mulierum* attributed to Albertus Magnus, concluding with Julian of Norwich's *Showings*.

189. *Ruodlieb*, lines 15, 1–33, ed. B. K. Vollmann (Wiesbaden: Reichert, 1985), 125.

190. Cited in Alcuin Blamires, ed., *Woman Defamed and Woman Defended: An Anthology of Medieval Texts* (Oxford: Clarendon Press, 1992), 175.

191. François Villon, *The Poems of François Villon*, ed. Edward F. Chaney (Oxford: Blackwell, 1940), 57–58.

192. Classen, 'Der alte Mensch', 233.

193. Ibid., 235.

194. Lucie Dolezalová, '*Nemini vetula placet?* In Search of the Positive Representation of Old Women in the Middle Ages', in *Alterskulturen*, ed. E. Vavra (Vienna: Verlag der Österreichischen Akademie der Wissenschaften, 2008), 181.

195. Ibid., 182.

196. *Dame Sirith*, lines 199, 306, 311, cited by Pearman, *Women*, 30; 'Dame Sirith', in *The Trials and Joys of Marriage*, ed. Eve Salisbury (Kalamazoo, MI: Medieval Institute Publications, 2002), 29–52.

197. "Tenus et repputee estre grant sorciere et mauvaise femme", Paris, Archive Nationales series JJ book 199 fo 276 no 441, cited by Pfau, *Madness*, 269.

198. Minois, *History of Old Age*, 191; *Egil's Saga*, trans. E. R. Eddison (Cambridge: Cambridge University Press, 1930), 219.

199. *Egil's Saga*, chap. 85, 219.

200. Shahar, 'The Middle Ages', 80. Examples in Aquinas, *Summa Theologiae* 3a, q. 72, art. 8; Matthew Paris, *Chronica Majora*, ed. R. Luard, Rolls Series 25 [57] (1877), 134.

201. Shahar, 'The Middle Ages', 88; Aegidius Romanus, *De regimine principum* (Rome, 1607), L. 1, pars 4, C. 1–4, 188–203.

202. Goodich, *From Birth to Old Age*, 42.

203. Coffman, 'Old Age', 264.

204. Ibid., 266.

205. *Parlement of the Thre Ages*, ed. M. Y. Offord, EETS 246 (London, 1959), 5, ll.154–55 and 158–59.

206. William Langland, *Piers the Ploughman*, rev. ed. Trans. J. F. Goodridge (Harmondsworth: Penguin, 1966), 94; "Ac olde men and hore that helplees ben of strengthe" (B-Text passus VII, line 98).

207. B-Text passus VII, line 100.

208. Langland, *Piers the Ploughman*, 248; "Elde the hoore; he was in vauntwarde, / And bar the baner bifore Deeth—bi right he it cleymede" (B-Text passus XX, line 95).

209. Ibid., 250; "And made me balled bifore and bare on the croune / . . . / And hitte me under the ere—unnethe may I here. / He buffeted me aboute the

mouth and bette out my wangteeth, / And gyved me in goutes—I may noght goon at large / . . . / For the lyme that she loved me fore, and leef was to feele / . . . / I ne myghte in no manere maken it at hir wille, / So Elde and he[o] haden it forbeten" (B-Text passus XX lines 183–98).

210. John Gower, *Confessio amantis*, ed. R A. Peck, Medieval Academy Reprints for Teaching 9 (Toronto: University of Toronto Press, 1980), Prologus, ll. 61–62.

211. Ibid., Liber octavus, ll. 3124–27.

212. Cited in Burrow, *Ages of Man*, 50.

213. *The Castle of Perseverance*, in *The Macro Plays*, ed. M. Eccles, EETS o.s. 262, 1969, ll. 2482–84.

214. Christine de Pisan, *The Treasure of the City of Ladies or the Book of the Three Virtues*, trans. S. Lawson (London: Penguin Books, 1985), part 3, chap. 7, 166.

215. Ibid., part 3, chap. 13, 179.

216. See Harry Peters, 'Jupiter and Saturn: Medieval Ideals of "Elde"', in *Old Age*, ed. Albrecht Classen (Berlin: Walter de Gruyter, 2007), 375–91.

217. On Saturn and/or Kronos as a decrepit old man, see Beauvoir, *Old Age*, 140; for an art historical treatment in connection with the imagery of old age, see Raymond Klibansky, Erwin Panofsky and Fritz Saxl, *Saturn and Melancholy: Studies in the History of Natural Philosophy, Religion and Art* (London: Nelson, 1964).

218. Cited by Burrow, *Ages of Man*, 198; Ptolemy, *Tetrabiblos*, trans. F. E. Robbins (Cambridge, MA: Loeb, 1940).

219. The topic of the ages of man in a philosophical, theological and artistic context is comprehensively treated by Sears, *Ages of Man*.

220. The text is transcribed and translated by Dove, *Perfect Age*, 80. The De Lisle Psalter, now sadly incomplete, forms the second part of MS Arundel 83, British Library. Other depictions of the 'Wheel of Life' in English art may be found in wall paintings, such as those at Saint Anthony's chapel in Leominster Priory, Herefordshire; Saint Mary's at Kempley, Gloucestershire; or Longthorpe Tower near Peterborough.

221. The text survives in a manuscript at Lincoln Cathedral library MS 66, fol. 84r/ p. 167.

222. Cited by Dove, *Perfect Age*, 85.

223. British Library MS Arundel 83, (II), fol. 126r; text given by Dove, *Perfect Age*, 92 (English) and 90 (Latin); a diagram in the context of a *Speculum Theologie* MS presents a similar poem on the ages of man in tabular layout, where the three stages of old age are also referred to as *senex, decrepitus, imbecillis* (Cambridge University Library MS Gg. 4.32, fol. 15v, fourteenth century; picture in Dove, *Perfect Age*, 93).

224. Thane, 'Geriatrics', 1094.

225. *The Travels of John Mandeville*, trans. C. W. R. D. Moseley (London: Penguin, 1983), 123, where the well is located in the forests near the city of Polumbum, sourced directly with waters from the Earthly Paradise.

226. Oxford, Ashmolean Museum, accession no. WA 1947.191.223, probably French, made c. 1440–1480.

227. Engraving in Vienna, Graphische Sammlung Albertina.

228. Image of old women being baked in an oven, by unknown artist, Augsburg, c. 1540, woodcut, Schlossmuseum Gotha. The story of Medea's rejuvenating magic was treated in the later Middle Ages in Gower's *Confessio amantis*, Book V, ll. 4068–4174.

229. In a scene set among a crowd of children, one could generally see a decrepit old woman, "with trembling limbs, whitened head, reddened forehead", reborn

in the sacred font as if renovated ("Videres plerumque inter multas infantium turbas anus decrepita valde aetate, cuncta tremula membra, canescente capite, rugata fronte, necnon viros eiusdem senectutis sub eius manibus in fonte sacro renasci quodammodo ac subito albis indutos renovari"), *Vita Eligii episcopi Noviomagensis*, 2,8, at 700; cited by Goetz, 'Alt sein', 31, note 77.

230. Demaitre, 'The Care and Extension', 21, citing the Salernitan *Flos medicinae*, verse 32, which stated that medicine may prolong life but not forever (*Vitam prolongat sed non medicina perennat*). Peter of Spain, later Pope John XXI, mentioned in his medical writings the putative existence of miracle waters to reverse or even cure the corruption and disintegration of bodily functions that ageing brought with it. For Roger Bacon and his ideas on how to use medicine and alchemy to prolong life, see Faye Getz, *Medicine in the English Middle Ages* (Princeton, NJ: Princeton University Press, 1998), 55–56; also the Middle English translation of two tractates by Bacon, *In debito regimine* and *Corpora Adae et Evae*, in Tavormina, *Sex, Aging, and Death*, 327–72, where it is argued that even post-lapsarian humanity has a potential natural life span much longer than that commonly found in Bacon's own time.

231. For an overview, see the collection of essays in Classen, *Old Age*.

232. Sarah Gordon, 'Representations of Aging and Disability in Early Sixteenth-Century French Farce', in *Old Age*, ed. Albrecht Classen (Berlin: Walter de Gruyter, 2007), 421.

233. Ibid., 422. Conversely, Tory Vandeventer Pearman, another literary scholar, has argued that "literary representations of femaleness, femininity, and disability—though they do not provide exact accounts of the lived experience of women or those with disabilities—are central to uncovering the social anxieties surrounding such Othered figures" (Pearman, *Women*, 2).

234. Classen, *Old Age*, 49.

235. A number of German nobility in the twelfth century 'retired' to monasteries, notably Count Gottfried of Cappenberg, who died as Premonstratensian canon in 1127, but in his active life not so long ago as a military leader had burned the cathedral of Münster in 1121; Jonathan R. Lyon, 'The Withdrawal of Aged Noblemen into Monastic Communities: Interpreting the Sources from Twelfth-Century Germany', in *Old Age*, ed. Albrecht Classen (Berlin: Walter de Gruyter, 2007), 143–69.

236. Dutton, 'Beyond the Topos', 91.

237. "Richtet sich, als er gegen Ende seines Lebens an den Füßen gelähmt wurde, eine bescheidene Wohnung zu daurendem Aufenthalte nahe beim Kloster ein" (*Die Zwiefalter Chroniken Ortliebs und Bertholds (1135)*, ed. Erich König and Karl Otto Müller [Stuttgart, 1941], 159, cited in Fandrey, *Krüppel*, 18).

238. Vincent of Beauvais, *Speculum naturale*, in *Bibliotheca mundi seu speculum quadruplex: Naturale, doctrinale, morale, historiale* (Douai, 1642), L. 31, C. 89, col. 2362; Shahar, *Growing Old*, 75.

239. Shahar, *Growing Old*, 75; Philippe de Navarre, *Les quatre ages de l'Homme*, ed. Marcel de Fréville (Paris: Didot, 1888), 194, 105.

240. "Es trifft also . . . gar nicht unbedingt zu, dass es im Mittelalter keine Vorstellung von Ruhestand gegeben hätte, vor allem wenn wir die soziale Schicht der reichen Kaufleute und Patrizier berücksichtigen" (Classen, 'Der alte Mensch', 227).

241. Elaine Clark, 'Some Aspects of Social Security in Medieval England', *Journal of Family History* 7, no. 4 (1982): 307–20, acknowledges that earlier historians had been quite aware of the existence of such records, e.g. George Caspar Homans, *English Villagers of the Thirteenth Century* (Cambridge, MA: Harvard University Press, 1941), 144–47. For an overview of different

types of retirement among elderly peasants, with a critical assessment of previous scholarship, see the article by Smith, 'The Manorial Court'. In Morris S. Arnold, ed., *Select Cases of Trespass from the King's Court, 1307–1399*, 2 vols., Selden Society Publications 100, 103 (London: Selden Society Publications, 1985, 1987), I, lii, Arnold suggests in his introduction that a variety of people attempted an early form of a modern trust, including ageing parents, uncles without children, or infirmed grandparents.

242. Elaine Clark, 'The Quest for Security in Medieval England', in *Aging and the Aged*, ed. M. Sheehan (Toronto: Pontifical Institute of Medieval Studies, 1990), 189; for a general study of manorial records and the role the court had to play, see Z. Razi and R. M. Smith, eds., *Medieval Society and the Manor Court* (Oxford: Clarendon Press, 1996).

243. Cited in E. Amt, ed., *Women's Lives in Medieval Europe: A Sourcebook* (London: Routledge, 1993), 184.

244. Clark, 'Some Aspects', 313–14; the widow and her sister-in-law lived together for six months, until the widow moved away, handing over the cottage, and with the house the obligation to care for the decrepit sister-in-law, to a local but unrelated man, who in turn sold the cottage and obligation of support to another villager after one year—not so much a care package as a veritable pass the parcel for the disabled woman.

245. Clark, 'Quest for Security', 190.

246. Ibid., reference to British Library, MS Add. 40625 (18 October 1336), where, according to an earlier section of the same manuscript (13 December 1317), 'enfeebled' peasants could petition the lord directly for help in such cases.

247. Shahar, *Growing Old*, 213, note 29.

248. Smith, 'The Manorial Court', 46.

249. H. S. Bennett, *Life on the English Manor: A Study of Peasant Conditions 1150–1400* (Cambridge: Cambridge University Press, 1965), 253.

250. Dyer, *Standards of Living*, 120, suggested it was "likely that many elderly women would have come to some arrangement by which other tenants worked the land for rent." Clark, 'Quest for Security', 194–95, argued that many childless peasants made arrangements with other relatives (brothers, nephews, etc.), servants, parish priests, neighbours and friends.

251. Cited in Homans, *English Villagers*, 146; cf. British Museum, MS Add 40167, fol. 50v: "Et predictus Iohannes in le Hale laborabit et deseruiet eidem Iohanni ate Barre in honestis seruiciis pro posse suo."

252. Although George Homans remarked that this provision was "uncommon" (*English Villagers*, 147) for these kinds of maintenance agreements, which tended to be more in favour of the person relinquishing their lands.

253. Document no. 1 in J. Z. Titow, *English Rural Society 1200–1350*, Historical Problems: Studies and Documents 4 (London: George Allen and Unwin, 1969), 110, citing Hampshire Record Office, MS Eccl. Comm. 2/159270A.

254. Ibid., 82.

255. Ibid. provides some comparative examples of manorial corrodies for the later thirteenth and early fourteenth centuries, ranging from the bare minimum needed for survival to the modest but adequate.

256. R. H. Hilton, *A Medieval Society: The West Midlands at the End of the Thirteenth Century* (London: Weidenfeld and Nicolson, 1966), 112. For her £93 the female corrodian could expect a daily ration of two monk's loaves, one small white loaf, two gallons of convent ale, also annually six pigs, two oxen, twelve cheeses, one hundred stockfish, one thousand herrings and twenty-four shillings' worth of clothing, which quantities indicate that she is extremely unlikely to have consumed all this herself, suggesting instead that she retained a number of servants in her retirement.

257. Borscheid, *Geschichte*, 86; after the death of the donors, the hospital became full owner of the land.

258. Bennett, *Life on the English Manor*, 253. For a recent study of land transactions among the peasantry in general, see John Mullan and Richard Britnell, *Land and Family: Trends and Local Variations in the Peasant Land Market on the Winchester Bishopric Estates, 1263–1415*, Studies in Regional and Local History 8 (Hatfield: University of Hertfordshire Press, 2010).

259. Thane, *Old Age*, 75. Older people in these records emerge as actively planning the use of whatever resources they had and driving as hard a bargain as they could get; in times of land scarcity, for instance, in the early fourteenth century in England, they could realise exceptionally beneficial maintenance contracts in return for relinquishing their holdings.

260. Smith, 'The Manorial Court', 56.

261. *Court Rolls of the Manor of Hales*, 166, cited in Bennett, *Life on the English Manor*, 253.

262. In another case the son had to promise to sustain his father *bene et competenter*, at *The Manor of Manydown*, 130, cited by Bennett, *Life on the English Manor*, 254, note 5.

263. Bennett, *Life on the English Manor*, 254, cites various other manorial rolls with specifications of the care and support of feeble elderly relatives, e.g. a son is to provide for his father "honorifice pro posse suo", *Halmota Prioratus Dunelmensis*, ed. Durham Halmote Rolls, W. H. D. Longstaffe and J. Booth (Durham: Surtees Society, 1889), 9; and F. M. Page, *The Estates of Crowland Abbey: A Study in Manorial Administration* (Cambridge: Cambridge University Press, 1934), 109–10.

264. Hilton, *Medieval Society*, 111.

265. Edward Miller and John Hatcher, *Medieval England: Rural Society and Economic Change 1086–1348*, Social and Economic History of England (London: Longman, 1978), 149.

266. Dyer, *Standards of Living*, 152 and 152–56, for further examples of maintenance agreements and types and quantities of foods consumed by retired peasants; also Christopher Dyer, 'English Diet in the Later Middle Ages', in *Social Relations and Ideas: Essays in Honour of R. H. Hilton*, ed. T. H. Aston, P. R. Coss, C. Dyer and J. Thirsk (Cambridge: Cambridge University Press, 1983), 197–203. The maintenance agreement made in 1352 at Gressenhale, whereby one Henry son of Stephen was to receive a large amount of produce and goods, seems to indicate that Henry intended to supplement his retirement by selling on some of them (Thane, *Old Age*, 77).

267. Dyer, *Standards of Living*, 175.

268. Clark, 'Some Aspects', 314.

269. Thane, *Old Age*, 79.

270. Clark, 'Some Aspects', 311.

271. Ibid., 310.

272. "Eine erste Institutionalisierung erfuhr das Ausgedinge bereits gegen Ende des 13. Jahrhunderts, als auf Veranlassung von Gutsherren vereinzelt alte, zur Leistung der Abgaben nicht mehr fähige Bauern den Hof verlassen mußten und dafür gemäß den Fürsorgepflichten des Herren für seine Untertanen auf ein Altenteil mit lebenslänglicher Versorgung gesetzt wurden" (Borscheid, *Geschichte*, 48).

273. Youngs, *Life Cycle*, 176.

274. Clark, 'Quest for Security', 192. "Put another way, the propertied old represented a potential source of credit for the young" (ibid., 197).

275. Thane, *Old Age*, 81.

276. Minois, *History of Old Age*, 218, citing his thesis, G. Minois, *L'Évêché de Tréguier au XVe siècle, Thèse de 3e cycle* (Rennes: Université Rennes, 1975).
277. Minois, *History of Old Age*, 138; the figure of Belisarius, a former general under Justinian, who was blinded in punishment for his part in a plot against the emperor and hence reduced to beggary came to represent a literary topos of the old man suffering from decline in fortune (Beauvoir, *Old Age*, 143–44). On poverty and the elderly in the early modern period, see L. A. Botelho, *Old Age and the English Poor Law, 1500–1700* (Woodbridge: Boydell Press, 2004), as a contrast to medieval mentalities.
278. Hanawalt, *Ties that Bind*, 237.
279. Peregrine Horden, 'A Discipline of Relevance: The Historiography of the Later Medieval Hospital', *Social History of Medicine* 1, no. 3 (1988): 370–72.
280. Nicholas, *Domestic Life*, 177–78.
281. Youngs, *Life Cycle*, 180; Rosenthal, *Old Age*, 186.
282. Thane, *Old Age*, 96.
283. Demaitre, 'The Care and Extension', 13; Henry H. Beek, *Waanzin in de Middeleeuwen: Beeld van de gestoorde en bemoeienis met de zieke* (Nijkerk: Callenbach, 1969), 145 and 268, note 7.
284. Minois, *History of Old Age*, 203.
285. A. Dirmeier, 'Armenfürsorge, Totengedenken und Machtpolitik im mittelalterlichen Regensburg. Vom *hospitale pauperum* zum Almosenamt', in *Regensburg im Mittelalter. Beiträge zur Stadtgeschichte vom frühen Mittelalter bis zum Beginn der Neuzeit*, ed. M. Angerer and H. Wanderwitz (Regensburg: Universitätsverlag Regensburg, 1995), 221–22.
286. Youngs, *Life Cycle*, 180–81; Brian Pullan, *Rich and Poor in Renaissance Venice* (Oxford: Blackwell, 1971), 208.
287. Minois, *History of Old Age*, 246.
288. Cited in Isabelle Chabot, 'Widowhood and Poverty in Late Medieval Florence', *Continuity and Change* 3, no. 2 (1988): 310, note 66; Archivio di Stato di Firenze, *Catasto* 24, fol. 1019r.
289. Cited in Chabot, 'Widowhood', 310, note 64; Archivio di Stato di Firenze, *Catasto* 15, fol. 59v.
290. Cited in Chabot, 'Widowhood', 310, note 57; Archivio di Stato di Firenze, *Catasto* 22, fol. 784. Retiring to live in just one single room, often a ground floor one, of one's house is a common phenomenon among contemporary elderly people trying to 'hang on' to independent living for as long as possible—in the modern case often for physical reasons (reduced mobility prevents access to upper floors), but in the Florentine one for financial ones, too.
291. Chabot, 'Widowhood', 303.
292. *Cartulary of St. Mark's*, xxxi and charter 302, at 194–95: "After he is freed from matrimony by the death of his wife (*post mortem uxoris sue solutus a coniugio*) the said Simon shall be able to enter the said almonry and there receive victuals like those of a chaplain of the same house for as long as he lives."
293. Harvey, *Living and Dying*, 179–209, presents a general overview of the problem of secular (and female!) corrodians resident in monasteries, with particular reference to the situation in the Benedictine abbey of Westminster.
294. Youngs, *Life Cycle*, 179.
295. As it is phrased in the charter issued by Bishop Konrad II, see Norbert Fromm, Michael Kuthe and Walther Rügert, '... *entflammt vom Feuer der Nächstenliebe'. 775 Jahre Spitalstiftung Konstanz* (Constance: UVK Universitätsverlag Konstanz, 2000), 9.

296. Ibid., 38.
297. Ibid.
298. Ibid., 57.
299. Ibid., 58.
300. Daniel Raths, *Sachkultur im spätmittelalterlichen Trier. Die Rechnung-süberlieferung des St. Jakobshospitals* (Trier: Kliomedia, 2011), 231 and 235.
301. Borscheid, *Geschichte*, 83: "alle die Lahmen und Hungrigen aufzunehmen, die in den Winkeln der Stadt herumlungerten, die Schiffbrüchigen der Gesellschaft und die alten Leute der untersten Schichten, die mit hohlen Augen durch die Gassen der Stadt schlurften."
302. Rawcliffe, *Leprosy*, 297; J. D. Mansi, ed., *Sacrorum conciliorum nova et amplissima collectio*, 53 vols. (Florence and Paris, 1759–1798), XXII, cols 835–36.
303. Harvey, *Living and Dying*, 191; also *Councils and Synods, with Other Documents relating to the English Church*, ed. F. M. Powicke and C. R. Cheney (Oxford: Clarendon Press, 1964), II, part ii, 788.
304. Rawcliffe, *Leprosy*, 298; *Calendar of the Patent Rolls Preserved in the Public Record Office, 1216–1509*, Public Record Office, 52 vols. (London: HMSO, 1891–1901), at *CPR 1374–1377*, 310.
305. *The Cartulary of St. Augustine's Abbey, Bristol*, ed. D. Walker (Bristol: Bristol and Gloucester Archaeological Society, 1998), charter no. 283; no. 284 recorded similar for the brother of the other corrodian.
306. Ibid., charter no. 523.
307. Harvey, *Living and Dying*, 183 and 242. Since Robert died 22 May 1298, he hardly became a long-term financial burden for the abbey.
308. *Cartulary of St. Mark's Hospital Bristol*, ed. C. D. Ross, Bristol Record Society 21 (Bristol, 1959), xvii.
309. Rotha Mary Clay, *The Medieval Hospitals of England* (London: Frank Cass, 1909; rpt. 1966), 156, points out that while in 1333 Saint Bartholomew's, Gloucester, "supported 90 sick, lame, halt and blind" people, two centuries later Leland observed there were now only thirty-two.
310. Dyer, *Standards of Living*, 254.
311. Davis, 'Preaching', 76; Carole Rawcliffe, 'Hospital Nurses and Their Work', in *Daily Life in the Late Middle Ages*, ed. Richard Britnell (Stroud: Sutton, 1998), 63.
312. Rosenthal, *Old Age*, 97; any possibility of scandal was mitigated by the age of both employer and servant: "No suspicion of the sin of incontinence can in future arise in regard to them, by reason of their age, all power of committing such things being on the contrary taken from them." *Calendar of the Papal Letters*, vol. X, *1447–54* (London: HMSO and Dublin, 1902–1986), 107, also 159 where another man pleads he is "seventy years old and impotent".
313. Esch, *Wahre Geschichten*, 49; *Repertorium Poenitentiariae Germanicum*, vol. VI (papacy of Sixtus IV, 1471–1484), ed. L. Schmugge (Tübingen: Max Niemeyer, 2005), case no. 3253.
314. Jane Laughton, *Life in a Late Medieval City: Chester 1275–1520* (Oxford: Windgather Press, 2008), 160, citing Cheshire and Chester Archives and Local Studies, ZSR 44, m.4d.
315. Youngs, *Life Cycle*, 180; Brian Pullan, *Rich and Poor in Renaissance Venice* (Oxford: Blackwell, 1971), 214–15; Frederic Chapin Lane, *Venetian Ships and Shipbuilders of the Renaissance* (Baltimore, MD: Johns Hopkins University Press, 1934), 76–77.
316. Lewin, *Pensions*, 54; P. E. Jones, *Calendar of Plea and Memoranda Rolls . . . AD 1458–1482* (Cambridge: Cambridge University Press, 1961), 108.

317. Borscheid, *Geschichte*, 44.
318. Shahar, *Growing Old*, 137.
319. Westlake, *Parish Gilds*, 149 and 236.
320. Rosenthal, *Old Age*, 186; Edith Rickert, ed., *Chaucer's World* (New York: Columbia University Press, 1948), 352.
321. C. M. Barron, 'The Parish Fraternities of Medieval London', in *The Church in Pre-Reformation Society: Essays in Honour of F. R. H. Du Boulay*, ed. C. M. Barron and C. Harper-Bill (Woodbridge: Boydell Press, 1985), 18, also remarks that "virtually all the fourteenth-century fraternities aimed to care for the sick and indigent members" (26), e.g. the *Salve* guild in Saint Magnus helped "brothers and sisters who were in prison, blind, fallen into decay and poverty, or sick of the palsy" (ibid.). Note that old age is not mentioned as such, yet again covering those people who were first and foremost sick or disabled and only assuming the presence of the aged if they happened to fall into one of the former categories as well.
322. Lewin, *Pensions*, 53; Cornelius Walford, *The Insurance Cyclopaedia* (n.p., 1878), article on guilds.
323. Reference in Rosenthal, *Old Age*, 218, note 82; Geoffrey Templeman, ed., *The Records of the Guild of the Holy Trinity, St. Mary, St. John the Baptist, and St. Katherine of Coventry* (Dugdale Society, 1944), II:45.
324. Shahar, *Growing Old*, 138; M. Bateson, ed., *Cambridge Gild Records* (Cambridge, 1903), 93.
325. Nicholas, *Domestic Life*, 177–78; apparently some elderly women of Ghent ended up living in inns, e.g. the case of a woman Jehane Ruwaerts, who found herself in trouble with the authorities in 1378 because both she and the keeper of the inn where she lodged were fined for carrying weapons at night (ibid.)— more of a battle-axe than an intimidated 'little old lady', one is led to assume.
326. Minois, *History of Old Age*, 245.
327. Ibid., 246.
328. Shahar, *Growing Old*, 137; also mentioned by Roux, *Paris*, 160; cf. G. B. Depping, ed., *Règlements sur les arts et métiers de Paris rédigés au XIIIe siècle et connus sous le nom du Livre des métiers de Etienne Boileau* (Paris, 1837), LXIX, 177.
329. M. R. McVaugh, *Medicine before the Plague: Practitioners and Their Patients in the Crown of Aragon 1285–1345* (Cambridge: Cambridge University Press, 1993), 93 and note 100.
330. Krötzl, *'Sexaginta vel circa'*, 114. In contrast, in the canonisation trials initiated in 1416 for Nicholas, bishop of Linköping, one of the witnesses was a woman aged over eighty, who was not only an honest matron (*honesta matrona*), but also an experienced surgeon still practicing her art (*multum famosa et in arte Cirurgica satis trita*) (ibid., 112).
331. Orme and Webster, *English Hospital*, 17.
332. Ibid., citing *Domesday Book*, vol. 13, *Buckinghamshire*, ed. John Morris (Chichester, 1978), section 57/6, and vol. 28, *Nottinghamshire* (1977), section 1/25, respectively.
333. Lewin, *Pensions*, 31; cf. *Calendar of Liberate Rolls I*, HMSO.
334. Lewin, *Pensions*, 32; cf. *Calendar of Liberate Rolls VI*, HMSO, 129. The pension was set at four pence daily for life, and, according to Lewin, the first old age occupational pension in a modern sense in English records.
335. Martyn Whittock, *A Brief History of Life in the Middle Ages* (London: Constable and Robinson, 2009), 89, citing *Calendar of the Close Rolls Preserved in the Public Record Office, 1227–1485*, Public Record Office, 45 vols. (London: HMSO, 1892–1954), Edward III, 1330–1333 (1898). Some more Whittoks, possibly related to the aforementioned family, received "two monks'

loaves of the largest size and a bottle of the best convent ale and a black loaf" every day for life, this being granted to John and Agnes Whittok in 1374, in an arrangement with the abbot of Sherborne (Dorset), where a land grant bought such a corrody (Whittock, *Brief History*, 89, citing *Calendar of the Patent Rolls*, Edward III, 1370–1374 [1914]).

336. Lewin, *Pensions*, 35; cf. William Campbell, *Materials Illustrative of the Reign of Henry VII*, 2 vols. (Rolls Series, 1873).

337. I. Jack, ed., *The Grey of Ruthin Valor*, Bedfordshire Record Society 46 (1965), 76, cited by Dyer, *Standards of Living*, 249, note 26.

338. Orme and Webster, *English Hospital*, 114. Between 1368 and 1515 records show only fifty-five of these so-called poor knights, and of these again only fifteen individuals had actually been knighted.

339. Ibid.

340. Hill, *King's Messengers*, 1994 edition; the earlier edition of 1961 (confusingly under the same title) devoted an entire chapter to provisions for sickness and old age, with 61–85 on pensions and corrodies.

341. Ibid. (1994), 22. John le Blak is "to have there for life the necessaries of life in food and clothing according to his estate".

342. Ibid., 65.

343. Ibid., 132.

344. Ibid., 168.

345. Ibid., 37–38.

346. Ibid., 99; non-specific "illnesses" are mentioned for several messengers, during which periods they were repaid any expenses incurred while sick on a journey (ibid., 6), as well as given time and paid leave to convalesce (7); on very rare occasions messengers were attacked, such as Alan and Douenald of Kinros 'Scotus', who were both sent on a mission in 1303–1304 during the Scottish wars, where they were wounded by the Scots, for which they received an additional allowance of five shillings (4 and 116).

347. Lewin, *Pensions*, 32; cf. *Calendar of Liberate Rolls VI*, HMSO, 237.

348. P. H. Cullum, *Cremetts and Corrodies: Care of the Poor and Sick at St. Leonard's Hospital, York, in the Middle Ages*, Borthwick Papers 79 (York: University of York, 1991), 15.

349. Shahar, *Growing Old*, 123; D. Knowles and R. N. Hadcock, *Medieval Religious Houses: England and Wales* (London: Longman, 1953), 308.

350. Irina Metzler, 'Liminality and Disability: Spatial and Conceptual Aspects of Physical Impairment in Medieval Europe', in *Medicine and Space: Body, Surroundings and Borders in Antiquity and the Middle Ages*, Visualising the Middle Ages 4, ed. Patricia A. Baker, Han Nijdam and Karine van 't Land, 273–96 (Leiden: Brill, 2012).

351. Orme and Webster, *English Hospital*, 117.

352. Ibid.

353. Jutta Grimbach, 'Hospitalgründungen des 15. und 16. Jahrhunderts am Niederrhein und im Herzogtum Westfalen', in *Norm und Praxis der Armenfürsorge in Spätmittelalter und früher Neuzeit*, VSWG-Beihefte 189, ed. S. Schmidt and J. Aspelmeier (Stuttgart: Franz Steiner, 2006), 195.

354. Shahar, *Growing Old*, 25. On noble widows and old age, see also the article by Margaret Wade Labarge, 'Three Medieval Widows and a Second Career', in M. Sheehan, *Aging and the Aged*, 159–72, which mentions Ela, founder and first abbess of Lacock, "retired [as abbess] in 1257 when she felt the pressure of old age [*senio et nimia debilitate affectam*], and died 24 August 1261 in her seventies" (168).

355. Thane, *Old Age*, 81; Richard A. Harper, 'A Note on Corrodies in the Fourteenth Century', *Albion* 15 (1983): 97–101.

356. Harper, 'A Note on Corrodies', 97 and 101.
357. *Charters of the Medieval Hospitals of Bury St. Edmunds*, ed. Christopher Harper-Bill (Woodbridge: Boydell Press, 1994), nos. 1–2, 56, 59, 224–51; Kealey, *Medieval Medicus*, 158, entry 83.
358. Orme and Webster, *English Hospital*, 114 and 116; the new and improved institution was to provide for an extra thirty-five brethren and three sisters, all to be unmarried, of gentle birth or members of his household.
359. Ibid., 117.
360. Nicholas Orme, 'Sufferings of the Clergy: Illness and Old Age in Exeter Diocese, 1300–1540', in *Life, Death, and the Elderly: Historical Perspectives*, ed. Margaret Pelling and Richard M. Smith (London: Routledge, 1991), 69. Wheatley, *Stumbling Blocks*, 59, makes the astonishing claim that such hospitals "strongly reinforce the religious model" that he advocates for medieval disability, thereby ignoring the simple fact that disabled priests are, first and foremost, disabled persons who cannot 'function' in their allocated role any longer—why singling out particular groups of deserving people should support the "religious model", when so many hospital founders singled out their 'pet projects' anyway, is unconvincing.
361. Shahar, *Growing Old*, 110.
362. Ibid.; *Concilium Aquisgranense*, C. 142, MGH Concilia II, pars I (Hanover, 1906), 417.
363. Shahar, *Growing Old*, 110; J. Mansi, *Sacrorum conciliorum nova et amplissima collectio* (Florence, 1759–1798; rpt. Graz, 1960), XXIII, col. 1105.
364. Rosenthal, 'Retirement', 183; *The Episcopal Register of Robert Rede, ordinis predicatorum, Lord Bishop of Chichester, 1399–1415*, 2 vols., ed. Cecil Deedes, Sussex Record Society 8, 10 (1908–1910), I:25–26 and 254.
365. Lewin, *Pensions*, 26; Edward L. Cutts, *Parish Priests and Their People in the Middle Ages in England* (London, 1898), 296.
366. Orme and Webster, *English Hospital*, 234–35; *The Register of John de Grandisson, Bishop of Exeter (A.D. 1327–1369)*, ed. F. C. Hingeston-Randolph, 3 vols. (London, 1894–1895), I:552.
367. Harvey, *Living and Dying*, 184, also referring to earlier parallels at Crowland and Thornton Abbeys.
368. Orme and Webster, *English Hospital*, 116.
369. Cited in Rosenthal, *Old Age*, 108; A. Hamilton Thompson, ed., *Visitations of Religious Houses in the Diocese of Lincoln*, Canterbury and York Society 29 (London, 1968), 380.
370. Thane, *Old Age*, 82.
371. Shahar, *Growing Old*, 105–6.
372. Ibid., 105; Harper, 'A Note on Corrodies', 95–101.
373. Harvey, *Living and Dying*, 189.
374. John R. H. Moorman, *Church Life in England in the Thirteenth Century* (Cambridge: Cambridge University Press, 1945), 46–47, 62–63, 269–71, 289, 306, 356, also on corrodies in general.
375. Harvey, *Living and Dying*, 243, Appendix V no. 27.
376. Ibid., 244, Appendix V no. 31.
377. Orme and Webster, *English Hospital*, 116.
378. Ibid., 58; unfortunately the source for Robert's disability, *Victoria County History*, ed. William Page et al. (London, 1900–), vol. *London*, 1 (1909), 532, note 30, simply states: "Robert de la Naperie, who had been maimed in the king's service, was sent there" on 17 November 1309; cf. *Calendar of the Close Rolls, 1307–13*, I:236.
379. Orme and Webster, *English Hospital*, 112 and 114; Clay, *Medieval Hospitals*, 99; other examples are John of Spain, who was sent to Tintern Abbey

by Edward II also in 1314; Gerard de Scissous sent to Ipswich Priory; Henry le Lounge to the hospital at Ospringe, Kent; and John de Scheperton to Saint John's hospital, Oxford.

380. Dyer, *Standards of Living*, 243–44. Henry III arranged for Helen, a blind woman of Faversham, to be maintained there in 1235 (Clay, *Medieval Hospitals*, 99). As a royal foundation Ospringe received a series of royal pensioners, e.g. Juliana, a damsel of Queen Eleanor, by 1278, Robert de Rideware in Juliana's place by 1307, to be followed by a royal servant John Le Chapman of Langley in 1314 (Orme and Webster, *English Hospital*, 114).

381. Thane, *Old Age*, 81. The royal habit of using monastic houses as retirement homes for royal servants placed increasing economic demands on these, until they worked out how to evade such demands by pleading poverty; Clay, *Medieval Hospitals*, 213–14.

382. Orme and Webster, *English Hospital*, 29; *Victoria County History*, ed. William Page et al. (London, 1900–,) vol. *Middlesex*, 1 (1969), 207; Risse, *Mending Bodies*, 168–69, also mentions cases of people feigning leprosy to gain admittance.

383. Clay, *Medieval Hospitals*, 219–20; *Calendar of the Patent Rolls* 16 Edward III, pt. ii. m. 22d; *Calendar of the Close Rolls* 20 Edward III, pt. i. m. 4d.

384. Borscheid, *Geschichte*, 89–90.

385. Demaitre, 'The Care and Extension', 13. See also Borscheid, *Geschichte*, 84.

386. Cited by Minois, *History of Old Age*, 131; Guigue I, *Coutume de Chartreuse* (Le Cerf, coll. 'Sources chrétiennes', 1984), 78.2.

387. Minois, *History of Old Age*, 131.

388. Ibid.; Salvian of Marseille, 'Les Livres de Timothée a l'Église', in *Oeuvres*, trans. G. Lagarrigue, 2 vols. (Le Cerf, coll. 'Sources chrétiennes', 1971 and 1975), IV.4.

389. Shahar, *Growing Old*, 123.

390. Joinville and Villehardouin, *Chronicles of the Crusades*, 175. The knight was among an assembly of clergy and Jews, which took place at Cluny; asking to speak first, the knight provoked "the most important and most learned rabbi" to assert that Mary is not Mother of God, whereupon the knight "lifted his crutch and struck the Jew such a blow with it near the ear that he knocked him down."

391. Clay, *Medieval Hospitals*, 8—regrettably without providing a source.

392. Thomas More, *Utopia*, trans. and intro. Paul Turner (Harmondsworth: Penguin, 1965), 44: "the case of the disabled soldier, who has lost a limb in the service of King and Country, either at home or abroad—perhaps in that battle with the Cornish rebels, or perhaps during the fighting in France, not so long ago. When he comes home, he finds he's physically incapable of practising his former trade, and too old to learn a new one."

393. On the general topic of women and arrangements for financial support in old age see Shahar, *Growing Old*, 126–30.

394. Ibid., 129; J. T. Rosenthal, 'Aristocratic Widows in Fifteenth-Century England', in *Women and the Structure of Society: Selected Research from the Fifth Berkshire Conference on the History of Women*, ed. B. J. Harris and J. A. McNamara (Durham, NC: Duke University Press 1984), 47.

395. Rosenthal, 'Retirement', 176; Helen M. Cam, 'Shire Officials: Coroners, Constables, and Bailiffs', in *The English Government at Work, 1327–1336*, vol. III, *Local Administration and Justice*, ed. James F. Willard (Cambridge, MA: Medieval Academy of America, 1950), 143–65.

396. Rosenthal, 'Retirement', 175–76.

397. Rosenthal, *Old Age*, 105; Rosenthal, 'Retirement', 176.

398. Rosenthal, 'Retirement', 176; *Calendar of the Close Rolls*, Henry IV, Vol. 1: 1399–1402 (London, 1927), 21.

399. Shahar, *Growing Old*, 132. Master artisans in particular, because of the structure of their trade with the family (and apprentices and/or journeymen) as a unit of production, were able to gradually phase out the more demanding roles and shift the more strenuous workload onto other members, so that a physically (but unlikely a mentally) disabled craftsman could still be the head of his workshop and remain in charge, as long as the other members of the production unit were able to maintain output and generate income.

400. Salzman, *Building*, 55; also Woodward, *Men at Work*, 83; the source is in *Fabric Rolls of the Minster of York*, ed. J. Raine, Surtees Society 35 (Durham, 1859), 161.

401. Jennifer I. Kermode, 'Urban Decline? The Flight from Office in Late Medieval York', *Economic History Review* 2nd series 35, no. 2 (1982): 192.

402. Attreed, *York Household Books*, I:61; John Tong, mayor of York in 1477, asked several times to be relieved of office since he was "broken by great sickness" before his demand was at last granted thirteen years later (Kermode, 'Urban Decline?', 192).

403. Rosenthal, 'Retirement', 179; *Calendar of the Letter-Books*, at *Letter-Book K* (1911), 86–87. Other exemptions were granted for "deafness and other infirmities', "failing sight and deafness", "deafness and increasing old age" and plain "deafness" (Rosenthal, 'Retirement', 179, note 19), also due to paralysis (*Calendar of the Letter-Books*, at *Letter Book I*, 87).

404. Rosenthal, *Old Age*, 102; Rosenthal, 'Retirement', 177.

405. Rosenthal, 'Retirement', 177. In the mid-fifteenth century, bishop Adam Moleyns was excused because "he is weak in body and sight" (ibid.).

406. Shahar, *Growing Old*, 30; also Rosenthal, 'Retirement', 177. Other nobles included the earl of Oxford, granted leave of absence due to his infirmities, or Ralph Boteler, Lord Sudeley, and John Lord Beauchamp of Powicke, granted exemptions due to "debility and age" (Rosenthal, 'Retirement', 178).

407. Rosenthal, *Old Age*, 127.

408. Shahar, *Growing Old*, 25.

409. Orme, 'Sufferings', 62.

410. Shahar, *Growing Old*, 102–3 and 106–7, provides some examples of monks, nuns and secular clergy remaining in office, and working, until the day they died.

411. Hrabanus Maurus, ed. Ernst Dümmler, MGH Epistolae 5 (Berlin, 1898–1899), ep. 28, 444, cited by Goetz, 'Alt sein', 35, note 93.

412. Hrabanus Maurus, ep. 50, 504–5, cited by Goetz, 'Alt sein', 35, note 94.

413. "Ecce ego duplici fatigatus molestia, id est senectutue et infirmitate." *Epistolae Alcuini*, Ep. 114, ed. Ernst Dümmler, MGH Epistolae 4 (Hanover, 1895), 169, cited in Dutton, 'Beyond the Topos', 77.

414. The letter is appended to Johannes Diaconus, *Life of St. Gregory*, a manuscript originally from Hereford, now Oxford, Jesus College MS 37, fols 156v–157r (reference provided by Chris Tuckley, paper 613b, Leeds International Medieval Congress, 2009).

415. Cited by Timothy Holme, *'Vile Florentines': The Florence of Dante, Giotto and Boccaccio* (London: Cassell, 1980), 2. The original Latin is in a passage of Boccaccio's famous Letter XII, addressed to Mainardo Cavalcanti: "Ex quibus fit ut michi sit celum inspicere grave, onerosa corporea moles, titubans gradus, tremule manus, pallor stigius, appetitus cibi nullus et rerum omnium displicentia; . . . animi remisse sunt vires, memoria fere nulla et hebes ingenium". Giovanni Boccaccio, *Opere in versi. Corbaccio . . . Epistole*, ed. Pier Giorgio Ricci (Milan: Riccardo Ricciardi, 1965), 1232.

416. Rosenthal, *Old Age*, 161, citing John H. Fisher, *John Gower, Moral Philosopher and Friend of Chaucer* (New York: New York University Press, 1964), 65: "senex et cecus . . . corpus et egrotum, vetus et miserabili totum."

417. "Omnes pene virtutes corporis mutantur in senibus, et, crescente sola sapientia, decrescunt caetera. Jejunia, chameuniae, huc illucque descensus, peregrinorum susceptio, defensio pauperum, instantia orationum, et perseverantia, visitatio languentium, labor manuum, unde praebeantur eleemosynae, et (ne sermonem longius traham) cuncta, quae per corpus exercentur, fracto corpore, minora fiunt", Hrabanus Maurus, *Commentarius in libros IV Regum*, 3,1, PL 109, col. 124, cited by Goetz, 'Alt sein', 36,note 97.

418. See R. N. Swanson, 'The Rolls of Roger de Meuland, Bishop of Coventry and Lichfield (1258–1295)', *Journal of the Society of Archivists* 11, nos. 1&2 (1990): 37–40.

419. Goetz, 'Alt sein', 39; Adam of Bremen, *Gesta Hammaburgensis ecclesiae pontificum*, ed. Bernhard Schmeidler, MGH Scriptores Rerum Germanicarum 2 (Hanover, 1917), 1, 52, at 50; Willibald, *Vita Bonifatii*, ed. Wilhelm Levison, MGH Scriptores Rerum Germanicarum 57 (Hanover, 1905), 5, 24. Similarly, coadjutors could be appointed in cases of the mental incapacity of clergy, see the case of an insane thirteenth-century rector: J. R. King, 'The Mysterious Case of the 'Mad' Rector of Bletchingdon: The Treatment of Mentally Ill Clergy in Late Thirteenth-Century England', in *Madness in Medieval Law and Custom*, Later Medieval Europe 6, ed. W. J. Turner (Leiden: Brill, 2010), 57–80; further cases of insane clergy in J. F. Kirby, ed., *Wykeham's Register, II*, Hampshire Record Society xiii (1899), 467–68.

420. Lewin, *Pensions*, 23; Edward L. Cutts, *Parish Priests and Their People in the Middle Ages in England* (London, 1898), 292.

421. All cases from papers held by the Borthwick Institute's archive, online at http://www.york.ac.uk/library/borthwick/projects-exhibitions/equality/disability/medieval-clergy-and-disability/ (accessed 1 March 2011).

422. In Orme, 'Sufferings', 64, citing from the register of Bishop Brantingham of Exeter.

423. Rosenthal, *Old Age*, 109; A. Hamilton Thompson, ed., *Visitations of Religious Houses in the Diocese of Lincoln*, Canterbury and York Society 29 (London, 1968), 158. Since the dean could not "undergo the burthens that lie upon him, he therefore prays that in his relief the other canons who are strong may visit the sick of the parish."

424. Even a late fifteenth-century chantry priest, described as old and ailing, was allowed a deputy, who was, however ,"removable at will" (Rosenthal, 'Retirement', 181).

425. Shahar, *Growing Old*, 109; Rosenthal, 'Retirement', 180. On the problem of unbeneficed, hence poor, clergy, see Orme, 'Sufferings', 69, who notes that curates in particular had to be active, that is able to lead parochial processions, visit the sick, or travel some distances within a parish, so that they "were unattractive to employ if they were disabled."

426. Rosenthal, 'Retirement', 182; Rosenthal, *Old Age*, 111.

427. Rosenthal, *Old Age*, 111, and Rosenthal, 'Retirement', 181; Bishop Rede of Chichester granted this priest twelve marks annually from the episcopal finances as a pension; *The Episcopal Register of Robert Rede, ordinis predicatorum, Lord Bishop of Chichester, 1399–1415*, ed. Cecil Deedes, Sussex Record Society 8, 10 (1908–1910), I:164. The rector of Lanreach retired because of "mental and physical infirmities *and* old age *and* blindness" (Rosenthal, *Old Age*, 110), and the aged prior of Bodmin suffered from "bodily weakness and blindness" (Rosenthal, 'Retirement', 183). This latter prior, Germanus, was retired in 1311, given the nearby Chapel of Saint Margaret and adjacent buildings to

live in and provided with ample food, drink and income, plus a canon of Bodmin "to keep him company" (Orme, 'Sufferings', 65).

428. Rosenthal, 'Retirement', 182; *The Episcopal Register of Robert Rede*, I:24.
429. Rosenthal, *Old Age*, 110 and 217, note 66; also Rosenthal, 'Retirement', 181.
430. Orme, 'Sufferings', 71. Of the total seventy-seven priests, a further eighteen were described as "infirm" without specifying their age, with eight of those also being blind, while another three were termed insane (but not due to senile dementia) and three as leprous.
431. Both cases of priests cited by Esch, *Wahre Geschichten*, 49; *Repertorium Poenitentiariae Germanicum*, vol. VI (papacy of Sixtus IV, 1471–1484), ed. L. Schmugge (Tübingen: Max Niemeyer, 2005), case no. 3342 for matutins and case no. 3404 for breviary.
432. Rawcliffe, *Medicine for the Soul*, 27–28, discusses institutional care offered to blind, aged and disabled priests. For further cases of deaf clergy, see Lincoln Archives Office, Episcopal Register iii, fols 366v–367r; for generally 'decrepit', see R. L. Storey, ed., *The Register of Gilbert Welton, Bishop of Carlisle, 1353–1362* (Woodbridge: Boydell Press, 1999), no. 431.
433. Shahar, *Growing Old*, 109; Rosenthal, *Old Age*, 110; Rosenthal, 'Retirement', 181, mentions the rector of Abbot's Ripton, who was "broken with age, infirm, blind, and unfit to exercise his office".
434. Shahar, 'The Middle Ages', 99.
435. Orme, 'Sufferings', 66. It seems almost as if the later Middle Ages were becoming somewhat embarrassed at the visibility, in society, of disabled priests; hence, obscurity in retirement became the preferred option. On visibility see also Chapter 4, this volume, with regard to disabled beggars being forced to cover up their physical blemishes lest they cause offence.
436. Cited by Rosenthal, *Old Age*, 145; A. T. Bannister, ed., *Registrum Thome Spofford, Episcopi Herefordensis, A.D. MCCCCXXII–MCCCXLVIII*, Canterbury and York Society 23 (1919), 165–67, 232–33, 251–52, 258–59.
437. Orme, 'Sufferings', 63.
438. Thietmar of Merseburg, *Chronicon* 4, 36, at 173.
439. Minois, *History of Old Age*, 167: for instance, Bishop Marbode of Rennes, aged eighty in 1120, who retired to Saint Abin d'Angers, or Bishop Arnoul of Lisieux who retired to the abbey of Saint Victor, Paris, aged eighty-one. Minois unfortunately does not provide details concerning the relative state of health of these bishops, so we do not know if they retired *before* old age disabled them or *because* they were already so disabled.
440. Montford, 'Fit to Preach', 104–5; also Montford, *Health*, 32–33.
441. Rosenthal, *Old Age*, 216, note 54, unfortunately without providing further detail of where the prior moved to.
442. Ibid., 109 and 216, note 56. According to the chamberlain in his statement to the episcopal visitation, apparently "religious discipline is well-nigh dead" due to the disability of the abbot, plus the age-related infirmities of the prior, and the sub-prior's "simpleness". A. Hamilton Thompson, ed., *Visitations of Religious Houses in the Diocese of Lincoln*, Canterbury and York Society 29 (London, 1968), 224, 272, 276.
443. Harvey, *Living and Dying*, 184.
444. Cited in Frances Beer, *Women and Mystical Experience in the Middle Ages* (Woodbridge: Boydell Press, 1992), 104; Shahar, *Growing Old*, 104.
445. Lewin, *Pensions*, 26.
446. Esch, *Wahre Geschichten*, 48–49; *Repertorium Poenitentiariae Germanicum*, vol. VII (papacy of Innocent VIII, 1484–1492), ed. L. Schmugge (Tübingen: Max Niemeyer, 2008), case no. 1604.

447. Rosenthal, 'Retirement', 181; *Calendar of Entries in the Papal Registers Relating to Great Britain and Ireland: Papal Letters*, Vol. 7: A.D. 1417–1431 (London, 1906), 456.

448. Shahar, *Growing Old*, 104.

449. Goetz, 'Alt sein', 47; Fructuosus, *Regula* 8, in Benedict of Aniane, *Concordia regularum* 46, ed. Pierre Bonnerue, Corpus Christianorum Continuatio Mediaevalis 168A (Turnhout: Brepols, 1999), 394–96.

450. Esch, *Wahre Geschichten*, 103; *Repertorium Poenitentiariae Germanicum*, vol. V (papacy of Paul II, 1464–1471), ed. L. Schmugge (Tübingen: Max Niemeyer, 2002), case no. 1975.

451. Esch, *Wahre Geschichten*, 103; *Repertorium Poenitentiariae Germanicum*, vol. IV (papacy of Pius II, 1458–1464), ed. L. Schmugge (Tübingen: Max Niemeyer, 1996), case no. 1550.

452. Esch, *Wahre Geschichten*, 103; *Repertorium Poenitentiariae Germanicum*, vol. IV (papacy of Pius II, 1458–1464), ed. L. Schmugge (Tübingen: Max Niemeyer, 1996), case no. 1370, or vol. II (papacy of Nicholas V, 1447–1455), ed. L. Schmugge (Tübingen: Max Niemeyer, 1999), case no. 451, for similar.

453. Shahar, *Growing Old*, 100; E. Gilliat-Smith, *St. Clare of Assisi* (London, 1914), Appendix, 288.

454. John T. Wortley, 'Aging and the Desert Fathers. The Process Reversed', in *Aging and the Aged*, ed. M. Sheehan (Toronto: Pontifical Institute of Medieval Studies, 1990), 64.

455. Cited by I. Sterns, 'Care of the Sick Brothers by the Crusader Orders in the Holy Land', *Bulletin of the History of Medicine* 57 (1983): 63–64.

456. Ibid.: "the master shall see to it that the brethren who are so old or so young or so feeble that they need it, shall receive better care than the others."

457. Ibid., 64.

458. K. Militzer, 'The Role of Hospitals in the Teutonic Order', in *The Military Orders*, vol. 2, *Welfare and Warfare*, ed. H. Nicholson (Aldershot: Ashgate, 1998), 59, argues that this appears to have been an isolated incidence in the records yet "there must have been" other such infirmaries despite lack of direct evidence; cf. L. Fenske and K. Militzer, *Ritterbrüder im abendländischen Zweig des Deutschen Ordens*, Quellen und Studien zur baltischen Geschichte 12 (Cologne-Weimar-Vienna: Böhlau, 1993), 757.

459. The Teutonic order was "des armen adelß dutscher nation spital und uffenthalt" (quoted in Borscheid, *Geschichte*, 99).

460. Nicholas, *Domestic Life*, 110, citing Stadsarchief te Gent, Ser. 330, register of *scepenen of gedele*, G 9,1, f.48v.

461. Pfau, *Madness*, 177, citing Paris, Archives Nationales series JJ book 130 fo 118v no 217.

462. Alexander Murray, *Suicide in the Middle Ages*, vol. I, *The Violent against Themselves* (Oxford: Oxford University Press, 1998), I:202–6; and Georges Minois, *History of Suicide: Voluntary Death in Western Culture*, trans. Lydia G. Cochrane (Baltimore, MD: Johns Hopkins University Press, 1999), 8. Murray (ibid., 218) cites the case of an old man of seventy in one of the French Letters of Remission of 1350 who had been "out of his mind and memory these last three years or thereabouts" and who, after many suicide attempts during those years, murdered his wife before taking his own life—whether due to *senile* dementia or just dementia we will never know.

463. Minois, *History of Suicide*, 30, for translation; Murray, *Suicide*, II:176, note 45, gives Latin: "Quod si taedio vitae aut pudore aeris alieni vel valetudinis alicuius impatientia hoc admisit, non inquietabuntur". This law collection

had possibly been made for Alaric II in 506, here using a citation from a
Roman jurist also found in Justinian's *Digest*.

464. Cited in Minois, *History of Suicide*, 40. 'Losing his body' referred to the
common practice of punishing the corpse of a suicide, by the same methods
as criminal execution, which Boutillier here argued against, saying "the body
has done no offense to justice, but [only] to itself" in cases of madness or illness (ibid.).

465. See ibid., 38–40, on the subject of insanity as excuse for suicide; and Murray,
Suicide, I:166–79, on suicide cases 'hidden' behind verdicts of insanity.

466. Siegfried Wenzel, *The Sin of Sloth: Acedia in Medieval Thought and Litera-
ture* (Chapel Hill: University of North Carolina Press, 1967), 82 and 123.
S. W. Jackson, *Melancholia and Depression: From Hippocratic Times to
Modern Times* (New Haven, CT: Princeton University Press, 1986), 46–77,
mainly follows Wenzel, *Sin of Sloth*, on *melancholia* and *acedia*, but additionally provides a useful overview of medieval medical texts on the subject.
On despair as a motive for suicide, see Susan Snyder, 'The Left Hand of
God: Despair in Medieval and Renaissance Tradition', *Studies in the Renaissance* 12 (1965): 18–59. On the association in medieval art between suicide
and the vice of Despair, an image often paired with the virtue of Hope, the
archetypal figure being Judas hanging from a tree, while later representations feature characters stabbing themselves with a knife, see Moshe Barasch, 'Despair in the Medieval Imagination', *Social Research* 66, no. 2 (1999):
565–76.

467. David of Augsburg, *Formula novitiorum*, 51, Marguerin de la Bigne, *Maxima Bibliotheca Veterum Patrum et Antiquorum Scriptorum Ecclesiastico-
rum*, 28 vols. (Lyon, 1677—Genoa, 1707), XIII, 438, cited by Wenzel, *Sin of
Sloth*, 160.

468. Roland of Cremona, *Summae Magistri Rolandi Cremonensis O. P. liber
tercius*, ed. Aloysius Cortesi. Monumenta Bergomensia 7 (Bergamo: Ediz-
ione "Monumenta Bergomensia", 1962); O. Lottin, *Psychologie et morale
aux XIIe et XIII siècles* (Louvain: Abbaye de Mont César/Gembloux: Ducu-
lot, 1948), II:527–37; on medieval theories of emotions generally, see Simo
Knuuttila, *Emotions in Ancient and Medieval Philosophy* (Oxford: Clarendon Press, 2004).

469. Bonaventura, *In II librum Sententiarum*, dist. 43, articulum 3, quaestio 2,
ad 1 in *Opera omnia* (Quaracchi, 1887), II, col. 995a: "tales desperatissimi
frequentissime sibi inferunt mortem.", cited in Murray, *Suicide*, I:366.

470. Murray, *Suicide*, I:337–38; *Dialogus miraculorum*, ed. J. Strange (Cologne,
1851), dist. 4, chap. 40, I:209–10.

471. Minois, *History of Suicide*, 9. Murray, *Suicide*, I:160–61, mentions several
other cases of suicide for reasons of severe or prolonged sickness, although
unfortunately it is impossible to tell from the wording in the sources whether
any of these 'illnesses' could be classed as disabilities.

472. Murray, *Suicide*, I:100–101, citing C. T. Gemeiner, *Die Regensburgische
Chronik*, 4 vols. (Regensburg, 1800–24), II:400: "Den andern Tag danach
war ein armer Kranker Mann Martel der Schweintreiber, von Geldschulden
wegen in grosser Armuth und Elend, frühe hinausgegangen, . . . und sich
mit einem strang . . . an die seitegehangen". Herding swine was apparently
a job often given to elderly people who had been pensioned off with one of
the 'cheaper' corrodies that was not a full retirement but still entailed some
lighter, less physically demanding work.

473. *Historia monasterii Villariensis in Brabantia, ordinis Cisterciensis*, book 3,
chap. 8, in E. Martène and U. Durand, *Thesaurus novus anecdotorum* 3
(Paris, 1717), 1368C–1369B, cited and trans. Murray, *Suicide*, I:321.

474. Murray, *Suicide*, I:322, Latin citing *Historia monasterii Villariensis*.
475. See Metzler, *Disability*, 163, for a discussion, including social status, of some disabled, albeit not elderly, people who wish for death to relieve them of the "hateful life" they linger in (*odibilis vite mora diu protractus*). It is mainly in the miracles of Saint Foy that one encounters narratives of various knights who were so wounded and disabled, such as Rigaud who wanted to die "rather than to drag out a disgusting and useless life with his body in such a shameful state" (ibid., 198 and 201). Also see Murray, *Suicide*, I:319–20.
476. Murray, *Suicide*, II:374–75, citing *Vita et miracula s. Edmundi*, MS Oxford, Bodleian, Fell 2, fol. 23r: "ad tantam deveneret miseram, quod nec mortui nec vivi effigiem pretenderet. Desperatus igitur a suis"; *Vita Wulfrici*, chap. 105, ed. M. Bell, Somerset Record Society 47 (1933): 132: "Medici desperaverunt eum"; *Vita s. Bernardi Poen*, *Acta sanctorum*, *Apr* 2 (1675), 692B: "desperabiliter aegrotasse"; *Miracula s. Fidis*, Book 4, chap. 24, ed. A. Bouillet (Paris, 1897), 221: "promerentur . . . vitaeque desperati celerem reparationem".
477. Murray, *Suicide*, I:124.
478. Ibid., I:403. However, earlier Murray had found that, unless coupled with mental illness, "on its own, [physical] sickness is rarer than we might expect, not least in view of its prominence in legal records and despite the bias in many of these for including it" (ibid., 320).
479. Among the vast literature concerning suicide according to geriatrics and gerontology two selective citations, one from each side of the Atlantic, may serve as arbitrary examples: M. L. Bruce et al., 'Reducing Suicidal Ideation and Depressive Symptoms in Depressed Older Primary Care Patients: A Randomized Controlled Trial', *Journal of the American Medical Association* 291 (2004): 1081–91; and George S. Alexopoulos, 'Depression in the Elderly', *Lancet* 365, no. 9475 (2005): 1961–70. The latter's abstract is worth quoting for its summary of modern medical opinion on the matter:

> In elderly people, depression mainly affects those with chronic medical illnesses and cognitive impairment, causes suffering, family disruption, and disability, worsens the outcomes of many medical illnesses, and increases mortality. Ageing-related and disease-related processes, including arteriosclerosis and inflammatory, endocrine, and immune changes compromise the integrity of frontostriatal pathways, the amygdala, and the hippocampus, and increase vulnerability to depression. Heredity factors might also play a part. Psychosocial adversity—economic impoverishment, disability, isolation, relocation, caregiving, and bereavement—contributes to physiological changes, further increasing susceptibility to depression or triggering depression in already vulnerable elderly individuals.

Plus ça change.
480. *Seneca's Letters to Lucilius*, trans. E. Phillips Barker, 2 vols. (Oxford: Clarendon Press, 1932), I:189–91, letter no. 58. In his *Letters* Pliny the Younger, too, praised instances in which several old men who had been beset by disability and illness had chosen to exit this life, including a friend of his who was lamed by gout and a seventy-five-year-old man labouring under an incurable disease (Minois, *History of Suicide*, 52).
481. Marie-Noëlle Lefay-Toury, *La tentation du suicide dans le roman français du XIIe siècle* (Paris: H. Champion, 1979).
482. Job 7:5 and 7:15, Vulgate: "induta est caro mea putredine" . . . "elegit suspendium anima mea et mortem ossa mea desperavi nequaquam ultra iam vivam". Gregory the Great's *Moralia in Job*, which was essential reading for "every serious medieval moralist" (Murray, *Suicide*, II:97) had to deal with this uncomfortable text.

483. Augustine, *Concerning the City of God against the Pagans*, trans. Henry Bettenson (London: Penguin, 1984), Book I, chap. 22, at 33.

484. Philippe Ariès, *The Hour of Our Death*, trans. H. Weaver (London: Allen Lane, 1981), 123; Alberto Tenenti, *La vie et la mort à travers l'art du Xve siècle*. Cahiers des Annales 8 (Paris: Armand Colin, 1952), 99.

485. *Fifteenth Century English Translations of Alain Chartier's* Le Traité de L'Esperance *and* Le Quadrilogue Invectif, ed. Margaret Blayney, vols. 1–2. EETS o.s. 270, 281 (Oxford: OUP, 1974 and 1980)—I am grateful to Julie Singer for this reference.

486. Cited in Ariès, *Hour of Our Death*, 123.

487. On the topic of visual representation of despair, see Moshe Barasch, *Gestures of Despair in Medieval and Early Renaissance Art* (New York,: New York University Press 1976); also J. A. Burrow, *Gestures and Looks in Medieval Narrative* (Cambridge: Cambridge University Press, 2002).

488. "I'non son brama-(che) di spenger (la) vita" (cited by Bolzoni, *Web of Images*, 39, note 63).

489. 'He' should be a 'she', since as was pointed out earlier, the allegorical figure of Death in this fresco is, in fact, represented by a monstrous old woman.

490. Barasch, *Blindness*, 117.

491. Heinke Sudhoff, *Ikonographische Untersuchungen zur 'Blindenheilung' und zum 'Blindensturz'. Ein Beitrag zu Pieter Breugels Neapler Gemälde von 1568* (PhD diss., University of Bonn, 1981), 94. More recently Bolzoni, *Web of Images*, 20–29, has specifically linked the theme of the desert fathers in the Thebaid, which is represented to the left of the fresco, with the spread of ideas about the ideal life via Dominican preaching.

492. For instance, the theory proposed by Millard Meiss on the change in Sienese and Florentine art as caused by the cataclysm of the Black Death; see Phillip Lindley, 'The Black Death and English Art. A Debate and Some Assumptions', in *The Black Death in England*, ed. Mark Ormrod and Phillip Lindley (Stamford: Paul Watkins, 1996), 125–46, especially 125–28 and 131–32, for a refutation of Meiss. On the ambiguity of the fourteenth-century crises in affecting mentalities and changing attitudes, in particular to poverty, begging and the disabled, see also Chapter 4, this volume.

493. Friederike Wille, *Die Todesallegorie im Camposanto in Pisa. Genese und Rezeption eines berühmten Bildes* (Munich: Allitera Verlag, 2002).

494. Sudhoff, *Ikonographische Untersuchungen*, 95.

495. Already in antiquity it had been observed that those who suffered a particularly misfortunate or brutal life were more ready to consider death as a relief, for instance, the mining slaves who were forced to labour in the Ptolemaic gold-mines, described by Agatharchides of Cnidus in the second century BC: "all these subject to the harsh lot just described consider death more desirable than life"; Stanley M. Burstein, *Agatharchides of Cnidus, On the Erythrean Sea*, Hakluyt Society, II, vol. 172 (Farnham: Ashgate, 1989), 63–64, §26a and 26b.

496. *The Book of Margery Kempe*, trans. B. A. Windeatt (London: Penguin, 1985), chap. 76, 221.

497. Cited in Amt, *Women's Lives*, 188.

498. Cited in ibid., 189–90.

499. It is the necessity for extended bed-rest and enforced immobility following a femoral head fracture in particular that is one of the prime causes of death in hospital after a fall, not so much because of the fracture, but because the long period of lying immobile in bed often leads to pulmonary disease, which then turns out to be the specific cause of death.

500. Cited in Getz, *Medicine*, 78; *Calendar of Coroners' Rolls of the City of London A.D. 1300–1378*, ed. Reginald R. Sharpe (London, 1913), 139–40.

501. Esch, *Wahre Geschichten*, 75–76. Johannes must have felt pangs of guilt, since he later wrote to the papal curia asking for dispensation for his involvement in this incident, which is how the event came to be recorded; *Repertorium Poenitentiariae Germanicum*, vol. VI (papacy of Sixtus IV, 1471–1484), ed. L. Schmugge (Tübingen: Max Niemeyer, 2005), case no. 3473.

502. "Die 'Normalität des Alters' tritt klar zum Vorschein, Alter wurde nicht gleichgesetzt mit Senilität oder Debilität, und abschätzige Bemerkungen über das Alter oder ältere Menschen fehlen in den untersuchten Quellen vollständig" (Krötzl, 'Sexaginta vel circa', 115).

503. Joinville and Villehardouin, *Chronicles of the Crusades*, 262–63.

504. Thane, *Old Age*, 7.

505. Rosenthal, *Old Age*, 100.

506. "Mit krachenden Beine und triefender Nase, kahlköpfig, taub und halb blind schleppt sich der alte Mensch aus dem Mittelalter heraus und kriecht auf Krücken gestützt, unter dem Spott der Jugend, über die Schwelle zur Neuzeit" (Borscheid, *Geschichte*, 13).

NOTES TO CHAPTER 4

1. Besides seminal work by Geremek and Mollat, Rubin and Farmer (see Bibliography), a useful overview of the subject is provided by O. G. Oexle, ed., *Armut im Mittelalter*, Vorträge und Forschungen, hg. vom Konstanzer Arbeitskreis für mittelalterliche Geschichte 58 (Ostfildern: Thorbecke, 2004) on poverty in medieval Germany.

2. Rubin and Henderson, plus Brodman in particular on charity and poverty (see Bibliography); for charity towards a particularly 'deserving' group, see P. Gavitt, *Charity and Children in Renaissance Florence: The Ospedale degli Innocenti, 1410–1536* (Ann Arbor, MA: University of Michigan Press, 1990); the German perspective may be accessed in the collection of conference proceedings edited by S. Schmidt and J. Aspelmeier, *Norm und Praxis der Armenfürsorge in Spätmittelalter und früher Neuzeit*, Vierteljahrschrift für Sozial- und Wirtschaftsgeschichte Beihefte Band 189 (Stuttgart: Franz Steiner, 2006).

3. Two important works are Brian Tierney, *Medieval Poor Law: A Sketch of Canonical Theory and Its Application in England* (Berkeley: University of California Press, 1959); and Brodman, *Charity*. For the interplay between literature and the moral/religious dimensions, see Crassons, *Claims of Poverty*.

4. Ephraim Shoham-Steiner, 'Poverty and Disability: A Medieval Jewish Perspective', in *Sign Languages of Poverty*, ed. G. Jaritz (Vienna: Verlag der Österreichischen Akademie der Wissenschaften, 2007), 80.

5. Fandrey, *Krüppel*, 17; image reproduced in A. Hauber, *Planetenkinderbilder und Sternbilder* (Strasbourg: Heitz, 1916), 117, plate 14.

6. Miri Rubin, 'The Poor', in *Fifteenth Century Attitudes: Perceptions of Society in Late Medieval England*, ed. R. Horrox (Cambridge: Cambridge University Press, 1994), 172.

7. Michel Mollat, *Die Armen im Mittelalter*, trans. U. Irsigler (Munich: Beck, 1987), 12.

8. Otto Gerhard Oexle, 'Armut und Armenfürsorge um 1200. Ein Beitrag zum Verständnis der freiwilligen Armut bei Elisabeth von Thüringen', in *Sankt Elisabeth. Fürstin, Dienerin, Heilige. Aufsätze—Dokumentation—Katalog* (Sigmaringen: Thorbecke, 1981), 82: "'Arm' sind Menschen, die immer oder zeitweise in einem Zustand der Schwäche, der Bedürftigkeit, des Mangels leben, wobei es nicht immer um das Fehlen physischer Kraft und materieller

Güter (Geld, Nahrung, Kleidung) geht, sondern insgesamt um einen Mangel an sozialer 'Stärke', die ein Ergebnis ist von sozialem Ansehen und Einfluß, von Waffengewandheit und Rechtsposition, von Gesichert-Sein durch soziale Bindungen, aber auch von Wissen und politischer Macht. Deshalb wird im Mittelalter der 'Arme' (pauper) nicht nur dem 'Reichen' (dives), sondern auch dem 'Starken' (potens) gegenübergestellt."

9. Dyer, *Standards of Living*, 235 makes a similar point concerning poverty as powerlessness.

10. Lester K. Little, *Religious Poverty and the Profit Economy in Medieval Europe* (London: Elek, 1978), 68.

11. Karl Bosl, 'Potens und Pauper. Begriffsgeschichtliche Studien zur gesell-schaftlichen Differenzierung im frühen Mittelalter und zum "Pauperismus" des Hochmittelalters', in *Frühformen der Gesellschaft im mittelalterlichen Europa. Ausgewählte Beiträge zu einer Strukturanalyse der mittelalterlichen Welt*, ed. Karl Bosl (Munich: R. Oldenbourg Verlag, 1964), 110.

12. Ibid., 107; also Otto Scherner, '"Ut propriam familiam nutriat". Zur Frage der sozialen Sicherung in der karolingischen Grundherrschaft', *Zeitschrift der Savigny-Stiftung für Rechtsgeschichte. Germanische Abteilung* 111 (1994): 330–62.

13. Bosl, 'Potens', 111–17.

14. Expanded on the period he studied by publishing a volume on poverty in the high Middle Ages: Karl Bosl, *Das Problem der Armut in der hochmit-telalterlichen Gesellschaft* (Vienna: Österreichische Akademie der Wissen-schaften, 1974).

15. Irsigler, '*Divites* und *pauperes* in der Vita Meinwerci', 449. The *vita* of Mein-werc, bishop of Paderborn (1009–1036), composed between 1155 and 1165, classified people according to *sexus, ordo* and *conditio*, where it is tempting to translate *conditio* as economic situation (ibid., 453).

16. Ibid., 450: "Jeder *potens* ist auch *dives*, umgekehrt gilt der Satz aber nicht. Bei *potens—pauper* ist also immer auch der Gegensatz *dives—pauper* mit-zudenken; dieses Begriffspaar begegnet schließlich in den früh- und hochmit-telalterlichen Quellen etwa ebenso häufig wie jenes".

17. Author's translation from German cited by Marie-Luise Windemuth, *Das Hospital als Träger der Armenfürsorge im Mittelalter*, Sudhoffs Archiv Beihefte 36 (Stuttgart: Franz Steiner Verlag, 1995), 23–24; Jerome [Hierony-mus], *Epistola 66*, in *Bibliothek der Kirchenväter* 15, ed. Otto Bardenhewer, Theo Scherman and Karl Weymann (Munich, 1914), 153–54.

18. *The Rule of St. Benedict*, 5th ed., ed. and trans. D. O. Hunter Blair (Fort Augus-tus: Abbey Press, 1948), 90, chap. 31 and 134, chap. 53; Julie Kerr, *Monastic Hospitality: The Benedictines in England, c.1070–c.1250*, Studies in the His-tory of Medieval Religion 32 (Woodbridge: Boydell Press, 2007), 25–26.

19. Le Goff and Truong, *Geschichte*, 131.

20. Frank Meier, *Gaukler, Dirnen, Rattenfänger. Außenseiter im Mittelalter* (Ostfildern: Thorbecke, 2005), 32.

21. "Der Arme, der auf die Unterstützung seiner Mitmenschen angewiesen war, stand im frühen und hohen Mittelalter durchaus nicht außerhalb oder auch nur am Rande der Gesellschaft, sondern war vielmehr integratives Glied der-selben" (Irsigler and Lassotta, *Bettler*, 18–20).

22. Janet Coleman, 'Property and Poverty', in *The Cambridge History of Medi-eval Political Thought, c.350–c.1450*, ed. J. H. Burns (Cambridge: Cam-bridge University Press, 1988), 629.

23. Cited in Minois, *History of Old Age*, 139; C. Mirabel, 'Les pauvres et la pauvreté en Italie du nord d'après Rathier de Verone', *Cahiers de la pauvreté* 6 (1967–1968).

24. Herlihy, 'Age', 144.
25. On the concept of 'need' as essential element for charitable assistance given to these groups, see J. Agrimi and C. Crisciani, 'Wohltätigkeit und Beistand in der mittelalterlichen christlichen Kultur', in *Die Geschichte des medizinischen Denkens. Antike und Mittelalter*, ed. M. D. Grmek (Munich: C. H. Beck, 1996), 182–215.
26. Frank Meier, *Gefürchtet und bestaunt. Vom Umgang mit dem Fremden im Mittelalter* (Ostfildern: Thorbecke, 2007), 134–35. Also in Renate Koos, 'Zu frühen Schrift- und Bildzeugnissen über die heilige Elisabeth als Quellen zur Kunst- und Kulturgeschichte', in *Sankt Elisabeth. Fürstin, Dienerin, Heilige. Aufsätze—Dokumentation—Katalog*, eds. Carl Graepler, Fred Schwind and Matthias Werner (Sigmaringen: Thorbecke, 1981), 236, note 285, where a similar list is given as "Cuidam ceco, uetulo pauperi, nudo garcioni, uago filio, uetute, peregrino, wallero giouago, duobus peregrinis, duobus infirmis". The random order and the rather strange inclusion of the morbidly fat (*pingues*), who most certainly did not suffer from malnutrition, just demonstrates the extremely wide definition of who deserved Bishop Wolfger's assistance.
27. Meier, *Gefürchtet*, 134–35. Incidentally, one of the *cantores* who benefited from the bishop's charitable handouts was a certain Walther von der Vogelweide, better known to posterity for his verses than for his poverty.
28. Coleman, 'Property', 619. Johannes Teutonicus (fl. 1210–1245) argued that people should only possess as much wealth as they needed (which of course begs the question of how much an individual person actually needs); *Glossa ordinaria* ad Dist. 86 c. 18. Possumus &.
29. Carole Rawcliffe, *The Hospitals of Medieval Norwich*, Studies in East Anglian History 2 (Norwich: University of East Anglia, 1995), 98; J. Willis Clark, ed., *The Observances in Use at the Augustinian Priory of St. Giles and St. Andrew at Barnwell, Cambridgeshire* (Cambridge, 1897), 175, 179.
30. Cited in Tierney, *Medieval Poor Law*, 101.
31. Coleman, 'Property', 620. Hostiensis, *Summa Aurea super Titulis Decretalium*, printed at Coliniae, 1612.
32. Dyer, *Standards of Living*, 236.
33. *Sancti Caesarii Arelatensis sermones*, ed. G. Morin (Turnhout: Brepols, 1953), I:112 (ep. 25), quoted by Anne M. Scott, *Piers Plowman and the Poor* (Dublin: Four Courts Press, 2004), 39. On the contractual aspects of almsgiving also Brodman, *Charity*, 36–37.
34. 'Protectorium Pauperis', ed. Arnold Williams, *Carmelus* 5 (1958): 132–80, at 141, cited by Crassons, 'The Workman', 89, note 27.
35. P. H. Cullum, 'Spiritual and Bodily Works of Mercy', in *A Companion to the Book of Margery Kempe*, ed. John H. Arnold and Katherine J. Lewis (Cambridge: D. S. Brewer, 2004), 180. Davis, 'Preaching', 73, has drawn attention to the question of why the corporal works of mercy resonated with hospital donors and personnel, and why people may have been motivated to found such institutions and work there by thinking about the works of mercy.
36. "Schwache ... erholen, Arme und Geistesgequälte getröstet, die eines Obdachs entbehrenden gastfreundlich aufgenommen, die Nackten gekleidet und noch andere Beweise der Liebe" (quoted in Borscheid, *Geschichte*, 83).
37. "Kann der Spendenempfänger dem Gebenden seinen Dank für die geleistete Hilfe nicht selbst aussprechen. Daher muss die vermittelnde spendensammelnde Instanz als Reziprozitätssubstitut einspringen, um die Spendengabe zu einem positiven Erlebnis für die Spender werden zu lassen" (Gabriele Lingelbach, 'Konstruktionen von >Behinderung< in der Öffentlichkeitsarbeit und Spendenwerbung der Aktion Sorgenkind seit 1964', in *Disability History*.

Konstruktionen von Behinderung in der Geschichte. Eine Einführung, Disability Studies, Körper—Macht—Differenz Band 6, ed. Elsbeth Bösl, Anne Klein, and Anne Waldschmidt [Bielefeld: transcript, 2010], 127–50, at 134, with reference to Marcel Mauss's theory of the reciprocity of the gift, first expounded in 'Essai sur le don', *L'Année Sociologique* [1923–1924]).

38. *Medieval Towns: A Reader*, Readings in Medieval Civilizations and Cultures XI, ed. Maryanne Kowalski (Quebec: Broadview Press, 2006), 263–64; G. Brucker, *The Society of Renaissance Florence: A Documentary Study* (New York: Harper and Row, 1971), 23–33. The fraternity of Orsanmichele provided further help to 228 individual paupers across Florence between 2 and 5 June 1347 alone, and in these activities differed from the majority of Florentine fraternities, which had a strictly limited focus on their own parish, e.g. the fraternity based in the parish of S. Frediano, whose prime concern was the burial of the dead poor—Orsanmichele tried to help the living poor instead; cf. John Henderson, 'The Parish and the Poor in Florence at the Time of the Black Death: The Case of S. Frediano', *Continuity and Change* 3, no. 2 (1988): 263.

39. Cited by Hilda Johnstone, 'Poor-Relief in the Royal Households of Thirteenth-Century England', *Speculum* 4 (1929): 156; *Red Book of the Exchequer*, II:759; Rawcliffe, *Leprosy*, 41.

40. Johnstone, 'Poor-Relief', 156.

41. "Pascantur autem omnes debiles et senes in magna aula et minori, minus debiles et mediocres in camera regis, et pueri in camera regine" (*Calendar of the Close Rolls*, 1242–1247, 150); see also Johnstone, 'Poor-Relief', 156.

42. C. Given-Wilson, *The Royal Household and the King's Affinity: Service, Politics and Finance in England 1360–1413* (New Haven, CT: Yale University Press, 1986), 69.

43. Ibid. In similar fashion Aethelwig, abbot of Evesham (1059–1077), had made provision for twelve so-called Maundy men, paupers who were obliged to pray and attend various monastic services in return for meals; some of these men were lepers, it seems, and when one died his place was taken by another; Kerr, *Monastic Hospitality*, 29; Thomas of Marlborough, *History of the Abbey of Evesham*, ed. and trans. J. Sayers and L. Watkiss (Oxford: Oxford Medieval Texts, 2003), 168–69, chap. 160.

44. Given-Wilson, *Royal Household*, 70.

45. For some preliminary thoughts on this topic, see Irina Metzler, 'Indiscriminate Healing Miracles in Decline: How Social Realities Affect Religious Perceptioní, in *Contextualizing Medieval Miracles*, ed. Matthew Mesley and Louise E. Wilson (forthcoming); on chantry chapels, for example, see H. Colvin, 'The Origin of Chantries', *Journal of Medieval History* 26 (2000): 163–73; Simon Roffey, *The Medieval Chantry Chapel: An Archaeology* (Woodbridge: Boydell Press, 2007); G. H. Cook, *Medieval Chantries and Chantry Chapels* (London: Phoenix House, 1947; rev. ed. 1963); Marie-Helene Rousseau, *Saving the Souls of Medieval London: Perpetual Chantries at St. Paul's Cathedral, c. 1200–1548* (Aldershot: Ashgate, 2011).

46. Roger Price with Michael Ponsford, *St. Bartholomew's Hospital, Bristol: The Excavation of a Medieval Hospital, 1976–8*, CBA Research Report 110 (York: CBA, 1998), 88; F. B. Bickley, ed., *The Little Red Book of Bristol* (Bristol, 1900), I:224. Edmund Blanket is popularly (but non-verifiably) credited with the 'invention' of the textile named after him in English.

47. "Diese Auffassung des Almosens wird seit dem 12. Jahrhundert deutlich ausgesprochen" (Bronislaw Geremek, *Geschichte der Armut. Elend und Barmherzigkeit in Europa*, trans. F. Griese [Munich: Artemis Verlag, 1988], 63).

48. Luke 14:16–24.

49. Heidelberg, Universitätsbibliothek, Codex Manesse, fol. 113v, first quarter fourteenth century. Hesse von Reinach was in minor clerical orders, but the main point is that the manuscript as a whole, depicting the most famous *Minnesänger*, was intended for a secular patron.
50. Christine de Pisan, *Treasure of the City*, part 3, chapter 13, 177.
51. Ibid., 178.
52. Ibid., 179.
53. Examples of charity in stained glass of Freiburg Minster dating from second half of the thirteenth century.
54. Livio Pestilli, 'Disabled Bodies: The (Mis)Representation of the Lame in Antiquity and Their Reappearance in Early Christian and Medieval Art', in *Roman Bodies: Antiquity to the Eighteenth Century*, ed. Andrew Hopkins and Maria Wyke (London: British School at Rome, 2005), 90.
55. Ibid., 90–91. On the particular resonance of orthopedically impaired beggars in the iconography of Saint Martin, see Irina Metzler, 'Bildliche Darstellungen des (nicht)behinderten Bettlers im Martinswunder aus der Perspektive mittelalterlicher Mentalitäten', in *Andere Bilder. Zur Produktion von Behinderung in der visuellen Kultur*, ed. Beate Ochsner and Anna Grebe (Bielefeld: transcript Verlag, 2013) and note 323 in this chapter.
56. Friedrich Zoepfl, *Mittelalterliche Caritas im Spiegel der Legende* (Freiburg: Caritasverlag, 1925).
57. Schubert, *Alltag*, 203. A relatively obscure Saint Johannes Elemosinarius (Saint John the Almoner) saves one Petrus Telonearius, who had persistently refused to give alms.
58. Langland, *Piers the Ploughman*, 132; "Ac calleth the carefulle therto, the croked and the povere" (B-Text passus XI line 192). This is a reference to Luke 14:12.
59. Piers Plowman, C-Text, passus IX lines 96–97: "These are almusse, to helpe þat han suche charges/ And to conforte such coterelles and crokede men and blynde." See Shepherd, 'Poverty', 172. Elsewhere in the C-Text the worthy poor are categorised as "Ac olde and hore, þat helpes ben and nedy, / And wymmen with childe þat worche ne mowe, / Blynde and bedredne and broken in here membres" (passus IX lines 175–77); see Geoffrey Shepherd, 'Poverty in *Piers Plowman*', in *Social Relations and Ideas: Essays in Honour of R. H. Hilton*, ed. T. H. Aston, P. R. Coss, C. Dyer and J. Thirsk (Cambridge: Cambridge University Press, 1983), 174; Crassons, *Claims of Poverty*, 81; also Derek Pearsall, '*Piers Plowman* and the Problem of Labour', in *The Problem of Labour in Fourteenth-Century England*, ed. James Bothwell, P. J. P. Goldberg and W. M. Ormrod (York: York Medieval Press, 2000), 128, who points out that "the old, blind, infirm, maimed, sick, all those unable to work through no fault of their own, the archetypally deserving poor, are alone worthy to receive Christian charity."
60. Siegfried Wenzel, ed. and trans., *Fasciculus Morum: A Fourteenth-Century Preacher's Handbook* (University Park: Pennsylvania State University Press, 1989), 541. One is reminded of the parable of the feast to which the poor, the maimed, the lame and the blind are invited (Luke 14:13). The *Gesta romanorum*, a collection of anecdotes and tales compiled at the end of the thirteenth or beginning of the fourteenth century, also mentions this episode; Schleusener-Eichholz, *Das Auge*, I:504. Barasch, *Blindness*, 93, misquotes this passage from Schleusener-Eichholz, erroneously reading the story as attributed to Hermann of Fritzlar, when in fact Fritzlar's text relates to the 'false' miracle of the frauds unwillingly healed by Saint Martin's relics—on which see the following.

61. *Decretum Gratiani*, D 45 c 13, ed. Emil Friedberg, 165, ref. following Schubert, *Alltag*, 203.
62. Miri Rubin, *Charity and Community in Medieval Cambridge* (Cambridge: Cambridge University Press, 1987), 62.
63. Marjorie K. McIntosh, *Controlling Misbehaviour in England, 1370–1600* (Cambridge: Cambridge University Press, 1998), 81–82.
64. Rubin, *Charity*, 68.
65. Schubert, *Alltag*, 205.
66. Ibid., 207: "Sehr widersprüchlich ist unser Ergebnis. Die Menschen helfen armen Blinden in der Not und die gleichen Menschen können über das Mißgeschick dieser Blinden auch Tränen lachen". The same ambiguity governed attitudes toward the orthopedically impaired as well: "Schon Moriz Heyne [writing in 1903] . . . war aufgefallen, daß der Krüppel gleichermaßen Gegenstand des Erbarmens, das sich in Almosen ausdrückte, wie des Spottes sein konnte" (ibid.); Moriz Heyne, *Fünf Bücher deutscher Hausaltertümer* (S. Hirzel, 1903), III:23–24.
67. Schubert, *Alltag*, 205; according to Elisabeth Sudeck, *Bettlerdarstellungen vom Ende des XV. Jahrhunderts bis zu Rembrandt*, Studien zur deutschen Kunstgeschichte 279 (Strasbourg: Heitz, 1931), 97, the scene is depicted in a painting by Hieronymus Bosch; more recently Edward Wheatley, 'The Blind Beating the Blind: An Unidentified "Game" in a Marginal Illustration of *The Romance of Alexander*, MS Bodley 264', *Journal of the Warburg and Courtauld Institutes* 68 (2005), 213–17, referring to fol. 74v, where on the left a boy leads four blind men, while on the right the same four men, now armed with clubs, are trying to beat the pig.
68. Schubert, *Alltag*, 205; Hermann Korner, *Chronica Novella*, ed. Jakob Schwalm (Göttingen, 1895), 83.
69. Schubert, *Alltag*, 205; Walter Schaufelberger, *Der Wettkampf in der alten Eidgenossenschaft* (Berne: Paul Haupt, 1972), 89.
70. "Alße waß solck ein lachendes vastelauent nicht geseen", *Johann Berckmanns Stralsundische Chronik*, cited in Gottwald, *Lachen*, 124.
71. "Mer ee si dat verken gevellen kunden, so wart mennich misselich slach van in geslagen: ir ein sloich den anderen, eindeils van in vielen over dat verken, dan sloigen die anderen up den gevallen. dat werde ein guede wile. intleste quamen si an dat verken ind sloigen dat doit, dat genuechlichen ind aventurlichen zo sien was" (cited in Irsigler and Lassotta, *Bettler*, 20).
72. Schubert, *Alltag*, 205; Werner Hofmann, ed., *Köpfe der Lutherzeit* (Hamburg: Hamburger Kunsthalle, 1983), 180.
73. *Journal d'un bourgeois de Paris de 1405 à 1449*, ed. Colette Beaune (Paris: Le Livre de Poche, 1990), 221: "Item, le dernier dimanche du mois d'août, fut fait un ébatement en l'hôtel nommé d'Armagnac en la rue Saint Honoré, qu'on mit quatre aveugles tous armés en un parc, chacun un bâton en sa main, et en ce lieu y avait un fort pourcel, lequel ils devaient avoir s'ils pouvaient tuer"; Geremek, *Margins*, 272 and note 10; Singer, *Blindness*, 157.
74. Huizinga, *Waning of the Middle Ages*, 24.
75. McCall, *Medieval Underworld*, 147.
76. Gottwald, *Lachen*, 44.
77. On laughter in the Middle Ages see Jacques Le Goff, *Das Lachen im Mittelalter* (Stuttgart: Klett-Cotta, 2004 [essays originally in *Un autre Moyen Âge*, Paris: Gallimard, 1999]); in contemporary culture, the problematic nature of medieval laughter and comedy has of course been popularised through the character of Jorge of Burgos in Umberto Eco's *The Name of the Rose*.
78. Incidentally, neither does Le Goff in his discussions of laughter. Gottwald, *Lachen*, 32, has very usefully typefied three kinds of historical sources on the

comic: a), fictional sources that elicit laughter about disabled people, e.g. jokes, images, farces; b), non-fictional sources that narrate laughter about disability, e.g. the chroniclers on the pig-beating events; and c), non-fictional sources that comment on and evaluate laughter about disability, e.g. theological texts—here conspicuous for their omission of blind beggars as spectacle. Aquinas, *Summa theologica*, Second part of the second part, question 72, article 1, reply to objection 3 (online at http://www.newadvent.org/summa/3072.htm, accessed 9 May 2012), rather bluntly states: "Hence if one man says spitefully to another that he is blind, he taunts but does not revile him".

79. Geremek, *Geschichte*, 39. Rather of Verona, *Praeloquiorum libri sex*, PL, vol. 136, col. 236; August Adam, *Arbeit und Besitz nach Ratherius von Verona* (Freiburg im Breisgau: Herder, 1927), 112.

80. Cited in Rubin, *Charity*, 86; *Die Exempla aus den sermones feriales et communes des Jakob von Vitry*, ed. J. Greven (Heidelberg, 1914), 38, no. 58.

81. Cited in Rubin, *Charity*, 86. "Elemosina est magis meritoria et virtuosa si fiat in sanitate et in vita", Thomas Brinton, *The Sermons of Thomas Brinton, Bishop of Rochester (1373–1389)*, ed. M. A. Devlin, Camden Society 3rd series (London: Royal Historical Society, 1954), 194, sermon 44.

82. As late as 1510 the last will and testament of Hermann Wyndegge and his wife, Peterse of Cologne, specifically mentioned the poor folk lying in the streets, being those with the pox, cripples, lame and blind (*armen mynschen up der straissen ligen, as mit den pocken, kropelen, lammen ind blynden*), cited in Irsigler and Lassotta, *Bettler*, 45.

83. Robert Jütte, *Poverty and Deviance in Early Modern Europe* (Cambridge: Cambridge University Press, 1994), 2.

84. Meier, *Gaukler*, 18.

85. Author's translation of Meier, *Gaukler*, 19–20.

86. Ibid., 20: "Erste Ansätze einer obrigkeitlichen Sozialfürsorge verdrängten schrittweise individuelles Mitleid und persönliches Erbarmen." See also Elaine Clark, 'Institutional and Legal Responses to Begging in Medieval England', *Social Science History* 26, no. 3 (2002): 447–73.

87. Jütte, *Poverty*, 2.

88. For instance, Rubin, *Charity*, 291; B. Pullan, *Rich and Poor in Renaissance Venice* (Oxford: Blackwell, 1971), 197–204; and Mollat, *Die Armen*, 82–96, 142–61.

89. Oexle, 'Armut', 84: "Hier zeigt sich die tiefe Kluft, welche die spätmittelalterliche und frühneuzeitliche Auffasung von der Armut und von den Armen grundsätzlich von der früh- und hochmittelalterlichen unterschiedet: Armut wurde nun nicht mehr durch den Zwang zur Arbeit definiert, sondern es wird jetzt Arbeit als Mittel gegen Armut verstanden, d.h. Armut als 'Nicht-Arbeit' definiert." A useful summary of these developments is given by Katharina Simon-Muscheid, 'Sozialer Abstieg im Mittelalter', in *Sign Languages of Poverty*, ed. G. Jaritz (Vienna: Verlag der Österreichischen Akademie der Wissenschaften, 2007), 100–102. On the topic of work and work ethic, how labour of itself came to be valued theologically as a means to salvation, see Postel, *Arbeit*. On work and medieval religion see Ranft, *Theology*.

90. Postel, *Arbeit*, 171. On notions and ethics of work more generally, see also Josef Ehmer and Catharina Lis, eds., *The Idea of Work in Europe from Antiquity to Modern Times* (Farnham: Ashgate, 2009). During the ninth century work came to be seen less as a punitive measure imposed on faulty, post-lapsarian humanity and more as containing a positive value in itself; see Janet L. Nelson, 'The Church and a Revaluation of Work in the Ninth Century?', in *The Use and Abuse of Time in Christian History*, Studies in Church History 37, ed. R. N. Swanson (Woodbridge: Boydell Press, 2002), 35–43.

91. *Commentariorum in Matthaeum libri octo* V, XV, PL, vol. 107, c. 982: "diversis virtutum opibus ditatos et fide robustos in divino servitio bene laborare", cited in Postel, *Arbeit*, 79.

92. Whatever the nature of the support, there was an "unspoken, unbreakable principle common to all European countries at all times of which we have knowledge. This laid it down that under no circumstances should anyone be allowed to die, the kinless and those without home and family along with all the rest", according to Peter Laslett, 'Family, Kinship and Collectivity as Systems of Support in Pre-Industrial Europe: A Consideration of the 'Nuclear-Hardship' Hypothesis', *Continuity and Change* 3, no. 2 (1988): 170.

93. Rubin, 'The Poor', 179; Dyer, *Standards of Living*, 243; F. W. Steer, 'The Statutes of the Saffron Walden Almshouses', *Transactions of the Essex Archaeological Society* 25 (1958): 161–83.

94. Windemuth, *Das Hospital*, 101–2.

95. Le Goff, *Medieval Civilization*, 239. For an overview of this order cf. Brodman, *Charity*, 127–36. In the fourteenth century, patient records of the abbey at Vienne mention an infirm woman without feet and "an infirm person with one foot" (ibid., 131).

96. Peter Laslett, *The World We Have Lost*, 2nd ed. (London: Methuen, 1971).

97. Coleman, 'Property', 629. For an interesting analysis of the connections between antimercantile ideology as reflected in literary texts and developments in medieval economic theory (and practice), see Roger A. Ladd, *Antimercantilism in Late Medieval English Literature*, The New Middle Ages (Basingstoke: Palgrave, 2010), chap. 'Langland's Merchants and the Material and Spiritual Economics of *Piers Plowman*'.

98. However, O. G. Oexle has argued that the contrast between voluntary, religious poverty, on the one hand, and involuntary, economic/social poverty, on the other hand, has been exaggerated; furthermore, poverty had come to be defined through manual labour in the high Middle Ages, so that in the case of Saint Elisabeth her aspirations to voluntary poverty included the real, involuntary poverty and physical work of the lower orders (Oexle, 'Armut', 79 and 92).

99. Meier, *Gaukler*, 23.

100. Bosl, 'Potens', 121.

101. Bynum, *Fragmentation*, 50. On voluntary poverty and the subsequent fourteenth-century debates over the ownership of property by Christ and by the Franciscans, see also David Burr, *Olivi and Franciscan Poverty: The Origins of the* usus pauper *Controversy* (Philadelphia: University of Pennsylvania Press, 1989); Hervaeus Natalis, *The Poverty of Christ and the Apostles*, MST 37, trans. John D. Jones (Toronto: PIMS, 1999).

102. Sharon Farmer and Barbara H. Rosenwein, 'Introduction', in *Monks and Nuns, Saints and Outcasts: Religion in Medieval Society. Essays in Honor of Lester K. Little*, ed. Sharon Farmer and Barbara H. Rosenwein (Ithaca, NY: Cornell University Press, 2000), 13.

103. On this topic, see the work of Oexle and Irsigler (see Bibliography), in particular on the life of Saint Elisabeth.

104. Brodman, *Charity*, 265. If, like the biblical Job or Lazarus, the poor readily accepted their condition, they were praised, but "precisely because they resisted their station and sought economic improvement", they were lambasted in sermons propagated by fourteenth-century mendicant preachers.

105. Thomas Aquinas, *Summa theologiae*, 2a 2ae, quaest. 186, art. 3, resp. ad 2, ed. and trans. Blackfriars (Cambridge: Blackfriars, 1973), XLVII, 108–11, cited by Farmer, 'Manual Labor', 273.

106. "Notandum quod pauperes raro veniunt ad ecclesiam, raro ad sermones, et ideo parum sciunt de pertinentibus ad suam salutem, et ideo instruendi sunt

ad suam salutem, cum inveniuntur congregati ad ecclesiam aliquam vel alibi, circa fidem, et circa ea, quae pertinent ad omnes Christianos, ut est confiteri semel in anno, et communicare, et scire Orationem dominicalem, et Ave Maria" (cited in Davis, 'Preaching', 81); Humbert de Romans, *De eruditione praedicatorum*, 1.2.86, in *Maxima bibliotheca veterum patrum*, ed. M. de la Bigne, 27 vols. (Lyon, 1677), XXV:499.

107. On Deguileville's life and works see Hagen, *Allegorical Remembrance*, 1–2. A Middle English translation was made by John Lydgate in 1426.

108. Hagen, *Allegorical Remembrance*, 21.

109. "Inter quorum pannos et illuviem corporis flagrans libido dominatur", Jerome, 'Against Vigilantius', 14, *The Principal Works of St. Jerome*. The Nicene and Post-Nicene Fathers 6, trans. W. H. Fremantle (Grand Rapids, MI, 1954), 422, cited by Farmer, 'Manual Labor', 273.

110. Thomas Aquinas, 'Contra impugnantes dei cultum et religionem', chap. 7, *Sancti Thomae Aquinatis Doctoris Angelici Ordinis Praedicatorum Opera Omnia*, 25 vols. (Parma, 1852–73), XV:43; and Bonaventure, 'Apologia pauperum', chap. 12, in *Doctoris Seraphici S. Bonaventurae Opera Omnia*, ed. College of St. Bonaventure (Quaracchi, 1891), VIII, 329.

111. Sharon Farmer, The Beggar's Body: Intersections of Gender and Social Status in High Medieval Paris', in *Monks and Nuns, Saints and Outcasts: Religion in Medieval Society. Essays in Honor of Lester K. Little*, ed. Sharon Farmer and Barbara H. Rosenwein (Ithaca, NY: Cornell University Press, 2000), 156. On the debate surrounding voluntary poverty of the mendicant orders, see Penn R. Szittya, *The Antifraternal Tradition in Medieval Literature* (Princeton, NJ: Princeton University Press, 1986), who traces the history of antifraternalist critique from the thirteenth century Parisian schools through William of Saint Amour into literature via the *Roman de la Rose*, to the polemic (*De pauperis salvatoris*) of Richard FitzRalph in the mid-fourteenth century and Langland's *Piers Plowman*; summarised in Scott, *Piers Plowman*, 55. On FitzRalph's theories and their influence, see Coleman, 'Property', 644–47.

112. 2 Thess. 3:10. The irony is that already in the thirteenth century both the Franciscan and Dominican mendicant friars started examining candidates for entry into their orders, admitting or refusing on the grounds of health in general and disability in particular (Montford, *Health*, 31–32).

113. Pestilli, 'Disabled Bodies', 90.

114. *Omne Bonum*, I:112.

115. Richard Firth Green, '"Nede ne hath no lawe": The Plea of Necessity in Medieval Literature and Law', in *Living Dangerously: On the Margins in Medieval and Early Modern Europe*, ed. Barbara A. Hanawalt and Anna Grotans (Notre Dame, IN: University of Notre Dame Press, 2007), 10. On Langland's anticlericalism, see W. Scase, *'Piers Plowman' and the New Anticlericalism* (Cambridge: Cambridge University Press, 1989), summarised in Scott, *Piers Plowman*, 55–56; also Crassons, *Claims of Poverty*, 41 and 89, for similar sentiments in a Wycliffite poem, *Pierce the Ploughman's Crede*, composed by an anonymous author after 1393.

116. Geremek, *Geschichte*, 44; English translation cited by Pestilli, 'Disabled Bodies', 96, note 43.

117. See the discussion in Metzler, *Disability*, 189; and Metzler, 'Indiscriminate Healing Miracles'. On harsh asceticism and self-mortification as crucial to shaping the soul's journey towards God, with particular reference to fourteenth-century Dominican convents, see David F. Tinsley, *The Scourge and the Cross: Ascetic Mentalities of the Later Middle Ages* (Leuven: Peeters, 2010).

118. This is why hermaphrodites are regarded as possessing worrying bodies, because they are positioned outside of the established concepts of male–female, and a male body can turn out to have female characteristics and vice versa. See Metzler, 'Hermaphroditism', 27–39.
119. Beate Althammer et al, 'Armenfürsorge und Arbeitswille von der Antike bis zur Gegenwart', in *Armut—Perspektiven in Kunst und Gesellschaft*, exhibion catalogue, ed. H. Uerlings, N. Trauth and L. Clemens (Darmstadt: Primus Verlag, 2011), 290; Katrin Dort and Christian Reuther, 'Armenfürsorge in den karolingischen Kapitularien', in *Zwischen Ausschluss und Solidarität. Modi der Inklusion/Exklusion von Fremden und Armen in Europa seit der Spätantike*, ed. L. Raphael and H. Uerlings (Frankfurt: Peter Lang, 2008), 133–64.
120. Officers were appointed at Aachen, see *Capitulare de disciplina palatii Aquisgranensis (ca. 820)* 7, ed. A. Boretius, MGH Capit. 1 (Hanover, 1883), 298; also Eric Shuler, *Almsgiving and the Formation of Early Medieval Societies, A.D. 700–1025* (PhD diss., University of Notre Dame, 2010), 356.
121. Johnstone, 'Poor-Relief', 150, note 1; *Verbum abbreviatum*, PL, vol. 205, col. 147–52 and 153–56.
122. "Sunt alii omni tempore calamitosi et inimici trivialiter se inflantes, tremulosi, et varias figuras aegrotantium induentes, vultum sicut protea mutantes" (Peter the Chanter, *Verbum abbreviatum*, c.48, PL, vol. 205, col. 152, cited after Farmer, 'The Beggar's Body', 160, note 24).
123. "[Mendici] numquam enim veniunt ad ecclesia causa orandi uel causa missis audiendi, sed causa extorquendi argentum per falsas lacrimas et per dolos et simulationes multas" (Thomas de Chobham, *Summa de arte praedicandi*, c. 3, ed. Franco Morenzoni [Turnhout: Brepols, 1988], 88, cited after Farmer, 'The Beggar's Body', 160, note 25.
124. "Sepe transfigurant se in habitu miserabili, ut videantur magis egeni quam sunt, et ita decipiunt alios ut plus accipiant" (*Thomas de Chobham Summa confessorum*, Art. 5, dist. 4, quaest. 6, ed. F. Broomfield [Louvain: Éditions Nauwelaerts, 1968], 297, cited after Farmer, 'The Beggar's Body', 160–61, note 26). Farmer also mentions Azo, a jurist at Bologna, who wrote a *Summa* on the *Corpus juris civilis* between 1208 and 1210, where he criticised able-bodied beggars "who simulate bodily infirmity by applying herbs or ointments to their bodies in order to make swollen wounds"; they could also make their bodies, arms and legs appear to be crooked and shrivelled (Farmer, *Surviving Poverty*, 66).
125. "Omnino qui eleemosynam dat non indigenti, non solum non meretur, sed et demeretur" (cited in Johnstone, 'Poor-Relief', 150, note 1).
126. Farmer, 'The Beggar's Body', 161, note 27. Farmer (ibid., 162) surmised that an almsgiver giving money to a fraudulent beggar faking a disability was "'buying' prayers, in a sense, from the wrong person"—but theologically it apparently did not matter *who* said prayers for the almsgiver's soul, so even if a fraudulent beggar received alms, as long as they returned the favour by praying for the donor, the spiritual accounts balanced and nobody lost out.
127. Farmer, 'Manual Labor', 277; H.-François Delaborde, ed., 'Fragments de l'enquête faite à Saint-Denis en 1282 en vue de la canonisation de Saint Louis', *Mémoires de la Société de l'Histoire de Paris et de l'Ille de France* 23 (1896): 57, 62 and 66.
128. On the image of fraudulent beggars in literature, see E. von Kraemer, *Le Type du faux mendiant dans les littératures romanes depuis le Moyen Age jusqu'au XVIIe siècle*, Societas Scientiarum Fennica. Commentationes Humanarum Litterarum 13, 6 (Helsingfors, 1944).

129. Shepherd, 'Poverty', 170; Crassons, *Claims of Poverty*, 75. In *Piers Plowman* C-Text, passus IX lines 61–281 are dedicated to beggars. So-called professional beggars are those who defraud the true poor, the needy who are "ymaymed in some member" (line 217), and cheat the giver (Crassons, *Claims of Poverty*, 77; Shepherd, 'Poverty', 171).

130. *Piers Plowman*, B-Text, passus VII, lines 92–93: "Or the bak or som boon thei breketh in his youthe,/ And goon [and[faiten with hire fauntes for everemoore after" ("Then you break their backs or their bones in childhood, and go begging with your offspring for ever after", Langland, *Piers the Ploughman*, 94). This is a theme already found in classical Latin texts. The elder Seneca (*Controversiae* 10.4) mentioned a man who "collects exposed children and cripples them so that they will be more effective at begging" (John Boswell, *The Kindness of Strangers: The Abandonment of Children in Western Europe from Late Antiquity to the Renaissance* [New York: Pantheon Books, 1988], 60), although Boswell has argued that this topos "could have arisen from faulty inference if, in fact, people exposed children born with some physical abnormality and someone else brought them up as beggars" (ibid., 106).

131. The *Journal d'un bourgeois de Paris*, ed. A. Tuetey (Paris, 1881), 389, mentions these horrific events: "Item en ce temps furent prins caymens, larrons et meurtriers, lesqulx par jehaine ou autrement confesserent avoir emblé enfens, à l'un avoit crevé les yeulx, à autres avoir coppé les jambs, aux autres les piez et autres maulx assez et trop." Cited by Geremek, *Margins*, 203 and note 183. Of the gang members, one man had put out the eyes of a child, another man had done the same to a second child and crippled a third child by cutting off his feet. According to various sources mentioned by Geremek (*Margins*, 204 and note 189) this third child had survived and was a ward of court at the time of the trial in May 1449, being two years old. Wheatley, *Stumbling Blocks*, 61, also mentions this case, relying on the literature cited, but fails to acknowledge Geremek's sources which do, contrary to Wheatley's assertion, mention "the fate of the blinded and lame children".

132. There are later associations of beggars and vagabonds with violently criminal elements. In late medieval London, for example, sources lead us to believe that people feared the existence of a quasi counter-society within the city, whose members were mainly active at night, roaming the city aimlessly and identifiable by their penchant for violence, sexual license and disinclination to work—this compares with the more generalised fear of marauding bands of real and/or fake beggars; Frank Rexroth, *Deviance and Power in Late Medieval London* (Cambridge: Cambridge University Press, 2007). More politically motivated associations of the poor with violence can be found in the revolutionary uprisings by peasants in southern Germany, the *Bundschuh* revolts of 1493, 1502, 1513 and 1517, preceding the better-known *Bauernkrieg* of 1524–1525. During the 1517 uprising one participant taken prisoner, Michel von Dinkelsbühl, gave an account of his fellow 'conspirators', who included vagabonds, among them many who could be recognised by their real or 'counterfeit' disabilities; one of three such beggars working for the *Bundschuh*, according to Michel, had "two bad legs" (but whether real or feigned we do not know) and wore pilgrim badges (A. M. Koldeweij, 'Lifting the Veil on Pilgrim Badges', in *Pilgimage Explored*, ed. J. Stopford [York: York Medieval Press, 1999], 182–83); Albert Rosenkranz, *Der Bundschuh, die Erhebungen des südwestdeutschen Bauernstandes in den Jahren 1493–1517*, 2 vols. (Heidelberg: C. Winter, 1927), II:269, note 41.

133. Eustace Deschamps, *Oeuvres complètes*, ed. Queux de Saint-Hilaire (Paris, 1878–1903), IX:81: "S'il est bossu ou s'il est borgne/ Boiteus, contrefait ou

calorgne / Et toy ou nul autre l'encontre / L'en juge que c'est un droit moustre / Et de veoir male l'Escripture / Et si tesmoigna l'Escripture / Que homs de membre contrefais / Est es sa pensée meffais / Plains de pechiez et plain de vices" (cited in Geremek, *Margins*, 210 and note 215).

134. *Miracles de Saint Geneviève*, in A. Jubinal, *Mystères inédits du XVe siècle* (Paris, 1837), I:281–82 (XIIIe miracle). The paralytic says: "Pour l'amour du doulz roy de gloire, / Donnez ou denier ou malette / Au povre enfant de la brouete. / Mielx ne le povez employer / Car, par m'âme, il ne puet ploier / Membre nu qu'il ait, ne estendre" (ibid., vv. 2617–22, cited by Geremek, *Margins*, 197).

135. Geremek, *Margins*, 196.

136. "Faytours, that getyn mete and monye of pyteous folk wyth wyles, as to makyn hem seme crokyd, blynde, syke, or mysellys, and are no3t so" (*Jacob's Well*, ed. Arthur Brandeis, EETS o.s. 115 [London: Kegan Paul, 1900], 134. *Jacob's Well* is a homily series now known under that name; on the text, see G. R. Owst, *Literature and Pulpit in Medieval England: A Neglected Chapter in the History of English Letters and of the English People*, 2nd ed. (Oxford: Blackwell, 1966), 32.

137. *Piers Plowman*, C-Text passus IX lines 98–101; Shepherd, 'Poverty', 172.

138. T. H. Jamieson, *The Ship of Fools Translated by Alexander Barclay*, 2 vols. (1874; rpt. New York: AMS Press, 1966), quoted in Arthur F. Kinney, ed., *Rogues, Vagabonds, and Sturdy Beggars* (Amherst: University of Massachusetts Press, 1990), 12; also Robertson, *Laborer's Two Bodies*, 184–85.

139. "Die Instrumentalisierung des Gebrechens macht die Bettlerwelt logisch zu einer verkehrten Welt: je schlimmer verstümmelt, desto reicher, je untauglicher, desto tauglicher" (Hölter, *Die Invaliden*, 82).

140. Shepherd, 'Poverty', 173. But the character of Piers the ploughman, trying to discern between rightful and fraudulent alms-seekers, learns in the course of the Hunger episode in B-Text passus VI "that he is not in a position to determine who is deserving or not . . . all beggars . . . are answerable to God individually. The onus is on the receiver" (Scott, *Piers Plowman*, 109). On the terminology used of fraudulent beggars, see Kellie Robertson, *Keeping Paradise: Labor and Language in Late Medieval Britain* (Basingstoke: Palgrave Macmillan, 2004). On beggars, vagabonds and other non-settled marginal types in general in England, see D. B. Thomas, ed., *The Book of Vagabonds and Beggars* (London: The Penguin Press, 1932); J. J. Jusserand, *English Wayfaring Life in the Middle Ages*, trans. Lucy Toulmin Smith (London: T. Fisher Unwin, 1888); and G. T. Salisbury, *Street Life in Medieval England* (n. p., 1939). More general is Jose Cubero, *Histoire du vagabondage du Moyen Age à nos jours* (Paris: Imago, 1998).

141. Langland, *Piers the Ploughman*, 84; "Tho were faitours afered, and feyned hem blynde; / Somme leide hir legges aliry, as swiche losels conneth, / And made hir [pleynt] to Piers and preide hym of grace: / 'For we have no lymes to laboure with, lord, ygraced be ye!'" (B-Text passus VI lines 121–4; C-Text passus VIII lines 128–30); Crassons, *Claims of Poverty*, 34, where Langland is interpreted as, in this section of his poem, endorsing the contemporary labour legislation.

142. Langland, *Piers the Ploughman*, 85; "But if he be blynd or brokelegged or bolted with irens, / He shal ete whete breed and [with myselve drynke]" (B-Text passus VI lines 136–37); in C-Text, passus VIII, line 129, Langland refers to frauds, as in beggars laying their legs *alery* to simulate disability (Pearsall, 'Piers Plowman', 125).

143. Langland, *Piers the Ploughman*, 86; "Blynde and bedreden were bootned a thousand, / That seten to begge silver, soone were thei heeled" (B-Text passus

VI lines 191–92). The C-Text, passus VIII lines 188–89, has Hunger driving everyone back to work including the disabled: "Blynde and broke-legged he botened a thousand / And lame men he lechede with longes of bestes" (cited in Pearsall, 'Piers Plowman', 125, discussed by Crassons, *Claims of Poverty*, 36).

144. Cited after Meier, *Gaukler*, 27.

145. Irsigler and Lassotta, *Bettler*, 53; text known as the *Notatenbuch* (Hölter, *Die Invaliden*, 84).

146. Irsigler and Lassotta, *Bettler*, 53, extant in a later Basle copy entitled "Dis ist die betrugnisse, damitte die giler und die blinden umbegand, und besunder von allen narungen, wie sy die nemment, damitt sie sich begant"; Hölter, *Die Invaliden*, 84.

147. Hölter, *Die Invaliden*, 84.

148. The types in the *Liber vagatorum* include beggars, charlatans and fake pilgrims. People described as *Bregren* were regarded as genuine beggars, who were begging out of necessity and modestly asking for alms. The next type, the *Stabüler*, were seen as not totally criminal but not exactly genuine either, since they were able-bodied but unwilling to work; these people moved around with their families as kind of professional pilgrims, wearing lots of pilgrim insignia (Koldeweij, 'Lifting the Veil', 181). There is also a text of 1484–1486, the *Speculum cerretanorum* by the Italian Teseo Pini, which lists about forty different 'occupational' groups of beggars (Jütte, *Poverty*, 181). On the *Liber vagatorum*, see R. Jütte, *Abbild und soziale Wirklichkeit des Bettler- und Gaunertums zu Beginn der Neuzeit. Sozial-, mentalitäts- und sprachgeschichtliche Studien zum 'Liber vagatorum' (1510)* (Cologne: Böhlau, 1988).

149. Regarding 'fake' pilgrims, who are mentioned frequently in the text, the *Liber vagatorum* has most concern about the practice of wearing pilgrim signs and badges, which fake pilgrims even trade amongst themselves to give the impression they have travelled widely and visited many holy places: "Christianern und Calmieren. Das sind Bettler, die Zeichen an den Hüten tragen, besonders römisch Veronika und Muscheln und andere Zeichen. Und gibt jeweils einer dem andern Zeichen zu kaufen, dass man glauben soll, sie seien an den Stätten und Enden gewesen, wovon sie die Zeichen tragen, obwohl sie doch niemals dorthin kommen. Und sie betrügen die Leute damit, die heissen Calmierer" (*Das Buch der Vaganten: Spieler, Huren, Leutbetrüger*, ed. and trans. H. Boehnke and R. Johannsmeier [Cologne, 1987], cited by Koldeweij, 'Lifting the Veil', 181, note 31). Pilgrims had privileged status, in that they were exempt from paying tolls, and they got free board and lodging in hospitals and monasteries. In the later Middle Ages pilgrims were identifiable by badges (made of shell or lead-tin alloy from the twelfth to the mid-fifteenth century). Koldeweij argues that one of the characters on the sketch by Hieronymus Bosch (variously also attributed to the elder Breughel), depicting a panoply of beggars, cripples and vagabonds, is wearing a pilgrim badge, which can be identified as originating from the town of Wilsnack in northern Germany. The emblem of three interlinked circles represented the Three Miraculous Hosts of Wilsnack. The fraudulent pilgrim in Bosch's sketch is misusing this easily drawn and therefore easily faked pilgrim-sign to gain sympathy and respectability. Wilsnack itself was regarded as a somewhat less than respectable pilgrimage site, and the wearing of a badge representing the Host was considered by some as a serious infringement of religious sensibilities, since it represented the body of Christ himself (Koldeweij, 'Lifting the Veil', 168).

150. Pestilli, 'Blindness', 110–11.

151. Jütte, too, observed this trend. He added that for the sixteenth century the pauper "was no longer characterized by physical deformities but was designated by begging gesture and a pathetic condition. This change reflects a new attitude to the poor. It was no longer a physical handicap that denoted a beggar, but something less concrete, less tangible: a gesture, a way of behaving, in short the physical and moral condition" (*Poverty*, 14).

152. Geremek, *Geschichte*, 64: "Für das Aussehen des Bettlers hat der Körper fundamentale Bedeutung. Zu den Techniken des professionellen Bettelns gehört vor allem, daß man seine Gebrechen, Krankheiten und körperlichen Mängel geschickt zur Schau stellt. [. . .] Die Berechtigung zum Betteln beruhte vor allem auf körperlicher Gebrechlichkeit, und sie in geeigneter Form zu betonen war ein Mittel, das Betteln zu legitimieren und Mitleid zu erwecken." As the status of beggars changed during the course of the Middle Ages, so a similar change in attitudes towards another group of people can be observed, in this case in the depiction of the Annunciation to the Shepherds in Danish wall paintings—shepherds are not exactly a marginal group, but apparently one that was subjected to a development from positive to negative connotations. While the twelfth-century wall paintings in Danish churches portray the shepherds in such scenes as well-dressed, well-behaved and socially integrated people, by the fifteenth century they are shown as badly dressed, rude and physically ugly, with some shepherds even portrayed in the same mocking gesture (baring their buttocks) as mockers of Christ have traditionally been shown (Axel Bolvig, 'Contrasts in Time and Space: The Use of the Image-Database "Danish Wall Paintings"', in *Kontraste im Alltag des Mittelalters*, Forschungen des Instituts für Realienkunde des Mittelalters und der frühen Neuzeit. Diskussionen und Materialien 5, ed. Gerhard Jaritz [Vienna: Österreichische Akademie der Wissenschaften, 2000], 236–37).

153. The miracles of Saint Louis are recorded in two texts, one being fragmentary remains of the examination of witnesses to the miracles during the canonisation proceedings (H.-François Delaborde, ed., 'Fragments de l'enquête faite à Saint-Denis en 1282 en vue de la canonisation de Saint Louis', *Mémoires de la Société de l'Histoire de Paris et de l'Ille de France* 23 [1896]: 1–71), the other being a *vita* (*Les miracles de Saint Louis*) written around 1303 by Guillaume de St.-Pathus who had been confessor to king Louis IX's wife.

154. Farmer, *Surviving Poverty*, 72.

155. Michael Goodich, *Miracles and Wonders: The Development of the Concept of Miracle, 1150–1350*, Church, Faith and Culture in the Medieval West (Ashgate: Aldershot, 2007), 81; on the deposition of Cardinal Colonna, cf. L. Carolus-Barré, 'Consultation du cardinal Pietro Colonna sur le IIe miracle de Saint Louis', *Bibliothèque de l'Ecole des chartes* 117 (1959): 57–72. Amelot de Chaumont was an unmarried servant who had become paralysed in her right thigh, leg and foot, and had been taken to Saint Louis's shrine at Saint Denis in 1277 on a stretcher, accompanied by two other women; she was given crutches on her first visit, and it took several more visits before a cure occurred. Her miracle is the second reported in the collection by Guillaume de St.-Pathus.

156. For the connection between the profit economy, the loss of status of poverty and a different view of begging, see Pestilli, 'Disabled Bodies', 96, note 45, and especially the work of Little, *Religious Poverty*.

157. The source for this story is tale no. 85 (78) of *Il Novellino*, written c. 1281–1300, cited in Le Goff, *Medieval Civilization*, 238; *Il Novellino: The Hundred Old Tales*, trans. Edward Storer (London: George Routledge and Sons, 1925), 192–93. It seems that the famine was a useful pretext for the civic leadership to rid themselves of all the unwelcome riff-raff in one fell swoop. If the Genoese

had enough cash to hire ships and rowers, surely they would have had equally enough cash to import foodstuffs, so the motivation for this mass transportation must have been for socio-political rather than economic reasons.

158. Pullan, 'Difettosi', VI:5.
159. John Henderson, *Piety and Charity in Late Medieval Florence* (Chicago: University of Chicago Press, 1994), 244; R. Davidsohn, *Storia di Firenze*, trans. G. B. Klein, 8 vols. (Florence: Sansoni, 1972–1973), III:682–83; V:325–26; VII:503–4; and F. Carabellese, 'Le condizioni dei poveri a Firenze nel secolo xiv', *Rivista Storica Italiana* 12 (1895): 416.
160. Henderson, *Piety*, 244. R. Mueller, 'Charitable Institutions, the Jewish Community, and Venetian Society: A Discussion of the Recent Volume by Brian Pullan', *Studi Veneziani* 14 (1972): 52–53.
161. L. B. Alberti, *L'Architettura (De Re Aedificatoria)*, ed. G. Orlandi and P. Portoghesi (Milan, 1966), I:367, cited by Henderson, *Piety*, 400.
162. Ibid., I:366–68, cited by Henderson, *Piety*, 405. Alberti also lambasted the 'advantages' gained by beggars, who are described as lazy parasites grazing on the sweat of other's labour, living a life of idle leisure, in his *Momus* (1443–1450); Pestilli, 'Blindness', 109.
163. Brodman, *Charity*, 41.
164. Geremek, *Margins*, 172. On the origin of the Quinze-Vingts, especially a debunking of the myth that the hospital was founded for 300 'war-veteran' crusaders, see Wheatley, *Stumbling Blocks*, 49–55; note Wheatley's suggestion that by recasting "disability as a personal tragedy for each crusader" (54), the myth displaced the possibility of treating blind inmates simply as 'impaired'.
165. Mark P. O'Tool, 'The *povres avugles* of the Hôpital des Quinze-Vingts: Disability and Community in Medieval Paris', in *Difference and Identity in Francia and Medieval France*, ed. M. Cohen and J. Firnhaber-Baker (Farnham: Ashgate, 2010), 159.
166. "Li rois a mis en I repaire / Mais ne sais pas por quoi faire, / Trois cens aveugles route à route / Parmi Paris en vat trois paires, / Toute ior ne fine de braire; / Au trois cens qui ne voyent goute, / Li uns sache, li autre boute" (Rutebeuf, *Oeuvres complètes*, ed. A. Jubinal [Paris, 1839], 163, cited in Geremek, *Margins*, 173).
167. O'Tool, 'The *povres avugles*', 173.
168. Geremek, *Margins*, 173.
169. Marcia Kupfer, *The Art of Healing: Painting for the Sick and the Sinner in a Medieval Town* (Pennsylvania: Pennsylvania State University Press, 2003), 39.
170. Brodman, *Charity*, 247.
171. Demaitre, 'The Care and Extension', 13, note 49; Henry H. Beek, *Waanzin in de Middeleeuwen: Beeld van de gestoorde en bemoeienis met de zieke* (Nijkerk: Callenbach, 1969), 147. The White Hall at Ilchester appears also to have been more of a 'short-stay' institution for transients, since the founder was concerned with supporting "poor, weak, and sick pilgrims" (Rosenthal, *Old Age*, 186).
172. Cited by Davis, 'Preaching', 85; *Catalogue général des manuscrits des bibliothèques publiques des départements*, ed. Félix Ravaisson et al., 7 vols. (Paris, 1849), I (Laon), 637.
173. Farmer, 'Young, Male and Disabled', 446; Guillaume de Saint-Pathus, *Les miracles de Saint Louis*, miracles 42, 17.
174. Geremek, *Margins*, 178, note 58. Clay, *Medieval Hospitals*, 17, notes that Bubwith's almshouse, Wells, "was to receive men . . . so decrepit that they were unable to beg from door to door."

175. On the changing attitudes in Germany to begging and poverty in the later Middle Ages as evidenced by regulations of begging, see O. Oexle, 'Armut, Armutsbegriff und Armenfürsorge im Mittelalter', in *Soziale Sicherheit und soziale Disziplinierung*, ed. Christoph Sachße and Florian Tennstedt (Frankfurt: Suhrkamp, 1986), 85–86. For a general history of the marginalised, poverty and criminality in Germany, see C. Sachße and F. Tennstedt, eds., *Bettler, Gauner und Proleten. Armut und Armenfürsorge in der deutschen Geschichte* (Reinbek bei Hamburg: Fachhochschulverlag, 1983).

176. A further or revised regulation seems to have been made in 1387. On begging laws and other public order proclamations in Nuremberg, see J. Baader, ed., *Nürnberger Polizeiordnungen aus dem 13.-15. Jahrhundert*, Bibliothek des literarischen Vereins in Stuttgart 63 (Stuttgart, 1861; rpt. Amsterdam, 1966).

177. Meier, *Gaukler*, 37. Tokens were widely used from the thirteenth century onwards as a method for administering charitable handouts; William J. Courtenay, 'Token Coinage and the Administration of Poor Relief during the Late Middle Ages', *Journal of Interdisciplinary History* 3 (1972): 275–95.

178. Evamaria Engel, *Die deutsche Stadt im Mittelalter* (Düsseldorf: Patmos Verlag, 2005), 241–42; C. Sachße and F. Tennstedt, *Geschichte der Armenfürsorge in Deutschland vom Spätmittelalter bis zum 1. Weltkrieg* (Stuttgart: Kohlhammer, 1980), 63–64.

179. Irsigler and Lassotta, *Bettler*, 25, citing Bettelordnung: "daz im daz almůsen notůrftig sey . . . die wol gewandern oder gearbeyten moechten, ůnd die des almůsens nicht notůrftig werden, den sol man niht erlaůben zů petteln, noch kein zeichen geben." In Regensburg, too, there were similar laws. The fifteenth century saw the introduction of a licensing system by issuing tokens that permitted the holder to engage in legitimate begging; pilgrims and foreigners or strangers were limited to begging permits of three days, later reduced to two days, duration (Dirmeier, 'Armenfürsorge', 230–31). At Strasbourg, distinctions were also made between local and extraneous beggars, whereby unlicensed or foreign beggars who were caught could be fined, removed from the city or imprisoned; signs and emblems, like at Nuremberg, were fixed to the clothing to identify the licensed beggars (Engel, *Die deutsche Stadt*, 241–42).

180. Dirmeier, 'Armenfürsorge', 231.

181. Geremek, *Geschichte*, 52.

182. Farmer, 'The Beggar's Body', 161. Farmer furthermore argues that poor people were also 'de-briefed' more thoroughly than wealthy people if they claimed to have been cured in a miracle, basing her findings on the *Miracles of Saint Louis*, an early fourteenth-century French text. "The elites were more likely to subject the poor, rather than other elites, to bodily tests in order to establish their actual state, or status" (ibid., 165). At the canonisation proceedings of Saint Louis the differing treatment by the clerical assessors of poor and noble/wealthy protagonists of the miracles does in fact have much in common with the differing treatment by and actions of *potentes* and *pauperes* outlined earlier.

183. O'Tool, 'The *povres avugles*', 168.

184. Meier, *Gaukler*, 37–38.

185. Rubin, *Charity*, 32.

186. Farmer, *Surviving Poverty*, 34. Apparently blind, deaf and "feeble" beggars in Paris did not habitually have regular 'pitches' from where they would beg (ibid.).

187. Geremek, *Margins*, 189.

188. The itinerant folk were described as: "Spielleute, Lotterpfaffen, Sprecher, Singer" (Dirmeier, 'Armenfürsorge', 230–31).

189. Irsigler and Lassotta, *Bettler*, 45.

190. Dirmeier, 'Armenfürsorge', 231.

191. Irsigler and Lassotta, *Bettler*, 47–48. The hospital accounts mention a donation to "den blynden vur dem doem". Foundlings and orphans were apparently also given privileged treatment, since they were allowed to beg inside the cathedral. The blind may have been the only group of beggars in Cologne who were organised under a 'king' similar to the French 'king of beggars', but it is not clear whether this was already the case in the fifteenth century, since Irsigler and Lassotta cite evidence from the late sixteenth.

192. "Diese Vertreibung der Bettler entzog sie dem kirchlichen Schutz und gab sie auf Gedeih und Verderb der Straße preis" (Meier, *Gaukler*, 39).

193. "Der starke Bettler war zugleich ein starkes Argument gegen das Almosengeben und damit gegen den im Alltag sichtbarsten Teil der Werkgerechtigkeit" (Ernst Schubert, *Fahrendes Volk im Mittelalter* [Bielefeld: Verlag für Regionalgeschichte, 1995], 365). On the topos of the sturdy beggar, particularly of crippled beggars feigning disability, see Ernst Schubert, 'Der "starke Bettler": das erste Opfer sozialer Typisierung um 1500', *Zeitschrift für Geschichtswissenschaft* 48 (2000): 869–93; and Ernst Schubert, 'Der betrügerische Bettler im Mittelalter und in der frühen Neuzeit', in *Festschrift für Dieter Neitzert*, ed. Peter Aufgebauer, Uwe Ohainski and Ernst Schubert (Bielefeld: Verlag für Regionalgeschichte, 1998), 71–107, crippled beggars at 90–91.

194. Laughton, *Life in a Late Medieval City*, 108.

195. Ibid.

196. Ibid., sources for all the preceding examples being Cheshire and Chester Archives and Local Studies: ZMB 1, f.16; ZMB 2, f. 19v; ZMB 4, f. 34; ZSB 1, f. 122; ZSB 4, f. 99v; ZSB 5, ff. 61, 63.

197. Ibid., 125; Cheshire and Chester Archives and Local Studies ZSB 5, f. 61.

198. Pullan, 'Difettosi', VI:9, 19 and note 32.

199. Brodman, *Charity*, 189, note 18.

200. See the studies by Rubin and Henderson, on charity and community in Cambridge and Florence, respectively, where guilds and religious fraternities are the principal focal points.

201. Geremek, *Geschichte*, 66; also Mollat, *Die Armen*, 163.

202. Brodman, *Charity*, 28. On the situation of the poor generally in late medieval Barcelona see Uta Lindgren, *Bedürftigkeit, Armut, Not. Studien zur spätmittelalterlichen Sozialgeschichte Barcelonas*, Spanische Forschungen der Görres-Gesellschaft 2, 18 (Münster: Aschendorff, 1980).

203. See later in this chapter on the theme of the blind person being duped, tricked and even abused by their sighted guide.

204. Quoted in Wheatley, *Stumbling Blocks*, 148, following Guillaume de Saint-Pathus, *Les Miracles de Saint Louis*, 180–81.

205. Epistle XVI, 7, *Letters of Old Age*, II:631, letter addressed to Donino, a grammarian of Piacenza, dated 12 May 1373.

206. Schleusener-Eichholz, *Das Auge*, I:508; cited by Barasch, *Blindness*, 100.

207. Barasch, *Blindness*, 100, following Schleusener-Eichholz, *Das Auge*, I:508; Dietrich Schmidtke, *Geistliche Tierinterpretationen in der deutschsprachigen Literatur des Mittelalters (1100–1500)* (Berlin: Freie Universität Berlin, 1968), 318.

208. Barasch, *Blindness*, 100, referring to Baltimore, Walters Art Museum, MS 82, fol. 207. The fifteenth-century wing of an altar from the workshop of Johann Koerbecke, *Legend of St. Leonard*, depicts a kneeling blind man

who holds a small dog by the leash, while a second blind man, possibly representing blind Lucillus from the *Legenda aurea*, is guided to this scene (cf. exhibition catalogue *Westfälische Maler der Spätgotik 1440–1490* [Landesmuseum Münster, 1952], no. 102 and plate 26); and in the *Bible of Jaromér* (cf. Bohatec, *Schöne Bücher*, Prague, National Museum, XII A 10, fig. 112) one finds the depiction of a blind man with his staff but also holding a dog on a long leash '"der sicher als Blindenhund gedient hat" (Georg Wacha, 'Tiere und Tierhaltung in der Stadt sowie im Wohnbereich des spätmittelalterlichen Menschen und ihre Darstellung in der bildenden Kunst', in *Das Leben in der Stadt des Spätmittelalters*, Veröffentlichungen des Instituts für mittelalterliche Realienkunde Österreichs Nr. 2 [Vienna: Österreichische Akademie der Wissenschaften, 1977], 243).

209. *Tales from Sacchetti*, trans. Mary G. Steegman (London: Dent, 1908; rpt. Westport, CT: Hyperion Press, 1978), 122, novel 38 (novel 140 in the original). The Italian, according to a critical edition, reads: "E movendosi ciascuno con un suo cane a mano, ammaestrato, come fanno, con la scodella" (Franco Sacchetti, *Il Libro delle Trecentonovelle*, ed. Antonio Lanza [Florence: Sansoni, 1984], 282).

210. *Tales from Sacchetti*, 122, novel 38 (novel 140 in the original). Italian: "Entrati questi ciechi con li cani e co' guinzagli a mano" (Sacchetti, *Trecentonovelle*, 282).

211. *Tales from Sacchetti*, 125, novel 38 (novel 140 in the original).

212. Barasch, *Blindness*, 121.

213. "Es soll in Zukunft kein Bettler einen Hund haben oder aufziehen, es sei denn, er wäre blind und brauchte ihn. Und wie oft jemand dagegen verstößt, der zahlt jedes Mal 1 Schilling Pfennige" (*Straßburger Bettelordnung*, in *Das Fürsorgewesen der Stadt Strassburg vor und nach der Reformation*, ed. Otto Winckelmann, 2 parts in 1 volume [Leipzig, 1922], at pt 2, Nr. 38, 84–85, cited in Engel and Jacob, *Städtisches Leben im Mittelalter*, 378).

214. Pullan, 'Support and Redeem', 185; Pullan, 'Difettosi', VI:9.

215. Pullan, 'Difettosi', VI:9.

216. Ibid.

217. Cited in ibid., 10.

218. Ibid.

219. From the statutes known as *Mariegola Zotti*, cited by Pullan, 'Difettosi', VI:10.

220. Ibid., 12.

221. Engel, *Die deutsche Stadt*, 241–42. The charitable organisations that Rubin and Henderson have analysed so thoroughly are essentially of this superimposed type: charity organised by non-marginal groups to be given out to people deemed worthy by the group.

222. For example, the governance of charity doled out by the fraternities in fourteenth- and fifteenth-century Italy was according to rules enacted by various statutes and constitutions, whereby officers of the fraternities were tasked with establishing need and scrutinising claims for assistance; Pullan, 'Support and Redeem', 180.

223. Quoted by Barron, 'Parish Fraternities', 27. Not only is the Kropotkinesque emphasis on mutual aid (a reference of course to the anarchist classic: Peter Kropotkin, *Mutual Aid: A Factor of Evolution* [London:Heinemann, 1902]) unusual in this parish organisation, but they also called themselves a *confraternity*, a term more often associated with sworn groups.

224. Meier, *Gaukler*, 31.

225. Irsigler and Lassotta, *Bettler*, 58, citing blind, lame and "ander bresthaftige lüt".

226. "Arme mynschen, die der Almosen levent, Krüppel, blynde und andere leut" (cited in Meier, *Gaukler*, 31).
227. Irsigler and Lassotta, *Bettler*, 58.
228. Cited in ibid., 60, source in the archives of the city of Cologne, Haupturkundenarchiv 12 547 a.
229. Ibid. The guild was not restricted to physically impaired members, as a document of 1471 demonstrates, in which Johan Ailbrecht and his wife, Ekell Zymmermans, incorporate themselves in the guild and leave their entire assets to it, also continuing to provide services to the fraternity in the form of keeping the accounts; in return the confraternity is obliged to sustain the couple until their deaths (Irsigler and Lassotta, *Bettler*, 62).
230. On the notion of disability as liminal, as in-between health and sickness but neither one nor the other, see the discussion here in the Introduction, and Metzler, *Disability*, 31–32, 155–57.
231. Fandrey, *Krüppel*, 32; Richard Laufner, 'Die "Elenden-Bruderschaft" zu Trier im 15. und 16. Jahrhundert', *Jahrbuch für westdeutsche Landesgeschichte* 4 (1978): 221–22. The fraternity had several thousand members in a wide area encompassing the cities of Essen, Paris, Lucerne and Regensburg (Ratisbon). By the end of the sixteenth century, following the changes in mentality that make the central theme of this chapter, this important fraternity was dissolved and subsumed into municipal poor relief (Fandrey, *Krüppel*, 48).
232. Geremek, *Geschichte*, 27: "Die Notwendigkeit, unter den Armen zu unterscheiden und die Arbeitsfähigen vom Anspruch auf Almosen auszuschließen, wurde sowohl von den Kirchenvätern wie von vielen mittelalterlichen Theologen und Kanonisten betont." The seminal work on this subject is Brian Tierney, 'The Decretists and the "Deserving Poor"', *Comparative Studies in Society and History* 1 (1958–9): 360–73; reprinted in Brian Tierney, *Church Law and Constitutional Thought in the Middle Ages*, Collected Studies Series 90 (London: Variorum, 1979), 360–73.
233. McCall, *Medieval Underworld*, 146. John Chrysostom had opined "that even laziness and feigned disability" should not become a discriminating factor (Brodman, *Charity*, 15); cf. *St. John Chrysostom on Repentance and Almsgiving*, 10.24, trans. G. G. Christo (Washington, DC: Catholic University of America Press, 1998), 147.
234. Mollat, *Die Armen*, 22.
235. Cokayne, *Experiencing Old Age*, 170. Furthermore, in antique Rome "the only 'legal' sort of beggar came to be one who was old and/or physically handicapped", according to Parkin, *Old Age*, 225. The *Codex Theodosianus* 14.18.1 stated: "Quos in publicum quaestum incepta mendicitas vocabit, inspectis exploretur in singulis et integritas corporum et robur annorum, adque ea inertibus et absque ulla debilitate miserandis necessitas inferatur, ut eorum quidem, quos tenet condicio servilis, proditor studiosus et diligens dominium consequatur, eorum vero, quos natalium sola libertas prosequatur, colonatu perpetuo fulciatur quisquis huiusmodi lenitudinem prodiderit ac probaverit, salva dominis actione in eos, qui vel latebram forte fugitivis vel mendicitatis subeundae consilium praestiterunt." This is repeated verbatim by the *Codex Justinianus* (see the following). More generally, see A. R. Hands, *Charities and Social Aid in Greece and Rome. Aspects of Greek and Roman Life* (London: Thames and Hudson, 1968).
236. Ambrose of Milan, *De officiis*, I. xxx. 158, in *Les Devoirs*, Latin ed. and French trans. Maurice Testard, Collection des Universités de France, 2 vols. (Paris, 1984, 1992), I:172, cited by A. Firey, '"For I Was Hungry and You Fed Me": Social Justice and Economic Thought in the Latin Patristic and

Medieval Christian Traditions', in *Ancient and Medieval Economic Ideas and Concepts of Social Justice*, ed. S. T. Lowry and B. Gordon (Leiden: Brill, 1998), 339.

237. Geremek, *Geschichte*, 25; *Codex Justinianus* 11.26.1, at 243, which repeats the Theodosian edict of 382. In the mid-thirteenth century the *glossa ordinaria* for Justinian's code (compiled at Bologna) mention people "who make themselves seem sick, applying herbs or something that causes them to swell" presumably so as to avoid having to work; Farmer, 'The Beggar's Body', 161, note 27.

238. Author's translation from citation in Windemuth, *Das Hospital*, 36; Alfred Müller, *Geschichte der Medizin im Prümer Land und das St. Joseph-Krankenhaus* (Prüm: Geschichtsverein Prümer Land, 1984), 15.

239. *Vita* written 1212 by Master Rufino, trans. in Diana Webb, *Saints and Cities in Medieval Italy* (Manchester: Manchester University Press, 2007), 78. However, after Raimundo at first sends the 'aggressive' beggars packing, telling them to beg "openly" as they usually do, not being sick and knowing no shame, he relents and disperses some of the alms, since the beggars had argued, "Yes, we beg; but we don't get anything" (ibid., 79).

240. Arnold Angenendt, *Religiosität im Mittelalter* (Darmstadt: Primus, 1997), 595.

241. 2 Thess. 3:10.

242. Rufinus, *Summa ad dist.* 42 ante C.I, quoted in Tierney, *Medieval Poor Law*, 59; *Die Summa Decretorum des Magister Rufinus*, ed. H. Singer (Paderborn, 1902), 100–101.

243. Quote in Jütte, *Poverty*, 159, citing Tierney, 'The Decretist', 363–64. The 'unlawful professions' are derived from Augustine, *Decretum magistri Gratiani*, in *Corpus Iuris Canonici I*, ed. E. Friedberg (Leipzig, 1877), at D.86 cc.7–9, 14–18; cf. Rubin, *Charity*, 69.

244. Cited in Rubin, *Charity*, 69. "Set hic intelligitur in eo casu cum quis potest laborare et suo labore sibi victum querere et non vult, set tota die ludit, in alea vel taxilis" (*Glossa ordinaria ad* C.5.q.5.C.2).

245. Cited in Rubin, *Charity*, 69. Tierney, *Medieval Poor Law*, 58 and 150: "Ei qui potest laborare, non debet ecclesia providere. Integritas [membrorum] enim et robur membrorum in conferenda eleemosyna est attenda" (*Glossa ordinaria ad* Dist.82 ante C.1).

246. Cited in Rubin, *Charity*, 70. "In elemosina autem delectus personarum habendus ut potius suis quam alienis, infirmis quam sanis, mendicare erubescenti quam effronti, egenti quam habenti, et inter egentes iusto prius quam iniusto des. Hec est caritas ordinata" (*Summa 'elegantius in iure divino' seu Coloniensis*, ed. G. Fransen, Monumenta iuris canonici ser. A: corpus glossatorum 1 [Vatican, 1969], C.54, 67).

247. "Nisi transeuntibus peregrinis senibus peris et aliis debilibus, qui illo tempore nequeunt laborare" (*The Account-Book of Beaulieu Abbey*, ed. S. F. Hockey, Camden Society 4th series 16 [Cambridge: Royal Historical Society, 1975], 174, also 172–82, 269–81); discrimination went so far that the poor sick people in the abbey's infirmary were to be fed the meat of animals that had died of disease (for comparison, in 1506 the household records of the bishop of Lincoln contain a note that charity given to the poor consisted of fish that had become "corrupt and defective" (Dyer, *Standards of Living*, 241). Dyer (ibid., 237) comments that this attitude of "attention to economy, the discrimination and the distrust of the poor would not have been out of place among the zealous administrators of the new Poor Law in the nineteenth century." The guild of butchers of Toulouse exercised similar charitable discrimination, in that the 1394 redaction of their statutes specified certain

kinds of dubious meat (including "flesh from pigs with leprous tongues and dead animals not properly slaughtered by butchers") to be confiscated by guild officials and if deemed still edible to be given to the poor, otherwise to be disposed of in the river; hence "at least one guild passed off its refuse as a charitable donation" (Epstein, *Wage Labor*, 168). Also Saint John's hospital, Oxford, which accommodated poor and sick people, in 1356 was assigned "all flesh or fish that shall be putrid, unclean, vicious or otherwise unfit", while Saint Giles's hospital, Maldon, received all confiscated "bread, ale, flesh and unsound fish" deemed commercially non-viable (Rawcliffe, *Leprosy*, 79; G. G. Coulson, *Medieval Panorama* [Cambridge: Cambridge University Press, 1939], 455–56).

248. Brodman, *Charity*, 33.
249. Barbara Tuchman, *A Distant Mirror: The Calamitous 14th Century* (Harmondsworth: Penguin, 1979).
250. McCall, *Medieval Underworld*, 147, citing Guillaume de Loris and Jean de Meun, *Romance of the Rose*, 199.
251. McCall, *Medieval Underworld*, 147, citing *Romance of the Rose*, 200–201. On William of Saint Amour, see Rubin, *Charity*, 73.
252. Rubin, *Charity*, 92.
253. Langland, *Piers the Ploughman*, 93; B-Text passus VII lines 74–78. Langland's reference to Gregory the Great is actually from Jerome's *Commentary* on Eccl. 11:6.
254. Langland, *Piers the Ploughman*, 94; B-Text passus VII line 82.
255. Langland, *Piers the Ploughman*, 260; C-Text, passus X lines 71–97.
256. Irsigler and Lassotta, *Bettler*, 53: false beggars go bent and lame along the road *(Sy gand krum und lam uf stras)*, and some can make themselves blind *(So kan sich menger machen blind)*.
257. Ibid., 56: "Die genannnten Quellen dokumentieren so bei kritischer Betrachtung vor allem den Entstehungsprozeß von Vorurteilen gegenüber dem genannten Personenkreis, wie sie letztlich bis in die Gegenwart fortleben."
258. Rubin, *Charity*, 268.
259. Ibid., 254; Westlake, *Parish Gilds*, 145.
260. F. F. Cartwright, *A Social History of Medicine* (London: Longman, 1977), 30.
261. Rawcliffe, *Hospitals*, 11.
262. The Middle Latin term *hospitale* is the origin of the later words; Pierre Riché, *Die Welt der Karolinger*, 3rd ed., trans. C. and U. Dirlmeier (Stuttgart: Philipp Reclam, 2009), 319.
263. Borscheid, *Geschichte*, 83.
264. Ibid., 84.
265. Cited by Jean Verdon, *Travel in the Middle Ages*, trans. G. Holoch (Notre Dame, IN: University of Notre Dame Press, 2003), 108, which regrettably omits to mention the source or the date of this complaint.
266. O'Tool, 'The *povres avugles*', 165.
267. Joinville and Villehardouin, *Chronicles of the Crusades*, 337.
268. Ibid., 342.
269. On poverty and the increased value placed on work:, see K. Bosl, 'Armut, Arbeit, Emanzipation', in *Beiträge zur Wirtschafts- und Sozialgeschichte des Mittelalters. Festschrift für Herbert Helbig* (Cologne: Böhlau, 1976), 128–29.
270. "In dem Maße, wie der Wert der Arbeit stieg, sank das Ansehen der Bettler" (Meier, *Gaukler*, 39).
271. The concept of a work ethic is most often associated with Protestantism, deriving from Weber's coining of the phrase 'Protestant work ethic' (Max

Weber, *The Protestant Ethic and the Spirit of Capitalism*, trans. T. Parsons [New York: Charles Scribner's Sons, 1950]). Dyer, 'Work Ethics', 21, argued that during the fourteenth century "the work ethic will influence ideas about social security and the entitlement of the poor, giving rise to the belief that charity can undermine or reinforce the motive to earn".

272. J. D. Dawson, 'Richard FitzRalph and the Fourteenth-Century Poverty Controversies', *Journal of Ecclesiastical History* 34 (1983): 315–44; Katherine Walsh, *Richard FitzRalph in Oxford, Avignon, and Armagh* (Oxford: Clarendon Press, 1981). For Wycliff and his influence on anti-begging notions, see the sermon he preached on the theme of the beggar Lazarus (Luke 16:19–31), English text given in Siegfried Wenzel, trans., *Preaching in the Age of Chaucer: Selected Sermons in Translation* (Washington, DC: Catholic University of America Press, 2008), 154–61.

273. "When thou makest a dinner or a supper, call not thy friends, nor thy brethren, neither thy kinsmen, nor thy rich neighbours . . . But when thou makest a feast, call the poor, the maimed, the lame, the blind: and thou shalt be blessed".

274. 'Defensio Curatorum', *Trevisa's Dialogus*, ed. John Perry, EETS o.s. 167 (Cambridge: Cambridge University Press, 1925), 88, cited by Crassons, 'The Workman', 82.

275. Crassons, 'The Workman', 82.

276. Ibid., 68; also Crassons, *Claims of Poverty*, 147.

277. Crassons, 'The Workman', 82.

278. 'The Sermon of William Taylor', *Two Wycliffite Texts*, ed. Anne Hudson, EETS o.s. 301 (Oxford: Oxford University Press, 1993), 15, lines 455–59; Crassons, 'The Workman', 82.

279. Crassons, 'The Workman', 83. The writings of both FitzRalph and Taylor are discussed in greater detail by Crassons, *Claims of Poverty*, 139–76.

280. Farmer, *Surviving Poverty*, 27.

281. Ibid., 144.

282. On the topic of female begging regarded as more dubious and morally reprehensible than male begging see ibid., 119–30.

283. Ibid., 32–33 and 35.

284. Geremek, *Margins*, 105.

285. Ibid.

286. Ibid., 31 and note 123. Peter I of Castile stated that in his kingdom of Murcia all people had to accept any form of work, with the exception of those who were sick, disabled, children under twelve years of age and the very old (Youngs, *Life Cycle*, 182). On the impact of English labour laws, in particular how the laws were enforced (or not, as legal disputes show) at a local level, see the essay by A. Musson, 'Reconstructing English Labor Laws: A Medieval Perspective', in *Middle Ages at Work*, ed. K. Robertson and M. Uebel (Basingstoke: Palgrave Macmillan, 2004), 113–32; also Chris Given-Wilson, 'The Problem of Labour in the Context of English Government, c. 1350–1450', in *Problem of Labour*, ed. J. Bothwell et al. (York: York Medieval Press, 2000), 85–100, especially 86–87 on the need to re-enact the labour laws as confirmations or modifications over a period of around one hundred years.

287. Geremek, *Margins*, 31–32. There was a sliding scale of penalties for people disobeying this ordinance, based on the 'three strikes and you're out' principle: four days in prison on bread and water at first offence, pillory for a second offence and branding on the forehead and banishment at the third count.

288. Ibid., 199. The notion of aggregating the disabled collectively as "miserable" people goes back to at least Innocent IV's commentary on the *Decretals* (c.

1250), where he classed widows, orphans, the old, blind or mutilated as *miserabiles personae*, with the restriction that "persons who were rich, although technically *miserabiles personae*," could not automatically appeal to canon law without having tried secular courts first (Tierney, *Medieval Poor Law*, 18).

289. Geremek, *Margins*, 39.

290. 25 Edward III, *Stat. 2*, in *Statutes of the Realm* (London: Dawsons, 1963), I:311–13.

291. Cited in Rubin, *Charity*, 31: "multi validi mendicantes, quandiu possent ex mendicantis elemosinis vivere, laborare renuunt, vacando ociis et peccatis ... latrociniis et aliis fiduciis"; cf. B. Putnam, *The Enforcement of the Statute of Labourers during the First Decade after the Black Death 1349–1359* (New York: Columbia University Press, 1908), 11 and 71–76.

292. F. F. Cartwright, *A Social History of Medicine* (London: Longman, 1977), 30.

293. On developments of poor relief and the concomitant change in conceptions of poverty, charity and the roles for the church, see Marjorie Keniston McIntosh, *Poor Relief in England, 1350–1600* (Cambridge: Cambridge University Press, 2011).

294. The topic of the visibility (and iterability) of the bodies of labourers has been discussed by Robertson, *Laborer's Two Bodies*, 17–18, who argues that prior to the labour regulations of the mid-fourteenth century "there is no laboring body" (18) that defines the cultural meaning of a "true" working body.

295. McCall, *Medieval Underworld*, 35; Statute 12 Richard II, cap. 7, in *Statutes of the Realm* (London: Dawsons, 1963), II:55–60. A general overview from the perspective of economic and social history of the effects of this legislation, arguing that the legitimate poor were henceforth to be maintained and cared for by their local communities, is given by Marjorie McIntosh, 'Local Responses to the Poor in Late Medieval and Tudor England', *Continuity and Change* 3, no. 2 (1988): 209–45. On the reception of the Statute of 1388 in Langland's *Piers Plowman*, cf. Anne Middleton, 'Acts of Vagrancy: The C Version "Autobiography" and the Statute of 1388', in *Written Work: Langland, Labor, and Authorship*, ed. S. Justice and K. Kerby-Fulton (Philadelphia: University of Pennsylvania Press, 1997), 208–388.

296. *Calendars of Close Rolls*, Edward IV, 1, 298–99, cited in Webb, *Pilgrims*, 211.

297. McCall, *Medieval Underworld*, 146; Tierney, *Medieval Poor Law*, 129. It is interesting to note that in the so-called Lollard Disendowment Bill of c. 1410, which makes reference to the 1388 statute, the problem of able-bodied beggars is also addressed, but with the addition that "only true beggars should be supported in almshouses" (Robertson, *Laborer's Two Bodies*, 101); Anne Hudson, *Selections from English Wycliffite Writings* (Toronto: University of Toronto Press, 1997), 135.

298. Irsigler and Lassotta, *Bettler*, 26: "die nit krüppel, lam oder plint sind".

299. Geremek, *Margins*, 192. For an analysis of the Parisian wills:, see ibid., 183–92.

300. Cited by Rosenthal, *Old Age*, 186; J. R. H. Weaver and Alice Beardwood, eds., *Some Oxfordshire Wills, 1393–1510*, Oxfordshire Record Society 39 (1958), 14.

301. Rawcliffe, *Hospitals*, 154.

302. Ibid.

303. Colin Platt, *Medieval Southampton: The Port and Trading Community, A.D. 1000–1600* (London: Routledge and Kegan Paul, 1973), 187; *The Black Book of Southampton*, ed. A. B. Wallis Chapman, 3 vols. (Southampton Record Society, 1912–1915), II:98–115.

304. Brodman, *Charity*, 29–30.
305. L. B. Alberti, *L'Architettura (De Re Aedificatoria)*, ed. G. Orlandi and P. Portoghesi (Milan: Edizioni Il Polifilo, 1966), I:336–37, cited by Henderson, *Piety*, 357.
306. Pelling, 'Illness among the Poor', 274, also mentions the first attempts at founding 'sheltered workshops' for the disabled during this period.
307. Farmer, 'The Beggar's Body', 154–55. For work particularly on female beggars and paupers, cf. Sharon Farmer, 'Down and Out in Paris', *American Historical Review* 103, no. 2 (1998): 344–72; and Farmer, 'Manual Labor', 264–65 and 272–80 (on the case of a disabled woman Jehanne, forced to beg and partially cured at the tomb of Saint Louis). In her expanded work on this topic (Farmer, *Surviving Poverty*, 64), Farmer equates the disabled male body with female bodies in general: according to medieval intellectual texts, men's bodies were meant to be strong and robust, particularly if they belonged to the lower classes (those who worked, not those who prayed); by contrast, male disabled bodies were weak and dependent, such as intellectual opinion held of female bodies.
308. S. M. Newton, *Fashion in the Age of the Black Prince: A Study of the Years 1340–1365* (Woodbridge: Boydell Press, 1980), 12; Thomas Aquinas, *Summa Theologica*, pt. II, 2nd part: Of modesty in outward apparel, clxix. The fourteenth-century Church also supported regulations on the use of false hair, cf. R. Trexler, *Synodal Law in Florence and Fiesole, 1306–1518* (Rome: Vatican Library, 1971), 116. On forbidding or allowing cosmetics in general during the middle ages, see Pierre Ruelle, ed., *L'Ornement des Dames (Ornatus Mulierum). Texte anglo-normande du XIIIe siècle. Le plus ancien recueil en français de recettes medicales pour les soins du visage* (Brussels: Presses de l'Université de Bruxelles, 1967).
309. Farmer, 'The Beggar's Body', 171.
310. Meier, *Gaukler*, 37.
311. "Alle, die mit Krankheiten behaftet vor den Kirchen sitzen oder auf der Straße ihre widerlichen Wunden und Gebrechen zeigen, sollen diese verdecken, damit die wohlgesetzten Bürger (gude lude) durch den Geruch und Anblick nicht belästigt werden" (cited in Irsigler and Lassotta, *Bettler*, 26).
312. "Es soll auch jeder Bettler, der eine offene, schlimme Verletzung an seinem Leibe oder seinen Gliedern hat, wovon die schwangeren Frauen durch Hinsehen Schaden erleiden können, diese Verletzung verdecken und nicht offen sichtbar zeigen oder zur Schau stellen, bei Strafe von einem Jahr Stadtverbannung" (cited in Fandrey, *Krüppel*, 20, following C. Sachße and F. Tennstedt, *Geschichte der Armenfürsorge in Deutschland. Vom Spätmittelalter bis zum 1. Weltkrieg* [Stuttgart: Kohlhammer, 1980], 65); Irsigler and Lassotta, *Bettler*, 26. On the concept of maternal imagination, pregnant women being influenced by what they see, cf. Metzler, *Disability*, 90–93, and Marie-Hélène Huet, *Monstrous Imagination* (Cambridge, MA: Harvard University Press, 1993). The notion of the maternal imagination as something that can have detrimental effects on the unborn fetus appears to be alive and well in twenty-first-century France: the Museum of Anatomy at Montpellier, founded in 1794 and today the oldest such institution still in operation worldwide, at time of writing offers visitors guided tours of its rich and varied collections, ranging from normal and pathological examples of human (and animal) anatomy via medical *moulages* (mock-ups of diseased body parts) to teratological exhibits, but expressly excludes the admission of young children and pregnant women.
313. Dirmeier, 'Armenfürsorge', 231. As late as the nineteenth century, notions of the maternal imagination were current in Victorian society. In his famous

London Labour and the London Poor (New York: Dover, 1968), IV:433, Henry Mayhew attested, "Instances are on record of nervous females having been seriously frightened, and even injured, by seeing men without arms or legs crawling at their feet"; furthermore, "a case is within my own knowledge, where the sight of a man without arms or legs had such an effect upon a lady in the family way that her child was born in all respects the very counterpart of the object that alarmed her. It had neither legs nor arms."

314. Farmer, *Surviving Poverty*, 157.
315. Mollat, *Die Armen*, 11. The preacher Guibert de Tournai (†1284) addressed one of his *ad status* sermons 'to lepers and the abject', reminding them that physical infirmity represented a divine test (Davis, 'Preaching', 82). In the *Leges Henrici Primi*, 108, c. 10,3, "abiectis" means literally people who have been cast out; such folk are lumped together with strangers, poor people and all persons in holy orders as deserving the king's protection if they have no one else who will take them.
316. Guy de Chauliac, *Inventarium* (or *Great Surgery*), cited in Wallis, *Medieval Medicine*, 420.
317. Wallis, *Medieval Medicine*, 421.
318. Farmer, 'The Beggar's Body', 159, note 19, who gives the date of the text cited earlier, *De reversione beati Martini a burgundia tractatus*, as probably written between 1137 and 1156. Latin text cited by Farmer after André Salmon, *Supplément aux chroniques de Touraine* (Tours, 1856), 52.
319. T. F. Crane, *The Exempla of Jacques de Vitry* (London, 1890), 112:52 and 182.
320. Jacobus de Voragine, *The Golden Legend: Readings on the Saints*, trans. W. G. Ryan (Princeton, NJ: Princeton University Press, 1993), chap. 166, II:300.
321. *Le mystère de la vie et hystoire de monseigneur sainct Martin*, featuring the blind Jolestru and the lame Haustebet; cf. Wheatley, *Stumbling Blocks*, 113–14.
322. On the literary topos of blind man and his guide and/or blind man and lame companion, see, most recently, Wheatley, *Stumbling Blocks*, chap. 4 and 171, relying on Jean Dufournet, intro. and trans., *Le garçon et l'aveugle: Jeu du XIIIe siècle* (Paris: Champion, 1989); older but still pertinent is G. Cohen, 'La scène de l'aveugle et de son valet dans le théâtre français du Moyen Age', *Romania* 41 (1912): 346–47; also G. Cohen, 'Le thème de l'aveugle et du paralytique dans la littérature française', in *Mélanges offerts à M. Emile Picot* (Paris: Damascène Morgand, 1913), II:393–404, who places the origin of the emblematic pairing blind-lame in hagiographic texts of around 1100; a drama performed in 1496 by André de la Vigne, *La Moralité de l'aveugle et du boiteux* (edition Paris, 1831), xi; for the topos in a fabliau 'De trois aveugles de Compiegne', ed. A. de Montaiglon and G. Raynaud, *Recueil général et complet des fabliaux*, vol. I (Paris, 1872), N. IV, 70–71. Some discussion of this theme in Geremek, *Margins*, 196, and Hölter, *Die Invaliden*, 93.
323. On this topos, see Metzler, 'Bildliche Darstellungen'. The aspect of solidarity between the two differently disabled persons, one blind and one lame, appears to originate in a first-century text, the *Apocryphon of Ezekiel* (Pestilli, 'Blindness', 107), where the two collaborate in order to get their revenge at not being invited to the king's feast. (Here, however, the story is used primarily as a moral to interpret the unity of body and soul, with the blind = body, lame = soul.) An interim example of the trope can be found in the thirteenth-century *vita* of Lame Margaret (Margareta contracta) of Magdeburg, who, as a young girl still living at home, helped guide a poor blind woman who had been given shelter by Margaret's mother, while the

blind woman supported her: "Ista contracta cecam duxit, ceca autem contractam sustentavit" (chap. 2, Johannes von Magdeburg, O. P., *Die Vita der Margareta contracta, einer Magdeburger Rekluse des 13. Jahrhunderts. Studien zur katholischen Bistums- und Klostergeschichte 36*, ed. Paul Gerhard Schmidt [Leipzig: Benno-Verlag, 1992], 3). Equally, this trope has an afterlife continuing long beyond the medieval period. To cite a few examples: in the emblem literature of the sixteenth and seventeenth centuries, generally consisting of a verbal motto, an image and a didactic poem, Andrea Alciati's *Emblemata* (various editions from 1542) uses the depiction of a blind man carrying a lame one to illustrate the motto "Mutuum auxilium", mutual assistance (Barasch, *Blindness*, 122, following Schleusener-Eichholz, *Das Auge*, I:504–5), exhorting people to help one another; in a poem by Wilhelm Busch published posthumously (*Unbeliebtes Wunder* [Unwelcome Miracle] 1909) the legend of Saint Martin is reworked in the comic verse Busch was famous for, the protagonists of this version being a blind and mute husband and his lame wife; and as recently as 2006 the topos found its way into popular culture via the animated film *Azour et Asmar* (English title: *The Prince's Quest*), screenplay/directed by Michel Ocelot, where the hero, feigning blindness so as to keep his "unlucky" blue eyes shut, falls in with an equally dissembling lame beggar. A real-life example, which also demonstrates historical awareness of this trope, stems from the anecdote told by a disabled German woman, Esther Bollag, who said that when one of her crutches broke her blind friend accompanied her to obtain a replacement, but since she could not walk with just one crutch, she leaned on her blind friend for support while she described the route they had to take; Bollag wrote: "At that moment we embodied the blind and the lame from the storybook (*Wir verkörperten in dem Moment den Blinden und die Lahme wie aus dem Bilderbuch*)" (Esther Bollag, 'Was denken da die Leut? Lachen und Behinderung—Grenzverletzend oder grenzüberschreitend?', *Zusammen* 22, no. 1 [2002]: 17, cited by Gottwald, *Lachen*, 273).

324. Geremek, *Geschichte*, 65.

325. Farmer, *Surviving Poverty*, 62–63. Examples include the blind man in the satirical piece *Le garçon et l'aveugle*, who promises the boy he enlists as guide that he will teach him the art of getting rich quick through his 'trade'; Thomas of Chobham's early thirteenth-century *Summa de arte praedicandi*, on beggars who "frequently collect alms in great quantity, and they do not use the money collected, but reserve it until their deaths, with great avarice" (Thomas of Chobham, *Summa de arte praedicandi*, chap. 3, ed. F. Morenzoni [Turnhout: Brepols, 1988], 88, cited by Farmer, 'The Beggar's Body', 63); and the story about a blind beggar who became so rich from alms that he became a professional moneylender, told by the Dominican preacher Stephen of Bourbon (*Tractatus de diversis materiis praedicabilibus*, ed. A. Lecoy de la Marche, *Anecdotes historiques, légendes et apologues tirés du recueil inédit d'Etienne de Bourbon Dominicain du XIIIe siècle* [Paris, 1877], 361, no. 414, cited by Farmer, 'The Beggar's Body', 63).

326. Barasch, *Blindness*, 120–21; Sacchetti, *Trecentonovelle*, novel 140.

327. For instance, Petrarch devotes an entire letter (*Rerum senilium* VI, 7) to the subject of avarice, highlighting this sin in old men, rich men and kings. Avarice in the old is slightly less culpable because of their "recollection of need and hardship" (*Letters of Old Age*, I:206).

328. *The Pilgremage of þe Lyfe of þe Manhode: Translated Anonymously into Prose from the First Recension of Guillaume de Deguilville's 'Le Pèlerinage de la Vie humaine'*, ed. A. Henry, EETS o.s. 288 (Oxford, 1985), 128, cited in Michael Camille, *The Gothic Idol: Ideology and Image-Making in*

Medieval Art (Cambridge: Cambridge University Press, 1989), 270. Avarice brags about her use of fraudulent relics (lines 18103–26 and 18156–65); Hagen, *Allegorical Remembrance*, 232, note 13.

329. Hagen, *Allegorical Remembrance*, 62.

330. Paris, Bibliothèque Nationale, MS fr. 829 (Guillaume de Deguileville's *Pèlerinage*: second recension), fol. 92v.

331. Camille, *Gothic Idol*, 271.

332. A theme that came to the fore in England not so long ago, when disabled people protested in London on 11 May 2011 against the government's spending cuts. A news report cited not just protest at loss of welfare benefits but "anger directed at benefit cheats." A placard read "I'm no scrounger, I have MS", and a blind protester worried that "people who already fiddle the system will go on receiving benefits, but honest people—who haven't learnt how to play the system—will end up with no help" (Marie Jackson, '"Hardest Hit" Speak Out about Spending Cuts', BBC News 11 May 2011, available at http://www.bbc.co.uk/news/uk-13365335, accessed 11 May 2011). Academic analysis did not lag behind, see K. Garthwaite, '"The Language of Shirkers and Scroungers?" Talking about Illness, Disability and Coalition Welfare Reform', *Disability and Society* 26, no. 3 (2011): 369–372.

333. "Item predicti menagerii heligentur laborantes terrarum et in aliis operibus panem suum lucrantes, non trutenni et trutenniter viventes nisi essent ceci vel alias debillitati vel antiqui quod propter hoc necessario haberent mendicare." The *Statutes* can be found in Astrik L. Gabriel, *Student Life in Ave Maria College, Medieval Paris: History and Chartulary of the College* (Notre Dame, IN: University of Notre Dame Press, 1955), 375, cited by Farmer, 'Young, Male and Disabled', 450.

334. Gerd Althoff, Hans-Werner Goetz and Ernst Schubert, *Menschen im Schatten der Kathedrale* (Darmstadt: Primus, 1998), 347.

335. Rubin, *Charity*, 68; *Decretum magistri Gratiani*, in *Corpus Iuris Canonici I*, ed. E. Friedberg (Leipzig, 1877), at C.2 q.1, X.20.32, X.1.6.22.

336. Coleman, 'Property', 627.

337. *Le Roman de la Rose*, l. 360.

338. Geoffrey Chaucer, *Troilus and Criseyde*, book 5 line 1222.

339. Guillaume le Roux (†1181), fourth master of the order of Saint Anthony of Vienne, had introduced this crutch-cross as emblem of the order; it was also the ownership sign branded onto the pigs belonging to the order; Windemuth, *Das Hospital*, 62.

340. "Item cuilibet . . . claudum, secum [caecum], vel impotentem, in cubiculo jacentem, xiijs iiijd". Testament of Sir Richard de Scrop, cited in J. Fowler, 'On a Window Representing the Life and Miracles of S. William of York, at the North End of the Eastern Transept, York Minster', *Yorkshire Archaeological and Topographical Journal* 3 (1873–1974): 260.

341. F W. Weaver, ed., *Somerset Medieval Wills*, Somerset Record Society 16 (1901), 404–5; cited in Rosenthal, *Old Age*, 186.

342. Smith, 'The Manorial Court', 47.

343. "And that no one shall glean who is able-bodied [*potens est*] and can earn 1d. a day and 1 ½ d. [*sic*] if any one within this demesne wishes to hire him." Document number 160 in Ault, *Open-Field Farming*. See Chapter 2, this volume.

344. *Statutes of the Realm*, ed. A. Luders, T. E. Tomlins and J. Raithby (London, 1810–28; rpt. 1963), I:307; Shahar, 'Who Were the Old?', 332.

345. Harvey, *Living and Dying*, 32, citing the Close Roll in Public Record Office C54/365, m. 5. Henry's mother, Margaret Beaufort, also stipulated alms for "the blind, the lame, the bedridden and the poorest of the poor" on her anniversary (ibid., 32, and Public Record Office C54/372, m. 23v.).

346. Cited by Jütte, *Poverty*, 11, following William Harrison, *Description of England in Shakespeare's Youth (1577/87)*, ed. F. J. Furnivall (London, 1877), 213.
347. Mollat, *Die Armen*, 117.
348. Farmer, 'Manual Labor', 276.
349. Crassons, *Claims of Poverty*, 174. On antifraternalism, see, most recently Guy Geltner, *The Making of Medieval Antifraternalism: Polemic, Violence, Deviance, and Remembrance* (Oxford: Oxford University Press, 2012); also Penn R. Szittya, *The Medieval Antifraternal Tradition* (Princeton, NJ: Princeton University Press, 1986).
350. Crassons, *Claims of Poverty*, 277, also 277–79 for further discussion of modern welfare reform in the US.
351. Geremek, *Margins*, 169.
352. Cited by Minois, *History of Old Age*, 120; Salvian of Marseilles, Letter IV.15, in *Oeuvres*, 2 vols, trans. G. Lagarrigue (Le Cerf, coll. 'Sources chrétiennes', 1971 and 1975).
353. Youngs, *Life Cycle*, 180.
354. Pestilli, 'Blindness', 107.
355. Henderson, *Piety*, 275. Additionally, Pestilli, 'Blindness', 124, note 5, points out that the 'traditional' role of blind and lame men as beggars goes back to antique stereotypes already encountered in Plutarch's *Life of Pelopidas* 3.4 (money is a necessity for Nicodemus, a man who was lame and blind) or Diogenes Laertius's *Life of Diogenes*, 56 (when asked why people give to beggars and not to philosophers, Diogenes said, "Because they think it possible that they themselves may become lame and blind, but they do not expect ever to turn out philosophers"). By the sixteenth and seventeenth centuries, "groups dubbed 'difettosi', 'impotenti' and 'inabili' . . . figure constantly in the ranks of the deserving poor in the relief schemes devised by Italian cities" (Pullan, 'Difettosi', VI:2).

NOTES TO THE CONCLUSION

1. Guillaume de Saint-Pathus, *Les miracles de Saint Louis*, 50–55.
2. Farmer, 'A Deaf-Mute's Story', who also translated from the French.
3. See Metzler, *Disability*, chap. 5, on disability in medieval miracle narratives.
4. Farmer, 'A Deaf-Mute's Story', 206, makes the unsubstantiated claim that Louis could have "been abandoned, as many disabled children were in the Middle Ages." This argument concerning the allegedly large quantity of abandonment is presumably based on Boswell, *Kindness of Strangers*, 168, 259–60, 337–39, although Boswell himself had pointed out the evidence concerning abandonment and/or infanticide of 'defective', hence disabled, children "does not support broader inference" (ibid., 212), and had cited many examples of the 'alternative' to abandonment, namely oblation to a monastery (ibid., chap. 8).
5. As Fandrey surmises: "Wahrscheinlich lebte so die große Mehrheit der behinderten Menschen des Mittelalters in normalen sozialen Verhältnissen und zumindest äußerlich wirtschaftlich und sozial integriert" (*Krüppel*, 15).
6. Cited by Farmer, 'A Deaf-Mute's Story', 203.
7. Ibid.
8. Louis's connection to the household of the count and countess is used by Farmer to construct the theory that aristocratic circles were "often" attractive potential employers of disabled people ('A Deaf-Mute's Story', 206).

The evidence for the frequency of this happening is rather sparse, as was pointed out in the Chapter 2 of this volume. Notably, the source text in the *Miracles of Saint Louis* is completely silent on the exact capacity in which Louis joined the court of Auxerre, other than mentioning his presence in the kitchen of the count—in terms of jumping to conclusions, it is a far cry from observing a deaf and mute man in the kitchen to constructing generalised statements concerning the cultural meaning of disabled people's presence in courtly households. When highlighting (Farmer, 'A Deaf-Mute's Story', 206 and 207, note 1) the presence of "the deaf man of the carriage" among the list of employees in the stables of the Countess Mahaut of Artois and Burgundy (accounts for 1304–1328), this is not evidence for the 'exoticism' of such an employee; rather it is evidence for the employability of disabled people in all sorts of routine and mundane tasks regularly carried out by the able-bodied.

9. Cited by Farmer, 'A Deaf-Mute's Story', 203.
10. Ibid., 204.
11. Ibid.
12. Ibid., 205.
13. Ibid.
14. On the subject of the change in types and frequency of thaumaturgic miracles from the earlier to the later medieval period, see the forthcoming article by Metzler, 'Indiscriminate Healing Miracles in Decline'.
15. Cited by Farmer, 'A Deaf-Mute's Story', 204.
16. Ibid., 207.
17. Ibid., 204.
18. Ibid.
19. Irina Metzler, 'Perceptions of Deafness in the Central Middle Ages', in *Homo debilis. Behinderte—Kranke—Versehrte in der Gesellschaft des Mittelalters*, ed. Cordula Nolte (Korb: Didymos-Verlag, 2009), 83–85.
20. Cited by Farmer, 'A Deaf-Mute's Story', 205.
21. 'Homesigns' are structured independently of speech, have evolved over a single generation and are generally restricted to a very small socio-linguistic community, as in this case here to just Louis, Gauchier and *familia*; cf. S. Goldin-Meadow and H. Feldmann, 'The Creation of a Communication System: A Study of Deaf Children of Hearing Parents', *Sign Language Studies* 8 (1975): 225–34.
22. Cited by Farmer, 'A Deaf-Mute's Story', 205.
23. Ibid.
24. One may think here of the famous ancient Greek maxim *gnothi seauton*, 'know thyself'. This part of the story therefore touches upon a very modern topic, namely, the almost obsessive preoccupation with identity.
25. *Aucassin et Nicolette*, ed. Jean Dufournet (Paris: Garnier-Flammarion, 1984), prose VI, in Pratt, '*De vetula*', 340.
26. Le Goff, *Medieval Civilization*, 321.
27. Langland, *Piers the Ploughman*, 138; "For be a man fair or foul, it falleth noght to lakke / The shap ne the shaft that God shoop hymselve" (B-Text passus XI ll. 394–95), with biblical reference to Genesis 1:31: "And God saw everything that He had made, and, behold, it was very good."
28. See the discussion in Metzler, *Disability*, 11–20, on the lack of historical examination of disability in periods prior to the nineteenth century.
29. Farmer, 'Young, Male and Disabled', 449.
30. Gottwald, *Lachen*, 287.
31. There is a vast literature on the question of what is illness/sickness/disease and on the position of chronic conditions within that discussion. A few

pertinent examples: George S. Rousseau et al., eds., *Framing and Imagining Disease in Cultural History* (Basingstoke: Palgrave, 2003); Ian Shaw and Kaisa Kauppinen, eds., *Constructions of Health and Illness: A European Perspective* (Aldershot: Ashgate, 2003); Stephen Platt et al., eds., *Locating Health: Sociological and Historical Explorations* (Aldershot: Ashgate, 1993).

Select Bibliography

ABBREVIATIONS

EETS   *Early English Text Society.* Cambridge: Cambridge University Press/ Oxford: Oxford University Press, 1864–.

MGH   *Monumenta Germaniae Historica.*

PL   *Patrologiae cursus completus: series latina.* Ed. J. P. Migne. 221 vols. Paris: Migne, 1841–1864.

PRIMARY SOURCES

The Account-Book of Beaulieu Abbey. Ed. S. F. Hockey. Camden Society 4th series 16. Cambridge: Royal Historical Society, 1975.

Adam of Bremen. *Gesta Hammaburgensis ecclesiae pontificum.* Ed. Bernhard Schmeidler. MGH Scriptores Rerum Germanicarum 2. Hanover: Hahnsche Buchhandlung, 1917.

Aelred of Rievaulx. *Opera omnia.* Ed. A. Hoste and C. H. Talbot. Corpus Christianorum Continuatio Medievalis. Turnhout: Brepols, 1971.

The Age of Bede. Rev. ed. Trans. J. F. Webb. London: Penguin, 1988.

Andreas Capellanus. *The Art of Courtly Love.* Intro., trans. and notes John Jay Parry. New York: Columbia University Press, 1960.

Annales Fuldenses sive Annales Francorum Orientalis. Ed. G. H. Pertz and Friedrich Kurze. MGH Scriptores Rerum Germanicarum 7. Hanover, 1891.

Annalista Saxo. Ed. Klaus Naß. MGH Scriptores 37. Hanover, 2006.

The Annals of Fulda. Trans. Timothy Reuter. Ninth-Century Histories II. Manchester: Manchester University Press, 1992.

Arnold, Morris S., ed. *Select Cases of Trespass from the King's Court, 1307–1399.* 2 vols. Selden Society Publications 100, 103. London: Selden Society Publications, 1985, 1987.

Attreed, Lorraine C., ed. *The York Household Books 1461–1490.* 2 vols. Stroud: Sutton, 1991.

Augustine. *Concerning the City of God against the Pagans.* Trans. Henry Bettenson. London: Penguin, 1984.

Bartholomaeus Anglicus. *On the Properties of Things: John Trevisa's Translation of Bartholomaeus Anglicus's De proprietatibus rerum.* Ed. M. Seymour. 2 vols. Oxford: Clarendon Press, 1975.

Bedfordshire Coroners' Rolls. Ed. R. F. Hunniset. Bedfordshire Historical Record Society 41, 1960.

Biblia Sacra iuxta Vulgatem Versionem. 4th ed. Ed. B. Fischer, I. Gribomont, H. F. D. Sparks and W. Thiele. Stuttgart: Deutsche Bibelgesellschaft, 1994.

The Book of Margery Kempe. Trans. B. A. Windeatt. London: Penguin, 1985.

Bracton on the Laws and Customs of England. Ed. George E. Woodbine. Trans. Samuel E. Thorne. 4 vols. Cambridge, MA: Harvard University Press, 1977.

Byrhtferth's Manual. Ed. S. J. Crawford. EETS o.s. 177, 1929.

Calendar of the Close Rolls Preserved in the Public Record Office, 1227–1485. Public Record Office. 45 vols. London: HMSO, 1892–1954.

Calendar of the Letter-Books of the City of London, 1275–1498, Books A–L. Ed. Reginald R. Sharpe. 11 vols. London, 1899–1912.

Calendar of the Patent Rolls Preserved in the Public Record Office, 1216–1509. Public Record Office. 52 vols. London: HMSO, 1891–1901.

The Cartulary of St. Augustine's Abbey, Bristol. Ed. D. Walker. Bristol: Bristol and Gloucester Archaeological Society, 1998.

Cartulary of St. Mark's Hospital Bristol. Ed. C. D. Ross. Bristol Record Society 21. Bristol, 1959.

The Castle of Perseverance. In *The Macro Plays,* ed. M. Eccles. EETS o.s. 262, 1969.

Charters of the Medieval Hospitals of Bury St. Edmunds. Ed. Christopher Harper-Bill. Woodbridge: Boydell Press, 1994.

Christine de Pisan. *The Treasure of the City of Ladies or the Book of the Three Virtues.* Trans. S. Lawson. London: Penguin Books, 1985.

Codex Justinianus. Ed. and trans. Gottfried Härtel and Frank-Michael Kaufmann. Leipzig: Reclam Verlag, 1991.

Cosmas of Prague. *Cosmae Pragensis Chronica Boemorum.* Ed. Berthold Bretholz. MGH Scriptores Rerum Germanicarum n.s. 2. Berlin, 1923.

Court Rolls of the Manor of Hales, 1272–1307. Ed. J. Amphlett. Worcester Historical Society, 1910–33.

Crime, Law and Society in the Later Middle Ages. Manchester Medieval Sources Series. Trans. and ed. Anthony Musson with Edward Powell. Manchester: Manchester University Press, 2009.

Dan Michel. *Ayenbite of Inwyt.* New ed. Ed. Richard Morris and Pamela Gordon. EETS o.s. 23. London, 1866, reissued 1965.

Dives and Pauper. Ed. P. H. Barnum. EETS o.s. 275. London, 1976.

Einhard. *Vita Karoli* 30. Ed. Oswald Holder-Egger. MGH Scriptores Rerum Germanicarum 25. Hanover, 1911.

English Gilds: The Original Ordinances of More than One Hundred Early English Gilds. Ed. Joshua Toulmin Smith and Lucy Toulmin Smith. EETS o.s. 40. London, 1870.

English Historical Documents, vol. 1 c. 500–1042. 2nd ed. Ed. Dorothy Whitelock. London: Eyre Methuen, 1979.

The English Manor c. 1200–c. 1500. Trans. and notes Mark Bailey. Manchester: Manchester University Press, 2002.

Geary, Patrick J., ed. *Readings in Medieval History.* Vol. I, *The Early Middle Ages.* Orchard Park, NY: Broadview, 1992.

Giraldus Cambrensis. *Speculum duorum.* Ed. Y. Lefèvre and R. B. C. Huygens. Trans. B. Dawson. Cardiff: University of Wales Press, 1974.

[Glanvill]. *The Treatise on the Laws and Customs of the Realm of England Commonly Called Glanvill.* Ed. and trans. G. D. G. Hall. Medieval Texts. London: Nelson, 1965.

Gower, John. *Confessio amantis.* Ed. R A. Peck. Medieval Academy Reprints for Teaching 9. Toronto: University of Toronto Press, 1980.

Gregory of Tours. *The History of the Franks.* Trans. Lewis Thorpe. London: Penguin, 1974.

Guillaume de Deguileville. *Le Pèlerinage de la vie humaine.* Ed. J. Stürzinger. London: Roxburghe Club, 1893.

Guillaume de Lorris and Jean de Meun. *Le Roman de la Rose*. Ed. Daniel Poirion. Paris: Garnier-Flammarion, 1974.

———. *The Romance of the Rose*. Trans. and ed. Frances Horgan. Oxford: Oxford University Press, 1994.

Guillaume de Saint-Pathus. *Les miracles de Saint Louis*. Ed. Percival B. Fay. Paris: H. Champion, 1931.

Halmota Prioratus Dunelmensis. Ed. Durham Halmote Rolls, W. H. D. Longstaffe and J. Booth. Durham: Surtees Society, 1889.

Helmold of Hirsau. *Chronicon*. Ed. Bernhard Schmeidler. MGH Scriptores Rerum Germanicarum 32. Hanover, 1937.

Hrabanus Maurus. Ed. Ernst Dümmler. MGH Epistolae 5. Berlin, 1898–1899.

Isidore of Seville [*Etymologiae*]. William D. Sharpe. 'Isidore of Seville: The Medical Writings. An English Translation with an Introduction and Commentary'. *Transactions of the American Philosophical Society* 54, no. 2 (1964): 3–75.

[Jean de] Joinville and [Geoffroy de] Villehardouin. *Chronicles of the Crusades (The Conquest of Constantinople* and *The Life of Saint Louis)*. Trans. M. R. B. Shaw. London: Penguin, 1963.

Justinian's Institutes. Trans. and intro. Peter Birks and Grant McLeod. Ithaca, NY: Cornell University Press, 1987.

Langland, William. *Piers the Ploughman*. Rev. ed. Trans. J. F. Goodridge. Harmondsworth: Penguin, 1966.

———. *The Vision of Piers Plowman: A Complete Edition of the B-Text*. Ed. A. V. C. Schmidt. London: Dent/New York: Dutton, 1978.

The Laws of the Earliest English Kings. Ed. and trans. F. L. Attenborough. Cambridge: Cambridge University Press, 1922; rpt. Felinfach: Llanerch Publishers, 2000.

The Laws of the Salian Franks. Trans. and intro. Katherine Fischer Drew. Philadelphia: University of Pennsylvania Press, 1991.

Leges Alamannorum. Ed. Karl Lehmann. MGH Leges I: Leges Nationum Germanicarum V.1. Hanover, 1888.

Leges Burgundionum. Ed. Ludwig Rudolf von Salis. MGH Leges I: Leges Nationum Germanicarum II.1. Hanover, 1892.

Leges Henrici Primi. Ed. and trans. L. J. Downer. Oxford: Clarendon Press, 1972.

Leges Langobardorum. Ed. F. Bluhme and A. Boretius. MGH Leges IV. Hannover, 1868.

Leges Saxonum. Ed. Claudius von Schwerin. MGH Fontes Iuris Germanici Antiqui. Hanover, 1918.

Lex Baiwariorum. Ed. Ernst von Schwind. MGH Leges I: Leges Nationum Germanicarum V.2. Hanover, 1926.

Lex Ribuaria. Ed. Franz Beyerle and Rudolf Buchner. MGH Leges I: Leges Nationum Germanicarum III.2. Hanover, 1954.

Lex Visigothorum. Ed. Karl Zeumer. MGH Fontes iuris Germanici antiqui 5. Hanover, 1894.

Liebermann, Felix. *Die Gesetze der Angelsachsen*. 3 vols. Halle: Niemeyer, 1898–1916.

The Life of Christina of Markyate. Trans. C. H. Talbot. Rev. and intro. S. Fanous and H. Leyser. Oxford: Oxford University Press, 2008.

The Lombard Laws. Ed. and trans. Katherine Fisher Drew. Philadelphia: University of Philadelphia Press, 1973.

Lotario de Segni (Papst Innozenz III.). *Vom Elend des menschlichen Daseins*. Philosophische Texte und Studien 24. Trans. Carl-Friedrich Geyer. Hildesheim: Georg Olms, 1990.

The Manor of Manydown. Ed. W. G. Kitchin. Hampshire Record Society, 1895.

The Mirror of Justices. Ed. J. Whittaker. Selden Society 7. London, 1895.

Omne Bonum: A Fourteenth-Century Encyclopedia of Universal Knowledge. Ed. Lucy Freeman Sandler. 2 vols. London: Harvey Miller, 1996.

Orderic Vitalis. *The Ecclesiastical History of Orderic Vitalis*. Ed. M. Chibnall. 6 vols. Oxford: Oxford University Press, 1969–80.

Otto of Freising and Rahewin. *Gesta Friderici Imperatoris*. Ed. A. Waitz and B. de Simson. MGH Scriptores Rerum Germanicarum 12. Hanover and Leipzig, 1912.

Parlement of the Thre Ages. Ed. M. Y. Offord. EETS 246. London, 1959.

Petrarch, Francis. *Letters of Old Age: Rerum Senilium Libri I–XVIII*. Trans. Aldo S. Bernardo, Saul Levin and Reta A. Bernardo. 2 vols. Baltimore, MD: Johns Hopkins University Press, 1992.

Petrus Damiani. Ed. Kurt Reindel. MGH Epistolae IV, 2. Munich, 1988.

Quadripartitus, ein englisches Rechtsbuch von 1114. Ed. Felix Liebermann. Halle: Niemeyer, 1892.

Robert Grosseteste. *De decem mandatis (de quarto mandato)*. Auctores Britannici medii aevi 10. Ed. Richard C. Dales and Edward B. King. Oxford: Oxford University Press, 1987.

Roger Bacon. *De retardatione accidentium senectutis cum aliis opusculis medicinalibus*. Ed. A. Little and E. Withington. Oxford: Clarendon Press, 1928.

———. *Opus majus*. Ed. J. H. Bridges. 3 vols. London, 1897–1900.

———. *Opus majus*. Vol. 2. Trans. R. Burke. Philadelphia, 1928.

Sacchetti, Franco. *Il Libro delle Trecentonovelle*. Ed. Antonio Lanza. Florence: Sansoni, 1984.

[Sacchetti, Franco]. *Tales from Sacchetti*. Trans. Mary G. Steegman. London: Dent, 1908; rpt. Westport, CT: Hyperion Press, 1978.

Sachsenspiegel. Landrecht und Lehnrecht. Ed. Friedrich Ebel. Stuttgart: Reclam, 1999.

The Saxon Mirror. Trans. Maria Debozy. Philadelphia: University of Pennsylvania Press, 1999.

Schwazer Bergbuch = Perkwerch etc. 1556. Facsimile of MS Codex 10.852 in Österreichische Nationalbibliothek, Vienna. Ed. Heinrich Winkelmann and Erich Egg. Graz: Akademische Druck- und Verlagsanstalt, 1988.

Tavormina, M. Teresa, ed. *Sex, Aging, and Death in a Medieval Medical Compendium: Trinity College Cambridge MS R.14.52, Its Texts, Language, and Scribe*. 2 vols. Tempe: Arizona Center for Medieval and Renaissance Studies, 2006.

Thietmar of Merseburg. *Chronicon*. Ed. Robert Holtzmann. MGH Scriptores Rerum Germanicarum n.s. 9. Berlin, 1955.

The Travels of John Mandeville. Trans. C. W. R. D. Moseley. London: Penguin, 1983.

Two Wycliffite Texts. Ed. Anne Hudson. EETS o.s. 301. Oxford: Oxford University Press, 1993.

The Usatges of Barcelona: The Fundamental Law of Catalonia. Trans. Donal J. Kagay. Philadelphia: University of Pennsylvania Press, 1994.

[Villon, François]. *The Poems of François Villon*. Ed. Edward F. Chaney. Oxford: Blackwell, 1940.

Vita Desiderii Cadurcae urbis episcopi 37. In *Passiones vitaeque sanctorum aevi Merovingici*, ed. Bruno Krusch. MGH Scriptores rerum Merovingicarum 4. Hanover, 1902.

Vita Eligii episcopi Noviomagensis. In *Passiones vitaeque sanctorum aevi Merovingici*, ed. Bruno Krusch. MGH Scriptores rerum Merovingicarum 4. Hanover, 1902.

Wallis, Faith, ed. *Medieval Medicine: A Reader. Readings in Medieval Civilizations and Cultures XV*. Toronto: University of Toronto Press, 2010.

Wenzel, Siegfried, ed. and trans. *Fasciculus Morum: A Fourteenth-Century Preacher's Handbook*. University Park: Pennsylvania State University Press, 1989.

――――, trans. *Preaching in the Age of Chaucer: Selected Sermons in Translation*. Washington, DC: Catholic University of America Press, 2008.

Willibald. *Vita Bonifatii*. Ed. Wilhelm Levison. MGH Scriptores Rerum Germanicarum 57. Hanover, 1905.

Bracton's *Laws and Customs of England* are available online at: http://hlsl5.law.harvard.edu/bracton/index.htm (accessed November 2008)

Justinian's *Digest, Code* and *Institutes* are available online at: http://www.umt.edu/law/original-understanding/roman.htm (accessed November 2008).

SECONDARY LITERATURE

Agrimi, Jole, and Chiara Crisciani. 'Savoir médical et anthropologie religieuse. Les représentations et les fonctions de la *vetula* (XIIIe–XVe siècle)'. *Annales Économies, Sociétés, Civilisations* 48 (1993): 1281–1308.

Alford, B. W. E., and T. C. Barker. *A History of the Carpenters Company*. London: George Allen and Unwin, 1968.

Althoff, Gerd, Hans-Werner Goetz and Ernst Schubert. *Menschen im Schatten der Kathedrale*. Darmstadt: Wissenschaftliche Buchgesellschaft, 1998.

Amos, Ashley Crandell. 'Old English Words for *Old*'. In *Aging and the Aged*, ed. Sheehan, 95–106. Toronto: Pontifical Institute of Medieval Studies, 1990.

Amt, E., ed. *Women's Lives in Medieval Europe: A Sourcebook*. London: Routledge, 1993.

Ariès, Philippe. *The Hour of Our Death*. Trans. H. Weaver. London: Allen Lane, 1981.

Ariès, Philippe, and Georges Duby, eds. *A History of Private Life II: Revelations of the Medieval World*. Trans. A. Goldhammer. Cambridge, MA: Belknap Press, 1988.

Aston, T. H., P. R. Coss, C. Dyer and J. Thirsk, eds. *Social Relations and Ideas: Essays in Honour of R. H. Hilton*. Cambridge: Cambridge University Press, 1983.

Ault, W. O. *Open-Field Farming in Medieval England: A Study of Village By-Laws*. London: George Allen and Unwin, 1972.

――――. 'Open-Field Husbandry and the Village Community: A Study of Agrarian Bye-Laws in Medieval England'. *Transactions of the American Philosophical Society* 55, no. 7 (1965): 5–102.

Bakhtin, Mikhail. *Rabelais and His World*. Trans. H. Iswolsky. Bloomington: Indiana University Press, 1984.

Barasch, Moshe. *Blindness: The History of a Mental Image in Western Thought*. New York: Routledge, 2001.

Baraz, Daniel. *Medieval Cruelty: Changing Perceptions, Late Antiquity to the Early Modern Period*. Ithaca, NY: Cornell University Press, 2003.

Barron, C. M. 'The Parish Fraternities of Medieval London'. In *The Church in Pre-Reformation Society: Essays in Honour of F. R. H. Du Boulay*, ed. C. M. Barron and C. Harper-Bill, 13–37. Woodbridge: Boydell Press, 1985.

Bartels, C., A. Bingener and R. Slotta, eds. *"1556 Perkwerch etc."*. *Das Schwazer Bergbuch*. 3 vols. Bochum: Veröffentlichungen des Deutschen Bergbau-Museum Bochum, 2006.

Bartlett, Robert. *Trial by Fire and Water: The Medieval Judicial Ordeal*. Oxford: Clarendon Press, 1986.

Beauvoir, Simone de. *Old Age* [*La Vieillesse*]. Trans. P. O'Brian. London: A. Deutsch and Weidenfeld and Nicolson, 1972.

Beer, Frances. *Women and Mystical Experience in the Middle Ages.* Woodbridge: Boydell Press, 1992.

Bennett, H. S. *Life on the English Manor: A Study of Peasant Conditions 1150– 1400.* Cambridge: Cambridge University Press, 1965.

Bildhauer, Bettina. *Medieval Blood.* Cardiff: University of Wales Press, 2006.

Binding, Günther. *Baubetrieb im Mittelalter.* Darmstadt: Wissenschaftliche Buchgesellschaft, 1993.

Blamires, Alcuin, ed. *Woman Defamed and Woman Defended: An Anthology of Medieval Texts.* Oxford: Clarendon Press, 1992.

Blamires, Alcuin, and G. C. Holian. *The Romance of the Rose Illuminated: Manuscripts of the National Library of Wales, Aberystwyth.* Cardiff: University of Wales Press, 2002.

Boissonade, P. *Life and Work in Medieval Europe (Fifth to Fifteenth Centuries).* Trans. E. Power. London: Kegan Paul, 1937.

Bolzoni, Lina. *The Web of Images: Vernacular Preaching from Its Origins to St. Bernardino of Siena.* Aldershot: Ashgate, 2004.

Boockman, Hartmut. *Die Stadt im späten Mittelalter.* 3rd ed. Munich: C. H. Beck, 1994.

Borscheid, P. *Geschichte des Alterns: 16.–18. Jahrhundert.* Stuttgart: F. Steiner Verlag, 1987.

Borst, Arno. *Barbaren, Ketzer und Artisten. Welten des Mittelalters.* Munich: Piper, 1988.

Bosl, Karl. 'Potens und Pauper. Begriffsgeschichtliche Studien zur gesellschaftlichen Differenzierung im frühen Mittelalter und zum "Pauperismus" des Hochmittelalters'. In *Frühformen der Gesellschaft im mittelalterlichen Europa. Ausgewählte Beiträge zu einer Strukturanalyse der mittelalterlichen Welt*, ed. Karl Bosl, 106–34. Munich: R. Oldenbourg Verlag, 1964.

Boswell, John. *The Kindness of Strangers: The Abandonment of Children in Western Europe from Late Antiquity to the Renaissance.* New York: Pantheon Books, 1988.

Bothwell, James, P. J. P. Goldberg and W. M. Ormrod, eds. *The Problem of Labour in Fourteenth-Century England.* York: York Medieval Press, 2000.

Bradbury, Jim. *The Medieval Siege.* Woodbridge: Boydell Press, 1992.

Brodman, James William. *Charity and Religion in Medieval Europe.* Washington, DC: Catholic University of America Press, 2009.

Brown, T. S. 'Urban Violence in Early Medieval Italy: The Cases of Rome and Ravenna'. In *Violence and Society in the Early Medieval West*, ed. Guy Halsall, 76–89. Woodbridge: Boydell Press, 1998.

Bruce, G. M. 'A Note on Penal Blinding in the Middle Ages'. *Annals of Medical History* 3 (1941): 369–71.

Brungs, Alexander. 'Die philosophische Diskussion des Alters im Kontext der Aristoteles-Rezeption des 13. Jahrhunderts'. In *Alterskulturen*, ed. Vavra, 91–107. Vienna: Verlag der Österreichischen Akademie der Wissenschaften, 2008.

Bührer-Thierry, Geneviève. '"Just Anger" or "Vengeful Anger"? The Punishment of Blinding in the Early Medieval West'. In *Anger's Past: The Social Uses of an Emotion in the Middle Ages*, ed. Barbara Rosenwein, 75–91. Ithaca, NY: Cornell University Press, 1998.

Burrow, J. A. *The Ages of Man: A Study in Medieval Writing and Thought.* Oxford: Clarendon Press, 1986.

Bynum, Caroline Walker. *Fragmentation and Redemption: Essays on Gender and the Human Body in Medieval Religion.* New York: Zone Books, 1992.

Bynum, W. F., and Roy Porter, eds. *Companion Encyclopedia of the History of Medicine.* 2 vols. London: Routledge, 1993.

Camille, Michael. *The Gothic Idol: Ideology and Image-Making in Medieval Art.* Cambridge: Cambridge University Press, 1989.

Chabot, Isabelle. 'Widowhood and Poverty in Late Medieval Florence'. *Continuity and Change* 3, no. 2 (1988): 291–311.

Clark, Elaine. 'The Quest for Security in Medieval England'. In *Aging and the Aged*, ed. Sheehan, 189–200. Toronto: Pontifical Institute of Medieval Studies, 1990.

——. 'Some Aspects of Social Security in Medieval England'. *Journal of Family History* 7, no. 4 (1982): 307–20.

Classen, Albrecht. 'Der alte Mensch in den spätmittelalterlichen Mæren: Die Komplexität der Alterserfahrung im Spätmittelalter aus mentalitätsgeschichtlicher Sicht'. In *Alterskulturen*, ed. Vavra, 219–41. Vienna: Verlag der Österreichischen Akademie der Wissenschaften, 2008.

——, ed. *Old Age in the Middle Ages and the Renaissance: Interdisciplinary Approaches to a Neglected Topic.* Fundamentals of Medieval and Early Modern Culture 2. Berlin: Walter de Gruyter, 2007.

——. 'Old Age in the World of the Stricker and other Middle High German Poets: A Neglected Topic'. In *Old Age*, ed. Albrecht Classen, 219–50. Berlin: Walter de Gruyter, 2007.

Clay, Rotha Mary. *The Medieval Hospitals of England.* London: Frank Cass, 1909; rpt. 1966.

Coffman, George R. 'Old Age from Horace to Chaucer: Some Literary Affinities and Adventures of an Idea'. *Speculum* 9 (1934): 249–77.

Cohen, Esther. *The Modulated Scream: Pain in Late Medieval Culture.* Chicago: University of Chicago Press, 2010.

Cokayne, Karen. *Experiencing Old Age in Ancient Rome.* London: Routledge, 2003.

Coldstream, Nicola. *Masons and Sculptors. Medieval Craftsmen.* London: British Museum Press, 1991.

Coleman, Janet. 'Property and Poverty'. In *The Cambridge History of Medieval Political Thought, c.350–c.1450*, ed. J. H. Burns, 607–48. Cambridge: Cambridge University Press, 1988.

Contamine, Philippe. *War in the Middle Ages.* Trans. Michael Jones. Oxford: Blackwell, 1984.

Crassons, Kate. *The Claims of Poverty: Literature, Culture, and Ideology in Late Medieval England.* Notre Dame, IN: University of Notre Dame Press, 2010.

——. '"The Workman Is Worth His Mede": Poverty, Labor, and Charity in the Sermon of William Taylor'. In *The Middle Ages at Work*, ed. Robertson and Uebel, 67–90. Basingstoke: Palgrave Macmillan, 2004.

Crawford, C. 'Medicine and the Law'. In *Companion Encyclopedia of the History of Medicine*, vol. 2, ed. W. F. Bynum and R. Porter, 1619–40. London: Routledge, 1997.

Crawford, Sally. *Childhood in Anglo-Saxon England.* Stroud: Sutton, 1999.

Cullum, P. H. *Cremetts and Corrodies: Care of the Poor and Sick at St. Leonard's Hospital, York, in the Middle Ages.* Borthwick Papers 79. York: University of York, 1991.

Davis, Adam J. 'Preaching in Thirteenth-Century Hospitals'. *Journal of Medieval History* 36 (2010): 72–89.

Dean, Trevor. *Crime in Medieval Europe 1200–1550.* Edinburgh: Longman, 2001.

Demaitre, Luke E. 'The Care and Extension of Old Age in Medieval Medicine'. In *Aging and the Aged*, ed. Sheehan, 3–22. Toronto: Pontifical Institute of Medieval Studies, 1990.

Der Sachsenspiegel. Ein Rechtsbuch spiegelt seine Zeit. Exhibition catalogue. Oldenburg: Idensee Verlag, 1996.

Dilg, Peter. 'Arzneimittel *ad longam vitam* aus Mittelalter und früher Neuzeit'. In *Alterskulturen*, ed. Vavra, 361–87. Vienna: Verlag der Österreichischen Akademie der Wissenschaften, 2008.

Dinzelbacher, Peter. *Europa im Hochmittelalter 1050–1250. Eine Kultur- und Mentalitätsgeschichte.* Darmstadt: Primus Verlag, 2003.

———. 'Über die Körperlichkeit in der mittelalterlichen Frömmigkeit'. In *Bild und Abbild vom Menschen im Mittelalter*. Schriftenreihe der Akademie Friesach 6, ed. Elisabeth Vavra, 49–87. Klagenfurt: Wieser Verlag, 1999.

Dirmeier, A. 'Armenfürsorge, Totengedenken und Machtpolitik im mittelalterlichen Regensburg. Vom *hospitale pauperum* zum Almosenamt'. In *Regensburg im Mittelalter. Beiträge zur Stadtgeschichte vom frühen Mittelalter bis zum Beginn der Neuzeit*, ed. M. Angerer and H. Wanderwitz, 217–36. Regensburg: Universitätsverlag Regensburg, 1995.

Dolezalová, Lucie. '*Nemini vetula placet?* In Search of the Positive Representation of Old Women in the Middle Ages'. In *Alterskulturen*, ed. Vavra, 175–82. Vienna: Verlag der Österreichischen Akademie der Wissenschaften, 2008.

Dove, Mary. *The Perfect Age of Man's Life.* Cambridge: Cambridge University Press, 1986.

Dunbabin, Jean. *Captivity and Imprisonment in Medieval Europe 1000–1300.* Medieval Culture and Society. Basingstoke: Palgrave Macmillan, 2002.

Dutton, Paul Edward. 'Beyond the Topos of Senescence. The Political Problems of Aged Carolingian Rulers'. In *Aging and the Aged*, ed. Sheehan, 75–94. Toronto: Pontifical Institute of Medieval Studies, 1990.

Dyer, Christopher. 'English Diet in the Later Middle Ages'. In *Social Relations and Ideas: Essays in Honour of R. H. Hilton*, ed. T. H. Aston, P. R. Coss, C. Dyer and J. Thirsk, 191–216. Cambridge: Cambridge University Press, 1983.

———. *Standards of Living in the Later Middle Ages: Social Change in England c. 1200–1520.* Cambridge: Cambridge University Press, 1989.

———. 'Work Ethics in the Fourteenth Century'. In *The Problem of Labour in Fourteenth-Century England*, ed. James Bothwell, P. J. P. Goldberg and W. M. Ormrod, 21–41. York: York Medieval Press, 2000.

Enderle, A., D. Meyerhöfer and G. Unverfehrt, eds. *Kleine Menschen—Große Kunst. Kleinwuchs aus künstlerischer und medizinischer Sicht.* Hamm: Artcolor Verlag, 1992.

Engel, Evamaria. *Die deutsche Stadt im Mittelalter.* Düsseldorf: Patmos Verlag, 2005.

Engel, Evamaria, and Frank-Dietrich Jacob. *Städtisches Leben im Mittelalter. Schriftquellen und Bildzeugnisse.* Cologne: Böhlau Verlag, 2006.

Epperlein, S. *Bäuerliches Leben im Mittelalter. Schriftquellen und Bildzeugnisse.* Cologne: Böhlau Verlag, 2003.

Epstein, Steven A. *Wage Labor and Guilds in Medieval Europe.* Chapel Hill: University of North Carolina Press, 1991.

Esch, A. *Wahre Geschichten aus dem Mittelalter. Kleine Schicksale selbst erzählt in Schreiben an den Papst.* Munich: C. H. Beck, 2010.

Evans, R. J. *In Defence of History.* London: Granta Books, 1997.

Eyler, J. R., ed. *Disability in the Middle Ages: Reconsiderations and Reverberations.* Farnham: Ashgate, 2011.

Fandrey, Walter. *Krüppel, Idioten, Irre. Zur Sozialgeschichte behinderter Menschen in Deutschland.* Stuttgart: Silberburg-Verlag, 1990.

Farmer, Sharon. 'The Beggar's Body: Intersections of Gender and Social Status in High Medieval Paris'. In *Monks and Nuns, Saints and Outcasts: Religion in Medieval Society. Essays in Honor of Lester K. Little*, ed. Sharon Farmer and Barbara H. Rosenwein, 153–71. Ithaca, NY: Cornell University Press, 2000.

————. 'A Deaf-Mute's Story'. In *Medieval Christianity in Practice*, ed. Miri Rubin, 203–9. Princeton, NJ: Princeton University Press, 2009.

————. 'Manual Labor, Begging, and Conflicting Gender Expectations in Thirteenth-Century Paris'. In *Gender and Difference in the Middle Ages*. Medieval Cultures 32, ed. Sharon Farmer and C. B. Pasternack, 261–87. Minneapolis: University of Minnesota Press, 2003.

————. *Surviving Poverty in Medieval Paris: Gender, Ideology, and the Daily Lives of the Poor*. Ithaca, NY: Cornell University Press, 2002.

————. 'Young, Male and Disabled'. In *Le petit peuple dans la société de l'Occident médiéval. Terminologies, perceptions, réalités*, ed. Pierre Boglioni, Robert Delort and Claude Gauvard, 437–51. Paris: Publications de la Sorbonne, 2001.

Farr, James. *Artisans in Europe, 1300–1914*. Cambridge: Cambridge University Press, 2000.

Feldmann, H. 'Die forensische Bewertung von Körperschäden im frühen Mittelalter—ein Vergleich mit heutigen MdE-Sätzen'. *Laryngo-Rhino-Otologie* 69 (1990): 166–70.

Fiorato, Veronica, Anthea Boylston and Christopher Knüsel, eds. *Blood Red Roses: The Archaeology of a Mass Grave from the Battle of Towton AD 1461*. Oxford: Oxbow, 2000.

Flint, V. I. J. *The Rise of Magic in Early Medieval Europe*. Oxford: Oxford University Press, 1991.

Frantzen, Allen J., and Douglas Moffat, eds. *The Work of Work: Servitude, Slavery, and Labor in Medieval England*. Glasgow: Cruithne Press, 1994.

Fromm, Norbert, Michael Kuthe and Walther Rügert. '. . . *entflammt vom Feuer der Nächstenliebe'. 775 Jahre Spitalstiftung Konstanz*. Constance: UVK Universitätsverlag Konstanz, 2000.

Frugoni, C. *A Day in a Medieval City*. Chicago: University of Chicago Press, 2005.

Geary, Patrick. 'Judicial Violence and Torture in the Carolingian Empire'. In *Law and the Illicit in Medieval Europe*, ed. Ruth Mazo Karras, Joel Kaye and E. Ann Matter, 79–88. Philadelphia: University of Pennsylvania Press, 2008.

Geltner, G. *The Medieval Prison: A Social History*. Princeton, NJ: Princeton University Press, 2008.

Geremek, Bronislaw. *Geschichte der Armut. Elend und Barmherzigkeit in Europa*. Trans. F. Griese. Munich: Artemis Verlag, 1988.

————. *The Margins of Society in Late Medieval Paris*. Trans. J. Birrell. Cambridge: Cambridge University Press/Paris: Editions de la Maison des Sciences de l'Homme, 1987.

Getz, Faye. *Medicine in the English Middle Ages*. Princeton, NJ: Princeton University Press, 1998.

Given-Wilson, C. *The Royal Household and the King's Affinity: Service, Politics and Finance in England 1360–1413*. New Haven, CT: Yale University Press, 1986.

Goetz, Hans-Werner. 'Alt sein und alt werden in der Vorstellungswelt des frühen und hohen Mittelalters'. In *Alterskulturen*, ed. Vavra, 17–58. Vienna: Verlag der Österreichischen Akademie der Wissenschaften, 2008.

Goldberg, Jeremy. *Communal Discord, Child Abduction, and Rape in the Later Middle Ages*. The New Middle Ages. New York: Palgrave Macmillan, 2008.

Goodey, C. F. *A History of Intelligence and "Intellectual Disability": The Shaping of Psychology in Early Modern Europe*. Farnham: Ashgate, 2011.

Goodich, Michael. *From Birth to Old Age: The Human Lifecycle in Medieval Thought, 1250–1350*. Lanham, MA: University Press of America, 1989.

———. *Miracles and Wonders: The Development of the Concept of Miracle, 1150–1350. Church, Faith and Culture in the Medieval West*. Ashgate: Aldershot, 2007.

———, ed. *Other Middle Ages: Witnesses at the Margins of Medieval Society*. Philadelphia: University of Pennsylvania Press, 1998.

Gordon, Sarah. 'Representations of Aging and Disability in Early Sixteenth-Century French Farce'. In *Old Age*, ed. Classen, 421–36. Berlin: Walter de Gruyter, 2007.

Gottwald, Claudia. *Lachen über das Andere. Eine historische Analyse komischer Repräsentationen von Behinderung*. Bielefeld: transcript Verlag, 2009.

Gragnolati, M. *Experiencing the Afterlife: Soul and Body in Dante and Medieval Culture*. Notre Dame, IN: University of Notre Dame Press, 2005.

Green, Richard Firth. '"Nede ne hath no lawe": The Plea of Necessity in Medieval Literature and Law'. In *Living Dangerously: On the Margins in Medieval and Early Modern Europe*, ed. Barbara A. Hanawalt and Anna Grotans, 9–30. Notre Dame, IN: University of Notre Dame Press, 2007.

Grimm, Jacob. *Deutsche Rechtsaltertümer*. 4th ed. 2 vols. Originally published 1828. Leipzig, 1899; rpt. Darmstadt: Wissenschaftliche Buchgesellschaft, 1994.

Groebner, Valentin *Defaced: The Visual Culture of Violence in the Late Middle Ages*. Trans. Pamela Selwyn. New York: Zone Books, 2004.

Hagen, Susan K. *Allegorical Remembrance: A Study of* The Pilgrimage of the Life of Man *as a Medieval Treatise on Seeing and Remembering*. Athens: University of Georgia Press, 1990.

Halsall, Guy, ed. *Violence and Society in the Early Medieval West*. Woodbridge: Boydell Press, 1998.

Hanawalt, B. A. *The Ties that Bound: Peasant Families in Medieval England*. Oxford: Oxford University Press, 1986.

Harvey, Barbara. *Living and Dying in England 1100–1540: The Monastic Experience*. Oxford: Clarendon Press, 1993.

Harward, V. J. *The Dwarfs of Arthurian Romance and Celtic Tradition*. Leiden: Brill, 1958.

Henderson, John. 'The Parish and the Poor in Florence at the Time of the Black Death: The Case of S. Frediano'. *Continuity and Change* 3, no. 2 (1988): 247–72.

———. *Piety and Charity in Late Medieval Florence*. Chicago: University of Chicago Press, 1994.

Hergemöller, Bernd-Ulrich, ed. *Randgruppen der spätmittelalterlichen Gesellschaft*. 2nd ed. Warendorf: Fahlbusch Verlag, 1994.

Herlihy, David. 'Age, Property, and Career in Medieval Society'. In *Aging and the Aged*, ed. Sheehan, 143–58. Toronto: Pontifical Institute of Medieval Studies, 1990.

Herlihy, David, and C. Klapisch-Zuber. *Les toscans et leurs familles*. Paris: Editions de l'Ecole des Hautes Études en Sciences, 1978.

Herrmann, Bernd, ed. *Mensch und Umwelt im Mittelalter*. Stuttgart: Deutsche Verlags-Anstalt, 1986.

Hill, Mary C. *The King's Messengers 1199–1377*. London: E. Arnold, 1961.

———. *The King's Messengers 1199–1377*. Stroud: Sutton, 1994.

Hilton, R. H. *A Medieval Society: The West Midlands at the End of the Thirteenth Century*. London: Weidenfeld and Nicolson, 1966.

Hinckeldey, C., ed. *Strafjustiz in alter Zeit. Band III der Schriftenreihe des mittelalterlichen Kriminalmuseums Rothenburg ob der Tauber*. Rothenburg-o.-d.-Tauber: Mittelalterliches Kriminalmuseum, 1980.

Hölter, Achim. *Die Invaliden. Die vergessene Geschichte der Kriegskrüppel in der europäischen Literatur bis zum 19. Jahrhundert*. Stuttgart: J. B. Metzler, 1995.

Homans, George Caspar. *English Villagers of the Thirteenth Century.* Cambridge, MA: Harvard University Press, 1941.

Horden, Peregrine. 'A Discipline of Relevance: The Historiography of the Later Medieval Hospital'. *Social History of Medicine* 1, no. 3 (1988): 359–74.

Huizinga, Johan. *The Waning of the Middle Ages.* Trans. F. Hopman. Harmondsworth: Peregrine, 1976.

Hurnard, N. D. *The King's Pardon for Homicide Before A.D. 1307.* Oxford: Clarendon Press, 1969.

Illich, Ivan. *Limits to Medicine. Medical Nemesis: The Expropriation of Health.* Harmondsworth: Penguin, 1977.

Irsigler, Franz. '*Divites* und *pauperes* in der Vita Meinwerci. Untersuchungen zur wirtschaftlichen und sozialen Differenzierung der Bevölkerung Westfalens im Hochmittelalter'. *Vierteljahresschrift für Sozial- und Wirtschaftsgeschichte* 57 (1970): 449–99.

Irsigler, Franz, and Arnold Lassotta. *Bettler und Gaukler, Dirnen und Henker. Außenseiter in einer mittelalterlichen Stadt. Köln 1300–1600.* Munich: DTV, 1989.

Jacquart, Danielle, and Claude Thomasset. *Sexuality and Medicine in the Middle Ages.* Trans. M. Adamson. Oxford: Polity, 1988.

James, R. R. *Studies in the History of Ophthalmology in England Prior to the Year 1800.* Cambridge: Cambridge University Press, 1933.

Jankrift, K. P. *Mit Gott und schwarzer Magie. Medizin im Mittelalter.* Darmstadt: Wissenschaftliche Buchgesellschaft, 2005.

Jaritz, Gerhard, ed. *The Sign Languages of Poverty.* Vienna: Verlag der Österreichischen Akademie der Wissenschaften, 2007.

Johnstone, Hilda. 'Poor-Relief in the Royal Households of Thirteenth-Century England'. *Speculum* 4 (1929): 149–67.

Jurasinski, Stefan. *Ancient Privileges: Beowulf, Law, and the Making of Germanic Antiquity.* Morgantown: West Virginia University Press, 2006.

Jütte, Robert. *Poverty and Deviance in Early Modern Europe.* Cambridge: Cambridge University Press, 1994.

Kay, Sarah, and Miri Rubin, eds. *Framing Medieval Bodies.* Manchester: Manchester University Press, 1994.

Kealey, Edward J. *Medieval Medicus: A Social History of Anglo-Norman Medicine.* Baltimore, MD: Johns Hopkins University Press, 1981.

Kermode, Jennifer I. 'Urban Decline? The Flight from Office in Late Medieval York'. *Economic History Review* 2nd series 35, no. 2 (1982): 179–98.

Kerr, Julie. 'Health and Safety in the Medieval Monasteries of Britain'. *History* 93 (2008): 3–10.

———. *Monastic Hospitality: The Benedictines in England, c.1070–c.1250.* Studies in the History of Medieval Religion 32. Woodbridge: Boydell Press, 2007.

King, A. '"According to the Custom Used in French and Scottish Wars": Prisoners and Casualties on the Scottish Marches in the Fourteenth Century'. *Journal of Medieval History* 28, no. 3 (2002): 263–90.

Kleinschmidt, Harald. *Understanding the Middle Ages: The Transformation of Ideas and Attitudes in the Medieval World.* Woodbridge: Boydell Press, 2000.

Knapp, Herman. *Das alte Nürnberger Kriminalrecht.* Berlin: J. Guttentag, 1896.

Knoop, D., and G. P. Jones. *The Medieval Mason: An Economic History of English Stone Building in the Later Middle Ages and Early Modern Times.* Manchester: Manchester University Press, 1933, rev. ed. 1967.

Knowles, D., and R. N. Hadcock. *Medieval Religious Houses: England and Wales.* London: Longman, 1953.

Koelsch, F. *Beiträge zur Geschichte der Arbeitsmedizin.* Schriftenreihe der Bayerischen Landesärztekammer Bd. 8. Munich: Bayerische Landesärztekammer, 1967.

Koldeweij, A. M. 'Lifting the Veil on Pilgrim Badges'. In *Pilgimage Explored*, ed. J. Stopford, 161–88. York: York Medieval Press, 1999.

Krötzl, Christian. '*Sexaginta vel circa*. Zur Wahrnehmung von Alter in hagiographischen Quellen des Spätmittelalters'. In *Alterskulturen*, ed. Vavra, 109–15. Vienna: Verlag der Österreichischen Akademie der Wissenschaften, 2008.

Kunitz, Stephen J. 'Medicine, Mortality, and Morbidity'. In *Companion Encyclopedia of the History of Medicine*, vol. 2, ed. W. F. Bynum and Roy Porter, 1693–1711. London: Routledge, 1993.

Lascaratos, J. 'The Penalty of Blinding during Byzantine Times: Medical Remarks'. *Documenta Ophthalmologica* 81 (1992): 133–44.

Laughton, Jane. *Life in a Late Medieval City: Chester 1275–1520*. Oxford: Windgather Press, 2008.

Lazda-Cauders, Rasma. 'Old Age in Wolfram von Eschenbach's *Parzival* and *Titurel*'. In *Old Age*, ed. Classen, 201–18. Berlin: Walter de Gruyter, 2007.

Le Goff, Jacques. *Medieval Civilization 400–1500*. Trans. J. Barrow. Oxford: Blackwell, 1988.

———. *Time, Work, and Culture in the Middle Ages*. Trans. A. Goldhammer. Chicago: University of Chicago Press, 1980.

Le Goff, Jacques, and Nicolas Truong. *Die Geschichte des Körpers im Mittelalter*. Trans. Renate Warttmann. Stuttgart: Klett-Cotta, 2007.

Letts, Malcolm. *Bruges and Its Past*. 2nd ed. Bruges: Desclée, De Brower and Co./ London: A. G. Berry, 1926.

Levy, H. 'The Economic History of Sickness and Medical Benefit before the Puritan Revolution'. *Economic History Review* 13 (1943): 42–57.

Lewin, C. G. *Pensions and Insurance before 1800: A Social History*. East Linton: Tuckwell Press, 2003.

Lewry, P. Osmund. 'Study of Aging in the Arts Faculty of the Universities of Paris and Oxford'. In *Aging and the Aged*, ed. Sheehan, 23–38. Toronto: Pontifical Institute of Medieval Studies, 1990.

Little, Lester K. *Religious Poverty and the Profit Economy in Medieval Europe*. London: Elek, 1978.

Luttrell, Anthony. 'The Hospitallers' Medical Tradition: 1291–1530'. In *The Military Orders: Fighting for the Faith and Caring for the Sick*, ed. Malcolm Barber, 64–81. Aldershot: Ashgate, 1994.

Lyon, Jonathan R. 'The Withdrawal of Aged Noblemen into Monastic Communities: Interpreting the Sources from Twelfth-Century Germany'. In *Old Age*, ed. Classen, 143–69. Berlin: Walter de Gruyter, 2007.

Maier, Johann. 'Die Wertung des Alters in der jüdischen Überlieferung der Spätantike und des frühen Mittelalters'. *Saeculum* 30 (1979): 355–64.

McCall, Andrew. *The Medieval Underworld*. New York: Dorset Press, 1979.

McGlynn, Sean. *By Sword and Fire: Cruelty and Atrocity in Medieval Warfare*. London: Phoenix, 2009.

McVaugh, M. R. *Medicine before the Plague: Practitioners and Their Patients in the Crown of Aragon 1285–1345*. Cambridge: Cambridge University Press, 1993.

Meier, Frank. *Gaukler, Dirnen, Rattenfänger. Außenseiter im Mittelalter*. Ostfildern: Thorbecke, 2005.

———. *Gefürchtet und bestaunt. Vom Umgang mit dem Fremden im Mittelalter*. Ostfildern: Thorbecke, 2007.

Metzler, Irina. 'Afterword'. In *Madness in Medieval Law and Custom*. Later Medieval Europe 6, ed. Wendy J. Turner, 197–217. Leiden: Brill, 2010.

———. 'Bildliche Darstellungen des (nicht)behinderten Bettlers im Martinswunder aus der Perspektive mittelalterlicher Mentalitäten'. In *Andere Bilder. Zur Produktion von Behinderung in der visuellen Kultur*, ed. Beate Ochsner and Anna Grebe, 1–23. Bielefeld: transcript Verlag, 2013.

———. *Disability in Medieval Europe: Thinking about Physical Impairment during the High Middle Ages, c.1100–1400*. Routledge Studies in Medieval Religion and Culture 5. London: Routledge, 2006.

———. 'Hermaphroditism in the Western Middle Ages: Physicians, Lawyers and the Intersexed Person'. In *Bodies of Knowledge: Cultural Interpretations of Illness and Medicine in Medieval Europe*. Studies in Early Medicine 1, ed. S. Crawford and C. Lee, 27–39. Oxford: Archaeopress, 2010.

———. 'Indiscriminate Healing Miracles in Decline: How Social Realities Affect Religious Perceptioní. In *Contextualizing Medieval Miracles*, ed. Matthew Mesley and Louise E. Wilson. Forthcoming.

———. 'Liminality and Disability: Spatial and Conceptual Aspects of Physical Impairment in Medieval Europe'. In *Medicine and Space: Body, Surroundings and Borders in Antiquity and the Middle Ages*. Visualising the Middle Ages 4, ed. Patricia A. Baker, Han Nijdam and Karine van 't Land, 273–96. Leiden: Brill, 2012.

———. 'Perceptions of Deafness in the Central Middle Ages'. In *Homo debilis. Behinderte—Kranke—Versehrte in der Gesellschaft des Mittelalters*, ed. Cordula Nolte, 79–98. Korb: Didymos-Verlag, 2009.

Mieszkowski, Gretchen. 'Old Age and Medieval Misogyny: The Old Woman'. In *Old Age*, ed. Classen, 299–319. Berlin: Walter de Gruyter, 2007.

Militzer, K. 'The Role of Hospitals in the Teutonic Order'. In *The Military Orders*. Vol. 2, *Welfare and Warfare*, ed. H. Nicholson, 51–59. Aldershot: Ashgate, 1998.

Miller, Edward, and John Hatcher. *Medieval England: Rural Society and Economic Change 1086–1348*. Social and Economic History of England. London: Longman, 1978.

———. *Medieval England: Towns, Commerce and Crafts 1086–1348*. Harlow: Longman, 1995.

Mills, Robert. *Suspended Animation: Pain, Pleasure and Punishment in Medieval Culture*. London: Reaktion Books, 2005.

Minois, Georges. *History of Old Age: From Antiquity to the Renaissance*. Trans. Sarah Hanbury Tenison. Cambridge: Polity Press, 1989.

———. *History of Suicide: Voluntary Death in Western Culture*. Trans. Lydia G. Cochrane. Baltimore, MD: Johns Hopkins University Press, 1999.

Mitchell, Piers D. *Medicine in the Crusades: Warfare, Wounds and the Medieval Surgeon*. Cambridge: Cambridge University Press, 2004.

Mollat, Michel. *Die Armen im Mittelalter*. Trans. U. Irsigler. Munich: Beck, 1987.

Montford, Angela. 'Fit to Preach and Pray: Considerations of Occupational Health in the Mendicant Orders'. In *The Use and Abuse of Time in Christian History*. *Studies in Church History 37*, ed. R. N. Swanson, 95–106. Woodbridge: Boydell Press, 2002.

———. *Health, Sickness, Medicine and the Friars in the Thirteenth and Fourteenth Centuries*. Aldershot: Ashgate, 2004.

Mullan, John, and Richard Britnell. *Land and Family: Trends and Local Variations in the Peasant Land Market on the Winchester Bishopric Estates, 1263–1415*. Studies in Regional and Local History 8. Hatfield: University of Hertfordshire Press, 2010.

Murray, Alexander. *Suicide in the Middle Ages*. Vol. I, *The Violent against Themselves*. Oxford: Oxford University Press, 1998.

———. *Suicide in the Middle Ages*. Vol. II, *The Curse on Self-Murder*. Oxford: Oxford University Press, 2000.

Neubert, Dieter, and Günther Cloerkes. *Behinderung und Behinderte in verschiedenen Kulturen. Eine vergleichende Analyse ethnologischer Studien*. 2nd ed. Heidelberg: Edition Schindele, 1994.

Nicholas, David. *The Domestic Life of a Medieval City: Women, Children and the Family in Fourteenth-Century Ghent*. Lincoln: University of Nebraska Press, 1985.

Nicolle, David. *Medieval Warfare Source Book*. Vol. I, *Warfare in Western Christendom*. London: BCA, 1996.

Oexle, Otto Gerhard. 'Armut und Armenfürsorge um 1200. Ein Beitrag zum Verständnis der freiwilligen Armut bei Elisabeth von Thüringen'. In *Sankt Elisabeth. Fürstin, Dienerin, Heilige. Aufsätze—Dokumentation—Katalog*, eds. Carl Graepler, Fred Schwind and Matthias Werner, 78–100. Sigmaringen: Thorbecke, 1981.

Ohler, Norbert. *Krieg und Frieden im Mittelalter*. Beck'sche Reihe 1226. Munich: C. H. Beck, 1997.

Oliver, Lisi. *The Body Legal in Barbarian Law*. Toronto: University of Toronto Press, 2011.

O'Neill, Ynez Violé. *Speech and Speech Disorders in Western Thought before 1600*. Contributions in Medical History 3. Westport, CT: Greenwood Press, 1980.

Orme, Nicholas. 'Sufferings of the Clergy: Illness and Old Age in Exeter Diocese, 1300–1540'. In *Life, Death, and the Elderly: Historical Perspectives*, ed. Margaret Pelling and Richard M. Smith, 62–73. London: Routledge, 1991.

Orme, Nicholas, and Margaret Webster. *The English Hospital, 1070–1570*. New Haven, CT: Yale University Press, 1995.

O'Tool, Mark P. 'Disability and the Suppression of Historical Identity: Rediscovering the Professional Backgrounds of the Blind Residents of the Hôpital des Quinze-Vingts'. In *Disability in the Middle Ages: Reconsiderations and Reverberations*, ed. J. R. Eyler, 11–24. Farnham: Ashgate, 2010.

———. 'The *povres avugles* of the Hôpital des Quinze-Vingts: Disability and Community in Medieval Paris'. In *Difference and Identity in Francia and Medieval France*, ed. M. Cohen and J. Firnhaber-Baker, 157–73. Farnham: Ashgate, 2010.

Page, F. M. *The Estates of Crowland Abbey: A Study in Manorial Administration*. Cambridge: Cambridge University Press, 1934.

Papayannopoulos, I. G. 'Information Revealed from the Old Testament Concerning Diseases of Old Age'. *Koroth* 8, nos. 5–6 (1982): 68–71.

Parkin, Tim. *Old Age in the Roman World: A Cultural and Social History*. Baltimore, MD: Johns Hopkins University Press, 2003.

Pearman, Tory Vandeventer. *Women and Disability in Medieval Literature*. The New Middle Ages. New York: Palgrave Macmillan, 2010.

Pearsall, Derek. '*Piers Plowman* and the Problem of Labour'. In *The Problem of Labour in Fourteenth-Century England*, ed. James Bothwell, P. J. P. Goldberg and W. M. Ormrod, 123–32. York: York Medieval Press, 2000.

Pelling, Margaret. *The Common Lot: Sickness, Medical Occupations and the Urban Poor in Early Modern England*. London: Routledge, 1998.

———. 'Illness among the Poor in an Early Modern English Town: The Norwich Census of 1570'. *Continuity and Change* 3, no. 2 (1988): 273–90.

Pelling, Margaret, and Richard M. Smith, eds. *Life, Death, and the Elderly: Historical Perspectives*. London: Routledge, 1991.

Pestilli, Livio. 'Blindness, Lameness and Mendicancy in Italy (from the 14th to the 18th Centuries)'. In *Others and Outcasts in Early Modern Europe: Picturing the Social Margins*, ed. Thomas R. Nichols, 107–29. Aldershot: Ashgate, 2007.

———. 'Disabled Bodies: The (Mis)Representation of the Lame in Antiquity and Their Reappearance in Early Christian and Medieval Art'. In *Roman Bodies: Antiquity to the Eighteenth Century*, ed. Andrew Hopkins and Maria Wyke, 85–98. London: British School at Rome, 2005.

Peters, Harry. 'Jupiter and Saturn: Medieval Ideals of "Elde"'. In *Old Age*, ed. Classen, 375–91. Berlin: Walter de Gruyter, 2007.

Pfau, Aleksandra N. *Madness in the Realm: Narratives of Mental Illness in Late Medieval France*. PhD diss., University of Michigan, 2008.

Phythian-Adams, C. *Desolation of a City: Coventry and the Urban Crisis of the Late Middle Ages*. Cambridge: Cambridge University Press, 1979.

Postel, Verena. *Arbeit und Willensfreiheit im Mittelalter*. Vierteljahrschrift für Sozial- und Wirtschaftsgeschichte Beihefte Nr. 207. Stuttgart: Franz Steiner, 2009.

Pratt, Karen. '*De vetula*: The Figure of the Old Woman in Medieval French Literature'. In *Old Age*, ed. Classen, 321–42. Berlin: Walter de Gruyter, 2007.

Prestwich, Michael. *Armies and Warfare in the Middle Ages: The English Experience*. New Haven, CT: Yale University Press, 1996.

Pullan, Brian. '"Difettosi, impotenti, inabili": Caring for the Disabled in Early Modern Italian Cities'. In *Poverty and Charity: Europe, Italy, Venice, 1400–1700*, ed. Brian Pullan, VI:1–21. Aldershot: Ashgate, 1994.

———. 'Support and Redeem: Charity and Poor Relief in Italian Cities from the Fourteenth to the Seventeenth Century'. *Continuity and Change* 3, no. 2 (1988): 177–208.

Ranft, Patricia. *The Theology of Work: Peter Damian and the Medieval Religious Renewal Movement*. The New Middle Ages. Basingstoke: Palgrave Macmillan, 2006.

Rawcliffe, Carole. 'Health and Safety at Work in Late Medieval East Anglia'. In *Medieval East Anglia*, ed. Christopher Harper-Bill, 130–51. Woodbridge: Boydell Press, 2005.

———. *The Hospitals of Medieval Norwich*. Studies in East Anglian History 2. Norwich: University of East Anglia, 1995.

———. *Leprosy in Medieval England*. Woodbridge: Boydell Press, 2006.

———. *Medicine and Society in Later Medieval England*. Stroud: Sutton, 1995.

———. *Medicine for the Soul: The Life, Death and Resurrection of an English Medieval Hospital*. Stroud: Sutton, 1999.

Renard, Georges. *Guilds in the Middle Ages*. London: G. Bell and Sons, 1918; rpt. New York: Augustus M. Kelley, 1968.

Riché, Pierre. *Daily Life in the World of Charlemagne*. Trans. Jo Ann McNamara. Liverpool: Liverpool University Press, 1978.

Risse, Guenter B. *Mending Bodies, Saving Souls: A History of Hospitals*. New York: Oxford University Press, 1999.

Roach, Andrew P. *The Devil's World: Heresy and Society 1100–1300*. Harlow: Pearson Education, 2005.

Roberts, Charlotte, and Margaret Cox. *Health and Disease in Britain: From Prehistory to the Present Day*. Stroud: Sutton, 2003.

Robertson, Kellie. *The Laborer's Two Bodies: Literary and Legal Productions in Britain, 1350–1500*. The New Middle Ages. Basingstoke: Palgrave Macmillan, 2006.

Robertson, Kellie, and Michael Uebel, eds. *The Middle Ages at Work*. The New Middle Ages. Basingstoke: Palgrave Macmillan, 2004.

Robinson, Daniel N. *Wild Beasts and Idle Humours: The Insanity Defense from Antiquity to the Present*. Cambridge, MA: Harvard University Press, 1996.

Roncière, Charles de la. 'Tuscan Notables on the Eve of the Renaissance'. In *A History of Private Life II: Revelations of the Medieval World*, ed. Philippe Ariès and Georges Duby, trans. A. Goldhammer, 157–309. Cambridge, MA: Belknap Press, 1988.

Rosen, George. *The History of Miners' Diseases*. New York: Schuman's, 1943.

Rosenthal, Joel T. *Old Age in Late Medieval England*. Philadelphia: University of Pennsylvania Press, 1996.

———. 'Retirement and the Life Cycle in Fifteenth-Century England'. In *Aging and the Aged*, ed. Sheehan, 173–88. Toronto: Ponticical Institute of Medieval Studies, 1990.

Rosenwein, Barbara, ed. *Anger's Past: The Social Uses of an Emotion in the Middle Ages*. Ithaca, NY: Cornell University Press, 1998.

Rosser, Gervase. 'Crafts, Guilds and the Negotiation of Work in the Medieval Town'. *Past and Present* 154 (1997): 3–31.

Rothauser, Britt C. L. 'Winter in Heorot: Looking at Anglo-Saxon Perceptions of Age and Kingship through the Character of Hrothgar'. In *Old Age*, ed. Classen, 103–20. Berlin: Walter de Gruyter, 2007.

Roux, Simone. *Paris in the Middle Ages*. Trans. J. A. McNamara. Philadelphia: University of Pennsylvania Press, 2009.

Rubin, Miri. *Charity and Community in Medieval Cambridge*. Cambridge: Cambridge University Press, 1987.

———. 'Medieval Bodies: Why Now, and How?' In *The Work of Jacques Le Goff and the Challenges of Medieval History*, ed. Miri Rubin, 209–21. Woodbridge: Boydell Press, 1997.

———. 'The Poor'. In *Fifteenth Century Attitudes: Perceptions of Society in Late Medieval England*, ed. R. Horrox, 169–82. Cambridge: Cambridge University Press, 1994.

Rubin, S. *Medieval English Medicine*. New York: Barnes and Noble, 1974.

Rushton, Peter. 'Idiocy, the Family and the Community in Early Modern North-East England'. In *From Idiocy to Mental Deficiency: Historical Perspectives on People with Learning Disabilities*, ed. D. Wright and A. Digby, 44–64. London: Routledge, 1996.

Ruys, Juanita Feros. 'Medieval Latin Meditations on Old Age: Rhetoric, Autobiography, and Experience'. In *Old Age*, ed. Classen, 171–200. Berlin: Walter de Gruyter, 2007.

Salzman, L. F. *Building in England Down to 1540: A Documentary History*. Oxford: Clarendon Press, 1952; reissued 1997.

Samson, Ross. 'The End of Early Medieval Slavery'. In *The Work of Work: Servitude, Slavery, and Labor in Medieval England*, ed. Allen J. Frantzen and Douglas Moffat, 95–124. Glasgow: Cruithne Press, 1994.

Schewe, Dieter. *Geschichte der sozialen und privaten Versicherung im Mittelalter in den Gilden Europas*. Sozialpolitische Schriften 80. Berlin: Duncker & Humblot, 2000.

Schleusener-Eichholz, Gudrun. *Das Auge im Mittelalter*. 2 vols. PhD diss., University of Münster, 1975/Munich: W. Fink, 1984.

Schubert, Ernst. *Alltag im Mittelalter. Natürliches Lebensumfeld und menschliches Miteinander*. Darmstadt: Wissenschaftliche Buchgesellschaft, 2002.

———. *Fahrendes Volk im Mittelalter*. Bielefeld: Verlag für Regionalgeschichte, 1995.

———. *Räuber, Henker, arme Sünder. Verbrechen und Strafe im Mittelalter*. Darmstadt: Primus Verlag, 2007.

Scott, Anne M. *Piers Plowman and the Poor*. Dublin: Four Courts Press, 2004.

Sears, Elizabeth. *The Ages of Man: Medieval Interpretation of the Life Cycle*. Princeton, NJ: Princeton University Press, 1986.

Sennett, Richard. *Flesh and Stone: The Body and the City in Western Civilization*. London: Faber and Faber, 1994.

Shahar, Shulamith. *Growing Old in the Middle Ages: 'Winter Clothes Us in Shadow and Pain'*. Trans. Yael Lotan. London: Routledge, 1997.

———. 'The Middle Ages and Renaissance'. In *The Long History of Old Age*, ed. Pat Thane, 71–111. London: Thames and Hudson, 2005.

———. 'The Old Body in Medieval Culture'. In *Framing Medieval Bodies*, ed. Sarah Kay and Miri Rubin, 160–86. Manchester: Manchester University Press, 1994.

————. 'Who Were the Old in the Middle Ages?'. *Social History of Medicine* 6 (1993): 313–41.

Sheehan, Michael M., ed. *Aging and the Aged in Medieval Europe*. Papers in Medieval Studies 11. Toronto: Pontifical Institute of Medieval Studies, 1990.

Sheer, J., and N. Groce. 'Impairment as a Human Constant: Cross-Cultural and Historical Perspectives on Variation'. *Journal of Social Issues* 44, no. 1 (1988): 23–37.

Shepherd, Geoffrey. 'Poverty in *Piers Plowman*'. In *Social Relations and Ideas: Essays in Honour of R. H. Hilton*, ed. T. H. Aston, P. R. Coss, C. Dyer and J. Thirsk, 169–89. Cambridge: Cambridge University Press, 1983.

Singer, Julie. *Blindness and Therapy in Late Medieval French and Italian Poetry*. Gallica 20. Cambridge: D. S. Brewer, 2011.

Smith, Richard M. 'The Manorial Court and the Elderly Tenant in Late Medieval England'. In *Life, Death, and the Elderly: Historical Perspectives*, ed. Margaret Pelling and Richard M. Smith, 39–61. London: Routledge, 1991.

Sprandel, R. *Das Eisengewerbe im Mittelalter*. Stuttgart: Anton Hiersemann, 1968.

Stahl, Alan M. 'Coin and Punishment in Medieval Venice'. In *Law and the Illicit in Medieval Europe*, ed. Ruth Mazo Karras, Joel Kaye and E. Ann Matter, 164–79. Philadelphia: University of Pennsylvania Press, 2008.

Sterns, I. 'Care of the Sick Brothers by the Crusader Orders in the Holy Land'. *Bulletin of the History of Medicine* 57 (1983): 43–69.

Sudhoff, Heinke. *Ikonographische Untersuchungen zur 'Blindenheilung' und zum 'Blindensturz'. Ein Beitrag zu Pieter Breugels Neapler Gemälde von 1568*. PhD diss., University of Bonn, 1981.

Swanson, Heather. *Building Craftsmen in Late Medieval York*. Borthwick Papers 63. York: St. Anthony's Press, 1983.

Swanson, R. N., ed. *The Use and Abuse of Time in Christian History*. Studies in Church History 37. Woodbridge: Boydell Press, 2002.

Sweetinburgh, Sheila. *The Role of the Hospital in Medieval England: Gift-Giving and the Spiritual Economy*. Dublin: Four Courts Press, 2004.

Thane, Pat. 'Geriatrics'. In *Companion Encyclopedia of the History of Medicine*, vol. 2, ed. W. F. Bynum and Roy Porter, 1092–1115. London: Routledge, 1993.

————, ed. *The Long History of Old Age*. London: Thames and Hudson, 2005.

————. *Old Age in English History: Past Experiences, Present Issues*. Oxford: Oxford University Press, 2000.

Tierney, Brian. *Medieval Poor Law: A Sketch of Canonical Theory and Its Application in England*. Berkeley: University of California Press, 1959.

Titow, J. Z. *English Rural Society 1200–1350*. Historical Problems: Studies and Documents 4. London: George Allen and Unwin, 1969.

Turner, Wendy J., and Tory Vandeventer Pearman, eds. *The Treatment of Disabled Persons in Medieval Europe: Examining Disability in the Historical, Legal, Literary, Medical, and Religious Discourses of the Middle Ages*. Lewiston, NY: Edwin Mellen Press, 2010.

van den Hoven, Birgit. *Work in Ancient and Medieval Thought: Ancient Philosophers, Medieval Monks and Theologians and Their Concept of Work, Occupations and Technology*. Dutch Monographs on Ancient History and Archaeology 14. Amsterdam: Gieben, 1996.

Vassberg, D. 'Old Age in Early Modern Castilian Villages'. In *Power and Poverty: Old Age in the Pre-Industrial Past*, ed. S. Ottaway, L. Botelho and K. Kittredge, 145–66. Greenwood, CT: Praeger, 2002.

Vavra, Elisabeth, ed. *Alterskulturen des Mittelalters und der frühen Neuzeit*. *Veröffentlichungen des Instituts für Realienkunde des Mittelalters und der frühen Neuzeit Nr. 21*. Österreichische Akademie der Wissenschaften.

Philosophisch-historische Klasse, Sitzungsberichte, Band 780. Vienna: Verlag der Österreichischen Akademie der Wissenschaften, 2008.

———, ed. *Bild und Abbild vom Menschen im Mittelalter. Akten der Akademie Friesach "Stadt und Kultur im Mittelalter" Friesach (Kärnten), 9.–13. September 1998*. Schriftenreihe der Akademie Friesach 6. Klagenfurt: Wieser Verlag, 1999.

Webb, Diana. *Pilgrims and Pilgrimage in the Medieval West*. London: I. B. Tauris, 1999.

Wenzel, Siegfried. *The Sin of Sloth: Acedia in Medieval Thought and Literature*. Chapel Hill: University of North Carolina Press, 1967.

Werner, H. *Geschichte des Taubstummenproblems bis ins 17. Jahrhundert*. Jena: G. Fischer, 1932.

Westlake, H. F. *The Parish Gilds of Medieval England*. London: SPCK, 1919.

Wheatley, Edward. *Stumbling Blocks before the Blind: Medieval Constructions of a Disability*. Ann Arbor: University of Michigan Press, 2010.

Windemuth, Marie-Luise. *Das Hospital als Träger der Armenfürsorge im Mittelalter*. Sudhoffs Archiv Beihefte 36. Stuttgart: Franz Steiner Verlag, 1995.

Woodward, D. *Men at Work: Labourers and Building Craftsmen in the Towns of Northern England, 1450–1750*. Cambridge: Cambridge University Press, 1995.

Wortley, John T. 'Aging and the Desert Fathers. The Process Reversed'. In *Aging and the Aged*, ed. Sheehan, 63–73. Toronto: Pontifical Institute of Medieval Studies, 1990.

Youngs, Deborah. *The Life Cycle in Western Europe, c. 1300–c. 1500*. Manchester: Manchester University Press, 2006.

Zanker, Paul. *Die Trunkene Alte. Das Lachen der Verhöhnten*. Frankfurt: Fischer Taschenbuch Verlag, 1989.

Zimmermann, Volker. 'Ansätze zu einer Sozial- und Arbeitsmedizin am mittelalterlichen Arbeitsplatz'. In *Mensch und Umwelt im Mittelalter*, ed. Bernd Herrmann, 140–49. Stuttgart: Deutsche Verlags-Anstalt, 1986.

Index